'This remains the go-to text for an understanding of the contemporary United States. It continues to be the leading source for information for my undergraduates who wish to gain an in-depth appreciation of the USA, its historical roots and those events which have shaped the America of today.'

– *Murray Leith, Professor of Political Science,*
University of the West of Scotland, UK

'This new edition of *Contemporary United States* mixes history, sociology and political science in a very fruitful way to produce a one volume introductory text that should be indispensable reading for undergraduate students of American politics and/or society.'

– *Ole Helmersen, Associate Professor of British & American Studies,*
Copenhagen Business School, Denmark

'*Contemporary United States* continues to be a one-stop shop for everything the aspiring student and scholar would want to know about the most complex and diverse nation on earth. Packed full of up-to-the-minute details and analysis, Goddard and Duncan do a remarkable job of condensing America's core elements. A brilliant synopsis that leads the way as a primer for the study of the United States in all its glorious, contradictory, and increasingly controversial ways.'

– *Ian Scott, Professor of American Film and History,*
University of Manchester, UK

'Tackling the further fissuring of the U.S. in an unflinching but balanced way, this edition provides the necessary overview to understand the complicated and complex reality of contemporary America. Written in clear prose and with academic breadth, it is certain to be a go-to resource for teachers of undergraduate courses.'

– *Steen Ledet Christiansen, Professor of Popular Visual Culture,*
Aalborg University, Denmark

Contemporary States and Societies Series

This series provides lively and accessible introductions to key countries and regions of the world, conceived and designed to meet the needs of today's students. The authors are all experts with specialist knowledge of the country or region concerned and have been chosen also for their ability to communicate clearly to a non-specialist readership. Each text has been specially commissioned for the series and is structured according to a common format.

Published

CONTEMPORARY AFRICA
Matthew Graham

CONTEMPORARY BRITAIN
(4TH EDITION)
John McCormick

CONTEMPORARY CHINA
(3RD EDITION)
Kerry Brown

CONTEMPORARY FRANCE
Helen Drake

CONTEMPORARY INDIA
Katharine Adeney and Andrew Wyatt

CONTEMPORARY IRELAND
Eoin O'Malley

CONTEMPORARY JAPAN
(3RD EDITION)
Duncan McCargo

CONTEMPORARY LATIN AMERICA
(3RD EDITION)
Ronaldo Munck

CONTEMPORARY RUSSIA
(3RD EDITION)
Edwin Bacon

CONTEMPORARY SOUTH AFRICA
(3RD EDITION)
Anthony Butler

CONTEMPORARY UNITED STATES
(6TH EDITION)
Russell Duncan and Joseph Goddard

CONTEMPORARY UNITED STATES

DEMOCRACY AT THE CROSSROADS

SIXTH EDITION

Joseph Goddard and Russell Duncan

BLOOMSBURY ACADEMIC
LONDON • NEW YORK • OXFORD • NEW DELHI • SYDNEY

BLOOMSBURY ACADEMIC
Bloomsbury Publishing Plc
50 Bedford Square, London, WC1B 3DP, UK
1385 Broadway, New York, NY 10018, USA
29 Earlsfort Terrace, Dublin 2, Ireland

BLOOMSBURY, BLOOMSBURY ACADEMIC and the Diana logo
are trademarks of Bloomsbury Publishing Plc

First published in Great Britain 2003
This edition published 2022

Copyright © Joseph Goddard and Russell Duncan, 2022

Russell Duncan and Joseph Goddard have asserted their right under the Copyright,
Designs and Patents Act, 1988, to be identified as Authors of this work.

For legal purposes the Acknowledgments on pp. xii–xiii constitute
an extension of this copyright page.

Cover design by Eleanor Rose
Cover images © Chip Somodevilla/Getty Images and © Ruslan Maiborodin/ Getty Images

All rights reserved. No part of this publication may be reproduced or transmitted in any form or
by any means, electronic or mechanical, including photocopying, recording, or any information
storage or retrieval system, without prior permission in writing from the publishers.

Bloomsbury Publishing Plc does not have any control over, or responsibility for, any third-party
websites referred to or in this book. All internet addresses given in this book were correct at the
time of going to press. The author and publisher regret any inconvenience caused if addresses
have changed or sites have ceased to exist, but can accept no responsibility for any such changes.

A catalogue record for this book is available from the British Library.

A catalog record for this book is available from the Library of Congress.

ISBN:	HB:	978-1-3503-4217-0
	PB:	978-1-3503-4216-3
	ePDF:	978-1-3503-4218-7
	eBook:	978-1-3503-4219-4

Contemporary States and Societies Series

Typeset by Integra Software Services Pvt. Ltd.
Printed and bound in Great Britain

To find out more about our authors and books visit www.bloomsbury.com
and sign up for our newsletters.

CONTENTS

List of Illustrative Material	viii
Acknowledgments	xii
List of Abbreviations	xv
Map of the United States of America: States and State Capitals	xviii
Introduction	**1**
1 History	**13**
The 1619 Project, Critical Race Theory, and the 1776 Commission	13
The Past as Prologue	15
The Rise of a Nation	16
The Rise to Power	25
From Isolation to Superpower	30
The Cold War	32
The 1990s	38
The Twenty-First Century	39
2 Land and People	**45**
The Land	45
Regions	53
The People	66
Immigration	72
3 Government	**83**
The Constitution	85
The Federal System	89
The Branches of Government	93
4 Politics and Democracy	**113**
The 2020 Election: Trump vs. Biden	113
Participatory Democracy	119
Political Parties	124
Politics	133

Contents

5	**Society**	**145**
	Class	148
	The American Family	156
	Women	160
	Race	164
	Crime and Punishment	168
6	**Religion, Education, and Social Policy**	**181**
	Religion	182
	Education	193
	Social Services	204
7	**Culture, Media, Sports**	**215**
	Borderlands	215
	Literature and the Rise of a Nation	221
	The Internet	222
	Social Media and Youth Culture	225
	Print Media and a Free Press	229
	Broadcast Media	233
	Leisure Time	236
	Sports	241
	Art	245
	Popular Music	249
8	**The Economy**	**255**
	The US Domestic Economy	260
	Labor Unions	266
	Business and Industry	268
	Government and Business	270
	The Global Marketplace	277
	The Dollar and the Renminbi	281
9	**Global Politics**	**285**
	An Upsurge of Nationalism	286
	Separation of Powers and Foreign Policy	292
	History of Foreign Policy	294
	The Cold War, 1945–1990	296
	The New World Order	302
	The Twenty-First Century	304
	September 11, 2001	304
	America's Longest War	305
	The War on Terror	308
	The War in Iraq and Syria	310

The US "Pivot" to Asia	313
Foreign Policy from Obama to Biden	314
The Invasion of Ukraine and a More Powerful Western Alliance	319

10 Prospects — **325**

Bibliography	335
Index	364

LIST OF ILLUSTRATIVE MATERIAL

Figures

2.1	Immigrants to the United States Gaining Legal Permanent Resident Status, by Decade, 1821–2019	73
3.1	The System of Checks and Balances	89
3.2	The Law-Making Process	104
3.3	The Court System	111
4.1	Voter Turnout Registration: Presidential Elections, 2000–2020	136
5.1	US Support for the Death Penalty, 2018	179
6.1	Education, Unemployment and Salaries, 2019	195
6.2	The American Educational System	199
6.3	Highest Level of Educational Achievement for Twenty-Five to Twenty-Nine-Year-Olds, 2020	201
6.4	HHS Budget by Sector, 2021	207
7.1	Time Use on an Average Weekday for Full-Time University and College Students	228
7.2	Time Use on an Average Work Day for Persons Aged Twenty-Five to Fifty-Four with Children	236
7.3	Leisure Time on an Average Day	237

Maps

0.1	The United States of America: States and State Capitals	xviii
1.1	US Territorial Expansion	21
2.1	Major Topographical Features	47
2.2	The South	54
2.3	The North	56
2.4	The Midwest	59
2.5	The West	61
2.6	The Pacific Rim	64
2.7	American Indian Reservations	70

List of Illustrative Material

Illustrations

0.1	A Not So Peaceful Transfer of Power	2
0.2	Fox Lies, Democracy Dies	6
0.3	The Murder of George Floyd and the Rising Power of #BLM	8
0.4	Biden Publicly Receives the Coronavirus Vaccination	9
0.5	Democracy at the Crossroads: The Flag is Bleeding, Dangerously	10
1.1	Slavery Is Not Marginal to American History	14
1.2	Manifest Destiny Crosses the Plains	22
1.3	The Central Problem of White Supremacy	24
1.4	One of History's Rhymes: Gilded Age Politics and Boss Tweed	27
1.5	President Barack Obama and Vice President Joe Biden	42
2.1	Climate Change—The Longest Drought in 1,200 Years: Lake Powell	50
2.2	Climate Change—Extraordinary Wildfires in the American West	63
2.3	American Indian Cultural Survival	69
2.4	Surging Latina/Latino Political Power	77
2.5	"Today I Am An American"	78
3.1	Polilticizing Public Health Guidelines	84
3.2	Seven Presidents	97
3.3	Democratic Lawmakers in White	100
3.4	US Supreme Court Justices Attend the Funeral of George H. W. Bush	109
4.1	Biden and a Bipartisan Alliance of Senators	115
4.2	Democratic Candidates Represent Diverse Factions	118
4.3	Biden Addresses a Joint Session of Congress	127
4.4	Gerrymandering: When Politicians Skew the Vote	131
5.1	The Politics of Gender: The Women's Movement	147
5.2	President Obama and Stacey Abrams Encourage Georgians to Vote	172
5.3	"I Don't Want To Die:" Students Protest Gun Violence	176
6.1	A National Day of Prayer: Trump, Pence, and Evangelicals	190
6.2	Corporate Profits and the Opioid Crisis	209
6.3	Progressives Want Biden to do Much More	211
7.1	LBGTQIA+ Identities, Subcultures, Inclusion	217
7.2	Juneteenth National Independence Day	240
7.3	Olympic Athletes, Sexual Assault, #MeToo, and the US Senate	243
7.4	NFL Players, Racial Equality, and #BlackLivesMatter	245
7.5	World Champions Demand Respect and Fair Pay for Women	246
7.6	Spotify Advances Latin Music and Hispanic Visibility	252
8.1	Joe Biden, Kamala Harris, and the American Jobs Plan	256
8.2	SpaceX: The Military Industrial Complex and the Space Race	271
8.3	USMCA and the Politics of the Border	280
9.1	"All Mouth, No Trousers": The G7 Fail to Reign in Climate Change	286
9.2	The G7 Confronts Trump's "America First" Plan	288
9.3	Domestic Protests Heavily Influence America's Soft Power Advantages	290

List of Illustrative Material

9.4	American Soldiers Killed in Afghanistan	306
9.5	Two Dictators, Same Results: A Stronger Western Alliance	321
10.1	A Generational, Racial, Gender, and Power Question	326
10.2	One Person, One Vote—Cast, Counted, Certified	329
10.3	The Youth Movement Understands the Connections	331

Tables

1.1	Selected Individual Federal Income Tax Brackets	34
2.1	Country and State Comparisons	46
2.2	The South	55
2.3	The North	57
2.4	The Midwest	59
2.5	The West	62
2.6	The Pacific Rim	65
2.7	Immigrants Gaining Green Cards in 2018—Sending Countries	73
3.1	Profile of the 117th Congress (2021–2023)	100
4.1	Ideological Self-Placement and Party Identification, 2020	128
4.2	Presidential Preference in 2020: Exit Polls	129
4.3	Presidential Elections, 2008–2020	135
5.1	Median Earnings for Full-Time Workers, Twenty-Five Years Old and Older, 2018	155
5.2	US Population by Age and Sex, Estimated, 2019	156
5.3	US Life Expectancy at Birth	156
5.4	American Population Diversity, 2000, 2019, and 2060 Projection	166
5.5	Executions and Death Row Inmates, January 1, 1976–January 1, 2020	178
6.1	American Religiosity—Adults (2019)	185
6.2	Foreign Students Studying in US Colleges/Universities in 2018–2019	196
6.3	Estimated Annual Costs for Four-Year College/University Students for 2020–2021	197
7.1	Primary Language Spoken at Home other than English or Spanish, by State	218
8.1	Unemployment Rates, November 2016–December 2020	261
8.2	Yearly Median Household (Family) Income by Selected Characteristics	262
8.3	Top Fifteen US Trade Partners, Exports and Imports, 2020	279
9.1	Countries with Nuclear Weapons: Number of Warheads	299
10.1	What's the Most Urgent Problem in America Today?	327

Boxes

1.1	Excerpt from *The Declaration of Independence*	19
1.2	*The Gettysburg Address*	25

List of Illustrative Material

1.3	*The Pledge of Allegiance*	29
3.1	The Constitution of the United States of America: A Summary	86
3.2	Federalism as Process	91
3.3	Constitutional Powers of Congress	102
4.1	The Path to the Presidency	134
7.1	Official Federal Holidays (purpose)	239

ACKNOWLEDGMENTS

First and most importantly, we would like to thank our families for the massive amounts of support given to us during the years of research and writing since the last edition in 2018. The world situation changed dramatically during that period. The challenges of discerning truth from fiction during the Trump presidency, the hideous expansion of partisanship in American society and politics, a grim global pandemic with its social quarantines, travel restrictions, massive numbers of deaths, and sheer fear for the future of family, community, nation, and world order made our newest edition a very different book from the previous one. Our families endured our struggles to interpret and balance the news and they served as sounding boards and inspiration for the final text in every chapter. Special cheers go to our partners Jytte Lindberg and Haini Zhong.

We are appreciative for the support given by our colleagues at the Institute for English, Germanic, and Romance Studies at the University of Copenhagen for the twenty years of research involved in writing previous editions. Unlike many textbooks, a text on the contemporary United States requires an almost complete rethinking and overhaul with each edition. Certainly, what we published in the first edition changed dramatically after 9/11 and with the advent of the internet and social media and the deterioration over time from dreams of global cosmopolitanism to the unfortunate rise of religious ethnonationalism and its cruelties. Any book on the contemporary United States has a life span of four years before it must be rethought. The University of Copenhagen provided funding and sabbaticals to support our latest efforts.

We are keenly grateful for the inputs by the unnamed—and unknown to us—peer reviewers who made the book better through their own insights into the Trump administration's mindset and actions. Their thorough reviews of the manuscript and recommendations undoubtedly made the book more valuable. Through conversations long and short in a variety of settings, many friends, acquaintances, and family offered ideas that have found their way into the text. Of particular help, Russell would like to thank Omar and Bonnie Bravo, Matias Frederiksen, Søren Storm, and Graham Hodges, Christopher Phillips, and Gregory Stephenson. Former colleague and monthly lunch partner, Professor Paul Levine, contributed enormously over sushi and by his daily blog on themes domestic and global as they intersect with US actions. Joe Goddard would like to thank the students who have taken different iterations of his recurring elective course in American politics and society, and helped enrich this book through passionate discussion. Also, thanks to colleagues and students past and present from the University of Copenhagen, Copenhagen Business School, and Aalborg University, and the wider Nordic American Studies community who have provided feedback and food for thought for the cumulative versions of this book.

Acknowledgments

The authors leaned on the expertise and guidance of the editorial and production staff at Bloomsbury Academic for the copyediting support and enthusiasm that pushed the book along as quickly as possible. We are especially beholden to Commissioning Editor Milly Weaver, Production Editor Elizabeth Holmes, and Assistant Editor Becky Mutton, copyeditor Dawn Cunneen and Project Manager Joanne Rippin at Integra, the design and marketing team, and the typesetters and staff.

Joseph Goddard has the overall editorial responsibility for the book and particular responsibility for writing Chapters 2, 3, 4, 5, 6, and 8. Russell Duncan has primary writing responsibility for the Introduction, Chapters 1, 7, 9, and the Conclusion. We dedicate this edition to our families.

Russell Duncan
Joseph Goddard

The authors and publishers are grateful to the following for permission to use copyright material: Getty Images for all illustrations except the following: Illustration 0.5 to Faith Ringgold / ARS, NY and DACS, London, Courtesy AGA Galleries, New York 2022 and Illustration 2.4 photograph by Bonnie Bravo.

Every effort has been made to trace all copyright-holders of third-party materials included in this work, but if any have been inadvertently overlooked the publishers will be pleased to make the necessary arrangement at the first opportunity.

LIST OF ABBREVIATIONS

ABA	American Bar Association
ACA	Affordable Care Act
ACLU	American Civil Liberties Union
ACT	American College Test
AFDC	Aid to Families with Dependent Children
AFL	American Federation of Labor
AFL–CIO	American Federation of Labor–Congress of Industrial Organizations
AIG	American International Group
AMA	American Medical Association
AMEX	American Stock Exchange
ARRA	American Recovery and Reinvestment Act
ASEAN	Association of Southeast Asian Nations
ATL	The Atlantic
BCRA	Bipartisan Campaign Reform Act
BI	Business Insider
BIA	Bureau of Indian Affairs
CC	Christian Coalition
CDC	Centers for Disease Control and Prevention
CEO	chief executive officer
CHIP	Children's Health Insurance Program
CIA	Central Intelligence Agency
CIO	Congress of Industrial Organizations
CNN	Cable News Network
CRT	Critical Race Theory
CSR	corporate social responsibility
DHS	Department of Homeland Security
DINKS	double income no kids
DOD	Department of Defense
DOE	Department of Education
DREAM	Development, Relief, Education for Alien Minors
EOP	Executive Office of the President
EPA	Environmental Protection Agency
ESA	Endangered Species Act
FCC	Federal Communications Commission
FDA	Food and Drug Administration
FDIC	Federal Deposit Insurance Corporation

List of Abbreviations

FDR	Franklin Delano Roosevelt
FEMA	Federal Emergency Management Agency
FY	fiscal year
GATT	General Agreement on Tariffs and Trade
GDP	gross domestic product
GRE	Graduate Record Exam
HBCU	Historically Black Colleges and Universities
HUAC	House Un-American Activities Committee
ICE	Immigration and Customs Enforcement
IT	information technology
JCS	Joint Chiefs of Staff
JFK	John Fitzgerald Kennedy
KOL	Knights of Labor
LGBTQIA+	lesbian, gay, bisexual, transgender, queer, intersex, and asexual +
LoC	Library of Congress
MAD	mutual assured destruction
MLBPA	Major League Baseball Players Association
MTV	Music Television
NA	National Archives
NAACP	National Association for the Advancement of Colored People
NAFTA	North American Free Trade Agreement
NAM	National Association of Manufacturers
NASA	National Aeronautics and Space Administration
NASDAQ	National Association of Securities Dealers Automated Quotations
NATO	North Atlantic Treaty Organization
NCLB	No Child Left Behind
NEA	National Education Association
NEA	National Endowment for the Arts
NPR	National Public Radio
NPS	National Park Service
NRA	National Rifle Association
NRDC	Natural Resources Defense Council
NSC	National Security Council
NYC	New York City
NYSE	New York Stock Exchange
OMB	Office of Management and Budget
OSHA	Occupational Safety and Health Administration
PAC	Political Action Committee
PBS	Public Broadcasting System
PISA	Programme for International Student Testing
PPP	purchasing power parity
RTTP	Race-to-the-Top
S&L	Savings and Loans

SALT I	Anti-Ballistic Missile (ABM) Treaty, Strategic Arms Limitations Talks
SAT	Scholastic Achievement Test
SCOTUS	Supreme Court of the United States
SDI	Strategic Defense Initiative
SEC	Securities and Exchange Commission
SNAP	Supplemental Nutrition Assistance Program
TANF	Temporary Assistance for Needy Families
TARP	Troubled Asset Recovery Program
TPA	Trade Promotion Authority
WP	Warsaw Pact
WTO	World Trade Organization
YMCA	Young Men's Christian Association

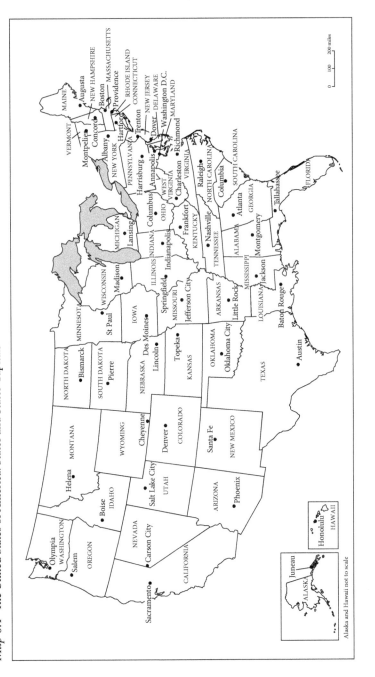

Map 0.1 The United States of America: States and States Capitals

INTRODUCTION

The alarm bells are ringing, have been ringing since the 1960s, when American society and politics were "atomized" as "things fell apart" in the new social movements that swept the country (Didion, 2017). In 2021, worried about the attacks on voting rights and the increased numbers of voting suppression laws being implemented across the United States, 150 eminent political scientists and historians of democracy wrote an open letter to Congress. They spoke in a unified voice: "The partisan politicization of what has long been trustworthy, non-partisan administration of elections represents a clear and present threat to the future of electoral democracy … Defenders of democracy in the United States still have a slim window of opportunity to act. But time is ticking away, and midnight is approaching" (Talev, 2021).

Something has gone wrong. There is a feeling that the center will not hold. The nation is offtrack, the political culture is fractured, the people have the jitters, and they are dangerously divided. Civic violence rules the day. In April 2021, President Joe Biden spoke to Congress about "the worst crisis in our democracy since the Civil War [1861–1865]" (Biden, 2021b). Neither Biden nor the 150 academics were exaggerating the situation. There is a real cause for concern. Disillusionment about the system has overtaken most Americans. Historically, there have always been disagreements in such a pluralistic society, but culture wars and political polarizations have gotten demonstrably worse in the twenty-first century and have been absolutely poisonous since the 2016 and 2020 presidential elections. An Age of Anger and Resistance has morphed into a more ominous era with Democracy at the Crossroads.

Realizing that majority rule is sometimes good and sometimes horrifying, Americans set up their democracy to protect the minority against any tyranny by the majority. But there are now powerful factions and institutions that are successfully pushing minority rule. A 2021 University of Chicago study found that 21 million American adults believe strongly that 1) Joe Biden is an illegitimate president who stole the election, and 2) Violence is justified as an acceptable way to overturn election results (Gellman, 2022). These 21 million are supported by millions more who believe Biden is illegitimate but will not pick up weapons.

On January 6, 2021, an armed mob of Republican vigilantes with a mean age of forty-two years broke into the US Capitol building in an insurrection to stop the certification of Joe Biden as the new president, to physically harm Speaker of the House Nancy Pelosi, and to "hang Mike Pence!" Trump was clearly involved in planning the attempted coup (Illustration 0.1). As a point of clarification, "insurrectionists" use weapons against a

Contemporary United States

Illustration 0.1 A Not So Peaceful Transfer of Power

On January 6, 2021, a mob of vigilantes violently stormed against the police barriers and lines protecting the US Capitol. Inside the building, elected Senators and Representatives were busy receiving and certifying the Electoral College votes from each state as they went about the peaceful transfer of power that had been the *sine qua non* of American democracy. Worldwide, viewers were stunned by what can only be deemed an insurrection to overthrow the workings of the American government. The images and aftermath of that riot are as memorable to many as the 2001 attacks on the World Trade Center, the assassination of John F. Kennedy in 1963 and of Martin Luther King, Jr., in 1968, and the bombing of Pearl Harbor in 1941 (see Illustration 1.3). Notably, as political strategist James Carville pointed out, 98 percent of the vigilantes in the Capitol and at the preceding rally were white. Carville added: "We need better white people in the United States" (Dowd, 2022).

Source: Brent Stirton via Getty Images

government that is repressive; "vigilantes" use weapons to support a government that is not strong enough. Chanting that they would "stop the steal" and use violence to restore Trump to power, the January 6 mob combined elements of both groups (Tanenhaus, 2021). Property was destroyed and the Capitol building was trashed. Five policemen died and 130 officers were wounded. It all played out live on global television and social media sites.

It may only have been Act One. Investigative journalist Barton Gellman's cover story in *The Atlantic* said that January 6 was not an isolated event: "January 6 Was Practice" (Gellman, 2022). Senate Republican Leader Mitch McConnell admitted:

> There is no question, none, that President Trump is practically and morally responsible for provoking the events … No question about it. The people who

stormed the building believed they were acting on the wishes and instructions of their President. And their having that belief was a foreseeable consequence of the growing crescendo of false statements, conspiracy theories and reckless hyperbole which the defeated President kept shouting into the largest megaphone on planet Earth.

(Gessen, 2021)

While McConnell dampened his criticism in the year that followed, Trump, Fox News, and at least 21 million Republicans continued his "big lie" that the election was stolen by illegal voters and election officials. Trump called for his supporters to take up arms again, if necessary, to prevent a similar steal in the 2022 midterms.

One of the biggest impediments to compromise is the fact that the federal judiciary is out of balance. The political makeup of the United States Supreme Court (SCOTUS) widened the partisan divide as the court lost its balanced four conservative, four liberal, one swing vote in 2013, then went 5–4 conservative, then became highly-unbalanced at 6–3 in 2020 (see Chapter 3). The power of the Court and belief in the rule of law is contingent on the people's faith in the fairness of the judicial decisions. If the people believe that the decisions do not represent equality and freedom for everyone, disorder rises as political divisions are exacerbated and democracy itself tumbles into crises. During his presidency, Trump appointed over 220 federal appeals court and district court judges, almost all white men—and nearly all opposed by the #MeToo and Black Lives Matter (#BLM) movements. In his first year in office, Biden named sixty-four judges, of whom forty-six were female and forty-one were people of color (Hulse, 2021). Senate Republicans vowed to block future Biden nominees whenever they have the power to do so.

Without exception, every recent poll shows that Americans have lost faith in the institutions and structures of government and society which have long sustained them. Congress cannot seem to pass legislation that is wanted by large majorities of the people. The national myths that bind the people together are under attack from competing, and seemingly irreconcilable narratives. Americans urgently need to regain the kind of patriotism that is expressed in the national motto "e pluribus unum" (from many, one), or more commonly: "we're all in this together."

Money matters. Class divisions and discrepancies in wealth are inextricably wound into political discourse because they are keys to life expectancies and opportunities for present and future happiness. Many people—especially those who land on top—hold the self-serving idea that a meritocracy of talent, brains, and hard work exists to divide winners from losers. They think that both people who gain great wealth and people who do not, deserve what they get. This idea of merit and hierarchy has damaged a loyalty to the common good. Philosopher Michael Sandel argues that the American dream is not meant to be an individual aspiration but is meant to invoke a broad and moral democratic nation-state where life is fuller and more rewarding for everyone (Sandel, 2020). Sandel concludes that if an individual or racial, gendered, talented, or moneyed meritocracy/plutocracy rules, then "solidarity [is] an almost impossible project" (Sandel, 2020). Political journalist Evan Osnos relayed a West Virginia coal miner's reaction to the

Contemporary United States

income differences between corporate CEOs and regular workers: "Do you know any man who is worth 400 to 500 times other men? I don't" (Osnos, 2021).

Race, LGBTQIA+ rights, religion, immigration, education, international relations, social services, women's equality, democracy, and national identity are among the issues under siege. The sociologist who invented the term "culture wars," James Davison Hunter, recently stated that fifty years ago the central issue of the culture war was abortion. In contemporary America, it is race (Hunter, 2021). But the abortion issue is far from resolved as the 6–3 conservative majority on the US Supreme Court continues to confront the #MeToo movement and the fight over a woman's right to control her own body. Feminists believe that if men could get pregnant, abortion would be a non-issue. The question is not whether a fetus is a person, but whether a woman is. Most conservatives focus on the fertilized egg and evangelicals put forward the argument of "fetal personhood" and "fetal citizenship." These ideas make a woman's body a "crime scene" with abortion being the murder of a person, a citizen. Most progressives focus on "my body, my choice" putting the woman first but not excluding the embryo. As SCOTUS determines a woman's right to privacy, the political passions become viscous cultural battles. The issue can galvanize voters in either, or both, directions. Liberals worry that because the Court in 2022 overturned a woman's access to abortion, it might also overturn the rights of same-sex marriage, transgender rights, and other civil rights issues.

Political sociologist George Packer analyzed the unwinding of national solidarity and the fracture into four socio-political groups who see reality very differently. "Free America" (conservative Republicans, free marketeers, libertarians, anti-communists) are joined by "Real America" (working-class white Christian nationalists). In opposition are those in "Smart America" (liberal meritocratic Democratic technocrats and globalists) and "Just Americans" (social-justice activists, minorities, and the "Values Generation" of Millennials and Gen Z who have just come of age). The Frees and the Reals against the Smarts and the Justs have the country divided into two powerful coalitions who see the other as not just mistaken, but as the enemy (Packer, 2014, 2021).

Ironically, democracy itself is a main proponent of partisanship as it organizes people into groups with different platforms, identities, and histories. The very ethnic and religious diversity of the American nation makes it difficult for democracy to work because of its principle of seeking majorities to decide issues (Mounk, 2022). In that way, American democracy is often at odds with the people its tenets embrace (Mounk, 2019). Fear, anger, and the lack of civility are growing as a majority of Americans agree that US culture is under attack, threatened by the actions of their opponents (PRRI, 2021). Republicans and Democrats have hardened their positions, but the Republicans have instituted a loyalty test that condemns members and removes them from committee posts and party support if they go against the leadership's dictates. Because of this, there has been a collapse of the Republican Party as a negotiating partner in the democracy. The same can be said of the media in general, as illustrated by the polarization of Fox News and MSNBC/CNN or the abyss between the *New York Times* and the *New York Post*. While good journalism aims to tell people what they want to hear, to be good also means to tell people what they need to know. The hyperactive media of Meta, Twitter, Instagram, TikTok, Spotify, and others, have overturned the balance. Internet and social media platforms really divide Americans because they work to gather people into partisan tribes. The technology itself is ambivalent in simultaneously promoting the spread of democratic information and global misinformation in supporting authoritarian, even fascist, ideas. On the positive side, technology has helped push the nation to a reckoning, as actor Will Smith noted about cell phone cameras, tweets, and police body cams: "Racism is not getting worse; it is getting filmed" (Smith, 2016). Simultaneously, the online seductions of fake news and greedy big media groups create a general chaos of conflicting "facts" and a groupthink loyalty (Illustration 0.2). The people join into what journalist David Brooks calls "the armies of certitude that march forth and dominate debate and politics" (Brooks, 2021b). It is an open question whether or not liberal democracy can survive social media.

In this environment, the public is exhausted by democracy and freedom of speech/press and the many claims to conspiracies against the truth. Shouting and clichés often give way to violence as partisans are stalemated and can't make democracy work in a conventional way of voting, declaring a winner, and accepting a loss. If an election, however honest, is held up as a stolen election, and a "stop the steal" group emerges to never concede the results, the nation is at a precipice. In 1800, when Federalist Party incumbent John Adams lost to the Democratic-Republican Thomas Jefferson, Adams conceded the election. Jefferson, acknowledging the importance of this peaceful transfer of power to the nascent democracy, called the concession the real American Revolution. Years later, on the eve of the American Civil War, President Abraham Lincoln addressed the loss of unity, rising segregation, and growing violence in America. He warned that "if destruction be our lot, we must ourselves be its author … We will be a nation of free men, or we will die by suicide." Lincoln warned that "a House divided against itself cannot stand."

Today, the US is in a crisis of legitimacy and the world is watching. As recently as 2016, the trust that foreign governments had in President Obama averaged 64 percent. With Trump elected and in charge, the level of belief that the United States could be counted upon to do the right thing fell to 22 percent (PEW quoted in Corchado, 2020). With Americans looking for reliability and a return to normalcy, Joe Biden was elected in 2020. By 2022, Biden's domestic poll numbers plummeted as he mishandled the end of the war in Afghanistan, failed to get the Covid pandemic under control, moved from moderate to progressive social programs, and was the "president of record" as inflation lifted gas and food prices to forty-year highs. The public feared the coming of a long Cold War, or worse, after Russia invaded Ukraine in 2022, bringing a massive shooting war to Europe for the first time since 1945.

Liberal democracy is always a fragile experiment. Historian Anne Applebaum said: "Polarization is normal. Scepticism about liberal democracy is normal. And the appeal of authoritarianism is eternal" (Applebaum, 2018). Even before 2016 there was a growing contempt for democratic institutions and divisions of power as set forth in the US Constitution. The necessity of a "loyal opposition by good-faith actors" had been replaced by non-negotiating stonewalling. Faith in the Constitution as "a machine that runs by itself" waned as people became aware that the fundament is not self-enforcing or

Illustration 0.2 Fox Lies, Democracy Dies

The majority of Republican voters turn on Fox News for basic Right-wing information that they supplement with Newsmax and/or One America News Network (OANN), conservative talk radio hosts such as Glen Beck, Mark Levin, Hugh Hewitt, and Michael Savage, online sources like Breitbart News, Alex Jones, and Joe Rogan, conservative political blogs such as RedState, HotAir, Michelle Malkin, and social media accounts that use algorithms to steer viewers to even more conservative sites. Donald Trump used Fox News as a main source for his information on policy and to broadcast his views to his base. For Democrats, Fox News hosts Tucker Carlson, Sean Hannity, and Laura Ingraham (shown above) are among the main sources for a pugilistic and paranoid style of misinformation and lies which lead to the partisan divides, increase racism, and help radicalize listeners to violence (Confessore, 2022). The more outrageous the claims made by Carlson, Hannity, and Ingraham, the more viewers they attract. A protester in front of News Corporation in Manhattan wants everyone to know that when "Fox Lies, Democracy Dies." For example, Fox hosts claim that vaccines kill you, Hillary Clinton heads a child sex-trafficking cabal, Biden stole the presidency, Kamala Harris is the "shadow president," leftist groups were responsible for the violence on January 6, Vladimir Putin is a shrewd role model, LGBTQIA+ and Feminists are dangers to greatness, climate change is a hoax, and immigrants are criminals or freeloaders (Milbank, 2022).

Source: Erik McGregor/LightRocket via Getty Images

permanent, or even necessarily an instrument of progress. The Constitution is imperfect, aspirational, and dependent upon the people to safeguard its protections.

Moreover, humans have trouble with self-government and political passions compete with reason in voting booths, legislatures, courts, and on Main Street in everyday America. Social media intensifies divisions among the body politic and an imperial president who does not adhere to norms and conventions that have been built up over time can quickly send the people out of control by challenging what they thought they knew. Technology often favors tyranny. For example, too many people rely on Google for fast and easy answers—a worrying technological authoritarianism of ambivalent information (Harari, 2018).

A culture of "WOKE-ness" confronts a culture of status quo "OK-ness" and pits change against both the forces of continuity and those of reaction. The #BLM and #MeToo movements focus on institutional racism and sexism (Illustration 0.3). Critical Race Theory (CRT) analyzes the structural dimensions of discrimination in law and public policy, including segregation, education, housing, distribution of benefits, voting rights, promotions and wages, and the national narrative. Republicans contort CRT to mean anything that re-examines race and racism; for them, CRT is un-American. Some things should not be talked about. It is not the evil but the knowledge of evil that offends Republican critics of CRT. The Right argues that a Cancel Culture restricts freedom of speech and exists to shame white men for the actions of their ancestors. The Right asks: Wouldn't it be better to be colorblind and genderblind when setting policy? The Left argues that the issue is one of racial and sexual accountability for historical errors that need to be called out, reconsidered, and fixed by reforms and reparations (Meckler and Natanson, 2021). Liberals and progressives believe that skin color and sex must be accounted for to reach equal justice.

The main debate stems from competing origin stories of the American experience. One narrative argues for a white European and Christian America; the other for the strength pluralism gives to a nation of immigrants. The conservative argument is one of exclusion and a theory of "replacement" by rapidly increasing minority groups who want to become part the nation's narrative. The historically white dominant group, which Fox News calls "legacy Americans," fears for its decline in population percentages—and thus its control over the democracy. Fox News headliner Tucker Carlson, who has the highest-rated cable show in TV history and has been suggested as the 2024 Republican nominee for president, rose to influence with extremist claims and conspiracy theories and a "flagrantly racist" mantra stoking white fear by claiming that the Left is pursuing a war against older white men (Confessore, 2022). In 2020, the Department of Homeland Security reported that white supremacy is "the greatest domestic terror threat to the United States." At the global level, the superpower that has been in the vanguard of the expansion of liberal ideas is increasingly mocked for the failures of its democratic system.

In *Democracy at the Crossroads*, we focus on the institutions of government and society, their unfolding, and the challenges and contradictions of those events. There is much to consider as the Biden administration works to flip Trump's white nationalism, "America First," and Christian-centered gospel of wealth to build a nation of domestic and global inclusion and distribution of rewards. Clearly, nationalism over globalization (Trump) differs from nationalism and globalization (Biden). Xenophobia, racism, and misogyny are still strong in public institutions and private lives, and the confused debates over "fake news" must be unraveled. This will be difficult because a mountain of evidence suggests that group loyalty interferes with reason. The group loyalty can be religious, national, family, or political in nature, or a combination.

Contemporary United States

Illustration 0.3 The Murder of George Floyd and the Rising Power of #BLM

On May 25, 2020, in Minneapolis, Minnesota, George Floyd used a counterfeit $20 bill to pay for some items in a convenience store. The clerk called 911 and Floyd was taken from his automobile by four police officers. The senior policeman, Derek Chauvin, handcuffed and pinned Floyd facedown on the pavement with a knee on his neck for nine minutes. Floyd repeatedly gasped "I can't breathe" and called out over and over for "mama." Pedestrians gathered, shouted that Chauvin was suffocating Floyd, and when they were held back by the "crowd control" tactics of the other policeman, used cell phone cameras to record the final moments of Floyd's life. The world soon watched those nine minutes over and over again. All the police officers were charged with Floyd's death. Chauvin was found guilty of murder, an almost unheard of result when a white policeman uses excessive force on a black man. Nationwide protests erupted in over a hundred cities and Floyd's death became a powerful engine for a nationwide conversation on police violence and the reality of "growing up black" in America. The *New York Times* reported that #BLM (established in 2013) had become perhaps the biggest mass protest movement in American history with nearly 5,000 demonstrations nationwide by July 2020 (Buchanan, Quoctrung, and Patel, 2020). The photograph shows a mural in Brooklyn by artist Kenny Altidor. In the foreground, Floyd's brother, Philonise, confronts viewers on his brother's behalf and to raise consciousness of #BLM's struggle against racism, inequality, and police violence.

Source: Stephanie Keith/Stringer via Getty Images

In 2016, America replaced its first black president with a man of a vastly different temperament and political philosophy. Where Obama did not have a single scandal during eight years in office, the four years of Trump rule were filled with jaw-dropping misdeeds. Congress impeached Trump twice. Lawsuits over sexual harassment and physical abuse, insider trading, illegal contacts with Russian emissaries, executive overreach, and unqualified and corrupt department heads and personal advisors were

Introduction

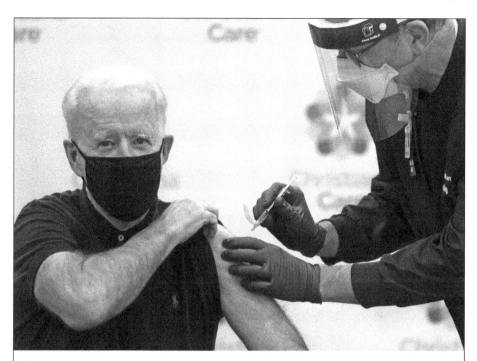

Illustration 0.4 Biden Publicly Receives the Coronavirus Vaccination

On January 10, 2021, demonstrating his difference from his predecessor, president-elect Joe Biden showcased his belief in science and the medical establishment by openly taking the second dose of the Corona vaccine. Biden had campaigned on the failures of Trump to take the pandemic seriously and to encourage the American people to save their lives and the lives of their loved ones—and strangers—by submitting to testing and the recommendations of scientists and doctors around the world. Biden and Democrats placed much of the blame for the vast numbers of deaths and hospitalizations on Trump's insistence that one day the virus would simply vanish. To vax or not to vax would divide families along political lines through the 2022 midterms and beyond (see Illustration 3.1). For politicians and the public alike, Covid has shown its complexity over how to go forward: trade-offs between government dictates and constitutional freedoms; between an "acceptable" number of deaths and family economies and international relations; between compassion and the Darwinian/Herbert Spencer ideas of survival of the fittest.

Source: Alex Wong via Getty Images

and are still being litigated in the courts. Biden navigated his first year in office without scandal or lawsuits but his falling poll numbers inflation, and the inability to corral the virus hurt Democratic chances to win in 2022 and 2024 (Illustration 0.4).

Democracy at the Crossroads takes clear perspectives on difficult discussions. Chapter 1 offers an important synthesis of American history over time, providing contextual complexity for the chapters that follow. Chapter 2 takes a geopolitical and sociological approach to the establishment of regions by immigrants from varying cultural nationalities. Chapters 3 and 4 explain the structure of American government and unravel the efforts by political parties to gain and retain power in an ever-polarized

9

Contemporary United States

Illustration 0.5 Democracy at the Crossroads: The Flag Is Bleeding, Dangerously

To illustrate the complex interdependencies of the issues and themes of all ten chapters in Democracy at the Crossroads, this painting is worth considering. The struggle for democracy in America began in the British colonies of the seventeenth and eighteenth centuries when colonists demanded representation in London, in Parliament, and pressed for the equal "Rights of Englishmen." It took an American Revolution and Constitution, 1776–1789, to secure the rights for resident white men over twenty-one years old. For 230 years, the basic law has been amended to include suffrage rights for black men, women, Native Americans, minority groups, immigrants, and the 18+ group. In the painting by Harlem, NY, artist Faith Ringgold, in the genre of "super Realism," the civil rights struggles of the 1960s reverberate in our own times. The American flag is transparent or opaque and is both protector and jailor. Three individuals are interlocked and looking out at us as they struggle and cooperate simultaneously. We see/feel violence, patriotism, compassion. The flag, representing much, is bleeding, and the people are wounded yet unblinking and resolute. They seem urgently to want something, to explain something. They want us to do something. It is not too late. This Minority Everyman, Everywoman, and White Everyman seek a way past their own histories and the restrictions of color and sex to stop the bleeding and to advance a social-justice agenda that reduces white privilege and advances black lives and women too, together. Ringgold's masterpiece echoes the realities of contemporary America and the search for the soul of American democracy.

Source: © Faith Ringgold / ARS, NY and DACS, London, Courtesy ACA Galleries, New York 2022

partisan system. Chapters 5 through 7 look into the contours of society, culture, and subcultures with statistics and trends focusing on families, class, race, gender, and generational differences. Religion, criminal justice, education, social welfare, sports, and social media are discussed at length. Chapter 8 focuses on economics, finance, capitalism, and the makeup and divisions in the American workforce. Chapter 9 expands into the international arena in a changing global order marked by a lost and then found cohesion in the EU, the spectacular gains by China, and the strained bonds of great power relationships affected by threats of terrorism, pandemics, environmental disasters, economic downturns, and the Russian war against Ukraine. Chapter 10 provides a leap into future possibilities.

Further Reading

Boyle, K. (2021) *The Shattering: America in the 1960s*, New York: W. W. Norton.
Didion, J. (2017) *Slouching Towards Bethlehem*, London: 4th Estate.
Gessen, M. (2020) *Surviving Autocracy*, New York: Riverhead.
Gitlin, T. (1995) *The Twilight of Common Dreams: Why America Is Wracked by Culture Wars*, New York: Henry Holt.
Gitlin, T. (2012) *Occupy Nation: The Roots, the Spirit, and the Promise of Occupy Wall Street*, New York: HarperCollins.
Hartman, A. (2015) *A War for the Soul of America: A History of the Culture Wars*, Chicago: University of Chicago Press.
Karl, J. (2021) *Betrayal: Final Act of the Trump Show*, New York: Dutton.
Mounk, Y. (2022) *The Great Experiment: Why Diverse Democracies Fall Apart and How They Can Endure*, London: Penguin.
Osnos, E. (2021) *Wildland: The Making of America's Fury*, New York: Gerard, Straus, & Giroux.
Snyder, T. (2017) *On Tyranny: Twenty Lessons from the Twentieth Century*, London: Penguin Random House.

CHAPTER 1
HISTORY

The 1619 Project, Critical Race Theory, and the 1776 Commission

Historians attempt to construct a useful narrative that is as fact-based as possible in a world of multiple viewpoints and complex ambiguities. Historians' findings do not please everyone. Many Americans do not like inconvenient memories, facts, or a history of collective cultural failures. They prefer the national story to be a heroic narrative of success, liberty, and justice for all.

In 2016 and 2020, Americans examined their high school textbooks and increasingly made a war on history. The textbooks were liberal, inclusive, and often ambivalent on discussions about slavery, gender discrimination, sexuality, class struggle, the fights for voting rights, failures in civil rights, imperialism, and the connection of community values with individual self-interest (Snyder, 2021). These issues quickly became political fights in an era when the national conversation about race was heightened by the murder of George Floyd by a white policeman, the rise of BlackLivesMatter (#BLM), and the continued killings of black men by public police forces and private vigilantes. The #MeToo movement joined the conversation by stressing the misogyny and sexual assaults by males and the fact that African American and other minority women are doubly victimized by the intersection of being non-white and female—or even face triple discrimination because so many of them are poor.

With the Republican Party composed of high percentages of white male voters who elected Trump and with Democrats usually having 85 percent or more of the African American and a large percentage of the ethnic minority vote, the debates over textbooks centered on the place of race and racism in the national story. Liberals endorsed a "1619 Project" to mark the date the first African slaves were brought to the British colony of Virginia (Illustration 1.1). Supporters believed that American history needed revision to reflect the fact that the country originated in slavery and racism and thus was something more than the patriotic narrative of white European immigrants finding and founding a new nation based on freedom (Jones, 2021b; Silverstein, 2021). Closely tied to this project and to incidents of racial violence, particularly the killing of George Floyd, 312 Confederate symbols and monuments were taken down by order of mayors, governors, or federal officers (SPLC, 2021).

President Trump responded with a "1776 Commission" to promote the restoration of a "patriotic education," freedom, and white nationalism. Trump denied the central

Contemporary United States

Illustration 1.1 Slavery is Not Marginal to American History

The "Ancestor Project" is a series of sculptures by Ghanaian artist Kwame Akoato-Bamfo which realistically portrays the machinery of slavery and resistance as his ancestors were captured, chained, and transported to America. On display at The National Memorial for Peace and Justice in Montgomery, Alabama, the sculpture is a strong statement of humanity among the slaves in the thralls of inhumanity by white slave traders and owners involved in the transatlantic slave trade. The National Memorial is the first and only memorial centered on enslavement, terror, lynchings, institutional segregation, and police violence. It opened in 2018 and quickly merged with efforts to embrace Critical Race Theory (CRT), #BlackLivesMatter, Voting Rights movements, the removal of Confederate monuments and slaveholding politicians from public spaces across the United States, the 1619 Project, and, in 2021, to bring about a new federal holiday, Juneteenth, to celebrate the emancipation of American slaves. The chains on the slaves rhyme in the metal handcuffs placed on the wrists of George Floyd, the circle around Biden, and the kneeling by NFL players depicted in Illustrations 0.3, 7.1, and 7.3.

Source: Raymond Boyd/Michael Ochs Archives via Getty Images

role of slavery and explained that "Critical race theory, the 1619 Project and the crusade against American history is toxic propaganda, ideological poison that, if not removed, will dissolve the civic bonds that tie us together" (Snyder, 2021).

When Biden took office in 2021, he immediately disbanded Trump's commission. But the battle continued as Republican politicians encouraged their voters to demonstrate against local school boards. Republican governors and state legislatures in twenty-seven states banned "divisive concepts" and allowed only readings and texts that upheld "the legacy of 1776" (Silverstein, 2021). Florida was the first state to enact a law making it illegal to teach about racism or discrimination against any group over time.

Conservatives insisted that discrimination is personal prejudice by an individual, not a systemic institutional problem (Snyder, 2021). That claim led more than 150 professional organizations to defend CRT, including the Society of Civil War Historians, the National Education Association, the American History Association, and the Organization of American Historians. Professional historians overwhelmingly agreed that teaching civics and the national story are important, but asked: "Should we set aside the best scholarship in favor of a unifying myth? Is history a science or a patriotic art? Should we reduce history to hero worship?" (Silverstein, 2021).

The Past as Prologue

Academics acknowledge that history is as convincing as it is contestable. The identity politics in the 1960s have been expanded on and joined to light-speed information access on internet sites since the 1990s and social media sites of the twenty-first century. Opinions are often confused with facts and there is a vast amount of conflicting information. Exemplifying this problem, annually, the *Oxford English Dictionary* (OED) and *Miriam-Webster's Dictionary* (MWD) select their "word of the year." It is instructive to consider the top words for the two latest presidential election years. In 2016 the OED picked "post truth" and the MWD went with "surreal." In 2020 MWD settled on "pandemic" and noted its Latin stem relationship to "democracy"—both of which affect "the people" (*dem*). The OED did not pick a single word in 2020 but offered up the following list: "Black Lives Matter," "cancel culture," "Critical Race Theory," "Coronavirus," "lockdown," "social distancing," "ZOOM," "mask," and "defund (the police)," among others. These words, except "ZOOM," quickly fed into finger-pointing partisan politics.

In 1941, President Franklin Roosevelt said that "past is prologue" and championed the preservation of historical documents because, he said, "… a Nation must believe in three things. It must believe in the past. It must believe in the future. It must, above all, believe in the capacity of its own people so to learn from the past that they can gain in judgment in creating their own future" (Roosevelt, 1941). In 2017, historian Timothy Snyder, an expert on the Second World War, Nazis, and Eastern Europe, wrote *On Tyranny: Twenty Lessons from the Twentieth Century* to remind us that to deny history and facts are the tactics of fascism. Snyder wrote that "history does not repeat, but it does instruct." He warned: "The European history of the twentieth century shows us that societies can break, democracies can fall, ethics can collapse, and ordinary men can find themselves standing over death pits with guns in their hands" (Snyder, 2017: 9, 12).

American history is long, reaching back to at least 10,000 years ago when the first group of humans struggled into the interior of a continent to become Native Americans. If dated from the Declaration of Independence in 1776, United States history is short—not yet 250 years old—and it is common for someone alive today to talk with people who remember Franklin Roosevelt and the 1930s, who, in turn, had known ex-slaves who could tell them firsthand about Frederick Douglass, Abraham Lincoln, and the 1860s, and who had known people who had shaken hands with Thomas Jefferson. Five people

Contemporary United States

linked together cover the entire life span of the United States, a nation born in modern times with a fast and furious history. There are rarer examples that compress the time gap to just three people. For example, in 2020, the grandson of President John Tyler (born in 1790) was alive, and Dan Smith, at eighty-eight, was the living son of a Virginia slave (born in 1864) (Brockwell, 2020; Trent 2020). This idea of history as present tense was succinctly described by novelist William Faulkner: "yesterday today and tomorrow are Is: Indivisible: One" (Faulkner, 1948: 194).

One thousand years or more before Europeans stumbled upon America, Pueblo Indians built their houses into high cliffs to protect themselves from their enemies, the Apaches (see Illustration 2.3). The Makah in Washington State had a highly developed culture based on salmon fishing. By 1492, the year of Italian navigator Christopher Columbus's "discovery" of a New World, between 10 and 50 million First Peoples already lived in what would become the United States.

On the eve of discovery, Europe had been transformed by the rise of nation-states, which were influenced by the twelfth-century Crusades' stimulation of commercial activities and an interchange of technology. Trade revolutionized commerce, changed the system from barter to coinage, and built banking houses, joint-stock companies, and cities. The Renaissance emphasized discovery and science, and the Protestant Reformation stressed individual freedom, and ignited competition and wars with Catholics. European mercantilist nations competed to control trade. Each needed a strong military and a rich treasury, which could be achieved through a favorable balance of trade, war and conquest, and colonies whose settlers fed raw materials to the mother countries.

As Europeans competed to colonize the New World, Native Americans became active participants in a web of commercial relations that made them into producers and consumers in a developing world market. While trade transformed cultures, disease wiped them out. The accumulated knowledge of the tribes was lost when the elders died and the death of the medicine men broke the spiritual edifice of Indian life. Contact with whites killed 90 percent of all Indians as pandemics of typhoid, influenza, smallpox, and tuberculosis took their toll. Many hoped for salvation by accepting the Christ thrust at them by missionaries. This trinity of trade, pandemics, and Christianity put Native American societies on the edge of oblivion.

The Rise of a Nation

Colonial America, 1607–1763

America was born in violence and change as Europeans fought Indians and each other for control of the land. World markets shaped development in terms of shipping, agricultural production, industry, and workforce. England established a line of colonies from Maine to Georgia. In 1607, Jamestown, Virginia, was financed by a joint-stock company and soldiered by professional mercenaries. Soon, immigrants were growing tobacco for the

European market. In 1619, a Dutch ship sold twenty Africans into indentured servitude in Virginia—an event that resonates in contemporary America as the "1619 Project" and puts the black experience at the center of the discussion of democracy and freedom. Soon, British, French, Portuguese, Spanish, Danish, and Dutch empires grew rich from the profits of the international slave trade. As cash crops expanded and workers were needed, plantation owners embraced racial slavery. By the time of the American Revolution, one of every five Americans was a slave (Indians excluded).

In 1620, religious dissenters who wanted to separate from the Anglican Church settled Plymouth Colony in Massachusetts. Indian tribes quickly developed trading ties with these Pilgrims and introduced them to corn, beans, turkeys, squash, and potatoes. Legend has it that the locals and the newcomers celebrated a huge feast in November 1621—the story behind the purest American holiday, Thanksgiving.

Other dissenters—in a group of 1,000 people aboard seventeen ships—who wanted to purify the Church of England arrived in Massachusetts in 1630. These Puritans engaged in an "errand into the wilderness" to establish a utopian religious community, a shining model for England and the world. Puritan leader John Winthrop defined the colony "as a city upon a hill. The eyes of all people are upon us." The Puritans were perfectionists who demanded order. They were so intent on living righteously in an evil world that they became intolerant and, in 1692, the excesses of the infamous Salem witch trials— marked as they were by community hysteria, the fear of women, rural–urban conflicts, and, simply, cultural change—highlighted the failure of the Puritan errand. And yet, American society owes much to Puritan patterns. Witch hunts fit neatly into the conspiracy theories of runaway government, fear of outsiders, border walls, or internal communist threats, and most Americans believe that the US is a chosen nation with a founding mission to enlighten the world. Insisting that hard work is its own reward, the Protestant work ethic is essential to capitalism. Higher education remains the best path to the American dream. The Puritans founded Harvard University in 1636.

Between 1660 and 1763, the colonies developed differently as immigrants created transnational and multicultural societies. The population increased rapidly from the steady arrival of European immigrants, African slave importation, and natural increase. There was a baby boom as families formed earlier due to the availability of land and need for labor. In England, the average marrying age for women was twenty-three; in America, nineteen. With every colonial woman giving birth to an average of seven children, the population reached 100,000 in 1660; by 1775, there were 2.5 million people, one-third of them native born.

Slavery has been the central paradox of American history and is linked to the rise of liberty and equality in America and the soothing of class conflict among whites. When Euro-Americans enslaved Africans, liberty expanded for white males (Morgan, 1995). Colonists transplanted social class hierarchies to the colonies, but as skin color began to mark caste, poorer whites demanded an expansion of voting rights and landholding privileges to which males could unite.

From 1734 to 1755, a populist evangelical revival swept through the colonies on the heels of Jonathan Edwards's sermon about "Sinners in the Hands of an Angry God,"

Contemporary United States

and Methodist cleric George Whitefield's colony-by-colony salvation tour. This Great Awakening was the first all-American cultural event, and it appealed to the Protestant sense of individual responsibility and anti-authoritarianism. This revival led many colonials to question the authority England was exerting over the colonies.

The American Revolution and the Constitution

While the colonies prospered, Britain engaged in a struggle for supremacy with Spain and France. In the Great War for Empire (also called the "French and Indian War"), 1754–1763, a victorious Britain gained Canada, all French possessions east of the Mississippi River, and Florida. With her rivals neutralized, the king tightened controls. Parliament increased taxes to pay the enormous war debt and from stationing 10,000 soldiers along the frontier to deter Indian attacks. The taxes took many forms and the colonists responded bitterly to every one of them. Staging riots and breaking laws, colonists claimed the "rights of Englishmen" to "no taxation without representation." Colonials adopted a conspiracy theory first advanced by English Whigs during the Glorious Revolution of 1688, and Thomas Jefferson argued that taxes and other recent events proved, "a deliberate, systematical plot of reducing us to slavery" (quoted in Wood, 1969).

Jefferson was just thirty-three years old when, in 1776, as a delegate from Virginia to the Second Continental Congress in Philadelphia, he wrote The Declaration of Independence (Box 1.1). The idea of revolution was not new, but the acts of a people, in an orderly manner, explaining and justifying their rights and establishing a new government was unprecedented. Jefferson was the first philosopher to place sovereignty, not just rights, in the people. The people had the power to create the government and the people had the power to tear it down. The war for independence lasted until 1783 when colonials under General George Washington, with crucial aid from France, prevailed. America became the first European colony to separate from its mother country.

After a brief period of ineffective government, a convention of delegates assembled in 1787 to write a document that British Prime Minister William Gladstone later praised as "the most wonderful work ever struck off at a given time by the brain and purpose of man" (quoted in Kammen, 1987: 162). The Constitution of the United States of America set up a federal system which shared power between the national government and the states and, ultimately, with the people. Because Americans feared central power, it took two years of intensive lobbying to convince the states to ratify the Constitution. This was accomplished by adding ten amendments, the "Bill of Rights," to protect individual liberty in ways that astonished European liberals and frightened monarchists. In 1789, the new government met in the nation's capital, New York City, and acclaimed George Washington president. Europeans were quickly distracted when Frenchmen stormed the Bastille. Acknowledging America's role in fomenting those events, the Marquis de Lafayette sent Washington the key to that prison. The liberal Enlightenment project of

Box 1.1 Excerpt from *The Declaration of Independence*

When in the course of human events, it becomes necessary for one people to dissolve the political bands which have connected them with another, and to assume among the Powers of the earth, the separate and equal station to which the Laws of Nature and of Nature's God entitle them, a decent respect to the opinions of mankind requires that they should declare the causes which impel them to the separation.

We hold these truths to be self-evident, that all men are created equal, that they are endowed by their Creator with certain unalienable rights, that among these are Life, Liberty, and the pursuit of Happiness. That to secure these rights, Governments are instituted among Men, deriving their just powers from the consent of the governed. That whenever any Form of Government becomes destructive of these ends, it is the Right of the People to alter or to abolish it, and to institute new Government, laying its foundation on such principles and organizing its powers in such form, as to them shall seem most likely to effect their Safety and Happiness. Prudence, indeed, will dictate that Governments long established should not be changed for light and transient causes; and accordingly all experience hath shown, that mankind are more disposed to suffer, while evils are sufferable, than to right themselves by abolishing the forms to which they are accustomed. But when a long train of abuses and usurpations, pursuing invariably the same Object evinces a design to reduce them under absolute Despotism, it is their right, it is their duty, to throw off such Government, and to provide new Guards for their future security …

We, therefore, the Representatives of the United States of America, in General Congress, Assembled, appealing to the Supreme Judge of the world for the rectitude of our intentions, do, in the Name, and by Authority of the good People of these Colonies, solemnly publish and declare, That these United Colonies are, and of Right ought to be free and independent states; that they are Absolved from all Allegiance to the British Crown, and that all political connection between them and the State of Great Britain, is and ought to be totally dissolved; and that as Free and Independent States, they have full Power to levy War, conclude Peace, contract Alliances, establish Commerce, and to do all other Acts and Things which Independent States may of right do. And for the support of this Declaration, with a firm reliance on the Protection of Divine Providence, we mutually pledge to each other our Lives, our Fortunes, and our sacred Honor.

(Thomas Jefferson, 1776)

Contemporary United States

expanding democracy throughout Europe and defeating authoritarianism throughout the world had its first major victories.

In 1793, when England again declared war on France, Washington immediately invoked neutrality. Americans were busy at home. Political parties had formed, dividing the supporters of stronger national power in the Federalist Party from the supporters of state power, Democratic-Republicans. By 1800, the population increased to 5.3 million, three new states had been added to the Union, and the value of exports was $71 million compared with $20 million in 1790. Twenty colleges had been established, there were 200 newspapers, and the technology of the cotton gin had increased production of "white gold" from 1.5 million to 36.5 million pounds in a decade—and with it, the demand for slaves. The country split between a free labor system in the North and a slave system in the South. Symbolizing the intersection of competing social systems, in 1800 Congress relocated the nation's capital to the District of Columbia—an area set free of the boundaries of any state—and named the city, Washington. The long war between England and France continued to disrupt the economy. In 1812, after the British seized American ships and impressed American sailors into the British navy, President James Madison declared war on England. The British burned Washington, DC, and during the siege of Baltimore, Maryland, Francis Scott Key wrote a poem, "The Star-Spangled Banner," that would become the US national anthem. The war was basically a drawn contest with the peace treaty ratified in 1815.

Westward Expansion and Reform

The nineteenth century was marked by the violence, power, and labor of territorial expansion (Map 1.1). In 1803, President Jefferson doubled the size of the United States by purchasing the Louisiana Territory from Napoleon. The US also purchased Florida from Spain in 1819.

By 1821, eight new states had entered the Union. And while the Northern states abolished slavery, white Southerners held tightly to their way of life. Jefferson, a prominent slaveholder, offered an apology that the institution was a necessary evil. He likened slavery to holding "the wolf by the ears." You don't like it, but you don't dare let it go (quoted in McPherson, 1982: 39). The principal American philosopher for freedom and equality clung to his slaves throughout his life as economic considerations trumped moral values. That collision of interests resonates strongly in contemporary America.

By 1838, all the eastern Indian tribes had been forced onto reservations west of the Mississippi River even though the US Supreme Court (SCOTUS) had ruled in favor of Indian sovereignty against state interventions. President Andrew Jackson, a noted slave trader and Indian killer, refused to enforce the judicial ruling—and in the most famous atrocity, 15,000 Cherokees were forcibly marched from Georgia to Indian territory in Oklahoma. Four thousand died along this "trail of tears." Complicating the land struggles, the area from Texas to California was claimed by Mexico, which had won its independence from Spain in 1821. In 1845, President James K. Polk, a fervent imperialist, proclaimed that the country should fill its natural boundaries and reach its

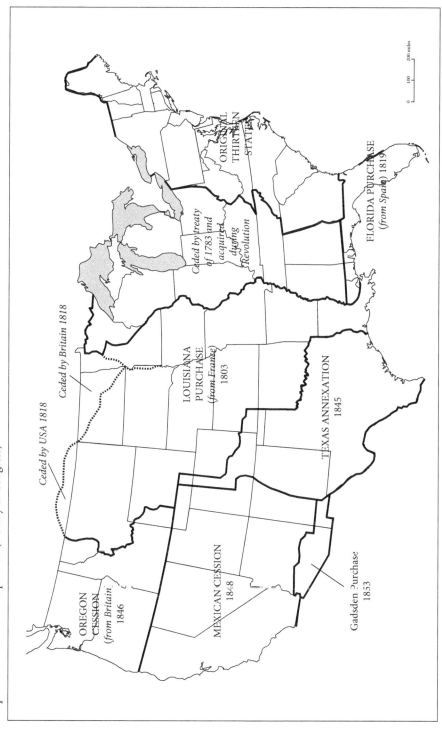

Map 1.1 US Territorial Expansion (Library of Congress)

Illustration 1.2 Manifest Destiny Crosses the Plains

Alternately titled "American Progress" and "Westward the Course of Empire," this 1872 illustration by John Gast captures the myth of the frontier and American expansion across the continent. Columbia—the female spirit of America—accompanies the explorers, covered wagon pioneers, communication and transportation systems, and pioneer farmers as they move westward. Her whiteness, the star in her headband to symbolize a new state and star in the American flag as she moves along, the power of floating barefoot as an angel or guiding spirit, and the Greco-Roman toga speak to the hierarchies of race, European background, and spread of Christianity. All Indians, buffalo, other wild "beasts," and the dark clouds retreat in the face of "civilization" as the "light" arrives to conquer the darkness. "Manifest" in being directed by God for his chosen nation. "Destiny" as future promise for success.

Source: Fotosearch/Stringer via Getty Images

"Manifest Destiny" of stretching from the Atlantic to the Pacific oceans (Illustration 1.2). The US absorbed Texas and, from 1846 to 1848, made war on Mexico, won, and took all Mexican land north of the Rio Grande. Then Polk bullied England into ceding the entire Northwest (part of Oregon territory) below the 49th latitude, thereby establishing the national border with Canada. The US bought a strip of land from Mexico in 1853 and reached its present size, excluding Alaska, Hawaii, and various small offshore possessions.

Rapid growth led to discussions concerning the social fabric. Reformers advocated institutional uplift. Workingmen's associations pulled laborers together. Most middle-class women supported a conservative ideology of separate spheres which posited that women should stay in the home and let men deal with the world. More progressive women argued for equality. Margaret Fuller's *Woman in the Nineteenth Century* (1844) helped inspire the first Women's Rights Convention (1848) at Seneca Falls, New York, where the delegates declared "All men and women are created equal." A temperance movement arose linking poverty and family violence with "Demon Rum" and called for bans, but not prohibition, on alcohol.

The Industrial Revolution reshaped the workplace and the market economy in the North to the demands of industrial capitalism, an agrarian empire was rising in the West, and a cotton kingdom ruled the South. Differing from the South, the North and West were becoming less Anglo-American and more Euro-American as immigrants poured in. Inventors pulled the country together with steamboats, railroads, and telegraph lines. Cities grew rapidly, especially New York City, whose population exceeded 200,000 in 1830, 1.1 million in 1860, and 4.8 million in 1900.

In politics, the Federalists were replaced by a party that soon called itself Whigs and favored stronger economic mercantilism. The Democratic-Republicans became the Democratic Party. The Democrats had a wider base but were weakened by their pro-slavery stance and emphasis "that slavery was a positive good." In 1854, the Whigs were replaced by the Republican Party, which organized a nationalist platform of antislavery to stop the extension of slavery into western lands. The Democratic and Republican parties—although greatly changed—have anchored the nation's two-party system ever since.

The American Civil War

In 1860, the election of the Republican antislavery advocate Abraham Lincoln so enraged the South that before he could take office in March 1861, there were seven—soon eleven—fewer states in the Union. The Southerners did not try to stop his inauguration because they recognized that he had legally won the election. Instead, they seceded. The Confederate States of America (CSA) formed a nation composed of South Carolina, Mississippi, Louisiana, Texas, Florida, Alabama, Georgia, Virginia, Arkansas, North Carolina, and Tennessee (Illustration 1.3). Many people hoped that Lincoln would let the states depart in peace, but he was firm in his conviction that the union could not be dissolved.

The crises were many. A constitutional crisis arose over the sovereignty question of state versus national power, of a written commitment to liberty and slavery, and of how to convert territories into states. A social crisis inherent in having the population double every twenty-five years since the 1700s and the reformist impulse of the abolitionist movement to improve the lot of slaves, women, Native Americans, and immigrants split communities. Economic interests questioned whether the transcontinental railroad should connect California with a southern or a northern terminus—the route picked would either spread slavery or free labor—and debated whether Southerners had the right to take slave "property" into the free states. A religious crisis split Protestant churches as abolitionists could not tolerate being in the same denomination as slaveholders, and vice versa. A moral crisis cast a hypocritical shadow over the contradiction in human bondage and the words of the Declaration of Independence that "all men are created equal."

Contemporary United States

Illustration 1.3 The Central Problem of White Supremacy

On January 6, 2021, a mostly white and male middle-class army of insurgents surged down Pennsylvania Avenue in Washington, DC, following their attendance at the "Stop the Steal" rally at the White House. Trump had given them instructions to go to the US Capitol and give strength to the weak Republicans to refuse the Electoral College count certifying Biden's win. Trump incited the crowd: "If you don't fight like hell, you're not going to have a country anymore." After physically assaulting policeman and breaking into the Capitol, thousands of protesters—some of them with clubs, knives, and other weapons—searched for legislators to threaten and maybe even to "hang Mike Pence." In one terrible and revealing image, a jubilant Trump activist parades a Confederate flag through the Senate lobby. The painting to the left of the protester is of US Senator and Secretary of State John C. Calhoun, the author of the pro-slavery argument that insisted on white supremacy and the humane moral value of slavery "as a positive good" for African laborers. The painting to the right is of US Senator Charles Sumner of Massachusetts. Sumner was a leading voice for the abolition of slavery. In 1856, US Representative Preston Brooks used a cane to club Sumner unconscious and near death for his efforts to free the slaves. The conflict between Calhoun and Sumner exemplified the central point of slavery and white supremacy in the coming of the American Civil War (1861–1865). The bust to the right is of President Richard Nixon. Nixon used a racist "Southern Strategy" to bring white voters into the Republican Party in 1968 and push minority voters toward the Democrats. Nixon's strategy was a model for Trump's rhetoric and political partisanship.

Source: SAUL LOEB/AFP via Getty Images

And then war came. The fighting lasted four years and more than 620,000 Americans died. It was a modern war with huge armies, rifled weaponry, forced enrolments, and widespread civilian casualties. Lincoln's speeches—the "Emancipation Proclamation" and his "Gettysburg Address" (Box 1.2)—are two of the most revered expressions of

Box 1.2 *The Gettysburg Address*

Four score and seven years ago our fathers brought forth on this continent, a new nation, conceived in Liberty, and dedicated to the proposition that all men are created equal. Now we are engaged in a great civil war, testing whether that nation, or any nation so conceived and so dedicated, can long endure. We are met on a great battle-field of that war. We have come to dedicate a portion of that field, as a final resting place for those who here gave their lives that that nation might live. It is altogether fitting and proper that we should do this. But, in a larger sense, we can not dedicate—we can not consecrate—we can not hallow—this ground. The brave men, living and dead, who struggled here, have consecrated it, far above our poor power to add or detract. The world will little note, nor long remember what we say here, but it can never forget what they did here. It is for us the living, rather, to be dedicated here to the unfinished work which they who fought here have thus far so nobly advanced. It is rather for us to be here dedicated to the great task remaining before us—that from these honored dead we take increased devotion to that cause for which they gave their last full measure of devotion—that we here highly resolve that these dead shall not have died in vain—that this nation, under God, shall have a new birth of freedom—and that government of the people, by the people, for the people, shall not perish from the earth.

(Abraham Lincoln, 1863)

American freedom, equality, and new beginnings. The "Gettysburg Address" uses biblical language, a progression of tenses from past to present, birth and rebirth metaphors, and Lincoln's contention that if America fails, freedom will fail.

The Rise to Power

Of Race and Frontiers

With the war over, the national government consolidated power and Americans changed a key verb. Before the war and in recognition of the power of the states, people used the plural form: "The United States are ...." After the war, with the nation achieved, they substituted the singular form: "The United States is ...." In 1867, the US purchased Alaska from Russia. The government sought to reconstruct the South in the national image. Three constitutional amendments (13th, 14th, 15th)—during the period called Reconstruction—freed the slaves, provided citizenship, and gave the vote to black men.

Southern whites responded by requiring literacy tests and poll taxes for voting, leasing convicts to private individuals, refusing to allow blacks to sit on juries, and organizing the white supremacist organization, the Ku Klux Klan. In 1877, Southern resistance had exhausted government efforts and led President Rutherford B. Hayes to end

Contemporary United States

Reconstruction and announce that the South would be left alone to deal with its "negro problem." By the 1890s, lynch mobs murdered over a hundred African Americans a year and courts sentenced many blacks to prison on the flimsiest evidence. SCOTUS ruled in the case of *Plessy v. Ferguson* (1896) that "separate but equal" school rooms, hospitals, libraries, hotel accommodations, and streetcars were legal under the Constitution. The nation was officially segregated.

During the last quarter of the nineteenth century, the government helped itself, railroad interests, and homesteaders to the land Indian tribes had believed to be theirs "as long as the wind blows, as long as the grass grows, as long as the rivers flow." The first transcontinental railroad connecting San Francisco with New York City was completed in 1869, and the government's resolve to finish the Indian wars was accelerated by an event that occurred during the nation's centennial celebration. In late June 1876, along the Little Big Horn River in Montana territory, a brash army colonel set out to destroy a group of Native Americans. Surprised by one of the largest concentrations of tribes in the history of the West, George Armstrong Custer and some 250 men were killed by the forces of Sitting Bull, Crazy Horse, and Rain-in-the-Face. Whites sought revenge. To destroy Indian resistance and culture—and to profit from the skins—professional hunters killed nearly 30 million buffaloes. The Indian wars ended in 1886.

The West belonged to the white man. Laws allowed homesteaders to settle on 160 acres, without cost, if they would cultivate the land. Settlers built little houses on the prairie and began farming. Railroad companies received enormous subsidies in the form of land grants, an area equal to one-sixth of all Western lands. Timber and mining companies were soon cutting and digging everywhere. During the cowboy era, herds of cattle were driven from the grazing fields in Texas to slaughterhouses in the Midwest.

In 1893, Frederick Jackson Turner's "frontier thesis" argued that the availability of free land had shaped American democracy and institutions (Turner, 1966). The frontier was the crucible where the American traits of individualism and acquisitiveness originated. While this is a contentious claim ignoring women, slaves, Indians, and immigrants of color, the myth is a central touchstone in the American imagination.

The Gilded Age

By 1900, the United States had built one-third of all the railroad mileage in the world. Railroad companies merged with investment banking firms and large corporate law firms to help create modern managerial capitalism. John D. Rockefeller's oil company and Andrew Carnegie's steel factories led the way by integrating production processes to control all aspects of the production of a single product (vertical integration) or to gain a monopoly over a single step in production (horizontal integration). In fact, developments sped along so fast that the industrialists and bankers, who saw themselves as "industrial statesmen," were seen to be "robber barons" to the general public. Writer Mark Twain called the period *The Gilded Age* (1873). Corrupt politicians built political machines to enrich themselves and to decide who should count which votes (Illustration 1.4). The

History

Illustration 1.4 One of History's Rhymes: Gilded Age Politics and Boss Tweed

At the beginning of what historians call the Gilded Age, William M. Tweed headed the NYC Democratic Party machine and gained the sobriquet "Boss Tweed" for his authoritarian and corrupt practices. He pandered to his base and operated as a cult leader. Tweed banked on his great wealth and insisted on pledges of loyalty from those he awarded patronage positions in city-wide offices. He paid off lawyers and police officials with "dark money." He bought and sold properties and became the third-largest owner of real estate in New York. His "Tweed Ring" used the Democratic Party as a gang to steal a sum reported at $200 million from taxpayers. The political cartoonist and journalist Thomas Nast brought down Tweed with a number of brave and pointed drawings highlighting Tweed's crimes and lack of stewardship for the people of New York. The two cartoons above depict Tweed's control over the ballot box. Tweed says, "As long as I count the Votes, what are you going to do about it?" Tweed was finally jailed, and died in prison, for the bribery and corruption he committed "Right Under Her Nose (New York's 'Justice' system) Every Day of the Week." Quoting Mark Twain, sociologist Todd Gitlin said that "history does not repeat, but it rhymes" in our own times. Trump's wealth, interests, control of his party, cult leadership, demands for loyalty, and charges of bribery and corruption highlight a "New Gilded Age" that Boss Tweed would recognize.

Source: Library of Congress/Interim Archives via Getty Images and Kean Collection via Getty Images

growth of huge industry, big cities, and commerce looked golden; but to scratch off the gold revealed the rawness of base metal.

The philosophy of the marketplace reflected the era's conservative free-market principles. This laissez-faire approach stressed self-sufficiency and self-interest with only limited governmental regulation, excepting tariff protection in international trade. The American creed of equal opportunity contributed to this, but so did the belief in natural selection and evolutionary change put forth by Charles Darwin and adapted into a philosophy of Social Darwinism that natural laws govern people's place in society. Herbert Spencer labeled this "survival of the fittest." Then, William Graham Sumner advanced the belief that the acquisition of private property was the most important goal for individuals. Carnegie promoted this "Gospel of Wealth" and agreed that any government interference—such as welfare or health care—hindered progress because in any free society operating under evolutionary principles, wealth and power would naturally go to those most deserving of it. This belief in private enterprise over public responsibility stresses the highly contested idea of "merit" and is seen in conservative initiatives in the twenty-first century.

Others longed for a more equitable distribution of wealth. As they have done throughout their history—in alternating cycles of liberal reforms and conservative retrenchments—Americans made adjustments. A new investigative journalism—"muckraking"—led the way as Americans searched for order, called for government action, and reformed society in the face of unprecedented immigration, industrialization, and urbanization. While maintaining white supremacy, reformers helped to ameliorate the problems of cities with pragmatic attempts to redistribute wealth, expand social services, and expand the middle class for whites. Rising wealth led to rising expectations.

The rural lifestyle of the nineteenth century gave way to the roaring urban machinery of the twentieth. In 1890, the same year that industries first earned more profits than farmlands, rural Americans formed the Populist Party to fight back. Populists favored an expansion of the money supply as one way to redistribute wealth, a graduated income tax so that the more you made the more you paid, nationalization of railroads in order to lower prices for farm products, voting reforms—including the secret ballot—to ensure democracy, and an eight-hour workday to protect laborers. Meeting the usual fate of third parties in American history, the Populist Party died in 1896. Its ideas survived and many were enacted into law during the Progressive Era.

The Progressive Era

Vast geopolitical economic resources made the United States the richest country in the world. Americans produced more than one-third of the world's coal, iron, and steel. Only Britain and Germany had bigger navies. And yet, America reflected a nervousness as patriots watched European imperialists divide Africa among themselves. Applying Darwinian ideas to nations, Americans viewed the United States as a superior race/nation which had the right to expand over lesser peoples/nations in the survival of the fittest. In 1898, in a war with Spain, the US spanned the Pacific and treated the Caribbean Sea like an American lake by taking the Philippines, Puerto Rico, and Guam, and establishing a base at Guantánamo Bay, Cuba. A flag cult arose with the ritual of standing for the playing of "The Star-Spangled Banner" and student recitation of the "Pledge of Allegiance" (Box 1.3) every day in school.

By 1910, six American cities had populations exceeding one million people. Massive overcrowding led to sanitation, sewage, and garbage problems. Economic competition flared up as every new wave of immigrants worked for whatever wages they could get, with wages kept low by the constant arrival of new workers. "Fresh-off-the-boat" immigrants sought out others of their own national origin and created ethnic enclaves with ethnic economies, including Little Italy, Little Norway, Little Russia, and Little Poland. Chinese, Koreans, African Americans, and others formed into ghettos of their own.

Box 1.3 The Pledge of Allegiance

I pledge allegiance to the flag of the United States of America, and to the Republic for which it stands, one nation [under God], indivisible, with liberty and justice for all.

Note: The Pledge was written by Francis Bellamy for the 1892 Columbian Exposition in Chicago. Congress adopted it officially in 1942 and added the words "under God" in 1954. In 2002, a federal court ruled the words unconstitutional by provisions separating church and state. President Bush defiantly responded: "no authority of government can ever prevent an American from pledging allegiance to this one nation under God" (Oppel, 2002). In 2004, the US Supreme Court reversed the decision by citing the Pledge as a patriotic oath, not a religious prayer.

Between 1890 and 1920, millions of non-English-speaking peoples from Southern and Eastern Europe entered America through the new federal immigration facility built in 1892 on Ellis Island in New York harbor. Towering over them stood the Statue of Liberty. This "Mother of Exiles" had been a gift from France in 1886. A plaque at the base proclaimed:

Give me your tired, your poor,
Your huddled masses yearning to breathe free
The wretched refuse of your teeming shore
Send these, the homeless, tempest-tossed to me,
I lift my lamp beside the golden door.

Activists, called progressives, instituted reforms. Instead of competitive Social Darwinism, these liberals promoted Social Gospel ideas of community first, individuals second. Social reformers achieved improvements in housing, labor, and health services. Structural reformers improved streetcar lines, railroads, state prison systems, and established a comprehensive school system. State legislators increased personal income taxes and taxed corporations for the first time. Labor inspectors monitored factory conditions, regulated the workdays of women and children, and supported a minimum wage. By 1916, most states had accepted the populist demands for election reforms: the secret ballot, initiative, referendum, recall, and direct election of US Senators.

Women's organizations grew to national prominence. Charlotte Gilman's *Women and Economics* (1898) challenged the right of men to the best jobs and supported the need for women's organizations, a position taken up again in the 1960s by Betty Friedan and the National Organization for Women. Feminists Elizabeth Cady Stanton, Susan B. Anthony, and Alice Paul demanded women's suffrage and eventually persuaded the country to ratify the 19th Amendment (1920). Emphasizing rights over their own bodies, Victoria

Contemporary United States

Woodhull advocated "free love"—sex for pleasure—and Margaret Sanger was put in jail for distributing birth-control information. These issues would continue well into the twenty-first century.

Calling for African Americans to pull themselves up by their bootstraps, the most powerful black leader in America, Booker T. Washington, reluctantly "lived with" segregation, while he pushed vocational education as the best way to advancement. His approach has been labeled "accommodation." Thousands of protesters reacted to the daily practices of racial discrimination by advocating confrontation and integration. W. E. B. DuBois helped found the National Association for the Advancement of Colored People (NAACP) in 1910. Black nationalist Marcus Garvey formed the Universal Negro Improvement Association (1919–1927), stressed a heroic African past, and promoted separatism. Alain Locke celebrated the "New Negro" and poet Langston Hughes pushed forward the Harlem Renaissance and its literary protests against the myth of American freedom and its promises as he holds up the idea of the word "America" as both aspirational and geographical: "O, let America be America again. The land that never has been yet …" (Hughes, 1994).

From Isolation to Superpower

The First World War and the 1920s

From 1901–1909, President Theodore Roosevelt helped establish the modern regulatory state. The federal government set rules and enforced standards to better the common good and expand executive power. In foreign policy, Roosevelt continued the Darwinian approach by dividing the world into "civilized" and "uncivilized" nations, the former defined as white and Western. Roosevelt built a canal in Panama to increase trade and security by linking the oceans. He championed reform by prosecuting corporate monopolies and safeguarding wilderness areas. His successors, William Howard Taft and Woodrow Wilson, advocated even stronger regulations.

Although protected by two broad oceans and a big navy, with a peaceful northern border and a weak neighbor to the south, the United States could not isolate itself from world affairs. When war erupted in Europe in 1914, Wilson declared neutrality. He was re-elected in 1916 on slogans of "He Kept Us Out of War" and "America First." But in 1917, after German submarines increased attacks on ships carrying US passengers, America entered the First World War. Anti-war protest was so strong that Congress enacted an Espionage Act to curb dissent. Draconian measures banned the teaching of the German language and the playing of Beethoven. Thousands of Americans had their civil rights abused and the US Supreme Court declared that freedom of speech could be limited if there was "a clear and present danger."

After the war, the war on German imperialism transferred to a "Red Scare" that the Russian Revolution of 1917 would spread to America. In 1919–1920, the US government went on a "witch hunt" for any foreigners who might be radicalized. Thousands had their constitutional rights abused as they were rounded up, mistreated, and deported. In response, activists organized the American Civil Liberties Union (ACLU)—still the most powerful NGO defending constitutional guarantees. Wilson supported a League of Nations, but ultimately failed to get congressional approval to join it. America witnessed its largest-ever race and labor riots.

The 1920s was an era of prosperity that has been described variously as: the "Jazz Age," the "Roaring Twenties," or the "Era of The Lost Generation." It was a hedonistic age marked by the pursuit of pleasure, pushed along by the rise of advertising and radio, stimulated by the writings of Sigmund Freud and F. Scott Fitzgerald, and changed by a revolution in manners and morals, movies, automobiles, and a "me generation" that stressed a live-for-today attitude. Young women—"flappers"—threw off the Victorian fashions of their mothers, cut their hair short, and reached for rayon stockings, silk panties, makeup, short dresses, a dance partner, a cigarette, and a beer. Americans sought "youth" and drank, even though the 18th Amendment (1919) prohibited the "manufacture, sale, or transporting of intoxicating liquors" anywhere in the United States. People flouted the law and bought from bootleggers until the 21st Amendment (1933) recognized the inevitable and nullified Prohibition.

The man behind Henry Ford's automobile assembly lines—efficiency expert Frederick W. Taylor—symbolized the 1920s. Manufacturing speed, standardized packaging, and a belief that there was only "one best way" led writer John Dos Passos to call the innovator "Speedy Fred," the man who died "with a watch in his hand" (Dos Passos, 1979: 48). In 1907, an automobile cost over $2,000. Taylor's methods built better cars and reduced the costs to $300 in 1924. Americans bought their dream machines on credit. Cars changed American patterns of mobility, settlement, and leisure time.

These changes led white Protestant America to invoke its jeremiad and reassert itself with a fundamentalist movement to root out advances by African Americans, the devil, and other communists. The worst race massacre by a white mob in American history, among many contenders, was the 1921 brutal murders and property destruction around "Black Wall Street" in Tulsa, Oklahoma. Hundreds of African Americans were killed and thrown into unmarked mass graves. The government was complicit.

The Red Scare gained strength when a racist twenty-five-year-old official in the Federal Bureau of Investigation (created in 1908) named J. Edgar Hoover was promoted to FBI director, a post he held from 1924 to 1972. The Ku Klux Klan rose up again, this time with five million dues-paying white supremacists who feared they might be replaced by immigrants. In this fearful anti-foreigner climate, the 1924 National Origins Act set quotas that favored white European Protestants over all other aspirants. The next year, the world watched to see if John Scopes would be put in prison for breaking a Tennessee state law prohibiting the teaching of evolution to high school students. These issues continue to polarize American society.

Meanwhile, business was booming. In 1928, soon-to-be-president Herbert Hoover announced: "We in America today are nearer to the final triumph over poverty than ever before in the history of any land … [P]overty will be banished from this nation." One year later, on October 29, 1929, the stock market crashed and the Great

Contemporary United States

Depression stalked the land. By January 1933, the economic situation entered its cruelest year with thousands of people dying from starvation and nearly 12 million others unable to find work.

A New Deal and The Second World War

No president in the twentieth century had a greater impact on American life than Franklin Delano Roosevelt (FDR). Voters elected him four times, 1932–1944. FDR used optimistic radio chats to persuade listeners that "The only thing we have to fear is fear itself." His New Deal economic recovery plan was a pragmatic approach—profoundly conservative and profoundly revolutionary. In his first "hundred days" in office, FDR sent over 100 pieces of reform legislation to Congress and, in so doing, created the American welfare state. He also "created" a strong progressive wing of the Democratic Party that provided a touchstone for the "Build Back Better" policies of Joe Biden (see Chapters 4 and 5).

In 1939, with the start of the Second World War in Europe, the United States again declared its neutrality. A nationalist and pro-German "America First" committee opposed the war. On December 7, 1941—in what Roosevelt called "a date that will live in infamy"—the Japanese attack on the US naval base at Pearl Harbor, Hawaii, rushed America into war. Bowing to racial hysteria, FDR ordered 120,000 citizens of Japanese-American backgrounds rounded up and incarcerated in guarded camps. It would not be the first or last time innocent non-whites suffered from the ethno-nationalist anxiety of their white countrymen.

National government power soared with new wage and price controls, rationed products, and increased taxes. Americans migrated to the cities and moved to the West, especially to California. Women and African Americans entered the workforce in large numbers as over 16 million men joined or were drafted into the military. FDR declared it illegal to discriminate in hiring for government jobs and Congress passed a Fair Employment Practices Act. By 1944, America produced twice as much war material as Germany and Japan combined. Government spending increased from $8 billion a year in 1936 to $98 billion in 1945. The Great Depression was over. American military units fought, killed, and died around the world before government scientists developed the two atomic bombs that were dropped on Japan to end the war. Three hundred thousand Americans died in the Second World War.

The Cold War

The 1950s

In 1945, the world entered into a "Cold War" divided into blocs led by the Soviet Union and the United States. Americans believed that Soviets were evil atheists out for world domination and concluded that the US was the only country capable of stopping them.

As the country accepted its superpower role, it moved to a strategy of sophisticated airpower, long-range missiles, nuclear submarines, and thermonuclear warheads.

Millions of military veterans used the new "G. I. Bill" to get university degrees and, in the process, increased the number of US research universities. As the middle class prospered, whites reached a consensus about values and culture. Sociologist David Reisman's *The Lonely Crowd* (1950) described this as a loss of individualism and the change to a new conformity of doing what others expected. The primary expression of wealth was the baby boom of 1945–1957 which saw the birth rate soar to twenty-five births per thousand people—about four million babies a year. Larger families demanded housing construction and the automobile allowed for far-flung communities. Americans created a consumer society. By 1960, the majority of Americans lived in the suburbs, commuted on the new interstate highway system, and bought what they needed in shopping malls.

The 1950s were conservative years. Americans returned to churches and listened to radio evangelists like Billy Graham who preached that true Americans were Christians, not "godless Communists." In 1954, Congress added the words "under God" to the Pledge of Allegiance, and the next year put the words "In God We Trust" on every piece of currency. Christians demanded order and pressured women to return to the domestic sphere to raise "decent" children. Thousands agreed or obeyed, but thousands more were reluctant to give up the freedom provided by a paycheck. The "two-income family" lifted the status of working women and increased disposable income so that most white Americans lived in what economist John Kenneth Galbraith called *The Affluent Society* (1958). The white poor, Native Americans, migrant laborers, and most African Americans continued to struggle. Many soon joined together into new social movements to force changes.

In *Brown v. Board of Education* (1954), the Supreme Court overturned the *Plessy* (1898) decision and ordered the integration of the nation's schools. The next year, protesters in Montgomery, Alabama, refused to ride the segregated bus lines and found a leader in a twenty-six-year-old preacher, Martin Luther King, Jr. Latinos, American Indians, and women protested their poverty and second-class citizenship in the richest country on earth.

During the 1950s, Americans grew hysterical over "Reds." The House Un-American Activities Committee (HUAC)—which was formed in 1938 to explore whether or not the New Deal welfare programs were "creeping socialism"—claimed to uncover conspiracies against the American way of life. HUAC's Richard Nixon headed the investigation into the stealing of atomic secrets by foreign spies. Actor Ronald Reagan accused Hollywood of harboring communists, and the "Red Scare" accelerated after Senator Joseph McCarthy claimed that communists had infiltrated the government. As McCarthyism and the Korean War increased the paranoia, voters in 1952 elected US Army General Dwight D. Eisenhower to the presidency. Eisenhower calmed fears by denouncing McCarthy and encouraging economic growth. He believed: "What is good for General Motors is also good for our country." Still, Eisenhower feared what he called the excesses of a "military-industrial complex."

33

Contemporary United States

The 1960s and 1970s

The era opened with a presidential election between Republican Vice President Richard Nixon and Democratic Senator John Kennedy (JFK). Both were anti-communists who had supported McCarthy's witch hunts. Nixon appealed to conservative Protestants and Kennedy, a Catholic, fought to downplay rumors that he was controlled by the Pope. In the first television debates in history, Kennedy's camera presence helped him win a very close election.

Immediately, Kennedy challenged Americans to "ask not what your country can do for you, ask what you can do for your country." His predatory womanizing—including Hollywood sex goddess Marilyn Monroe—was not high media drama in days well before the #MeToo movement. JFK insisted on a balanced budget and put forth a domestic program, the "New Frontier," which raised the minimum wage, built low-cost housing for the poor, sponsored a redevelopment program for poverty-stricken Appalachia—the mountainous area of twelve states from southern New York to northern Alabama—and appointed more minorities to federal jobs than anyone had done before. This was done through a historically progressive tax system (Table 1.1).

Table 1.1 Selected Individual Federal Income Tax Brackets (1963 and 2019 tax years)

Income ($)	Tax Rate (%)	Tax Owed (before deductions) ($)
0	**10**	**0**
0	16	0
9,700	**12**	**970**
9,700	30.5	2286
39,475	**22**	**4,543**
39,475	61	24,080
84,200	**24**	**14,383**
84,200	73.5	47,490
160,725	**32**	**32,749**
160,725	76.5	105,813
204,100	**35**	**46,629**
204,100	77	139,015
510,300+	**37**	**153,799**
510,300	77	374,789
1,000,000 (for example)	**37**	**334,988**
1,000,000 (for example)	77	751,858

[*Note:* Tax rates are for individual taxpayers. The 2019 tax rates are shown in **bold**. There were only 7 tax brackets in 2019 with the highest bracket of 37 percent on all income over $510,300. There were 27 tax brackets in 1963 when the highest rate was 77 percent on all income over $204,100. The chart excludes 20 of the 1963 brackets in order to compare the taxes owed in column 3.]

Source: IRS (1964) and IRS (2020b)

In foreign affairs, a CIA-planned invasion of Cuba failed, and a few months later the world awoke to a Soviet victory, the Berlin Wall. In October 1962, the USSR placed nuclear missiles in Cuba. Kennedy ordered a naval blockade and threatened war if the missiles were not removed. When the Soviets capitulated, Kennedy's popularity soared. JFK's establishment of the Peace Corps fit into the historical missionary zeal of spreading democracy and "American know-how" to developing countries. Americans liked his determination to win the space race by putting a man on the moon and supported his order sending 16,000 combat advisors to Vietnam. Then, on November 22, 1963, a sniper—or, according to a proliferation of conspiracy theories, snipers—assassinated him in Dallas, Texas.

JFK-the-martyr myth became a shining promise of what might have been. His beatification eased the way for Lyndon Baines Johnson (LBJ) to declare a "war on poverty" and to promote "Great Society" programs. LBJ pushed through Medicare, Medicaid, and Social Security programs to expand health care and provide pensions—three of the most important entitlement programs in American history. In the West, farmworkers Dolores Huerta and Cesar Chavez organized migrants into the United Farm Workers Union. The African American Civil Rights Movement hit high gear, and mass protests brought world opinion to bear on discrimination and racism. Congress passed the landmark 1965 Immigration and Nationality Act to overturn the racially biased 1924 National Origins Act and open up immigration worldwide.

Significantly, in terms of racial equality, Congress passed the 1964 Civil Rights and 1965 Voting Rights acts. Martin Luther King, Jr. used non-violent moral pressure while Malcolm X and the Black Panthers increasingly believed that violence could be a revolutionary tool. From 1964 to 1968, race riots enflamed urban America before and after the assassinations of movement leaders: Malcolm X (1965), King (1968), and presidential candidate Robert Kennedy (1968).

The nation divided sharply along generational, philosophical, gender, and racial lines. A struggle for the soul of America saw anti-war protests grow as women, environmentalists, blacks, Latinos, gays, Native Americans, hippies, students, and new immigrants demanded change. Two general sides existed with one group stressing individual liberty and limited government and the other wanting equality, strong community, and government-regulated social programs. Johnson was besieged by the incessant chanting outside the Oval Office: "Hey, Hey LBJ! How many kids you kill today?" and "Two, Four, Six, Eight, We don't want to integrate!" and "Power! Black Power!" He decided not to run for re-election.

Richard Nixon saw an opening in promising "peace with honor" in Vietnam and a return to "law and order" at home. White conservatives—whom Nixon called "the Great Silent Majority"—elected him to the presidency in 1968 and 1972. He did pull US troops out of Vietnam, but only after casualties doubled and a savage US escalation of bombing forced the peace. Nixon made overtures to Russia and China, and foreign policy entered an era of détente. In domestic affairs, he promoted a "New Federalism" to reduce the role of the national government by returning power to the states and placed thousands of police in America's streets to re-establish domestic order.

Contemporary United States

The scandals came quickly. Daniel Ellsberg, a Pentagon official, leaked top-secret documents, the Pentagon Papers, to the *New York Times*. The *Washington Post* uncovered a story about the 1972 burglary of the Democratic National Headquarters in the Watergate building. The first story revealed the misinformation campaign and outright lies the Johnson administration told the American people about Vietnam. The second story revealed that Nixon had directed and covered up a felony crime. Threatened with impeachment, Nixon resigned. While a triumph for a liberal press, the checks and balances system, and the American people, the revelations increased fears of government conspiracy and corruption. After years of social turmoil and assassinations, the lost war, a stagnant economy with high inflation, and two presidents dishonored, Americans suffered a crisis in confidence.

By law, the vice president becomes president when a vacancy occurs, but Nixon's VP had been found guilty of tax evasion and had resigned. Michigan congressman Gerald Ford was confirmed to replace him. One month later when Nixon resigned, Ford took office and quickly issued an executive pardon freeing Nixon from criminal prosecution. Ford said he wanted to end "our long national nightmare" (Ford, 1974). Most Americans saw this as another misuse of executive privilege. A year later, the last American soldiers unceremoniously escaped from Vietnam as the world watched on television. Runaway inflation and recession marked the post-Vietnam years, as did a "Vietnam Syndrome" against military adventurism in foreign wars.

In 1976, Georgia Governor Jimmy Carter defeated Ford by making a single campaign promise never to lie to the American people. In domestic affairs, Carter could not stop inflation, which rose to 14 percent as unemployment topped 7 percent for the first time since the Depression. An energy crisis came when Islamic states cut oil exports in protest of US–Israeli actions in the Middle East. Two disasters also indicated governmental failures and environmentalists' fears. In 1978, at a housing development in Niagara Falls, New York, called "Love Canal," hundreds of people suffered when dioxin—one of the deadliest poisons ever made— rose up from the toxic waste dump nearby. The next year, at Three Mile Island in Pennsylvania, a nuclear power plant released radioactive gases into the atmosphere. As disasters piled up and the economy continued to tumble, Carter spoke about a "crisis in the American spirit" and of "self-indulgence and overconsumption" (Carter, 1979). The speech was ill-received. The people faulted presidential actions and a lack of leadership.

Carter did better in the global arena, deftly handling a treaty returning the canal zone to Panama, officially recognizing and opening up the People's Republic of China, brokering the peace between Egypt and Israel that ended their thirty-year war, and campaigning worldwide for human rights. But those successes were overcome in the long year of 1980 when Iranian jihadists held fifty-two Americans hostage in Tehran after the overthrow of the US-backed Shah. Carter's diplomatic and military efforts failed and Americans fumed over Islamic terrorists and oil embargoes.

History

The Reagan Era

In 1980, voters opted for the governor of California, a former B-level actor and charismatic cowboy who was threatening war with Iran if it did not return the hostages. Ronald Reagan beat Carter by a landslide Electoral College vote of 489–49 after promising to return the country to greatness. He stressed patriotism and a stronger military. At sixty-nine, Reagan was the oldest president ever elected; his grandfatherly chuckle and acting ability gained him the sobriquet "the Great Communicator" [note: Trump was seventy, a Twitter star, and not the "grandfather" type. Biden, another grandfather type, was seventy-eight, but he lacked the cult status and communication skills of the others].

On Inauguration Day, Iran released the hostages—there had been a secret deal. Reagan quickly labeled the Soviet Union "an evil empire" and vowed to intervene militarily if US interests were threatened by anyone. He increased the military budget to an amount four times greater than during the Vietnam War. But Reagan did not bring peace or security. When terrorists used a truck bomb to kill 239 marines in Lebanon in 1993, Reagan immediately withdrew all US soldiers.

Then, after Reagan sent the CIA to help the "Contras"—a Right-wing group in Nicaragua trying to overthrow an elected socialist government—Congress worried about another Vietnam and ordered all funding stopped. Reagan approved the use of money from a secret arms deal with Iran to fund the revolution in Nicaragua. Patently illegal, the press called the events "Irangate" and a congressional investigation revealed executive overreach. Reagan said he knew nothing of it and the matter faded away.

Domestically, Reagan sliced into the welfare programs of the New Deal and Great Society. He criticized individual "lifestyle choices" to explain away poverty, failure, and multiculturalism. Meanwhile, Reagan got tax breaks for the rich, and pushed for an accelerated schedule of capital punishments, harsher penalties for drug use, more prisons, and bigger police departments.

In 1988, Reagan's vice president, George Herbert Walker Bush, was elected on a pledge of a "kinder, gentler America" while he continued Reagan's economic policies. There were breathtaking global developments: the Berlin Wall fell, Germany reunited, and the Soviet Union broke into several national states. The Warsaw Pact no longer existed and Eastern Europe moved toward free-market capitalism, something Bush called "the New World Order." China made real gains in developing its economy and opening its society to broader freedoms even as the killings of students in Tiananmen Square in 1989 ominously foreshadowed the survival of Maoism.

In August 1990, Iraq invaded Kuwait, only to be surprised by Bush's order dispatching over 500,000 US soldiers to the Persian Gulf. The quick victory in "Operation Desert Storm" boosted his popularity and gave him the opportunity to further reduce government welfare programs. But when the economy slowed, Bush reneged on his earlier campaign promise, "Read my lips! No new taxes!" In 1992, the tax increase caused disgruntled Republicans to defect to a third-party candidate, Texas computer billionaire Ross Perot

37

Contemporary United States

and his "flat" tax plan where everyone pays the same rate. Hereafter, the Republican Party drew a line in the sand against even the smallest tax increase. This split in the conservative vote elected the Democratic nominee, William Jefferson Clinton.

The 1990s

Coinciding with Clinton's presidency, the US economy entered a long period of expansion, unemployment fell to historic lows, inflation bottomed out, crime rates plunged dramatically, civil disorders nearly ceased, and world leaders generally approved of the change in leadership styles and rhetoric. Clinton and his wife, Hillary Rodham, were baby boomers who were equal partners in political strategy. The Clintons put forth a "third way" mixing conservative and liberal agendas to boost health care, fix the economy, end deficit spending, reduce discrimination, flatten violence, and give more power to the states.

Immediately, Clinton was in trouble. With his first executive order, he removed the ban preventing homosexuals from enlisting in the armed forces. The backlash by military leaders and homophobic Americans was so great that the president switched to a "don't ask, don't tell" policy, meaning that recruiters would not ask about sexual preference and gays should not reveal themselves. Simultaneously, the allegation that the Clintons had received insider treatment in a real-estate deal ("Whitewater") was coupled with lawsuits charging the president with sexual misconduct while he was Governor of Arkansas.

By 1994, media attacks on the Clintons created enough of a backlash to elect a Republican majority in the House and Senate for the first time since the 1950s. House Republicans pushed a "Contract with America" to demand tax cuts, set term limits for politicians, expand capital punishment, restrict social welfare, and pass a constitutional amendment to balance the budget. They refused to negotiate any of those terms. The Senate refused to agree to the contract and the president vetoed the House's budget proposal because it sliced into Medicare payments, reduced environmental safeguards, and cut taxes too much. Without a budget, no money is available. Twice, in efforts to force Clinton to sign the budget, the government shut down, delaying payroll checks to civil service employees, soldiers, and politicians. The public sided with the president; Congress fell into line. In 1996, the roaring economy re-elected the president.

A twenty-one-year-old White House intern, Monica Lewinsky, told a friend that she had been having sex with the president and that she had a sperm-stained dress to prove it. On television, Clinton looked the country straight in the face, and stated, "I did not have sexual relations with that woman, Miss Lewinsky" (quoted in Campbell, 1998). When he later admitted that he had lied under oath, the House voted for impeachment. The American people were titillated but forgiving; nearly 80 percent disapproved of the trial and the Senate deadlocked 50–50 along party lines. Since a two-thirds majority, sixty-seven votes, is necessary to remove a president, the vote was a victory for Clinton.

The Twenty-First Century

The election of 2000 featured the Democratic Vice President Al Gore against the Republican Texas Governor George W. Bush. With the economy booming and no foreign crisis pressing, the election turned on personalities with the press framing Bush as a likeable but "empty suit" ignoramus and Gore as a robotic, congenital, "know-it-all" exaggerator. Gore won the popular vote nationally by a narrow margin, but Bush won enough states—and Electoral College votes (271–266)—to declare victory. Both Bush and Gore filed lawsuits contesting the Florida vote. When the Supreme Court judged Bush the winner, Democrats complained about a "stolen" election. But Gore soon conceded and spoke of reconciliation and a peaceful transfer of power: "Partisan feeling must yield to patriotism ... [I]t has ended, resolved, as it must be resolved, through the honored institutions of our democracy ... Just as we fight hard when the stakes are high, we close ranks and come together when the contest is done."

Bush expected his presidency to be dominated by domestic affairs. Early on, he massively cut taxes and supported immigration reform to provide an easier path to citizenship. While he called for "compassionate conservatism," his party disagreed and took hard-line stances with immigrants. Bush also voided the Kyoto Protocol on climate change and carbon reduction goals that had been signed by Clinton.

The terrorist attacks of September 11, 2001, on New York and Washington brought on a national trauma. Bush promoted a global "War on Terror." He expanded executive power, created the Department of Homeland Security to coordinate intelligence information, and signed a "Patriot Act" to override privacy laws and civil liberties in favor of national security.

NATO and the UN agreed that Afghanistan was the "breeding ground for terrorists" supported by the Taliban and the mastermind of the 9/11 attacks, Osama bin Laden (see Chapter 9). Bush accused Iraq of complicity and vowed to force a "regime change" and destroy Iraq's "weapons of mass destruction" stockpile. The US military quickly defeated the Iraqi army and executed the Iraqi president. No weapons stockpile was found. The war turned into a civil conflict that spread into Syria and beyond.

In 2004 Bush was re-elected because Americans overwhelmingly rally to a president during wartime. Bush emphasized an "ownership society" whereby Americans took a stronger stake in their communities and control of local institutions and social welfare (Rosenbaum, 2005).

The worst financial crisis since the Great Depression struck suddenly in 2007/2008 and thrust the ownership society into reverse. Millions of people lost jobs, homes, and savings due to dangerous banking practices involving mortgage loans. Government policies of deregulation since the Reagan years and overconfident consumer spending spree were at the root of the crisis. Bush responded quickly, agreeing to a massive economic bailout program ($700 billion) just to keep the US solvent. Americans almost always blame the sitting president for the economy, so Bush's approval ratings tumbled. In 2021 a C-SPAN survey of presidential historians ranked Bush 29th of 44 US presidents (Obama 10th, Trump 41st, Biden unranked) (C-SPAN, 2021).

Contemporary United States

The people wanted change and hope—and in 2008 they shattered a racial barrier to achieve these goals. As journalist Andrew Sullivan explained: "Barack Hussein Obama [born in 1961] is the new face of America. A brown-skinned man whose father was an African, [whose white mother is from Kansas], who grew up in Indonesia and Hawaii, who attended a majority-Muslim school as a boy" (Sullivan, 2008). New Yorker magazine editor David Remnick added that

> Obama's family, broadly defined, is vast. It's multiconfessional, multiracial, multilingual, and multicontinental … He has a Kenyan step-grandmother in a village near Lake Victoria who speaks only Luo and Swahili; a biracial half-brother who speaks fluent Mandarin and trades in southern China; a cousin-by-marriage who is an African-American rabbi in Chicago determined to forge closer relations among Jews, Muslims, and Christians of the South Side.
>
> (Remnick, 2010)

Obama confronted the racism and racial imaginations of 250 years of American slavery (1619–1865), Social Darwinism, discrimination, violence, and struggle for equal treatment (1865–present). He gave the world hope that a post-racial America might be possible. Obama got ten million more votes than Republican nominee John McCain and had an Electoral College victory of 365–173. In 2012, Obama won again in a slightly closer contest over Senator Mitt Romney of Utah. To be a black man with Obama's diverse family and to be elected *twice* confirmed Obama's oft-stated American dream: "In no other country on Earth is my story even possible" (Obama, 2004).

Obama wanted higher taxes, more government regulation, gun control, welfare expansion, multilateral decision-making, globalization, and laws that included non-traditional families and LGBTQIA+ rights. In governing he hoped for bipartisanship, but this was not possible in the increasingly polarized political era. Consequently, Obama often used "executive orders" to get things done when Congress deadlocked. His major successes on the domestic front were in the American Recovery and Reinvestment Act (ARRA) which was a stimulus package that kept the US economy from failing, and the Affordable Care Act (see Chapter 5) which expanded health care to millions of Americans. No Republicans voted for either act. Obama appointed two women to SCOTUS. He extended immigration visas for thousands. He won the Nobel Peace Prize in 2009 and ended combat operations in Iraq in 2011. He suffered many failures domestically and in global affairs, including gun control, immigration policies, failure to end the war in Afghanistan, substantial losses to China in the world order, and increased partisanship in American society and politics.

Analysts spoke often of "No Drama Obama," a quality that can be contrasted with his successor, who was all drama all the time. In 2016, most pundits expected that the Democratic nominee, former First Lady, New York Senator, and Secretary of State Hillary Clinton, would shatter a gender barrier and continue Obama's program, taking the country into a New Progressive Era. Clinton won the popular vote by three million votes, but when she lost close counts in three traditionally liberal states, the Electoral

College belonged to Trump, 306–232. The New York businessman, reality TV star, and a leader of a New Gilded Age had campaigned directly on a promise to repudiate Obama's legacy and return America to Reagan's vision. Much of his victory came from what journalist Ta-Nehisi Coates described as "a horrifying and simple reality: A significant swath of this country did not like the fact that their president was black" (Coates, 2017a). The essential meaning of the 2008 and 2012 elections was inclusion; the 2016 election was a return of white male supremacy.

Other reasons cited by Trump's supporters included the deindustrialization and the loss of working-class jobs to Mexico and China, a fear of refugees, immigrants, and foreigners in general, belief in male leadership, grievances against those who condemn non-politically-correct speech, a sense of being looked down upon, the progressive disrespect for traditional family values, liberal condescension for Christian beliefs and patriotic nationalists, and a whole range of complaints against the Democratic nominee, the female Hillary Clinton.

National polls, respected political analysts, and TV talk shows had overwhelmingly predicted a Clinton victory. Changing demographics in America pointed to gains by every liberal group and Obama's approval rating on election day stood at 55 percent. Trump beat all the odds. Analyst John Heilemann explained: "Our failing was that we [pundits] took Trump literally but we didn't take him seriously. People in the country took him seriously but they didn't take him literally" (Heilemann, 2017).

Trump promised heightened security, lower taxes, drastic cuts to government regulations and entitlement programs such as health care, unilateral decision-making, a more muscular military, and a withdrawal from global commitments to bring back jobs and focus on America First. In his Inaugural Address, Trump spoke of "American carnage" and continued his dark campaign themes of danger, fear, and failure—a chilling and "dystopian picture of a United States in decline" (Kakutani, 2017). On a victory tour, Trump said: "There is ... no certificate of global citizenship. We pledge allegiance to one flag and that flag is the American flag. Never again will anyone's interests come before the interest of the American people." It was to be the highly competitive nationalism of "America First."

There is a Janus-faced twoness/duality to American society in terms of political partisanship. This is evidenced by the quick reversal from the highly progressive cosmopolitanism of Obama to the authoritarian nationalism of Trump then back to the Obama agenda under Biden. Philosopher Reinhold Niebuhr imagined a "Children of Light, Children of Darkness" society in which community idealism faced off against greedy self-interest. The country is divided and the presidency swings back and forth. Some optimistic analysts argue that the Left–Right dance is an overlapping and a rebalancing of political ideas, programs, and values in a diverse society trying to satisfy complex cultural nationalities and ambivalences under a single federal government (Walzer, 1992). But too often the dance is to the beat of racist and sexist tunes and veers toward constitutional crises. The second decade of the twenty-first century is such a time.

In the 2020 election, Trump lost to Biden by over seven million popular votes and by an Electoral College vote of 306–232. But, for the first time in American history, the loser did not accept the results and did not concede. This had been unthinkable. Instead of following convention, Trump filed over sixty lawsuits asking to overturn the results. After re-counting millions of ballots and finding very few or no indications of voter fraud, multiple courts in seven states and the District of Columbia ruled against Trump. The cases were dropped, dismissed, or denied because they were "without merit" or "frivolous." Trump appealed to the Supreme Court but it refused to hear the case. Joe Biden had won.

Biden embraced a progressive (some say "socialist") agenda and promoted a "Build Back Better" program which promised the biggest expansions in the welfare state since LBJ in the 1960s and FDR in the 1930s (Illustration 1.5). His ability to make changes faced the reality of an evenly split Senate (50 Republicans and 50 Democrats) and a 3-vote Democratic majority in the House (219 Democrats and 216 Republicans). Additionally, Biden would have to fight SCOTUS and its 6–3 conservative Republican majority. Still,

Illustration 1.5 President Barack Obama and Vice President Joe Biden

In mid-2012, Obama and Biden enjoyed the respite of a basketball game during a re-election campaign in which they would prevail. The image shows their real friendship beyond the political posturing by politicians who guard their personal lives beyond the public's ability to penetrate. For Biden the friendship and strong connections with Obama increases his success among black voters and all wings of the Democratic Party. The support of Obama, Representative Jim Clyburn of South Carolina, Vice President Kamala Harris, grassroots organizer Stacey Abrams, and others has pushed Biden to make a record number of federal appointments for African American office seekers, including Biden's pick of Ketanji Brown Jackson as the first black women on the United States Supreme Court.

Source: Patrick Smith/Stringer via Getty Images

History

in his first two years, Biden had the support of Democratic Senate Majority Leader and the Speaker of the House to control which legislative proposals were brought to a vote in their chambers. And the power of the executive is no small thing.

In the chapters that follow, *Democracy at the Crossroads* examines key efforts by the Biden administration in overturning or reshaping the Trump agenda. Overwhelmingly, analysts see a worldwide trend toward a decline in democracies, rise of authoritarian leaders, and ethno-nationalism that threatens globalization and the cosmopolitan world order. The Covid-19 pandemic and the problems of social media and internet algorithms, along with the challenges from China and Russia must be controlled as much as possible. The 2022 invasion of the sovereign nation of Ukraine and the open confrontation with NATO by Russian President Vladimir Putin was a move directly taken from eighteenth-century imperialist playbooks where the strong simply took what they wanted from weaker nations. Republicans continue to rally to Trump. Few doubt that he will run again for president in 2024 and be bolstered by the changes made to voting tabulation and rights by Republican state legislatures using gerrymandering and states' rights arguments to control their own Electoral College certifications.

There is a reason for pessimism. But Biden is an heir to Obama, and to Obama's admonition: "To be optimistic about the long-term trends of the United States doesn't mean that everything is going to go in a smooth, direct, straight line. It goes forward sometimes, sometimes it goes back, sometimes it goes sideways, sometimes it zigs and zags" (Coates, 2017b). Biden wants compromise and civility. But the democratic verity is that the next election is always just two years away and the challenges of democracy are growing as an unnerved citizenry and uneasy world looks on. Authoritarian and hyper-nationalistic tendencies have grown. The fragility and strengths of American democracy are the focal points for our discussion.

Further Reading

Anbinder, T. (2016) *City of Dreams: The 400-Year Epic History of Immigrant New York*, Boston: Houghton Mifflin.

Branch, T. (2007) *Parting the Waters: America in the King Years, 1954–1963*, New York: Simon & Schuster.

Coates, T. (2015) *Between the World and Me*, New York: Spiegel & Grau.

Foner, E. (2011) *The Fiery Trial: Lincoln and American Slavery*, New York: W. W. Norton.

Foner, E. (2020) *Give Me Liberty! An American History*, 6th edn, New York: W. W. Norton.

Goodwin, D. (2006) *Team of Rivals: The Political Genius of Abraham Lincoln*, New York: Simon & Schuster.

Hannah-Jones, N. and *NYT* Magazine (2021) *The 1619 Project*.

HBO (Home Box Office) (2021) *Four Hours at the Capitol*, HBO Documentary, October.

Lewis, J. (1998) *Walking with the Wind: A Memoir of the Movement*, New York: Simon & Schuster.

McPherson, J. (2003) *Battle Cry of Freedom: The Civil War Era*, Oxford: Oxford University Press.

Obama, B. (2020) *A Promised Land*, New York: Generic.

Packer, G. (2021) *The Last Best Hope: America in Crisis and Renewal*, New York: Gerard, Straus, & Giroux.

Contemporary United States

Remnick, D. (2010) *The Bridge: The Life and Rise of Barack Obama*, New York: Vintage.

Rucker, P. and C. Leonnig (2020) *A Very Stable Genius: Donald J. Trump and the Testing of America*, London: Bloomsbury.

Ruiz, V. (2008) *Unequal Sisters: An Inclusive Reader in U.S. Women's History*, 4th edn, London: Routledge.

Tocqueville, A. (1994) *Democracy in America*, London: The Everyman's Library.

Turner, F. (1966) *The Significance of the Frontier in American History*, Ann Arbor: University of Michigan Press.

Wilentz, S. (2005) *The Rise of American Democracy: Jefferson to Lincoln*, New York: W. W. Norton.

Woodward, B. (2020) *Fear: Trump in the White House*, New York: Simon & Schuster.

CHAPTER 2
LAND AND PEOPLE

The United States has a diverse and expansive population and geography. In 1790, the first US Census counted 3,929,214 people on 891,364 square miles (2,308,622 sq. km) of land. By 2021, with 330 million people and a total area of 3,794,100 square miles (9,826,675 sq. km), the US is the third-largest country in population and in land size. The continental distance is immense. Between New York City and San Francisco, it is 3,200 miles (5,200 km), about the same distance as from New York to London. Alaska alone covers 586,412 square miles (1,518,807 sq. km) and is 2,300 miles (3,700 km) long.

The United States has a wide hue of ethnic, racial, and cultural variations. The nation's physical environment includes Arctic tundra, subtropical rainforests, natural harbors, arid deserts, fertile prairies, three continental mountain ranges, active volcanoes, swamplands, geysers, great inland seas, multiple networks of lakes and rivers, and three ocean borders. Excepting Hawaii and Alaska, the nation is confined geographically by the same latitudes stretching between northern France and Egypt and is as large as the whole of Europe combined. America's highest point is Mt. Denali (McKinley) in Alaska at 20,320 feet (6,194 m), and the lowest and hottest point is Death Valley in California–Nevada at 282 feet (86 m) below sea level and a record-high temperature of 134 degrees Fahrenheit (57°C).

There are more than 300 cities with 100,000 or more people. Over 80 percent of the national population lives in metropolitan (urban and suburban) areas. This leaves vast open spaces and a feeling of "emptiness." In 2021, 31 of the 50 states had smaller populations than did Denmark, with 5.8 million people. Additionally, the population density of the US is 36 people per square kilometer as compared with Denmark's 138, China's 148, Germany's 237, Britain's 275, Japan's 347, and India's 455 (Worldbank, 2020b). Table 2.1 indicates the actual and relative sizes of the United States and selected states, plus GDP, in comparison with selected countries. Gross Domestic Product for rich states such as New York is close to double that of poor states, such as Mississippi. State/country comparisons are indicative, due to different statistical practices.

The Land

The landmass of the contiguous forty-eight states (see Map 2.1) is framed by the Pacific Ocean and Sierra Nevada mountain range on the west and the Atlantic Ocean and Appalachian mountain range on the east. The Gulf of Mexico and the Rio Grande River

Contemporary United States

Table 2.1 Country and State Comparisons

Entity	Area (sq. km*)	Population (in millions**)	National GDP PPP (in billions of $; 19,490 = $19,490,000,000,000***)	Per capita GDP PPP (in $ ***)
Russia	17,098,242	141.7	$4,016	$27,900
Canada	9,984,670	37.7	1,774	48,400
USA	**9,826,675**	**333.0**	**19,490**	**58,180**
China	9,596,960	1,394.0	25,360	18,200
Brazil	8,514,877	211.7	3,248	15,600
Australia	7,741,220	25.4	1,248	50,400
EU 27 nations	4,236,351	453.0	20,850	40,900
India	3,287,263	1,326.1	9,474	7,200
Mexico	1,964,376	129.2	2,420	19,130
South Africa	1,219,090	56.5	767	13,600
Afghanistan	652,230	36.7	69	2,000
France	643,801	67.8	2,856	44,100
Texas	692,244	27.5	1,891	61,682
Spain	505,370	50.0	1,778	38,400
Sweden	450,295	10.2	518	51,200
Iraq	438,317	38.9	649	16,700
California	411,469	39,1	3,164	70,662
Japan	377,915	125.6	5,443	42,900
Germany	357,022	80.2	4,199	50,800
Montana	380,847	1.0	52	44,145
Finland	338,145	5.6	245	44,500
Norway	323,802	5.5	381,2	72,100
Vietnam	331,210	98.7	649	6,900
Poland	312,685	38.3	1,126	29,600
Italy	301,340	62.4	2,317	38,200
Philippines	300,000	109.2	877	8,400
New Mexico	314,937	2.1	103	46,304
UK	243,610	65.8	2,925	44,300
Oregon	251,571	4.0	254	52,726
North Korea	120,540	25.6	40	1,700
Cuba	110,860	11.1	137	12,300
Florida	155,214	20.3	1,104	47,267
New York	139,831	19.8	1,730	75,131
South Korea	99,720	51.8	2,035	39,500
Denmark	43,094	5.8	288	50,100
Taiwan	35,980	23.6	1,189	50,500
Israel	20,770	8.7	317	36,400
Maryland	31,849	6.0	432	61,926

*   1 sq. km = 0.3861 sq. miles. *Source*: CIA (2020)

**   Population estimates for 2020 are rounded to the nearest 100,000. *Source:* CIA (2020)

***   PPP = in purchasing power parity (which takes relative price levels into consideration) from 2018–2020

Source: CIA (2020). State GDP/GDP per capita 2018/2019 (BEA, 2020)

Source: Statista (2020) Note that state and country comparisons are indicative

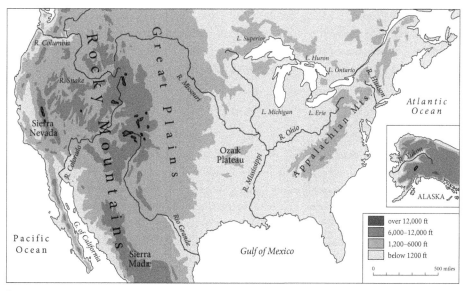

Map 2.1 Major Topographical Features

mark the border with Mexico; the St. Lawrence Seaway and the Great Lakes establish much of the border with Canada. The country is bisected by the world's third-longest river, the Mississippi (3,740 m/6,020 km), which begins in Minnesota, irrigates and drains half the continent, and pours into the Gulf of Mexico just south of New Orleans. The United States is further dissected by the Rocky Mountains, a high range stretching southwards from Alaska to New Mexico.

Most of the United States is in the temperate zone and enjoys four distinct seasons, though in recent years weather events have become more extreme, attributed to climate change. All US cities outside Alaska experience hot summers. The warm water of the Atlantic Gulf Stream spawns hurricanes and thunderstorms from Texas to Maine. Hot weather in the country's midsection combines with flat land to produce over 1,000 tornadoes every year. Droughts have aggravated wildfires. In August and September 2020, more than four million acres of the northwest were aflame in "megafires," stoking the environment as a 2020 election issue (Carlisle, 2020). At the pinnacle of the political system, President Biden is convinced of the climate crisis' "emergency," in stark contrast to his predecessor.

As a consequence of global warming, the frequency and power of hurricanes has increased, with the 2020 season one of the busiest on record. In 2005, the costliest natural disaster in US history, Hurricane Katrina, hit New Orleans, destroying lives (1,836) and buildings amounting to $81 billion. In winter, an Arctic or "Canadian" jet stream brings severely cold and disruptive weather and heavy snows to the Northern states.

East of the Rockies and along most of the Pacific coast, the United States has adequate to above-average rainfall, punctuated in recent years by intense periods of drought as

Contemporary United States

shown in Illustration 2.1. This combines with the rich soil of the Midwest, the South, and California to provide a bountiful agricultural production in grains, fruits, and vegetables. Where the rainfall is less—but is still sufficient to grow grass—cattle farmers and cowboys operate massive livestock businesses on a monotonous landscape.

Natural Resources

Natural resources are important to national security and global power. The United States has vast concentrations of timber, oil, natural gas, coal, iron ore, bauxite, uranium, gold, copper, and silver. It also controls nearly 12,500 miles (20,000 km) of coastline from which to import and export products, and to send out fishing fleets. For over 200 years, European immigrants wrote about what seemed to be limitless forests and of their own handiwork in using an axe for taming the wilderness. Today, US timber companies clear-cut whole areas of woodlands and fight with environmentalists over the destruction of old growth forests, most of which are protected by law. The companies also plant more trees than they cut each year, ensuring a growth cycle which renews the forests every twenty years.

America has rich reserves of energy, including abundant supplies of the natural gas used for electricity, heating, and petrochemicals. The vast iron ore deposits in Wisconsin and Michigan, and the world's largest coal mines—in West Virginia and Pennsylvania—ensure that the country's steel mills are well supplied. Coal production has declined due to cheaper oil, natural gas prices, increasing use of solar panels, windmills, and CO_2 emission policies, and seems likely to continue to do so moving forward. Wind and sun power promise cleaner energy and are supported by environmentalists despite often costing more. Two-thirds of the world's known uranium deposits are located under the Navajo Indian reservation in Arizona. The United States uses the uranium for its military and to power over 100 nuclear power reactors in thirty-one states.

The biggest oilfield is in Alaska and a trans-Alaskan pipeline carries crude oil to coastal shipping and refining firms. Still, the American love for the automobile means that the country currently consumes more oil than it produces. The US imported around 9.14 million barrels of oil a day in 2019 (EIA, 2021b). Yet, overall US energy imports have fallen due to the growing use of "hydraulic fracturing"—called "fracking." Fracking involves the pumping of water, sand, and chemicals into artesian basins to force out fossil fuels that provides needed energy, but at a cost to the environment due to the use of water and potential artesian water pollution. Renewable energy, fracking, and conservation helped establish the US as an energy exporter in 2019 (EIA, 2021c).

From its colonial beginnings, America has held a wealth in resources that created a mindset of unlimited abundance. Americans ran roughshod over the land, depleting the soil, over-killing animals, polluting the environment, and wasting resources. Fur traders and soldiers slaughtered millions of bison; by 1889, fewer than 1,000 animals remained alive. Old growth forests were lost through logging practices that scalped whole areas, strip mining scarred the earth, the dumping of chemicals into waste heaps caused health problems, and rivers and lakes became so polluted that whole ecosystems were changed.

The Environmental Protection Agency and Global Warming

In 1970, the Nixon administration established a national policy for the environment and created the Environmental Protection Agency (EPA). The EPA tries to achieve a balance between population size and resource use and sets national standards for the emissions of greenhouse gases, supports anti-pollution activities, regulates the disposal of toxic wastes, monitors noise levels, pesticide use, ocean dumping, and provides Environmental Impact Statements on the possible consequences of new building sites. A staff of 14,000 employees research and set national standards for water and air quality, test compliance, and issue sanctions against any corporation, individual, state, or Indian tribe which violates the standards. Staffing has reduced slowly since 2000, indicating that economic growth mostly wins over environmental protection (EPA, 2020). On January 20, 2001, in his first day in office, President Biden signed an executive order "to immediately confront the climate crisis," marking a reversal of four years of President Trump's denudation of climate and environmental policy (White House, 2021b).

The United States is awash with environmental groups that hold environmental protection as a key American value. Groups such as the Sierra Club carefully monitor air and water pollution levels and alert the EPA and politicians to violations or oversights in government policy. Politicians are keenly aware of their power. When BP's Deepwater Horizon Oil Well, located a mile deep in the Gulf of Mexico, became the biggest oil disaster in history, President Obama's response was closely observed. The well spewed 15,000 barrels of oil daily from April 20 to July 15, 2010, fouling wildlife habitats and ancient swamps, hurting the fishing and tourist industries, killing whales and other sea life, and polluting waterways from Mexico to Europe because of Gulf Stream currents (Dailygreen, 2012). In 2015, BP agreed to pay out over $18 billion in damages (Gilbert and Kent, 2015). Obama suspended all new offshore oil drilling along the main east and west coasts but allowed wells in Alaska and the Gulf (Meyer, 2016). In 2020, the Trump administration announced plans to allow oil drilling in the environmentally fragile Alaskan Arctic Refuge—an action Biden stopped on Inauguration Day.

The giant oil company TransCanada's construction plans for the 1,700 mile-long Keystone XL pipeline from Canada to the refineries along the Gulf of Mexico stalled during Obama's second administration. Environmentalist and health groups fear for the contamination of holy sites and ground water in sensitive ecosystems—such as on Sioux lands at Standing Rock—and had hoped to close down the pipeline permanently. Trump planned to hasten the project, but a Supreme Court order in June 2020 insisted that deliberative process must precede work to complete the pipeline (Liptak, 2020a). With thousands of jobs and US energy security in the balance, the issues of the economy, national security, and the environment are continually debated by presidential administrations. Republican presidents more often line up with Big Oil by favoring fewer restrictions on oil extraction and transportation than Democrats, though both are susceptible to lobbying. Biden halted Keystone in January 2021.

The year 2016 was the warmest on record; 2020 was the second warmest; and 2019 the third. Global temperatures were hotter than at any time in the last 150 years (NASA, 2020a). Most scientists agree that manmade causes of climate change are overwhelming the natural changes caused by weather variations, volcanoes, shifts in ocean currents, and wind patterns. In Alaska, ice and permafrost melted at an unsurpassed rate, causing problems for people and the environment. Drought conditions and hot weather have repeatedly scorched the lower half of the United States in recent summers (Illustration 2.1). Polls suggest that 59 percent of Americans see global warming as a major threat to the US, while 16 percent saw no threat (Fagan and Huang, 2019). There is less agreement on the causes and consequences of this

Illustration 2.1 Climate Change—The Longest Drought in 1,200 Years

The 220-meter-long Glen Canyon Dam across the gorge of the Colorado River holds back the waters of Lake Powell, the second largest reservoir in the US. Construction began in 1956. The dam took over twenty years to complete and fill. Lake Powell serves the power and water needs of tens of millions of people in seven states. During construction, environmentalists worried about the effects of the dam on the marine ecosystem. Over the last years, persistent drought has seen Lake Powell's water level drop by 40 m. Scientists insist that intensified climate variability is a symptom of climate change.

Source: Justin Sullivan via Getty Images

warming, allowing deniers "wiggle room." In 2021, on Inauguration Day, President Biden rejoined the Paris COP-21 climate protocol agreement, after Trump's earlier withdrawal (White House, 2021a).

Since 2005, the US has reduced greenhouse gas emissions causing global warming by 10 percent (EPA, 2021). Projections based on current policy suggesting emissions will fall further towards 2050 (EIA, 2021b). This will change as incoming administrations address the climate emergency more seriously. The US emits more carbon dioxide per capita than most other developed and developing countries: 15 percent of the total world emissions—only surpassed by China's 28 percent (UCS, 2020).

While Obama ended fifteen years of world criticism that the US was a climate pariah, Trump's Make America Great Again (MAGA) philosophy put American economic concerns before global environmental ones. Biden reversed course, confirming the presidential stop–go nature of environmental policy. Growth interests at home and emerging economies abroad resisted the extra costs of regulation needed to stop the planet warming more than 2 degrees centigrade and claimed that global warming had non-human causes or was the product of developed world industry over two centuries. Rising nations led by China and India insisted that Western nations should bear the brunt of emission cuts instead of the developing nations. For such nations, economic progress mattered more than environmental warnings.

While Trump weighted economic growth over the environment, climate change mitigation did not gain much substantive support in Washington—even though it has enthused many young climate activists. These activists with increasingly mainstream supporters have pulled the Democrats leftward on climate issues, led, among others, By US Representative Alexandria Ocasio-Cortez. Most environmentally conscious Americans were thrilled to have Biden in the White House.

While catastrophes like Hurricane Katrina or Sandy demonstrate the increased thermal energy in the global weather system, they are seldom remembered for long, fading into a background of cold winters (2014–2015) and hot summers (2016, 2020), droughts (2008–2015, 2020) and deluges (2016–2017). Weather comes before climate in the public's mind, despite the testimonies of experts. Yet, humanity's effects on the planet are so profound that geologists argued for the start of the "Anthropocene" age, where virtually every aspect of planetary life had been changed (Carrington, 2016).

National Parks

In 1871, Congress established the nation's first national park, Yellowstone, in Montana and Idaho. The National Park Service (NPS) was created in 1916 to administer lands put into the public trust. The NPS controls 84 million acres (34 million hectares) in 419 parks visited by over 328 million tourists each year. The NPS employs approximately 20,000 people (NPS, 2022). In addition to the NPS, each of the fifty states has a state park system for recreational and conservation purposes, for a total of more than 10,000 state parks protecting another 18 million acres and serving over 700 million visitors a year (America's State Parks, 2021).

Contemporary United States

Generally, Democratic presidents have supported programs protecting public lands. Recent Republican presidents have resisted the creation of more parks and wanted existing reserves opened to private enterprise. For example, the Clinton administration banned road-building and commercial logging on 60 million acres (24 million hectares) of forests, increased the size of many national parks, established eleven new national monuments and adopted tougher standards for automobile emissions. The Sierra Club and the Wilderness Society praised Clinton and hailed 2000 as the best year for conservation since the Carter administration (Booth, 2001).

George W. Bush's policies reversed long-standing protection trends. Congress enacted a Clean Air Act (1970) and Water Pollution Control Act (1972) to ban pesticides, require unleaded gasoline and levy huge fines for dumping waste. Since then, thousands of laws nationwide provided environmental protection. Bush opened parks and Indian reservations for oil exploration, power plants, logging, and mining. He believed that the economy, jobs, and national security outweighed environmental concerns. Obama went further than his predecessors, protecting an extra 265 million acres of water and land from development. The Trump administration dialled back conservation and protection programs to America's wild places, but still supported the bipartisan Great American Outdoors Act in August 2020, directing around $9 billion to that institution for infrastructure projects (Vasquez and Klein, 2020). On entering office, Trump promised to review land protections established since 1996, such as the Bears Ears and Staircase Escalante monuments which he ultimately reduced in size by 85 percent. Biden reversed Trump's orders. State politics matter on environmental protection, with Republican Western states favoured by large energy reserves wanting less regulation for federal lands.

In addition to the land set aside for parks, the federal government has designated more than 150 million acres (61 million hectares) as National Wildlife Refuges (FWS, 2016). These refuges protect animals and plants, restrict sightseeing, and prohibit fishing, hunting, and rock collecting. In 1973, Congress passed the Endangered Species Act (ESA) to provide guidelines for the protection of certain animal and plant species. One of the more recent successes has been the recovery of the American Bald Eagle, one of the world's largest soaring birds and the long-time symbol of the American nation. While its survival is a striking success story, only forty or so other species have been removed from the endangered list in three decades and 1,115 remained or were new on the list in 2012 (FWS, 2012). United Nations' reports suggesting that around one million animal and vegetable species risked becoming extinct over the next few decades was reported by the business-friendly *Wall Street Journal* (Abbott, 2019).

Enacted in response to the Love Canal catastrophe, since 1980 the EPA has operated a Superfund program to clean up toxic waste dumps. The program was funded by an annual tax of $1 billion on the industrial corporations responsible for the pollution. From 1994 to 2009, Republican-dominated Congresses reduced the tax and cut the budget. With the Superfund lacking money, the Bush administration limited clean-up operations, including the New Jersey dumping ground for Agent Orange, the Vietnam War era cancer-causing defoliant. President Obama sought a more activist, interventionist, and costly environmental policy, but often experienced strong congressional opposition to policy initiatives—not least the EPA-driven 2015 Clean Power Plan to reduce carbon emissions. In 2019, the Trump administration effectively repealed the plan, with EPA Administrator Andrew Wheeler arguing that the costs of the plan fell disproportionately on low- and middle-income Americans (Irfan, 2019). Biden's 2021 infrastructure bill promises renewed carbon reductions.

Regions

While the United States of America is a nation, its name indicates the simple fact that it is a union of different states. Each state has a particular personality based upon its peculiar history of settlement and immigration, as well as according to its geography. Americans often describe their country by regions. There is a general, but not complete, agreement over which states belong to which regions and, of course, regions contain sub-regions which are also contested. We have divided the country into five basic areas which generally conform to a contemporary understanding: South, North, Midwest, West, and Pacific Rim. Note that there is tremendous economic diversity within regions and states (see the following tables). Living costs in Connecticut, for example, are much higher than in Mississippi, decoupling per-capita purchasing power from per-capita income.

The South

As the area closest to Columbus's discovery, the South (Map 2.2 and Table 2.2) has cities dating from the struggles of Spain, England, France, and American Indian tribes for dominance in the New World. The oldest permanent European settlements in the United States are the Spanish cities of San Juan, Puerto Rico (1508), and Saint Augustine, Florida (1565), the English settlement at Jamestown, Virginia (1607), and the French city of New Orleans, Louisiana (1718). Indian tribes were mostly removed west of the Mississippi River by the 1840s, but the Cherokee Indian Reservation in the Appalachian Mountains in North Carolina remains the largest Indian land-base east of Oklahoma. The "father of his country" (George Washington), the author of The Declaration of Independence (Thomas Jefferson), the principal writer of the Constitution (James Madison), and the nationalist who claimed the entire Western Hemisphere for American hegemony (James Monroe)—four of the first five presidents—were Virginians.

Much of the South's regional identity comes from its way of life based upon the legacies of slavery and racism, its failed attempt to separate from the United States, and its warm climate. Spanish remains the official language in Puerto Rico and the Southern drawl—a speech pattern which mixes African and Scottish influences—is widespread. This creates a division, real as well as psychological, that defines the South.

Contemporary United States

Map 2.2 The South

Since colonial times, the South has delivered staple crops—tobacco, cotton, rice, sugar—to a world market. The earliest settlers were mostly English and Scottish Protestants (and Spanish Catholics in Puerto Rico and French Catholics in Louisiana) who imported Africans and set up a hierarchical society with slaveholding aristocrats at the top and black slaves at the bottom. White Southerners developed a pro-slavery argument based upon genetics, history, religion, and anti-capitalism. They used pseudo-scientific theories to argue that whites were superior, that the classical democratic city of Athens and the republican city of Rome incorporated slavery, that the Bible sanctioned slavery, and that the system was a positive good when contrasted to the outrages of Northern manufacturing capitalism with its degradation of white workers. The Confederate States of America (1861–1865) consisted of all the states in this region, plus Texas, excepting only Kentucky—and West Virginia, which seceded from Virginia in 1863 to form a new state. Precisely because the South lost and the slaves attained freedom, much of white Southern identity is still marked by the "Lost Cause" and by the intimate interaction and family ties of blacks and whites.

Jimmy Carter's 1970 election as governor of Georgia and his subsequent 1976 election to the presidency marked the South's rise to regional power. Until then the region operated

Land and People

Table 2.2 The South

State, District, Territory, or Commonwealth	Date joined US	Area (sq. miles*)	Population (2019 est.)	Personal income ($ per capita 2020)
Georgia	1788	58,977	10,607,000	51,780
South Carolina	1788	31,189	5,149,000	48,021
Virginia	1788	42,326	8,536,000	61,958
North Carolina	1789	52,672	10,448,000	50,305
Washington, DC	1791	68	706,000	86,567
Kentucky	1792	40,411	4,468,000	47,339
Tennessee	1796	42,219	6,829,000	51,076
Louisiana	1812	49,651	4,649,000	50,874
Alabama	1817	52,237	4,903,000	46,479
Mississippi	1817	48,286	2,976,000	42,129
Arkansas	1836	53,182	3,018,000	47,235
Florida	1845	59,928	21,478,000	55,675
West Virginia	1861	24,231	1,792,000	44,994
Puerto Rico**	1898/1917	3,508	3,194,000	34,518 (2019)
US Virgin Islands***	1917/1927	171	105,000	35,938 (2019)

*   1 square mile equals approximately 2.6 square kilometers.

**   Of these, an estimated half (two million) of all Puerto Ricans live in the US and their numbers are distributed among the states in which they live. Puerto Rico is a commonwealth whose people are citizens of the United States. Puerto Ricans are not allowed to vote in US presidential elections, neither are they required to pay income taxes, unless they live inside US national boundaries. *Source:* World Bank (2020a), note figures are in per capita GDP.

*** The US Virgin Islands are unincorporated territories which were purchased from Denmark in 1917. Citizens of the Virgin Islands became non-voting citizens of the United States in 1927.

Sources: CIA (2020); US Census Bureau [USCB] (2020b); BEA (2020)

mostly as an internal colony of the North, supplying cheap labor and raw materials to feed the nation's growth. For the last half century, the "New South" has been part of the "Sunbelt"—a broad cross-regional area from Virginia to California—which continues to enjoy high immigration, massive job growth, and sunny, hot weather. Illustrating its political strength, Sunbelt candidates won every presidential election from 1964 to 2004. While Washington, DC, is a decidedly Southern city, the key city in the modern South is Atlanta, Georgia. Immigrants—particularly those from Vietnam and Mexico—have changed the dynamics of the Southern population, as has the return migration of African Americans from Northern cities since the 1970s. Foreign industries invest heavily in building factories in Southern cities in exchange for tax relief, pollution waivers, and non-unionized workers. The National Aeronautics and Space Administration (NASA) and the Defense Department are significant contributors to the Southern economy,

55

Contemporary United States

with the main space launch pad at Cape Canaveral, Florida, the nuclear research lab at Oak Park, Tennessee, the principal army bases in North Carolina and Georgia, and the Marine Corps training facility at Parris Island, South Carolina. Warm sunshine promotes the South's huge tourism business, with more than a thousand miles of beaches and resorts, pristine islands protected against development, and many large amusement parks, including Florida's Disneyworld and Universal Studios theme park. Prominent universities such as Emory, Georgia Tech, Duke, Vanderbilt, and Georgetown help the South past its long-time image of slow-talking and slow-thinking, even while the region remains the most religious, least-educated, and lowest-paid area in the country.

The North

The North (Map 2.3 and Table 2.3) has long been associated with core American values of religious freedom, cultural diversity, liberty, capitalism, democracy, work, and education. Most of the prominent symbols of American nationalism—apart from those in Washington, DC—are located in the North. The buildings in which congresses

Map 2.3 The North

Land and People

Table 2.3 The North

State	Date joined US	Area (sq. miles*)	Population (2019 est.)	Personal income ($ per capita 2020)
Delaware	1787	2,396	974,000	56,097
Pennsylvania	1787	46,058	12,802,000	61,700
New Jersey	1787	8,215	8,882,000	73,460
Connecticut	1788	5,544	3,565,000	78,605
Massachusetts	1788	9,241	6,893,000	78,458
Maryland	1788	12,297	6,046,000	66,799
New Hampshire	1788	9,283	1,360,000	67,097
New York	1788	53,989	19,454,000	74,472
Rhode Island	1790	1,231	1,059,000	60,825
Vermont	1791	9,615	624,000	59,187
Maine	1820	33,741	1,344,000	54,211

* 1 square mile equals approximately 2.6 square kilometres.

Sources: CIA (2016); USCB (2020b); BEA (2020)

wrote the Declaration of Independence and the Constitution are in Philadelphia, Pennsylvania. Massachusetts has the landing spot of the Pilgrims—Plymouth Rock—Puritan graveyards, and the houses and churches where patriots planned the American Revolution. The Statue of Liberty, Ellis Island Immigration Museum, and United Nations Headquarters stand in New York harbor.

Puritan beliefs in the middle-class values of hard work, education, individual uplift, democracy, religiosity, and America as a "city upon a hill," defined an American ideology. English Puritans built homogeneous communities in the sub-region of New England: Massachusetts, Connecticut, New Hampshire, Vermont, and Maine. Yet, the arrival of Swedes, Germans, Dutch, Catholics, Quakers, and other dissenters throughout the Mid-Atlantic sub-region of New York, New Jersey, Maryland, Pennsylvania, Rhode Island, and Delaware foreshadowed the future of American cultural pluralism.

With the exception of Vermont, all the states in this region have direct access to big Atlantic harbors from which trading and fishing ships have always operated. Additionally, with the Appalachian Mountains pushing the fall line near the coast, Northern cities benefit from water power available to supply electricity and run factories. The Industrial Revolution which began in England first arrived in Boston. Textile and flour mills, factories making interchangeable parts for weapons, shipbuilding, and insurance firms have long been mainstays of the region. By the mid-nineteenth century, the United States led the world in the number of merchant ships—and these operated almost entirely out of Northern ports. As trade was orchestrated from this region, banking houses such as JP Morgan, Chase Manhattan, and the New York Stock Exchange financed America's business expansion and built New York City (NYC) into the world's leading financial center.

57

As NYC established itself as the main port for immigrants from Europe, various waves of ethnic groups gave the North an even more polyglot society. "Chain migrations" reached into Europe as one immigrant family from a single town would cause a linkage, pulling scores of relatives, friends, and former neighbors to America. Starting in 1892, immigrants were processed at Ellis Island before most of them settled in ethnic enclaves of their own cultures. Here, the immigrants found people, language, food, churches and other self-help organizations, and historical knowledge which kept alive Old World cultures while they made the transition to the overarching American culture. Today, people from all over the world, even those who could never imagine themselves as Americans, identify with New Yorkers.

Iron and oil deposits in Pennsylvania led to the rise of Andrew Carnegie's steel company and John D. Rockefeller's Standard Oil monopoly. Pennsylvania, New Jersey, and New York surpassed Massachusetts as centers of heavy industry. Industries, trade, and the finance capitalism of the region mean that even though the North is geographically smaller, it is more densely populated and urban than the other regions. NYC is the nation's largest city and a sprawling urban network—a megalopolis—connects Boston to Washington, DC. State populations in the north are mostly stagnant, as seen in Table 2.3.

The universities in this region are renowned and include the oldest American university, Harvard (1636), as well as Yale, Princeton, Brown, Columbia, NYU, MIT, and literally hundreds of others. Education is big business, employing millions, and supplying vital knowledge to American undergraduates and to the foreign nationals who help US graduate programs excel (see Chapter 6). Universities also provide many of the innovations in scientific and technological advances.

The Midwest

The Midwest (Map 2.4 and Table 2.4) is largely an extension of the North and was mostly settled by immigrants streaming westward from Northern states in the aftermath of the American Revolution and War of 1812. After the 1848 European revolutions restored conservative monarchies, many Northern Europeans saw the chance to get a farm, work, and to be free by immigrating to the United States. The Midwest has huge populations descended from Germans, Irish, Scandinavians, Poles, Russians, and Ukrainians.

Residents still see the region as the "heartland" of America, mostly untainted by the history of slavery in the South, and overcrowded moneychangers and capitalists in the Northeast and Middle Atlantic states. Midwesterners are known for their honesty and down-to-earth directness and they speak a dialect best described as "flat." They view themselves as classic liberals who conserve American values. Beginning in 1862, the Homestead Act allowed families to claim 160 acres of land (equal to one-quarter of a square mile) by living on it. The area expanded rapidly. As Russian and Ukrainian immigrants came into the region, they brought wheat seeds from the Steppe, which quickly took to the soil and gave the region its major crop.

Bordering Canada or the Mississippi River system, the Midwest is further serviced by direct access to the largest freshwater lakes in the world, the Great Lakes, which provide

Land and People

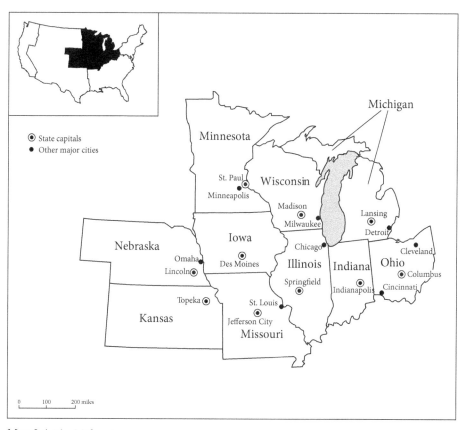

Map 2.4 The Midwest

Table 2.4 The Midwest

State	Date joined US	Area (sq. miles*)	Population (2019 est.)	Personal income ($ per capita 2020)
Ohio	1803	44,828	11,689,000	53,641
Indiana	1816	36,420	6,732,000	51,926
Illinois	1818	57,918	12,672,000	62,930
Missouri	1821	69,709	6,137,000	51,697
Michigan	1837	96,705	9,987,000	53,259
Iowa	1846	56,276	3,155,000	53,478
Wisconsin	1848	65,499	5,822,000	55,593
Minnesota	1858	86,943	5,640,000	62,005
Kansas	1861	82,282	2,913,000	56,099
Nebraska	1867	77,358	1,934,000	57,570

* 1 square mile equals approximately 2.6 square kilometers.

Sources: CIA (2016); USCB (2020b); BEA (2020)

Contemporary United States

drinking water as well as shipping links to the Atlantic Ocean. The land has gentle hills east of the Mississippi and an increasing flatness west of the river. This is farming country, the agricultural breadbasket, meatpacking, and dairyland of the nation. It is also a region of great industrial and manufacturing cities, including Chicago, Detroit, Cleveland, Cincinnati, St. Louis, Minneapolis-St. Paul, Indianapolis, and Milwaukee. Heavy factories near these cities produce automobiles, chemicals, steel—and pollution. In the 1980s, the Great Lakes ecosystem was heavily fouled and the Cuyahoga River running through downtown Cleveland frequently caught fire due to its high oil and chemical content. In 2014, the systemic pollution of Flint, Michigan's drinking water— the product of corrosive river water, leaching lead piping, bacterial buildup, and anti-bacterial chemical cocktails—burst onto the nations headlines and helped fuel the anti-establishment revolution that swept Donald Trump to victory and the White House (M-Live, 2016).

Between the world wars, the cities of the Midwest (and North) proved an irresistible magnet for African Americans emigrating from the South to the promise of better lives. As the economy expanded after the Second World War, blacks continued to arrive in large numbers. The competition for jobs and housing led to ugly racial incidents and to the establishment of inner-city ghettos with maximum crowding and high crime rates. By the 1980s, the Midwestern automobile and steel industries had come under pressure from foreign competitors. Critics labeled the region the "Rust Belt" when many companies collapsed, workers were laid off, and millions relocated to better opportunities and less polluted cities in the Sunbelt. Still, the agricultural prowess of the region kept it in business until the industries could rebound.

For twenty years prior to the 2008 financial crisis, the Midwest prospered from the resurgence of the automobile industry and the success of urban renewal projects as economic highs brought prosperity, better jobs, more police protection, and lower crime rates, which made the cities attractive again. Cleveland built the Rock & Roll Hall of Fame next to two new sports stadiums and a technology museum adjacent to where the cleaned-up Cuyahoga River flows into Lake Erie. Chicago remains central to the region as the third-largest city in America and home of the nation's commodities exchange. Overall, however, Midwestern state populations are largely stagnant, as shown in Table 2.4.

The West

The West (Map 2.5 and Table 2.5) is the region of big states and small populations. Even with the recent decade of rapid population growth coming from Mexico, the region's leading state, Texas, is relatively unpopulated outside the major cities of Dallas-Fort Worth, Houston, San Antonio, and Austin. The West is also "Indian Country," with sizeable populations of Native Americans both on and off the reservations. Because the West—except Texas—came into the Union after the American Revolution created a nation and the American Civil War decided what sort of nation it would become, it is often said to be defined by its lack of an Anglo-American history and its newness. And

Land and People

Map 2.5 The West

yet, the West looms large in the popular perception of Americans as movies tell the tales of immigrant wagon trains crossing the frontier, the adventures of cowboys, and the wars between the US cavalry and the Native Americans. The West of the imagination is also vast in territory and it is that open space, the frontier still waiting to be filled that continues the expansive dreams of the country and draws in people from near and far.

The West is dryer than the rest of the country with many parts of it described as the Great Plains and the Great American Desert. It contains a vast open landscape and dramatic scenery including the Grand Canyon in Arizona, the Badlands in South Dakota, the largest cave in the United States at Carlsbad Caverns, New Mexico, ancient Mesa Verde cliff dwellings in Colorado, and petrified forests made up of trees turned into stone. Since the 1920s, when engineers built giant dams to tame the region's rivers—such as Hoover Dam on the Colorado River—the cities of Phoenix, Arizona; Las Vegas,

Contemporary United States

Table 2.5 The West

State	Date joined US	Area (sq. miles*)	Population (2019 est.)	Personal income ($ per capita 2020)
Texas	1845	267,277	28,996,000	55,129
Nevada	1864	110,567	3,080,000	53,720
Colorado	1876	104,100	5,759,000	63,776
Montana	1889	147,046	1,069,000	53,361
North Dakota	1889	70,704	762,000	61,530
South Dakota	1889	77,121	885,000	59,281
Idaho	1890	83,574	1,787,000	48,759
Wyoming	1890	97,818	579,000	61,855
Utah	1896	84,904	3,206,000	52,204
Oklahoma	1907	69,903	3,957,000	49,878
Arizona	1912	114,006	7,279,000	49,648
New Mexico	1912	121,598	2,097,000	46,338

* 1 square mile equals approximately 2.6 square kilometers.

Sources: CIA (2016); USCB (2020b); BEA (2020)

Nevada; and Albuquerque, New Mexico have grown large as irrigation systems provided a more accommodating environment. Even with the great forests and lakes in the Rocky Mountains, the region is marked by hot, dry summers and lightning storms that set off forest fires every year (Illustration 2.2). In this heat and drought, Americans turn up their air-conditioners and spread what little water they can spare over their lawns. This adds to the demand for electricity, increases calls for nuclear power, puts further pressure on precious water supplies, and endangers wildlife.

The West has a different ethnic mix than the rest of the country because of the large numbers of Native Americans and large resident Latino population. Migration to the West remains strong, with population growth bringing rapid change to the political dynamic of the states—particularly in the region's southernmost states (see Table 2.5).

For years, most white Americans saw the West as too rocky and dry for successful farming operations. The wagon trails that rolled westward from St. Louis headed for the Pacific Rim states. Except for Texas and the states of Nevada and Colorado, which were settled by prospectors mining gold, silver, lead, and copper, the Western states are among the latest additions to the United States. Utah was settled by Mormons following leader Brigham Young to territory outside the United States, founding what is perhaps the country's most culturally homogeneous city: Salt Lake City (1847). The Mexican War brought Mormons back under US control by the land transfer agreed to in the peace treaty.

Much of the land in the West is owned or administered by the federal government. Indian reservations, most of the nation's national parks, and large areas of national

Illustration 2.2 Climate Change—Extraordinary Wildfires in the American West

Our planet is on fire. In 2022, the UNEP issued a seminal report about "the rising threat of extraordinary fires" that can destroy ecosystems and species, cause refugee crises, and damage national economies. The UNEP cited annual economic costs to the US of up to $358 billion (UNEP, 2022) with long-term risks in the vast amount of toxic CO_2 emissions forest fires release into the atmosphere. A global response is needed, now. In the US, the 2021 wildfire season saw more than 45,000 occurrences nationwide with the largest and most destructive fires in the west and Pacific Coast regions. California alone had 8,835 registered incidents burning over two million acres (Calfire, 2021)—the most since 2017. In 2021, among the thirteen large uncontained fires burning simultaneously, the Alisal Fire near Santa Barbara had the attention of 1,300 firefighters, four of whom are shown in the photograph. Overall, the wildfire season in California claimed hundreds of homes and businesses. Twin explanations for wildfires are the repeated failure of the winter rain season and the pressures of human development in tinderbox-dry environments. Beyond climate change, causes include faulty out-of-date electrical lines, automobile exhausts, lightning strikes, and the human factors of cigarettes, campfires, overturned stoves, and malicious arsonists.

Source: Qian Weizhong/VCG via Getty Images

mineral and forest reserves keep populations thin, as do the deep canyons and rugged landscapes of the Rocky Mountains. Private individuals also control vast areas of the West. For example, CNN founder and pioneer of rolling news services Ted Turner owns around two million acres (8,094 square miles: an area bigger than Delaware or Rhode Island) on eight ranches in Montana, New Mexico, and Nebraska, swears to hold the land as an undeveloped trust, and grazes the nation's largest buffalo herd (50,000 head) on prairie grass (Turner, 2021). Most white Westerners disagree with Turner and want US

Contemporary United States

land policies aimed less at conservation and more at development. These citizens have been politically influential in the rise of the New Right, which has demanded more states' rights and less federal government intervention. In the 2020 presidential election, many of these white conservatives voted Republican, sending a majority of Western states' electoral votes to Donald Trump. Republicans continue to advocate for the conveyance of federal lands to the states.

The Pacific Rim

The states and Pacific island territories in this region (Map 2.6 and Table 2.6) are tied together by their common orientation to the Pacific Ocean. The US Navy, Marine Corps, and Air Force have some of their largest strategic bases in these states, with the facility at Pearl Harbor, Hawaii, being the best known. The histories of the Pacific Rim states differ dramatically but their commerce is interwoven and is oriented more toward Asia than to Europe. Alaska has a large Inuit population, Hawaii has a large Polynesian population supplemented by at least 25 percent of Japanese ancestry, and California is the primary port of entry for Asian immigrants. California was taken from Mexico in 1848, Oregon and Washington were ceded by Britain in 1845, Alaska was purchased for $7 million

Map 2.6 The Pacific Rim

Land and People

Table 2.6 The Pacific Rim

State	Date Joined US	Area (sq. miles*)	Population (2019 est.)	Personal income ($ per capita 2020)
California	1850	158,869	39,512,000	70,172
Oregon	1859	97,132	4,218,000	56,312
Washington	1889	70,637	7,615,000	67,126
Guam**	1898/1950	217	167,292	35,712 (2019)
American Samoa***	1929/1967	90	55,000	11,467 (2019)
Alaska	1959	615,230	732,000	63,502
Hawaii	1959	6,459	1,416,000	58,655

*   1 square mile equals approximately 2.6 square kilometers.
**   Guam is an unincorporated territory whose inhabitants are US citizens without the right to vote in US elections. Guam has an elected legislature of its own. The large US Navy base at Guam provides most of the island's economy. GDP Per capita. *Source:* World Bank (2020a)
***   American Samoa is an unincorporated, unorganized territory whose citizens are US nationals, but not US citizens. American Samoa has a non-voting representative in the US Congress. The US administration is the main employer, followed by an American tuna firm, and tourism.

Sources: CIA (2020); USCB (2020b); BEA (2020)

from Russia in 1867, Hawaii was wrenched from independent Hawaiian control in 1891, Guam was ceded by Spain in 1898, and American Samoa was incorporated by mutual agreement in 1929. For many Americans, Alaska's huge territory and tiny population marks it as the "last frontier" within the boundaries of the United States—and the state and national governments control 99 percent of Alaskan land.

Historically, the Spanish settled in California and sponsored expeditions into the entire Southwest. The cities of Santa Barbara, Monterey, San Francisco, San Diego, and Los Angeles began as religious missions that claimed the land for Spain and the people for the Catholic Church. The year California was ceded by Mexico, settler John Sutter found gold near Sacramento and the "gold rush" that followed brought so many settlers—from 15,000 in 1848 to 260,000 in 1852—that by 1850, California was a state. Its Mediterranean like climate, location, and scenic beauty have beckoned millions since 1945.

California contains one eighth of the total American population and Los Angeles rivals NYC as the nation's biggest city. Its most famous industry, Hollywood, glues Americans together via mass culture while computers, telephones, and devices made or inspired by Apple, Google, and other tech pioneers have revolutionized lifestyles. In 2000, California's non-white population surpassed the white population for the first time since 1860 as Hispanics and Asian immigrants flooded into the state. In presidential elections, California usually supplies millions of surplus votes for Democratic candidates. Up the coast in Seattle, Washington, Amazon delivers goods and services that span the globe, Microsoft reaches into global world markets, and Boeing makes aircraft

65

Contemporary United States

that tie these two industries to the high-tech research and development in California's "Silicon Valley"—home of computing gargantuans and fellow trillion dollar capitalized companies, Apple and Google.

The Pacific Rim states are mountainous and sit atop geological fault lines or alongside active volcanoes. Earthquakes are common and volcanoes sometimes erupt, spewing lava and starting forest fires. The Hawaiian Islands in the mid-Pacific are actually the tops of volcanoes. The Pacific Ocean provides an enormous harvest of fish and the states' large rivers are full of salmon and shellfish. Washington and Alaska employ thousands in the salmon industry. Huge agricultural areas—excepting Alaska—grow large portions of the nation's vegetables, fruits, and nuts. There are vast forests of fir trees and the logging industry is strong. The California Redwood or Giant Sequoia is the world's largest species, growing to a height of 400 feet (120 m), having a diameter of 30 feet (nearly 10 m), and being approximately 4,000 years old. Besides protecting the Giant Sequoias, the US government has control over a forest area of approximately 45,000 square miles in California, Oregon, and Washington alone—an area equal in size to the entire state of Pennsylvania.

The People

Race, ethnicity, and gender remain important factors in American life, defining a person and opportunity as much as gender, age, and economic class. Barack Obama's 2008 election led many analysts to hope for a post-racial America; but the 2012, 2016, and 2020 elections and the striking inequalities along the color line testified to the continuing tension as Republicans remained the party dominated by older, white men and Democrats assembled a female, multiracial, more educated, and youthful coalition. The killings of young black men by security guards and the police electrified sensitivities and punctured whatever hopes existed for a post-racial America. Starting in 2012 with Trayvon Martin in Florida, Michael Brown and Eric Gardener in 2014 in Ferguson, Missouri, and New Jersey respectively, the activist Black Lives Matter movement responded to the killings and the transparent injustices. In July 2016, five police officers were shot by Micah Johnson in Dallas. Johnson had mental health issues but was radicalized in part in response to police heavy-handedness, recalling the violent Black Power struggles of the late 1960s.

The year 2020 saw repeated killings by police offers of purported perpetrators, cementing race's position at the apex of national problems. On March 13 emergency medical technician Breonna Taylor was shot and killed by eight police bullets as officers executed a search warrant at the wrong address—her Louisville apartment (BBC News, 2020). Breonna's boyfriend had fired shots, fearing a home invasion. A Kentucky Grand Jury found that police gunfire was justified (Williams, Craig, and Iati, 2020). George Floyd's murder on May 25 particularly inflamed tensions. Floyd had passed a counterfeit $20 bill in a store, after which he was subdued by police officers using a neck knee-hold which crushed his air passages. Floyd begged the four officers for air but was left unresponsive after six minutes and dead on a Minneapolis sidewalk after eight.

Floyd's murder invigorated the #BlackLivesMatter (#BLM) movement and led to over 7,750 demonstrations in nearly 2,500 locations across the nation to August 22, 2020 (Craig, 2020). The *New York Times* reported that the summer's protests could have drawn the most participants in the nation's history (Buchanan, Bui, and Patel, 2020). In September 2020, two police officers were shot in Compton, California, in what may have been an echo attack. Americans held their breath as calls for calm and peaceful demonstrations were answered by President Trump, chasing re-election, on what many regarded as a racially charged "Law and Order" platform. Underlying these examples, from January 1 to mid-September 2020, over 1,000 people were shot and killed by police. African Americans were more than twice as likely to encounter deadly force than whites, while Hispanics were nearly twice as likely to meet the same fate—leading many to conclude that policing was racialized. Smartphones have made it much easier to document injustices, with a lens click and a "share" on social media.

While Americans increasingly identify themselves to census takers as having more than one race/ethnicity, the categories of "African American," "American Indian," "Hispanic/Latino," "Asian American," "White-non-Hispanic," "Pacific Islander," and "Other" continue to inform the daily activities of the people of the United States. These identifying categories are used by the United States Census Bureau for descriptive and policy monitoring purposes.

Native Americans

When Europeans arrived in America, they found it already occupied. Through European eyes, the Native Americans were living upon the land but did not possess or use it according to biblical injunctions to "Be fruitful, and multiply and replenish the earth, and subdue it; and have dominion … over every living thing that moveth upon the earth" (Genesis 1:27–8). Religious immigrants saw the land both as a place where danger lurked and as a source of redemption and wealth. Soon Euro-Americans were using Royal grants, legal deeds, squatters' rights, vigilante justice, and military force to subdue the "Red Man" and the land.

In contemporary America, a few million people are descended from the Native Americans, but the vast majority is of European, African, or Hispanic ancestry. Europe's primary export for the last 400 years has been people, and Europeans have been especially effective as agents of rapid ecological change and in reproducing societies which mirrored their origins. As soon as they had transplanted colonies, the interplay of other immigrant cultures, the land, and climate changed them.

Somewhere around 12,000 years ago or earlier, the people who came to be called "Native Americans" migrated across the Bering Straits from Asia to settle on land unclaimed by precedent or legal deed—or even by humans at all. These Asians advanced ten or so miles yearly until they stretched out in different groups across the North American continent. As time and distance separated them from their roots in Mongolia and Siberia, these immigrants accommodated their cultures to the land and became "Indians"—as the early Europeans called them. Prior to the arrival of the Europeans,

Contemporary United States

thousands of Indian tribes were widely distributed across America. The Anasazi culture of Colorado built a thousand homes into cliffs at Mesa Verde and Chaco Canyon. The Adena-Hopewell culture built huge ceremonial mounds in Ohio. In New Mexico, the oldest continuously occupied town in the United States is the Acoma Pueblo village. At Cahokia, near St. Louis, the Mississippi culture built a massive pyramidal city of 10,000 inhabitants that had to be abandoned due to overcrowding and pollution problems about the time of Columbus's voyages. From Canada to Georgia, the Iroquoian peoples hunted, farmed, and warred against their neighbors for supremacy over the land.

In 2019, around four million Americans identified themselves primarily as American Indians or Inuit; an additional 2.3 million more cited a partial ancestry (USCB, 2020b). Indians are fully assimilated into the national culture. In 2020, for example, 24,000 of these "first Americans" were on active duty with the US military, joining the 150,000 living veterans (NCAI, 2021). Nearly one-quarter of all Indians reside on land set aside exclusively for their tribe (nativepartnership.org, 2021). The other three-quarters live in urban or suburban areas nationwide. Generally, an individual must have at least one-quarter blood quantum measurement to be classified as "Indian" under tribal and US government rules. Many tribes allow exceptions of various types, with the Cherokee, for example, believing that a person either is or is not a Cherokee—blood cell counts being less relevant than identity and culture. The American Indian Movement was established in 1968 and has continued to keep pan-Indian issues alive—even while insisting that the correct reference is "American Indian," not "Native American." Most people use the terms interchangeably (Illustration 2.3).

There are 574 officially recognized tribes/clans and over one million people living on 325 reservations comprised 56 million acres of land (see Map 2.7) (BIA, 2021). The US Constitution places sovereignty in three places: the federal government, states, and Indian tribes. Tribal affairs are administered by elected chiefs and tribal councils who act in ways similar to mayors and city councils. Tribal councils hear complaints, settle disputes, and decide how to spend the money earned by tribal enterprises or distributed to them by the federal government under the Department of the Interior's Bureau of Indian Affairs (BIA). Thirty-five tribes oversee community colleges on seventy-five campuses within their reservations, educating around 30,000 students (AIHEC, 2017). Forty-eight tribes are involved in oil or natural gas production and perhaps fifty tribes have mining operations. Many tribes have opened casino gambling parlors and built tourist hotels and golf courses on reservations to attract capital for jobs and improvements. The total casino intake in 2018 was estimated at $33.7 billion (NIGC, 2020). Some tribes manage all the profits for the collective communities and others transfer money directly to tribal members.

Despite these success stories, most Indian tribes are located on isolated reservations where tourists rarely travel. Tribal members remain poorly educated, and impoverished. Indians have social problems that far exceed the national average in rates of alcoholism, low life expectancy, high unemployment, and inadequate health care. In 2018, the official overall Native American unemployment rate—6.8 percent—was nearly double the 3.9 percent national average; reservation unemployment was substantially higher

Illustration 2.3 American Indian Cultural Survival

Among the newest museums on the National Mall in Washington, DC, is the Museum of the American Indian. It celebrates the survival of American Indian tribes nationwide and brings Native American history into the national narrative. Many other museums add to the story. The New Mexico Museum of Indian Arts and Culture in Santa Fe, New Mexico, narrates and promotes an extensive archive of native art and material culture, while also supporting native folkways. In the photograph taken outside the main entrance to the collection, dancers of Navajo origin are foregrounded in front of "The Mountain Dancer," a contemporary sculpture by Craig Dan Goseyun of the Eastern White Mountain Apache tribe. Mountain Dancers are important to Apache and other First People cultures and symbolize the power to protect and heal. Every year across "Indian Country"—the reservations and cultural sites where Indians live—tribes hold tribal and multi-tribal PowWows to keep traditions alive, to honor ancestors, and to organize activists in the service of Indian progress.

Source: Robert Alexander/Archive Photos via Getty Images

Map 2.7 American Indian Reservations

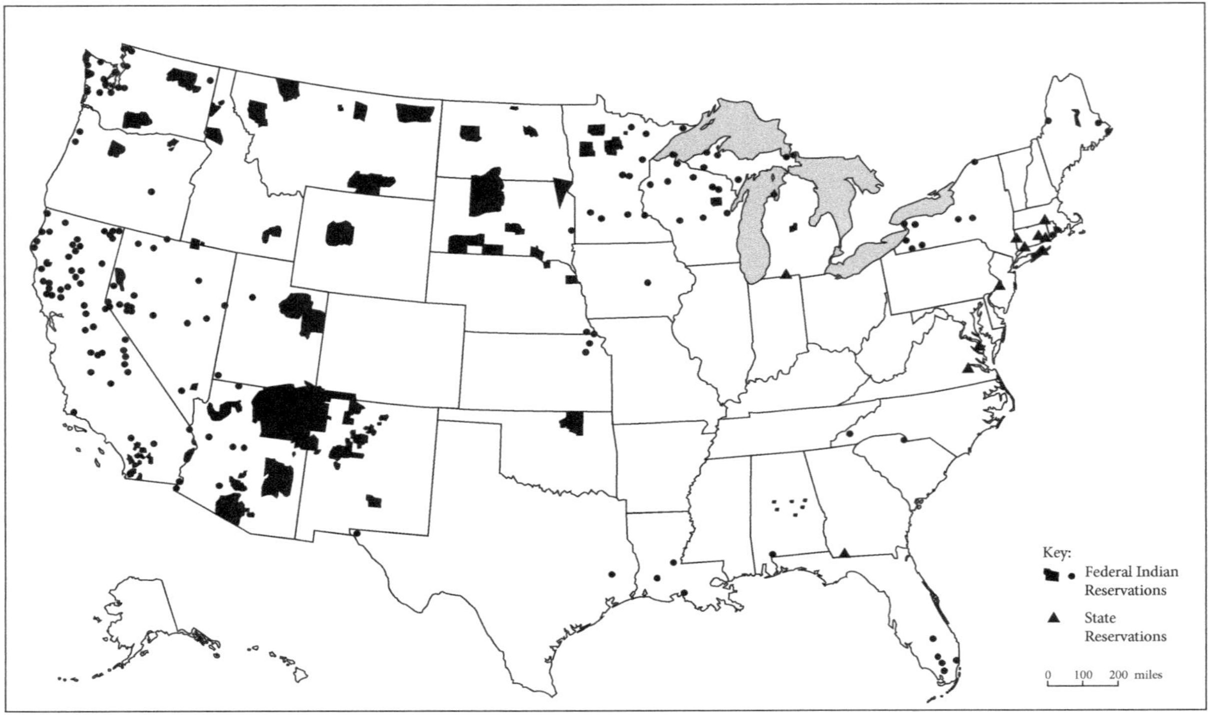

(BLS, 2019a). Another failure is cultural; by 2050, perhaps only twenty of the 139 spoken native languages will remain in everyday use (NCAI, 2020).

While Indians are proud to be Americans, the major disputes with the federal government are over the sense of Indian-ness that is tied to the land. Without the land, some have said, there are no Indians. As an example of the interconnectedness, in the Apache language, the word for land is the same as the word for mind; the issue of sovereignty is tethered to that construction. Many of the disputes are over who has the right to the natural resources, as in the case of the 2016 Standing Rock pipeline dispute. The Obama administration denied the pipeline a permit. Work resumed when the incoming Trump administration overturned Obama's order. In July 2020, Standing Rock Sioux won a court ruling halting work on the pipeline pending a full environmental review. At stake was the risk of water pollution from the pipeline work and its petrochemical cargo, and ultimately a sense of environmental injustice where the least resourced suffer dire environmental consequences (Earthjustice.org, 2020). Public dams redirect water supplies and conservation policies restrict the number of fish that may be caught. Both of these infringe on traditional patterns and livelihoods, and Native Americans have mostly won lawsuits to control water and fishing rights.

Other land disputes concern the rich mineral deposits and oil under reservation lands which have been leased to private corporations or, in the name of national security, have been mined under contracts with the US Bureau of Land Management. The US government currently allows private contractors to operate coal-burning power plants on or near sacred lands. Obama consistently supported Indian rights over sub-surface resources under reservation lands. The Trump administration had a more "utilitarian" approach to tribal and western national monument lands. In 2020, one tribe, the Massachusetts Mashpee Wampanoag, had their reservation designation rescinded. Other tribes feared similar erosions of rights (*Guardian*, 2020).

African Americans

African Americans as a group do not share the common defining historical experience of voluntary immigration to the United States which most other Americans share; instead, their ancestors were kidnapped, or sold into slavery and forced to adapt to a country with established racial hierarchies. This substantial difference still affects race relations as other racial and ethnic groups feel themselves more authentically American because of the original intent of their ancestors to make a new and better life for themselves from the one they were leaving behind. It is important to remember that the United States had no feudal past and thus no established peasantry. For African Americans, the continent of origin, slavery and its confrontation with America's stated moral vision, and the long-standing status as the nation's central minority set them apart—as Ta-Nehisi Coates correctly noted (Coates, 2015).

After decades of struggle, the Civil Rights Movement of the 1950s and 1960s mobilized the African American community in line with the actions and words of leaders such as Martin Luther King, Jr. ("Agitate, Litigate, Legislate!") and Malcolm X

Contemporary United States

("By any means necessary!"). While still facing discrimination by private individuals, in job promotions, and by financial institutions, much has changed as blacks have succeeded in wiping away all rules and regulations that denied equality before the law. A good deal of the split in American society is now as much a function of class as race, with a large portion of African Americans still, using King's words, "wrapped in an airtight cage of poverty in the midst of an affluent society" (King, 1963). This is neither to downplay the discrimination nor exaggerate the advances that have been made. Signs of black progress are everywhere apparent in the sheer numbers of prominent business people, actors, sports figures, politicians, military personnel, and university graduates in every US state. In his May 2016 Howard University Commencement Address, President Obama underlined how much better things had become for people of color (NPR, 2016). At the same time, discrimination and poverty are apparent and the United States is increasingly divided into the haves and have-nots where race and class intertwine. The many failings catalogued by Black Lives Matter attest to manifestly unequal policing, as does the high African American murder rate in Chicago and elsewhere. Racism and unequal opportunities have much to do with what seems to be a rising caste system (see Chapters 5 and 6).

According to the US Census Bureau, African Americans account for around 13.4 percent of the total population—or 44 million people (USCB, 2020b). Being African American is more than visual as blacks define themselves as much by self-choice and societal definition as by ancestry. Social definitions count. For example, Americans consider white women to be capable of conceiving black babies, but generally deny that black women can have white babies. In a reversal, Haitians have defined anyone with one part of white blood as "white," which is the opposite of the historical American insistence that one drop of black blood made a person "black."

Whether defined in racial, ethnic, or cultural terms, Americans have long experienced a phenomenon just beginning in many societies in the world: the ability to blur the differences between culture groups and fuse them into a national group. Many would like to see the old racial classification pentagon of white, black, red, yellow, and brown, and cross-cultural definitions such as Muslim, Hispanic, Asian American, or Jew, deleted for a post-racial or post-ethnic idea of simply being "American" or not. Intermarriages push different groups closer to this idea as does the concept of "symbolic identity," which allows a feeling of ethnicity or race as a sub-region of the whole. And, of course, in contemporary America, immigration issues affect every race, but none more decisively than Hispanics/Latinos and Asian Americans, who are demanding entry and equality in striking numbers (see Table 5.4).

Immigration

The movement of peoples from other nations into the United States has been unsurpassed and the country continues to be the preferred destination for nearly 20 percent of all immigrants worldwide (Figure 2.1 and Table 2.7) (Budiman, 2020; MPI, 2020). Since

Land and People

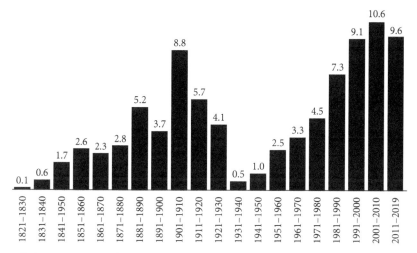

Figure 2.1 Immigrants to the United States Gaining Legal Permanent Resident Status, by Decade, 1821–2019 (in millions)

Source: DHS, 2020b

Table 2.7 Immigrants Gaining Green Cards in 2018—Sending Countries

Americas	Asia and Middle East	Africa	Europe
1. Mexico (161,858)	2. China (65,214)		
4. Cuba (76,486)	3. India (59,821)		
5. Dom. Rep. (57,413)	6. Philippines (48,633)		
8. El Salvador (28,326)	7. Vietnam (33,834)		
9. Haiti (21,360)			
10. Jamaica (20,347)	11. S. Korea (17,676)		
12. Columbia (17,545)	13. Pakistan (15,802)		
15. Guatemala (15,638)	14. Bangladesh (15,717)		
16. Brazil (15,394)	17. Syria (14,686)		
20. Honduras (13,794)	18. Iraq (14,351)	19. Nigeria (13,952)	
	21. Afghanistan (12,935)		
25. Venezuela (11,762)	23. Nepal (11,953)	22. Ethiopia (12,403)	24. Ukraine (11,879)
26. Ecuador (11,472)			
	27. Iran (10,116)	28. Dem. Rep. Congo (9,941)	29. UK (9,908)
30. Canada (9.898)			
31. Peru (9,878)		32. Egypt (9,826)	33. Russia (8,621)
34. Guyana (8,394)			
**Totals by Continent:	35. Burma (8,182)		
Americas (497,460)	Asia and Middle East		
World Total 1,096,611*	(397,187)	Africa (115,736)	Europe (80,024)

* Includes 4,653 from Oceania, of which Australia is highest at 2,693.
** Totals for continents do not add up to the world total exactly because of a double count, at times, between Asia and Europe and some unspecified origins.

Source: DHS (2020b)

Contemporary United States

1607, immigrants have come with their own ideas of what they would do if they could claim a piece of land for themselves. America's population doubled every twenty-five years in the nineteenth century and every fifty years in the twentieth century. In 1965, one in every twenty Americans was foreign-born. In the twenty-first century, one person in eight (over 40 million people) was born abroad. The United States is currently having both its strongest period of immigration and its highest percentages of immigrants in the total population—at 13 percent (MPI, 2020). The consistently strong immigration has kept America younger than many other nations. Projections for 2050, for example, put the US median population age at thirty-five years, in comparison with a 52-year-old European Union and an even older China. The US naturalizes—grants citizenship to—nearly 2,000 people each day (DHS, 2020c) and granted green cards—permanent residence status—to around one million people in 2018 (DHS, 2020b).

Beyond the original colonists, early immigrants, and the 400,000 Africans brought as slave laborers during what might be called the first wave of immigration, there have been eras marked by the influx of different groups. Between 1820 and 1890, ten million "Old Immigrants" came. These peoples were overwhelmingly English, German, Irish, and Scandinavian. The Irish came from different religious and economic backgrounds as they fled persecution for their Catholicism and starvation from the widespread potato famine. From 1890 to 1924, Europeans from Eastern and Southern Europe poured into New York. These "New Immigrants"—many of them of Italian, Polish, Hungarian, Russian, Czech, Greek, and Middle Eastern origins—were mostly unlettered, poorer, religiously different, and politically unwanted in their countries of origin. But whatever their economic status or home culture—and surviving the multitude of hatreds and fears from among the "Old Immigrants"—these individuals quickly gathered themselves into a new and somewhat homogeneous group recognized as Americans. This does not mean that assimilation was easy. In the face of a coercive conformity, many immigrants struggled to hold onto, even to re-establish, the world they left into the world they entered. However much they may have wanted to isolate or segregate themselves into distinct ethnic enclaves, they were affected by the seething tide of humanity, technology, and change all around them. Probably most immigrants kept one foot in each world, forming a transnational culture whose economic interactions shaped the minority experience in the United States. The current wave of immigrants, overwhelmingly from Latin America and Asia, is once again changing the way America defines itself and is defined by others.

The immigration policy of the United States has been both inclusive and discriminatory. There have been efforts to bar some groups and stop immigration entirely. Critics, including President Trump, say that immigrants have a profoundly harmful effect on a high-tech society if they are poor, under-educated, and economically marginalized, and union representatives sometimes complain that immigrant labor keeps down wages while increasing welfare payments. Both arguments are echoed in US immigration debates. When the economy is growing, the call is for more immigrant workers; but financial downturns lead quickly to fundamental questions about immigration policy and the very nature of America. Immigration—formal and informal—is intensely politicized and was a major issue in the 2016 election campaign and Trump's single term in office. In an era of endless campaigning, Trump repeatedly targeted cultural difference, economic competition, and alleged immigrant criminality. Latin Americans were especially denigrated, with the idea of a wall to separate the US from Mexico and Latin American immigration as Trump's central coordinating theme, some argued (Hirschfeld-Davis and Shear, 2019). Immigrants are found in all levels of work, from the lowest farm and blue-collar laborers to the upper echelons of white-collar business firms. Immigrant billionaires include Google's Sergei Brin and Tesla's Elon Musk. Public laws and private acceptance bring in more skilled and richer foreigners in a transnational and global economy, despite hostility from cultural conservatives.

Immigrants have sometimes faced a "100 percent Americanism" backlash by xenophobes who want everyone to speak the same language, to be of a certain ancestry, and to have an accepted religion and cultural folkways. Even the way people dress has come under criticism. Catholics, Jews, and others have been singled out in the past but are generally accepted in modern America. Since the September 11, 2001, attacks, bias has grown against Muslims—much of it fanned by radio talk shows and social media—but the vast majority of Americans have always rejected neo-Nazi or Ku Klux Klan ideology and they continue to favor the individual variations of a multicultural society. Most Americans realize that first-generation adult immigrants rarely break free of their old habits or become fluent in English. Most of these immigrants are transnationals with loyalties and customs honored in the country of origin and the country of residency. Their children are less transnational because they often assimilate with a vengeance that mutes the "foreign" ways of their parents; by the third generation, very few children can speak the foreign language of their grandparents. More than any government action or voluntary help programs, popular culture and intermarriages turn immigrants into Americans.

The National Origins Act of 1924 limited immigration to a quota system based upon country of origin. The Act favored Northern and Western Europe and reduced total immigration from over 800,000 to 164,000 per year. The Great Depression, the Second World War, and the Cold War had a great impact on policy, which has been in flux ever since. In 1965, the quota system was revised, as Congress allowed a more equitable distribution of immigration visas by hemispheres, totaling 290,000 per year and stressing the reunification of families instead of job qualifications. The Immigration Act of 1986 granted general amnesty and, sometimes, citizenship to those who could pass the tests about general US history and laws to illegal immigrants who would register. In 1990, Congress raised the number of legal immigrants per year to 700,000. The 2000 Immigration Act allowed "commuter green cards" to people who live in Mexico or Canada but who are in the US daily or often on work-related business. The result has been a surge in the numbers of women, rich business people, and two new immigrant minorities: Latinos (including Hispanics) and Asians.

"Latinos" is an inclusive term for people from Central and South American origins: Brazilians who speak Portuguese are Latinos, not Hispanics. Hispanics are so-called because they speak Spanish as their first language. In contemporary America, "Latinos" means both groups. Before the Second World War, there were just three million Latinos

Contemporary United States

counted in the US, mostly in the southern parts of the Sunbelt and among the Puerto Rican community in NYC. In 2020, the 60 million Latinos made up 18.5 percent of the total population (USCB, 2020b). The majority of Latinos are Chicanos—as immigrants from Mexico identify themselves.

Many Latinos provide substantial support to communities in their country of origin. For example, in 2016, $74 billion was wired south of the border, with Chicano immigrants alone sending approximately $29 billion (Budiman and Conor, 2018). The newest wave of immigrants is made up of transnational commuters who frequently travel back and forth, and who feel immense loyalty to their country of birth and their country of residence. When these groups establish themselves in America, they tend to settle together among relatives and friends they have known all or most of their lives.

The rapid rise in the percentage of Hispanics has caused concern in some circles. Political Scientist Samuel Huntington warned that this "persistent inflow of Hispanic immigrants threatens to divide the United States into two peoples, two cultures, and two languages" (Huntington, 2004). Privileging Europeans, Huntington argued that the American idea and policies toward immigration have been symbolized by the Ellis Island immigration facility—or even John F. Kennedy Airport in NYC—where immigrants come into America by air. Mexican immigration is different because of Mexico's contiguity with the United States and because of the demographic scale which includes legal and illegal immigration of so many people with a similar language, Spanish, as opposed to a diversity of languages in the past.

While no other immigrant group could ever claim original title to American soil, the area from Texas northward to Utah and westward to California was part of the Mexican homeland until 1848. Former Mexican President Vicente Fox called Mexican emigrants "heroes" and called himself "president of 123 million Mexicans, 100 million in Mexico and 23 million in the United States" (quoted in Huntington, 2004). Both Huntington and Fox underscore the rise of transnationalism among immigrant groups and the growing political influence of America's largest minority population (Illustration 2.4). Meanwhile, Donald Trump fanned frustration over Latin America's cultural, social, and economic penetration of the US, demonizing Latino immigration, replacing trade deals, repatriating undocumented immigrants, and began building "a great, great, wall" between the US and Mexico, for which—contrasting with Trump's insistence that Mexico would pay—the US financed. Millions supported him, because of worries over the ten million undocumented immigrants living within the nation's borders and concerns among older and less educated whites over demographic change. Still, little construction on a new wall happened on Trump's watch.

Asian Americans are designated as a group not by language, culture, history, or ethnicity, but by the fact that they arrive from Asia. There is little cohesion among the group as Vietnamese, Indians, Afghans, Chinese, Japanese, Burmese, Koreans, and others have little to bind them together. In the past, discriminatory immigration laws prohibited the Chinese from immigrating in 1882 and the Japanese in 1924. The Japanese attack on Pearl Harbor (1941), the Korean War (1950-1953), Vietnam War (1954–1975), and the rise of communist, modern China maintained fears of Asians. In the 1980s, Congress voted monetary compensation to the thousands of Japanese-Americans concentrated

Illustration 2.4 Surging Latino/Latina Political Power

The United States is ever more diverse in its ethnic and racial identities. The twenty-first century has benefited from an ever-increasing multicultural populace driven both by immigration and high birth rates in minority communities. Some have called the surge a "browning of America." And clearly the country is split by those welcoming the integration into the global community and those fearing that "they will replace us" and change the culture from white privilege to a broader equality. On January 20, 2021, Kamala Harris was sworn in as Vice President of the United States. She was the first person of color and first female to achieve the position. Her South Asian (India) and African American (Jamaica) ancestry punctuated the change that came with the 2020 presidential election and certified the rising strength of minority voting groups, young people, and women. The photograph highlights her power to gain the attention of three multi-ethnic girls, Andrea Reese, Liliana Ami, and Alexis Isabella Bravo, who see someone like themselves in her identity and similar to the strong female Chicana, Maribel Valdez Gonzalez, pictured on the right side of the wall in a poster by artist Shepard Fairey. With birth rates among Hispanics leading all ethnic groups in America, these future voters—plus their two brothers and their politically active parents—herald a new dynamic for the American experience.

Source: Bonnie Bravo

into work camps during the Second World War. Nearly half of all immigrants to America since 1965 have been Asians who initially settled together in Pacific Rim states and big cities in the Sunbelt. In San Diego, the world's largest community of Vietnamese immigrants lives in "Little Saigon" and makes up a major part of the more than 711,000 Vietnamese Americans living in California and the 1.9 million nationwide.

Asian immigrants have been dubbed the "model minority" by the press because of their admirable work ethic, low crime rate, strong families, focus on education, rapid acquisition of English, and quick assimilation into the broader culture. In fact, Asian Americans—notably Japanese, South Koreans, Chinese, and Indians—now score higher than all other groups on standardized exams, attend the finest universities in numbers out of proportion with their percentage of the population, and earn higher salaries than European Americans (Illustration 2.5).

The government agency which oversees immigration is the Department of Homeland Security (DHS). The DHS was created in 2002 and given cabinet-level status to strengthen security, as part of the war on terrorism. With a budget of $92 billion in 2020, the DHS employs over 240,000 people (DHS, 2020a). Within the DHS, Immigration and Customs Enforcement (ICE) employs over 20,000 people; analysts and officers patrol the Canadian and Mexican borders of the United States. Agents monitor visas, investigate visitors, test and administer naturalization oaths, arrest, detain, and deport illegal aliens (DHS, 2020a). In 2014, the DHS processed over 374 million travelers. Additionally, asylum

Illustration 2.5 "Today I am an American"

On May 27, 2021, at a Maryland Naturalization Ceremony, Patricia Chung took her Oath of Allegiance and became an American—by choice. In Fiscal Year (FY) 2020, even while the pandemic held down the numbers, 625,000 people attained citizenship. Women between the ages of thirty and forty made up the largest age group. The top five countries of origin were Mexico (13.3 percent), India (7.7 percent), Philippines (5.3 percent), Cuba (5.0 percent), and China (3.7 percent). (USCIS.GOV, 2022)

Source: Kevin Dietsche via Getty Images

seekers and refugees also apply to the DHS for permission to stay in the US—among them were more than one million Vietnamese, Laotians, and Cambodians applying from 1975 to 1993 in the wake of the US war with Vietnam.

In 2019, Customs and Border protection agents made over 859,000 apprehensions, predominantly along the southern border. Border Patrol officers also stopped over 288,523 inadmissible aliens at the nation's 300-odd official points of entry (USCBP, 2022). Reasons for refusing entry include criminal and immigration violations. The separation of thousands of children from parents of accompanying adults during Trump's term was particularly contentious (Aguilera, 2019). Trump increased budget requests for DHS—by 24 percent in 2020 alone—signaling the importance the administration vested in border law and order (DHS, 2020a). Biden must decide how to confront continued undocumented border crossings as the issue remains politically potent.

Government policy is often contradictory in its treatment of undocumented immigrants. The 1996 Immigration Law requires that foreigners facing deportation be jailed while they are processed—from murderers to students who overstay their student visas. Conversely, those who are not apprehended are protected by a federal law requiring schools to educate all children, irrespective of their status. The government insists on minimum wage and safety guidelines to protect these immigrants from unfair hiring practices by employers. Of course, the law is one thing and practice is another. Many undocumented immigrants are afraid to challenge employers for fear of being found out and deported. They accept less than a minimum or competitive wage in order to remain at work in the United States, feeding the perception that they are undercutting American labor. Many states offer welfare benefits and hospital services on a need basis, not by legal status. Other states take a harder line. For example, California has barred state money for education, health care or other services for undocumented aliens—though this has in part been overturned by the courts.

Obviously, the US immigration system is broken and has needed fixing for a long time. Encouraged by the Trump administration, a bipartisan group in the Senate came close to an agreement in early 2018 midterms on regularizing the status of young, undocumented migrants. This plan ultimately failed when Trump amped up a hard-line approach. Immigration policy remains unreformed, where some cities and states pursued "Sanctuary City" policies protecting immigrants while the federal government and ICE seeks deportations. Emotions about immigration enforcement will continue to run high.

The American people, by overwhelming majorities, say they want two things: a tough enforcement policy, and leniency for the millions of undocumented people already in the US. Nearly 60 percent of Americans oppose substantially expanding the border wall (Bialek, 2019). The political debate focuses on unauthorized Mexican immigrants, possible Muslim terrorists, and border management. Trump focuses on negative elements, such as supposed cultures of criminality fed by undocumented migration, yet more than three-quarters of Americans acknowledge the striking economic benefits immigrants bring by taking the jobs that Americans do not want (Krogstad, Lopez, and Passel, 2020).

Contemporary United States

Americans must compromise over competing concerns to strike a balance between national security and national cohesion, between economic impact and human rights issues, between compassion for immigrants and constitutional law and order. With ideological and practical deadlock over how to solve the problem—amnesty, permanent citizenship, crackdowns on employers, work visas, renewable permits, deportation, stronger border controls, and imprisonment—many Americans see merit in Trump's wall with Mexico and deportations of those already here. Millions of pro-immigrant protesters, meanwhile, have marched through American cities in some of the largest mass protests in US history. Sociologist Alan Wolfe noted that for a nation that defines itself as a liberal democracy built by immigrants, "There is something ugly about criminalizing illegal aliens, rounding them up, and deporting them" (Wolfe, 2006). The incendiary sentiments advanced by President Trump in office fueled nativist sentiments. Perhaps Biden's quieter approach will quell them.

President Obama acknowledged that Americans were "a nation of laws as well as a nation of immigrants," worked unsuccessfully on legislative immigration reform, and when that failed in 2012, acted through executive orders to protect young Hispanics who called themselves "Dreamers." Obama agitated for a "DREAM Act" (Development, Relief, Education for Alien Minors) to allow immigrants who had been brought to the US as children to be granted amnesty and permanent resident or citizenship status. In 2018, Trump attempted to dismantle DACA (Deferred Action for Childhood Arrivals), resulting in legal challenges that reached the Supreme Court in June 2020. The Court blocked Trump's actions, despite its 5–4 conservative majority, and drew the accusation from Trump that the decision was "horrible and politically charged" (Totenberg, 2020). Biden has pledged to offer all Dreamers a path to citizenship; fulfilling that pledge will probably have to wait until the 2023–2024 Congress convenes.

It seems probable that with strong immigration from Asia and the Americas, the United States will continue its historic pattern of expansion and diversity. The country's wealth and power remain dependent on the nation's ability to attract and assimilate foreigners. The land and resources are sufficient to accommodate a much larger population. Both the internal birth rate and immigration sources favor non-white groups as a more culturally diverse and multiracial America continues to unfold. African Americans, American Indians, Asian Americans, and Latinos are increasing at double and quadruple the rate of white ethnics. About 48 percent of the nation's population growth in the last decade has come from immigration (Adamy and Overberg, 2019).

Demographers and economists recognize the need for willing hands and minds to work in the US, as population growth—bar immigrants and their offspring—is markedly below the replacement level. America beckons to people across the globe because it continues to offer a dream of a better future—even if that dream is not realized. Administrations on the Left and Right must ensure that nativist worries neither strangle economic needs, nor dampen the promise of a fresh start. Trump wished to advance immigration reform by attracting highly skilled and self-supporting immigrants on terms similar to those offered by Canada, Australia, and other countries, but attracting highly skilled immigrants in the Covid-19 era proved difficult. Both presidential candidates in the 2020 election sought to attract white working class votes who often see immigrant labor as a threat, so border control will remain an issue—whether via Trump's symbolic physical structure or Biden's "smart border enforcement" (Taylor and Smallberg, 2020). The tension between the labor needs of the American economy and nativist resistance among older Americans seem likely to persist as an issue central to governance.

Further Reading

Bishop, B. (2008) *The Big Sort: Why the Clustering of Like-Minded America is Tearing US Apart*, Boston: Houghton Mifflin Harcourt.

Coates, T. (2015) *Between the World and Me*, New York: Spiegel & Grau.

Desmond, M. and M. Emirbayer (2020) *Race in America*, 2nd edn, New York: W. W. Norton.

Friedman, T. (2008) *Hot, Flat, and Crowded: Why We Need a Green Revolution–And How It Can Renew America*, New York: Farrar, Straus, & Giroux.

Huntington, S. (2004) *Who Are We: The Challenges to America's National Identity*, New York: Simon & Schuster.

Paik, N. (2020) *Bans, Walls, Raids, Sanctuary: Understanding U.S. Immigration for the Twenty-First Century*, Los Angeles: University of California Press.

Wright, E. and J. Rogers (2015) *American Society: How It Really Works*, London: W. W. Norton.

CHAPTER 3
GOVERNMENT

The Corona outbreak of 2019–2021 confirmed that Americans expect presidents to rise to the occasion in the hardest of times. In the presidential election, Donald Trump claimed a competent, hands-on approach where timely action by his administration had prevented perhaps two million deaths and kept Americans safe. Challenger Joe Biden, meanwhile, counter-argued that too little executive action, organization, and direction caused many needless deaths among the hundreds of thousands of fatalities, the ensuing economic crisis and mass-unemployment—the deepest since the 1930s—and a social and cultural crisis that threatened to fray the fabric of the nation (Illustration 3.1).

Before Corona, Trump could point to a booming economy fueled by debt-driven government spending and tax cuts that saw asset values soar. Trump claimed minorities had particularly benefited by economic growth and historically low unemployment. Senate and House Republicans accepted Trump's leadership of their party—some more than others—while universally rejoicing over the conservative restructuring of the Supreme Court. Democrats countered that the "Trump" economic boom continued the sound economy inherited from Obama, and that boom-cycle deficit spending threatened the ability of government action should things go awry—as they did in March 2020. Having won a solid blue-wave House majority in the 2018 midterms, Democrats coveted Senate control and the keys to the White House for Joe Biden, both of which they achieved in 2020.

Liberal Supreme Court Justice Ruth Bader Ginsberg's death in September 2020 gave Trump the opportunity to pick a third justice, to create a durable 6–3 conservative Supreme Court majority. Democrats were fired up, fearing another conservative voice on the Supreme Court would imperil the right to abortion, same-sex marriage, and health system protection provided by Obamacare. The stakes had never been higher in the fall of 2020, as all three branches of government—the White House, Congress, and the Supreme Court—were evidently in play.

Both Trump and Biden accepted that government played important roles in the lives of Americans. Trump perceived that role negatively, as constricting individual choice and a limiting of the executive's ability to act, where the "deep state"—the semi-permanent and everyday echelons of government—thwarted the executive. Trump saw law, order, and the military as government virtues, requiring increased funding to "Keep America Great." Biden, meanwhile, maintained that collective action and government could do more for ordinary folks, and help American society "Build Back Better" from Covid

Contemporary United States

Illustration 3.1 Politicizing Public Health Guidelines

In this photograph, President Trump is flanked on the left by White House Coronavirus Response Coordinator, Deborah Birx, and on the right by National Institute of Allergy and Infectious Diseases Director Anthony Fauci. On March 20, 2020, the Covid Task Force held one of many briefings on the Covid situation. At that briefing, Trump talked up hydroxychloroquine as a potential therapy while Fauci doubted that therapy would work. Later Trump supported the injection of ultra-violet light, the swallowing of a disinfectant bleach, and a deworming drug used for horses and cows. His scientific advisors were appalled. In February 2022, the US Covid death toll exceeded one million and climbing.

Source: Jabin Botsford/*The Washington Post* via Getty Images

and a generation of increasing economic and social inequality. Republicans usually argue that government should be limited and local in focus; Democrats contend that the federal government is a force for good and can solve problems that local government cannot. Though the 2020 election united the federal government's three elected branches under the leadership of the Democrats, much is decided by the state, county, or city governments.

Deliberate divisions of power typify America's governing structures. The federal government is split and shared among three branches, comprising the executive, the legislative, and the judicial—each with specific areas of responsibility. Yet, they were not set up to control fully their own spheres. The division of power is complicated by checks and balances, amounting to mutual surveillance and limitation, while allowing the federal government to make, enact, and interpret laws. While divided powers are grounded in the Constitution, they also rely on custom to persist. A further division of government exists in the overlapping relationship of federal and state governments. Each state resembles the federal government, with separate executive, legislative, and judicial branches. Beyond this, governmental power fractures again to create local, county, and district levels of authority. The separation of powers and the checks and balances give access points to individuals or groups who are not always represented by the principle of majority rule. Access allows a plurality of interests to be heard and appeased, though some argue the system is so complex that understanding it is left solely to the truly interested. This access brings the diverse peoples together under the Constitution, formally amended only seventeen times since the inclusion of the first ten amendments as the Bill of Rights in 1791. The branches must cooperate for government to work effectively. Though divided government has been the rule for much of the last generation, in 2020 the Democratic Party united all three elected branches.

The Constitution

The Constitution is the founding document of American government. The intention of the Founders was to guarantee political freedom, promote social order, and install a degree of equality among citizens. The division of power in this federal system is determined both by the Constitution and through a mix of practical compromises made during the 230 years since the republic was founded.

In the formative years of the nation, the idea of apportioning authority was seen as the best method of ensuring benevolent government. When the American Revolution ended in 1783, the Founders—including Benjamin Franklin, John Adams, James Madison, and Alexander Hamilton—needed to establish a system to do the business of government. This meant creating institutions to run what was, even then, a vast territory along the Eastern seaboard from Massachusetts to Georgia, and beyond to the Mississippi River. Preserving order and protecting the nation from external threats were uppermost in their minds. At the same time, each state believed itself to have established its own identity in colonial times and wanted a system to protect its sovereign power while limiting national power. The Founders developed a double plan. The Constitution (Box 3.1) sets out the structure of the federal government, explaining how it should carry out its business. The Bill of Rights, appended during the ratification process, guaranteed protections under law for state and individual rights. Essentially, three sets of sovereignty were confirmed: federal, state, and popular.

The debate over government power reflected the differing concerns of the states. Larger states, such as Virginia, would get more influence simply through the size of their populations. Smaller states, such as New Jersey, wanted the numbers in the legislature to be the same for all states, regardless of size. The Founders agreed to mesh the interests of small and large states by establishing a bicameral legislature, collectively called "Congress," and consisting of a House of Representatives and a Senate. The number of representatives each state placed in the House—above a minimum of one representative

Box 3.1 The Constitution of the United States of America: A Summary

Preamble

We the People of the United States, in Order to form a more perfect Union, establish Justice, insure domestic tranquility, provide for the common defence, promote the general Welfare, and secure the Blessings of Liberty to ourselves and our Posterity, do ordain and establish this Constitution for the United States of America.

Articles

I Legislative Branch. Sets a bicameral legislature, membership and election rules, privileges, areas of authority and limitations.

II Executive Branch. Sets election and eligibility stipulations for President, the powers of the presidency, relations with Congress and impeachment.

III Judicial Branch. Establishes Supreme Court and sets jurisdiction.

IV Federalism. Provides mutual recognition and citizenship rights, creation, and governance of new states.

V Amendment Procedures. Establishes procedure for amending the Constitution.

VI Supremacy Clause. Establishes federal laws over State laws. Prohibits religious tests for officeholders.

VII Ratification. Provides conditions for initial ratification of Constitution.

Bill Of Rights [Amendments 1–10 (1791)]

1st Establishes freedom of religion, speech, press and assembly

2nd Confirms right to bear arms

3rd Prohibits quartering of military troops in private houses in peacetime

4th Prohibits unreasonable searches and seizures

5th Gives freedom from double-jeopardy or self-incrimination

6th Maintains rights of accused to speedy jury trial, witnesses, and lawyer in criminal trials

7th Establishes right to jury trial in civil cases

8th Prohibits cruel and unusual punishments; requires reasonable bail

9th Retains unlisted rights for the People

10th Reserves unlisted powers for the States or the People

Subsequent Amendments:

11th Limits lawsuits between states (1795)

12th Revises presidential Electoral College system (1804)

13th	Abolishes slavery (1865)
14th	Grants citizenship to ex-slaves and all children born in the US. Provides for *due process* and *equal protection* (1868)
15th	Protects voting rights regardless of "race, color or previous condition of servitude" (1870)
16th	Authorizes federal income tax (1913)
17th	Provides for direct election of US Senators (1913)
18th	Prohibits the manufacture or sale of alcohol (1919)
19th	Grants voting rights for women (1920)
20th	Sets accession dates for President and Congress. Establishes presidential succession (1933)
21st	Repeals 18th Amendment (1933)
22nd	Sets two-term limit for President (1951)
23rd	Grants electoral votes to citizens of Washington, DC (1961)
24th	Prohibits poll taxes in federal elections (1964)
25th	Revises presidential succession procedure (1967)
26th	Lowers voting age to eighteen years old (1971)
27th	Sets timing limits on congressional pay raises (1992)

Note: For full text see United States Citizenship and Immigration Services: https://www.uscis.gov/sites/default/files/document/guides/M-654.pdf

per state—would be in direct proportion to its percentage of the total national population. In the Senate, each state would be equally represented by two senators.

This compromise gave—and still gives—over-representation to the small states, because no matter how low a percentage of the national population, each would have two senators and one representative. Presidential elections have always been influenced by this advantage as the numbers of electors each state has in the Electoral College matches its total number of representatives (proportional according to decennial census population) and senators (always two). This arrangement puts geographical sovereignty above popular sovereignty. Note that Americans do not vote for their president directly and nationally. they vote indirectly and by state, with votes transformed into Electoral College delegates. The victorious candidate in each state—except in Maine and Nebraska, where votes are split—wins all the state's electoral delegates. Because there are 538 electors—100 senators, 435 representatives, and 3 delegates from the District of Columbia—it takes 270 votes to win an election. In 2000, despite getting 400,000 fewer votes than Al Gore, George W. Bush won the Electoral College by 271 to 267. In 2016, Hillary Clinton (48.3 percent) beat Donald Trump (46.2 percent) by over 2.8 million popular votes but lost the Electoral College 302–238. These anomalies, between the popular vote and the electoral vote, have fueled calls for electoral reform.

Contemporary United States

Division of Powers

The Constitution, as originally devised, divided power between law-making, law-enforcing, and law-interpreting branches: legislative, executive, and judicial. This separation of powers limited each branch of government to its own specific area of authority. The executive branch had the power to administer laws and to represent the state in foreign affairs. Congress was designed to pass laws, with its authority split between the House and the Senate. Through its control of the budget and taxation, the House focused on domestic policy. Because treaties with other nations need approval or refusal, the Senate would oversee foreign policy. The Founders imagined the Supreme Court as the weakest branch and did not define it or the federal court system in clear terms. The judiciary would act as a court of appeal to mediate among different legal interpretations, and, eventually, to decide the constitutionality of government actions.

The division of government into three branches along with strict written definitions of the range of federal and state power worked to soothe fears of a rogue executive, or of a conspiracy by a legislative majority to take away fundamental rights. The Trump administration tested the complex machinery of governance by asserting executive pre-eminence within the federal government and over the states, by ignoring tempering norms of governance, and by attacking semi-independent institutions (Levitsky and Ziblatt, 2019). In fact, although executive, legislative, and judicial authority overlap on most issues, Americans split the functions of government so dramatically that no branch occupies the central space on the field of power unopposed. This situation strongly contrasts with most parliamentary systems, where the biggest party or governing coalition forms the government, appoints and directs the executive, and controls chief judicial appointments. Even the layout of Washington, DC, reflects the separation of powers by physically separating the three branches in a long, acute triangle. The large buildings command a view of the Mall, the grassy 3-mile (5 km) long rectangle in the heart of the city, yet no branch has an uninterrupted view of the other two. Both spatially and conceptually, their gaze meets outside the locale of individual power.

The constitutional separation of powers creates a checks and balances system with each branch dependent on the others. Although these checks and balances will figure prominently in a later discussion of what each branch can or cannot do, their overlapping nature makes it difficult, if not impossible, for unrestrained power to accrue to any one branch: for example, a rogue executive. Divisions of power are designed to avoid precipitous change and to promote stability; however, some commentators argue that checks and balances on political power create paralysis or rule-by-bureaucracy, making the business of government a hard task when the branches are unable to compromise due to ideological polarization. As demonstrated in Figure 3.1, each branch can check the actions of the other branches. This balance encourages compromise as the most effective strategy for achieving results. One consequence of the division of powers is that it can be difficult for ordinary citizens to pin down who does what and can feed into a generalized dissatisfaction and distrust of government.

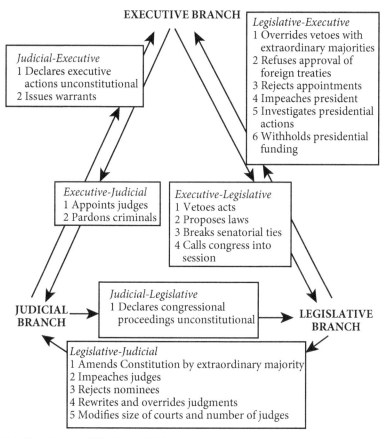

Figure 3.1 The System of Checks and Balances

The Federal System

The original idea of the relationship of the states and the federal government is contained in Article V of the Constitution. Additionally, the 10th Amendment states: "The powers not delegated to the United States by the Constitution, nor prohibited to it by the States, are reserved to the States respectively, or to the people." Today, the reality is quite different. Constitutional arrangements satisfactory for a small republic of four million people in thirteen semi-sovereign agricultural states do not meet the needs of 325 million people living in an integrated, service-based, post-industrial, globally integrated economy. Defining what is local, state, and national is much more difficult and any clear-cut division of power is vague.

Modernization has replaced the static relationship of power with a dynamism that makes federalism as much a process as an institution. The process of federalism has accelerated over the last century and has moved power from the states to the national government, despite persistent rhetoric to the contrary. This process was helped by

Contemporary United States

the generality of the Constitution and Amendments, leaving room for interpretation when circumstances change. Box 3.2 outlines federalism as process, showing how the enumerated powers of the government have been changed by delegated powers.

Historians have used many metaphors to describe federalism. These metaphors present pictures of how power is shared, separated, checked, and balanced. Layer Cake, or Dual, federalism evokes an image of separate and somewhat equal layers of sovereignty. The powers of the national government are contained within its single layer, over and above the distinct powers in the layer of state government, which are over and above the powers of local governments. The United States clearly matched this model from 1790 to 1865 and continued to be influenced by it until 1932.

Marble Cake federalism best illustrates the period 1933–1969. In this model, state and national power swirl around each other, rising and falling and being supreme according to where the cake is sliced. Power is not set firmly above or below, but is cooperative and fluid, allowing for expansion and contraction of federal power and programs according to the beliefs of a specific president and Congress. In 1933, during the worst year of the Great Depression, President Franklin D. Roosevelt (FDR) greatly expanded the role of the federal government with his "New Deal" program of welfare, social security, and jobs. In the 1960s, President Lyndon Johnson's "Great Society" further expanded services. From 2009, President Obama's stimulus and health care policies made strides in the same direction. And, Trump's 2020 expansive avowal of the powers of the executive over the rest of the system pushed for federal supremacy over states issue (Flynn and Chiu, 2020).

In 1969, President Richard Nixon proposed "New Federalism." Nixon believed that the government's main role was in foreign policy and that, in domestic affairs, the federal government had become too intrusive in everyday lives. He wanted to allow the states more power to decide how much to spend and on what to spend it. The Nixon administration pushed a states' rights position just as Americans were discovering the conspiratorial and imperial workings of Nixon and his henchmen in the Watergate affair and Vietnam. Still, this model of New Federalism matched the people's fears that the national government had gotten too big and self-indulgent, a fear shared in contemporary America by libertarian Tea Party and Freedom Caucus Republicans. After a hiatus during the term of Jimmy Carter, administrations since Ronald Reagan in 1981 enacted a "New" New Federalism which provided less finance, more tasks and, thus, more control to the states.

In the 1990s, Bill Clinton pioneered a subtle change in the model. Called "Rhetorical Federalism" by political scientists, Clinton downsized the federal government by allowing the states to decide how to spend money transferred from the national treasury to them. While the federal government reduced funding to the states, it still mandated policy regulations to assert its will without costing it dollars in such areas as communications, transportation, education, and environmental protection.

George W. Bush continued to devolve power to the states, even while the events of September 11, 2001, and the new Department of Homeland Security strengthened the federal government's role in welfare and police power within each state. The

Box 3.2 Federalism as Process

Eighteenth Century

Interstate Commerce: Article I Section 8 grants Congress the right to regulate commerce between the states. As the domestic economy expanded, congressional power was magnified.

Necessary and Proper Clause: Article 1 Section 8 contains the "elastic clause" which empowers Congress to "make all laws which shall be necessary and proper" to govern. For instance, the Constitution enumerates the power of Congress to raise taxes. The elastic clause allows Congress to establish a bureaucracy, the Internal Revenue Service, to fulfil this obligation.

Nineteenth Century

Supremacy Clause: Article VI declares the Constitution to be the "Supreme Law of the Land," trumping the powers of state constitutions. However, it was only in cases such as *Marbury v. Madison* (1803), and *Fletcher v. Peck* (1810) that the supremacy of federal law was accepted and made enforceable. As the final adjudicator of the law, the Supreme Court has the potential to be the most powerful branch, if it chooses to exercise this potential.

Citizenship: At the end of the Civil War, the 13th Amendment freed the slaves, the 14th provided citizenship to black males, and the 15th promised the vote, thereby transferring the power over citizenship and voting from the states to the national government.

Twentieth Century

Business Regulation: The Progressive Era brought about an increased regulation of industry and industrial ownership. The federal government began to exercise greater control over the economy to ensure fair prices and high-quality products in a competitive environment.

Trust in Government: The First World War, the Great Depression, and the Second World War redefined the government's role in managing national economic and human resources for a common purpose. The successful outcome of the wars and the Depression-era legislation provided public support for expanded government.

Stronger Government: The Cold War struggle in space, nuclear armaments, and world power aided the public perception and need for a stronger federal government to direct the national defense.

Global Village: The communications revolution of internet computers decreased the importance of distance and frontiers, and let corporations, not national governments, dominate trade and commerce. Nixon and Reagan returned some power to the states.

Twenty-First Century

The War on Terror and the Rise of the National Security State: Governmental power increased through inter-agency cooperation, enhanced surveillance, and public support for security measures. There was an emergence of executive-directed "unitary government" and massive defense-led increases in government spending.

A Globalized World: The rise of non-governmental actors and complex economic interdependence gives transnational corporations more power to relocate businesses and workers, maximize profits, and reduce the tax-raising and standard-regulating effectiveness of the federal government.

2019–2021 Corona Pandemic: Reconsidering federal power to surmount the Corona pandemic meshed with the instincts of a personalized and authoritarian president.

Bush administration encouraged the view that federal powers should be focused and coordinated by the executive. Overstretched federal budgets helped pay for the "War on Terror," Iraqi reconstruction, and to fund federal tax cuts—leaving the states responsible for welfare programs without funding to implement them.

How these models are applied determines whether each state or the nation provides each particular public service and, of course, who pays for it. The Obama administration promised activity and coequality without arm-twisting from the executive and the federal government. Yet, critics saw Obama's health care reform as evidence of strong-arm control and critiqued that administration's Race to the Top (RTTP) education policies as they imposed responsibility on states without sufficiently increasing funding. Meanwhile, the increasingly transnational mobility of capital and people globally hollowed out what the federal government could do, as global competition over tax rates and regulation encouraged corporations to avoid national tax jurisdictions. The Trump administration followed a patchy strategy on federalism, treating federal tax largesse as a reward for political friends in the states, while denying it from political enemies (Rubin, 2017). In this way, Trump's pressured the federal remit on state policy. Democratic states lashed back, protecting the rights of residents via Sanctuary Cities (Lind, 2018), and by insisting that the 2020 Black Lives Matter protests could be dealt with by dialogue on a city or state level and not by calling in the national guard (Dinan, 2020). Generally, Democrats see federal government action more favorably than Republicans—who often prefer state action over federal. State and local politics, however, make these philosophical preferences "rules of thumb."

Every state has its own written constitution establishing governing practices within its borders. This is not surprising since the original thirteen states were in place before there was a United States and their representatives framed the US Constitution. The states mirror the federal division of powers, with popularly elected governors, bicameral legislatures (except Nebraska), and separately functioning court systems topped by state supreme courts. In ten larger states, state senators and representatives are virtually full-time legislators. In some states, state senators and representatives are part-timers and return home from the state capitols once legislative sessions are over to attend to their regular jobs (NCSL, 2021a).

States decide on taxes, maintain their own police forces, and set laws for people living within state boundaries. When permitted, they may decide on how policies—such as healthcare including abortion and Corona vaccines—are implemented within their borders. Most states limit state executive power by having the people elect state government cabinet members and judges—even state supreme court justices—unlike the federal Constitution, which leaves those selections to the president and confirmations to the Senate. Thus, there is often more internal anarchy in state government as the officials within the state executive branch are responsible to the people who elected them and not necessarily to the political party of the governor.

Local government at the county and municipal levels is much more idiosyncratic. The US Constitution does not provide a guide for how states should distribute their internal power, and the tradition of local autonomy resulting from the existence of self-governing communities in colonial times continues to thrive. Across the country, there are 89,004 units of local government (USCB, 2012). Gallup polls show that American opinions are consistently favorable towards state and local governments, awarding them job approval ratings of around 70 percent (McCarthy, 2018). Mayors, city councils, and city courts—all elected—have responsibility and power in geographically defined municipalities. County commissioners decide policy, enforce the law, and provide services to areas outside of city borders. Tribal councils with tribal police set policies in Indian country. Elected school boards direct school districts which establish local curricula and have decision-making and spending powers over local property taxes. Big cities like New York often straddle state boundaries and state power relationships, spreading cooperative local jurisdictions interstate. Many other types of government entities exist, from wildlife protection areas to military bases.

The Branches of Government

The Executive Branch

President Harry S. Truman (1945–1953) remarked that his days in office were spent persuading people who should have known better what they ought to do (Neustadt, 1990). Embedded in Truman's lament is the complaint that the presidency is not as powerful as is sometimes supposed, meaning that the chief executive often must be chief lobbyist. Presidential influence relies on hard constitutional and legal sources of power, as well as softer, personality and communicative powers such as persuasion and likeability. Reagan portrayed a grandfatherly demeanor and a camera presence that caused him to be dubbed "The Great Communicator." Clinton had an affability and boyish charm that

Contemporary United States

few could resist. They contrast sharply with the tough images put forth by the "imperial" presidents of the 1960s: Kennedy, Johnson, and Nixon.

Obama projected a cool rationality to support his position. He combined reforming zeal with the belief that social media such as Facebook and Twitter could allow him to sidestep traditional media conduits and communicate directly with the nation, signaling that social media savvy communication had become essential in governance. Presidents must navigate between the pragmatic need to accommodate changing circumstances, such as in a recession, and the fundamental need to follow their moral compass by doing what they judge right, such as expanding health care coverage or defense spending despite funding difficulties. In his second term, Obama used executive orders—instructions based in current law—to overcome "gridlock" in Congress. While legislators claimed he had exceeded his constitutionally defined powers, Obama did not use executive orders more than his predecessors had done.

Trump promised an active presidency with firm executive leadership to deal with the nation's growing health, economic, and security challenges. Illustrating contemporary hyperpolarization, Republicans saw that promise fulfilled whereas Democrats found it wanting. Using established media, mass rallies, and social media—especially Twitter—Trump was omnipresent, communicating with everyone, everywhere, all the time, whether they liked it or not. Trump used an unorthodox and personalized communication beyond that seen by previous presidents. This communication seemed immediate and reactive, rather than considered and cerebral. Some called Trump un-presidential, while others saw honesty in his communication avalanche.

Other than in a national emergency, there is a mismatch between what a president can do and what most people think s/he can do—and sometimes what a president himself thinks s/he can do. A president is limited by the separation of powers and the system of checks and balances, as well as by the watchdog attention of the world media. Moreover, much of the deep, administrative state of government is beyond their immediate reach. Further, Congress is often controlled by the opposition party, making it difficult for a president to act, and allowing opposition politicians to berate his leadership abilities. Wars, economic crises, and epidemics influence a president's range of options as the American public will blame or support him in often unpredictable ways.

While any increase in national power certainly strengthens the power of the presidency, short-term issues can wreck a president's ability to influence legislation or conduct foreign policy. Power rises and falls. FDR had enormous power as his energetic resolve coincided with the national emergencies of the Great Depression and the Second World War—emergencies that demanded and warranted extensions of government responsibility into the daily lives of American citizens. Contingencies matter, as they add to or subtract from political capital—as does the proximity of the next election. Obama's approval ratings rose remarkably towards the end of his final term, as his political power was declining. Trump's approval ratings began at around 50 percent, before idling in the high 30s/low 40s for most of his term. In 2022, Biden's initial rating of 55 percent fell to the thirties and forties, fed by the collapse of Afghanistan, rising inflation, and seeming inability to pass signature programs.

Government

Whereas no one before FDR served more than two terms, the American people elected FDR president four times. Congress, fearing a concentration of power and wanting to prevent this from happening again, voted for term limits. The 22nd Amendment, ratified in 1951, limited any single president to two four-year terms. Underlining how power is divided, neither a president nor his cabinet officers are members of Congress. In fact, the vice president is the only member of the executive branch who can cast a vote on legislation—and only in the Senate if one vote is necessary to break a tie, as was the case from 2021. Kamala Harris can use her decisive vote to break a Senate impasse.

With only a few years to make a difference, a newly elected president traditionally has enormous momentum and congressional goodwill to get his programs enacted— though this can evaporate quickly. By convention, outgoing presidents are gracious and advise incoming executives in the seventy-odd days between the election and the inauguration as the new administration decides who will staff what office. Though, this was decidedly not the case in the transition between Trump and Biden. Bill Clinton saw his post-inaugural momentum seep away, due to the defeat of his health care reforms, flip-flopping support for gays in the military, and after re-election, the Lewinsky affair— and impeachment. Bush started with less goodwill due to his polarizing 2000 victory. Before Bush's first year in office ended, the 9/11 terrorist attacks showed that Americans rally around the flag and the person of the president in a crisis. The war in Iraq increased Bush's power and led to his 2004 re-election victory. Obama's 2008 victory promised new directions, but health care reform battles and the continuing economic crisis eroded his authority—before his 2012 re-election victory replenished his power. Trump enjoyed united Republican control but held limited political capital due to his loss of the popular vote, resistance from his own party and Democrats, and low poll ratings. The perception of effective leadership matters. World events such as Corona, the economy, competence, the media, popularity, and personality combine to enhance or limit the constitutional power of a president. These factors are beyond a president's control to a large degree.

The legal power of the presidency comes from the enumerated, inherent, and delegated powers provided by law and precedent. Article II of the Constitution sets forth the presidential powers in approximately 500 words, including the role of commander-in-chief of the armed forces and senior diplomatic officer, the authority to appoint federal officers, ministers and Supreme Court Justices, and the power to pardon criminal offenders. Additionally, the president must annually inform Congress about the state of the Union: this address is a powerful agenda-setting tool. He or she is expected to initiate legislation in the nation's interests and to serve as the chief executive officer of the corporate whole of the United States, as well as being the chief bureaucrat formally responsible for every action of government agencies.

While the American people might hope that all presidents would follow Truman's famous maxim "The buck stops here," they expect political finger-pointing and even admire a person's ability to wriggle out of bottom-line responsibility. While Nixon, Carter, and Ford were blamed for almost everything they did or did not do, Reagan's talent to elude blame was so pronounced that nothing seemed to stick to him—"the Teflon President." Clinton proved so politically astute as to be labeled "Slick Willie" and

Contemporary United States

"the Comeback Kid." Bush's mistake in believing that Saddam Hussein had weapons of mass destruction and links with al-Qaeda, the enormous budget deficit and ballooning national debt, and the loss of three million jobs did not stop his re-election. Obama acknowledged that voters expected their leaders to project a sense of adeptness and confidence; yet, he was blamed for increasing the national debt without fully solving the economic crisis or bringing back prosperity for blue-collar Americans. It was different for Trump. He survived intense and deserved scrutiny, because of the hyperpolarized nature of American politics and partly because the American public did not damn him for not measuring up to the yardstick used on a "traditional" politician.

In addition to the powers enumerated in the Constitution, presidents have gathered or accrued powers, which have been buttressed by Supreme Court rulings that "inherent powers" reside in the duties and responsibilities of the Chief Executive. Presidents need such authority to make decisions concerning territorial, economic, and demographic expansions. George Washington expanded presidential power by taking on a ceremonial role as head of state, receiving foreign diplomats, signing treaties, and "embodying" the nation. Thomas Jefferson's purchase of Louisiana (1803) was an obvious example of the exercise of inherent powers, as the Constitution nowhere mentions the right to buy territory. This loose interpretation of presidential prerogative set a precedent for future land deals. Abraham Lincoln pushed the limits of constitutional powers by calling forth and increasing the size of the army in 1861, freeing the slaves with an "Emancipation Proclamation," and denying the citizens' rights to *habeas corpus*. Teddy Roosevelt claimed it as the president's duty to do anything that the needs of the nation demanded, unless expressly prohibited by the Constitution or Congress—including building the Panama Canal, making executive agreements with leaders abroad, and establishing regulatory agencies.

Delegated powers are responsibilities transferred to the president by Congress, often in times of crisis, or in his role as head of the bureaucracy. An example of crisis delegation was Roosevelt's "New Deal" program, whereby the Congress temporarily relinquished its law-making role to give the executive the kinds of power usually reserved for a president in wartime. FDR swiftly enacted a public works program to relieve unemployment. Other delegated powers reflect the president's role as chief administrative officer. Presidents appoint the heads of all federal agencies and thereby create policy according to the political and ideological stance of the appointee on issues such as racial justice, law enforcement, or use of natural resources. Occasionally, potential nominees look likely to get such a harsh reception in confirmation hearings that they either do not get nominated or they are forced to withdraw their candidacies. Importantly, the precise extent of presidential power also originates from shallower norms, precedents, and deference-based sources, for example as when a president may nominate candidates for vacant spots on the Supreme Court (Levitsky and Ziblatt, 2019).

Presidential power also increased during the Cold War as the role of war manager led to a more focused and imperial presidency. That power receded with revelations of corruption concerning Vietnam and Watergate, a non-elected president (Ford), and Carter's powerlessness to stop double-digit inflation, or return the hostages from Iran.

Government

Illustration 3.2 Seven Presidents

On December 5, 2018 a state funeral was held for President George H. W. Bush at the Washington National Cathedral. The five living presidents paid their respects, from right to left on the front row: Jimmy Carter (1977–1981); Bill Clinton (1993–2001); Barack Obama (2009–2017); Donald Trump (2017–2021); and George Walker Bush (2001–2009), the son of the deceased. Future president Joe Biden (2021–2025) is seen behind Clinton. The 2000 Democratic nominee Al Gore is standing beside Jill Biden and the 2016 Democratic nominee Hillary Clinton is next to her husband. Vice President Mike Pence is standing behind Trump's empty chair. The seven presidents, three Republicans and four Democrats, commanded the world stage for more than forty-five years and bent American policies in liberal and conservative ways that made many compromises but also shaped partisan factional politics.

Source: Matt McLain/*The Washington Post* via Getty Images

Trust matters. With the end of the Cold War, presidential power softened again before the attack on the World Trade Center stiffened presidential authority, giving George W. Bush the opportunity to rebuild the imperial presidency—or at the very least a strong and unitary executive with fewer limits (Brinkley, 2009). In terms of organization and control, Obama maintained a tight hold upon the Executive branch, not least because Democrats lost their grip on Congress in 2011 and the nation was threatened by gridlock. Sometimes the expectations of parties victorious—such as the Democrats in 2020—can be the hardest for a president to meet, as Biden quickly learned.

Simultaneously, the role of the media in sanctioning or condemning presidential actions affects a president's strength. After the Watergate affair, reporters, who had traditionally shown discretion concerning presidents' private lives, were willing to tell all. The media

Contemporary United States

frenzy surrounding Bill Clinton's extra-marital escapades entertained audiences with open discussions that would not have been acceptable before the collapse of media deference. A disgraced President Nixon described executive failure in 1977: "Anybody who is in that [presidential] office who does something that reduces respect for the office makes America a little weaker, a little less admirable, and most important, a little less able to be the leader of the free world" (Birt and Frost, 2002). The postmodern presidency emerged. To be president was to be fragile and assailable from all directions. The occupant of the Oval Office became more ordinary. But this situation also played into the hands of experts and spin doctors, who could use the media to gain public sympathy even while reporters were tearing at personal lives and language blunders (Kurtz, 1998). Modern presidents recognize the media's influence. Reagan, Clinton, Bush, and Obama were masters of the photo opportunity and the effective use of choreographed images. Until banned, Trump employed social media like no predecessor: in 2019, Trump could be everywhere at the same time via 6,934 tweets and re-tweets. Illustration 3.2 shows the six living presidents—Jimmy Carter, Bill Clinton, George W. Bush, Barack Obama, Donald Trump, and Joe Biden—mourning the 2018 passing of a seventh—President George H. W. Bush.

A president needs a large staff to manage the duties and personnel of the executive branch, which currently totals more than three million employees. The Executive Office of the President (EOP) is composed of over 1,500 people specializing in various fields. Employing suitable candidates takes up a great deal of the incoming administration's time—as witnessed by the 2021 transition. Solving this staffing conundrum explains the length of a presidential "interregnum": the time from Election Day (early November) and Inauguration (late January). The president's most trusted advisors make up an informal group called the White House Staff. The Chief of Staff is a facilitator who protects the president, acts as his most savvy political advisor, literally manages the president's schedule, has influence over who gets to see the president and when, and may be the last voice the president heard before making decisions.

The vice presidency has evolved from "stand-by equipment," as Vice President Nelson Rockefeller quipped in the late 1960s, to become more important. Vice President Dick Cheney held immense influence under George W. Bush, and Vice President Joe Biden wielded much influence as Obama's policy "point" man. Vice President Mike Pence was likely an exception. The National Security Council (NSC) is the executive's most influential group in dealing with internal and external security. Membership is determined by the sitting president, but it usually includes the vice president, Secretaries of State and Defense, and various senior members of the armed forces and intelligence communities (see Chapter 9). The Office of Management and Budget (OMB) deals with the president's program, recommends the federal budget, and oversees federal spending programs.

Beyond the EOP, thousands of administrative jobs change hands with every new president. Senior bureaucratic positions in domestic and foreign affairs are filled by presidential nominees who give the president extensive support and influence over national affairs, politicizing such positions. The president's cabinet is made up of a second body of advisors who are appointed by the president—and confirmed by the

Senate—to head federal departments. The significance of the cabinet changes according to the managerial style of the president, but the US does not practice a cabinet-style government of collective responsibility and decision-making common to many parliamentary democracies. The power of the department heads for Trade, Housing, Energy, Education, Defense, State, and the others stems directly from the president. Cabinet members are not elected and cannot hold elected positions, even if many have established political power bases of their own. Critics have claimed, perhaps unfairly, that the cabinet is simply an advisory body with real decisions being made within the EOP and appointments made to showcase diversity rather than competence. Trump appointees sat at the pleasure of the executive and risked being fired when the president was displeased. Biden's cabinet radiates diversity and his leadership style is more inclusive, with lower staff turnover.

The presidency is resilient and the world is unstable enough to provide opportunities for power to rise or fall according to circumstance and will. The presidency provides a focal point for the American people and the world—a central and unified institution in the body of one person which is powerful, but not all-powerful. The Constitution originated this role for the executive, but years of discovering inherent rights and adding delegated powers have created a much more powerful office than the Founders imagined or desired. The prominence of the office is reflected by its central position in media attention, public consciousness, and popular culture. This is also a weakness: public expectations of the presidency can be unrealistic. After the December 2012 Newtown school shootings, Obama acknowledged that he was not omnipotent, stating that he would use the powers at his disposal to counter gun tragedies (*WP*, 2012). In truth, he could do little. Traditionally, the American public has been impatient with presidents who have failed to bring troops home, to create growth, to stem unemployment, or to keep them safe. Public opinion ebbs and flows.

The Legislative Branch

Congress is a bicameral legislature made up of 435 representatives (commonly called "congressmen" or "congresswomen") and five delegates in the House of Representatives and 100 senators in the Senate. The Constitution sets two-year terms for representatives and six-year terms for senators. Every even-numbered calendar year, the entire membership of the House and one-third of the Senate stand for re-election. This election cycle makes the House more chaotic as representatives are always on the campaign trail. The staggered election cycle in the Senate means that even if all the incumbents were to be defeated and replaced by new faces—a highly unlikely scenario—two-thirds of the body would be experienced and provide a certain measure of stability to the national government. Women make up a small but quickly growing minority of federally elected officials (see Illustration 3.3 and Table 3.1).

The legislative process is tempered by different term lengths, leading to a more divided government because voters vote at two-year intervals. Thus, the president, senators, and representatives are expressions of the electorate's will at different times

Contemporary United States

Illustration 3.3 Democratic Lawmakers in White

At Donald Trump's 2019 State of the Union Address, female Democratic lawmakers dressed in white, in solidarity with the suffragettes who had successfully fought for the right to vote ninety-nine years earlier, in 1920, and to show unity with women everywhere. The white clothing of the female lawmakers stood in stark contrast to dark suited and overwhelmingly male majorities in Congress. At the center of the image, on the front row, is progressive Democrat, Alexandria Ocasio-Cortez. These women were declaring their solidarity with the #MeToo movement and using political theater to visibly confront the victory of Donald Trump, who stood behind the podium delivering his Address.

Source: Alex Wong via Getty Images

Table 3.1 Profile of the 117th Congress (2021–2023)

Gender/Ethnicity	US Population	Representatives		Senators
	(%)	(no.)	(%)	(no. and %)
Male	49.2	312	71.2	76
Female	50.8	123	28.8	24
African American	13.4	57	13.0	3
Latino (Hispanic)	18.5	47	8.7	7
Asian American	5.9	19	3.8	2
American Indian	1.3	5	1.1	0
Average age	38.3	58.4		64.3

All percentages rounded. Includes delegates and vacancies.

Sources: CRS (2020a); USCB (2020b)

Government

and can all claim separate mandates. Until the twenty-first century, voters often "split tickets": by voting for candidates of both parties for different offices. Recently, party voting has become more common. Majorities in one election can turn into a minority in the next election. Midterm elections—two years after a presidential election— frequently serve as "presidential plebiscites," where the voters confirm, or more usually, condemn presidential actions by electing or defeating members of his party. In contrast to parliamentary systems, a midterm defeat for a president's party cannot translate into a formal vote of no confidence in the president because he or she still has two years more to serve, even if it complicates governance or encourages cooperation. Relative approval ratings for the president and for Congress also affect legislative dynamics. For example, in September 2020 Congress held job approval ratings of 17 percent (Gallup, 2021b)— less than the 45 percent of President Trump (Gallup, 2021g).

It has been quite normal for American government to be divided, with different parties controlling different elected branches. Divided government and different term lengths weaken the role of the parties, making cooperation necessary. Traditionally, this created strong pressures towards bipartisanship, where representatives and senators made decisions and created durable compromises on policy across party lines. In 1994, and then again in 2010, however, ideologically invigorated anti-tax Republicans took the House in a manifestation of increasing interparty polarization and rancor, which made law-making more difficult, and, some said, government dysfunctional (Kornacki, 2018). Congressional Democrats, meanwhile, began championing greater federal governmental action. Voters returned Republican majorities: in the House from 2011 to 2019, and in the Senate from 2015 to 2021. While united government disguised ideological division between the parties in Washington, the degree to which polarization extends beyond the political elite to the wider population remains a point of discussion. Polarization can paralyze government. If Congress refuses to provide the funds that the executive branch needs in order to function, crises may lead to limited government shutdowns, such as occurred in 1995, 1996, 2013, 2018, and 2019. The government shut down in the winter of 2019 for thirty-five days— underlining the difficulties of bipartisanship in the hyper-partisan Trump era. Every two years the midterms provide opportunities for greater polarization.

The working atmosphere varies as the House is brusque and the Senate historically somewhat more collegial in spirit. House rules are much stricter overall with debating time severely limited, while the Senate allows more time for deliberation. The sheer number of people in the House chamber explains some of the difference, as does the effect of term lengths on the internal community of politicians. Senators see things from a larger and longer-term perspective because their six-year terms protect them from wild swings in public opinion and because of their enhanced stature in representing an entire state instead of a congressional district within a state. States are more diverse than congressional districts and senators are used to combining disparate views into a majority opinion. These advantages give them far more media attention than representatives who must usually decide—with their re-election hanging in the balance every twenty-four months—between local issues and national opinion. The House chaos reflects its members' close attention to immediate, rather than long-term, public opinion.

Contemporary United States

John F. Kennedy noted that a politician's wish to be elected might push him to "flatter every public whim and prejudice ... to put public opinion ahead of public interest" (Safire, 1978). Often, voters hold contradictory opinions, believing one thing at any given moment and something quite different over the long-view. The way the question is framed matters too. In the abstract, most Americans agree that action should be taken to reduce the difference in life opportunities between people; but they overwhelmingly oppose specific, concrete actions such as tax policy which could affect their own personal lifestyles. For example, gun ownership has been at around 40 percent for a generation, even as majorities of Americans support more gun controls (Gallup, 2021d). Insurgent forces with deep human and financial resources, such as #BLM, #MeToo, and climate activists also focus the attention of politicians who seek re-election. Social media can be a powerful weapon.

Both the House of Representatives and the Senate are fully involved in making the law and making sure the bureaucracy implements and enforces the law as intended. The House is more specialized and the Senate is generalist. The prime responsibility of the House of Representatives is initiating legislation for the collection and distribution of money through its control over taxes and spending. The Senate is specifically charged with approving or rejecting all presidential appointments and treaties with foreign countries. The original powers of Congress as enumerated in Article I of the Constitution are shown in Box 3.3. The work of the House and Senate is coordinated along lines of party affiliation. The legislative agenda of the House chamber is set by the Speaker—the leader of the party with the greatest numerical representation, called the "majority party."

Box 3.3 Constitutional Powers of Congress

- Levy and collect taxes
- Borrow money for the public treasury
- Make rules and regulations governing interstate and foreign commerce
- Make uniform rules for the naturalization of foreign citizens
- Coin money, state its value, and provide for the punishment of counterfeiters
- Set weights and measures standard
- Establish bankruptcy laws
- Establish post offices and post roads
- Issue patents and copyrights
- Set up a federal courts system
- Punish piracy
- Declare war, raise and support armies, provide for a navy
- Call out the militia to enforce federal laws, suppress lawlessness or repel invasions
- Make all laws for the seat of government-
- Make all laws necessary to enforce the Constitution
- Power of Impeachment

Government

The longest-tenured committee member representing the majority party generally sets the working agenda of each of the committees. Party leaders go to considerable lengths to enforce voting discipline among their members, and they are often successful due to their ability to provide campaign money, information, and expertise.

All the same, party affiliation has not always been the decisive factor for American politicians. For example, representatives vote to improve the economy of their home district by building a military base, establishing a national park, or constructing a dam. This is called "bringing home the pork" or "pork-barrel" legislation—that is, keeping the home folks fed. The amount of pork and the constant electioneering let voters focus on politicians as individuals rather than as party members, personalizing elections in such a way that they take on more of a candidate-centered hue. This strengthens the independence of elected officials somewhat, though in recent years, the parties have become more homogeneous due to primary challengers from within that keep incumbents in line.

One unique power of the Congress is that of impeachment of a president and other high officials. In 1999, Clinton was tried for perjury and obstruction of justice. He was acquitted and his presidency survived. The Constitution stipulates "treason, bribery, or other high crimes and misdemeanours" as grounds for impeachment. The House of Representatives charges the accused and the Senate functions as a court in which cases are heard. A conviction requires a two-thirds majority of senators present to avoid overly political or trivial impeachments. Proceedings are chaired by the Chief Justice of the Supreme Court. The imminent threat of impeachment for obstruction of justice, abuse of power, and contempt of Congress was enough for Nixon to resign office in 1974. In 1999, Clinton was tried and acquitted of perjury and obstruction of justice over the Monica Lewinsky affair, but his presidency survived. On December 18, 2019, Donald Trump was impeached in the Democrat majority-held House of Representatives on charges of high crimes and misdemeanors, by which Trump abused his power to force Ukraine to deliver information on the activities of Joe Biden's son, Hunter. On February 5, 2020, the Republican-controlled Senate acquitted Trump by a 52–48 near-party line vote, ending the process. Again, from January to February 2021, Trump was impeached for his part in the January 6 storming of the Capitol. Although 57 of 100 senators voted to impeach, it takes a supermajority of 67 votes to remove a president. Trump was again acquitted.

Committees are at the heart of law-making. Legislators spend much more time involved in process, in the production of the actual wording of the law—based on debate and expert help—than they do voting in chambers. A century ago, President Woodrow Wilson contrasted committee work with full House proceedings as the difference between "Congress at work," and "on public exhibition." Committee work is a slow and unglamorous process.

The large number of representatives enables a division of labor which produces specialists within policy fields. The small number of senators translates into fewer and broader committees. On any given day, there are 200 committees of the four various types operating—standing, select, joint, and conference. The twenty-six House and sixteen Senate standing committees in each chamber are a fixed feature of congressional life in that they are involved both in the formulation of law and the feedback of its effects from the departments and agencies implementing the law (United States Congress, 2021). Committees also exert oversight over specific areas of policy implementation, such as the Senate Committee on Foreign Relations. Select committees are temporary, created with a single task in mind. One example is the House Select Committee on the January 6th Attack on the U.S. Capitol. Joint committees include members from both houses, such as the Joint Economic Committee. For a bill to become a law, both houses must agree to the exact wording and details. Conference committees, including both Senators and Representatives, are set up specifically to reconcile differences in legislation passed in each of the houses. The need for discussion based on specialist knowledge of particular issues means that committees often have to set up subcommittees. The House Subcommittee on Livestock and Foreign Agriculture with twenty-one members, for example, is a subcommittee of the forty-nine-member House Agriculture Committee. Subcommittees discuss the specifics of a law and conduct hearings with expert witnesses to ensure that the detailed drafting of a law is consistent with intended policy outcomes. Figure 3.2 shows the time-honored procedure of how a bill becomes a law.

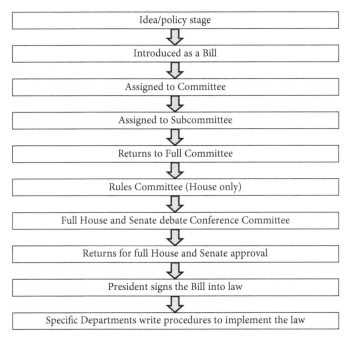

Figure 3.2 The Law-Making Process

Note: Bills go through the stages shown in Figure 3.2 in both houses (Rules Committee excepted). This figure shows the route of a successful bill. At any stage, the bill can fail and perish. Even when it survives the Congress, a president can veto the bill and return it to Congress for revision or oblivion. Congress can then overturn the veto by a two-thirds majority vote. The procedure is time-consuming and can be curtailed in an emergency.

Ideas for legislation come from any branch or level of government, interest group, community, or individual. To initiate the legislative process, the idea must be sponsored by a member of Congress who formally introduces it on the floor of the House or Senate as a "bill." Each bill is assigned to a relevant committee. Its chair—usually the senior (longest-serving) member of the majority party who is attuned to the political desires of his party—structures the work of a committee. Chairs have considerable power and decide which bills to consider or ignore; for many politicians being chair represents the pinnacle of their career. There are far more bills introduced than committees can handle. Thus, the majority party controls the legislative agenda both through the committees and through the leadership offices of Speaker of the House and of the Senate's President "*pro tempore*"—for the "time being." The vice president is the formal President of the Senate and breaks ties in votes where senators are evenly divided. The Speaker and Senate President decide on legislative priorities and appoint committee chairs.

The strength of party affiliation and the influence of the House Speaker or Senate President has hardened since Newt Gingrich became Speaker of the House (1994–1998). Committee Chairs can exert significant independence—a result of the seniority principle and, consequently, having worked within committees for a long time, and of a feeling of collegiality among all committee members.

Subcommittees study bills and listen to advice and critique from experts both in and out of government. Once convinced of the merits of a bill, the subcommittee reports to the full committee which, when satisfied, reports it ready for debate by the full House or Senate. In the House, the Rules Committee sets rules and time limits for debate. After debate and changes, members vote on the bill. Unless there are compelling local or ideological reasons not to cast a party line vote, members usually rely on their party's advice and vote accordingly. If voted down in either chamber, the bill is dead; if passed, the bill goes to a Conference Committee to iron out differences between the bills passed in different chambers. The revised bill is sent back to both houses again. If approved, it goes to the president for final approval, which he usually gives, signing it into law. If the president does not like the bill and less than ten days remain in the legislative session before recess, he can kill the bill by refusing to sign it. This is called a "pocket veto." The president can also veto the bill and return it to Congress, where it is either modified and returned to the president or simply dies. Trump exercised veto power ten times (US Senate, 2021). If there is support from at least two thirds of Congress, the legislators can override the president's veto. The bill now becomes law and is called an Act. Committees have the right of oversight—keeping a watchful eye to ensure that the Act is applied as it was meant and that its effects match legislative intent.

Most of the time the legislative process is deliberate and slow. However, Congress can act promptly during times of national crisis or when popular opinion clearly backs a course of action. In early 2020, the Coronavirus Aid, Relief, and Economic Security Act (CARES ACT) went from proposal on the floor to presidential assent in about six weeks, pumping $2.2 trillion into an economy hurt by the Corona virus (J. P. Morgan, 2020). From 2017, Republicans altered the steps in making a bill into a law. Procedural changes include drafting bills in the Senate Republican caucus and bypassing the committee stage to introduce the bills directly on the Senate floor, where they can be voted on and passed by a simple majority. Under circumstances less afflicted by partisanship and crisis, this shortened process that circumvents the norms of governance may be reconsidered (Levitsky and Ziblatt, 2019).

Congress has never been a mirror of American society, but during the last generation, officeholders have become more representative of American society in terms of gender, age, race, and ethnicity. However, there has been less change in terms of education, occupation, and income levels of officeholders. As Table 3.1 shows, older white males still dominate the 117th Congress. On the other hand, a generation of effort by feminist organizations such as Emily's List have campaigned successfully to increase pro-choice female representation, especially within the Democratic Party, which has benefited from over $700 million in campaign support (Emily's List, 2022). Democratic women used the 99th anniversary of women's right to vote at the 2019 State of the Union (see Illustration 3.3) by donning white, highlighting their presence in Congress while emphasizing their relatively modest numbers among a sea of men in suits.

In all democracies there is tension in the way elected officials view their responsibilities toward the people: should they act as delegates or trustees? Delegates treat the policy wishes of their supporters as instructions. Trustees are freer to follow their own views on how to best help their district and nation. Most elected officials mix and match these two approaches. If an issue exerts strong passions among constituents back home, it is almost certain to bring out the delegate; if the issue is not particularly important locally, the trustee appears. The national political climate also matters. The general ideological reinvigoration of the parties and polarization over the last generation, and Trump's 2016 presidential victory more specifically, encouraged politicians on both sides to vote along party lines. In early 2021, opposing philosophies were complicated by a resurgence in nationalism and populism among both Democrats and Republicans. For the last two decades, populist, affective division, and anti-systemic forces have driven greater economic and social polarization in the nation.

Collectively, Congress represents a synthesis of models of government. Candidates are elected by the will of the majority, yet their effect is diluted by the plurality of districts and institutions within the three elected branches. Mandates overlap. Additionally, the social profile of elected officers, and the vast expense of getting elected, suggests that legislators' lives are far removed from the daily concerns of ordinary citizens. Legislators are much older, whiter, richer, and male than the mean voter. The bifocal nature of representation (local and national) forces lawmakers toward compromise and gives access to different groups of voters and interests. Occasionally majority opinion gets decoupled from the policy process, leaving legislators and sectional interests to develop private or "elite" policy outcomes.

The Judicial Branch

In contemporary America, the judicial branch is the equal of the others, but this has not always been the case. The Founders imagined the Supreme Court as the "least dangerous" branch and the Constitution devotes just three short paragraphs in Article III to establish the Court and to empower Congress to construct a federal judicial system. The real power of the Court came in the early 1800s when Chief Justice John Marshall used the Constitution's Supremacy Clause to declare the federal courts superior to the state courts. Marshall also established the principle of judicial review to make the Supreme Court the final arbiter on whether congressional acts, state laws, lower court judgments, and executive actions follow the rules set out in the Constitution.

The US Supreme Court is predominantly an appeals' court which rules on the constitutionality of a law or action, and in that way establishes the law for all courts. Using the power of judicial review, the Court is always involved in the most politically sensitive issues, including racial integration, prayer in the schools, abortion rights, handgun control, death penalty decisions, and fairness issues. Most cases before the Court deal with 1st and 14th Amendment freedom and equality protections. For example, in the case of *June Medical Services v. Russo* (2020), the Supreme Court ruled 5–4 that women's rights to abortion in Louisiana would be subject to an undue burden because of new regulations which insisted that abortion providers should offer similar levels of medical coverage as offered in hospitals. This echoed the Court's 5–3 ruling in *Whole Womens' Health v. Hellerstedt* (2016), which applied to a virtually identical Texas law. These new rules would have drastically reduced the number and geographic spread of abortion clinics in both states (Liptak, 2020b). In 2021–2022, the Court considered the validity of a Mississippi State law restricting the right to abortion to the first fifteen weeks of pregnancy (Liptak, 2021). On June 24, 2022 in Dobbs v Jackson Women's Health Organization the Supreme Court repatriated the right to abortion to the states by a 6–3 majority. Nine states banned abortion.

No discussion of liberties and rights would be complete without the strong voice of the Supreme Court in the resolution of an issue. This judgment has the result of politicizing appointments. This contrasts markedly to most other Western countries, where such issues are often handled by the elected legislatures. Judicial activities are divided into separate federal and state jurisdictions. The system of federal courts includes a tripartite division among US District Courts, US Courts of Appeal, and the Supreme Court. The federal courts hear appeals from judgments rendered by lower courts, but mostly they work with original disputes over federal law, suits by or against the federal government, or cases between citizens of different states.

The Supreme Court consists of nine judges—called "justices"—who are appointed by the president and confirmed by the Senate. Because justices serve for life and because a president can only appoint a new justice when a vacancy occurs, each president's influence is limited. When a justice retires, changes career, or dies, as Antonin Scalia did in 2016, the Justice Department creates a list of likely candidates which will be reduced to a shorter list by senior White House advisors. The president selects his nominee and sends the name to the Senate, where the Judiciary Committee conducts hearings to determine the candidate's background qualifications, approach to the law, and judicial philosophy. Senate approval is not automatic. In 2016, the Republican-controlled Senate refused to conduct hearings for Obama's nominee to replace Scalia (Everett and Kim,

Contemporary United States

2015). Senate Majority Leader Mitch McConnell insisted that a president with less than a year to serve should not have the right to appoint anyone.

Two months before the 2020 election, McConnell acted differently. The death of Ruth Bader Ginsburg allowed Trump to nominate Amy Coney Barrett. Senate Democrats insisted that McConnell's final-year proviso still stood, but a Republican majority in the Senate allowed Barrett's confirmation. The power of Court nominations loomed large in the 2020 elections. Barrett was Trump's third appointment and created a 6–3 conservative-liberal split that has pressed calls for court reform—such as the expansion of the number of Justices—by Democrats. In reality, rules change with circumstances. Two recent reforms include the introduction of simple majority for nomination confirmations instead of a 60–40 supermajority in 2017, and the no-election-year-nominations claimed by Senate Republicans in 2016 and unclaimed in 2020.

Trump selected justices for their appeal to his conservative base and their judicial philosophy limiting interpretations of the Constitution and role of the federal government, whereas Obama appointed justices for their gender, liberal stances, and to reach out to a changing demographic of voters. The Roberts Court—all Supreme Courts are named after their Chief Justice—is a relatively conservative body which reflects an adherence to individual and states' rights over the national collective. In 2022, Ketanji Brown Jackson replaced retiring Justice Stephen Breyer, to become the first black woman confirmed to the Supreme Court. Voices for reform—more justices and term limits—have not yet won mainstream support.

Judicial politics are dynamic and the Court is active in politics by nature of its selective and interpretive judgments. The law may be the law, but interpretations of the law vary. In deciding a case, justices have considerable discretion and are influenced by ideas of judicial method and judicial philosophy. Judicial method can be traced along a line with procedural ideas at one extreme and substantive ideas at the other. Put simply, a procedural view is based on a justice's strict adherence to accepted rules when formulating judgments. A substantive approach concentrates more on outcomes than process, with judgments made for the effects they will have, rather than strictly according to precedent. Justices also must balance judicial restraint against judicial activism. Judicial restraint stems from a philosophy that elected legislators should make the law and that justices should closely follow the original intent of statutes. Judicial activism assumes that justices, even though not elected, should make judgments in line with an ever-changing society. These differences in politics and philosophy explain why nominations to the Supreme and federal courts are so fiercely contested.

The current Court is divided into a conservative group which claims it emphasizes restraint, states rights, established process, and the letter of the law on the one hand, and a liberal group of judicial activists more concerned about the spirit of the law on the other hand. Until recently, consensus was difficult to obtain and many verdicts from the Roberts Court split 5–4 in favor of restraint and established process. That changed with Barrett's appointment. The Supreme Court's conservative majority of 6–3 overturned fifty years of federal abortion rights stemming from *Roe v. Wade* (1973). While unanimity of opinion among justices is not required, lower courts can more easily

Illustration 3.4 US Supreme Court Justices Attend the Funeral of George H. W. Bush, December 5, 2018

The Supreme Court Justices paid their last respects to late President George H. W. Bush. From left to right are Sonia Sotomayor (appointed by Barack Obama in 2009); Steven Breyer (appointed by Bill Clinton in 1994 and retired in 2022); Elena Kagan (appointed by Barack Obama in 2010); Neil Gorsuch (appointed by Donald Trump in 2017); Clarence Thomas (appointed by George H. W. Bush in 1991); Chief Justice John Roberts (appointed by George W. Bush in 2005); Brett Kavanaugh (appointed by Donald Trump in 2018); former Justice Anthony Kennedy (appointed by Ronald Reagan in 1987, and retired July 2018); and Samuel Alito (appointed by George W. Bush in 2006). Justice Ruth Bader Ginsburg (appointed by Bill Clinton in 1993 and died in 2020) is not pictured.

Source: Jonathan Ernst-Pool via Getty Images

follow precedent when the Supreme Court is unified. Additionally, the more contentious the issue, the better a unanimous or near-unanimous verdict works to convince the public on a certain point. For example, the 9–0 decision on school desegregation in 1954 convinced Americans that the federal government would enforce integration. Splits of 5–4 ensure that more cases will arise in hopes of swinging one or more justices to the other side and overturning the decision.

The Supreme Court has the flexibility and freedom to decide which cases to hear. Justices select around seventy-five cases each year from the approximately 6,500 cases discussed in Court conferences (USSC, 2019). If at least four justices agree to hear a case, it is placed on the docket. Choosing its own cases allows the Court to direct the law in areas it wants and ignore it in others—even though the Court often adds cases the administration or national media push strongly. Of course, just how the justices interpret the law depends on their legal philosophy and personal beliefs.

Contemporary United States

Legal adjudication is based on the principles of constitutional and statute law, and, in their absence, common law (or judge-made law). The adjudication of statute law—especially that which is newly enacted—is less problematical than common law. The intent of legislation is usually more obvious, either from the legal text itself, or from the records of the committee or government department primarily responsible for the drafting of the text. Exceptions occur when cases are heard which are based on contradictory or clashing pieces of law. Common law is based on the principle that if there is no existing written or statute law on an issue, the uniformity of the law will be enforced by using earlier judgments—especially those from higher courts—called "precedents." The briefness of the Constitution, the large number of states, the abundance of laws that need to be reinterpreted as time and conditions change, and the fact that the US is the most litigious society on earth, give the Supreme Court enormous leverage to shape society through its decisions.

The federal court system also includes fourteen appellate courts and ninety-four district courts with over 800 judges. Presidents have a great impact at these levels, leaving a durable legacy by filling vacancies with personal choices. Democrats Carter, Clinton, Obama, and Biden changed the courts dramatically by eschewing middle-class and middle-aged white men and appointing hundreds of women and minorities. Their choices have made the judicial branch far more diverse than the legislative branch. George W. Bush underlined the importance of legal philosophy of his nominees, and selected them he said, to "faithfully interpret the law, not legislate from the bench" (OPS, 2004). By September 2020, Trump had appointed over 217 judges to the federal bench, reshaping the courts in a conservative direction (Shubber, 2020). Of the fifty or so appeals judges appointed and confirmed under Trump, none were black (Nelson, 2020).

In addition to the president's power to select judges, the executive branch has other ways to influence the judicial branch. The Department of Justice deals with the day-to-day management of judicial affairs. The Attorney General, who is appointed by the president, is the nation's chief law enforcement officer. The Attorney General—currently Merrick Garland—is a powerful aide to the president because of the authority to select cases to push the political agenda into the federal courts. The president also has an officer, the solicitor general, who represents the federal government in dealings with the Supreme Court. The solicitor general decides which lower court judgments the government should appeal. Parallel to the federal system of courts are the state courts, which adjudicate the overwhelming majority of the approximately 84 million lawsuits tried each year (Court Statistics Project, 2020). State inferior courts—often divided into city or county jurisdictions—deal with routine cases of traffic violations, divorce, child custody, or other relatively minor cases and civil suits. State superior courts preside over multi-county districts and convene juries to try criminal cases—such as burglaries, murders, rapes, and assaults (see Chapter 5).

Each state has its own appeals courts, topped by a state supreme court. States vary in the number of courts and in terms for judges who are either appointed by state governors or elected by the people. Elected judges who must stand for re-election may feel pressure to follow public opinion, which can lead to popular but legally dubious decisions. Appeals courts are in place to rectify possible errors.

With separate federal and state systems (see Figure 3.3), each with three levels of courts, groups who want to reform the laws have multiple points of access. "Class action suits" bring people in similar circumstances together to have a verdict rendered which will apply to everyone. Tobacco companies (Phillip Morris), Opioid drugmakers (Purdue Pharma), credit card companies (Visa and Mastercard), car makers (Volkswagen), silicone implant manufacturers (Dow Corning), and oil companies (British Petroleum) have all incurred multi-billion dollar punitive verdicts for selling products or operating in manners that failed to meet safety standards. Environmental groups have originated cases against factories for polluting air and water resources. Access to the courts requires money and expertise, which favor powerful interests in the private and political realms, but multiple levels of courts give access to groups and citizens who can challenge the laws or the political majority. Ease of access helps explain the high numbers of lawsuits in the United States and the way in which the courts provide cultural glue for the many interests of a diverse population. A converse argument acknowledges the expense and expertise required to access the court system, privileging those with greatest resources.

The Supreme Court is often heavily criticized for being an unelected branch of government which has an oversized impact on people's lives. Controversy surrounds some judgments, yet the predominant role of the Court is to guard and mediate the Constitution in the present and to bring about closure. Until recently, some commentators maintain that Supreme Court Justices are reluctant to move far from public opinion, despite their political or legal philosophies. This hesitance has influenced multiple

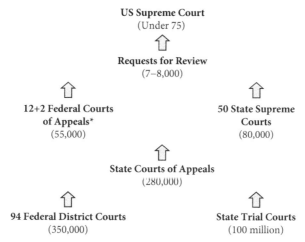

Figure 3.3 The Court System
* There are twelve regional United States Court of Appeals, one United States Court of Appeal for the federal circuit, and one United States Court of Military Appeals. Figures in brackets indicate the approximate number of cases heard yearly.

Sources: USSC (2019); Court Statistics Project (2020)

Contemporary United States

verdicts on abortion, civil rights, and immigration. The verdict in *June Medical Services v. Russo* scaled back reductions in abortion rights in Louisiana by a 5–4 verdict. In an amalgamated verdict covering three cases, a 6–3 verdict ruled that gay and transgender people were protected from workplace discrimination by the 1964 Civil Rights Act. In the 5–4 ruling *in Department of Homeland Security v. Regents of the University of California*, the Supreme Court ruled that DACA (Deferred Action for Childhood Arrivals) could not be immediately shut down by the Trump administration. This decision shielded young immigrants from deportation (Liptak and Parlapiano, 2020). In 2022, the Supreme Court's influence was demonstrated by the overturning of federal abortion rights stemming from *Roe v. Wade*, the confirmation of the right to carry hand guns for self defense, the reduction of the ability of the administration to combat climate change, and decreased separation of church and state in education.

American government is an institution in motion. The three branches are dynamic, and their relative strengths are affected by diverse factors as they compete for influence on the federal stage. The states and the federal government are likewise interdependent and competitive, with power overlapping and flowing among jurisdictions. Legitimacy aggregates from ballot boxes and informs government at all levels. Observers have claimed that the genius of the American system is in its flexibility to accommodate to new circumstances. This discussion of power transitions and continuities brings us into the realm of politics and democracy.

Further Reading

Janda, K., J. Berry, J. Goldman, D. Schildkraut, and P. Manna (2022) *The Challenge of Democracy: American Government in Global Politics*, 15th edn, Boston: Cengage.

Kornacki, S. (2018) *The Red and The Blue: The 1990s and the Birth of Political Tribalism*, New York: Echo Press.

Levitsky, A. and M. Ziblatt (2019) *How Democracies Die: What History Reveals about Our Future*, New York: Penguin.

McKenzie, R. (2021) *We the Fallen People: The Founders and the Future of American Democracy*, Westmount, IL: IVP Academic.

Meacham, J. (2018) *The Soul of America: The Battle for Our Better Angels*, New York: Random House.

Milkis, S. and M. Nelson (2019) *The American Presidency: Origins and Development*, 1776–2014, Los Angeles: SAGE.

Toobin, J. (2007) *The Nine: Inside the Secret World of the Supreme Court*, New York: Doubleday.

CHAPTER 4
POLITICS AND DEMOCRACY

The 2020 Election: Trump vs. Biden

Usually, elections deliver conclusive presidential election results speedily after polls close on the first Tuesday in November. TV channels call a winner, and the candidate with the fewest projected Electoral College votes concedes gracefully. But, not in 2020. Though Biden won a majority of votes cast and a significant majority of Electoral College delegates, Donald Trump refused to concede, and said he would never concede. Trump publicly maintained that the election was stolen, fraudulently, as a result of ballot rigging and illegal voting. Worse, in April 2022, a sizeable majority of Republicans still believed Trump's "Big Lie" that the election had been stolen (Ipsos, 2022). In living memory, never have so many people disputed a presidential election for so long, so loudly. American democracy has the loser's concession as a central feature in uniting the nation.

Though the election result was clear, the process behind Election 2020 was more complex. Endpoints include that first post-election Wednesday in November; the Electoral College declaring and certifying a winner state-by-state on December 14; the formal certification of results by Congress on January 6; and the final inauguration of President Joe Biden on January 20. Trump and his supporters still disputed the result wherever they could. On December 23, and in a telling slip in his managerial style, Trump argued that he could remain in the White House despite the popular and Electoral College tallies, claiming "maybe that administration will be me" (Gerstein, 2020). Two weeks later on January 6, in the most dramatic and distressing of events, Trump supporters stormed Congress—killing three people and leading two more to commit suicide a week later. The insurrectionary events came because Trump refused to accept defeat. As a consequence, Trump was impeached for the second time. At noon on January 20, 2021—Inauguration Day—Chief Justice John Roberts administered the oath of office to Joseph Robinette Biden. Former Vice President Mike Pence, Vice President Kamala Harris, and the whole world watched. The process of Democracy had survived.

Joe Biden was in some ways an unlikely choice for the presidency. He turned seventy-eight shortly after the election, the oldest man ever elected president. A three-time candidate, he had pursued the Democratic nomination unsuccessfully in 1988 and 2008. Biden's support stemmed from Democrat moderates—a wing in decline as the party's grassroots turned youthful and leftwards. What made his choice likely was his long career in politics. In 1973, a twenty-nine-year-old Biden was elected to represent

Contemporary United States

Delaware in the Senate—where he stayed until 2009, holding leadership positions on the Senate Judiciary and Foreign Affairs committees. Biden served as Obama's Vice President from 2009–2017. In an environment that usually prefers outsiders, Biden was the first Washington "insider" to win the presidency since George H. W. Bush in 1989. Given the Corona crisis, Biden's familiarity with what government can and cannot do may have been a determining factor for the 2020 electorate. Meanwhile, Trump's strengths—disrupting comfortable consensuses—did not help as Covid-19 took 400,000 American lives while he was in office.

Yet, even as something approaching normality seemed to be re-established, it is instructive to recall the dimensions of Trump's 2016 upset. Trump triumphed in large part because of the communication and entertainment skills he learned as a TV personality. In the 2016 Republican primaries Trump crushed fifteen skilled opponents, and in the general election he defeated a very prominent, politically astute, and well-financed opponent in Hillary Clinton. Trump won by promoting a populist ethno-nationalism that included higher spending on security issues and lower taxes. By securing a Republican victory in the House, Senate, and in state governments along with his own triumph, Trump tried to overturn the Obama legacy. Inexperience and ineffectiveness at using the governing apparatus made radical change impossible, with no cancelation of Obamacare and relatively limited reform on trade (see Chapter 8). Trump's enduring legacy may be in his three Supreme Court appointments and in the liberal world order he so readily attacked.

In 2021, some saw the resurgence of the 1992–2016 Democratic Age of Clinton–Obama. Others saw an end to an "Age of Reagan," arguing that the magnitude of victory, coupled with the opportunity to "build back better" due to the Covid crisis, granted a unique opportunity to promote the role of government and expand social and infrastructure agendas. Such progressive ideas had been unfashionable. Biden moved the ideas further Left. The 2022 midterm and 2024 presidential elections will fuel the debate on how much government spending Americans are willing to embrace.

Victories in presidential elections are often not clear-cut, due to the effect of the Electoral College, which considers territoriality. While Biden's popular vote victory by seven million ballots was decisive, a few tens of thousands votes placed strategically in specific states: Georgia, Arizona, and Pennsylvania, for example, would have delivered delegates for a second Trump term. In fact, in only one (2004) of the last eight elections have Republicans won the national popular vote for the presidency. Despite this, the electoral system delivered victories for Republicans three times (in 2000, 2004, and 2016)—due to the Electoral College rules (see Chapter 3).

Biden's policy intentions for his administration were largely moderate during campaigning but developed a more radical edge as Covid ravaged the economy and society. The crisis made more progressive ideas palatable and, arguably, necessary, to bolster the economy and to rebuild social cohesion. Within his first hundred days, Biden promoted emergency proposals to resuscitate the economy, massive and generational physical infrastructure spending, and landmark human capital investment to the tune of $6 trillion. In March 2021, cash payments and enhanced unemployment benefits brought

Politics and Democracy

extra purchasing power to ordinary Americans. Renewing infrastructure—roads, bridges, seaports, broadband, and other public goods—would make the economy more efficient and provide jobs. Human capital enhancement—education—would provide two years of free kindergarten before K-12, and free community college education. Soon these infrastructure spending proposals had been scaled back. Spending $6 trillion on a diverse basket of programs would represent a rejection of a generation of limited government ideas—explaining why getting an agreement in Congress was hard (Illustration 4.1).

Unlike the social media ubiquity of Trump, Biden used the media sparingly—addressing the press for the first time some two months into his term. Biden replaced Trump's continual stream-of-consciousness social media communication to govern effectively by making sure Americans were vaccinated. Opinion polls suggested that

Illustration 4.1 Biden and a Bipartisan Alliance of Senators

On June 24, 2021, Joe Biden met with senators from both parties to discuss an infrastructure deal. Five months later, on November 15, Biden signed the Infrastructure Investment and Jobs Act into law. The bipartisan law earmarked a total of $1.2 trillion in spending, including money for transport and transit investment, broadband access, electric grid updates, and clean water projects. Flanking Biden from right to left are senators: Mitt Romney (R-UT); Mark Warner (D-VA); Joe Manchin (D-WV); Kyrsten Sinema (D-AZ); Susan Collins (R-ME); Lisa Murkowski (R-AK); John Tester (D-MT); Bill Cassidy (R-LA); Rob Portman (R-OH); and Jeanne Shaheen (D-NH). Many held hopes that congressional bipartisanship (cross-party cooperation) could remerge and lessen polarization between Republicans and Democrats.

Source: Win McNamee via Getty Images

Contemporary United States

Biden's head-down-and-get-to-the job approach worked. For the first few months of his administration, Biden enjoyed popularity ratings of around 55–57 percent—much higher than his predecessor. These numbers fell back dramatically after the August 2021 defeat and withdrawal from Afghanistan (see Chapter 9). Twitter and Facebook banned Trump over his involvement in the January 6 insurrection, reducing one source of opposition by silencing Trump from his eighty million followers (Burke, 2017). Normally outgoing presidents limit critiques of new presidents, but Trump showed no signs of following tradition. In any case, Trump's Twitter silence allowed Biden to concentrate on the job.

As Biden's agenda developed in 2021, some semblance of politics as usual returned. Biden's "Build Back Better" trinity of Covid-related legislation (stimulus, human, and physical capital) was debated at length. Under pressure from moderate Democrats, the new administration attempted to reach a deal with centrist Republicans by paring back the budget for infrastructure spending. But as the year progressed, bipartisan agreement beyond physical infrastructure seemed unlikely. Meanwhile progressive Democrats insisted that Biden's original number—totaling $6 trillion—was a minimum. Republicans argued that huge spending would be a wasteful return to bigger and intrusive government, lead to deficits and inflation, and would make the economy less dynamic (DeBonis, 2021).

Biden's progressive flank saw redistributive legislation as necessary—to provide public goods and diminish inequality, mostly to be paid for by revoking Trump's tax cuts for wealthy Americans. Usually, navigating priority bills into law is easier in an administration's first year, as a president's power and goodwill—political capital—ebbs as midterms approach. With the Senate split 50–50 and the House held by a majority of three, the margins were miniscule. Deaths or fractious defections could erode control of the Senate, so getting the best possible policy outcomes quickly was vital. Future perils include restrictive voter laws passed by Republican-controlled states—for example in Texas, Florida, and Georgia—which will almost certainly make it more difficult to vote and make holding control of the Senate and House more difficult for Democrats.

Biden's November 2020 victory stemmed from multiple factors but was also dependent on Trump's mishandling of the Covid crisis (Geller and Haar, 2021). First, Biden was not, like Trump, a leader suffering with high disapproval ratings. Second, Biden seemed considered, whereas Trump spoke before he had formulated his thoughts. Moreover, Biden was seen as experienced, he knew how Washington worked, and he understood the importance of policy. Biden's instinctive pragmatic centrism attracted independent voters. Fourth, Biden ran an organized campaign that targeted the rustbelt states he needed for victory. He was effective, calm, and composed in public communications. Empathy, authenticity, and a low-key approach were his strongest attributes. Fifth, Biden brought in ex-rivals early, ensuring that Democrats remained on message. Sixth, Biden offered more coherent policy options, which Trump didn't important as it left open the question of what a second Trump administration could offer—beyond more-of-the-same pragmatism, allied to an instinctively authoritarian mindset. Finally, Democrats were highly motivated to dump Trump and their enthusiasm ensured strong Democratic turnout (Burns, Martin, and Glueck, 2020).

Politics and Democracy

But Biden's victories in Congress did not seep down to the states. Republicans maintained power as state governors and kept their disproportionate control of state legislatures. State elections have consequences, evidenced in the restrictions added in 2021 and 2022 to state voting laws in the face of the Biden administration's opposition. One argument for this mismatch between national and state control of political offices is that Republicans may concentrate their energy more strongly on state and local governments. Democrats spend more efforts at the federal than at the state level, reflecting a philosophy that rates federal government action higher. Consequently, Biden gained over seven million more votes than Trump in the presidential election, while still performing quite poorly in state gubernatorial and legislature races.

As president, Trump argued for a smaller government, accepted deficit spending, and reduced taxes—all three of which Biden opposed. And Biden supported a redistribution of wealth, greater economic security for citizens, and more opportunities for poorer Americans, for example through universal preschool and community college, continued and extended support for healthcare, and higher real wages. Overturning the Trump tax cuts for the wealthiest Americans and closing tax loopholes would pay for these policies. Rhetorical difference saw Trump's "Drain the Swamp" slogan in contrast with Biden's call for activist government to "Build Back Better." Trump complained of an inflexible deep state opposition from within, whereas Biden saw the bureaucracy as a useful tool for the formulation, implementation, and monitoring of policy.

Many observers claim that the US is in an age of partisan realignment, certainly since 2016. Parties are dynamic, complex coalitions and change elements of their electorates and policies over time. For example, in 2022 Republicans count pro-Trump diehard groups loyal to the ex-president, such as Florida Governor Ron DeSantis and Texas Senator Ted Cruz, and smaller fractions of never-Trumpers like Illinois Representative Adam Kinzinger and Utah Senator Mitt Romney. Other Republican groups include post-Trump conservatives, such as Wyoming Representative Liz Cheney. Democratic factions, meanwhile, include traditional blue-collar moderates like Corey Booker, red-state stalwarts such as West Virginia Senator Joe Manchin, coastal radicals including Vermont Senator Bernie Sanders, and youthful insurgents such as New York Representative Alexandria Ocasio-Cortez. These factions often collide, and were on full display in the 2020 Democratic primaries (see Illustration 4.2).

During the last four decades some blue collar Democrats, often older and white, have increasingly backed Republicans over cultural issues such as abortion and a more permissive society, whereas many educated, suburban voters have left the Republican Party for the Democrats. These trends continued in 2020 (Chinni, 2021). In the wake of victory, such as 2020 for Democrats, these coalitions can be perilous as groups jostle for real policymaking influence and less compromise. Fighting to reassert control usually provides a focus for parties out of power, especially after they have performed autopsies over their losses. The Republicans began this post-2020 process haltingly, by blaming overly-lax voting rules. In a two-party system, adjustments are necessary as giving the people what they want is imperative for dreams of regaining power.

117

Contemporary United States

Illustration 4.2 Democratic Candidates Represent Diverse Factions

The 2019–2020 campaign for the Democratic presidential nomination showed how the major parties are diverse in regional representation and coalitions housing multiple viewpoints, interests, identities, and factions, including black, Hindu-Samoan American, Army Reserve, second-generation immigrant, gay, progressive, mainstream, socialist, African-East Indian, Chinese American, and billionaire environmental activist. There were six men and four women among the top tier candidates, as well as others with slimmer prospects. The candidates portrayed above held diverse experience: as vice president, senators, representatives, mayors, and businesspeople. To win in the general election, candidates must bring these factions together—as Joe Biden succeeded in doing. Pictured at the November 20 televised MSNBC/Washington Post debate from left to right are candidates: Cory Booker of New Jersey, Tulsi Gabbard of Hawaii, Amy Klobuchar of Minnesota, Pete Buttigieg of Indiana, Elizabeth Warren of Massachusetts, Joe Biden of Delaware, Bernie Sanders of New Hampshire, Kamala Harris of California, Andrew Yang of New York, and Tom Steyer of California.

Source: Joe Raedle via Getty Images

Voters turned out in droves in 2020. Biden attracted more voters by offering a credible alternative and Trump enthused Republicans enough for them to cast ballots. Nearly 258 million voters were qualified by age; over 239 million voters met voter eligibility criteria; and nearly 160 million voters—or nearly seven out of ten eligible voters—cast votes (USEP, 2020). Only three of ten eligible voters stayed home, a number much lower than in recent elections. Ninety-seven million people voted early or by mail (Walsh, 2020). All age groups saw higher turnout, with more than half of eighteen-to-thirty-four-year-olds voting. Nearly 72 percent of whites, nearly 66 percent of blacks, and nearly 53 percent of Hispanics voted (USEP, 2020). The weight of whites as a proportion of the electorate fell by over two percent, to 71.2 percent. In sum, both Biden and Trump successfully posted higher numbers of voters for their respective parties, but Biden was more successful.

Since 2002 many analysts saw demographic change (see Chapter 2) as presenting an "emerging Democratic majority" (Judis and Teixeira, 2002). Working against this trend, Latinos vote less than other demographic groups. Moreover, Latinos do not vote as a bloc, and are becoming somewhat more attracted to the Republican Party over time. Migration from traditionally Democratic Northern states to usually Republican Southern states has also been argued as a Democratic advantage, without taking into account the possibility that relocated white northerners might navigate within Southern political norms, rather than change them. And yet the relocation to Georgia shows the change migration can yield.

Perhaps twelve to fourteen states were in play in 2020. Biden needed to retake the "northern blue wall" of Minnesota, Wisconsin, Michigan, Ohio, and Pennsylvania; Trump needed to retain these states. Biden hoped to wrest "red" (Republican) states in the South and Southwest that Trump was defending or hoped to win, including Florida, Georgia, North Carolina, Arizona, New Mexico, Colorado, and Nevada. As had been expected, Biden convincingly won the popular vote and the Electoral College vote (see Table 4.3). Biden also swept the swing states—excepting Ohio and Florida—with voters hoping he would offer less-confrontational and more effective political stewardship that would aid the nation in a pandemic. Once elected, Biden showed greater reforming zeal than expected.

Participatory Democracy

Voters and Voting

American citizens generally register to vote at the local courthouse in their hometowns when they turn eighteen years of age. Voter rules are determined by the states. Some states require registrees to state their political affiliation, usually Democrat, Republican, or Independent. Citizens in some states can also register at libraries when they sign up for a lending card, at police stations when they get a driver's license, or by mail when they move outside the city, county, or state. Because Americans move a great deal, they must often re-register in a new city or state. Once on the electoral roll, Americans can vote in the many separate or combined elections to pick local dogcatchers, local and state school board members, mayors, members of city councils, sheriffs, judges, Secretaries of State, lieutenant governors, governors, highway commissioners, state legislators, US Senators and Representatives, and the President of the United States, to name only a few of the elected posts.

In the contemporary United States, voting is a near-universal right, whereas in the past it was viewed more as a privilege. Even though the Constitution declared "We the People," the Founders had real reasons to fear "mob rule" and so restricted voting rights to those who owned property and met residency requirements. "We the People" was an

Contemporary United States

elite idea of representative rule before the agitation by free whites increased in 1828 and led to the expansion of the suffrage and establishment of the Democratic Party. By mid-century, all white male citizens could vote. Black men received the vote in 1870 only to have it removed on a state-by-state basis in the South; women were included in 1920; and American Indians were classified as citizens in 1924.

There were important Voting Rights acts in the 1960s and 1980s which finally ensured that every citizen who wanted to vote could vote—except the several million people disqualified by committing felony crimes. Progressives argue that the differing state rules on voter registration and on participation for citizens who have not pre-registered can suppress the vote. Conservatives counter that the validity of the ballot suffers where pre-registration rules and identity controls are lax. Since 2010, twenty-five states, predominantly in the South and Midwest and with Republican governors have modified the right to vote (BCJ, 2019), a process that intensified after the 2020 Election. Restrictions included reduced early voting possibilities, additional obstacles to registration, and stricter requirements on voter identification—in addition to the redrawing of electoral boundaries (ACLU, 2010).

Many people fear that Republican actions to tighten voting restrictions in states they control could influence the outcome of elections by suppressing the turnout of marginalized groups. Others, on the Right, continued to insist that illegal voting was a problem. "Stop the Steal" campaigns drew support from up to two-thirds of Republicans who considered Trump's 2020 loss the result of voter fraud—despite the complete lack of evidence. Taking fraud allegations at face value, on a state-by-state level Republicans worked in 2021 and 2022 to limit early voting and mail-in voting, scrubbed voter rolls, and gave legislators the power to overturn election results by simple majority votes. Pointing out that voter fraud in 2020 was virtually non-existent, and fearful that state measures would limit legitimate citizens from voting in the future, Democrats unsuccessfully sought to introduce and enforce uniform national rules for voting, including the John Lewis Voting Rights Act.

In addition to choosing leaders, voters vote directly on the issues. Nearly half the states allow their citizens to vote for or against state laws and forty-nine states require a popular vote on any change to a state's constitution. When state legislatures put a proposal to the people's vote—instead of deciding matters themselves—the vote is called a "referendum." In addition to a legislature's power to call for a referendum, twenty-six states allow the people to initiate a referendum from the grassroots level without going through a city council decision, state legislature, judicial ruling, or congressional procedure (Ballotpedia, 2021c). Advocates for a new law often go door-to-door, collecting signatures on petitions. Once enough signatures are gathered—from 1,000 to 60,000 according to jurisdiction—the "initiative" is placed on the ballot. People vote on such issues as whether or not to hike or lower sales taxes, whether or not alcohol can be sold in their counties, to build sports stadiums, to decriminalize marijuana, and to allow gay or lesbian adoptions. For example, in 2020, voters in Mississippi and South Dakota approved ballot measures allowing medical marijuana use; Arizonans voted down a measure banning abortion; localities in Alabama approved stand your ground gun

Politics and Democracy

laws, and Missourians supported Medicaid expansion in that state. In September 2021, California Governor Gavin Newsom prevailed in a recall vote that would have installed a Republican replacement. In all, thirty-two states held 120 ballot referenda—passing 88—in conjunction with the 2020 election (Ballotpedia, 2021b).

Additional concerns plague the question of who votes. In the 1830s, Alexis de Tocqueville wrote glowingly of American democracy: "In countries in which universal suffrage exists, the majority is never doubtful, because neither party can reasonably pretend to represent that portion of the community which has not voted" (Tocqueville, 1994). Tocqueville could not know that nearly one-third of eligible voters would abstain from casting their votes in US presidential elections. Americans have long agreed on the principle that all citizens have the right, but not the obligation, to vote. People see it as a freedom and an equal opportunity to do with as they wish.

Does it really matter if Americans decide not to vote? Some political scientists acknowledge that individual Americans and various organizations have ways to participate in and make an impact upon political decisions without stepping into a voting booth. Moreover, some specialists even believe that voting is one of the least influential forms of political participation available. Others point out that people who are lower on the socio-economic scale are the least likely to register to vote by a large margin (McElwee, 2015). In recent elections, turnout has increased as many Americans have seen the power of the ballot (as Figure 4.1 indicates).

Interest Groups

There are two basic forms of participatory behavior for individual or group action: conventional and unconventional. Conventional behavior includes the regular voting and party systems that legitimize existing institutions. Unconventional participation includes such activities as the November 2016 protests against the election of Trump. Internet and social media activity, increasingly a vector of political participation, can fall into either form—though people are more likely to vent outrage online than to praise politicians. In contemporary America, everyday individual political behavior spans the spectrum from the supportive to the disruptive. Opinions are often aggregated through interest groups, not by individual voters. For instance, a member of the American Federation of Teachers (AFT)—a union with a qualified membership and specific interests—may abstain from voting in a local, state, or national election but still be intimately involved in the political process through the collective influence of the AFT. As a national organization representing 1.7 million members, AFT spent over $20 million in the 2020 election cycle, endorsing Joe Biden (Open Secrets, 2021b). AFT state chapters endorsed candidates further down the ticket.

Another example of conventional behavior is when a busy chief executive officer (CEO) decides not to take an hour off to vote but influences policy decisions when engaged in management decisions through a business group, such as the National Association of Manufacturers, representing 14,000 companies (NAM). NAM spent $24 million on lobbying in 2019–2020 (Open Secrets, 2021c). NAM's members also

Contemporary United States

bankroll political campaigns directly and in coalitions. NAM's website lists the many ways it aids its members, by "standing up for manufacturers" and "providing news and intelligence about the industry" (NAM, 2016). NAM members employ nearly 13 million Americans.

The AFT and NAM have exhibited conventional behavior in the two examples. However, they could also be involved in disruptive actions through strikes, illegal monopolies, tax efficiency plans, or insider trading schemes that affect the entire US economy by damaging confidence in the political system's ability to regulate trade. Interest group politics are growing while individual voting participation remains modest—this development can incite voter frustration with the political system as a whole.

An interest group, often called a "lobby," is made up of people or businesses who organize themselves to influence public policy on certain issues. They link civil society (see Chapter 6) and the market to political institutions by supporting or declining to support particular politicians. Legislators are lobbied directly by experts who present them with detailed research or opinion polls, and often contribute money to a politician's (re)election fund. Interest groups have narrow policy focuses and goals, whereby politicians and parties face broad and varied constituencies. An evaluation of the role of social media organizations like Facebook/Meta and Twitter as deliverers/providers of content for groups—such as Antifa on the Left and Proud Boys on the Right—depends on a person's point of view. In a pre-social media world, interest organization was less click-a-button. Addressing how social media affects the ability of interests to communicate is up for discussion, with successful groups needing thoughtful strategies to engage people in a time of information and attention overload.

Traditionally, interest groups comprised two types: open, and closed. Open groups allow anyone to join, claim to work for the public good, and have mass memberships consisting of individuals with limited resources. For them, social media outreach is vital. Such open groups are varied, as the following examples indicate. The Natural Resources Defense Council (NRDC) has "over three million members and online activists," well over a million Twitter and Facebook/Meta followers, and online activists dedicated to curbing global warming and pollution (NRDC, 2021). The American Civil Liberties Union (ACLU) has around 1.7 million members and over four million total Twitter and Facebook/Meta followers, who especially focus on the First Amendment's protection of freedom of speech (ACLU, 2021). The Christian Coalition (CC) supports pro-family and anti-Christian bigotry policies and claims 290,000 Facebook/Meta fans. The National Rifle Association (NRA) claims five million members supporting "America's longest standing civil rights organization" and protection of Second Amendment rights (NRA, 2022b). Additionally, the NRA has over five million Facebook and Twitter followers.

These open interest groups have large and disparate memberships and followers, rely on dues, merchandise, or private contributions to support their lobbying efforts, and more often than not provide voters, instead of dollars, to politicians who support their causes. Typically, open groups grow rapidly when the political environment is adversarial: the Natural Resources Defense Council (NRDC) called for donations and new members following Trump's 2016 election, to "Protect our Planet," while the ACLU solicited for donations to "Protect the Rights and Freedoms We Believe In." The NRA is currently pushing for members and dollars to stop the "Biden-Pelosi-Schumer Gun-Ban Agenda."

The second type is the closed interest group, which promotes action to benefit very specific organizations or groups of people. These closed groups include labor unions such as the American Federation of Labor (AFL), the Major League Baseball Players Association (MLBPA), the American Bar Association (ABA), and the American Medical Association (AMA). Closed interest groups use money and the promise of votes as a way to lobby for candidates who support their interests. The 12-million-member AFL spent over $6 million in the 2020 federal elections, and endorsed Biden's campaign (OpenSecrets, 2021a; AFL, 2020). With the exception of unions and professional associations, closed interest groups usually have small memberships, but their strong financial resources and laser-like focus on preferential policy ensures that politicians will listen to them. The AMA is influential in health care reform. The growth of lobbies focuses attention on issues which are too small to be effectively promoted by parties but are vital to their members and are promoted by groups through support, candidate endorsement, and campaign contributors' cash. Some commentators worry that "interest" democracy and "voter" democracy are incompatible.

The ideological and socioeconomic contrasts between the parties are also reflected in interest groups. Commercial interest groups like NAM and its associate Business-Industry PAC (BIPAC) more often support the Republicans over the Democrats, who gain more support from unions and public interests. Lobbyists provide ideas for legislation and give feedback to politicians on the effects of legislation and of voters' responses to it. Money collected by interest groups flows towards incumbents or to challengers likely to be elected. Partisan interest is tempered by the need to be heard. The influence of interests gained through campaign contributions has come under repeated scrutiny over the last generation.

The existence of interest groups illuminates the intentionally pluralist nature of American civil society. Interest groups allow Americans to express their views and preferences constantly, not just in voting booths on election days every two years. They give citizens with particular concerns many points of access to the political process. In a society with over 330 million people divided into thousands of subcultures and many classes with varying religious, educational, and occupational interests, lobby groups help broaden democracy by giving voices to minorities otherwise stifled by a majority-rule system. With interest group politics, various minority groups or minority interests can be heard and might succeed on issues that would never survive a majority vote. Critics argue that groups with greater resources in terms of members, expertise, and money have disproportionate influence on policy debates, arguably short-circuiting electoral democracy. Additionally, interests increasingly work in transnational ways, linking human and financial interests in a global era. Political scientists posit that this lack of international transparency can fuel the claims of populists who say they speak for the "forgotten majority" of voters (Müller, 2016).

Contemporary United States

Recent decades have seen the rise of think-tanks which link interest groups and policymaking to academia. Think-tanks populate broad swathes of the political landscape and cover more policy ground than single interest groups. Think-tanks are funded by private gifts from individuals and organizations, through publishing, grants, and endowments. Prominent think-tanks, like the Brookings Institution (founded 1927) and the Heritage Foundation (founded 1973) employ hundreds of top scholars, assistants, and administrators to produce credible research for governments and media as a way to shape public opinion. Academics use think-tanks to apply research to policy formulation, implementation, and monitoring. Brookings produces research and background papers on health care, foreign policy, urban issues, transnational and migration issues, economic studies, globalization, and governance studies from a liberal point of view. Heritage covers healthcare, tax, globalization, defense, and all other issues, from a conservative perspective.

Among the several hundred influential think-tanks that have offices in Washington, DC, are the Institute for Policy Studies, the Progressive Policy Institute, the American Enterprise Institute, and the Cato Institute (Singer, 2012). Every week, the breadth and depth of policy outreach think-tanks offer in lectures, talks, roundtables, and other events open to the general public is impressive.

Interest groups have the financial resources to push legislation and ensure that they are heard in another way, through litigation. Groups often file "class action" lawsuits in American courts to stop big business or to overturn legislation that does not give every person "equal protection" under the law, as demanded by the 14th Amendment. Some scholars argue that the use of lawyers to override the will of a legislature is hardly democratic; others contend that lawsuits and interest groups help ensure that all those citizens who want to be heard are heard and that the law is applied fairly.

Political Parties

Over and above the interest groups, political parties gather the electorate into large coalitions of voters that affect the governing structure of the country. Parties and their candidates support ever-changing plans for the administration of government in order to balance freedom, order, and equality, and to provide national security for the state. Parties usually propose and nominate candidates and offer general policy platforms to help voters make choices. The Democratic and Republican parties dominate the political landscape, yet they are not alone. Many smaller parties exist—the Working Families Party, Libertarian Party, and Green Party are prime examples—but their influence is normally limited, as the winner-takes-all electoral system discards all the votes of losing candidates. Voting rationally means voting Democrat or Republican for most people.

Since the 1860s and until recently, the stability of the Republicans and Democrats as structuring organizations for civil society has been striking. The two major parties bring together disparate and sometimes conflicting views. The longevity of the parties indicates a high degree of flexibility on issues and the ability of the parties to transform themselves

Politics and Democracy

to meet changing circumstances and attitudes. Otherwise, the rise of strong third parties or insurgencies, such as the Reform Party in 1992 or the Tea Party in 2009, might supplant them. The elections of 1896, 1932/1936, and 1980 were transforming elections for the two parties, as they fused ideas from other/lesser platforms and switched constituencies. Republicans in 1896 dropped the mantle of reform and equality that had been Abraham Lincoln's legacy and became the conservative party of big business interests. Democrats in 1932 were able to build a coalition of Northern workers and unions with Southern and Western farmers and African Americans to redistribute wealth a little. In 1980, the Republicans drew Southern and Western white voters away from the Democrats and transformed their party around Ronald Reagan's conservative response to the cultural turmoil of the 1960s and his promise to limit government.

In 2016, both parties experienced insurgent campaigns: outsider Donald Trump and independent Senator Bernie Sanders shook the political establishment, as Trump won the Republican, and Sanders came very close to winning the Democratic nomination. Republicans and Democrats exchanged a few voters; Trump harnessed disaffected blue-collar voters, older white men, and sympathizers of the nationalist and Christian Right, while Hillary Clinton made gains among educated suburban voters. This process, of Republicans netting erstwhile Democratic voters in the northeast, and Democrats capturing previously Republican voters continued in 2020, signposting future voter dynamics.

To win elections, candidates must convince the component groups within their parties. Dominant groups within the Democrat Party include socially liberal and economically big-government Left-leaning party activists like Bernie Sanders, pro-choice, centrist reformers like the Clintons, as well as conservative Democrats supporting President Joe Biden. Protests against the Trump administration's confrontational style and policy goals encouraged both mainstream suburbanites and more radical and youthful voters to vote Democrat in greater numbers in 2020 than in 2016. The Republican Party is also composite and contains remnants of the liberal eastern Republicans who once dominated the party like Senator Mitt Romney and former Governor Chris Christie, fiscal conservatives like Congresswoman Liz Cheney and Congressman Adam Kinzinger, nominal libertarians like Senator Rand Paul, the religious right including Senator Mike Lee and Senator Ted Cruz, and neo-Conservatives like Senator Marco Rubio, and the currently dominant new white nationalist coalition around Trump and Governor Ron DeSantis. Free-market or regulated economic philosophies, religious or secular cultural values, individualistic or communitarian social ideas, nationalism or cosmopolitanism, and regional preferences and traditions mix within both parties to produce a dizzying and diverse set of policy options which force the parties to accept great internal compromise. But despite earlier practices, political polarization means bipartisan overlap between individual politicians in the two parties is much less common in contemporary America.

Both parties must deal with conflict between the strong support of their bases and the softer support of the center, which collectively make up a ruling coalition. Balancing the beliefs of the grassroots and the more moderate views of swing voters is often

Contemporary United States

difficult—and sometimes impossible. In 2021, Democrats felt this tension as Biden attempted to fashion cross-aisle compromises for human infrastructure reform without losing support from his progressive base. Meanwhile, and defending their positions, Republicans in opposition have begun to practice a lockstep strategy to maximize pressure on the Biden administration. Voters may reward an opposition party's blocking strategy by deeming the in-power administration ineffective and voting for the out-of-power party next time or staying away from the polls. That is the bet Senate Minority Leader Mitch McConnell has made in 2022, and that Democrats will make again next time they are in opposition, perhaps with continuing dissatisfaction and polarization among voters.

Elections like 2020 bring fresh starts, but they are often time-limited. Biden's victory imagined a bipartisan rush to the middle but saw Republicans rally round Trump. There are certainly bipartisan initiatives propelled by centrists in both parties, but ideological and affective polarization between the parties seems likely to remain strong. Agreement on the need to build the future breaks into discord on taxes, deficits, infrastructure loans and user fees, social policy, cultural policy, diplomacy, military action abroad, immigration policy, criminal justice reform, and a host of other issues. Even issues where consensus is possible, such as on infrastructure, how to invest, how much to invest, and who gets what, divide the parties.

By 2022, Democrats had held the majority in the House of Representatives for four years and the Senate for two years. Illustration 4.3 shows this control by the presence of Democrats Nancy Pelosi and Kamala Harris as House Speaker and president of the Senate respectively, behind President Biden in his 2021 address to a Joint Session of Congress. But the Democrat majority in the House was less than ten and the party was not monolithic. When majorities are small, individual members of the governing party hold real tradable power on specific issues. Presidents propose legislation—such as the infrastructure bills of 2021, and then must negotiate with legislators in their own parties. Simultaneously, congressmen in the minority party understand power and know they can inflict damaging strategic defeats on a president through a united partisan front and a hope to attract a few votes from the other party. There is a downside to this strategy. Such political positioning feeds into the popular mistrust of government. In late 2021, polls suggest that only one in five Americans approve of the job that Congress is doing (Gallup, 2021b).

Analysts offer a "median" voter theory in explaining how the two-party system often creates somewhat similar stances on issues, despite the practical politics and strong trends towards heightened polarization. Because there are a number of voters in the center, and because American elections are based on a winner-takes-all system—as opposed to proportional representation—politicians usually seek to attract middle-of-the-road independent voters, who often straddle liberal and conservative issues. While other theories see economic, gender, North–South, rural–urban, cultural, or value-laden coastal–heartland divides as pre-eminent factors in voter behavior, median voter theory helps to understand the variation in election outcomes from one year to the next.

Votes from the center might decide elections if candidates maintain strong bases. Median voter theory helps explain why candidates embrace the independent voters

Politics and Democracy

Illustration 4.3 Biden Addresses a Joint Session of Congress

Presidents address a Joint Session of Congress (year one of their terms) or a State of the Union speech (years two, three, and four of their term) at least once a year, usually in late January or early February. Well over 20 million Americans watched Biden's 2021 address. Main themes included a fresh start after the previous four years, that Americans should listen to one another, and that Americans should work towards unity instead of division. The Covid-induced economic crisis loomed large, rekindling unity. The image shows Biden flanked by the Speaker of the House of Representatives Nancy Pelosi to the right and president of the Senate, Vice President Kamala Harris, to the left. This was the first time that two women had officiated a Joint Session of Congress.

Source: Chip Somodevilla via Getty Images

who number up to one-third of the electorate. Table 4.1 indicates how Americans view themselves on a simple Left–Right spectrum, with "Left" expressed as liberal and "Right" as conservative. Most voters put themselves in the center—at least when responding to a pollster. Whether centrist self-identification conforms with the position people actually take on specific issues is another matter, complicating strategy choices for politicians. Occasionally, candidates can taste success by negative campaigning, enthusing their base, and turning off their opponents, as Trump did in 2020. But this risks further polarization. Trump won more votes than any other Republican nominee in history—over 74 million—but it was not enough to top Biden's 80 million votes and retain office. Biden held his base and won over Independents (Lindsay, 2020).

The Democratic and Republican parties navigate between three core values: individuality (freedom), community (order), and fairness (equality). When asked whether they prefer absolute freedom or absolute equality, Americans by a wide

Contemporary United States

Table 4.1 Ideological Self-Placement and Party Identification, 2020

Ideology/party	2020
All respondents	
Liberal	25
Moderate	35
Conservative	36
Republicans	
Liberal	4
Moderate	20
Conservative	75
Democrats	
Liberal	51
Moderate	35
Conservative	12
Independents	
Liberal	20
Moderate	48
Conservative	29

Source: Saad (2021)

margin choose freedom; thus, they are choosing diversity and wide class differences over conformity, homogeneity, and social equality. Republican voters tend to stress the maintenance of order as the highest aim of government, with freedom second, and equality, third. Democrats usually put equality issues first, freedom second, and order third—but centrist Democrats generally mean equality of opportunity while progressives want equality of outcome. Conservatives favor less government intervention except in demanding harsher penalties for crimes and stronger militaries and police forces, while liberals expect activist governments to work for minority and women's legal rights. Communitarians who want equality of outcome generally vote with the Democrats, while libertarians who want the least possible government—except where necessary to protect life and property—vote on the Republican side. Table 4.1, "Ideological Self-Placement and Party Identification," suggests that voter ideas and self-understanding cohere. Since 2000, ideological self-placement polls indicate modest growth for liberals and modest declines for conservatives and moderates (Saad 2021).

Ideological self-placement and party support largely correspond. A voter's upbringing, gender, race, age education, religious fervor, and income also determine voting behavior, as is indicated in Table 4.2. Voting patterns remain more complex than socioeconomic Left–Right splits suggest.

Politics and Democracy

Table 4.2 Presidential Preference in 2020: Exit Polls (percentage of 2020 electorate in parentheses)

Voting Group (%)	Dem.: Joe Biden %	Rep.: Donald Trump %
Males (48)	45	52
Females (52)	53	42
White (67)	41	58
Black (13)	87	12
Latino (13)	65	32
Asian (4)	61	34
No college degree (59)	48	50
College degree (41)	55	43
Income: under $100,000 (74)	56	43
Income: over $100,000 (26)	42	54
Liberals (26)*	89	10
Moderates (39)*	64	34
Conservatives (35)*	14	85
Vote for president mainly:		
For your candidate (71)	46	53
Against the opponent (24)	68	30
Area Type		
Urban (29)	60	38
Suburban (51)	50	48
Rural (19)	42	57
Party Identification		
Democrat (37)	94	5
Republican (36)	6	94
Independents (26)	54	41
Age		
18–24 (9)	65	31
25–29 (7)	54	43
30–39 (16)	51	46
40–49 (16)	54	44
50–64 (30)	47	52
65+ (22)	47	52
Religion		
Protestant or other Christian (43)	39	60
Catholic (25)	52	47
Other religious affiliation (8)	69	29
No religious affiliation (22)	65	31

Contemporary United States

Voting Group (%)	Dem.: Joe Biden %	Rep.: Donald Trump %
Issues: which mattered?		
Racial inequality (20)*	92	7
Corona pandemic (17)*	81	15
Abortion legal (51)/illegal (42)	74/23	24/76
The economy (35)*	17	83
Crime and Safety (11)*	27	71
Character traits		
Can unite the country (19)*	75	24
Is a strong leader (33)*	28	72
Cares about people like me (21)*	49	50
Has good judgment (24)*	68	26
Marital Status		
Married (56)	46	53
Not married (44)	58	40
Personal financial situation		
Better than four years ago (41)	26	72
About the same as four years ago (39)	65	34
Worse than one year ago (20)	77	20
Condition of the nation's economy		
Excellent (13)	16	84
Good (36)	24	75
Not so good (31)	76	22
Poor (19)	87	10
Confident votes counted accurately?		
Confident (86)	54	45
Not confident (12)	45	63

Sources: CNN (2020); NYT (2020)

Recent elections suggest that both parties have had trouble adjusting to voter volatility. Democrats had hoped that Obama's 2008 popularity would strengthen the party nationwide. In sheer numbers of party members, it did, but the Democratic Party became a minority party in terms of its control over state government and it became increasingly embattled in Washington. More accurately, neither party has been able to conquer disaffected public opinion despite the gerrymandering of congressional districts (the drawing of borders to gather as many like-minded voters as possible), while both parties reactively and pragmatically tailor their platforms to opinion polls as they battle for any voters they can convince. Gerrymandering makes election outcomes more predictable, and undercuts democracy, engendering court challenges and protests (see Illustration 4.4). Although they vote less than their elders, the views of young people must be taken into account, as they represent changing opinions and future concerns which parties must confront if they expect

Illustration 4.4 Gerrymandering: When Politicians Skew the Vote

On October 3, 2017, the Supreme Court heard arguments regarding gerrymandering: a technique used by both Republicans and Democrats to manipulate congressional district results by cracking (splitting up voters) or packing (corralling) voters to create electoral fortresses that are virtually unwinnable for the other party. These practices thwart the spirit of democratic elections. Claims that elections are rigged stem back to the nineteenth century but have become more acute since 2000. Democrats argue that voting is made deliberately difficult via the lack of polling places, limited mail-in and drop-off voting, and in-advance-of-elections voter registration rules. Republicans claim that lax state laws allow the ineligible to vote, feeding into Trump's 2021 "Stop the Steal" claims. Reliable expert studies have consistently found that the number of ineligible people able to cast votes is negligible. In 2021, Democrats introduced and narrowly passed HR 1, "For the People Act," to make voting easier, reform campaign finance rules, and stop partisan gerrymandering. In the Senate, however, the Bill lacked the filibuster-proof 60-vote supermajority needed to pass. While most Democrats advocated abolishing the filibuster rules to pass the bill, others fretted over the long-term consequences of reorganizing rules that favored the minority parties—especially as the prospect of the Democrats losing the Senate in the 2022 midterms loomed.

Source: Bill O'Leary/The Washington Post via Getty Images

Contemporary United States

to maintain influence. No party wants to be seen as "out of new ideas." Obama excited young Americans in 2008 and retained the youth, Hispanic, Asian, and African American vote in 2012. Clinton failed to charge up young and African American voters in 2016, partly due to Sanders's socialist appeals. Younger voters also supported Biden disproportionately. Commentators have noted how voters have become more faithless in recent years, raising speculation that independent voters may see themselves beyond party or community bounds. The base, however, remains enthusiastic towards the parties, while those who say they are independent have increased (Pew, 2019c).

The 2020 presidential election results recorded in Table 4.2 indicate that younger adults tend to prefer Democrats more than their parents and grandparents. People under fifty said they voted for Democrats, whereas the over-fifty groups favored Republicans. The reform spirit and relative disenchantment of younger Americans stems from disconnect over what they feel government can deliver and illustrates the generation chasm between them and older citizens. Federal politics are dominated by a gerontocracy of the middle aged and elderly. Trump (seventy-four) and Biden's (seventy-seven) combined age in 2020 was 151. Speaker Nancy Pelosi was eighty-one. In 2020 voters over fifty years old cast 52 percent of the vote.

In the 1960s and 1970s political behavior was highly unconventional—many citizens marched, burned draft cards, sat-in, and rioted to demand government responsibility toward equality. In the 1980s and 1990s citizens often chose not to vote, or they voted to dismantle social programs that increased taxes. In 2016 Trump's support overwhelming came from white people, the biggest group of voters. This suggests that if whites vote together, they could avert the consequences of increasing diversity. Other observers argued that voting trends are unclear. America's growing outer-suburbs and "penurbs" (rural, outer suburbs) tend to vote Republican. Education and a better job may make a person more sympathetic to a Democratic ticket. However, getting ahead by getting away to the bigger houses, better schools, lower taxes and a green, countryside environment in outer penurban suburbs pushes voters towards the Republicans.

2020 exit polls presented in Table 4.2 suggest that Biden prevailed in the presidential election because he was effective in portraying himself as a unifier with good judgment. While Trump's 2016 campaign as the antithesis of an insider worked that year, 2020 voters saw Biden as a better bet in the fight against Covid and as the candidate most likely to further equality—even though they saw the Trump administration as reliable on the economy. Trump appealed to whiter, older, rural and Protestant voters; Biden appealed to younger, urban, Catholic, non-white and non-religious voters. In truth, Biden's specific action program for the economy and society helped. Trump's program was non-specific and based on a "not-Democrat" stance—a difficult stance to defend during the transformative Covid crisis.

Traditionally, successful politicians had to adapt their messages to different audiences while avoiding obviously contradictory fifteen-second soundbites on the national news. Because issues that hit home in Washington, DC, may not matter much elsewhere, candidates usually rely on a party's national platform for stability, devising specific strategies for local campaigns. Biden was somewhat traditional and reticent in communicating with the public, probably reflecting a belief that under the circumstances, the election was his to lose. Biden used social media, targeting Facebook moms and celebrity endorsements. Trump was again untraditional and omnipresent on Twitter, his campaign based around himself. Estimates suggested that the 2020 election cycle spending surpassed $14 billion. The Democrats had a huge financial advantage, of $8 billion to $6 billion (Evers-Hillstrom, 2021). Money buys campaign expertise, organization, and media time.

While contemporary politicians are often more ideological (or less ideological) than the voters to whom they cater, and their votes on specific issues sometimes contradict, or go far beyond, campaign promises, this is probably not the case with Biden. Grabbing the Covid moment, Biden may have overpromised. The administration got caught between the enthusiasm of voters and the party's young and diverse grassroots, and the art of the possible with fragile control of Congress. Many voters are likely to be disappointed—a factor that feeds into the pervasive view that politicians cannot be trusted and that government does not benefit the public as much as it should. Such a split between expectations and results may determine the 2022 midterms and the 2024 general election. Biden has a narrow window to prove that decisive and effective government can legislate, implement, and heal the nation.

Politics

Elections

Ordinary American voters are given the final say over who should represent the parties in elections, unlike in many other Western democracies. Before the general election is held between one Republican and one Democrat—and a few Independents or others—a primary election takes place to pick the party candidates. Although presidential primaries are the most widely reported, primaries are held for almost all the country's elected offices. In a primary, voters elect one candidate from a field of hopefuls who have simply announced that they are candidates for the particular office and wish to run as Republicans or Democrats. Some states allow for open primaries whereby voters from either party can vote in either the Republican or Democratic primary. Other states hold closed primaries, restricting the vote in each primary to registered party members. The primary system increases the depth of democracy by giving the people the power to determine the official party candidates over the entire spectrum of political offices. Recently, primaries have been used in both parties to challenge moderate congressional incumbents by splitting the votes in a way to make sure the most partisan nominee wins.

Presidential elections illustrate the complexity of the election process (Box 4.1), even though variations are of different scales for each public office. The visible process starts well before the presidential elections take place, when hopefuls declare

Box 4.1 The Path to the Presidency

1　Election Day minus 4–8 years. A future president has usually first been elected as a state governor, US senator, or vice president; sometimes a military hero or a reality TV host will do.

2　Election Day minus 2 years. Hopefuls fundraise the tens of millions of dollars needed to begin a campaign. Contributors give money directly to the candidate and not to a political party.

3　Election Day minus 18 months. Individuals announce that they are actively campaigning to be president of the United States. They begin to visit states with early primaries.

4　Election Day minus 12 months. Opinion polls in state primaries usually identify a field of two or three favorites in each party. Unpopular candidates begin to concede.

5　Election Day minus 10 months. Results from the state primaries usually point to a clear frontrunner from each party.

6　Election Day minus 5 months. The winners are virtually assured the nominations of their parties.

7　Election Day minus 3–4 months. Party conventions officially name their presidential candidates. The parties now begin to fund the nominee's campaign. Candidates announce their choices for vice-presidential running mates, visit states they can win, avoid those they will surely lose, and pour money into the toss-up states.

8　Election Day minus 6 weeks. Hard campaigning and head-to-head television debates by which media pundits, viewers, and voters decide who performs best under the spotlights. Mail-in voting begins.

9　Election Day. Voters nationwide cast ballots and electoral votes are tallied in a state-by-state fashion to name the winner. Losers usually concede quickly.

10　Election Day plus 6 weeks. The Electoral College officially declares the winner.

11　Election Day plus 10 weeks. Inauguration of the President.

their candidacies, as Biden did in April 2019. Starting in January in the year of the general election, states hold primary elections or closed political meetings called "caucuses." Primaries and caucuses receive massive media coverage, and voters often turn out in significant numbers—as was the case in 2020. Delegates are awarded according to a kaleidoscopic mix of criteria that guarantee only a rough overall form of proportionality in regard to population and some influence for senior party members—called "superdelegates."

During the summer before an election, the parties hold conventions where their presidential candidates are officially chosen and the campaigning accelerates. This long transition from being a hopeful to becoming the nominee helped to "personify" the political structure in the pre-Trump era by focusing attention on the personal attributes of each candidate. Voters select candidates with whom they identify, or by habit of party affiliation, mixing the personal with the political. Overall, local interests and primaries put candidates in stronger positions towards their parties than in other countries where voters choose parties, not candidates. When casting ballots, voters have traditionally weighed personality as much as ideology—though this may be changing. They are more likely to ask, "Is he like me, and do I like him?" than "Is he the best leader possible?" Emotional intelligence and empathy are usually seen as important assets. Table 4.3 shows that control of the White House has split fairly evenly between Democrats and Republicans since 1980, and how minor parties sometimes help determine the outcome of the elections—for instance, in 1992 and 2000, and, some argue, in 2016.

Because elections to the House of Representatives occur every two years, representatives must constantly be on the campaign trail. All 435 representatives pay closer attention to their home districts than to the wants of their parties, even though they tend increasingly to vote along party lines so long as an issue does not disadvantage

Table 4.3 Presidential Elections, 2008–2020

Year	Candidate	Popular votes (million)	%	Electoral College Votes
2008	Barack Obama (Dem)	69.5	52.9	365
	John McCain (Rep)	59.9	45.6	173
	Ralph Nader (Ind)	0.7	0.6	0
	Bob Barr (Lib)	0.5	0.4	0
2012	Barack Obama (Dem)	62.6	50.6	332
	Mitt Romney (Rep)	59.1	47.8	206
	Gary Johnson (Lib)	1.3	1.0	0
	Jill Stein (Green)	0.5	0.4	0
2016	Donald Trump (Rep)	62.4	46.3	306
	Hillary Clinton (Dem)	64.6	48.0	232
	Gary Johnson (Lib)	4.3	3.3	0
	Jill Stein (Green)	1.4	1.0	0
2020	Joe Biden (Dem)	81.3	51.3	306
	Donald Trump (Rep)	74.2	46.8	232
	Jo Jorgensen (Lib)	1.9	1.2	0
	Howie Hawkins (Green)	0.4	0.3	0

Rep = Republican; Dem = Democrat; Lib = Libertarian; Ind = Independent.

Source: Leip (2021)

Contemporary United States

the folks "back home." Politicians who "go native" and support compromise over their own constituents are usually punished in the next election as disloyal.

The size of Congress has not changed since 1912, when the number was set at 435. Because of population growth, each representative represents an average of 740,000 people, instead of the 60,000 people in 1789. In 2020, House candidates raised around $1.1 billion total—over $2 million per district, making fundraising as important as legislative work (Levine and Funakoshi, 2020).

The 100 senators, elected on six-year cycles, represent large and changing state-wide electorates. The states have vast differences in population with the result that California's Senators represent nearly 40 million people, while Wyoming's only represent 578,000 (USCB, 2021e, 2021j). Until 1913, senators were appointed by state legislatures rather than being elected by the voters, emphasizing the point that senators were intended to be ambassadors for sovereign states, rather than representatives of the people. Senatorial election campaigns are far more expensive than House elections, costing more than $30 million each in 2020, for a total surpassing $1 billion (Levine and Funakoshi, 2021). The twin Georgia runoff contest between Republicans David Perdue and Kelly Loeffler and Democrats John Ossoff and Raphael Warnock to determine which party would control the Senate cost over $300 million (Montellaro, 2020). Democrats won both runoffs and secured Democrat control.

Historically, the frequency of democratic elections and the spectacle of politics have helped knit civil society together. Even though campaigns may be bitter, Americans have usually rallied around the victors once the results are known and certified. That did not happen in 2016 as a massive resistance arose to contest Trump's victory. In 2020, polls indicated that over half of Republicans felt that the election had been stolen. *Newsweek* magazine reported that 59 percent of Republicans saw the belief in a rigged election as a tenet of Republican faith (Zhao, 2021).

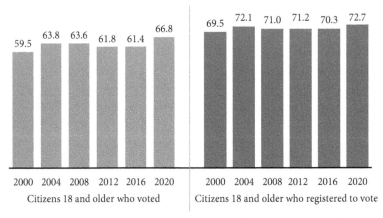

Figure 4.1 Voter Turnout and Registration: Presidential Elections, 2000–2020 (percentage)
Source: USCB (2021f)

Media

The media—print, broadcast, internet, and social—exert a powerful influence and offer a conduit for communications between the people and their politicians. Today's fractured politics and society feed personalized social media universes in the plural, a revolution which has been underway for at least a decade. Separate media universes increase polarization as consumers are less likely to be confronted with views that oppose their own. Conversations fragment to become internally Democrat or internally Republican, rather than to address society as a whole.

The media are influenced by the profit motive and offer questionable stories to attract and retain viewers, instead of informing them on the issues. The 2016 Trump campaign so arrested media attention that it lost its objectivity, though that was not the case in 2020. At other times, the media acts like a government mouthpiece or, contrarily, can serve as a populist megaphone where ordinary people call for conventional or unconventional actions to change a political situation. In 2020 Trump waged a second outsider "disruption" campaign, whereas Biden used a "return to normalcy" media strategy on the back of a massive funding advantage.

In the year between the first presidential primaries and the final election, journalists are relentless in exposing the lives of the likely winners. Primaries are both "beauty contests" and forensic marathons, with every deviant feature of the candidate's lives and family backgrounds exposed until the unrelenting exposure of personal details convinces some candidates to quit. Many people do not enter political life simply because their private lives cannot bear the scrutiny from professional reporters or talk show pundits. For the American public, this is greatly entertaining, and more people closely follow the campaigns than actually vote.

Most media organizations in the US are privately owned; thus newsworthiness must be balanced against market forces to maximize profits. The First Amendment protects free speech and freedom of the press, but also gives shelter to gossip pages that lie or stretch the truth to sell papers or attract viewers. Mostly, though, the established media take pride in the truthfulness and trustworthiness of their stories and are quick to retract or correct a falsehood, despite claims of bias. Recently, more partisan, energized, and often less reliable media have thrived on the internet, displacing traditional sources. Examples of new players include the *Huffington Post* on the Left, *Axios* and *Politico* in the center, and *Breitbart News* on the nationalist Right.

The media are essential tools for politicians: hence candidates develop press strategies to connect with potential voters. Franklin Roosevelt showed the power of radio in the 1930s, John Kennedy proved the effectiveness of television in the 1960s, and Obama demonstrated the importance of the internet and smart phones. Since Clinton in 1992, candidates have used somewhat unscripted appearances on late night TV, judging the benefits in popularity will outweigh the risk of uncontrolled media exposure. This is risky for candidates, but it can help poll ratings.

Candidates increasingly use social media to connect with supporters directly and let peer-to-peer networks promote the benefits of a candidate or policy change. Political

Contemporary United States

advertising is increasingly moving on to social media, such as Facebook/Meta. Although Biden out-fundraised Trump, the ex-president remained a master of the media and understood the value of celebrity. For example, in January 2021, Trump had over 80 million Twitter followers, whereas Biden had only 30 million (Murdock, 2021). Internet sites permit candidates to connect directly with many times the viewership of a TV show, as well as letting supporters connect in real time outside traditional organizations.

Prominent politicians spend a great deal of money and expertise shaping media moments to attract voters, stay in the public eye via a TV "photo opportunity," or by spinning—interpreting favorably—a negative story to diminish its impact. In 2020, the two televised presidential debates (a third one was canceled) attracted between 63 and 73 million viewers—numbers equal to half of those who voted and not including those who watched later. As soon as the debates were over, the respective campaigns began the job of spinning their candidate's "victories"—regardless of how pundits and commentators scored the performances. Breaking with tradition, President Trump did not confer legitimacy to President-Elect Biden by meeting with him after the election and did not attend Biden's inauguration. Trump broke with a tradition of photo ops that are intended to help unite the country, celebrate the people's vote, and coalesce support for the president-elect.

The national and local scope of the media presents an ambiguous picture. The connection of media to politics is complicated by localism as no printed newspaper successfully reaches a national audience, even though the *Wall Street Journal*, *Washington Post*, *New York Times*, and *USA Today* come close in digital versions. The media—television, radio, and newspapers—are increasingly owned by large corporations. Jeff Bezos's Amazon.com owns the *Washington Post*, has a firm hold on the publishing business, and has recently expanded to internet TV via *Prime*. Carlos Slim owns the *New York Times* as well as a diversified basket of communications industries. Comcast, Time, and Fox consolidate media and communications. Yet new digital media continue to emerge, in both the broadcasting (Netflix) and publishing (*Quartz*) worlds—suggesting that technological innovation and new media models (online) and titles counteract traditional media consolidation (see Chapter 7).

Traditionally the media have acted the role of gatekeeper, controlling the flow of information to and from politicians and the people and determining its spin. But the new media—the internet, smart phones, social media, streaming services, satellite television and radio channels, segmentation of FM and medium-wave radio by ideology and religious views, and the growth of cable TV news complicate analyses of media influence as the proliferation of types of outlets clearly erodes news control. While older media consumers watch "flow TV" and read physical and electronic iterations of traditional media, younger Americans increasingly personalize their news consumption to create their own "liberal" or "conservative" media universes. More than four in five Americans get news from electronic devices (Shearer, 2021).

The 2020 election campaign saw a dramatic rise in un-curated online, multisource news, alongside the "dark marketing" of manipulated or purely "fake" news which was intended to influence the electoral process. After five years of political discourse afflicted by a "post-truth" and "alternative facts," respectable media attempted to push back against false media by offering more in-depth analyses. The outgoing administration had slated traditional media as "biased" and "failing." In February 2017, Trump called the fake press the "enemy of the people," but directed this phrase at the established media (Higgins, 2017). By 2020, the novelty of Trump's media onslaught had worn thin, allowing more space in reporting which probably was a factor in high turnout levels and awareness of the importance of the election.

Increased competition has made the media hungry for news and aggressive in acquiring it. To keep viewers or subscribers, reporters feel that they must be the first to break the news. The media need a candidate's headline-making ability and advertising money. In 2016, Trump's unconventional behavior and outrageous statements entertained viewers, and encouraged news studios to provide him with over $2 billion of free media time. However, in 2020 voters tired somewhat of Trump's war of attrition against the media. The 2024 election is likely to see Trump again in the mix and will demonstrate the depth of the connection between newer forms of media and campaigning and untraditional candidates.

The popular vote opinion polls in Election 2020 were fairly consistent in projecting Biden as the winner. However, the distribution of votes—with large Democrat majorities stacked up on the east and west coasts, and large Republican majorities in the heartland—portended a much closer Electoral College result, allowing the media to trumpet a horse race between Biden and Trump. Ultimately, however, Biden won with a strong majorities in both tallies.

The influence the media have in voter education and political socialization—helping people determine how they should vote and where they fit into government—is clear. A week before the election, the Center for Responsive Politics estimated that presidential, house, and senatorial candidates collectively spent around $14 billion on election campaigns in the 2019–2020 election cycle (OpenSecrets, 2020a). Over 200 billionaire donors invested indirectly in support of candidates' campaigns, with 131 favoring Biden and 91 Trump (Tindera, 2020). The "Super PAC" supportive campaign funding allowed by the *Citizens United* Supreme Court ruling (see the following section) has arguably pushed the political system in a more conservative direction. Meanwhile the increase in small online donations probably pushed the other way. Precise dollar estimates in the wake of *Citizens United* are hard to make (and do not include free media coverage), yet it is clear that a large proportion of campaign money paid for media exposure.

Campaign Finances

Election costs are paid by the candidates, the federal government, political parties, interest groups, and private contributors. The system favors the affluent because of the start-up money required to begin and the inadequacy of public funding to run an effective campaign. The idea that the candidate who spends the most money for advertising can buy the election, rubs against long-standing myths that anyone can rise to be president. But the biggest concern among Americans is that private contributions

Contemporary United States

to campaign coffers give the donor too much access and influence, thereby damaging the democratic process.

In 1971, Congress passed the Federal Election Campaigns Act and, in 1974, created the Federal Election Commission to require candidates and donors to make full disclosures on contributions and spending. The 2002 Bipartisan Campaign Reform Act (BCRA) attempted to tighten election finance laws, to control the use of soft money by parties and candidates, and to make financing more transparent. While limits and matching governmental campaign contributions were available and readily used by candidates from the 1970s to the 2000, by 2008, candidates were able to use the internet to raise enough money online from a grassroots army of small donors, making them able to refuse the limitations on government contributions. Having given once, online donors created a community which could be revisited for future contributions. Campaign limits did not apply to a candidate's personal money. In the 2016 Republican primary, Trump partly self-funded—allowing him to claim that he wasn't dependent on special interest or donors. Still, the self-funding of presidential elections is not usually successful—as Mitt Romney found out in 2012. Billionaires such as Starbucks founder Howard Schulz and media tycoon Michael Bloomberg considered running for president in 2020 but accepted the reality that their wealth would not buy the results they wanted.

The outcome of the 2010 *Citizens United v. Federal Elections Commission* case changed the way campaigns were financed. The case emerged from *Hillary: The Movie*, a film accessible via the internet and hostile to Clinton's 2008 primary run against Obama. This film had been banned, as it contravened regulations barring corporations from direct candidate endorsements or oppositions. The Supreme Court overturned the ban by a 5–4 decision and judged that any restrictions on corporations—classed as legal "persons"—unconstitutionally broke First Amendment guarantees. The judgment allowed corporations "to spend freely to support or oppose" candidates' contributions to campaigns (Barnes and Eggen, 2010). Critics argued that corporations would now be able to flood campaigns with money. Many fretted that soft money bought access, and a politician's judgment could be clouded. Candidate Trump pinpointed the problem between campaign donations and access in the August 11, 2015, Republican debate, remarking: "I will tell you that our system is broken. I gave to many people … [when] I was a businessman … And do you know what? When I need something from them two years later, three years later, I call them, they are there for me" (*Time*, 2015).

As stated above, ordinary people also contribute to campaigns. In 2020, Trump outraised Biden in his percentage of small donor contributions: 49 percent to 39 percent (OpenSecrets, 2020b). The charitable status of donations gives the contributor tax breaks and the feeling that they "own" part of the campaign. Traditionally, Political Action Committees (PACs) have raised and distributed contributions for candidates from interest groups, religious organizations, and private citizens. FEC rules do change, but politicians and interests quickly adapt to the new environment and divert money so that it follows the rules and keeps flowing. *Citizens United*-enabled "Super-PACs" raised $2 billion. This "outside" money could be used for issue advocacy in explicit support of candidates, or for negative advertising, although it is illegal to give money directly to a candidate. The liberal "Priorities USA" raised $123 million for Biden, while the largest conservative PAC, "America First Action," provided $95 million in support of Trump. Biden outpaced Trump in access to Super PAC money (Hillstrom, 2020).

Analysts have pointed out the dangers of PACs, but these organizations also give strength to civil society by allowing groups of people to gain access to a politician's office and ear. Whether they can be heard over the din of corporate interest donations is another matter. While Americans may be uneasy about the mix of money and politics, the 2020 campaign demonstrated that fundraising remains important, even if Trump's 2016 victory demonstrated that charisma and entertainment also count.

Pluralistic Democracy

In America, where the winner-takes-all system determines election outcomes, the question of how to safeguard minority and class-based representation is difficult to resolve. In the 1980s, Congress encouraged states to redraw election districts to group minority voters together so as to give a group a majority in a district. This "gerrymandering" of voters into minority–majority districts succeeded, as minority representation in Congress rose by 50 percent. Sometimes gerrymandering created snakelike districts to ensure a majority, wriggling in and out of black neighborhoods and going down interstates to incorporate another community of African Americans, like the North Carolina 12th District. When the media printed maps of these districts, many Americans were outraged by the obvious prejudice inherent in such a system and criticized the moves as favoring one group of citizens over another. Supporters argued that this was the only way to put more minorities and thereby more diversity into seats in Washington.

Congressional efforts to increase minority representation were initially supported by the Supreme Court under the equal protection provisions of the 14th Amendment. But in the case of *Shaw v. Reno* (1993), concerning "racial gerrymandering" in North Carolina, the Court ruled that creating minority districts amounted to political apartheid. In *Easley v. Cromartie* (2001), the Court modified its stance, allowing race as a factor, as long as it was not the "dominant and controlling one" (Greenhouse, 2001). The issue remains controversial, especially to those who prefer a proportional system of representative democracy or honest competitive districts. In 2013, in the case of *Shelby v Holder*, the Supreme Court struck down preclearance rules for electoral practices changes that had been introduced by the 1965 Voting Rights Act. Preclearance rules effectively extended a federal mandate over changes in specific jurisdictions and in spirit more generally. Unlike in some congressional districts, there is no gerrymandering in a presidential election.

Whether or not citizens feel better represented by a candidate of their own ethnicity, there is certainly more proportionality between the number of women, African Americans, Asian, and Latinos in Congress than in the past (as shown in Table 3.1). Some commentators argue that class is more important than demography, as most

Contemporary United States

politicians of all colors, races, ethnicities, or gender come from the privileged upper middle class or higher.

Gerrymandering has also had the effect of making "safe districts" for incumbents who can rely on war chests, name recognition, and ideological conformity to win re-election campaigns. This, in turn, allows polarization, as incumbents do not need centrist voters. Confirming the power of gerrymandering, only sixteen House and Senate seats changed hands in 2020 (Williams, 2020).

With migration, and with some states and districts growing faster than others, redistricting on the basis of decennial census findings is a necessity to safeguard the equal value of each vote. While race, ethnicity, and identity are acceptable as factors in the redistricting of voting districts in a democracy, partisan concerns are not. In 2011, on taking over of all branches of state government Wisconsin Republicans redrew their state electoral map, cementing two-thirds control of the state legislature despite roughly equal shares of the vote for the two major parties. In 2016, a panel of federal judges ruled the redistricting unconstitutional. On appeal in 2018, the Supreme Court found the charges of partisan gerrymandering unproven and sent the case back to the lower courts (Liptak, 2018). This example demonstrates the power of state governments over redistricting, but also that excessive gerrymandering risked Supreme Court action. Redistricting remains under the spotlight of all three branches of government and by the media, given the claims of stolen elections.

Incumbency is clearly important in the US, with some voices arguing for the imposition of term limits. The obvious legal precedent for this is the constitutional two-term limit on American presidents. Theoretically, citizens in democracies should be able to vote for any politician of their choice for as many terms as they want. This has led some to argue that the whole concept of limiting terms is anti-democratic and threatens to weaken government by removing the most competent leaders and replacing them with inexperienced newcomers, or with candidates who have independent means. Conversely, many argue that democracies require turnover to bring forward new ideas and to involve more and younger people in politics.

Many voices call for direct "accountability" and suggest that politics should not be a career-in-itself. This promotes the idea of citizen-politicians who do something else first and are legislators second. In 2020, term limits for state legislators had been approved and enacted in fifteen states and approved but rejected by state supreme courts or legislatures in six others (NCSL, 2020b). Some states have also placed term limits on US Senators and Representatives, though the Supreme Court ruled in 1995 that putting term limits on federal office holders was unconstitutional.

Overall, the American political system is a cacophony of direct democratic, majoritarian, plural, and elite interests. The more savvy, influential, or determined an individual or interest group is, the more the system adjusts to the pressure. A rogue candidate, a single dissenter, or a mass movement can still bring about change through the electoral system, the court system, or by taking to the streets. The powerful use of dissenting voices has always played an integral part of American political culture, from the throwing of tea into Boston Harbor in 1773, to marching on Washington against

Politics and Democracy

the Vietnam War or for civil rights in the 1960s, blockading abortion clinics in the 1980s, marching for immigrant rights in 2006, gathering to support #BLM in 2016, participating in the universal women's march in 2017, or demonstrating against new immigration and visa policy in 2017. The January 6, 2021, riot inside the US Capitol to overturn a legal election went well beyond anything American political culture had ever seen before.

As this chapter has shown, Americans' belief in the federal government has remained consistently low since the early 1970s, excepting the brief upsurge after the 9/11 attacks. In the twenty-first century, between one-quarter and one-fifth of Americans believed that they could trust the government all or most of the time, and trust is much higher among those whose party is in power. In a clear expression of political polarization, in 2021 Republicans currently have less trust in government than Democrats (Pew, 2021e). In late 2021, Congress held approval ratings of around 25 percent (Gallup, 2021b). Biden's approval ratings had fallen from 57 percent on inauguration to 42 percent at the end of 2021—similar to those of Trump during his last year in office (Gallup, 2021a; Jones, 2021). Approval for the Supreme Court was at 40 percent (Gallup, 2021e). Government is not universally unpopular: state and local governments scored 20 to 30 points higher. The positive response towards local government is an enduring a feature of US politics (McCarthy, 2018).

Americans vote, or have the opportunity to vote, more times and for a wider range of officials than probably anyone else in the world. Some observers claim that this "hyper-democracy" explains apathy and reduces voting rates. Politics that serves-the-base-but-seeks-the-center also dampens voter interest, as does the belief that big-money controls politicians no matter what the voter does. The adversarial tone of campaigns turns some people off, even as it entertains others. The traditionally limited ideological spread within party constituencies means that some feel unrepresented, doubt if their votes make any difference to ordinary people living ordinary lives, and thus make populism of all ideological types more attractive. An opposite argument is that the widespread use of polling may convince many voters that their views are already known and that candidates will obey the dictates of that public opinion.

American social behavior tempers American voting behavior as the middle class pursues lifestyles centered on work, homeownership, long commutes, and the good life provided by double-incomes. School and work-based activities crowd out free time and many people are too busy to bother with political activities, especially when they believe the government is unresponsive to their needs anyway. However, Election 2020 presented stark choices for the nation. Biden's "Build Back Better" agenda signposted a change in social and spending priorities and a return to an era of greater civility in American life. Trump's "Keep America Great" indicated a consummation of the Trump reforms and accompanying communicative noise. Biden's message appealed to more middle-class voters than previously, whereas Trump's slogan attracted ethno-nationalist and evangelical white working-class voters. Biden prevailed, though commentators asked whether or not Biden's middle-class support would return to Republicans in the future. Long-term voter dynamics will continue to unfold.

Contemporary United States

Decisive elections in one cycle can change quickly in the next. Until Trump in 2020, no first term incumbent had failed to be re-elected since George H. W. Bush in 1994. Voters' patience is short because they expect to see results quickly. Even when elected on a unified ticket, most recent administrations have experienced an attrition in the strength of their congressional seats. History supports this verdict, and it happened to Trump in the 2018 midterms and looks likely to happen to Biden in 2022 unless political circumstances change dramatically. A defeat in the congressional midterms always brings more divided government and a tarnished mandate to an incumbent president. Which party's base will be the most fired up in the 2024 presidential election is anybody's guess. Divided and ineffective government, financial and legislative impasses over the budget and policy, and a lack of direction for the nation lead to more dissatisfaction with the political system and leadership. Democracy in America is at a difficult crossroads. The political system is distrusted by the majority of Americans and is under scrutiny by leaders and peoples worldwide. The efforts to rewrite voting rules, relieve the anxiety of the Corona pandemic, restore domestic and global leadership, expand economic opportunities, regulate social media, and mend the social fabric continue to test the resilience of the system and of American society.

Further Reading

Leonnig, C. and P. Rucker (2021) *I Alone Can Fix It: Donald J. Trump's Catastrophic Final Year*, London: Penguin.

Levitsky, S. and D. Ziblatt (2018) *How Democracies Die: What History Reveals about Our Future*, London: Penguin.

Müller, J. (2016) *What is Populism?* Philadelphia: University of Pennsylvania Press.

Nelson, M. (2019) *Trump: The First Two Years*, Charlottesville: University of Virginia Press.

Obama, B. (2020) *A Promised Land*, New York: Crown.

Rucker, P. and C. Leonnig (2020) *A Very Stable Genius: Donald Trump's Testing of America*, London: Penguin.

Woodward, B. (2020b) *Rage*, New York: Simon & Schuster.

CHAPTER 5
SOCIETY

The polarization that afflicted American politics in 2020 also affected American society. During the Trump administration, the rifts of class, race, and gender grew wider. Meanwhile, many younger Americans questioned American "growthism" by supporting environmental causes and planetary protection. In 2016, Donald Trump had appealed to blue- and white-collar white voters in rural and rustbelt areas, promising them a brighter future described in mid-twentieth century terms: breadwinner jobs, male respect, and racial and gendered hierarchies. In 2020, "Average Joe" Biden harnessed mid-twentieth-century liberal values of equality, social-justice, decorum and civility (Flegenheimer and Glueck, 2020).

American society fissured under Trump. Unemployment was low, but income and life opportunity inequality remained. One example: during the ongoing opioid epidemic, life became harder for poorer Northern whites as families collapsed, petty crime rose, and overdoses skyrocketed. More Americans died of overdoses in 2018 than died during the whole of the Vietnam War, with opioid deaths for that year alone at 47,000 (CDC, 2021d). Over 1.7 million Americans suffered substance abuse addiction; the CDC estimated the economic cost of the epidemic at over $78 billion a year, with heavier social costs (ScienceDaily, 2016; McGreal, 2018). Racism boiled to the top of the national agenda, again. Police shootings of African Americans reinvigorated the #BlackLivesMatter (#BLM) movement (Bote, 2020), including March 2020 Louisville, Kentucky, victim Breonna Taylor, killed by a barrage of thirty-two police bullets, and of George Floyd in May 2020 in Minneapolis, Minnesota, suffocated by a policeman kneeling on his neck and crushing his windpipe—despite having told officers over twenty times that he could not breathe. Public anger and anguish over these killings transcended race, drawing support from Americans of diverse ethnic and racial background and fueling a summer of protest, and counter-protest, unrest, and lootings. Protests peaked on June 6 as an estimated 500,000 people assembled in 550 locations nationwide (Buchanan, Bui, and Patel 2020).

While most protests were peaceful, some attracted white nationalist extremists looking to incite civil unrest. Experts noted, and the Department of Homeland Security confirmed, that far-Right white supremacist groups represented the greatest terror threat and perpetrated a majority of attacks and plots (Gross, 2020). On August 25, in Kenosha, Wisconsin, one violent protest saw seventeen-year-old self-appointed nationalist "militiaman" Kyle Wittenhouse kill two people with an AR-15 assault rifle

Contemporary United States

(Frosch and Levy, 2020). Trump claimed—incorrectly—that leftist "Antifa" activities matched those of white supremacists. Commentators and state politicians complained that Trump fed turmoil by inciting division and polarization so that he could claim law-and-order credentials and enhance his re-election chances—a tactic that worked for his predecessor, Republican Richard Nixon, towards the end of the first civil rights era in 1968 (Mahshie, 2020).

Gender also rose to the top of the national agenda under Trump. While the #TimesUp and #MeToo movements protesting exploitation of females predated the administration, that atmosphere of protest thickened after the 2016 election. Infamously, in 2016 Trump admitted unwanted sexual advances on the "Access Hollywood" tape: "… when you're a star, they let you do it. You can do anything … Grab 'em by the pussy. You can do anything" (*New York Times*, 2016). Several witnesses came forward to attest to his advances, and several more claimed they had been paid off—including Stormy Daniels and Karen McDougall in 2016, who were paid $130,000 and $150,000 to keep quiet about "alleged" affairs (Palazzolo, Hong, Rottfeld, O' Brian, and Bullhaus, 2018). Trump's attitudes of male sexual entitlement, objectification of women, and the clear commodification belief that he could buy silence for his behavior outraged many people—though not his conservative base. Indeed, one evangelical pastor said, "I think President Trump is a miracle" (Thompson, Sarlin, and Dean, 2021).

While Trump survived marches (see Illustrations 5.1), lawsuits, impeachment, and public disapproval, other predators did not. On October 5, 2017, *New York Times* reporters Kantor and Twohey revealed that Hollywood producer Harvey Weinstein had preyed upon female actresses, promising careers for sex and exploiting the power-gap between himself and his victims. Kantor and Twohey won the 2018 Pulitzer Prize for their work. Weinstein apologized, but did not seem apologetic. Weinstein's crimes dated back at least three decades and involved at least eight legal settlements and an unknown number of victims. Women were first stunned, and then galvanized into action. Alyssa Milano, one of Weinstein's victims, implored all female survivors of assault and predatory behavior to retweet the #MeToo hashtag. Milano's appeal triggered an avalanche of evidence from women and testimony—69,000 comments and nearly 40,000 re-tweets—that questioned accepted norms of behavior between men in positions of power and women. Gwyneth Paltrow, Rosanna Arquette, Cara Delevingne, and Angeline Jolie, among others, attested to Weinstein's harassment and assaults (*Vogue*, 2017). Beyond Weinstein, media stars Matt Lauer, Al Franken, Charlie Rose, Kevin Spacey, Woody Allen, and Jeffrey Epstein were among the men brought down by rising moral consciousness over years of abusive male privilege.

The new social movements focusing on class, race, and gender were joined by burgeoning movements against climate change and pollution. Media and popular attention and tens of thousands—some said 250,000—of concerned participants took to the streets of New York in September 2019 to draw attention to an existential crisis (Sengupta, 2019). Arising out of the global environmental movement, protesters warned that extreme weather patterns (see Chapter 2), elevated sea levels, and mass extinctions beckoned. Anger at the inability of the world's leaders to address climate change found a foil in Swedish activist Greta Thunberg's September 2019 speech to the United Nations: "We

Society

Illustration 5.1 The Politics of Gender: The Women's Movement

On January 21, 2017, over 500,000 women marched in Washington in support of gender equality and civil rights, and against newly installed President Donald Trump. Parallel marches held in other cities across the nation attracted millions more. From 2017, #MeToo exploded. Previously unreported incidents of sexual harassment came to light as women acknowledged and voiced that they too had been victims of sexually predatory behavior. Film producer Harvey Weinstein, Fox Corporation Mogul Roger Ailes, TV Host Matt Lauer, and financier Jeffrey Epstein were among those found guilty. President Trump's sexist language, stage setting, and multiple allegations of sexual misconduct against him provided kindling for the #MeToo movement (see also Illustration 7.3).

Source: Mario Tama via Getty Images

are in the beginning of a mass extinction and all you can talk about is money and fairy tales of eternal economic growth. How dare you!" *Time Magazine* named the teenager its 2019 "Person of the Year" (Alter, Haynes, and Worland, 2019). Environmental sacrifices that had been made for economic growth were no longer acceptable considerations of race, class, gender, and environment intersected for many activists in America society, most especially the younger generations. Invented during the first civil rights era of the 1960s, the catchall term, "Youthquake," garnered so much popularity in 2017—arguably in the midst of a second civil rights era, that it was declared "word of the year" by Oxford Dictionaries. On taking office, presidents Trump (seventy years old) and Biden (seventy-eight years old) were the oldest in the nation's history and not, by age at least, representative of youth. Sclerotic attitudes by many established politicians towards hot button issues echoed of the 1960s generation gap. But it was far from a one-way street. Many older white Americans feared the direction of the nation as Trump opportunistically tailored his understanding of society to garner mass popular support from this group. Trump's Republican populism

Contemporary United States

spoke of a war against white men and believed that since the 1960s American society had drifted too far to the multicultural liberalism of civil rights issues. The black and/or female bodies of Barack Obama, Kamala Harris, and Hillary Clinton displayed social change. Representative Alexandria Ocasio-Cortez and Georgia activist Stacy Abrams were vilified and feared for their progressive leadership and non-white and female bodies. Meanwhile, Democratic populism pushed for leftist and equality-enhancing solutions for the nation's problems, in a renewal of a process instigated in the 1960s. As we saw in Chapter 4, many of these issues came together individually, and through the social and economic fallout over the Corona epidemic, in Election 2020, and in partisan fears over whether American democracy could survive.

Joe Biden prevailed in the 2020 campaign in no small part because he was able to bridge the issues. Biden highlighted the importance of a vital middle in American politics as a unifying factor for the American people in terms of class, race, and gender, family, work, community, fairness, law and justice. After the election, Biden pushed his "Build Back Better" agenda leftwards and expressed a desire to be seen as a figure like 1930s progressive pragmatist President Franklin D. Roosevelt.

Class

There has been a long-standing myth among Americans that social classes do not exist in the United States. Except for ubiquitous references to an undefined mainstream "middle class" and its well-being, the word "class" has been historically treated as a pejorative, a forbidden lusty and loathsome thought—a descriptor more useful for talking about European Marxists, Russian Leninists, or Chinese Maoists. For most Americans, the dream and opportunity of a better life outweighed the need to create a society where everyone had economic equality. Even the most dynamic struggles of the 1960s were primarily over racial and sexual, not economic, equality (Alterman and Mattson, 2012). Until November 2016, most people argued that Americans supported cultural liberalism but questioned economic liberalism. Four years of Trump-led culture wars may have changed that. In September 2020, at a Constitution Day speech, Trump raged against the "liberal indoctrination of America's youth" and blamed the summer 2020 social protests as springing from decades of leftist school indoctrination. Trump's comments attested to the cultural divides that afflicted the nation as much as economic inequality, and cultural politics displacing class-based politics (Vasquez, 2020).

Whichever way the nation's cultural divides play out under Biden, Americans usually support individual freedom over movements for economic parity and community responsibility. Historian E. J. Dionne says that Americans have "a divided political heart" that cherishes both individualism and community values (Dionne, 2012). Historian John Meacham supports this idea and argues that despite division, the nation's essential soul usually leads Americans to understanding and unity—eventually (Meacham, 2018).

The American creed that all men and women are created equal has five main components: liberty, egalitarianism, individualism, populism, and laissez-faire. This philosophy highlights individual control of personal property and has made little room for socialism—in theory. Egalitarianism is mostly defined in terms of political and merit-based equality. Still, in very real terms, socialism punctuates American history in the moments of creedal consciousness that historians call: Progressive Era, New Deal, and Great Society. Today, the case for democratic socialism is advanced by Bernie Sanders, Elizabeth Warren, and Alexandria Ocasio-Cortez.

Americans have always been able to see that there are rich and poor people, but they usually play down the reality of social classes. The Marxian concept that class division and inequality work to promote class consciousness and conflict has not been true in the American experience. Until recently, there has been no particular envy of the rich and the enduring myths of equal opportunity, individual responsibility, and the examples of those who have gone from "rags to riches," have deflected class tensions which do arise. The traditional assertion of mobility, that a person can succeed with education, hard work, and by individual determination has been challenged in contemporary America.

Americans increasingly believe that they have been sorted into two classes, "winners and losers." The post-Covid economic crisis may accentuate this trend. With a few exceptions, median incomes have lagged behind wealth for a generation, threatening the American dream. Meanwhile, Conservatives who dislike social programs often call those who fail the "takers, not the makers." Liberals are more likely to highlight inequality and the unequal distribution of wealth between most people and the top 1 percent. Starting in 2011, protests by the "Occupy Wall Street" movement confirmed the viability of a rising class consciousness (Gitlin, 2012). Social mobility has declined over the last thirty years as society has become more economically unequal than at any time since the Second World War (Putnam, 2015). A rising percentage of Americans are "working poor"—in poverty despite working forty-hour-a-week jobs. As early as 2004, economist Paul Krugman maintained that the dream of "income mobility has always exceeded the reality," with reduced rates of intergenerational mobility (Krugman, 2004).

The Middle Class

Americans elected Joe Biden to make government a more effective and consistent tool in people's lives, and as a response to Trump's indecisive handling of the 2020 Corona crisis. Biden's mandate included keeping Americans safe and prosperous with a steady hand to ensure aid for the unemployed and the furloughed to fuel the economy, strengthening health care, rebuilding infrastructure, improving the environment—or, in a slogan, "Build Back Better." Elections in which incumbents seek re-election usually function as votes on the job done by the officeholder. While many Americans judged Trump competent on economic policy, his administration came across as chaotic. Voters across most demographic groups saw Biden—part of the political establishment for two generations—as a safer "anti-Trump" steward. However, the anger over politics as usual which had propelled the victory of the outsider Trump in 2016 has not receded among partisans.

Contemporary United States

In a highly convincing study, economic historian Robert Gordon detailed the rise and fall of US living standards since the latter half of the nineteenth century. He concluded that from 1870 to 1970, the American economy produced a miracle that justified the world's praise for the American way (Gordon, 2016). Gordon showed how most of the scientific, technological, managerial, and social innovations that supported a relatively equitable middle-class country (for white families) accelerated in the period 1920–1950 and were all in place by 1970. Since then, changes have been incremental and the rewards systems of society have helped racial and ethnic minorities but increasingly hollowed out the middle class, pushing a few into the top 10 percent and the many into the working class.

Investigative journalist George Packer concurs with Gordon but places the "unwinding" of middle-class society in the period since 1978, when wages and salaries for most Americans did not rise in relation to inflation (Packer, 2013). Moreover, Packer argued that manners and morals failed civility tests, while organized money interests took over to reward winners and hurt losers in the new "global" economy. With the fall of old institutions and civic virtue, society was challenged by both sentimental and angry voices who wanted a return to "the dimly remembered past—telling a joke above the noise of the assembly line, complaining behind window shades drawn against the world, thundering justice to a crowded park or an empty chamber, closing a deal on the phone, [and] dreaming aloud late at night on a front porch as trucks rush by in the darkness" (Packer, 2013: 4).

Despite wide disparities in income, the vast majority of Americans have always self-defined themselves as middle-class—a self-designation sometimes at odds with economic status. Beyond paychecks, other factors leading to middle-class claims could include having a good-paying blue-collar or regular white-collar job, a university education, home ownership, economic security, and certain social values. For half a century, the numbers of adults in middle-class households (measured by income) have fallen steadily, from 61 percent in 1971 to 52 percent in 2020. Nineteen percent are in the upper class, and 29 percent in the lower class. Perceptions matter, but so do incomes. In 2018, the PEW Research Center set middle-class economic standards for households. A family of three (close to the average household size of 2.5) must take in between $48,500 and $145,500 a year, with the lower threshold designating lower status and the higher indicating higher status (Bennett, Fry, and Kochhar, 2020). Some analysts add a class below the lower class: the underclass—a marginal group in extreme poverty and lacking the skills or education necessary to rise into the lower class or higher (Wright and Rogers, 2015). Additionally, married couples tend to have higher household incomes than singles, people aged eighteen to twenty-nine lost the most in the last forty years, and unmarried women with children are a high percentage in the lower class, followed closely by unmarried men. Asians and Whites outperform blacks and Hispanics, US-born adults (non-black) outpace foreign-born adults, those over sixty-five are most likely to be lower class, and the college-educated are more likely to be upper class (Bennett, Fry, and Kochhar, 2020).

One problem in grasping what it is to be middle class is that having $150,000 per year while living in Manhattan and having $50,000 in rural Utah amount to similar material rewards and quality of life—certainly, the housing would be much bigger in Utah. It might be easier to think of the middle class as being composed of those people who have, at least, a college degree, some real choice as to where to live and work, and who can live with a minimum reliance on government aid.

Historically, the chief source of American wealth has been the equity in homes, followed by various forms of savings/retirement plans. Median family wealth tumbled from $146,000 in 2007 to $89,000 in 2013; by 2016 it had recovered somewhat to $102,000 (Horowitz, Igielnik, and Kochhar, 2020). In recessions, mortgage holders can see their house values plummet, leaving them in negative equity, or owing more than the houses were worth. In the first quarter of 2020 the US housing stock counted 141 million, of which around 124 million were occupied. The homeownership rate in the fourth quarter of 2021 was 65.5 percent, slightly lower than the 2004 high of 69.2 percent (FRED, 2021c, 2021d; USCB, 2021i). Looking at different demographic groups, white families had an ownership rate of 75.8 percent, Asians 61 percent, Hispanics 50.9 percent, and blacks 46.4 percent. While homeownership rose under the Trump administration, African Americans and Hispanics still have markedly lower rates than whites, as do the young (USCB, 2021h). The idea of owning a home of one's own has always been central to the middle-class ideal.

The 2008–2010 recession is now a decade distant, but many people remain bitter. Even though average incomes and wealth levels have scraped back most of their losses, many feel the benefits of a decade of recovery remained absent, especially in the rustbelt. The recession left people feeling cheated by banks, Wall Street, and politicians as they lost their homes or saw their home equity evaporate. A breakdown of trust in economic and political institutions helped frame the people's anxiety during the 2020 Covid crisis. With the strong memory of the recession, many Americans wondered whether they would lose their incomes and homes due to the Covid lockdown and the following economic crisis. Following the opposing twin American ideals of helping a neighbor in distress, and not wanting to make that neighbor a dependent, government came together to temporarily fund economic relief, including furlough schemes and business support though the Coronavirus Aid, Relief, and Economic Security Act (CARES Act) and subsequent legislation to March 2021—to the collective tune of $5 trillion.

Returning to homeownership and the young, for many, renting is trending upward as a necessary option. This is especially true among White Millennials (born 1981–1996) and Generation Z (born after 1996) without a college degree (ages eighteen to thirty-five). This group is caught squarely in the lingering effects of wage stagnation, continue to rent from or live with their parents, and they delay marriage (Parker, Graf, and Igielnik, 2019). Moreover, younger Americans do not believe that they will do as well as their parents in terms of realizing the Dream. Millennials are more pessimistic than previous generations about being able to freely decide how to live their lives or about their chances to move up the social ladder.

Contemporary United States

In America, race informs class as most minority groups tend to make significantly less than whites. The 2020 elections demonstrated that minority groups will support candidates who promise to work to raise living conditions through government programs that help redistribute wealth from the rich to the poor. Biden accomplished this in his $2 trillion addition to earlier Covid relief packages in March 2021. The inclusion of minority members into the upper echelons of university faculties, professional sports, law firms, religious organizations, and government are among the successes in race relations and more equal opportunities to gain a part of the American dream. The historic election and re-election of Barack Obama clearly marked how the national conversation about race can be changed, as did the 2020 election of the nation's first woman and first person of color—Kamala Harris—to the vice presidency.

However, claims of a "post-racial" America are double-edged when Republicans use them to confront Democrats. Conservatives say that a quick look around American society shows minority members at the highest levels of government and business, thus proving that those who work hard under the American creed have no barriers to their success beyond their own ambition and work ethic. In this view, it is good to have "makers" but there are still too many "undeserving takers" on Medicaid and unemployment programs, for example. Many conservatives blame the victim or cite a culture of poverty, and the impact of racial prejudice has not declined. In 2019, polls indicated that people expressed racist or racially insensitive remarks more commonly (65 percent) during the Trump administration; over eight in ten (84 percent) blacks said they suffered from discrimination—from police, by the criminal justice system, and at work (Horowitz, Brown, and Cox, 2019; Newport, 2020).

Rural and Urban America

While America is increasingly divided between "haves" and "have-nots," other divisions arise in the conceptions of self and in where people live. Place matters, and for most everyday life is local. Rural Americans outside the mega-cities often criticize the transformations wrought by the 1960s countercultural, multicultural, and feminist movements. They want to return to traditional, hierarchical, patriotic, small government, and religious family values to rebuild America. Urban Americans are more likely to have a more flexible moral code, to be uneasy with open displays of patriotism, and to describe themselves as "non-religious." Radio programs are saturated with local fundraising activities, lodge meetings, sports events, and church services. Rural dwellers more often tune into *Fox News* and talk radio, want to be left alone, and vote largely for Republicans. Urbanites read the *New York Times*, balance freedom with equality, and vote Democratic.

Basically, Americans do not bother themselves with the lives constructed or believed in by other Americans, so long as the others do not infringe on their lives. But a middle-class withdrawal syndrome has led to a loss of community as Americans go "bowling alone," eschewing traditional big-membership organizations and spending their free time within small circles made up of family, friends, and co-workers that make them comfortable (Putnam, 2000). Sociologist Eric Dunkelman adds that the dramatic cultural shift is a result of "quick hit interactions" on social media that has reordered networking priorities by creating "friends" and like-minded groups (Dunkelman, 2014). David Brooks noted that "every place becomes more like itself" as people relocate into neighborhoods where they have a political and cultural affinity. In America, this presents a "cafeteria choice" of options (Brooks, 2004).

Since 1975, key factors of affluence and educational level led Americans to cluster themselves into communities of sameness dominated by class levels, a phenomenon Bill Bishop labeled "the big sort" (Bishop, 2008). There has been a "white flight" since the 1960s integration and fair housing standards, but there is an accelerating geographical isolation by the privileged class. This sorting has socio-cultural consequences, with the conclusion that inherited advantages of class have now made it very difficult to go from "rags to riches" (Putnam, 2015).

Others argue that it is precisely the freedom of selecting a different lifestyle that binds the community and nation together. Perhaps "binds" is the wrong word because of what Dunkelman calls "the interpersonal erosion occurring in American neighborhoods and the gradual fade out of … collaboratively minded townships" (Dunkelman, 2014). The rich, who live in their own enclaves, towers, and gated communities, lack the empathetic interaction with others and do not have as much self-interest in funding neighborhood improvements the way they did when classes were less divided and living closer together. The effect of "spill over" benefits to the middle and lower classes are drying up (Edsall, 2016). The "big sort" of upper-class enclaves and lower class marginal spaces fracture the US by class (and often by gender and race) to undermine social connectedness.

Poverty and Affluence

Poverty has been omnipresent in American history with Native Americans, slaves and their descendants, poor whites, single mothers, and successive waves of low-paid immigrant laborers working at whatever jobs they could find. Until recently, there has been a steady decline in the percentages of citizens in poverty as the rising economy lifted wages and, more importantly, as wives entered the labor force and created two-income families. However, Nobel laureate Joseph Stiglitz wrote that "Inequality is greater here than in any other advanced country" and "matters may get worse" (Stiglitz, 2012). In 2018, the poverty rate reached 12 percent—or over 38 million people.

In 2020, the official poverty line for a family of four was $26,200 and for an individual, $12,760 (about 20 percent higher in Alaska and Hawaii) (ASPE, 2021a). However, unofficial rates are closer to the truth of poor people's lives and relative deprivation is a more useful analytical tool. Here are a few points to consider. In 2017 if the official poverty line for individuals was set at half of the median household income level ($68,703 in 2020), the percentage of poor Americans in 2017 would jump to almost 17 percent for Americans as a whole and 21 percent of children (Pressman, 2018). Removing government social security payments to the elderly poor would add millions more, as would the inclusion of undocumented aliens. If the "near poor" are added, the numbers would reach an appalling 100 million people, or one American in three. The "near poor" are those above the official poverty line but whose taxes, medical expenses,

Contemporary United States

and adjusted regional or urban living costs considerably reduce their economic situation and keep them in a state of daily crisis (DeParle, 2012). In 2020 and 2021 government aid to mitigate the Covid-fueled economic downturn lifted many Americans out of poverty. Though these benefits were temporary, they helped people substantially until the economy began to produce jobs again (Giannarelli, Wheaton, and Acs, 2020).

Even in normal times, too many people suffer from food insecurity. The non-profit organization Feeding America estimated that 54 million Americans face hunger on a daily basis. The near poor and the poor both rely on private-sector charities, including the 200 food bank distributors working with Feeding America to serve over four billion meals yearly. In 2019, Feeding America served 40 million people. One of every eight Americans used a food bank to offset costs so that they have money for rent, electricity, and gasoline (Feeding America, 2019). When polled about what they would do if they suddenly had a $400 expense they had not foreseen, 47 percent said that they would have to borrow the money from family or friends, or sell something; $400 is a very small expense (Gabler, 2016). Many people live from paycheck to paycheck in the best of times, juggling creditors, and have no savings for a rainy day.

Much of the gap between rich and poor is due to the changing nature of work, the loss of industrial jobs to countries with cheaper labor costs, the unequal distribution of personal income, changes in the tax burden that favor the wealthy, the growing number of single-income families, and an increasing emphasis on a well-educated workforce. Social mobility has flattened out. The poor are concentrated into inner-city neighborhoods, mobile home parks throughout the South and West, Indian reservations, rented farmhouses across the Midwest, or sleep homeless. They struggle quietly to make ends meet and to keep their lives together. Low-waged workers are generally younger, female, and less educated, and they work without the safety nets of health insurance or retirement benefits. The key factor in poverty seems to be the education level of the primary wage earner, which also ties into the income and location of schools. For example, kids in poorer urban schools are less likely to develop educational capital than kids in richer, suburban schools. Table 5.1 and Figure 6.1 indicate the link between education level and pay. Pay rates for those with less education have lagged relative to the more highly educated.

In terms of affluence, the richest 1 percent of all Americans have nearly as much wealth (30.5 percent) as the bottom 90 percent combined (31 percent), with the latter group comprising not only everyone in the lower and middle classes but also half of those in the upper class (FRED, 2019). By themselves, the ten richest people in America—Jeff Bezos ($179 billion: Amazon); Bill Gates ($111 billion: Microsoft); Mark Zuckerberg ($85 billion: Facebook); Warren Buffett ($73.5 billion: Berkshire Hathaway); Larry Ellison ($72 billion: Oracle); Steve Ballmer ($69 billion: Microsoft); Elon Musk ($68 billion: Tesla); Larry Page ($67.5 billion: Google); Sergei Brin ($65.7 billion: Google); and Alice Walton ($62.3 billion: Wal-Mart) have a total known wealth of around $800 billion (mostly from information technology). In terms of income, the top 1 percent receives around 20 percent of the annual total (Stebbins and Commen, 2020). It should be no surprise that they own several luxury houses, each, worldwide—or even whole clubs

Table 5.1 Median Earnings for Full-Time Workers, Twenty-Five Years Old and Older, 2018

Degree level	Median earnings	
	Males	Females
No High School diploma	$33,919	$21,755
High School diploma	$45,188	$31,123
Some college, no degree	$39,940	$31,100
Associate (two-year) degree	$59,223	$39,239
Bachelor's	$87,399	$59,260
Master's and above	$114,054	$76,009
Professional	$176,443	$119,616
PhD	$157,252	$119,778

Source: Statistica (2020)

like Trump's Mar-a-Lago resort. Many upper-class families have clustered into "gated" communities where high fences, heavy security, and ultra-expensive houses keep them protected and isolated in luxury. The upper middle class is moving beyond suburbia and exurbia, into penurbia—areas that, while not quite rural, invoke the powerful ideas of reinvention and frontier community, as well as protection from the pandemic.

Trump's approach on poverty took a rising-tide-lifts-all-boats approach. Deregulation, tax cuts, and a growing economy helped bring more Americans into the labor market during his first three years. Rising real wages made a difference by reducing the number of Americans in poverty. However, the decade-long economic recovery, begun under the first Obama administration, reversed during the Corona crisis in the first quarter of 2020. The response by the elected branches of government led to some of the most effective poverty mitigation policies in a generation—thanks to the CARES Act and its successors. One provision of the CARES Act saw unemployment benefits extended by thirteen weeks, along with a $600 a week on top of existing benefits. Additionally, the federal government issued checks of $1,200 for each individual and $600 for children—signed by Trump (JP Morgan, 2020). While temporary, federal checks significantly helped many Americans in need. Conversely, the political rancor over their reduction/discontinuation threatened to send millions back into poverty (*WSJ*, 2020).

The United States has nearly 30 percent of the total global personal wealth (China is second with nearly 18 percent, but also has high rates of wealth inequality among its citizens (Desjardins, 2020)). Obviously, America is rich enough to redistribute income in such a way as to make the country a comfortable and generally middle-class nation from top to bottom. In the 1950s and 1960s bipartisanship produced a "democracy of prosperity" in contrast to the "democracy of financial insecurity" of the twenty-first century (Gabler, 2016). A tax reform setting a maximum and minimum income could raise the 99 percent; but, until recently, Americans would fight such an effort tooth and claw, calling it immoral, un-American, socialistic, and, possibly, Satanic. Critics

Contemporary United States

of redistribution point to figures showing the poor living as long, growing as tall, and having as many mobile devices as the rich. Still, rising inequality and the differential effects of the Covid crisis have strengthened voices for redistributive reform, even as fiscal conservatives insist that federal spending balances with tax receipts.

The American Family

Family dynamics (Tables 5.2 and 5.3) have changed over the past few decades. Maternal health and childcare have improved significantly, helping infants survive into adulthood. Generally, adults are living longer and enjoy "decades of life after children," as some realists put it. Since around 2013, however, longevity rates have fallen somewhat. This is partly due to the prescription drug, or opioid crisis, mentioned at the beginning of this chapter, which, coupled with Covid deaths, has claimed enough victims directly or indirectly to depress life expectancy.

While the divorce rate has fallen since 2000 (CDC, 2018), many Americans circumvent the statistics by not getting married in the first place. Currently, 53 percent of Americans are married (Horowitz, Graf, and Livingstone, 2019). All told, the proportion of Americans living alone, or in single-parent families has risen. Causes include longer

Table 5.2 US Population by Age and Sex, Estimated, 2019 (millions, rounded to nearest 100,000)

Age Group	Males	Females	Total
0–14	31.0	29.7	60.7
15–24	21.3	20.8	42.1
25–64	82.9	85.9	168.8
65 and over	23.9	28.9	52.0
Total	159.1	165.3	324.4
Median age	37.1	39.5	38.3

Source: USCB (2021c: Table 1)

Table 5.3 US Life Expectancy at Birth (all races, foreign and native-born), 1950, 1995, 2016

Year of Birth	1950	1995	2016
Male	65.6	72.5	76.1
Female	71.1	78.9	81.1
Overall	68.2	75.8	78.6

Source: CDC (2017: Table 15)

life spans (seen over the long term) and changing attitudes toward marriage. Single parents are three times as likely to be living in poverty as married people with or without kids—a gap that continues as they grow older, live alone, and pay premium costs for not sharing housing, utilities, food, and other expenses (Livingstone, 2018).

At present, there are 128.6 million households nationwide of which 83.5 million are families of two persons or more, and 62 million of those are composed of married couples with or without children present. The average household size is 2.5 people and the average family (two or more people) size is 3.2 people (USCB, 2019b). Americans increasingly accept that no single family model is dominant among the many variations, some of which are: married couples, remarried couples, cohabitating couples, single parent with child, and no parent (Thomas, 2020). Americans are marrying later and having fewer children. This trend is part of the liberalization of the 1960s, but it also comes from a need for income and job security before embarking on procreation.

Financial stability helps build relationships and economic recessions hurt them. Females continue to place very high importance on having an employed spouse and as Robert Gordon points out, "There are only 65 employed men for every 100 women of a given age" (among whites) and the numbers fall to 51 employed per 100 for black males (Gordon, 2016). The male preference to have employed wives is also rising as the economy insists upon it and as marriages based on equality and companionship are seen as more desirable and durable.

Part of the "big sort" is to find a partner similar in education, earnings potential, and lifestyle interests—something sociologists call "assortative mating" (Miller and Bui, 2016). The 1950s practice of employers paying a "family wage" to males was based on the idea that husbands would and should be the "breadwinner" able to cover all the expenses of a family and shelter the wife at home with the housework. This philosophy also maintained the hierarchy of the patriarchy and caused females to want to marry richer men. Since the 1970s, as women have entered paid employment in large numbers, companies have eliminated the family wage. This change increased the class divide as assortative mating patterns, enhanced by media dating apps and sites, reduce cross-class partnerships, segregate people geographically, and further class divisions (Miller and Bui, 2016). For example, as the professional class intermarries and has dinner conversations at home, their kids grow up hearing 19 million more words than middle-class children and 32 million more words than working class kids—by the time they are six years old (Putnam, 2015). Putnam points out that place is a powerful factor in determining opportunities and multigenerational advantages or disadvantages. "What is truly American is not so much the individual but neighborhood inequality" (Putnam, 2015: 215). Where inequality is concerned, class origins matter at least as much as race or gender constructions—even though those factors contribute strongly to outcomes.

The average age for new mothers has increased to 26.9 years old as teenage pregnancies have fallen dramatically and as women are better educated than before (CDC, 2016, 2021c). The median age at first marriage continues to rise: nearly thirty years for men and twenty-eight for women (USCB, 2021g). The number of families with both husband and wife present continues to shrink. Single-parent households have skyrocketed to 28

Contemporary United States

percent—the world's highest percentage—and this, together with rising divorce rates and continued gender pay inequities, puts more women with children into poverty because two incomes are increasingly essential to middle-class lives (Kramer, 2019). Conservatives voice nostalgia for the "good old days" when women stayed home, men went to work, children were manageable and "above average," and there were two cars in every driveway. But a return to a world of male privilege would require women to give up the gains of a lifetime. Most females and all feminists are manifestly unwilling to do that, and especially so given hardening conceptions of gender equality.

Still, individuals experience a "culture war within" as they are torn between traditional and modern family models and are deeply ambivalent about the one they should construct for themselves. American society is marked by an increasing number of adults who prefer neither to marry nor to cohabit. The number of Americans living alone is 35.7 million, of whom 13.6 million are over sixty-five years old (USCB, 2018a). Traditionalists call for limiting divorce, living near other family members, children obeying their parents, women focusing on domestic duties and motherhood, and families being involved in church or spiritual activities. But the reality of liberal families is an absence of strict rules, both spouses as free agents in the labor market, children who are not the biological offspring of the adults they live with, and a culture dominated by entertainment and the emphasizing of rights and sexual freedoms (Wolfe, 2006). Affluence, too, can contribute to the breakup of families, as many young people grow up faster with smartphones, internet, streaming, and social media. However, while many folks are frustrated with the modern family, few seem willing to revert to earlier models.

The issue of homosexual marriage threatens long-held ideas of manhood and gender norms. In 1996, Republicans passed the Defense of Marriage Act (DMA) to define a legal marriage as a union between one "born-that-way" man and one "born-that-way" woman. The Act only intensified the debate over love, marriage, and government entitlements. By 2011, when the Obama administration announced that it would seek a repeal of the DMA, thirty-one states had constitutional amendments and six states had laws against gay marriages. Unsurprisingly, conservatives blocked Democratic repeal efforts; but they could not block public opinion. After Vice President Joe Biden came out in support of gay marriage, Obama made a clear, if tepid, statement to a nationwide audience: "it is important for me to go ahead and affirm that I think same-sex couples should be able to get married" (Calmes and Baker, 2012). This was a calculated move in line with rapidly evolving public attitudes. In June 2015, after several US District Courts had ruled against the DMA, the US Supreme Court ruled 5–4 that same-sex couples have a constitutional right to get married and to have their marriage recognized throughout the United States, its territories and possessions worldwide. A poll taken a week after the ruling showed a 58 percent approval rating.

By 2019, the Census Bureau's American Community Survey recorded just under a million same-sex couple households (980,000), of whom 568,110 had exchanged wedding vows, a development celebrated by the Lesbian Gay Bisexual Transsexual (LGBTQIA+) community. Fifteen percent of same-sex couples' homes counted children: almost 300,000 in all (Schneider, 2020). But the issue is still red hot, especially for social conservatives. In 2018, the FBI ranked the number of victims of "hate crimes"—some with multiple biases, including 2,426 African Americans, 1,445 LGBTQIA+, 1,038 anti-white, 920 anti-Semitic, and 236 anti-Islam (FBI, 2018).

More than one in four American children (27 percent) live with a single adult, usually their mother; but that can be said another way: nearly seven in ten under eighteens (69 percent) live with two adults (USCB, 2017). Eighty-four percent of Asian children live with two adults, as do 73 percent of whites, 57 percent of Hispanics, and 33 percent of blacks (NCES, 2019a). The 3,971,712 recorded live births and a birth rate of 11.6 per 1,000 people in 2018 represented the lowest rate ever among US women (CDC, 2021a). Of these, 40.1 percent, 1.5 million were to single mothers (CDC, 2021e). Minority births surpassed majority births for the first time in December 2012. The United States is a multicultural nation that continues to see a rising number of interracial and/or interethnic unions producing babies who will check two or more racial/ethnic categories on future census forms. Additionally, many families are actually "blended families" of stepparents, stepchildren, and stepsiblings or multigenerational families with grandparents present.

In 2015, the costs of raising a child from birth to eighteen years of age varied by geographical region, rural or urban setting, single versus multiple children in same house, race, ethnicity, gender, and other factors. Generalizing, and after adjusting for inflation, a family with a low annual income (under $59,200) should expect to spend $212,300 over seventeen years; a middle-income family ($59,200–$107,400) will pay $284,570; and the upper income family (over $107,400) will spend $454,770 (USDA, 2017). Costs can easily double if the child pursues a university education.

Financial matters continue to be the biggest concerns for Americans, even more than terrorism, war, or education. In 2019, Pew recorded that over twice as many Americans (45 percent) thought family incomes would fall over the next generation as those that believed they would increase (29 percent). Of course, from a world perspective, the United States has been a rich country for a long time, and is likely to remain rich. The median yearly income for an American household in 2018 was $60,293 (USCB, 2019c). The problem is not the world comparison, but the domestic relative inequality.

The World Bank uses a GINI Index to rank countries on a most equality to less equality scale. The United States lags behind virtually all other developed countries and has seen GINI levels of inequality increase since 1980 (OECD, 2021a; World Bank, 2021b). The haves and the have-nots live vastly different lives.

Americans are caught in a work-and-spend cycle that weakens family and community ties. The last generation has witnessed an increase in competitive acquisition and conspicuous consumption and reinforcement of the long-standing American notion that "more and newer" is better. One key manifestation: homes have grown in size by 40 percent and cars have become markedly bigger (Pinsker, 2019). Breakneck technological gain has reinvigorated complaints that Americans are caught in a costly net of planned obsolescence, where product life cycles shorten. Keeping up with the Joneses next door, or even their own kids to acquire the latest fashion or flashing the latest smartphone, means more parents must work longer hours to make the additional disposable income necessary to fund their own and their children's new gizmo addictions. Most are overworked and overspent (Gabler, 2016).

The United States has always been a competitive society that expects that the next generation will live better than the previous one. The idea of intergenerational progress is central to the American dream. Parents might want to downsize their own lifestyles but cannot, and will not, because to do so would threaten the status and opportunities of their children. In the recent past, most American families neither adhered to a family budget nor saved much money for the future; instead, they spent their entire salaries between paychecks and acquisitively bought on credit, or by using the equity in their homes to take out second mortgages. However, the Covid-19 economic crisis saw savings skyrocket as Americans grew fearful for the future (FRED, 2021b). Still, credit card balances carried month by month average $6,847 per household and are part of the total household debt including mortgages in 2019 of $137,729, a 20 percent rise in the last five years (Issa, 2022).

Single women and minorities lead the categories of those who owe much more than they can afford to pay, oftentimes because they have less home equity. Two-income middle-class families with children and DINKS (double income no kids) have two salaries to help pay the bills, but their expectations and upscale spending patterns often lead to debt. It is therefore not surprising that poorer Americans are less optimistic about the future as prices rise faster than incomes. From 2009–2019, household income increased by 30 percent; living costs went up by nearly 19 percent, leaving Americans slightly better off for the decade (Issa, 2022). Yet, those reliant on the federally mandated minimum wage—$7.25 an hour since 2009—saw real incomes and spending power reduced. In 2020, Joe Biden campaigned on raising the minimum wage to $15 an hour, though passing that in Congress will probably not be possible. Some economists argue that hikes in the minimum wage would result in pricing low-cost labor out of work and fuel inflation; others claim the economy would power up on the increased spending power.

Women

American women have long been a majority within the nation's population; but until the last three decades, they have faced limited choices in the job market. Moreover, the divisions of race, class, marital status, political philosophy, and immigration divide women as much as they do men. One thing is certain: since Betty Friedan wrote *The Feminine Mystique* (1963) women have come a long way in every field of private and public life. In contemporary America, women have risen to near-equality in access to jobs, education, and aspirations; and yet, "near-equality" is not equality. Males are still richer and have maintained a dominant class status based upon privileged gender roles; women have always been much more likely to be poor. The #MeToo movement illuminated countless examples of toxic masculinity and male privilege which were used to get sexual favors and which demonstrated the hollowness of claim that substantive equality in workplaces had been reached.

The rise of paid labor and industrialization in the early nineteenth century simultaneously gave women avenues to self-sufficiency outside marriage while it circumscribed their choices by funneling them into "women's work" and lesser salaries. Women were seen as helpmates to men, secondary wage-earners, and, primarily, as homemakers. This "separate sphere" philosophy held out the roles of piety, purity, submissiveness, and domesticity as the realm of true womanhood. Feminists from the 1830s and 1840s protested this inequality, but it would take until 1920 for women to push through the 19th Amendment to win women's suffrage in national elections. Most of the gains focused on white women, with minority women stigmatized by race.

Women had long been regarded as "weaker vessels" whose physical frailty needed protection. Even though the government had called for "Womanpower" to fill industrial jobs during the Second World War, until the 1960s court decisions and social convention limited work hours as a way, they said, to keep women safe and healthy. Of course, these "protections" provided rationalizations for paying women less, limited their occupational choices, and maintained their dependence upon men. As early as 1923, feminists believed that, to change things, the country needed to adopt an Equal Rights Amendment (ERA): "Equality of rights under law shall not be denied or abridged by the United States or by any State on account of sex." Efforts to get Congress to consider such an amendment fell flat until it was resurrected in 1972, with Congress quickly passing the ERA and sending it to the states for ratification by 1983. But it was not ratified because it fell three states short of the thirty-eight required for a constitutional amendment. At the state level, it was symbolically important that on January 15, 2020, Virginia became the thirty-eighth state to ratify the ERA: passing the three-quarters-of-states threshold that would have seen it come into law, had it not lapsed (Cohen and Codrington, 2020).

Partly, the ERA failed to be ratified in time because conservative women fought vehemently against it, afraid that it would change conventions on child custody, which favored mothers, change bathroom segregation, or that it would make females available for a wartime draft into the military. Biological explanations for discrimination abound with their insistence that it is "natural" for women to be domestic, take care of babies, and be less aggressive, while apologists for men argue that is "natural" for them to be more sexually predatory. Feminists respond that it is also "natural" to die of smallpox but that vaccines are available; after all, "natural" is a social norm taught and acted upon (Wright and Rogers, 2015).

Some women argued that equal pay would not lift women's pay but would be used by corporations to lower men's pay—hurting both the men and the families (Hartman, 2015). Highly religious women clung to biblical admonitions that a woman should support her husband and be subordinate to him. Others believed that women would lose their femininity by becoming "men" or being "shrill"—the "feminazi" charge was often used against strong women, including Hillary Clinton, Michelle Obama, and Kamala Harris. Big businesses fought the ERA because of the costs of higher salaries. Many liberals argued that the amendment was unnecessary because the 1964 Civil

Contemporary United States

Rights Act had explicitly banned discrimination based on sex or race and that the "equal protection" clause of the 14th Amendment was increasingly being used to overturn discriminatory practices.

Laws have made workplace environments safer. Sexual harassment lawsuits against employers for making unsolicited sexual advances and for withholding promotions and pay raises if a woman refuses sex, have overwhelmingly been settled in favor of the woman filing the claim. Despite progress, the #MeToo movement catalogued and broadcast the continuing abundance of sexually predatory behavior by men, as discussed previously. What shocked the nation was the scale and depth of male sexual harassment and sexual entitlement. On hearing prominent cases, more and more women came forward on social media and elsewhere, explaining the "#MeToo" moniker.

#MeToo played out against the background of the 2016 presidential candidacy of Donald Trump. In 2020, Trump faced over twenty allegations of sexual misbehavior. Trump's response when the allegations first became public in 2016 was "No one has more respect for women than I do" (Jamieson, Jeffrey, and Pugliese, 2016). The allegations seemed to wash off Trump, though some saw this as the result of a weaponization of the Department of Justice to protect the president (Zhou, 2020).

The #MeToo movement has invigorated younger generations of women into action in a manner almost unimaginable a decade ago. On January 21, 2017, the Women's March on Washington attracted nearly half a million counter-inaugural protesters raising their voices in support of civil rights, immigration rights, and reproductive rights (Hartocollis and Alcindor, 2017). In 2020, over half of women (61 percent) labeled themselves "feminists." Whether politics and activism will decouple in the future is unclear, but currently most women (68 percent) see feminism as empowering freedom and rights. A small majority (52 percent) of men disagree, seeing feminism as a polarizing stance (Barroso, 2020).

Returning to the progress made by women in society, social scientists define the enhanced personal freedom experienced by women as an "intersectionality" of sexual expression, gender identity, and career-plus-family choices with or without marriage. Only one in five women in the twenty–twenty-nine-year-old category is married—compared to six in ten in 1960, when the birth control pill first hit the market and ramped up the sexual revolution. Sociologist Patricia Traister argues that no one today is foregoing marriage to prove equality (Traister, 2016). New feminists herald the rise of the single woman who is whole in her belief that it is okay for women to live parental, sexual, financial, and social lives independent of marriage (Traister, 2016). Traister cites multiple studies showing that educated single women make more money than married women and have near-parity with men, while uneducated women comprise two-thirds of all minimum wage workers (Traister, 2016). Counter studies indicate that money is not everything and that married people of all educational levels are happier and live longer than singles (Putnam, 2015).

Women are employed in increasing numbers in every profession, and across racial and ethnic lines. In the most traditional of male bastions, the US armed forces, women make up 16 percent of enlisted forces and 19 percent of officers (CFR, 2020). Over

Society

700,000 women served between 2001 and 2015 (CRS, 2020c; USDV, 2020). By 2018, over 300,000 females had seen action in either Iraq or Afghanistan, or both, with 165 killed in combat or hostile actions and 678 wounded (VA Blog, 2018). Female Secretaries of State include Madeleine Albright (1998–2001), Condoleezza Rice (2005–2009), and Hillary Clinton (2009–2013). Nancy Pelosi was the first woman to be Speaker of the House of Representatives (2007–2011 and 2019–2022). Women have led the Department of Justice, served as US Ambassador to the United Nations, gained the highest ranks in the military, and headed FBI field offices. Four women are presently US Supreme Court Justices: Sonia Sotomayor, Elena Kagan, Amy Coney Barrett, and Biden-appointee Ketanji Brown Jackson. Women surpass men in obtaining bachelor's, master's, and doctoral degrees.

Glass ceilings for promotion still exist, as do "pink collar" jobs where women are predominant, such as secretarial work, nursing, elementary-school teaching, waitressing, and as librarians. This keeps the issue of equal pay and ideas of "comparable worth" rightfully in the headlines. Women still earn only 82 cents for every dollar a man earns and are forced to choose between career and family because of the wide-spread practice of "equality without protective oversight" (Sheth et al., 2021). While there have been significant gains in the number of child daycare facilities, these are costly, privately owned businesses. Many working mothers are forced to leave their children with grandparents, or home alone. The Family and Medical Leave Act of 1993 mandates twelve weeks of maternity leave for pregnant and new mothers at companies employing fifty or more people. However, with no provisions for paid leave, most women cannot afford to take unpaid absences for very long. Biden's 2021 "Build Back Better" bill proposed to increase access to pre-kindergarten childcare and provide twelve weeks of paid family leave (*Guardian*, 2021).

The abortion controversy is a volatile political issue tied up with premarital sex, birth control, and traditional religious family values. Margaret Sanger founded the non-profit American Birth Control League (ABCL) in 1921 to promote women's health issues. The ABCL changed its name to Planned Parenthood Federation (PPF) and, in 2022, is the nation's largest provider of reproductive health care services, including sterilization and abortion. Stressing dedication "to bringing high-quality, affordable care to every member of their community," PPF's mission supports the provision of "comprehensive reproductive and complementary health care services in settings which preserve and protect the essential privacy and rights of each individual" (PPF, 2021). PPF includes HIV/AIDS testing, STD treatments, birth control pills, pregnancy planning, and other matters dealing with reproduction and sexual activity. Democrats traditionally strongly supported budgetary funding for the organization. In 2017, Trump signed legislation defunding Planned Parenthood, despite condemnation from liberals and women's rights organizations nationwide (Davis, 2017). However, Trump's action had little effect on PPF's government income stream, which actually rose from $544 million to $617 million between 2017 and 2020—mostly via Medicaid payments (Cunningham, 2020).

Nearly half of all pregnancies are unintended (CDC, 2021c). The Supreme Court often hears cases to decide between the constitutional rights of women to control their

163

Contemporary United States

own bodies and the rights of society to protect human lives. Even though most of its rulings are by 5–4 votes, the Court had continued to rule in favor of a woman's right to choose to give birth or have an abortion, a rule it established in the *Roe v. Wade* (1973) decision. However, in 2022, in the aftermath of Trump's reconfiguration of the bench, the Supreme Court has overturned *Roe* and returned abortion regulations to the states (McCann and Johnson, 2022). Nine states have banned abortion, with more likely to follow, deflecting some women who exercise their right to choice to states in which abortion remains legal.

Between 1973 and 2017, close to 60 million legal abortions were performed in the United States (Guttmacher, 2017). In 2017, the number of reported abortions declined to 862,000, the lowest since *Roe* (Nash and Dreweke, 2019). Part of this decline is explained by the ever-increasing use of a pill, RU-486, which has been available since 2000, and which makes abortion more private and less a matter of statistics. In 2016, more than one in five pregnancies ended in abortion, with 75 percent being low-income women, 61 percent among women twenty–twenty-nine years old, 94 percent by heterosexuals, 39 percent by non-Hispanic whites, 28 percent by non-Hispanic blacks, 25 percent by Hispanics, and 8 percent by other women (Guttmacher, 2017).

Americans have made progress to level the field for women, but there remains much to be done. In 2018, women made up a majority of law school students (52.4 percent) for the third straight year (ABA, 2019). The rising numbers of women in politics and universities portends well for future gains. Still, when all the numbers are added up women earned less, are much more likely to live in poverty, and are barely visible at the highest levels of corporate life (Semega, 2019).

Race

Historian W. E. B. DuBois said it in 1903: "The problem of the twentieth century is the problem of the color line" (DuBois, 1903). That remains true in the twenty-first century. Even in the best of times, America is a society deeply divided and conscious of skin color and ethnic groups. In the worst of times when economic security and personal safety issues over crime and terrorism are highlighted, white fears of blacks, browns, and Asians can rise up quickly, heightened by politicians willing to point fingers and blame Islam, Mexicans, or Chinese for the problems of American decline. Laws banning Muslims, dog-whistles on race and crime, a wall against Mexico, or a focus on "the yellow peril" all have deep roots in racism and racial inequalities.

Two-thirds of Americans believe that racially insensitive speech became more common during the Trump administration. Conservative calls for a colorblind society compete with the dilemma cited by liberal Critical Race Theorists who say that not seeing color (race) is a barrier to equal treatment because reform is not possible unless inequality is identified. In a 2019 PEW poll, 75 percent of Republicans and 21 percent of Democrats said that too much attention is paid to race (Horowitz, Brown, and Cox, 2019). There is a link between race and citizenship in the United States stretching from exclusions of American Indians, slaves, Chinese and others in the nineteenth century, up to the voting ID laws and harassment of undocumented aliens gaining favor since 2012.

It is useful to remember that race and human classifications of all kinds are constructed social categories, not strictly biological ones. As discussed in Chapter 2, Americans used the one-drop-of-black-blood formula to designate a person as black. Historian Barbara Fields and others ask us to imagine the difference if the rule was that one-drop-of-white-blood makes a person white: Michael Jackson, Beyoncé, and Barack Obama, for example, not to mention the millions and millions of people with varying gene pools.

Obama's presidency started with great optimism that a post-racial society was near. Trump's election doubled down on deep racial divides, some of them exposed by the fact of a black man recently in the White House (Dyson, 2016). In terms of black and white, there are questions of whether or not the country can make the changes necessary to achieve "America." These questions have been underscored by the killings of African Americans by police, by the resultant violent protests against police brutality, and by Trump's connection of race with crime and unrest. The failures of race relations are obvious: racially tinged inner-city poverty, crime, strong-arm police behavior, neo-Nazis, militant anti-immigrant groups such as the "Proud Boys," and ethnocentric politicking. There are prejudices that need to be overcome and true equality remains a dream deferred. Racial preferences remain in hiring and promotion practices, in home loan availability, in buying homes in certain neighborhoods, and in myths about intelligence and criminality.

On the other hand, the successes of Kamala Harris, Barack Obama, Colin Powell, Clarence Thomas, Oprah Winfrey, Ta-Nehisi Coates, Morgan Freeman, prominent African American mayors, sixty members of Congress (2021), over 10,500 black elected officials, and thousands of others living solidly middle-class lives point to a society that respects equal opportunity and merit (Wright and Rogers, 2015). African Americans alive in the 1950s could not have imagined the successes they and their children would achieve, even while those gains are not evenly distributed across class or locational lines. If we were to mark the start of gaining a more equitable society from the end of the 1954–1968 Civil Rights Movement, African Americans have had 359 years of brutal oppression (1609–1968) and fifty years of increasing opportunities. Blacks say the main three impediments are racial discrimination, poor schools, and lack of well-paying jobs (Horowitz, Brown, and Cox, 2019). The NAACP, National Urban League, and the congressional Black Caucus continue to monitor, protect, and advocate for positive changes in American society.

White Americans have generally expected an individual to succeed or fail on his or her own merits. But when a minority group claims rights (and legal entitlements), many in the privileged group hesitate. Racism compounds problems, such as achieving universal health care, because many whites do not like the idea of helping "the takers"—people Ronald Reagan called "welfare queens." The lack of health care for whites is thus bound up in white racism against others. The tough question is whether or not Americans should discriminate against single individuals for the benefit of a group—socialism. Not surprisingly, majorities of white Americans traditionally support the

Contemporary United States

Table 5.4 American Population Diversity, 2000, 2019, and 2060 Projection (in millions)

| Year/Total | 2000 (281.4) | | 2019 (328.2) | | 2060 (404.5) | |
Group	No.	percent	No.	Percent	No.	Percent
Non-Hispanic White	211.5	75	197.2	60.1	179.2	44.3
Hispanic/Latino (any race)	35.3	13	60.7	18.5	111.2	27.5
African American	34.0	11	44.0	13.4	60.7	15.0
Asian American	10.1	3	19.4	5.9	36.8	9.1
American Indian and Inuit	2.1	0.7	4.2	1.3	5.6	1.4
Native Hawaiian/ Samoan	0.8	0.3	0.7	0.2	1.1	0.3
Two or More Races/ Ethnicities	6.8	2.4	9.2	2.8	25.3	6.2

Note: Beginning in 2000, the US Census Bureau allowed individuals to mark more than one category for race. Most of the double markings are non-Hispanic White plus one other category. The figures for 2060 are estimates and reflect the loss of the baby boom generation and declining birth rates among whites. Numbers are rounded.

Sources: USCB (2020b); Vespa, Medina, and Armstrong (2020)

small government-advocating Republican Party, while majorities of other voters favor the Democratic Party which traditionally accepts a greater role in redistributive policies. The answer is hard to reconcile with the Constitution and with the racial progress of the last century. American racial diversity is shown in Table 5.4.

Before the Second World War, 87 percent of the black population was mired in poverty and were poorly educated. That has changed dramatically. Today, 81 percent are above the poverty line, 88 percent hold high school diplomas, and 26 percent hold bachelor's degrees (Cheeseman Day, 2020; USCB, 2020a). Despite great progress, a racial divide remains and the economic outcome is not equal. Household wealth for whites in 2016 was $171,000; for blacks, about one-tenth as much, at $17,150 (McIntosh, Moss, Nunn, and Shambaugh, 2020). The poverty rate for blacks is 18.8 percent; for whites it is 7.2 percent (Cheeseman Day, 2020). In October 2020, the unemployment rate for blacks was 10 percent; for whites, 6 percent (BLS, 2021b). In the fourth quarter of 2021, median white male earnings amounted to $1,030 weekly; black males earned $805—over 20 percent less; and black females brought home just $802 (BLS, 2021g).

The incarceration rate for blacks is five times that of whites, which has led to some commentators and academics arguing the criminal justice system was "racialized" (Alexander, 2012; BJS, 2020b). Higher unemployment, lower wealth and earnings, greater incarceration rates, and a higher incidence of single-family households together increases the socioeconomic precariousness of blacks. Even when non-white men are released from jail, their criminal records make it hard to find good jobs. Additionally, in 2020, only Maine, Vermont, and the District of Columbia allowed unrestricted voting by prisoners. Sixteen states allow voting once a prisoner is released from jail. Twenty-one states restore rights once a sentence and parole are completed and any fines/costs are

Society

paid. Eleven states permanently disfranchised people who committed felonies and ten states restricted some people with misdemeanors from voting (NCSL 2021b).

Glass ceilings and discriminatory practices also exist for upwardly mobile individuals. In November 2000, the Coca-Cola Company was compelled to pay $192 million to African American workers who had been "passed over" for promotions. In 2011 and 2012, the Bank of America and Wells Fargo Bank agreed to pay out $335 million and $175 million, respectively, for discrimination against African American and Hispanic customers (Rothaker and Ingram, 2012). The American legal system has been a most useful tool in moving the country toward less discrimination and more opportunity.

Analysts note that whites live "here" and blacks "there," but even if neighborhoods were integrated proportionally, only thirteen of every 100 households would be black. When African Americans speak of integration, they refer to a mix of 50–50; when whites speak of integration, they mean the proportional representation reflecting American society. Not wanting to break up the culture of black communities, black families continue to buy houses near other black families and—as whites do the same—this form of self-segregation continues. One-third of all African Americans live in the suburbs, sometimes completely integrated with whites, but more often in a checkerboard pattern of black street, white street, reflecting strong preferences to live in cultures within cultures. While it is misleading to claim, as some do, that the United States has residential racial apartheid, America does have a society heavily sorted by subcultures, sorted by race and class.

Asian Americans have an easier time integrating, even though there is a long history of mistreatment by racists. Chinese immigrants surpassed Indian immigrants as the largest group coming to America in 2018, followed closely by Mexicans (Budiman, 2020). Asian Americans are often described as a "model minority" because they have the highest education levels and salaries and most stable family structures. In 2020 Asians Americans exceeded the median weekly income for whites, $1,499 to $1,030 for men and $1,165 to $939 for women (BLS, 2021g). Put differently, Asian American women earn more than white men. In 2017 Asian Americans enjoyed annual household incomes of $81,331 versus $68,145 for whites (USCB, 2018b). High incomes probably result from high levels of human capital: education. In 2016, over half of Asian Americans twenty-five and over held bachelor's degrees and fully one in five held advanced degrees—much higher than the US average (USCB, 2016). Asian Americans are also the most urban centered group, living in higher-paying cities and not in rural areas (Guo, 2016).

Hispanics are now the country's largest minority group. Most Hispanics/Latinos have family ties to Mexico, the Caribbean, and South America. The sub-group Chicanos are made up of families who lived in areas before those areas were brought into the US by wars. Others emigrated from Mexico as legal or undocumented persons. It is hard to imagine "A Day Without a Mexican" as a 2004 film title had it, because of the social impact and number of workers who support the American economy. Recently, Mexican and other Hispanic immigrants have come under attack from racists who want all undocumented workers deported and a border wall along the 2,000-mile-long US–Mexican border. The fact that transnational South American crime rings operate

167

Contemporary United States

a huge drug and smuggling trade in the United States (discussed later) does not help law-abiding families. Additionally, many American workers claim that Mexicans take jobs away by working for less and sending most of their earnings back to Mexico—thus hurting the US economy.

In 2015 Trump announced his candidacy for president by saying that Mexican immigrants were "bringing drugs. They're bringing crime. They're rapists" (Trump, 2015). The border wall was central to his thinking (Hirschfeld-Davis and Shear, 2019). This rhetoric is as disturbing as it is all too common. Hispanics are increasingly numerous, will double their voting power by 2030, and will have an enormous impact by 2060, when they will make up between 25 and 30 percent of the population (see Table 5.4). Some commentators have argued that Hispanic voter influence will benefit Democrats. However, the 2020 election attests to tremendous diversity among Hispanics that reduces the clarity of the term. Most Hispanics self-identify as white or brown; Hispanics are often as socially conservative as other religious Republicans, including Cuban-Americans, for example (Chavez, 2020).

Crime and Punishment

Americans rely on legal remedies to maintain order, equality, and freedom in a multicultural society. The approximately $200-billion-a-year US criminal justice system has three components: law enforcement, courts, and corrections (prisons and parole). The loss of lifetime earnings as the result of incarceration adds another $300 billion or so (Craigie, Grawert, and Kimble, 2020). With more lawyers than any other nation in the world, Americans use the court system to settle disputes, large and small. They put real faith in the ability of the judges to ensure that constitutional guarantees overcome unfair actions by individuals, groups, the government, or even the law itself. The courts follow federal and state law, the Constitution, and decisions from similar cases, called precedents, to establish verdicts and set sentences.

The Constitution has much to say about the legal rights of Americans charged with crimes. Amendments 4–8 provide the basics of due process of law, speedy and public jury trials, no cruel or unusual punishments, an adversary system, the right to remain silent, the right to a lawyer, the right to call and confront witnesses, no second trial for the same offense, no excessive bail, and no police coercion of witnesses. The Supreme Court has further ruled that police must advise a person of these rights when he or she is arrested. Called the "Miranda Rights" after the name of the court case, a police officer must say:

> You have the right to remain silent. If you give up the right to remain silent, anything you say can and will be used against you in a court of law. You have the right to an attorney and to have an attorney present during questioning. If you cannot afford an attorney, one will be appointed for you without charge. Do you understand these rights as I have explained them to you?

If the arresting officer fails to advise the prisoner of these rights or does not follow the exact procedure in searching for and finding evidence, the courts will free the accused person, even if the evidence points to guilt.

During their lives, most Americans are involved in at least one court case. The legal system is adversarial, pitting defendant(s) against accusor(s), while a judge and jury listen to evidence presented according to formal rules. Civil law cases account for the bulk of legal actions as individuals sue each other for financial compensation arising from accidental destruction of property, divorce and child custody, psychological "pain and suffering," accidental physical injury, breach of contract, or discriminatory acts of a racial, ageist, or sexual nature. Most cases involve minor irritations: neighbors who play loud music, dogs that bite, or fences that are too high. Civil cases include suing McDonald's for selling dangerously hot coffee, class action suits against makers of faulty breast implants, and claims for general reparations to contemporary African Americans who suffer post-slavery stress syndrome. Civil courts often award compensation above the actual loss in property or medical costs, including punitive financial damages against companies for "negligence." In 2020, states sought damages totaling \$2.3 trillion from Purdue Pharma as a result of their marketing of the highly addictive opioid, OxyContin (Spector, 2020). The US government sought another \$11 billion in criminal and civil compensation (Feeley, 2020) (see Illustration 6.2). For the most part, civil cases do not involve prison time—although failure to pay child support or follow court judgments can land the offender in jail. Jury verdicts in civil cases are usually decided by majority vote.

Criminal cases are brought against those who are charged with committing a crime against individuals and, by extension, society. Murder, rape, assault, burglary, use of illegal drugs, theft, insider trading, embezzlement, child molestation, kidnapping, and arson are a few of the most common felonies. For the most part, these cases are kept within the state court systems, with appeals available to the Supreme Court (see Figure 3.3). In forty-eight states, criminal cases are settled with a trial by a jury of twelve citizens, who, after listening to the evidence, must unanimously agree that the person is guilty beyond a reasonable doubt. If even one juror dissents from the opinion, the prisoner is released. Louisiana and Oregon allow for verdicts by ten of twelve and eleven of twelve, respectively, in criminal cases that do not result in a death penalty conviction.

Capital punishment requires a unanimous verdict. Defendants can skip the jury trial by agreeing to a "plea bargain" agreement with the prosecutor, typically agreeing to plead guilty to a lesser charge in exchange for a shorter prison term and/or financial penalty in lieu of a long trial and an undetermined verdict. If the defendant is too poor to hire an attorney, the state is required to appoint and pay the costs for a "public defender." These lawyers have enormous caseloads, are the most poorly trained, youngest, and the least paid of trial lawyers. Because 80 percent of all defendants are poor, and defended by appointed counsel, the US clearly has a wealth-based justice system favoring the middle and upper classes. Additionally, most juries are drawn from lists of registered voters on which the poor are underrepresented, a practice which keeps the middle class and elderly in charge of deciding verdicts.

Contemporary United States

The United States retains a notoriously high crime rate and the vitality of the legal system makes most observers believe that America has even more crime than it does. Nearly every Hollywood movie revolves around a crime or includes a crime in the plot. The news media attract viewers and readers with stories of one misfortune after another, knowing that tragedy sells better than feel-good stories: "if it bleeds, it leads." Viewers want to see dramas that let them watch the courts and police in action. There is a love affair for violent spectacle. The insatiable appetite for crime fiction, TV series, and film may explain the clash between falling actual crime rates since 2000 and rising public perception of crime rates (Koerth and Thomson-DeVeaux, 2020).

America has 18,000 separate state and local police departments with over 700,000 full-time police officers; there are also 250,000 civilians involved in law enforcement. Additionally, there are approximately 100,000 federal officers in twenty-four agencies authorized to make arrests and carry weapons. The four biggest agencies are the US Customs and Border Protection (UCBP), Immigration and Customs Enforcement (ICE), Federal Bureau of Prisons (FBP), and Federal Bureau of Investigation (FBI). Other agencies with law enforcement functions include the Bureau of Indian Affairs Reservation Police, Drug Enforcement Administration, US Marshall Service, Bureau of Alcohol, Tobacco and Firearms, and US Secret Service. Overall, the police are well funded.

The FBI is part of the Department of Justice and has a dual mission responsibility of law enforcement and intelligence collection. This includes the protection of the United States and its citizens from terrorist attacks, foreign espionage, cyber technology crimes, corruption by public officials, civil rights and hate crime violations, transnational criminal gangs, white-collar crime, and "significant" violent crime (FBI, 2021a). The FBI has 35,000 employees in field offices in every major US city and in sixty US embassies around the world. The Director of the FBI is one of the most powerful and independent officials in government, but he/she can be removed by the president or by Congress under extraordinary conditions. This has happened twice. President Clinton removed Director William Sessions for misusing travel funds (and likely for partisan political reasons) and President Trump fired James Comey for not halting an investigation into Russian interference in the 2016 election. FBI directors are appointed by the president and confirmed by Congress to a ten-year appointment and has primary responsibilities to ensure the mission is accomplished and to brief the executive and legislative branches. In 2016, Comey had fed the ire of Democrats by announcing days before the general election that Hillary Clinton was under investigation, possibly influencing the outcome. As Secretary of State (2009–2013) Clinton had allegedly risked national security by storing mail on her private server. In 2016 and 2017, Comey was heavily involved in investigations of Russian cyber hacking of the 2016 presidential election and into public corruption at the highest levels of the Trump administration.

The United States has the highest proportion of its population in prison among major nations and around one in five of all reported prisoners worldwide (ICPR, 2018). The sentences ordered by American courts are double and triple the years ordered for similar offenses in the rest of the developed world. Punishment is tied to the idea that freedom has serious responsibilities. People are free to act, but if they decide to break the social compact, they are judged to "deserve" to be punished. In 2018, there were over two million people behind bars in the United States: 738,000 in county and city jails and 1,456,200 in state and federal penitentiaries. However substantial, these numbers are falling: the result of efforts to reduce prison populations for non-violent and non-sex offenses and because crime rates have until recently been dropping for two decades (Maruschak and Minton, 2020). Prisoner demographics include: 93 percent male in federal jails, 33 percent black, 50 percent white, and 15 percent Hispanic in federal and state jails (BJS, 2020b; Gramlich, 2020b; FBP, 2021). A further breakdown is revealing: one in every 57 black men, one in 122 Latinos, and one in 320 white males are behind bars (BJS, 2020b). Some 4.5 million more people are on probation or parole (Maruschak and Minton, 2020). The prisons are overcrowded, and more than 8 percent are now run by private-for-profit corporations which contract services to federal and state governments. Prisons function mainly to detain people and to exact retribution, instead of rehabilitating them.

Why are so many locked up for so long? In 1993, a crime wave fueled by drug wars and an economic downturn swept over the country. Eleven million people were victimized and the number of robberies and burglaries rose to more than 32 million incidents. With fear increasing, President Clinton used widespread bipartisan support to enact the 1994 Crime Act. The Act put 100,000 more police officers on the streets and set tougher penalties for drug offenders. Part of this get-tough-on-crime policy expanded the death penalty and another part instructed judges to impose harsher sentences for small offenses, including drug abuse, street corner fights, and shoplifting (Yassky, 2016). The focus on cutting crime led to "stop-and-frisk" laws that were passed in many states allowed police to search anyone exhibiting suspicious behavior. Many young African American and Latino males were detained even though "racial profiling" is illegal, feeding into high incarceration rates and the loss of voting rights (Alexander, 2012). Arrests for DWB (Driving While Black)—as satirists called it—became commonplace. Rates of incarceration for males twenty–twenty-nine years old per 100,000 people in each group were 8,932 blacks, 3,892 Hispanics, and 1,437 whites (Wagner, 2012).

Low-level, non-violent offenders soon overcrowded American jails, their lives ruined in the process. Conservatives praise the "Great American Crime Decline" in the number of criminal cases, as the total number of violent criminal offenses was reduced by 50 percent, from 79.8 incidents per 100,000 people in 1993 to 23.2 per 100,000 in 2018 (Gramlich, 2019). The number of homicides, rapes, robberies, and assaults remained close to the lowest levels in four decades (BJS, 2020a). Some cities, such as Chicago, had notably higher rates of violent crime.

Still, the focus on non-white American males and the overzealousness by police officers led to civil rights violations and social disorder. In an era of social media interconnectedness and smartphones that allow real-time streaming of police arrests, the level of public scrutiny of misbehavior quickly went viral. A Facebook-driven group arose to organize protests. #Black Lives Matter (#BLM) first appeared after the Travyon Martin verdict in 2013. #BLM became a viable new social movement for non-violent civil rights protests, and garnered support from outrage over the killings of Breonna

Contemporary United States

Taylor and George Floyd mentioned at the beginning of this chapter. Radicals wondered whether police forces could counter systemic racism in their midst and argued for a fresh start and redirected funding of monies to promote softer, sensitive policing. Republicans latched on to this "defunding" of police departments, claiming it would lead to lawlessness.

Commentators saw law and order as an important, below-the-line issue in Election 2020, which helped to explain the high national vote for Biden, but greater conservatism in congressional, senatorial, and state and local elections (Illustration 5.2). Even before George Floyd's murder, there was a deep racial confidence gap between whites and blacks over police performance. Fifty-six percent of black Americans said they had at least some confidence that police officers acted in the best interests of the public, compared to fully 84 percent of whites. Among Republicans, 43 percent thought that blacks were treated less fairly in dealings with the authorities. Eighty-eight percent of Democrats—more than double—felt that blacks were treated less fairly (DeSilver, Likpa, and Fahmy, 2020).

Illustration 5.2 President Obama and Stacey Abrams Encourage Georgians to Vote.

While Stacey Abrams lost her historic 2018 bid to become Georgia Governor, Democrats succeeded in enthusing people to register to vote and cast their ballots. Democrats Raphael Warnock and Jon Ossoff won both Georgia Senate seats in the 2020 elections, with get-out-the-votes campaigns among the African American community almost certainly decisive. Abrams's organization "Fair Fight" led the way. In this November 2 image taken at Morehouse College, President Obama is campaigning for Abrams. She was the Democratic nominee for governor in 2022 and is being mentioned for the Democratic presidential nomination in 2024.

Source: Jessica McGowan/Stringer via Getty Images

The current salience of #BLM emerged towards the end of the Obama presidency, as a pattern of deaths followed Trayvon Martin's murder and his killing which still resonates ten years on. In 2014, videos of the police chokehold-induced death of Eric Garner in New York and the shooting of twelve-year-old Tamir Rice on a Cleveland, Ohio, playground came just after a white policeman killed black teenager, Michael Brown, in Ferguson, Missouri. Peaceful protests turned violent, sparked incidents across the country, and commanded the news cycles. Then-President Obama addressed the convergence of race, violence, and unity in a national broadcast: "There is never an excuse for violence against police" but "there's also no excuse for police to use excessive force against peaceful protests" (Shear and Alcindor, 2017).

A year later, Freddie Gray, hands cuffed behind him and not wearing a seat belt, had his spinal cord snap while being transported in a police car in Baltimore, Maryland. Riots erupted over police negligence. Then, a young white supremacist killed nine black congregants and their pastor in an evening Bible class in a church in Charleston, South Carolina. Obama went to the church, spoke of healing, praised the victims' families who "forgave" the killer, and led the singing of "Amazing Grace"—one of the most poignant televised moments in US history of a president comforting the wider American community (Kaufman, 2015). Police began to wear body cameras as a way to show their view of situations as a complement to the webcams of bystanders, and as a way to bolster their credibility among communities of color.

During the Trump administration tensions between #BLM and anti-racist protesters on the one hand and Alt Right white nationalist on the other heightened, exploding on August 11–12, 2017 at a "Unite the Right" torchlight rally in Charlottesville, Virginia. A Ku Klux Klan rally had been held at the same location previous month, in favor of retaining Civil War statues like that of Confederate commanding General Robert E. Lee (Spencer and Stevens, 2017). Progressives saw the celebration of Confederate heroes as a shameful reminder of a racist past and insisted on their removal. Traditionalists, meanwhile, saw the removal as severing them from their history, and wanted their retention. These two views illustrate the two cultural opposites at war in the US today and in its history: which past should we celebrate, and which pasts should chasten us? As exponents of these ideas clashed in Charlottesville, one person died and at least nineteen suffered injuries as twenty-year-old white nationalist James Alex Fields, Jr., torpedoed his car into the crowds; Fields was sentenced to life in jail on twenty-nine counts of hate crimes (Fieldstadt, 2019).

Many people believed that Trump aggravated the situation in the aftermath to Charlottesville by suggesting equivalence between the protesters and counter-protesters. Trump declared that there was an "egregious display of hatred, bigotry and violence on many sides" and were "very fine people on both sides" (Astor, Caron, and Victor, 2017; Kessler, 2020). Some Republicans defended Trump, claiming that white supremacists and anti-Fascist "Antifa" leftists threated public order and the right to free speech (Stockman, 2017). Racial tensions remained high for the rest of Trump's presidency.

The United States has had highly structured criminal gangs since the early nineteenth century. Gangs often have social as well as criminal functions. An immigrant society of

Contemporary United States

diverse ethnic groups almost institutionalizes such affiliations. The gangs are expanding in number and are responsible for at nearly 50 percent of violent crimes (FBI, 2015). There are 33,000 different gangs with 1.4 million members nationwide in 2015, divided into street, prison, motorcycle, and US border groups (FBI, 2015, 2021c). Organized primarily by race, ethnicity, or language, these gangs commit most of the drive-by target-of-opportunity crimes and a significant portion of the murders in contemporary America.

Additionally, Mexican, Chinese, Italian, Somali, Russian, and other gangs are part of transnational or globally organized crime networks. These gangs are highly skilled in social media and internet and are responsible for most of the drug trafficking and prostitution, credit card fraud, identity theft, and money laundering. Gang members have infiltrated all major law enforcement agencies—including ICE and UCBP—and the US military to provide useful inside information to help their gangs (FBI, 2015). The most violent gang is the notoriously misogynistic Mara Salvatrucha 13 (MS-13), a Los Angeles affiliate of a transnational El Salvadorian gang that began in the 1980s and has 10,000 members and operations in at least forty US states (BJS, 2017). MS-13 operates as a crime school for young boys who are expected quickly to master lesser offenses before moving to more violent acts.

Historically, Americans grew up with weaponry, and killed the French, Spanish, British, Native Indians, Mexicans, and each other, as they shot their way westward. So many weapons currently exist that they seem certain to remain a fixed feature in American life. There are actually more guns than there are people in the US—nearly 400 million (Karp, 2018). Americans buy more than eight million firearms yearly, with upticks in the millions during crises like the Covid-19 outbreak. Shooters use firearms to kill over 14,500 Americans annually (BJS, 2019; Gramlich, 2019; Levine and McKnight, 2020). In 2020, gun related homicides killed more than 45,000 people, the highest level ever recorded in the US (Rabin & Arango, 2022).

From 1994 to 2004 the sale of military style semiautomatic assault weapons was banned. As the weaponry returned to the marketplace, shootings increased. The 2017 Las Vegas mass killing of 58 people and injuring of over 850 more at a country music festival appalled the nation. The shooter, sixty-four-year-old Steven Paddock, had used a "bumpstock" modification, making one of his weapons virtually automatic, increasing its firepower greatly (Corcoran, Baker, and Choi, 2019). In the aftermath, as with every mass shooting, many argued for tighter gun legislation. Bumpstop modifications were banned in March 2019.

The most powerful interest group in America used to be the pro-gun lobby, led by the National Rifle Association (NRA). The NRA—which claimed a near-five-million-voter-strong membership in 2018—uses snappy slogans such as "Guns don't kill people; people kill people!" and "If guns were outlawed, only outlaws would have guns!" to lobby for individual, not government, responsibility (NRA, 2022a). The NRA's influence and reputation were shredded due to alleged multiple examples of financial malfeasance including "a culture of self-dealing, mismanagement and negligent oversight" causing losses of up to $64 million dollars, according to New York Attorney General Letitia

James who is seeking to have the organization banned (Mak, 2020). Were the NRA to be dissolved, a successor organization would likely be established, catering to the interests of gun owners, gun sellers, and gun manufacturers. In June 2008, in a 5–4 decision, the US Supreme Court interpreted the Second Amendment as giving individuals the constitutional right to own a gun for personal use and to keep loaded handguns at home for self defense (Law.gov, 2008).

The issue of gun ownership remains contentious, even at the highest levels. In 2020, Trump favoured less restrictive gun ownership policies than Biden, who sought a reintroduction of the ban on assault style weapons and high capacity magazines, and effective regulation of private and gun show sales currently uncontrolled (Pearce, 2020). The public is split. Polls indicate that slightly more than half of Americans (57 percent) support tougher laws, while around one-third (34 percent) support less regulation—a slight fall in support for stricter gun policies since 2016 (Gallup, 2021d).

Nine states have waiting periods from the hour of purchase to taking possession of a weapon. Florida requires three days, but, in most states, a buyer who clears the FBI check can walk out of the store with the gun. Concealed handguns are legally carried in most states (Giffords, 2021). In 2019, well over 18 million Americans had concealed carry permits—an 8 percent increase over the previous year. The highest rates for permits were in Alabama (26.3 percent of adults), Indiana (16.9 percent), and South Dakota (16 percent). Twenty-five states have "Stand Your Ground" self-defense laws, often termed "shoot first" laws. Eight more states have stand your ground provisions via judicial decisions. Twenty-three states protect gun owners from civil litigation of actions taken in self defense (NCSL, 2020b). Over thirty states allow the "open carry" of handguns, with different degrees of exceptions. Anti-gun activists worry that more guns openly carried lead to a raw and representative violence and more homicides (Harvard, 2021b). Pro-gun advocates maintain the ability to self defense is itself a deterrent to violent crimes. While a causal link between higher gun ownership and higher homicide rates is hard to prove, recent research suggests a correlation between gun ownership and domestic violence, usually against women, but not more violence outside of the home (Mervosh, 2019).

Since November 1998, when background checks to purchase guns were mandated, the FBI has handled over 300 million checks. This does not equate to the total of guns bought, which can't be known because of private sales and gun show sales that do not require FBI approval. And, even with the checks, only 1.5 million applications have been rejected (FBI, 2021b). Significant reforms would have to come from within American society; the issue is much too hot and polarizing for politicians who must play to the pro- or anti-control bases—unless the Supreme Court were to emphasize the provision for regulation as a demand of the 2nd Amendment: "A well-regulated Militia, being necessary to the security of a free State, the right to bear Arms, shall not be infringed." Worldwide, only the US, Guatemala, and Mexico protect the right to bear arms (Weiss and Pasley, 2019) (Illustration 5.3).

Horrific shootings in 1999 in the high schools at Columbine in Colorado and Heritage in Georgia increased debate and triggered national mourning. Major incidents included the killing of five Amish girls in a Pennsylvania schoolhouse in 2006; the gunning down

Illustration 5.3 "I Don't Want to Die:" Students Protest Gun Violence

On April 20, 2018, like the Chicago students shown here, kids across the country left their desks to participate in National School Walkout Day. The march coincided with the nineteenth anniversary of the shocking Columbine High School Massacre in which nineteen died and also one month after the shootings in Parkland, Florida, left seventeen students dead and created a nationwide "March For Our Lives" day in which 3,300 protests were held nationwide. In every march, the students used clear language to confront the NRA and to encourage their parents and politicians to regulate firearms. But the shootings continued and firearms were not regulated. From 2018 to December 2021, Education Week recorded ninety-two school shootings (Edweek, 2021).

Source: Jim Young/Stringer via Getty Images

of thirty-two students at Virginia Tech University in 2007; and the killing of twenty six- and seven-year-old children and their teachers at Sandy Hook Elementary School in Newtown, Connecticut, just before Christmas 2012. Further public shootings tore people's feeling of safety and compassion, including: the Charleston Church shooting in 2015 claiming nine lives; the Orlando nightclub attack killing forty-nine; the Las Vegas shooting of fifty-eight in 2017; the Parkland, Florida, murder of seventeen in 2018; and the Robb Elementary School shooting of 21 in Uvalde, Texas, in 2022. Gun control advocates prayed that maybe the atrocities could bring reform, while gun advocates, the NRA, repeatedly opposed any bans, saying "The only thing that stops a bad guy with a gun is a good guy with a gun" (Overby, 2012).

In the school massacres, "average" white male students shocked the nation by killing teachers and other white students. The perpetrators in the Charleston and Las Vegas shootings were also white males. It is worth observing that if the killers had been black and the victims white, the response would have been quite different, with talk of criminality among young blacks rather than of the individual tragedies of both perpetrators and victims. It is a continuing feature of American society that whites are treated as individuals without blaming all whites, but blacks bear the onus of being blamed as a group for failures or crimes perpetrated by individuals. This same pattern of prejudice applies to Muslims, Mexicans, and others. The court system continues to hand out harsher penalties to black men than to whites who commit similar crimes as skin color, plea bargains, and higher-qualified lawyers reduce sentences for whites.

On November 20, 2020, Kyle Rittenhouse, who had shot two demonstrators in Kenosha, Wisconsin, in August, posted full bail of $2 million and was released from custody to a private ex-special forces security detail paid to protect him. Among others, money to spring Rittenhouse from custody and defend him was posted by the #Fightback organization, the National Association for Gun Rights, and American Wolf 689. One of Rittenhouse's attorneys, Lin Wood, called Rittenhouse a "political prisoner" (Guarino, 2020). #Fightback claims it fights "back for forgotten America ... ready to protect and defend the constitutional rights, livelihoods and property of people and businesses that are being targeted and destroyed" (Fightback, 2021). Many wondered whether Rittenhouse would have been offered $2 million bail, or could have afforded to post it, had he been born black.

The death penalty is disproportionately imposed against black Americans convicted of murder than against other groups. Perhaps not surprisingly, Figure 5.1, US Support for the Death Penalty, shows that African Americans, Democrats, and the highly educated are among the demographic groups least supportive of capital punishment, whereas Republicans and white evangelicals are most in favor. While more than half of Americans support the death penalty (54–55 percent), support has fallen dramatically from four out of five since 1994 (Gallup, 2021c). In 1998, the United Nations Commission on Human Rights charged that "race, ethnic origin and economic status appear to be key determinants of who will, and who will not, receive a sentence of death" in the United States (Olson, 1998). The key factor seems to be the race of the victim, not the race of the defendant. Over 75 percent of court-ordered executions involve a white victim, even though just 56 percent of victims are white (DPIC, 2021a). State governors have the authority to pardon anyone for any crime, but they rarely overturn judicial decisions supported by the electorate. US presidents can pardon prisoners held in federal prisons but cannot overrule state court decisions and executions.

The morality of capital punishment continues to be the subject of debate. In only one instance, *Furman v. Georgia* (1972), did the Supreme Court outlaw the death penalty by judging it "cruel and unusual punishment" prohibited by the Eighth Amendment. Four years later, in 1976, the Supreme Court reversed itself and some states began executing people again. As of October 2, 2020, 1,526 people had been put to death and there were

Contemporary United States

Table 5.5 Executions and Death Row Inmates, January 1, 1976–January 1, 2020

Category	Executed (2019)	Executed since 1976	On death row
Non-Hispanic White	14	853	1,102
African American	7	519	1,078
Hispanic/Latino	1	129	352
Asian	0	6	47
Native American	0	17	27
Other Race	0	3	1
Male	22	1,502	2,554
Female	0	16	53
Totals	22	1,518	2,607

Sources: DPIC (2019; 2021c; 2021d)

2,591 people on death row (Table 5.5). The average time spent awaiting execution is close to twenty years (DPIC, 2021e). Since 1973, more than 185 people on death row were released when new evidence proved their innocence (DPIC, 2021b). In a recent PEW poll, 63 percent of Americans said that capital punishment was "morally justified"; but many of these people still opposed it on the grounds that an innocent person may be wrongly executed (Oliphant, 2018).

In 2019, juries nationwide imposed thirty-four death sentences, compared with 279 in 1999, one of the lowest numbers since 1976 (DPIC, 2019). Also in 2019, the Supreme Court heard *Bucklew v. Precythe*, which centered on whether a painful execution was banned by the Constitution's "cruel and unusual" clause. Writing for the 5–4 majority, Trump-appointee Neal Gorsuch interpreted the clause as not guaranteeing a painless death for Bucklew, who had fatally shot his ex-girlfriend. Bucklew suffered a rare blood vessel disease which would cause unnecessary pain should death be administered by lethal injection (Savage, 2019). Gorsuch argued that the Bucklew's appeal attempted to delay the execution needlessly. The liberal minority on the bench led by Justice Steven Breyer maintained that the medicinal circumstances would make Bucklew's execution "excruciating and grotesque" and therefore broke the ban on "cruel and unusual" punishments (Liptak, 2019). Bucklew was executed on October 1, 2019.

Twenty-two states and the District of Columbia do not have a death penalty and three states have gubernatorial moratoria. Thirty-two states plus DC and the US military have not executed anyone since 2010 (DPIC, 2021d) and prefer "life sentences without the possibility of parole" as the ultimate punishment.

And yet, in the face of national trends, in April 2017, in the space of ten days, the state of Arkansas rushed to execute eight men—four black and four white—who might have to wait because of the looming expiration date and lack of future availability of a drug used for lethal injections. Arkansas had suspended executions since 2005 by gubernatorial moratorium, but when pharmaceutical companies began to prohibit the use of their drugs to induce death and when no other states would share or sell their own

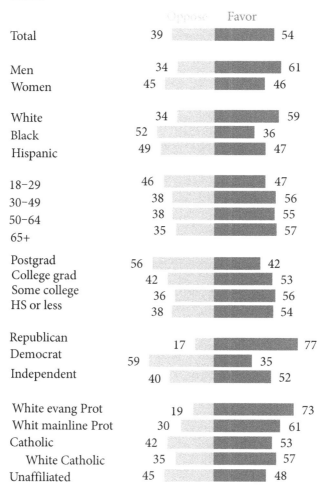

Figure 5.1 US Support for the Death Penalty, 2018
Source: Pew (2018b)

Contemporary United States

supplies, the Republican governor decided to execute the men (Haag and Fausset, 2017). The US Supreme Court stopped four of the executions on appeal; Arkansas executed three black men and one white man (AP, 2017).

To describe American society, the cohesion or culture wars in its midst, and the speed of change due to large-scale continuing immigration is a complex proposition. Inequities in race, gender, and class abound—the first two categories moving toward more equal treatment, and the latter category widening the distance between the richest and the poorest citizens. New immigrant groups continue to arrive and, in their transition to American society, force compromises and new understandings that reinvigorate contemporary society. The institutions of education and religion are highly significant portions of the story, as are the social programs put in place by government to provide for the general welfare of the citizenry. A real understanding of the workings of society depends upon acknowledgment of the power of the overarching culture. These discussions continue in the following chapters.

Further Reading

Alexander, M. (2020) *The New Jim Crow: Mass Incarceration in the Age of Colorblindness*, New York: New Press.

Coates, T. (2015) *Between the World and Me*, New York: Spiegel & Grau.

Gordon, R. (2016) *The Rise and Fall of American Growth: The US Standard of Living since the Civil War*, Princeton: Princeton University Press.

Hinton, E. (2021) *America on Fire: The Untold History of Police Violence and Black Rebellion since the 1960s*, New York: Liveright.

Packer, G. (2021) *Last Best Hope: America in Crisis and Renewal*, New York: Farrar, Straus, & Giroux.

Putnam, R. (2015) *Our Kids: The American Dream in Crisis*, New York: Simon & Schuster.

Reeves, R. (2017) *The Dream Hoarders: How the American Upper Middle Class Is Leaving Everyone Else in the Dust, Why That's a Problem, and What to Do about It*, Washington DC: Brookings.

Wright, E. and J. Rogers (2015) *American Society: How It Really Works*, London: W. W. Norton.

CHAPTER 6
RELIGION, EDUCATION, AND SOCIAL POLICY

Before Covid-19, the USA had "The greatest economy in the history of our country." At least, that's what Donald Trump claimed. By many economic measures he was right, in that the booming economy lifted salaries for most workers and reduced unemployment across most demographic groups (Casselman, 2019). In a way, Trump was echoing a comment made by Barack Obama in 2016. Obama said: "If you had to choose any time in the course of human history to be alive, you'd choose this one. Right here in America, right now" (Obama, 2016a). Crime, poverty, and teen pregnancies were down; education and workforce participation rates for women and minorities were up. Trump's statement measured material progress whereas Obama saw both economic and social progress, but both played to an American theme of improvement and expectations that material, social, and spiritual progress would continue. In office, Biden wanted to convince Americans that good times could return, despite the Covid era.

There are pronounced differences in how recent presidents have seen civil society, the "soft" voluntary center of life sandwiched between the worlds of work and politics, comprising religion, schooling and social policy. The roots of civil society are often local— the church you attend, the school your kids go to, and the people who promote social welfare through locally delivered governmental and voluntary systems. Often the three are intertwined, such as with food drives in schools, food banks run by churches, and through secular organizations strengthening local communities where help is needed. Biden manifestly believes in government as a force for good in society, where the federal government provides policies and services that individuals and states cannot, such as protective gear provision, a national mask policy, and aid to state and local governments. Biden also knew about limits. In the effort to combat Covid in November 2020, he argued that "the federal government can't do this alone. Each of us has a responsibility in our own lives, to do what we can do to slow the virus." Put differently, governments act with the consent of the people. Americans needed to accept that the Covid crisis touched everyone and required all Americans to accept social distancing and mask wearing to help the nation to overcome the crisis.

Trump's approach was different. The 45th president believed that for ordinary Americans, Covid decisions—to wear a mask or to isolate—were best made by the people themselves. Yet in many other ways Trump's policies to "Make America Great Again" presupposed decisive, certainly paternal, and likely authoritarian direction. Trump claimed that crime was increasing, faith and education systems had broken

Contemporary United States

down, and that programs like Obamacare strangled the free market. Trump believed that less government in the spheres of religion, education, and social policy would benefit the nation more effectively, but he often undermined his ability to be an effective leader by lowering staffing numbers. For example, he distrusted the State Department because of his suspicion of the bureaucracy (Gramer, 2019). Beyond Trump's policy positions, his rhetoric bore distinct traces of apocalypticism, where "I alone can fix it."

Biden's victory contained a significant "business as usual" component, building a bridge back to the last "normal" administration. Unlike Hillary Clinton four years earlier, Biden did not need to challenge the Obama legacy. Trump's term in office made the election more about Trump than a "third" Obama term. But once Biden won, his early cabinet picks of Obama-era alumni and Biden's executive order to effect instant, visible change fueled accusations of a restoration of the Obama era. Examples of policy priorities included: refunding the World Health Organization, rescinding the Muslim ban, rolling-back environmental deregulations, working on DACA, reintroducing protections for transgender students, rejoining the Paris climate accord, and "normalizing" foreign relations (Stalley, Ossola, Palmer, Bain, Epstein, and Campoy, 2020). This politics-as-usual claim would be contested in the 2022 midterms. Even before Biden's inauguration, 2024 Republican presidential hopefuls Marco Rubio fed anti-establishment sentiment tweeting "I have no interest in returning to the 'normal' that left us dependent on China" (Mascaro and Daly, 2020). Obamaian (Obama/Biden) and Trumpian (Trump/Rubio) continuities and changes (Trump/ Biden) are easy to see.

Religion

The American experience displays an uneasy tension between individual advancement and a belief in equality. Religion, education, and government services are marked by this tension, and each of these institutions helps to reconcile personal success and failure with ideas of the work ethic. In the United States, secular and religious faiths remain strong, and often clash. For the last generation religion has played out on the political stage, with abortion, medical research, and ethics debates prominent in elections and policy formulation.

Trump's appointment of a pro-life conservative Christian, Amy Coney Barrett, to the Supreme Court in October 2020 accentuated religion as an issue in the election that year. Religious Republicans praised the conservative turn of the federal courts resulting from Trump's appointments, whereas Democrats wished to ensure that Trump's judicial revolution would not continue into a second term. Voters were enthusiastic on both sides, a factor in the high turnout levels recorded in Chapter 4. Religion is more than a matter of worship. In many districts, faith-supported schools offer an alternative to public schools. Religion, education, and social policy provide avenues by which Americans maintain their faith in uplift, advancement, individualism, and equality

Religious Freedom

The United States is both remarkably religious and remarkably secular. The country's semi-official motto "In God We Trust" is located on every piece of currency, and the Pledge of Allegiance has long included the words "One Nation, Under God." The United States military employs chaplains and builds churches on military bases. Religious groups are supported by having tax-exempt status. All of this clashes with the historical American rejection of an established religion, as does the continuing tradition of lighting a Christmas tree on the White House lawn even though Congress cannot sanction any religious holiday.

Religion has always found fertile soil in the United States, from Native American shamanism to Euro-American myths of providential foundings in a New Eden and manifest destinies to subdue the earth. The concurrent timing of the Protestant Reformation and the discovery of the New World compounded matters. While the Puritans and Pilgrims in Massachusetts, Anglicans in Virginia and Georgia, Jesuits in California, Mormons in Utah experimented at different times with official government-established religions, American history is punctuated by religious diversity and freedom. The mixture of large numbers of believers of different faiths has demanded tolerance and helped persuade the Founders to state in the First Amendment: "Congress shall make no law respecting an establishment of religion, or prohibiting the free exercise thereof."

The First Amendment dampens ethno-religious conflicts, even if it has caused a two-centuries-long struggle over the use of the Bible in public institutions. In fact, the First Amendment seems to want it both ways, allowing neither the establishment of nor interference with religion. This ambivalence has proven successful in that both government and religion have prospered by being independent of each other. After all, the political views of religious people vary. To establish a religion in a country of immigrants would endanger the survival of the nation while simultaneously making for "bad religion"—too formal, authoritarian, and undemocratic. Americans associate churches with community spirit and self-help, and they want to keep them free from the European associations with oppressive, established classes, state churches, and governments.

Religious infighting still occurs within the United States. The arrival of each group of immigrants whose faith is new to the towns or regions in which they settle often results in fear and hostility among people already settled. Catholics, Jews, Transcendentalists, Amish, Shakers, Quakers, Muslims, black Muslims, Buddhists, Mormons, Jehovah's Witnesses, Pentecostals, Fundamentalists, Moonies, Christian Scientists, Scientologists, Branch Davidians, and others have been treated with suspicion, ridicule, and violence. Since the late 1960s, theologians have noted the extraordinary rise of what they call the New Religious Movement connecting with a "Fourth Awakening," which is a creation of faiths even more diverse than before. Associated trends include "New Age" spirituality, which influences the religious and secular alike (Gecewitz, 2018). With hundreds of denominations active in the United States, it might be difficult to imagine more diversity.

Contemporary United States

Historically, Americans have practiced a "quiet faith," are non-judgmental and acknowledge the fundamental right of all individuals to believe in the god of their choice, as long as they abide by the law (Wolfe, 1999: 39). This is a classic Enlightenment view of tolerance and non-interference in the lifestyles of other people. Open religious prejudice is rare as Americans have faith in faith, and believe that regardless of doctrine, good people are rewarded and do not go to hell. In one 2015 poll, two-thirds of believers held that a belief in any religion could lead to eternal life. Nearly 40 percent of Americans believe that even atheists could go to heaven (Pew, 2015a, 2021a) Religion is laissez-faire and is discussed in everyday conversation, in greater or lesser amounts according to the community and region in which a person resides. Writer David Brooks says that Americans seek a "flexidoxy," which he defines as "the hybrid mixture of freedom and flexibility on the one hand and the longing for rigor and orthodoxy on the other" (Dionne, 2008). When polled, 89 percent of those asked say that they believe in God or a universal spirit (Hrynowski, 2018), 61 percent believe in the devil, and 64 percent in hell. Nearly three-quarters of Americans (71 percent) believe in heaven, angels (72 percent), and miracles (NPR, 2010; Newport, 2016). This is clearly a part of American optimism. A growing proportion, about one-quarter of Americans, are "Nones"—atheists, agnostics, or unaffiliated to any specific church or group (Pew, 2019a) and many more practice their faiths in private. Atheists and agnostics are not discriminated against, though it is hard to imagine a successful presidential candidate who does not profess faith.

Most Americans believe in a personal God who performs daily miracles. Americans believe more or less equally in the virgin birth of Jesus (66 percent) and in the creation of the world by God or via divine intervention. A third of Americans (33 percent) believe in evolution alone (Pew, 2015a). Forty-five percent attend church at least once a month (Pew, 2019a). Twenty-eight percent say that God speaks directly to them (Pew, 2018c) and nearly half (49 percent) pray at least once a day (Diamant, 2019), with around 20 percent of Christians uttering unintelligible language—called "speaking in tongues" (Pew, 2015b). Often, prayers ask for good grades, a higher salary, a nice boyfriend, or a victory in the ice-hockey game. Concurring with Alan Wolfe, Americans are believers, but accept that there may be many paths to an eternal paradise.

Main Religious Groups

In 2020, Protestant denominations were in a generation-long decline, fragmented into thousands of congregations, and, at 43 percent, had lost majority status (see Table 6.1) (Pew, 2019a). Claiming one in five Americans, the Catholic Church is the largest single religious group with its membership augmented by predominantly Catholic Latino immigration. Christopher Columbus brought Catholicism with him to the New World in 1492 and Jesuits soon worked across the continent. The colony of Maryland was established as a refuge for French Catholics, and large numbers of Irish Catholics poured into east coast cities after the potato famine in the 1840s. A larger, and different, group came during the massive influx of the 1880s–1920s. Some Protestants formed into xenophobic, nativist groups, and they used mob violence and rioting to protest against

Religion, Education, and Social Policy

Table 6.1 American Religiosity—Adults (2019)

Affiliation	% of American adults
Protestant	43.0
Evangelical	25.0
Mainline	18.0
Historically Black Protestant	6.5
Catholic	20.0
Mormon	2.0
Jewish	2.0
Muslim	1.0
Buddhist	1.0
Hindu	1.0
Other non-Christian	3.0
Agnostic	5.0
Atheist	4.0
Nothing in particular, "Nones"	17.0

Sources: Pew (2015a, 2019a)

the culture of the newcomers and their cheap labor. These conflicts between Catholics and Protestants largely disappeared from America after the Second World War, and certainly stopped after the election of John F. Kennedy to the presidency in 1960. Many American Catholics practice birth control, many have divorced, and some churches have asked that priests be allowed to marry and that women be elevated to the priesthood; others are more traditional in their beliefs and follow the lead of the Vatican. In 2020, Joe Biden became the second Catholic president (after Kennedy). Kamala Harris was brought up in black Protestant and Hindi traditions. Her husband is Jewish. Donald Trump was raised as a Presbyterian, Mike Pence as a Catholic, and Hillary Clinton as a Methodist.

Upwards of 167 million adult Americans are Christians, divided among denominations and thousands of self-identified congregations. Nearly 80 percent of African Americans adhere to Protestant denominations (Masci, Mohamed, and Smith, 2018). Two of the largest groups, Baptists and Methodists, spread rapidly among the lower and middle classes during the Great Revival of the 1830s. The evangelical message of appealing directly to an all-powerful God soon translated into an anti-authoritarian individualism that bypassed clergy, government officials, and the upper classes. In modern America, Baptists and Methodists divide into approximately 250,000 local congregations worshipping in various ways according to history, ethnicity, race, class, or particular preacher. Even with the gains in equality and societal acceptance by minority groups, American churches are, with a few exceptions, not multiracial. In 1963, Martin Luther King, Jr., said that 11 a.m. Sunday morning was the most segregated hour in America. In 2022, this is still overwhelmingly true.

185

Contemporary United States

Founded in 1830, the Church of Jesus Christ of Latter Day Saints—commonly called the Mormon Church—is the largest indigenous religious group in America. Its early attempts to establish a religious government in Utah, as well as the widespread practice of polygamy, confronted the First Amendment's ideas of religious pluralism, separation of church and state, and the common belief in sanctity of the family, defined as one husband, one wife. The result was long years of religious persecution with congressional and constitutional insistence that Utah be free of church control. By 1890, Mormon leaders agreed officially to stop polygamy, even though unsanctioned plural weddings continue in contemporary America. In 2019, there were over 6.5 million Mormons in the United States—primarily in Utah and surrounding states (Pew, 2019a). Mormons are well represented in Congress, with six Mormon Representatives and three Senators in 2021 (CRS, 2021b).

There are approximately six million American Jews divided into Orthodox, Conservative, or Reform groups, with most feeling solidarity with Israel and a common history of persecution both within and without the United States. Most Jews came to America from Germany (1820–1880) and Russia or Poland (around 1900). Emigration also ticked up after the fall of the Soviet Union. Jewish scientists and intellectuals, including Albert Einstein in 1933, immigrated in the 1930s and 1940s. Supporting one another and pursuing education as the way to success, American Jews have risen economically and politically to become the most influential Jewish group in the world. They enter the professions in large numbers and are leaders in obtaining doctorates and teaching positions in American universities. Additionally, in rural areas, where evangelism is strongest, the population is strongly pro-Israel and a large number of Protestant ministers have made pilgrimages to Jerusalem.

In recent decades Orthodox views have become more pronounced, not least as intermarriage by Reform (liberal) Jews to Christians is common—potentially reducing the size of the Reform community. Jewish Americans are often politically prominent. Well-funded political action committees affect foreign policy—as do the twenty-five US congressional seats and the nine Senate seats held by Jews in 2019. The 2021 Senate includes twenty-four Catholics, fifty-eight Protestants, the three Mormons recorded above, one Buddhist, and three senators who did not specify their faith (CRS, 2021b).

Islam has grown from having 52 mosques in 1945 to over 2,100 mosques in 2018 and approximately 235 schools in 2016 (Thurston, 2016; Fadel, 2018). In 2018, estimates suggested that the Muslim population in the United States was probably around 3.5 million people, though more may be undercounted by the statistics (Fadel, 2018). Even though over half of adult Muslims are first-generation immigrants (58 percent), they are highly assimilated and support integration into the larger society, rather than separating themselves (Pew, 2018d).

The origins of American Muslims are fairly equally divided between African Americans, South Asians, and those from the Middle East. Over 90 percent say they are proud to be Americans and Muslims (Pew, 2018d). The majority of Muslims are Sunnis and nearly nine in ten Muslims are traditionalists of whom 96 percent believe in "One God, Allah." Two-thirds of American Muslims say religion is very important in their lives. Muslims are not more religious than other Americans, with similar proportions considering religion important and slightly fewer attending mosques weekly than Christian churchgoers do (Lipka, 2017; Pew, 2018d). A majority of Muslims say that since 9/11 it has been more difficult for them because of prejudices, being seen as part of al-Qaeda, general ignorance about Islam, stereotyping, and increased religious profiling by government agencies. Yet, just under 80 percent are overwhelmingly satisfied with their lives in the US (Pew, 2018d).

It might still be too soon to sift through how Trump's presidency affected life satisfaction and created a perception of prejudice towards Muslims, but actions such as the 2017 Muslim bans on travel from seven named countries and long legal battles scapegoated Muslims. In 2021, three Muslims hold congressional seats, including Ilhan Omar who openly called Trump a "racist xenophobic" in 2020 (Stracqualursi, 2020).

Another indigenous religion, the Native American Church, has about 250,000 members in 100 branches. This church blends Christianity with the use of peyote cactus—which contains the hallucinogen mescaline—in worship services. In 1990, the Supreme Court ruled that states could prohibit the use of peyote, but twenty-eight states have allowed the practice to continue, in private. In 1978, Congress passed the Religious Freedom Act to allow Indians to use sacred tribal places on public land. Most American Indians are Christians wholly, or have combined Jesus with traditional spiritualism of prayers, dancing, and singing. Native spirituality and environmentalism often combine, as exemplified in the 2016–2017 Standing Rock protests against the oil pipeline threatening native lands.

Revivalism

Periodically, America has experienced widespread evangelical movements which turn people back to God. Grounded in the core claim of Christianity that God sent his only Son to redeem the sins of the world, these "liberation" revivals occur during times of large-scale immigration, fears of war, or economic uncertainties. The First Great Awakening, in the 1730s, witnessed the arrival of Methodist Reverend George Whitefield who preached up and down the colonies. His oratorical power made hell so vivid that some listeners searched for it on an atlas. Whitefield helped bind the colonists together and his message of salvation made a substantial contribution to inciting the American Revolution. The Second Great Awakening, in the 1830s, lit a religious fire that thrust thousands into Baptist and Methodist churches and formed others into groups to end slavery, set up communes, or join Mormon, Shaker, or Seventh Day Adventist churches. A third great revival, in the 1920s, pitted the traditional agricultural and white nineteenth-century values of creationism against the industrial, urban, multicultural twentieth century and its embrace of the theory of evolution. This debate between fundamentalism and modernity played out spectacularly in the 1925 Scopes Monkey Trial, when a young teacher was jailed for teaching the scientific theories of Charles Darwin.

For the last generation, America has been in the midst of a fourth great revival, which arose from the anxiety over contemporary themes of multiculturalism, feminism,

Contemporary United States

post-modernism, terrorist threats, nationalist movements, and globalization (Fogel, 2000; Jenkins, 2002; Hartman, 2015). Some of the thrust for the revival is explained through generational theory, which maintains that children of the 1960s generation rebelled against their parents by becoming more conservative. This generation, in turn, faces an individualistic turn from Millennials. The new revival also benefits from the ending of the Cold War and the gradual fading of the memory of a bipolar world, when the Soviet Union, six-decade-long arch-enemy of the United States disappeared suddenly, leaving Americans to renew their focus on an older enemy, Satan. George W. Bush's division of the world into good and evil fueled his political support by attracting religious conservatives to vote for him; this became an important aspect of domestic and foreign policy agendas. Manichaean worldviews won more ground on the Right, certainly after 2001, and again during the 2016 election campaign as Right-wing populism flared up.

Simultaneously, there is a "New Atheism" rising and using the lessons of evangelical "born-again" activities. These new atheists also link themselves with "Nones," in that both groups are spiritual and highly secular liberals. New Atheists even rent churches for their lectures, and a few traditional churches have hired New Atheist ministers as well. Liberal believers have also started to network in order to increase their political heft and advance progressive causes (Bush, 2019).

Nationalist Republicans were substantially more concerned by radical Islamic terror than were liberal Democrats, explaining why many Republicans supported the Muslim travel ban. Incidents like the shocking terrorist attacks in Bataclan, Paris, in November 2015 turbocharged Trump's primary campaign. Trump's "America First" universe, built on fear of a host of threatening "others," appealed to many—as his 74 million 2020 votes attested. While in office, Trump delivered on issues the religious Right considered important, such as by appointing over 200 conservatives to the federal judiciary and installing three new Supreme Court justices. Religious conservatives supported Trump in return for future influence in the courts, which Trump had promised to transform (Shubber, 2020). The conservative turn of the Supreme Court was underlined by Court's decisions of 2022 (see page 130).

Abortion presents a pre-eminent example of clashes over absolute values and has fed into the "culture" and "religion" wars since the 1973 *Roe* decision enabled abortion. Liberals and non-believers tend to accept the right of a woman to choose whether to bring an embryo to term; most socially conservative Christians insist on the sanctity of life from conception. Pregnancy is seen as an expression of God's will—regardless of the reasons for the pregnancy. The 2017 confirmation of Justice Neil Gorsuch, 2018 confirmation of Brett Kavanaugh, and 2020 confirmation of Amy Coney Barrett to the Supreme Court resulted in the overturning of the right to abortion.

Religion has long been a part of American pop culture, placed prominently on display in a century of Hollywood film and literature. Christian fiction has its own listing on Amazon, with popular titles selling in excess of one million copies, following in the footsteps of blockbuster authors such as Tim LaHaye. The 2018 film *I Can Only Imagine* directed by the Erwin bothers grossed $83 million in the US and Canada. Glossy, media-savvy Christianity in the form of Mel Gibson's blockbuster film *The Passion of the Christ*

(2004) grossed over \$370 million domestically. The religious entertainment market is well-developed and profitable, catering to a clientele that range in faith from liberal to fundamental.

The Fourth Awakening is led by dedicated evangelical Protestants who put God up front in their lives. In 2019, well over half of all Protestants and a quarter of the total American population defined themselves as evangelicals (Pew, 2019a). Revivals have been held in America since the 1730s to bring sinners back to Christ. It must be noted that fundamentalists—those who believe in the literal truth of the Bible—are not in the majority among evangelical groups, who run the gamut between extreme liberalism and radical conservatism. Pentecostal groups—formerly known as "holy rollers" for their habit of speaking in tongues and belief that some people are blessed by God with the ability to heal—have gained adherents over the last generation, especially among Hispanics. Pentecostals are famous for tent revivals in which the lame are made to walk again through faith healings.

Perhaps the greatest gap between the US and other developed nations is over American faith in an active God. Religion remains one of the main ways by which Americans have tried to retain their balance. Many Christian groups are promoting a return to "Ten Commandment morality" and have exploited the war on terrorism to push their conservative agendas of putting prayer back into the schools and expanding the role of religion in the public sphere. As various court decisions and government programs –such as Obamacare—continue to blur the line separating an expansive role for churches and a circumscribed state, liberals hope that the nation's secular faith in the Constitution will ultimately prevail. Biden has written that he believes in equality before God and in a divine imperative to serve the community in a pursuit of religious and secular improvement, for example by helping the poor. Biden has clearly grappled with the notion of faith in adversity, not least in the loss of his first wife and two of his children. His faith forms a cornerstone in his private and public lives (Biden, 2020).

Religion's foray into the political realm is the most controversial contemporary aspect of religion. This is not new, even if it has been discouraged by the constitutional separation of church and state, and by the common assent of most Americans. How people see themselves in relation to the cosmos will clearly affect their deepest attitudes and, ultimately, their political views. Martin Luther King, Jr. liked to say, "God isn't going to do all of it by Himself" (quoted in Dionne and Dilulio, 2000). King understood the complex balance of individual and collective responsibilities in a liberal society, and the interplay between individual freedoms and social order.

Since the election of Jimmy Carter in 1976, presidents have increasingly invoked religious sentiments, thereby setting aside the taboo of keeping religion out of politics. Bill Clinton repeatedly employed biblical language; George W. Bush spontaneously referred to his deep religious beliefs; and Barack Obama linked faith with policy. Capturing the votes of four out of five white evangelical voters, Trump's actions in the courts, in moving the US Embassy to Jerusalem, and in addressing March-for-Life protesteors spoke louder than any public expression of religious sentiment (Gjelten, 2020; Jenkins, 2020). Trump called himself a "non-denominational Christian" (Garger, 2020).

Contemporary United States

A present controversy is over conservative usurpation of liberal methods. Protestant and Catholic conservative Christians, reacting to the social upheavals of the 1960s and the anxiety of a globalizing and uncertain world, have created an interfaith cooperative under the general idea of social action by a Christian Right. Conservatives joined with fundamentalists in a small-government, big-faith alliance to elect politicians more favorable to banning abortion, to allow prayer and the teaching of creationism in public schools, to make it unconstitutional to burn the American flag, to return power to the states by reducing federal taxes, and to get the government out of the welfare business. Christian activists worked to link evangelicals to politics and voting (Illustration 6.1). And the National Prayer Breakfasts held yearly meetings which connect religious leaders with sitting presidents, for example as President Trump did in February 2020.

Illustration 6.1 A National Day of Prayer: Trump, Pence, and Evangelicals

On September 1, 2017, President Trump declared the following Sunday a day of prayer for the victims of Hurricane Harvey, a superstorm which claimed 100 lives in Texas and Louisiana. In this image, Trump receives a benediction from faith leaders while Vice President Mike Pence prays to his right. Evangelicals could ignore Trump's moral failings as his three Supreme Court appointees delivered a solid conservative majority on that body and the prospect of restricting or removing abortion rights. Moreover, there is a growing "dominionism" or "divine sanction of authoritarian methods" in the Trump wing of the Republican Party. These evangelicals believe that God requires believers to assert a "Christian nationalism" over family, religion, education, economic matters, arts and culture, media, and governments (Edsall, 2021; McCrummen, 2021).

Source: Alex Wong via Getty Images

Religion, Education, and Social Policy

Trump's takeover of the Republican Party and capture of the White House by mobilizing a populist coalition did not reduce the influence of religious and cultural conservatives, even as it certainly did see a weakening of economic conservatives. Just as religion is often largely a local matter decided by local congregations, so is social policy—which is often decided by states and local communities in referenda. Election Day 2020 saw voters approve 88 of 120 state ballot issues in thirty-two states, including measures on election policy, tax policy, and the reintroduction of wolves, amongst others. Four more states approved the use of recreational marijuana (Arizona, Montana, New Jersey, and South Dakota), bringing the national total to eleven. Medicinal marijuana is legal in thirty-four states (Ballotpedia, 2021b). By 2015, thirty-seven states had approved same-sex marriage, contributing to the Supreme Court ruling in favor, in *Obergefell v. Hodges* (2015). In 2022, the Roberts Court proposed to renew that decision.

A Portable Civil Society

The United States has both a highly educated citizenry and a heavy emphasis on religion; this has been the case for a century. Some argue that the more technologically advanced a country becomes, the more religion is downgraded. This secularization thesis suggests that religion fades as modernization and globalization expand. Other observers suggest that the more complex and abstract life becomes, the greater the need for religion even as the form religion takes may change. In contemporary America, religion is a growth industry, adapting, crossing denominational boundaries, and expanding. The country oozes religion: nearly nine out of ten Americans believe in God; nearly two in three believe in God with absolute certainty (Hrynowski, 2019). There are nearly 500,000 physical churches, temples, mosques, or gathering sites. Billboards and church locations can be seen along major interstates and in city shopfronts. Street corner preachers, handbills attached to trees and radio and television programs spread the good news or apocalyptic prophecy to anyone who listens, reads, or tunes in.

The megachurches, where from 2,000 to 40,000 members convene every weekend and thousands more are actively involved during the week, have grown from 700 congregations in 2003 to more than 1,500 in 2018 (Fieldstadt, 2018). Some megachurches offer radio and television ministries, and preachers reach many more people through podcasts. The churches encourage religion, rootedness, and convenience where people can live lives around church activities on a "24/7" basis—open all day, every day. These fellowships vary between evangelical, denominational, and independent, entrepreneurial, market driven non-denominational entities. They are mostly middle-class. Lakewood Church in Houston, Texas, welcomes around 40,000 or so worshippers a week in a church adapted to the Covid era with the installation of "touchless faucets, touchless soap dispensers and touchless flush valves." Lakewood offers shuttle busing in normal times from its huge car parking facilities, childcare, life training courses, dance classes, charity work, singles classes, and biblical financial tuition (Lakewood, 2021)

Other megachurches offer up to eighty different activities each evening, including groups involved in Bible study, legal clinics, basketball games, financial planning, marriage

Contemporary United States

counseling, drug recovery support groups, and teenage dance parties. Conveniences include on-property or in-church McDonald's, credit unions, schools, daycare, AIDS clinics, language courses, sports facilities, fitness centers, libraries, food courts, movie theaters—basically, self-contained small towns. While convenient, scholars warn that megachurches can become isolated "gated communities" of like-minded people who lose touch with the wider community. To be successful, these ambitious "big-box" chains of megachurches must raid the smaller churches for believers. Many small churches relocate or close.

Instead of holding to dogmatic beliefs, Americans often change denominations, explaining this faith hopping as a spiritual journey toward individual fulfilment. One in three Americans has changed faiths—and well over 40 percent of all Protestants had switched to another denomination (mostly to either evangelicalism or to being unattached) (Pew, 2015a). This is populist, not hierarchical, and is marked by "privatism." Religion provides a portable civil society for a mobile nation. Because there is little direct state support for US churches—except for the benefit of tax breaks for non-profit groups, money for schoolbooks to church-sponsored schools and some funding to "faith-based initiatives" aimed at welfare support for the poor—religion is supported via private donations. Churches need a competitive product and they must promote it successfully to attract money. Many churches and individual preachers have expanded their congregations by live-streaming, television and radio ministries, or online cyber-sites which appeal to those who are sick, or find it too difficult to travel, or who want to "attend" more services every week. Religious Americans can tune in to online services. When Americans move, they seek out new churches, explore the market, and make choices based upon convenience, class, race, preaching style, beauty of the church structure, childcare, sports leagues, and position on conservative or liberal issues. For example, after winning the 2008 election and moving from Chicago to Washington, DC, the Obamas naturally "shopped" around before they committed to a congregation that suited them. The Obama family's example helps describe religious pluralism in America, the ever-expanding numbers of churches, and the competitive business of American religion.

Polls consistently find that churches are as social and secular as they are religious. Churches succeed in getting up to half of all Americans to work two to three hours every week in volunteer service to the community. In a nation that believes in private—not public—sector responsibility for social problems, churches are vitally important civil society institutions doing jobs that business and the government do not. They distribute free food and clothing services to the poor, house the homeless, care for the sick, set up daycare facilities for children of working mothers, and reach out internationally to victims of natural disasters or wars—such as sending shoes, eyeglasses, and money to Ukrainians displaced and suffering from the Russian invasion in 2022. So, while many academics have seen religion as irrational, primitive, or superstitious, Americans continue to join churches for spiritual, social, and practical reasons. Bigger churches offer more services, factors which some worshippers take into account when they move to new areas such as the rapidly expanding south and west where megachurches have proliferated.

Education

Colleges and Universities

In 1944, Swedish sociologist Gunnar Myrdal identified the essence of the American belief in advancement, remarking that education had "been the major hope for improving the individual and society" (Blanck, 2002). It is a fundamental part of the American dream and a part of the social compact idea that democracies require educated citizens. American education developed from European traditions, centered originally in families, and entered the public sphere when Puritans established the first community and Church-related schools just after arriving in the New World. Religious piety required adherents to know God by reading the Bible. By the American Revolution, every colony had public and private schools and there were nine universities, with a total of 731 students: Harvard (Puritan Congregational, 1636), William and Mary (Anglican, 1693), Yale (Puritan Congregational, 1701), Princeton (Presbyterian, 1746), University of Pennsylvania (non-sectarian, 1751), Columbia (Anglican, 1754), Brown (Baptist, 1764), Rutgers (Dutch Reformed, 1766), and Dartmouth (Congregational, 1769). America's university system is one of its greatest achievements and soft power assets.

After the Revolution, Americans developed a more nationalistic syllabus for students—this was done privately and was neither sanctioned by law, nor mandatory—with texts emphasizing constitutional freedoms and the sacrifices of heroes such as George Washington, Thomas Jefferson, and Benjamin Franklin. Students continued to study Greek and Latin, and primarily read British literature. Noah Webster compiled an American dictionary to stress differences in spelling and pronunciations from British English. He sold his product with a promotion that "NOW is the time, and *this* the country … Let us then seize the moment and establish a national language, as well as a national government" (Webster, 1789). American leaders insisted that girls receive a thorough primary education so that they could fulfill their roles as "republican mothers" to the new nation. It was widely hoped that education would ease social tensions and provide upward mobility and equal opportunities for all free, white Americans in the marketplace.

Teaching expanded quickly in the North, but public schools in the South and West were not generally available until around 1900. African Americans and American Indians were widely deprived of anything beyond elementary education, apart from a few missionary schools. With large-scale immigration around 1900, public schools expanded as a way to rid immigrants of foreign influences, and to assimilate and integrate them into Americans. The number of universities grew remarkably from 119 in 1850 to 356 in 1876, the year Johns Hopkins University became the first college to insist that research and graduate classes take precedence over undergraduate teaching. In contrast to all other nations, America educated the masses. This unparalleled commitment to education gave rise to American power and has provided a gigantic global advantage in favor of the United States. Today, many worry that the source of American greatness is in danger as its school system declines. Observers note that meritocratic social mobility through education is harder today than two generations ago (Putnam, 2015). At the same time, economic globalization makes technological prowess and human skills more valuable than ever, in a global competition for well-paid work.

Contemporary America has roughly 2,800 universities which grant bachelor or higher degrees. There are around 20 million enrolled students and around 1.5 million faculty members (NCES, 2019b). In 2017, the federal government funded higher education to the tune of $75 billion; states added another $87 billion (Pew, 2019b). State-supported colleges were established immediately after the Revolution, with the University of Georgia (1785) and the University of North Carolina (1789) leading the way. Today, every state has at least one central four-year university and most states have a university system with many campuses. There are about 1,500 two-year public community colleges, often called "junior colleges" with the states providing more funding than any other single source. In 2019–2020, the average annual tuition fee was $3,730 (NCES, 2019b).

Community colleges provide education for the 11.8 million students who cannot afford the higher costs of four-year institutions, who are generally older (the average age in 2020 was twenty-eight), who have responsibilities of children or work, or who seek to improve their academic credentials in hopes of being admitted to a university (AACC, 2021). Students successfully completing the requirements at community colleges are granted an Associate degree. More than two-thirds received some aid towards their courses. Additionally, since the 1960s, vocational-training colleges have been established to provide skills to students in specific occupations, or to provide English language classes to immigrants. This public system operates alongside and in competition with the large number of private universities and colleges.

Overall, the system is market-driven, decentralized, and pluralistic, providing opportunities for students of different abilities, income levels, family responsibilities, and goals. Enrolment has skyrocketed from 3 percent of college-age students attending in 1890, to 25 percent in 1950, to around 65 percent in 2020. The largest increase came after the Second World War, when the US government's G. I. Bill (1944) offered subsidies to veterans who wanted to obtain college degrees. The Cold War increased the need for scientists and specialists, and Congress passed the National Defense Education Act of 1958, which linked the nation's security to the brain power and skills of university students.

With globalization and the compelling need to absorb, process, and combine information, education is vital. Universities are clearly the gatekeepers to the most lucrative jobs and occupational mobility. Much of the income division in America stems from how much or how little education an individual has obtained (Figure 6.1). In the 1960s, college attendance doubled as the baby boom generation reached eighteen years of age. The African American, Chicano, and American Indian Civil Rights Movements, the Feminist Movement, and the deferment granted from the war in Vietnam for active students, further expanded enrolments. As more students experienced equal access to universities, the attitude toward higher education changed from being seen as a privilege to being claimed as an equal right. In 2020, around 88 percent of Americans had a high school diploma, and more than 60 percent of all Americans over twenty-five had

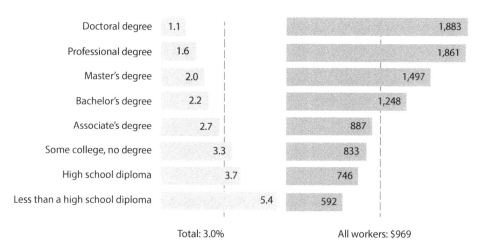

Figure 6.1 Education, Unemployment, and Salaries 2019
Source: BLS (2021h)

attended some college or taken some college courses or more. Approximately a third of the population have completed a bachelors' degree or better. Asian Americans top the category: 54 percent had university degrees as compared with 35 percent for whites, 21 percent for blacks and 15 percent for Hispanics (NCES, 2019b). These numbers are likely to grow if the trend for states to offer tuition free teaching continues (Dickler, 2019). Women accounted for 57 percent of bachelor degrees, 59 percent of master's degrees, and 53 percent of doctoral degrees in 2013–2014 (NCES, 2018).

Universities compete for students and students compete for acceptance into universities. Most American students take a standardized Scholastic Achievement Test (SAT) and/or American College Test (ACT) to determine their competitiveness against all students graduating from high school in a given year. Prestigious private universities accept under 10 percent of all applicants, while some state and private colleges have an open admissions policy (US News, 2020). Even at most public four-year universities, less than 50 percent of the applicants are admitted. Those rejected must apply elsewhere or go directly into the labor market, mostly at minimum wage. About 65 percent of all students enroll in public colleges.

Since the 1960s, universities have been sensitive to past discrimination, diversity, and minority needs, and have selected students based upon Affirmative Action policies in relation to race, gender, and class. Supposedly, fairness to minorities and academic achievement determines placement. However, observers note that better-off Americans like to "believe that their success is due entirely to brains and hard work." Merit is a "self-justification" (Menand, 2019). Elite college tuition costs can run to over $200,000 over four years, not including living expenses. Average private college costs $37,650 a year and average fees have roughly doubled over the last generation (College Board, 2020).

Contemporary United States

In 2020, total student debt topped $1.5 trillion, shared among 45 million borrowers who owe an average of $32,731 (Friedman, 2020). Differential access to funding turned college selection into a "new caste system" (Ferguson, 2012). As education provides a path to social and economic advancement, the expense of elite colleges—and indeed tertiary education more generally—can reduce social mobility. If enacted, Biden's progressive plan to make community college free, double federal Pell Grants, and reduce loan repayments for lower-paid workers would reduce costs markedly (Biden/Harris, 2020).

An undergraduate degree takes a minimum of four years to complete and consists typically of thirty-six to forty different courses. American colleges are uniform in requiring that one-third of a student's curriculum be in general classes in science, philosophy, history, literature, math, and language, so that students will be broadly informed democratic citizens. After completing these required courses, students select a major and take nine to twelve specialized courses. The remaining classes needed for graduation are electives which students choose to supplement other areas of interest, or to concentrate on a minor field which strengthens the major. Lately, the trend is away from traditional disciplinary study in the arts and humanities, and toward business administration.

In 2020, American universities dominated the respected London *Times Higher Educational Supplement* (*THE*) rankings, placing fourteen universities among the world's top twenty. These included: California Institute of Technology (2nd); Stanford (4th); MIT (5th); Princeton (6th); Harvard (7th); Yale (8th); Chicago (9th); University of Pennsylvania (11th); Johns Hopkins (12th); University of California—Berkeley (13th); Columbia (16th); University of California—Los Angeles (17th); Cornell (19th); and Duke (20th) (*THE*, 2020). Those rankings, as well as high rankings in science and social sciences, pull hundreds of thousands of talented foreign students to American classrooms, many from Asia, and represent a tremendous "brain-gain" for the nation. In 2018–2019, 1.1 million foreign students studied at US universities. They contributed over $44.7 billion to the US economy, double the 2010–2011 impact. Table 6.2 lists the top five countries with students studying in the United States. Complementing these numbers, 341,000 American students studied abroad in 2017–2018 (IIE, 2019). The Corona pandemic reduced enrolments from overseas students (Silver, 2021).

**Table 6.2 Foreign Students Studying in US Colleges/
Universities in 2018–2019**

1 China	369,548
2 India	202,014
3 South Korea	64,000
4 Saudi Arabia	60,000
5 Canada	27,000
Other countries	408,285
World total	1,095,299

Source: IIE (2019)

Religion, Education, and Social Policy

If a student wants to go on to graduate school, he or she first takes a standardized test, the Graduate Record Exam (GRE), which does what the SAT did at the undergraduate level. The competition for placement begins again. A master's degree usually means an additional six to eighteen courses plus a thesis, and a PhD could add another six to eighteen courses plus a dissertation, depending upon the specific program and whether or not classes are on the quarter or semester system.

Most state universities charge substantial fees to residents of their states—over $40,000 for four years, while surcharges on students from other states more than double the cost (AACC, 2021). Rising costs threaten to price higher education beyond the ability of many to pay, and thereby imperil the American dream of personal, familial, and societal betterment. Many students can only afford to attend public universities, as they, or their parents, generally must finance their courses. Average university costs for the 2020–2021 academic year are compared in Table 6.3.

Nationwide, there are US government "need-based" scholarships for poorer students. Pell grants of up to $5,815 a year, with supplementary hardship and subject-specific grants of up to $4,000 are available. Tax credits, state grants, and student loans are also possible—at low interest rates. Based on family circumstances, the precise level of support varies dramatically. In 2016, 7.6 million students received Pell grants of $3,685 each for a total of $28.2 billion overall (College Board, 2016). Top athletes are given scholarships to matriculate while they compete in intercollegiate sporting contests. Both public and private "merit-based" scholarships are offered by every university to attract the most academically gifted students. While complex, the funding system currently provides some support for most needy students.

Thousands of private foundations or individual donations promote education. The Bill and Melinda Gates Foundation has provided over $1.2 billion for the United Negro College Fund, including the financing of full scholarships for twenty years (1999–2019). The Gates Foundation has dispensed over $54 billion since it began (Gates, 2021a). In 2019, the Lilly Endowment donated $161 million to education

Table 6.3 Estimated Annual Costs for Four-year College/University Students for 2020–2021

	Public (in state) (in $)	Public (out of state) (in $)	Private (in $)
Tuition and fees	10,560	27,020	37,650
Room and board	11,620	11,620	13,120
Books	1,240	1,240	1,240
Other expenses	2,170	2,170	1,810
Transportation	1,230	1,230	1,060
TOTAL	26,820	43,280	54,880

Note: The actual costs vary widely according to which of the 6,500 institutions a student attends, individual student economies, and scholarship grants. Personal expenditures are not included above.
Source: College Board (2020)

Contemporary United States

programs, with Native Americans, African Americans, and Hispanic Americans targeted (Lilly Endowment, 2021). One of the beneficiaries, the American Indian College Fund to help improve tribal community colleges supported more than 4,000 new scholarships, and over 143,000 since 1989 (AICF, 2021). In 2008, there were some 30,000 students in thirty-five accredited tribal colleges representing 250 North American tribes (Nelson, 2017).

Historically Black Colleges and Universities (HBCU) held less endowment funding than America's richest universities: Howard's total $691 million endowment (the richest HBCU) was matched more than twice over by Mike Bloomberg's 2018 donation of $1.8 billion to his alma mater, Johns Hopkins University (Quintana, 2018; Howard, 2019). Jeff Bezos's wife Mackenzie Scott's 2020 grant of $40 million to Howard was described as "transformative," part of a larger wave of giving to black universities (Howard, 2020). More than half (60 percent) of students embarking on a four-year degree program completed their studies within six years (Hess, 2019). In 2017–2018, American universities awarded around one million associate (two-year) degrees, two million bachelor's (four-year) degrees, 800,000 master's degrees, and 180,000 doctorates and professional degrees (NCES, 2020b). Half of MA degrees and 56 percent of doctoral degrees in STEM (science, technology, engineering, and mathematics) were awarded to non-US citizens.

A State Responsibility

The United States does not have a national system of primary and secondary education, even if the government sometimes makes land available, provides funding for special projects, and ensures that all citizens have equal access to schools. While the US Department of Education (DOE) has very limited supervisory powers, it does research, makes suggestions for national standards, and directs money toward programs deemed essential to national interests. In 2020, President Trump requested $66.6 billion to fund DOE K-12 programs in 2021 (DOE, 2020), around 8 percent of the total school spending (CBO, 2020b).

The states have constitutional authority over education. This gives them the flexibility to meet the demands of a variety of citizens and ways of life. State Boards of Education set minimum requirements for teacher qualifications, student attendance, and course offerings, but real control devolves to the local community. The day-to-day management of 56.3 million students in the 98,300 public and 33,600 private schools and over 3.1 million teachers is delegated to 16,800 independent school districts. For 2021–2022, funding averaged $14,484 per annum per student (EDI, 2020; Hanson, 2021). The private schools which divide between religious and class-based college-preparatory institutions are outside of state control—except that they are required to meet minimum accreditation guidelines for course offerings. They receive very little state, federal, or local funding, and must raise money from endowments, donations, churches, and tuition. The structure of education in the US is summarized in Figure 6.2 (NCES, 2016a).

Religion, Education, and Social Policy

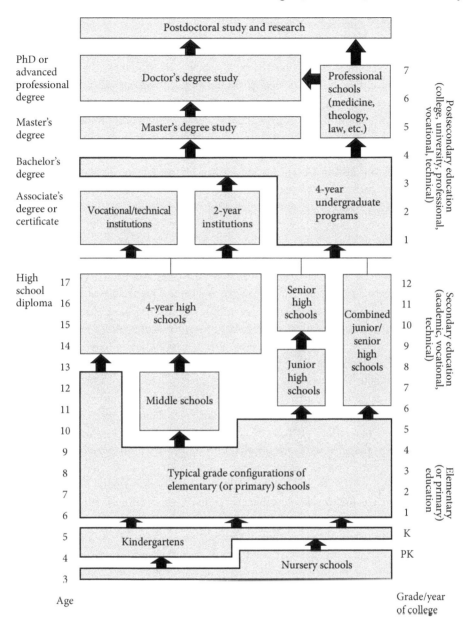

Figure 6.2 The American Educational System
Note: Adult education programs may provide instruction at the elementary, secondary, or higher education levels. The chart reflects typical patterns of progression.
Source: NCES (2016a)

Contemporary United States

School Districts and School Boards

School districts are administered by school boards elected or appointed from the local communities or counties. School boards decide what will be taught in their schools and administer the funding. Generally, nearly half the money to operate schools comes from the state and a similar proportion is raised through local property and sales taxes, as decided by each community. Localism cuts two ways. Those communities which have high property values, or a willingness to increase their taxes, can provide high-quality facilities, the newest software, and the best teachers for their schools. Poorer districts find it difficult to fund the basics and are marked by inadequate supplies, burned-out teachers, absent students, old computers, and older buildings. The federal government offers financial assistance for under-funded public schools. Since the 1960s, an Upward Bound program aids poor high school students and Project Head Start provides pre-school education to help nearly one million disadvantaged children improve their basic skills, with around 37 million having benefited in all (HHS, 2021b). First Lady Jill Biden has a PhD in education and teaches at North Virginia Community College.

School boards decide which textbooks to buy and which courses to mandate—choices made with community needs in mind. Agricultural communities, African American communities, urban areas, Muslim groups, fundamentalist Christian groups, immigrant communities, liberal and conservative communities all have differing ideas of appropriate textbooks and courses. Reflecting demographic change, in 2020, just over half of students in public primary and secondary schools were from racial/ethnic minorities: 27 percent Hispanic, 15 percent African American, and 6 percent Asian (NCES, 2020a). Selection of texts and courses can be a daunting task in urban areas, especially where the variety of students often consists of those speaking up to ninety first languages at home, while concentrating on English at school. More than one-fifth speak a language other than English at home, and fully 10 percent were classified by the National Center for Education Statistics as "English Language Learners" (NCES, 2021a).

Studies indicate that while suburban areas have good schools, inner-city urban areas and the country's rural districts produce less well-prepared students. Americans research the differences among schools when they make decisions on home purchases or job relocation, often making the final decision exclusively on the school district their children will enter. Of course, poorer Americans have much less choice as they may not be able to relocate to access better schools. Middle- and upper-class Americans can pay to place their children in private schools if the public schools do not meet their expectations for discipline, safety, and intensive education. Educational ambition thus feeds into socioeconomic clustering.

Americans expect their high schools to give comprehensive educations, wide-ranging and unspecialized. The educational philosophy is that everyone should receive twelve years of schooling, whether or not the student is motivated to study or is academically qualified for the task. This philosophy of not selecting among students aims at providing equal opportunity for everyone, to ensure literate workers, and to make the complex variety of ethnic, racial, and cultural peoples into Americans. This inclusion of students

Religion, Education, and Social Policy

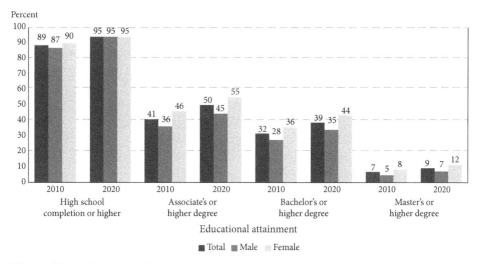

Figure 6.3 Highest Level of Educational Achievement for Twenty-Five to Twenty-Nine-Year-Olds, 2020
Note: High school completion includes equivalency programs, such as a General Educational program. Details may not sum to totals because of rounding.
Source: NCES (2020c)

of varying abilities in the same school and same courses can hold back the academic potential of individual students as teachers face the challenge of trying to teach everyone. Most schools have tried a "tracking" system that places students in classes by ability, still teaching everyone but often at vastly different levels. Tracking is controversial for those who want fairness over academic challenge.

The most exclusive private "college preparatory" schools select only students with certain IQ scores and/or proven ability, as well as those whose parents stand high in the community, or who will donate sizeable monetary gifts to the school. Whether educated publicly or privately, by 2020, 92 percent of Asians, 89 percent of whites, 79 percent of blacks, and 81 percent of Hispanics completed high school within four years, for a national completion rate of 85 percent, with others taking longer (NCES, 2019b). Recent challenges to the public school system have focused on increasing competition to attain a higher standard, and the use of vouchers to pay for education—which parents may use in the schools of their choice. Defenders of public schooling respond that funds are limited, and anything that dilutes the resources going to public schools will cause them to decline. Figure 6.3 shows the level of highest educational attainment of Americans aged between twenty-five and twenty-nine in 2020.

American schools are professionally run by administrators and teachers, who generally hold college degrees. It is not uncommon to find primary and secondary teachers with master's degrees, and a few have gained PhDs. Prospective teachers must pass state written examinations to be certified to teach in the public schools; certification in one state does not necessarily transfer to another. Overall, Americans have built a system that is decentralized, comprehensive, universal, and professional. And with all

201

Contemporary United States

these students, faculties, and administrators engaged on a full-time basis—representing around 25 percent of the American population—education is big business.

Debates over what happens in the schools and the quality of education are constant. Americans are competitive and dislike reports that students in other countries, states, or school districts are achieving more. In recent years, there has been much concern over the scores of fifteen year olds in tests, and on SAT/ACT examinations. The Programme for International Student Testing (PISA) comparisons of student scores worldwide indicate that the US performs averagely among developed nations in science and math (OECD, 2018b). Finger-pointing occurs as parents hold teachers and administrators responsible; teachers respond with studies that indicate that the presence or absence of family support and issues of poverty are key determinants to test scores.

Teachers argue that the top-half of American students compares with any students anywhere. Most suburban parents are content with their schools and say that it is the inner-city numbers or new immigrants who reduce the national scores; their own children are achieving. Asian Americans are held up as the model minority, receiving much support at home, excelling in testing, and comprising more than one-quarter of the student population at some prestigious universities, such as MIT and Berkeley (Jaschic, 2017). Americans accept the role of government in providing monetary support and in intervening, sometimes, to uphold minority rights.

Integration and Affirmative Action

In the landmark case of *Brown v. Board of Education* (1954), the US Supreme Court ruled that separate schools for different races were "inherently unequal" and that the states had to desegregate all educational facilities. The struggle to integrate schools met with strong local resistance and sporadic violence, but schools were integrated. The government persuaded universities to use Affirmative Action guidelines to bring in minority students even when their test scores were below those of white students who were being denied admission. The government provided money to those universities which showed progress in integration; federal marshals and private organizations such as the NAACP brought lawsuits against universities which discriminated against minority students. These actions were highly successful in integrating universities—even while there have been setbacks.

The *Bakke* (1978) decision ruled that it is "reverse discrimination" and unconstitutional to set quotas for minorities at the expense of qualified white students. This begs the ironic question: Does the Equal Protection Clause of the 14th Amendment perpetuate racial supremacy when it is used to stop Affirmative Action? The Court ruled that diversity could be taken into account in admissions decisions, but quotas could not be mentioned. In 1991, Congress outlawed the practice of "race-norming," where universities compared only black student scores with each other before adjusting them upward to match white student scores for admissions decisions; the Supreme Court agrees that race-norming hurts white students. With the white backlash in the 1990s against the claims of "preferential treatment" for minority students, President Clinton

Religion, Education, and Social Policy

reiterated his support for Affirmative Action, saying, "Mend it, don't end it." This encapsulates the majority view that history requires some strategy favoring minority uplift, but that previous discrimination against one group does not warrant present discrimination against another.

In 2016, the Supreme Court completed its judgment of *Fisher v. University of Texas*. Abigail Fisher was denied entry to the University of Texas, she argued, because of her white race and as a result of the Texas "Top Ten" program, designed to attract the best students from each high school rather than the brightest state-wide. Fisher said she "probably would have got a better job" if she had gone to the University of Texas. The Court found narrowly against *Fisher*, arguing that her rights had not been violated, and that the interest of demographically descriptive diversity could be served where justified, or supported by state law. In 2002, the Court forecast another review of the constitutionality of Affirmative Action.

Clearly, it is difficult to balance equal protection and equal opportunity with a history of disadvantage and discrimination in a multicultural society. Community schools are located in suburbs and cities, reflecting the race, ethnicity, and class of the homeowners, which are often the result of deliberate residential choices. In the 1960s, the Supreme Court tried to solve this residential segregation dilemma—partly caused by "white flight" from cities—by ordering school districts to use "busing" to transport inner-city children to suburban schools, and vice versa. Because public schools are funded primarily by property taxes, the middle class—many of whom had recently chosen to live in the suburbs—resisted this practice of taking students from well-financed school environments and placing them in schools in adjacent school districts which lacked the basics. African Americans protested that busing destroyed their inner-city neighborhoods and asked instead for more financial support to keep their children in local schools. Whites increasingly put their children in private schools or fled further into the suburbs.

In 1974, the Court reversed itself by deciding that local control of the schools should be upheld and that busing between school districts must stop. But that was not the end to questions concerning *Brown*. In 2007, the Court ruled that the school boards were not to make decisions assigning students living *within* individual school districts to schools based upon the race of the student (Bazelon, 2008). Americans continue to self-sort themselves into "clusters" by class, race, ideology and, increasingly, by language (Bishop, 2008). Interpretation of the upcoming 2020 census data will likely suggest that communities and thus schools remain segregated.

In 1962, the Court ruled that prayer has no place in public schools, because it violates the separation of church and state, and abridges the rights of non-Christians. States responded with "moments of silence" to allow students to sit quietly in their own thoughts. The Court has ruled against prayers at open football games and commencement ceremonies, even though groups of people often protest the order by simply reciting the Lord's Prayer aloud. In 2022, the Court reversed itself and allowed prayers at public high schools. Since 1925, the courts have consistently ruled out the teaching of creationism as an alternative or complement to the teaching of Darwin. In 1987, the US Supreme Court

Contemporary United States

ruled that the inclusion of religious materials in science classes was unconstitutional. Controversy continues. Creationism has been dubbed by adherents as "the theory of intelligent design" to match the theory of evolution. Recently, climate change deniers have doubted the need to act in defense of a warming planet, citing divine design and intention—part of a wider move to discredit scientific authority and put trust in a metaphysical God instead. For similar reasons, many on the Christian Right denied the seriousness of the Corona virus in 2020–2022.

While most people accept a role for evolution, only 22 percent of Americans believe human life evolved without some form of divine intervention; 33 percent maintain evolution was guided divinely; and 40 percent believe God created the human race as it is today (Brenan, 2019). Some twenty states have textbooks approved by a state board of education which can then be selected by local school boards. In 2010, Christian conservatives in Texas insisted on changes to the approved texts, including the redefinition of capitalism as the "free enterprise system," the acceptance of conservative economic theories, history texts promoting "American Exceptionalism," discussions of whether the separation of church and state is valid, and the qualification that evolution is only one theory of origin. Critics argued that these changes affected others, because with five million schoolchildren, Texas is the nation's second biggest textbook market. As these texts are used nationally, what happens in Texas does not stay in Texas (Koppelin, 2014). The nation's leading textbook market, California, pushes publishers and authors in a more liberal direction. In contemporary America, polarization can seem pervasive, with states insisting on different editions of authoritative textbooks (Goldstein, 2020). As in the discussions over religion, the education debates will continue to define the American experience.

Social Services

Seen from a global perspective, the United States is a limited welfare state with an infrastructure designed to distribute services to those who qualify and to the poor, sick, aged, and unemployed. Historically, local communities and churches provided help for the needy. Over the last fifty years, government has been influential in increasing incomes and life spans, primarily through subsidies for education, pensions, and public health intended to improve well-being and social mobility. This redistribution of tax money is highly controversial in a nation that promotes individual and family self-reliance, has a diversity of racial and ethnic groups, and consists of fifty states governed by elected politicians of varying conservative or liberal philosophies. Some people argue that middle and upper earners have gamed the redistributive system to their benefit. Mostly, the government's social services attempt to alleviate suffering and to provide a minimum living standard for the poor and disabled.

In addition to public assistance, there are church, charity, and private organizations which deliver social services. Moreover, many Americans feel the need to insure themselves privately, buying health care and contributing to pension plans over and above government provision, religious handouts, or employer–employee benefit packages. These programs overlap. Many Americans dislike the idea of a dependency culture, arguing that people are the architects of their own fortune. However, in 2020, the highest number recorded—54 percent of Americans—favoured increased government intervention to manage the nation's problems, while under half expressed more limited views on the purview of government. This high number may be a result of the Covid crisis, or the product of longer-term attitudinal change.

Traditionally, conservatives believed that self-reliance was a mark of independence and freedom, while liberals believed that federal or states' governments should help provide for the poor and infirm (Brenan, 2020b). Two American dreams coexist in social service provision: that of the value of individual agency and that of community compassion. There is a clear understanding of who makes up the deserving or undeserving poor. Children, the elderly, war veterans, and disabled persons are seen to deserve assistance and are fairly well-provided for. People who consistently lose their jobs, drop out of high school, have children outside of marriage, or rely on assistance too often are dismissed as undeserving, irresponsible, and part of a dependency culture that must be put to work.

Major events change attitudes. Under the 2020–2021 Covid crisis, a bipartisan consensus formed that the government should aid those suffering from Corona-related unemployment and economic dislocation. Nearly $6 trillion was injected into the economy—in unemployment benefits, child credits, and health care via the 2020 CARES ACT, the 2021 American Rescue Plan Act (ARPA) and other measures. Spending at this level lifted millions out of poverty, however temporarily that might last (COPSPCU, 2020; DOL, 2022).

Government Assistance

From 1789 until the 1930s, the United States did not provide public assistance. Most of the government aid programs available in contemporary America are rooted in the social policies of Franklin Delano Roosevelt's New Deal (1933–1939) and the 40 percent unemployment rate of 1932. About one-half of all American families had someone employed by a New Deal agency. Roosevelt maintained that poverty was not a moral failure but arose from social and economic conditions not always in a person's control— an argument that was hard to contradict at that time due to systemic crisis and massive widespread poverty. He promoted the understanding that, given the opportunity, any American would take a job instead of a handout.

In the end, the New Deal changed laissez-faire welfare policies by taking the responsibility for aiding the poor and placing assistance squarely onto federal government regulatory and social agencies. The Wagner Act protected labor's right to collective bargaining, the Works Progress Administration put hundreds of thousands of people to work in government programs, and the Fair Labor Standards Act mandated a minimum wage and restricted the hours of allowable work. Critics have argued that New Deal welfare provisions targeted white working class men as the model recipients, and this disadvantaged women and minorities.

Contemporary United States

The most important New Deal era program proved to be the Social Security Act, which established the pension system, unemployment insurance, and a forerunner to what became, in 1962, Aid to Families with Dependent Children (AFDC). The old-age pension portion of the Social Security Act is compulsory and is raised by taxes paid into a trust fund by employers and employees during an employee's working years; it does not come from general tax revenues and it is not distributed equally to the elderly. The more an employee and employer pay in—usually corresponding to higher incomes—the bigger the individual's retirement pension. Social Security is a "pay-as-you-go" system whereby present-day workers' pay present-day retirees' pensions; in 2020, 65 million Americans received social security benefits.

The Social Security Trust Fund disbursed over $1 trillion in 2020, with an average monthly check to retirees and their dependents of over $1,514 (SSA, 2020). As the number of retirees grows, more workers are required to cover the costs. Given the continuing debt crisis resulting from inadequate taxation to cover spending, retirement ages will likely be raised, pensions might be lowered, and taxes and contributions will rise. The pension age for those currently under sixty years old is sixty-seven.

With the New Deal, the government committed itself to supporting those who were down on their luck through no fault of their own. This helped to change attitudes toward the unemployed. Since the New Deal, various groups of workers, consumers, and minorities have been able to press for government intervention, something formerly only available to big business interests. This transformed the nation into a "broker state" adjudicating claims among various interest groups in society and giving rise to "rights talk"—the notion that social programs are "entitlements" which Americans are guaranteed under the Constitution. In 2021 cost-of-living adjustments saw social security benefits increase by 5.9 percent starting in December 2021, adding an average of $115 a month to payees (SSA, 2021).

In the 1960s, President Lyndon Johnson announced a "War on Poverty" and rewrote New Deal programs to include the creation of the US Department of Housing and Urban Development, Department of Transportation, Corporation for Public Broadcasting, Office of Economic Opportunity, and two education acts to fund school districts and to provide college funding for poor students. Johnson's War on Poverty measures were more universally targeted across gender, racial, and ethnic lines, factors which fed resistance from white nationalists. All these programs are still in force.

A federal program of food stamps, now called the Supplemental Nutrition Assistance Program (SNAP), provides an electronic debit card that works like an ATM card and can be used in grocery stores nationwide (USDA, 2021c). Even though students, people convicted of drug felonies, and married couples without children are generally excluded, most households with a monthly gross income below 130 percent ($2,839) of the national monthly poverty line ($2,184) for a family of four in 2021 are eligible (USDA, 2021d). In 2019, 35.7 million Americans used the program each month and the average monthly aid for a family of four was $519 (USDA, 2021a). The Trump administration pinpointed a booming economy providing more jobs as one reason why nearly ten million SNAP recipients departed the rolls from 2016–2020. A less chest-beating reason was the

Religion, Education, and Social Policy

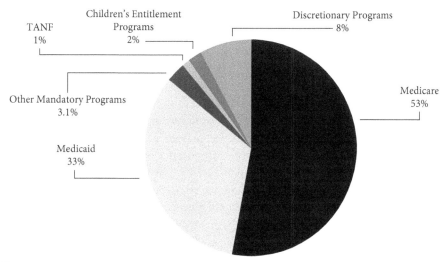

Figure 6.4 HHS Budget by Sector, 2021
Source: HHS (2021a)

reintroduction of time limits on benefits for childless couples (Rosenbaum and Jennings, 2019). Further food support is provided by a School Breakfast and Lunch Program which serves free or reduced-cost meals for poor children (where family incomes are below 185 percent of the poverty line, or $48,470 for a family of four in 2020) in public schools. Over 29 million students benefited from daily support in 2019 (ASPE, 2021b; USDA, 2021b).

In 1965, the federal government established Medicare to fund health care costs for the disabled and for everyone aged over sixty-five years, regardless of need; the following year, Medicaid expanded those health benefits to anyone living under the poverty line. Medicaid is administered by each state, has wide variations in the quality of service, and is funded by a combination of federal and state monies. The Children's Health Insurance Program (CHIP) aimed to ensure that no children would be without health care coverage, and covered 8.9 million children in 2016 (AHA, 2021). Total outlays on Department of Health and Human Services (HHS) programs are projected at around $1.37 trillion in 2021. Figure 6.4 shows how this sum is divided. About one in every four tax dollars is spent by HHS. This figure predates March 2021 American Recovery Plan Act (ARPA) reforms.

As the numbers in Figure 3.4 indicate, despite historically preferring limited government, many Americans have accepted an extensive role for government. Moreover, the incoming Biden administration fulfilled initial campaign pledges by spending larger sums on Americans' welfare, witnessed by ARPA. By way of comparison, total US military spending in 2019 was 3.2 percent of GDP, or $676 billion (Duffin, 2021). By 2027, national health expenditures costs are expected to reach nearly 20 percent of GDP (CMS, 2018). This percentage will rise if the Biden administration is able to expand health care coverage to include currently uninsured Americans.

Contemporary United States

Since the 1930s, various administrations have attempted to provide a comprehensive and inclusive health care system. In 2008, over 46 million Americans such as workers just above the poverty line in minimum wage jobs fell through the cracks and remained without health insurance—inspiring President Obama's attempt to introduce health care for all (NPR, 2009). The Affordable Care Act (ACA)—known as "Obamacare"— passed in 2010 by a Democratic majority Congress markedly increased the percentage of Americans with health care coverage, while also throwing up one of the most important and rancorous points of polarization between Democrats and Republicans. While Obamacare was intended to create a more cost-effective and less expensive health care system, the system quickly came under financial strains. Health care premiums rose markedly for users and for federal and state governments because fewer healthy young people bought insurance, leaving a pool of older people to share the expensive burden. Despite ACA, 20 million or so Americans remain without coverage (USCB, 2019a).

Government health plans like Obamacare are unpopular among Republicans because they influence the health care sector's command of nearly one-fifth of national economic activity. Health care is a lightning rod for discontent against more government and higher taxes, as it is a touchstone among Democrats towards creating a more inclusive and comprehensive society.

In 2017, Congress and the Trump administration began the process of repealing, modifying, and replacing ACA with a new frame, the American Health Care Act (AHC). Despite the rhetoric of hostility from the administration, Trump was unable to repeal and replace ACA, not least as the program garnered support from a small majority of Americans (Younis, 2020). Instead, Trump opted for scale-backs, such as less federal and more states responsibility for health care markets. Biden, meanwhile, has promised— but not yet delivered—a federal "public option" that would resemble Medicare and that people could opt-in on.

Obesity is a significant factor in the high costs of health care. The Centers for Disease Control and Prevention (CDC) estimates that 42.5 percent of American adults are obese—10 percent more than in 2000 and more than in most other major nations, resulting in $147 billion a year in extra medical costs (CDC, 2021b). The fast food culture and sheer abundance of products supersize everything. Obesity has affected longevity rates, which fall dramatically in relation to how low Americans are in the class hierarchy. Life spans of the poorest one-fifth of Americans average 76.1 years for men and 78.3 years for women; life spans for the richest one-fifth average 88.8 years for men and 91.9 for women (Ehrenfreud, 2015). From 2014–2018, average life spans fell by 0.3 percent, and will certainly fall further due to the more-than-one-million Covid death toll and the continuing opioid crisis (McGreal, 2018) (Illustration 6.2).

Health care problems—particularly the explosive increase in dementia, diabetes, colon problems, AIDS-HIV, and heart diseases—put further stress on the health care system, especially for poorer Americans. Falling life expectancy even before Covid astonished many observers (McKay, 2018). Additionally, some portions of society have experienced increasing mortality rates, partly due to lifestyle related illnesses stemming from smoking and alcohol.

Religion, Education, and Social Policy

Illustration 6.2 Corporate Profits and the Opioid Crisis

On November 17, 2021, the Centers for Disease Control and Prevention indicated that the yearly death toll for drug overdoses had surpassed 100,000. For opioids alone by 2021, the tally had risen to over 70,000 more than those fallen in the entire Vietnam War (58,000) and more than all the deaths from firearms, murders, suicides, and car crashes combined. On December 3, 2021, bereaved Americans from across the nation rallied at the Federal Department of Justice in Washington—some carrying placards with the images of those lost to the crisis. Their aim was to persuade Attorney General Merrick Garland to issue criminal charges against the Sackler family, owners of opioid manufacturer Purdue Pharma, for false marketing claims that suggesting that OxyContin—the opioid they manufactured—was harmless. Previously Purdue had agreed to pay between six and eight billion dollars in compensation.

Source: Michael Nigro/Pacific Press/LightRocket via Getty Images

Beyond policy spending, the federal government subsidizes the whole economy. It is the nation's single biggest employer, with around four million workers in jobs such as the military, immigration, foreign service, post office departments, federal law enforcement, and janitorial staffs. Including local and state government employees, the government is responsible for about one-eighth of the total workforce. Additionally, tax money in the form of housing and education loans, business bailouts, and tax breaks to start businesses help the middle and upper classes—especially in times of crisis.

The women and men who select careers in the armed services receive the most comprehensive packages. Military personnel receive free medical and dental care, housing, high-tech training, and shopping benefits for themselves, their spouses, and children. If stationed overseas, they receive income supplements, cheap insurance rates

Contemporary United States

and tax breaks on most purchases. For those who decide to quit the military after their enlistment period is up—usually three to six years—the government provides money to help underwrite a college education and offers low-cost housing loans (USDV, 2021a). Personnel who serve twenty years accrue retirement benefits worth about 40 percent of their normal salaries (Hanc, 2019). Retirees retain most of the special benefits which they had on active duty (USDV, 2021b).

Social Security, Medicare, and Medicaid are presently the costliest programs in the social insurance system, consuming nearly half of the entire federal budget (CBPP, 2020). Until recently, politicians rarely dared to support changes because of the political strength of the elderly who claim the programs as entitlements and are protected by strong civil society groups like the American Association of Retired People, representing nearly 38 million people over fifty (AARP, 2021). The "graying of America"—the huge, aging baby boom generation combined with higher life expectancies—threatens the entire system, as there are too many retirees for present workers to support without raising taxes significantly. In 2020, approximately 52 million Americans were over sixty-five years old. By 2060, this group is projected to number over 95 million (PRB, 2019). The combination of longer healthy life spans and ballooning medical costs may see retirement ages increase (pandemics notwithstanding), with further increases designed to cap pension and health care system costs.

Additionally, advances in biotechnology seem close to matching drugs to individual genotypes, thereby saving lives and extending working spans, but at greater costs. Health care costs outstrip the rate of inflation.

Plans to prune back the welfare state to cut the current or future budgets have proven difficult to pass in Congress. Traditionally Democrats, citing public benefits, have supported case-based (and not comprehensive) expansions of the welfare state; meanwhile Republicans have argued for scale-backs to reduce deficits. Two factors have muddied these positions. In practice, Trump's "economic populism" ran on a defense of social welfare programs, largely accepted by Republican deficit conservatives. Secondly, Covid's oversized effects on older Americans disrupted health spending by spending on an episodic event rather than a systemic reform of health care provision. Calls for greater fiscal limits will almost certainly return once the Corona crisis has passed, making significant increases in spending by the Biden administration on reducing gaps in health coverage more difficult to fund. For Biden hard choices loom, between campaign pledges and funding opportunities, while Republicans rev up their opposition to comprehensive health care. Medicare and Social Security programs dominate federal budget expenditures and are at the heart of the paralyzing partisan debates over fiscal solvency.

Workfare

Americans continue to debate the issue of what should be done to help the poor. Many argue that private-sector economic growth will eradicate poverty; others want higher taxes coupled with a redistribution of income and job training. Some claim that the poor lack the will to rise, while others argue that all societies are marked by class inequalities

Religion, Education, and Social Policy

Illustration 6.3 Progressives Want Biden to Do Much More

During the 2020 presidential primary debates among Democratic candidates, Joe Biden often found himself at odds with the Progressive, Socialist-leaning, Left candidates Senator Elizabeth Warren of Massachusetts and Senator Bernie Sanders of New Hampshire. The Progressive side of the Democratic Party was stronger than ever before and had made significant inroads into power since the 2016 campaign when Sanders narrowly lost the nomination to Hillary Clinton. And in the House of Representatives, Alexandria Ocasio-Cortez had been very active pushing a "Green New Deal" to confront climate change and to support Sanders's democratic socialist agenda (see Illustration 3.3). Biden prevailed in his moderate, just-left-of-center campaign. But once elected, Biden moved quickly leftward with infrastructure programs, social spending plans, and job plans that caused credible comparisons to the New Deal programs of Franklin Roosevelt. He imagined himself as a transformational president. Biden was also transactional, but not like Trump. He was willing to be persuaded by progressives to get things done. And with the Republican Party being unwilling to compromise, Biden continued to move Left (Giridharadas, 2021). Where Trump represented a New Gilded Age, Biden represented a New Progressive Era, if only for a short time (see Chapter 1). The photo is from the December 19, 2019 debate in Los Angeles.

Source: Justin Sullivan via Getty Images

that disadvantage large groups. Critics claim that government has never had the will to invoke real programs that work and has simply done the minimum to control the poor. Conservatives say that government programs have been adequate but that poverty and dependency are tenacious among various groups. There are strong historical attitudes toward giving or taking "handouts" from a government, a clear attachment to the work ethic, and strong ethnic, religious, and racial prejudices in the way.

Contemporary United States

For over a generation, conservatives have blamed welfare programs for creating a cycle of dependency and a culture of poverty that would keep new generations on welfare. The New Deal AFDC program was formulated in the 1930s, when families were more traditional. It was largely targeted at white women, especially widowed or divorced mothers who were raising children alone. From the 1960s onward, the number of divorced and single mothers has expanded claimants to four million adults and nine million children, with eligibility more universal. Since Ronald Reagan, presidents have been taking the federal government out of the welfare business by returning authority (and less funding) to the states.

In line with his emphasis on economic freedom not economic equality, Reagan pushed through substantial cuts in food stamps, housing assistance, and job-training programs. These were some of the first efforts to move the poor from welfare to "workfare." In 1996, Clinton agreed with the Republican Congress "to end welfare as we know it," by creating a program of Temporary Assistance for Needy Families (TANF). TANF ended AFDC, set time limits on welfare recipients, set up strong work requirements, and devolved power over welfare monies to the states, territories, and Indian tribes, each with a different program.

In 2020, TANF funds sent to the states remained constant at $16.5 billion for the twenty-fourth straight year; states contributed $10 billion extra. In 2020, over one million families received various amounts as determined by individual states, territories, or tribes (CRS, 2021a). Each recipient, unless disabled, is limited to lifetime benefits of five years, although some exceptions have been introduced. New immigrants to the US were made ineligible for any benefits under the law, but the states stepped in to support jobless immigrants under the same general conditions provided by TANF.

Across the United States, once taxpayers see the poor as deserving workers who are temporarily unemployed, instead of as undeserving "welfare cheats," they have become more generous. With everybody willing to work, everybody is willing to help. The flood of single women into the labor market has been a solid achievement; but TANF has not created more two-parent families. The Trump administration froze TANF funding and time limits while pursuing regulatory measure to reduce claims. Biden is likely to roll back Trump's restrictions, and progressive Democrats like Bernie Sanders and Elizabeth Warren (see Illustration 6.3) will try to persuade Biden to increase funding and eligibility (Reiley, 2020).

In the United States, there is as much to condemn as to praise. The country has not been able or willing to eradicate poverty, or to move closer to an equality of outcome for all its citizens. Cries of hypocrisy abound as critics point out that the nation says one thing and does another. There are layers and layers of objections and problems when it comes to equalizing treatment for an increasingly diverse population of citizens. The "classless society" has failed to eradicate class, race, gender, and age divisions. Class consciousness has increased, now infused by the clash between locally and globally minded Americans. Race consciousness has also risen, epitomized in the conflicts between police and the #BLM movement. Gender and sexuality awareness has also grown—a product on the one hand of the #MeToo movement, and on the other of the collision between the restrictive views of the traditionally and biblically minded, and the more open and progressive identity categories more prevalent among the young. Debates over the role of science versus the belief in God, or religion, continue at a strong pace. What civil society and government can do to improve people's lives clearly depends on the willingness of politicians to cooperate and legislate. The economy is, of course, a third factor.

Further Reading

Hinton, E. (2017) *From the War on Poverty to the War on Crime: The Making of Mass Incarceration in America*, Cambridge, MA: Harvard University Press.

Peters, C. (2017) *We Do Our Part: Toward a Fairer and More Equal America*, New York: Random House. Survey, Nov. 1.

Putnam, R. (2015) *Our Kids: The American Dream in Crisis*, New York: Simon & Schuster.

Rauch, J. (2021) *The Constitution of Knowledge: A Defense of Truth*, Washington, DC: Brookings.

Reeves, R. (2017) *Dream Hoarders: How the American Upper Middle Class Is Leaving Everyone Else in the Dust, and What to Do about It*, Washington, DC: Brookings.

Stewart, K. (2020) *The Power Worshippers: Inside the Dangerous Rise of Religious Nationalism*, London: Bloomsbury.

Sutton, M. (2016) *American Apocalypse: A History of Modern Evangelicalism*, Cambridge, MA: Belknap.

CHAPTER 7
CULTURE, MEDIA, SPORTS

American culture is an overarching term covering a multitude of cultures and subcultures, at times similar one to the other, and at other times so estranged or peculiar that they are Manichean. There is not a single source or recipe because American culture pulls from the global diaspora. There are multiple meanings and complex "blended" interdependencies.

While nativists often insist on an exceptional and hegemonic master narrative, both different from and better than competing ones, very few people exist in places untouched by multiculturalism, transnationalism, and the global marketplace. Still, nationalistic zealots claim a cultural superiority and aggressively push an American model as heroic and in need of defending against "un-American" values. In his 2014 political film, *America*, neo-conservative moviemaker Dinesh D'Souza asserts that US cultural values are responsible for all the good things put forth in the world for the past 200 years (D'Souza, 2014). His hubris even reaches the conclusion that slavery was good for African Americans because without it, blacks would have still been in Africa, and would not have had a better life. Trump used crude nationalist language to openly disparage Haiti, El Salvador, and much of Africa as "shithole countries" (Barron, 2018). D'Souza, Trump, and their allies want a dominant white nationalistic culture to hold and cherish. Liberals prefer to mix and match, add and subtract, and take on roles that fit with one or more of the many subcultures under the umbrella term "American culture." Variations play out simultaneously and independently in changing ideas of "Americanness."

Borderlands

Writers have described American culture as a crossroads, a jumble of conflicting discourses, a place of contact zones, and a geography of borderlands where a person ventures into, encounters the Other, experiences disorientation, gains perspective, merges, defines, and contests identities. A voyager learns to represent himself/herself/themself as a majority person at the center, or as a minority person on the margins of power, or as someone with a foot in each camp, or neither. There are multi-layered perspectives and concurrent meanings to contemporary American cultures. Self-definition is as possible as it is impossible in a nation where control, oppression, strategies of dissent, and everyday activities must be negotiated and ruled upon. There are many

Contemporary United States

bodies and many voices. Generational legacies and family echoes are also major factors to cultural continuities and changes for many people (Singh, 1994).

American culture varies widely by locale, region, ethnicity, and race in a nation with fifty states as diverse in historical subcultures and personal identities as the French Quarter in New Orleans, Pine Ridge Sioux Reservation in South Dakota, Muslim Detroit, casino-rich Las Vegas, Japanese Honolulu, Irish Boston, African American Atlanta, Blues-bound Chicago, Chinatown in San Francisco, Inuit Alaska, Jewish Colorado, Elvis-afflicted Memphis, Mormon Utah, Cuban Miami, Protestant Indiana, Chicana Texas, Quaker Philadelphia, Scandinavian Minnesota, Puerto Rican New Jersey, Gun-toting Arizona, LGBTQIA+ New York City, Amish Pennsylvania, Hollywood-starred Los Angeles, corn-fed Iowa, monument-crushed Washington, and Rock & Roll Cleveland (Illustration 7.1). If your identity does not match the subculture around you, there are possibilities to explore.

There has never been an official national language, even though thirty states and nineteen cities mandate American English grammar and punctuation rules for governmental correspondence. Most people speak the American dialect in one of its regional variations in public and either English, Spanish, or one of 300 other languages at home (see Table 7.1). A hybrid "polyvocality"—a many-voicedness—can be heard in multi-ethnic and multiracial marriages and families (Campbell and Kean, 2016). There has never been an official national religion, even though the country is known for its evangelical Protestants. The US Constitution has always been a secular deity for many Americans, although faith in its "scriptures" has fallen dramatically as political polarization has surged. There are no bans on flying the flags of other nations alongside, or instead of, the national banner in private locations. All government offices fly the American flag exclusively, or along with state or municipal flags.

The United States is a nation of immigrants whose personal histories multiply as they reach back into national histories and ethnic rivalries on every continent, each with different cultural memories. Long-standing notions of individualism, self-reliance, and freedom of action further divide people from a common community. America in its chaotic blend of multiculturalism and transnationalism is the world in its postmodern diversity. Simultaneously, America in its closed-border nationalism is the world in its tribal ethnocentrisms. This is not new. Cultural conflicts have always been a part of the culture of discontent that is America and the current round of culture wars has long roots in American society. In colonial America, red, white, and black cultures and subcultures contested, compromised, and yielded lifestyles, languages, and religions—not to mention gender, class, power, ethnic, sexuality, and national cultural differences. As the twenty-first century approached, two sociologists asked: "Whose culture shall be the official one and whose shall be subordinated? … Whose history shall be remembered and whose forgotten? … What voices shall be heard and which shall be silenced?" (Jordan and Weedon, 1995).

Over the last decade, calls to make America great again and the rising nationalist and authoritarian tendencies the world over held up particular kinds of identity and cultures as preferable to others. In 2015, Ta-Nehisi Coates won the National Book Award for *Between the World and Me*, an exploration into the American dream, "bone-deep"

Culture, Media, Sports

Illustration 7.1 LGBTQIA+ Identities, Subcultures, Inclusion

President Biden is an ally in the cause for equal justice and full inclusion for all people. He has been named the most pro-transgender president in American history. As Obama's VP, Biden was a key supporter of the Equal Marriage Act and social benefits for couples who did not meet the one born-that-way man and one born-that-way woman requirement insisted upon by religious conservatives. In 2021, one of Biden's first acts as president was to overturn the Trump–Pence ban on transgendered soldiers in the military. There was a backlash as partisan politicians focused on transgender people who wanted to live according to their identities and not to a biologically determined category on a birth certificate of male or female, with heterogeneity assumed by most Americans. Two percent of high school students in the US identify as trans. Republican politicians found a culture war issue and made laws banning restrooms for transgendered people, cast doubt over the fairness of sports competitions, fanned hysteria over trans kids educated alongside "my kids," and made claims that trans people were child molesters. Dozens of state legislatures passed restrictive laws demonizing kids in hopes of attracting conservative votes. Similar laws had been used against gays and lesbians since the 1960s. In 2021, as the photograph shows, large crowds from fifty LGBTQIA+ organizations, including the National Center for Transgender Equality gathered outside the Stonewall Inn in New York City, a hallowed spot for progress over the last fifty years, renewed the demand that "Gay Rights are Human Rights," and as one acknowledged "Trans People Started Our Movement."

Source: Erik McGregor/LightRocket via Getty Images

identities, and "the politics of personal exoneration" in a dominant culture where "'safety' was a higher value than 'justice'" (Coates, 2015). Coates reminded us that there is always a struggle for memory, identification, and cultural survival in the American experience.

Contemporary United States

Table 7.1 Primary Language Spoken at Home other than English or Spanish, by State, Numbers of Speakers

Language	States
Chinese (2,200,000)	Delaware, Missouri, New York, North Carolina, Pennsylvania, Washington, Wyoming
Tagalog (Filipino) (1,800,000)	California, Nevada, New Jersey
Vietnamese (1,500,000)	Arkansas, Georgia, Iowa, Kansas, Nebraska, Oklahoma, Oregon, Texas
Arabic (1,300,000)	Idaho, Michigan, Ohio, Tennessee, Virginia, West Virginia
French (1,200,000)	Louisiana, Maine, Maryland, New Hampshire, Vermont, District of Columbia
German (862,000)	Alabama, Colorado, Indiana, Kentucky, Montana, North Dakota, South Carolina
Haitian Creole/French (833,000)	Florida
Portuguese (801,000)	Connecticut, Massachusetts, Rhode Island, Utah
Polish (517,000)	Illinois
Hmong (233,000)	Wisconsin
Somali (178,000)	Minnesota
Navajo (American Indian) (167,000)	Arizona, New Mexico
Ilocano (Filipino) (105,000)	Hawaii
Aleut (Alaskan) (27,000)	Alaska
Lakota (American Indian) (15,000)	South Dakota
Muskeogean (American Indian) (14,000)	Mississippi

Sources: Kiersz, De Luce, Hoff (2020) and USCB (2019d)

E Pluribus Unum

And yet, everyday it is possible to locate a single, dominant American culture—and the reality of Americanization is true. Were this not so, we would hardly hear the multitude of fearful voices arguing that American cultural exports are neo-colonialism and neo-imperialism, making all the world's languages subservient to the linguistic-debasement of American slang, and all the world's people conform to cheap and transient American tastes. Well before the supremacy of the internet and social media, Historian Richard Pells wrote that Americanization included "the world-wide invasion of American movies, Rock 'n' Roll, mass circulation magazines, best-selling books, advertising, comic strips, theme parks, shopping malls, fast food, and television programs" (Pells, 2000). Perhaps the 1960s slogan advocated by Dr. Timothy Leary could be remade to express world fears or praise for American dominance: "Tune in! [to the American idea],

Turn on! [to Hollywood movies], Drop out! [of your own culture]." Many foreigners fear cultural appropriation, standardization, and homogenizing consumerism of "Americanization," which is also corrupted into "McDonaldization" to acknowledge the power of multinational corporate capitalism.

But the transmission and reception of culture is not a one-way process; it is reciprocal. America is transnational at its core with its beginnings in the diversity of European, African, and Native American lifestyles. American culture does not stay "American" very long because local and national cultures around the world adapt US culture to their own wants and needs (Campbell and Kean, 2016). Americanization that is global and local is called "glocalization"—where local traditions negotiate with other cultures and adapt them (Pells, 2012). Korean K-Pop and Japanese J-Pop derived from American influences but they have local rhythms. Even when anti-Americanism rises in the Middle East, North Korea, China and elsewhere, American popular culture continues its appeal. The American military or American democracy can be hated, and are, but hip-hop is not and neither are "Game of Thrones," "The Queen's Gambit," and other TV epics that streamed in Iranian homes and elsewhere. One Hollywood director explained, as paraphrased here: "Batman is Batman, Jason Bourne is Jason Bourne, and the Avengers are the Avengers regardless of who is in the White House" (Arango, 2008). Perhaps the same cannot be said for Wonder Woman or Lovecraft Country if the viewer is politically astute.

American culture is loud and American culture is fast. It advertises itself as perpetually young and somehow still innocent in its boisterous enthusiasm for itself, its language, clothes, music, food, and sense of entitlement. Critics sometimes dissolve the whole into a McCulture, boring in its one-dimension homogeneity, cheapness, and ubiquity—a "fast food nation," eating out as much as four nights a week, eager for immediate service, and demanding cheap food prices, while paying scant attention to how the burgers got to the drive-thru window in the first place (Schlosser, 2001). Covid restrictions and fears changed this only temporarily.

America is an "idea state" held together as much by a promise as by geography and law. The promise not only shaped the culture; it is older than the government and thus provides the impetus for nationalism. In 2001, George W. Bush expressed this understanding in his Inaugural Address: "America has never been united by blood or birth or soil. We are bound by ideals that move us beyond our backgrounds." In his Farewell Address eight years later, Bush spoke of the "proud moment of hope and pride" for America that would come on January 20 when "standing on the steps of the Capitol will be a man whose history reflects the enduring promise of our land." A few days later, Barack Obama told the nation: "Our patchwork heritage is a strength, not a weakness. We are a nation of Christians and Muslims, Jews, and Hindus—and non-believers. We are shaped by every language and culture, drawn from every end of this Earth." Trump stoked a partisanship that disagreed with Bush and Obama. From 2015 and continuing well after he lost the 2020 election, Trump blamed liberals and non-whites for taking away American greatness and he promised that "only I know how to

Contemporary United States

fix it" (Rucker and Leonnig, 2020). His solution was conservative values, a support for Christian nationalism, and racial and class hierarchies.

The election of Obama had been partially due to the changes in the pop culture of the 1990s, when, in the words of Jeff Chang, "American culture became colorized" (Hsu, 2009). Golfer Tiger Woods exemplified an ethnic/racial ambiguity; Denzel Washington was one of Hollywood's leading men; Asian and Hispanic populations were rising; Oprah commanded daytime talk show audiences; and the victory of hip-hop culture and the ethic of diversity in network and cable television shows were obvious. But it was that very colorization that led many white dissenters to react and to support the election of Trump.

Clearly, differences in "red rural state" Republicans and "blue city" Democrats describe the partisan divides along geographical lines. The culture wars can be seen as a separation of African Americans, Latinos, Native Americans, Asian Americans, Whites, and Women, into six competing tribes. Multiculturalism and deep divisions exist but Obama sought compromise: "There is not a liberal America and a conservative America. There is a United States of America" (Obama, 2009b). In 2012, Obama reiterated this theme (Obama, 2012):

> It doesn't matter whether you're black or white or Hispanic or Asian or Native American or young or old or rich or poor, abled, disabled, gay or straight. You can make it here in America if you're willing to try … We are greater than the sum of our individual ambitions and we remain more than a collection of red states and blue states. We are, and forever will be, the United States of America.

Notwithstanding Obama's cheerleading for unity, chaotic heterogeneity is the American cultural norm. Identity questions are inherent in a society that emphasizes redemption, rebirth, reinvention, and renewal. The national motto, *E Pluribus Unum*, stresses diversity and unity at the same time. The American creed promises equal opportunity and there is a strong belief in both individual freedom and community responsibility. America-the-dream is the self-conscious invention that has molded a huge population with varying, local folkways into a national culture. From the beginning, in a time when the American Revolution was not yet settled, French soldier and new American immigrant Hector St. John de Crèvecoeur asked "What is this American, this new man?" Here is his answer:

> I could point out to you a family whose grandfather was an Englishman, whose wife was Dutch, whose son married a French woman, and whose four sons have now four wives of different nations. He is an American, who, leaving behind him all his ancient prejudices and manners, receives new ones from the new mode of life he has embraced, the new government he obeys, and the new rank he holds … Here are individuals melted into a great new race of men, whose labours and posterity will one day cause great changes in the world.
>
> (Crèvecoeur, 1782)

Culture, Media, Sports

Literature and the Rise of a Nation

Since Crèvecoeur, Americans have created art, literature, and music to meet their idea and sense of being "American." Borrowing heavily on European masters, portraitists John Singleton Copley, Gilbert Stuart, Benjamin West, and John Trumbull painted and repainted the heroes of the Revolution. Their efforts made myth, helped tie the nation together, and elevated George Washington into a symbol of the new America. Patriots wanted to assimilate Indians and immigrants into an Anglo-American culture praying in Protestant churches and learning the English language. In the nineteenth century, painters Thomas Cole and Albert Bierstadt located the American difference in the Native Americans, wagon trains full of settlers, and the sublime landscape stretching westward across the continent. In the twentieth century, between the period of the Armory Modern Art Show in 1913 to the Second World War, New York City became the undisputed world capital of modernism, with a heresy that mocked classical traditions and establishment understandings, and whose "heroes" were the machines, industry, and skyscrapers that gave rise to a superpower. Regionalists disputed the "hero" and honored rural Americans who believed in the small towns and vast agricultural farms that made Americans a "people of plenty." Later, abstract expressionists located the "frontier" within the individual, pop artists celebrated consumerism, and trash artists protested the masculinity, materialism, and nationalism of the dominant culture.

From the middle of the nineteenth century, American literary expression was filled with clear American dialects in the works of Cooper, Thoreau, Emerson, Dickinson, and Twain. Herman Melville's complex precursor to the modernist novel, *Moby Dick* (1851), is the story of Captain Ahab's obsession with killing the great white whale that had bitten off his leg in a previous encounter. Melville shows the futility of assuming any single explanation of the truth and offers multiple meanings of the whale and of Ahab's desperation. Nathaniel Hawthorne's *The Scarlet Letter* (1850) is another characteristic example of American dissent. Hawthorne spun the witches and judges of Salem on their heads, offering several suggestions for Hester Prynne's seduction of the Puritan cleric. Opposition to institutional power, racism, sexism, and conspiracies has remained at the heart of American literature for over 150 years.

American literature also followed the trends of urbanization, industrialization, and westward expansion. Mark Twain's *Adventures of Huckleberry Finn* (1885) faces up to the tension between nature and civilization, Stephen Crane's *Maggie: A Girl of the Streets* (1893) looks at poverty and sexuality in immigrant America, and Kate Chopin's *The Awakening* (1899) explores issues of sex and gender in middle-class life. These themes would continue to fill the great American novels of the twentieth century. Between 1900 and 1945, American artists and writers did locate "the Great American Thing" in the tension between the past and the new gods of technology all around them with the class, race, and gender divisions of modern industrial capitalism and the boom-and-bust cycles of hope and desperation. They illuminated the tensions of a "wasteland" (Sinclair Lewis) or among "the grapes of wrath" (John Steinbeck) and with those whose "eyes were watching god" (Zora Neale Hurston) or in recognition that "all right we are two nations"

Contemporary United States

(John Dos Passos) or that the "bell tolls" (Ernest Hemingway) of death confront the hopes that "the sun also rises" (Ernest Hemingway).

American literature became increasingly multicultural during the Cold War. Minority authors gained audiences and told stories of hyphenated racial and ethnic cultures. Among the best are James Baldwin, Ralph Ellison, Toni Morrison, August Wilson, Amy Tan, Maxine Hong Kingston, Richard Rodriguez, Sandra Cisneros, Oscar Hijuelos, Junot Diaz, Scott Momaday, Michael Dorris, Louis Erdrich, and Sherman Alexie. Social realism and redress of grievances took center stage. Philip Roth, E. L. Doctorow, Tim O'Brien, Jonathon Frantzen, and Richard Powers must be mentioned for their excellent novels. Their stories of growing up, societal change, men at war, and physics/technologies expose the central cultural themes of good and evil, failure and success, ethnocentrism and the Other that have been at the center of American writing since Crèvecoeur. Powers's prize-winning masterwork, *The Overstory* (2018), is a vast landscape of activism and resistance where humans and the natural world are in conflict for survival. The only hope for both competitors is cooperation. *Bewilderment* (2021) detailed a world imperiled by man-made climate changes.

Among the twelve Americans who won the Nobel Prize in Literature was songwriter Bob Dylan in 2016. Dylan combined folk and rock music, anti-racism, anti-war, and youth rebellion in songs aimed directly at the heart of American culture, including. "Blowing in the Wind," "The Times They Are A'Changin'," and "A Hard Rain's A-Gonna Fall." "Masters of War" is the most powerful anti-war song in American history with its finger-pointing anger against the older generations in the military, industrial, government, capitalist establishment. Dylan's last verse is aimed at these powerful white men and includes the verse: 'And I hope that you die/ And your death will come soon/ I'll follow your casket/ By the pale afternoon/ And I'll watch as you're lowered/ Down to your death bed/ And I'll stand o'er your grave/ Til I'm sure that you're dead.'

The Internet

The internet is a mostly unregulated cultural tool that simultaneously reflects and changes society by allowing people to communicate and do old things in more convenient ways. The internet aids social interaction, different perspectives, wider cooperation, and individual development. The cost, and it is huge, is the loss of privacy through the data collection by service providers and government or criminal interests. The system was born in 1969 as a Department of Defense surveillance project linking together government agencies and research universities. The National Science Foundation provided the R&D funds to incorporate new hardware and software innovations into a commercial network. In 1993, only fifty websites existed worldwide. The babysteps toward a worldwideweb (www) developed with CompuServe file sharing and the innovation of email with its @ symbol. Email predated mobile phones and provided a much quicker way for people to communicate than the old post office letter system. It is useful to remember that sending a letter across time zones or across continents could take weeks, phone calls were prohibitively expensive, and often calls went unanswered. Suddenly, anyone with an email address could contact anyone else who had an email address. Email set the precedent for open access and allows unacquainted individuals to contact each other.

The system was so efficient for both business and social connections, that, by 1995, 14 percent of Americans had an internet connection. SPAM filters quickly followed and made email even more powerful. Consumer interest accelerated when Yahoo and Amazon were founded and as corporations advertised and made personal computers (PCs) more affordable and desirable. Bill Gates's Microsoft Company (since 1976) was a key factor, starting with IBM PCs and quickly becoming the central software for fast, cheap computers. America Online (AOL) considerably quickened the net, making email nearly instantaneous and cheap. By 1998 there were millions of sites and billions of users as the internet became the world's largest communications network. Google and Bing were the most popular search engines. In 2016, one study found that white-collar workers are anxious and compulsive in checking emails an average 77 times a day, and, with some, over 300 times a day (Brooks, 2016). This reflects the shame culture of not responding fast enough, or perhaps, the psychological need to erase emails as fast as they arrive (Brooks, 2016).

Internet users began to sort themselves into sites, which began to sort the users in return. MiGente.com (for Latinos), AsianAvenue.com, and BlackPlanet.com were early favorites. Soon, Friendster (gaming), LinkedIn (business), and Facebook/Meta (social, then musicians and bands) had large followers. In 2020, there were one billion internet hosts (Statista, 2021i) and nearly five billion users in a global population of 7.9 billion people. Among Americans, there is a significant disparity in online access among those in suburban/urban areas, and with different education and income levels (Pew, 2017b). About five million children in low-income families do not have access at home, or have slow connections, and thus have a "homework gap" (Pew, 2017b). Sociologist Robert Putnam pointed out that access itself bridges neither the networking gap nor the inequality gap because of the way the internet is used (Putnam, 2015). Upper middle-class kids are highly sophisticated in digital literacy on the newest devices. They know how to search and how to evaluate what they find. These kids use the internet to gather news, connect and join different political and social-issue organizations, build résumés, find jobs, and look for travel opportunities. Poorer kids do not seek "mobility enhancing" sites but focus mostly on entertainment and recreation (Pew, 2015). Putnam concludes that "the Internet seems more likely to widen the opportunity gap than to close it" (Putnam, 2015). In 2021, the Infrastructure Investment and Jobs Act, a bipartisan plan pushed by the Biden administration, provided $65 billion to provide new broadband capabilities to ensure overlapping coverage with high-speed fiber so that the 30 million Americans in rural areas and poorer Americans everywhere would have better access to information and opportunities

The internet has spread American culture and its format is stereotypically American: informal, consumer-oriented, competitive, individualistic, disrespectful, decentralized, and diverse. In the early days, in 1999, the World Bank predicted an "end of geography"

Contemporary United States

as the internet helped to democratize information by breaking down the border walls of class, caste, and nationalism, and bringing economic progress to isolated countries (Knowlton, 1999). That prediction has not been accomplished. But the internet has shown its boundary-breaking effectiveness, proved with the victorious campaigns of Obama and Trump, the undermining of information censorship by China and others, and the spread of both real and fake news via social media sites everywhere.

Even as people are increasingly dependent on online services, the internet has an increasing number of problems due to personal privacy, data sharing, and copyright violations. Because anything that is ever posted will become public at some point, the hacking of private financial and biographical information from online archives is a serious problem. The proliferation of hate and pornography sites and their accessibility to children is a clear danger. The courts have sided with the sites by ruling that the 1st and 14th Amendment protections of free speech and right to privacy are guarantees that also protect books and magazines. In 2008, the US Supreme Court (SCOTUS) overturned several communications indecency acts by ruling that the federal government could not limit the internet with legislation that it felt was "harmful to minors" (EPIC, 2008). In 2017, the controversies over what could be "appropriate and decent" reached new heights with live postings of rapes, kidnappings, child porn, gruesome beheadings, suicide, and erotica.

The internet is clearly Janus-faced. It can be a positive force for multiculturalism and cosmopolitanism as it helps establish a "network nation" and "global civil society" empowering individuals and "crosscutting social groups" via Metaverse (Meta), Instagram, Twitter, TikTok, YouTube, YikYak, WeChat, Spotify, and thousands of blogs (Hsu, 2009). These platforms have promoted civic awareness among all groups, but especially Millennials and Gen Z through "We Count On Us" and "Sunrise Movement" voting coalitions, among others (Lee, 2020). Most of the tweets, posts, and net blogs are creative, happy, sweet, and unproblematic. At the same time, the net can damage physical person-to-person contacts, increase anxiety, and lead to online addictions. Communications Professor Thi Nygun explains that Twitter, and other social media platforms, "gamify conversation ... by offering immediate, vivid and quantified evaluations of one's conversational success" by scoring likes and dislikes that are addictive to users (Klein, 2022). Presently, every social media platform is facing public criticism and congressional investigations because of the algorithms that can be vastly destructive. For example, Instagram algorithms and social media influencers have been linked to mental health problems and suicides among teenage girls. Meta says it is innocent, but parents and politicians demand oversight and regulation, calling Instagram and other sites a deadly addiction, "the new tobacco" (NPR, 2021). In the recent past, men's magazines and women's magazines, beauty contests, and advertising by such companies as Victoria's Secret have been criticized for creating unattainable beauty, body, and lifestyle standards that have made girls feel inadequate and negative about their own bodies (Marikar, 2019). And, obviously, Instagram provides easy targets for male lust, sexist or otherwise, sought after or manipulated by those uploading explicit photos, or posted and then exploited by the male gaze (Swisher, 2021). The same is true of the female gaze but with less violence and gender hierarchy involved.

One dilemma is how to sift through the enormously vast amounts of material at your fingertips where information competes with misinformation. Misinformation leads often to animosity, combined with the light speed at which outrage can spread. The hopeful idea of the net as "a marketplace of ideas" to spread democracy, has changed, as journalist Farhad Manjoo explained: "the internet has loosened our collective grasp on the truth" (Manjoo, 2016). Social groups organize, publish, and broadcast their preconceptions and, often, biased interpretations of events, tethered or untethered to facts. Marginalized groups, hoaxers, and conspiracy theorists suddenly find that they have a larger number of people who agree with their views than could have been imagined without the net's ability to find and consolidate them. Progressive groups like #MeToo or Black Lives Matter (#BLM) can organize, but so can any other like-minded network, including criminal gangs and fascists. Foreign and domestic entities can carry out plans to shake up elections as was seen with Russian cyberhackers in 2016 and Trump supporters, the Proud Boys, in 2020. There are "trolls" who send out rumors trying to get a response from sycophants who tune-in only to sources with which they already agree.

Truth and documentary evidence are not the important factors; it is the point-of-view narrative that constructs social reality. Trump is famous for his quick tweets and interview responses and for his commitment to "echo chambers." He said, "All I know is what's on Internet" (Bruni, 2016). Also, "I didn't make an opinion on it. That was a statement made by a very talented lawyer on Fox. And so you shouldn't be talking to me, you should be talking to Fox" (Otterson, 2017). Other viewpoints can be muted, blocked, un-followed, ridiculed, or denied (Friedman, 2016b). Sociologist Clay Shirky analyzed the change that came in 2016 after social media exploded everywhere: "Before, white ethnocentrism was kept at bay ... Every person who was sitting in their basement yelling at the TV about immigrants or was willing to say white Christians are more American than other kinds of Americans—they didn't know how many others shared their views" (Friedman, 2016b). *Atlantic* editor Jeffrey Goldberg ominously added that the organizing power of the internet to increase hatreds is in its infancy and the future is approaching (Goldberg, 2017). Goldberg's prophecy came true in 2021 when the Proud Boys and others organized online and violently stormed the US Capitol.

Social Media and Youth Culture

It is difficult to discuss youth culture because of all the subcultures in a nation as diverse as America. There is also the trend that subcultures are giving way to a more individualized, post-subculture grouping based not on gender, sexuality, race, power, class, or location, but on "collectivities" defined by lifestyles and picking and choosing from many groupings. What is clear is that young people are quick to challenge, collide with, and violate established social directions as they immerse themselves and become sophisticated with the use of new technologies and cultural forms (Campbell and

Contemporary United States

Kean, 2016). There is the peer pressure involved and social media platforms provide continuous contact and a sense of co-presence (Mesch, 2009). And it is not just young people.

Sociologist Gustavo Mesch explained that technological change leads to social reorganization, whether the society resists the change or not (Mesch, 2009). This is technological determinism. Young adults who came of age in the twenty-first century have lived wholly within the internet era with its media-saturated computer and mobile electronic environment. It is hard for Millennials (Generation Y or Generation Next, born 1982–1994) or Generation Z (b. 1995–2014) to imagine a time when instantaneous social networking did not exist. What Generation Alpha (b. 2015–) will experience is anybody's guess. The older generations—Traditionalists (b. 1900–1945), the "Me" Generation of Baby Boomers (b. 1946–1964), and Generation X (b. 1965–1981)—had much fewer viewing choices to make and when they did choose, television viewing and telephone calls were done in the private spaces of their homes (WMFC, 2017). Things are more public now. All age groups were soon using SMS texting on mobile phones before the invention of smartphones and smartwatches. Texting is still the most popular way for instant contacts.

Personal "multimedia privatization" has become standard. Young people live more public lives due to the amount of material posted to the net or on social media platforms, but they also have created private spaces in their own rooms, away from parental supervision—this "bedroom culture" is a subset of youth culture (Mesch, 2009). This culture got stronger during the Covid-19 pandemic. Teenagers and young adults have an array of media choices as part of "bedroom culture," including video games, DVDs, HDTVs, computers, Skype and Zoom links, tablets, MP3 players, and smartphones with high-quality camera and video capabilities. They consume mightily but they are also active participants who create content as they post material online. YouTube's original slogan, "Broadcast Yourself," has been taken to new levels with millions of apps (applications) available to get voice, face, videos, and photographs into the virtual reality of cyberspace. There is a chance at fame and fortune. And to be ignored is devastating for young people.

Social media and youth culture come together in the cult of celebrity. Entertainment stars must now nurture their online presences, via media such as Twitter, Instagram, and Meta. For example, among the top fifty worldwide Twitter hosts: 1) Barack Obama had 130 million followers; 3) Katy Perry had 109 million; 6) Taylor Swift had 89 million; 13) Elon Musk had 66 million; 35) Oprah Winfrey had 43 million (Wikipedia, 2021). As a note, Donald Trump had 88 million followers on January 8, 2021, when Twitter announced: "After close review of recent Tweets from the @realDonaldTrump account and the context around them we have permanently suspended the account due to the risk of further incitement of violence" (Collins and Zadrozny, 2021). Trump had been temporarily suspended several times before that, particularly for his tweets that mostly African American demonstrators who gathered to honor the memory of George Floyd were "THUGS" and he would use military intervention because "when the looting starts, the shooting starts" (Room and Chiu, 2020). Social media companies are under increasing pressure to censor if public safety is involved.

After Facebook (Meta) built a platform in 2007 that allowed almost any app to work, it immediately soared to the top of the social media world in the US. In 2021, Meta had 2.9 billion active monthly users worldwide, with India leading with 349 million users and the US second at 194 million (Statista, 2021h). While there are millions of fake profiles, the lure of Meta is in being able to be open about yourself and your activities and letting the world in to see you. On the other hand, anonymity can also free people to show their inner selves, free themselves of their bodies, and thereby experiment in what sociologist Sherry Turkle calls "identity play, but it is very serious play" (Mesch, 2009). Others argue that these virtual relationships are "more intimate, richer, and more liberating than offline relationships because they are based on genuine mutual interest rather than the coincidence of physical proximity. It is a zone of freedom, fluidity, and experimentation" (Mesch, 2009). Youth culture has rejected much of the adult culture of privacy and, instead, openly engages in self-expression and shares personal information varying from highly intimate to banal activities as they dissolve the space between offline and online, off work and at work.

Young people have learned to find and process information differently than their elders. The Net-generation actively and fearlessly experiments with new programs and has grown up with the idea that any information can be acquired quickly online, even while multitasking among different devices and programs. Generations Y and Z are empowered by being able to reach local, national, and global audiences virtually anywhere they can get an internet connection.

Smartphones (cell phone PCs) were invented in 2002 and by 2015, two-thirds of all Americans relied on them, thus making Apple the world's largest corporation (PEW, 2015c). New developments came quickly, including Snapchat (private images that disappear after ten seconds if not screen-shot), Instagram (public images), Photobucket (digital photos), Twitter tweets and livestreams, Buzzfeed and 9GAG (viral videos and livestreams). Unsurprisingly, matchmaking services were very popular, and by 2021 included Zoosk and Match.com (all inclusive), OkCupid (the rating and dating market), Grindr (LGBT), YikYak (teenage confidential), BlackPeopleMeet (African American), Sugardaddie (college girls seeking affluent partners), ChristianMingle (faith based), AgeGapDating (significant age difference dating), OurTime (mature women), Silver.com (the over-fifty crowd), and thousands of others. Filters help users find partners based on ethnicity, race, religion, income, education level, location, age, body types, and more. Virtual reality headsets offer even better augmented reality apps. Beeps, music, and vibrations demand quick responses. And because Meta, Google, Twitter, and others allow it, users can choose to post to multiple platforms at the same time.

For most American teenagers in normal times, life outside the family revolves around school, part-time jobs, bedroom culture, college applications, athletics, and friends. Most middle-class teens have the philosophy of their own potential drilled into them by parents and teachers—an achievement ethos that makes them anxious about failing. The Covid-19 pandemic that started in 2020 brought even more anxiety as teen life outside their homes was heavily restricted, classes moved online, clubs were closed,

Contemporary United States

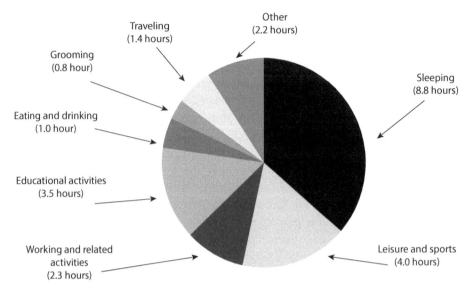

Figure 7.1 Time Use on an Average Weekday for Full-Time University and College Students
Source: https://www.bls.gov/tus/charts/students.htm

part-time work fell off, travel was nearly non-existent, and relationships suffered from quarantines and mask mandates.

As pandemic restrictions ebbed and flowed, teens returned to regular patterns. Most teens get driver's licenses when they are sixteen and, quickly thereafter, a car of their own. Middle-class teenagers have many social engagements in after-school athletics, clubs, volunteer organizations, music or dance lessons, and work. School days begin at or before 8 a.m. and end at 3 p.m. College students must manage their own schedules. Their various activities are depicted in Figure 7.1.

Social patterns are hard to characterize but have definitely changed. Previously, couples had formal dates, most often going out to dinner and a movie before committing to sex. Generations Y and Z commonly have sex before they commit to dating. While nearly half of all teenagers have had intercourse, it has become common in parts of the South and West for teens voluntarily to agree to an abstinence pledge—popularly called a "Virginity Oath"—abstaining from vaginal sex until they enter college or get married. The Silver Ring Thing has thousands of "I'm with Jesus" teens wearing a silver ring and promising that upon marrying, they will present the ring—and their virginity—to their betrothed (SilverRingThing.com, 2017; Unaltered, 2021). Even though more Americans say that sex among unmarried people is "not wrong at all," and the society is more tolerant about sex than ever before, this delay is part of a broader trend among young people to wait longer to begin having sex, to have fewer partners, and to have intercourse less frequently than previous generations (Julian, 2018). Researchers attribute this withdrawal of physical intimacy to declines in dating and couplehood, rise in consensual sex, rise in asexuality, obesity, anxieties over body image, porn and "the vibrator's golden age" in the doubling of masturbation rates among men and tripling among women. Social media sites like Grindr and Tinder (OkCupid is an exception) have a lot of users, but very few swipe rights unless the user is particularly handsome. It takes about 300 tries to have one in-person conversation (Julian, 2018). Additionally, one of the fallouts from the #MeToo movement is the decrease in men approaching women in public anymore. Seventeen percent of Americans aged eighteen to twenty-nine say that inviting a woman to have a drink is "always" or "usually" sexual harassment—a conclusion that makes them wary of males. Adults over twenty-nine do not agree with this conclusion but are a bit more tentative and hesitant than before (Julian, 2018).

Smartphone sexting is now normal with teenagers, mostly girls, sending nudes to boyfriends and others, who quickly share them around, of course (Sales, 2016). Peer pressure and popularity issues, experimentation during the "emerging adulthood" period, a selfie culture that teaches self-objectification, and some blackmail is often involved (Orenstein, 2016). So is the widespread "hook-up"-instead-of-dating culture and the easy availability of pornography as a sex instruction manual for many adolescents (Sales, 2016). Sociologists worry that porn is primarily about male lust and the objectification of females which makes it more about sexism than sex.

With or without understanding the underlying issues of gender equality and violence, teenagers rebel against adults who describe them as "victims." Teens argue that they are self-determining actors who will not be bound by "old-school" constraints (Orenstein, 2016). Increasingly, parents monitor their children's digital activities by checking viewed websites, using monitoring tools to track physical locations, and insisting on having passwords to all accounts (PEW, 2016).

Print Media and a Free Press

The growth of the United States corresponded closely with the rise of newspapers. In 1775, the English colonies published thirty-seven papers, which were important political organs carrying the debate over revolutionary ideas. The *New York Times* was founded in 1851 and competed with the news empires of Joseph Pulitzer and William Randolph Hearst in mixing accurate news, inaccurate sensationalism—termed "yellow journalism," and politically oriented social causes. In the 1880s, America had 971 daily papers and 8,633 weeklies. Urban dwellers had a wide choice of local papers. New Yorkers, for example, picked among twenty-nine and Chicagoans had eighteen. With the advent of radio and television news programs, many newspapers went out of business while others consolidated to survive. In 2021, most readers prefer digitalized news sources available anywhere, online. Printed papers continue to lose readerships.

Americans have always had a trust–distrust relationship with government and other institutions. The three historical "estates" are the church, the state, and the people, which are organized by the constitutional division of powers: judicial, executive, legislative in their incarnations at federal, state, and local government levels. The press has been referred to as the "fourth estate" and is expected to be a check on power by acting as a

Contemporary United States

watchdog alerting the public to possible corruption and outright lies by elected officials. The press touts its objectivity and likes to say that it speaks truth to power, even as it has become more partisan.

The American media became more truth-oriented in the twentieth century and jealously guarded its reputation of checking facts before and after stories were published. In the 1950s, newsman Edward R. Murrow was instrumental in crushing the excesses of McCarthyism and the Red Scare. In 1974, reporters from the *Washington Post* (est. 1877) relentlessly chased leads and exposed Nixon administration lies and the Watergate scandal, bringing down a corrupt president in the process. Nixon declared: "The press is the enemy" (Grynbaum, 2017). Both Joseph McCarthy and Richard Nixon were notorious for reversing the stories by lying and accusing their accusers—but the press won. The TV news program *60 Minutes* (1968–present) led the way with credible investigative exposés. The national press treated truth and false as binaries to be corrected instead of as negotiable transactions "up for grabs." But in the most recent decades, the culture wars placed the binaries in political partisans not in the accuracy of the stories (Gitlin, 1995; Hartman, 2015).

In the 2016 and 2020 elections, Donald Trump used the most sophisticated understanding ever of what might be called the "Twitter Democracy." Trump recognized that conservative Americans overwhelmingly believed in a "rigged system" by a "liberal media." He understood the power of groupthink loyalty. He could say and do anything. Trump famously claimed: "I could stand in the middle of 5th Avenue and shoot somebody and I wouldn't lose any voters. Okay? It's like incredible" (Trump, 2016b). When the news media called him out for statements he had made on record, Trump turned the tables by using what he called "truthful hyperbole"—which is defined as "an innocent form of exaggeration." He then leveled repeated charges of "fake news" at anyone who disagreed with him. His advisors supported him with "alternative facts" that appealed to his supporters. Key advisor Stephen Bannon put it bluntly, telling the press to "keep its mouth shut and just listen for a while … The media here is the opposition party. They don't understand this country" (Revesz, 2017). Once inaugurated, Trump doubled down on his use of social media lies to lambaste the fourth estate.

As discussed above, the internet and social media are responsible for much of the confusion over truth and lies. Even the most cherished American value of protecting freedom of speech puts democracy at risk by allowing con-artists and one-issue groups to discombobulate the masses with false or divisive claims. The people's trust in the press as an institution of fact and fairness has been essential to the democracy. One problem is the mixture of information with entertainment—"infotainment"—not only in the late night comedy shows and reality TV but also to maintain subscriptions and profits. Overwhelmingly, media corporations are private business ventures who answer to stockholders. And while the *New York Times* employs 1,300 journalists, newspaper companies overall employ 271,000 fewer workers than in 1990. The result is that, as a PEW poll found, only two in ten citizens trust the news "a lot" (Bishop, 2017). Talk radio and other formats rely on echo chambers of loyal followers. Historian Timothy Snyder calls this affirmation aspect dangerous because it is an "anticipatory obedience" to political spin (Snyder, 2017). Snyder adds: "To abandon facts is to abandon freedom. If nothing is true, then no one can criticize power … then it is all spectacle" (Snyder, 2017). This is dangerous because the primary point in having "news" is that it be factual and useful to democratic civil society decision-making. If the public accepts the modifiers "real news" and "fake news," then the shared culture is shattered as the people lose trust in the media. For all the conformity of the 1950s and the limited media choices available until the new media era, most Americans were reading the same newspapers and watching the same TV programs and movies. This sameness helped to unify the culture and society. The advent of "fake news" and a "confirmation bias" undermines facts, the *sine qua non* of democratic decision-making (Weisberg, 2019).

Many voices worried about the change from Obama to Trump. In 2017, Republican Senator John McCain understood the danger to US democracy: "When you look at history, the first thing that dictators do is shut down the press. And I'm not saying that President Trump is trying to be a dictator. I'm just saying that we need to learn from history" (McCain, 2017). George Shultz, the former Secretary of State for both Nixon and Reagan, reflected on Trump's lies and the democracy: "truth is the coin of the realm" and must be safeguarded by presidents (Shultz, 2017). British historian Simon Schama tweeted: "Indifference about the distinction between truth and lies is the precondition of fascism. When truth perishes so does freedom" (Cohen, 2017). Democracies require virtue and faith by winners and losers in political and social contests, and those attributes depend upon knowing fact from fiction. The *New York Times* changed its motto to "The truth is more important than ever." The *Washington Post*'s masthead also changed: "Democracy dies in darkness." Columnist Charles Blow expanded: "The press is the light that makes the roaches scatter" (Blow, 2017).

In 2021, only 3 percent of Americans said that printed papers were their primary source for news (PEW, 2021b, 2021d). The top four US papers, both digital and print, were led by the popular tabloid *USA Today*, which, like most papers, buys its stories from agencies that sell and distribute worldwide: Associated Press (AP), Bloomberg, and United Press International (UPI). The three others were a step higher, offering the highest quality articles by editorially independent investigative journalists: *Wall Street Journal, New York Times*, and *Washington Post*. Still, these three have clear political stances in conservative and liberal politics.

Magazines and periodicals remain widely popular, though less in print and more in online editions. Consumers have a choice among the current issues of nearly 7,500 magazines. In 2020 there were 222 million subscribers (Statista, 2021g). *American Association of Retired Persons* (AARP) and AARP *Bulletin* are bought by older persons at the rate of 23 million copies each per month. *Game Informer* caters to video gamers and is second to AARP with six million copies per month. *Southern Living, Consumer Reports, Time, Newsweek, Good Housekeeping, People, Better Homes and Gardens, Reader's Digest, Cosmopolitan, Women's Day, Women's Health, Men's Health, Sports Illustrated, American Rifleman, Car and Driver, Essence, Rolling Stone, Vogue, and Vanity Fair*, among others, cater to a broad readership. *National Geographic, The Atlantic, The New Yorker,*

The Economist, Wired, Smithsonian, and Forbes lead the pack of high quality, essential reads for the informed, professional classes (Magazine, 2021).

Starting in 1939, when the publisher Pocket Books made cheap editions available, a paperback revolution helped democratize culture. Believing that literacy and reflection are essential to a democracy, twenty-first-century analysts worry over the downward trend in book consumption, even though Americans are purchasing around two billion books per year in one form or another. During the Covid pandemic book sales in all categories, except educational texts in K-12 and universities, rose. In 2020, US sales of printed books were $26 billion, audiobooks $1.3 billion, and digital e-books $191 million (Statista, 2021d). The rise in self-publishing or "published on demand" increase the totals. Because consumers often feel overwhelmed at the long lists of "just released" books, people rely on bestseller lists and familiar authors. The worry is that everyone ends up reading the same books, thereby diminishing the diversity of viewpoints necessary for nuanced contributions to democracy. Others say that at least Americans can unite over a few popular authors, most likely those whose books are turned into movies.

American public libraries provide books and the physical space for community activities, such as individual study, immigrant language classes, literacy study activities for the homeless, book club meetings, and speaker/author lectures. Library use is the most common American cultural activity. Computers with internet connections are available to users for research into global resources, with printers available. Before the pandemic, every day, about four million people visited one of the 16,557 public libraries and, in total, checked out 1.5 billion books a year. During the pandemic, libraries quickly expanded their e-book offerings and loaned out 289 million e-books via the internet in 2020 alone (ALA, 2021). There are approximately 104,000 other kinds of libraries. Each of the nation's schools and universities has at least one library, and most have many. The Bureau of Indian Affairs operates 106 reservation libraries and the US military has 280 collections on bases worldwide. Overall, the two biggest collections are in the New York Public Library (21 million printed holdings), which is the world's largest city library, and Harvard University (16.8 million books plus 10 million microforms), which is the world's largest university library. There are also hundreds of private collections available to researchers and readers nationwide, among them the Henry H. Huntington Library in San Marino, California, and the world's best financially endowed library, the J. Paul Getty Museum in Malibu, California.

Each state has its own archives and history collections and many cities have local history collections. The federal government maintains two of the biggest libraries in the world in the Library of Congress (LOC) and National Archives (NA). Established in 1800 and secured in 1814 when Congress purchased 7,000 volumes from the private collection of Thomas Jefferson, the LOC is the largest library in the United States, with more than 38 million books and over one billion items of all types (ALA, 2017). The NA houses the documents of government agencies and owns such items as the original copies of the Declaration of Independence and the Constitution, soldiers' records, photographs, Indian treaties, and most of the official correspondence among government officials.

Culture, Media, Sports

Former presidents since Herbert Hoover (1929–1933) also have a federally funded presidential library in their home state. The latest, the Obama Presidential Library, began construction on September 28, 2021 in Chicago (Malloy, 2021). In the groundbreaking ceremonies, Obama said that he hoped the library would strengthen democratic ideas at a time when Americans are "seeing more division and increasingly bitter conflict" (Malloy, 2021).

Broadcast Media

Radio

Radio was first broadcast commercially in the 1920s and, by 1935, almost every American family owned a receiver. The radio helped immigrants learn English, the language of the airwaves, by standardizing the language and unifying the population. Perhaps the most famous use of the radio was by President Franklin Roosevelt, whose "fireside chats" in the Depression and the Second World War helped the nation through hard times. Two other highlights include the live broadcast of the arrival and "on-air" explosion of the German airship *Hindenburg* in New Jersey in 1937 and the 1938 transmission, without explanation, of the H. G. Wells's novel, *The War of the Worlds*—a broadcast that caused panic and hysteria in listeners who thought the earth was actually under attack by spacemen from Mars.

In contemporary America, every major city has dozens of privately owned stations. Public radio stations are operated mostly on college campuses or by National Public Radio (NPR), an association funded primarily by private subscriptions. NPR presents high-quality programming and news specials similar to those presented by its television counterpart, the Public Broadcasting System (PBS). Radio is accessible on the internet and satellite stations provide nearly 200 highly focused channels from which listeners can choose. The most popular formats are talk, country music, oldies, rock, news, religion, Hispanic, and Sports. "Talk radio" began in 1970 and has continued to proliferate. Listeners make the radio an interactive medium simply by calling the host or posting an opinion—the more outrageous the opinion, the more likely to get it aired.

Radio targets partisan audiences with Right-wing talk dominating the AM-radio stations. Syndicated nationwide from 1988 until his death in 2021, Rush Limbaugh built a weekly following of an estimated 15.5 million listeners for his three-hour-long politically oriented program. Limbaugh held enormous influence with Republican Party voters who believe in flag, country, low taxes, pro-life, anti-gay, and other traditional values. He and other conservative talk radio hosts became prominent players in Republican Party politics and especially strong in their support for Trump with their insistence that, for example, the mainstream press is fake news; Christians are persecuted in America; the government wants to take your guns away; abortion is murder; Obama is a Muslim who hates white people and democracy; Hillary is the devil; global warming is a hoax; schools are liberal propaganda agencies; and evolution is a lie.

Contemporary United States

FM-radio stations target different audiences. Many channels—like WAMU (American University)—are linked into the more liberal NPR networks. Here, the talk format is neutral or Left-leaning, involving various stakeholders and experts in informal debates and with news coverage often drawn from international organizations like the BBC. Religious radio also airs extensively on FM. Satellite radio is a fully subscription-based service picked up at home or in cars and contains a dazzling array of programming that can satiate virtually any taste or language. When they are driving, about 40 percent of Americans listen online through their smartphones via internet and radio apps.

Television

France experimented with television in the early 1900s, but the phenomenon grew fastest in the US, with twenty-three stations broadcasting in 1940 and 98 in 1950. In 1951, experimental broadcasts in color began and the first simultaneous coast-to-coast broadcast marked the rise of mass culture with an "everyone-knows-this-at-the-same-moment" phenomenon. By 1960, nine out of ten American families owned a TV set. Mass culture was reinforced by the dominance of three national channels: CBS, NBC, and ABC, before cable arrived in the mid-1970s and was available nationwide a decade later. In 1980, Cable News Network (CNN) provided continuous news simultaneously to all Americans and Music Television (MTV) fed youth culture. Other channels proliferated as television became even more popular with programs aimed at specific interests. Netflix, Home Box Office, Disney, Hulu, Amazon, and many others offer subscription viewing and archives of programs that allow for binge viewing. There are more excellent TV programs than ever before and the "on-demand" nature of cable, satellite, internet TV, and smartphones diversifies programs and democratizes viewing styles. Watching television is participatory and interactive. Viewers record and delete at will and gain flexibility in "time-shifted" schedules of work and play, becoming less dependent on broadcast schedules. American adults spend an average 13 hours and 12 minutes daily on media devices of all kinds, of which 3 hours and 17 minutes is traditional TV time (Schomer, 2021). Many programs reach across political divides, including some highlights in 2021: *The Beatles: Get Back*; *Succession*; *Squid Game*; *Mare of Easttown*; *What We Do In the Shadows*; *Emily in Paris*; and *Lupin* (IMDb, 2021). Sports is also mostly non-partisan with millions watching the National Football League Super Bowl game, College Basketball Final Four, Major League Baseball World Series, National Basketball Association Finals, Dayton 500 Stockcar Race, Masters Golf Tournament, US Open Tennis, and the hundreds of games leading up to those finals.

Americans increasingly go online for news, although 52 percent use television, cable, or network as the primary source (PEW, 2021b). There is a "graying" of television news watchers as younger people are more likely to be mobile with Twitter and Meta leading the way (PEW, 2021b). Television newscasts are increasingly partisan. Fox News advertises itself as a "fair and balanced" alternative to biased liberal media, when, in fact, Fox is a political force that openly pushes a neo-conservative agenda (see Illustration 0.2). Trump accepts Fox and does not include it on his fake news tweets.

Culture, Media, Sports

Government Activities

Since the relationship between government and culture often conflicts, Americans are content to leave the media to private businesses because they view government ownership as unacceptable to freedom of speech and freedom in general. The nearly 1,800 full-power commercial television stations are paid for by advertisers or by cable subscriptions. Much commercial broadcasting is "trash TV" because the profit motive makes it focus on the lowest common denominator in order to maximize audience appeal, and because of the sheer number of hours of broadcast time to fill. There are also high-quality programs and a wide range of more specialized channels, like Discovery, which concentrates on nature and scientific phenomena. Americans also support nearly 350 public television stations and 900 public radio stations broadcasting locally or regionally. The Public Broadcasting System (PBS), founded in 1967, is non-profit and educational, non-partisan but center-Left in news programs, has no advertising, and is funded by small contributions from thousands of viewers, large foundation grants, and government support.

Even while believing in private ownership and freedom of speech, most Americans want the government to safeguard children from the programming of violent, dirty language, or sexual content, something almost impossible to do in the era of internet smartphones and US Supreme Court (SCOTUS) decisions upholding freedom of speech. Hollywood has always been involved in controversies. In 1915, SCOTUS refused to ban the showing of *The Birth of a Nation* (1915), a film praising the violence of the Ku Klux Klan while stereotyping African Americans as brutish. In the 1930s, Hollywood introduced a production code to self-censor its films, but films became bland and ridiculous, to the extent of demanding that married couples sleep separately in twin beds in the same room. This changed in the 1960s and was thrown out entirely with cable TV subscriptions and the internet. In 1947, during the apex of the Red Scare, the House Un-American Activities Committee (HUAC) investigated Hollywood for films that might influence people toward communism. The Federal Communications Commission (FCC), an independent regulatory agency created by Congress in 1934, has five members appointed by the president to grant station licenses, maintain an acceptable—non-pornographic—broadcast, and regulate media ownership. The Telecommunications Act of 1996 relaxed restrictions on media ownership, a measure that reduced diversity and brought more homogeneity to mass media.

Americans still debate whether or not television affects behavior and generally believe that some impressionable viewers mimic what they see on TV, mostly of a sexual or violent nature. While Americans worry over racial and gender stereotyping and other offensive programming, there is little in the way of content regulations or direct government censorship. The entertainment industry polices itself, mostly effectively. In 1996, a conservative Congress pushed through the Communications Decency Act to require a labeling system to advise parents of programs suitable for children (G-rated), unsuitable for children aged under fifteen (R-rated) or eighteen (X-rated). In 2004, after singer Justin Timberlake partially ripped off Janet Jackson's leather bustier to

Contemporary United States

expose a breast during the live broadcast of the Super Bowl, the Bush administration challenged public broadcasts that it viewed as indecent. Timberlake claimed a wardrobe malfunction, but Congress passed the Broadcast Decency Enforcement Act of 2005, which increased penalties up to $325,000 for each broadcast incident of indecency. In June 2012, SCOTUS overturned all sanctions against profane language and nudity on television because restrictions violated 1st Amendment protections (Schatz and Kendall, 2012). Since it is not broadcast over the airways, cable television and internet sites can air nearly anything, with the exception of child pornography.

Leisure Time

Americans are not good at relaxing. Laziness confronts the work ethic and, in a society rife with traditional homilies like "time is money," "don't leave for tomorrow what you can do today," "the early bird gets the worm," and "a rolling stone gathers no moss," Americans weigh the costs of leisure against the rewards of work. In the seventeenth century, Puritan clerics warned that "idleness is the devil's workshop" and preached a gospel of "work as its own reward." This attitude filters into all aspects of American life and combines democracy, religion, and capitalism into a belief that "God helps those who help themselves." The effects of the 2008 recession still lingered when the Covid-19 pandemic swept across the world in 2020. Due to the pandemic, reliable statistics are not yet available and many agencies did not make reports in 2020 or 2021. Figures 7.2 and 7.3 are instructive for detailing the daily activities of pre-Covid American adults.

Beliefs in equality of opportunity and in a constantly rising living standard based on merit and "by the sweat of one's brow" have long marked American society. Americans

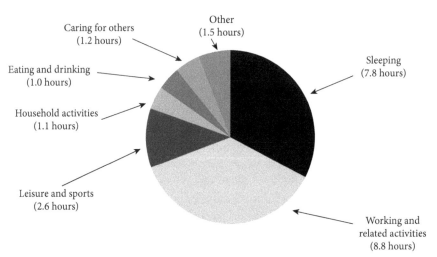

Figure 7.2 Time Use on an Average Work Day for Persons Aged Twenty-Five to Fifty-Four with Children

Culture, Media, Sports

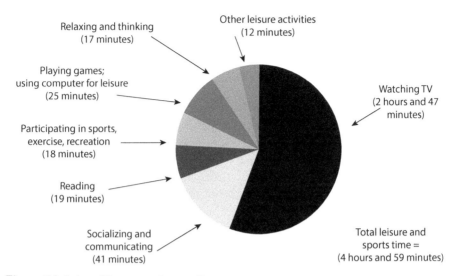

Figure 7.3 Leisure Time on an Average Day

generally expect all able-bodied adults to work to support themselves and their families and to manage their own expenses. Additionally, the "winner takes all" ethic of the workplace pays the most successful workers the highest salaries. This unequal distribution of rewards makes most workers struggle harder so as not to fall. Since 2008, Americans have told pollsters that they fear for the future and think that, for the first time ever, their children will not be as well off as they themselves have been. Thus, they are uneasy with leisure as they find themselves in a work-and-spend cycle of increasing wants, needs, and debts. In a "he-who-dies-with-the-most-toys-wins" mentality (consumption as utopia), the more he works, the more money he has available to buy the newest item, the more he owes, the more he wants, the more he works, the more he makes, and so on. Even with the overwork ethic deeply rooted, Americans believe that "all work and no play make Jack a dull boy." On an average day, adults spend about five hours in leisure activities (Figure 7.2).

Part of the American dream involves home ownership and so, when they have free time, most Americans work at domestic chores associated with maintaining and improving their property. Even after the loss of equity during the mortgage and financial crisis, a majority still strives for the status and success of owning a home of one's own: "a man's home is his castle." In 2008, foreclosures increased, the number of new houses being built drastically diminished, and, in the midst of bank failures and government bailouts (see Chapter 8), potential borrowers were unable to secure loans to buy new homes, even if their credit was good. The market showed some signs of recovery in 2016, but the median house price had dropped to $212,000 from $284,012 in 2012. Informing those prices is the fact that the number of foreclosures fell from 1.53 million to 810,000 as buyers purchased houses at bargain rates (RealtyTrac, 2017). With the pandemic, families sought security and real-estate prices rose as bidding wars drove house prices higher than ever. Many families supersize their homes and it is commonplace to find

Contemporary United States

a middle-class family of three living in a house with over 3,500 square feet and five bathrooms. The new homes have three-car garages, which American families use as a storage center for overflow purchases. Whether lounging or working, home life has become more private, as mass culture is experienced less in community and more in solitude, or with a few relationships.

While mocked as a "no vacation nation" because there is no nationally mandated vacation law, American workers generally get between one week (business and manufacturing firms) and four weeks (teachers and government workers) of paid vacation a year. Governments elsewhere require employers to fund official holidays, "bank holidays," and paid vacations for employees. Details vary, but roughly, some comparisons include: Brazil, Lithuania, Sweden—41 days; Finland, France, Russia—40 days; UK—36 days; Denmark, Germany, Spain—34 days; Ireland—29 days; India—28 days (Yonatan, 2016; Ray and Schmitt, 2017). Many US companies grant time off, but without pay, an offer most Americans cannot afford. Nationwide, private companies have downsized their workforces and maintained the "vacation fiction." With Covid, working patterns changed quickly to allow more people to do their jobs from home, thus blurring "at work" and "at home" differences and increasing the willingness to play. Until 2020, the majority of Americans took only 30 percent of the possible vacation time enumerated on their contracts. One reason was that a downsized workforce increases work per worker and many people refuse vacation so they can finish their work and keep their jobs. There are also growing numbers of people either trapped in the work-and-spend cycle, or who have not just a work ethic but an overwork ethic and so opt for nothing longer than a weekend getaway now and then. In lieu of longer vacation periods, Americans have some vacations on federal holidays (Box 7.1), most of which have been placed to give three-day weekends.

In 2021, Biden signed the "Juneteenth National Independence Day Act" to add a permanent official holiday to honor the final emancipation of African Americans from slavery on June 19th, 1865 (CRS, 2021d) (Illustration 7.2). Biden used the moment to support critical race theory: "I call upon the people of the United States to acknowledge and celebrate the end of the Civil War and the emancipation of black Americans and commit together to eradicate systemic racism that still undermines our founding ideals and collective prosperity" (Biden, 2021a).

Hollywood

The American movie industry was created in 1908 when Jewish American filmmakers moved production studios from NYC to a suburb of Los Angeles. Hollywood had its first studio by 1911 and its first prominent company, Universal City Studios, in 1917. Today, there are hundreds of independent film makers complementing the big six studios of Columbia, Paramount, Warner Brothers, Fox, Disney, and Universal. Over the years, the exceptionally large US domestic market allowed companies an economy of scale matched by no other country. India and China are now realizing the enormous power of their own domestic markets and are starting to compete globally. Hollywood still uses its reputation and market control mechanisms to retain a lion king's share of profits.

Box 7.1 Official Federal Holidays (purpose)

January 1	New Year's Day (Provides order; celebrates survival and a new beginning)
Third Monday in January	Birthday of Martin Luther King, Jr. (Honors equality and dissent)
Third Monday in February	Presidents' Day (Celebrates Washington and Lincoln as secular heroes)
Last Monday in May	Memorial Day (Honors slain soldiers and past wars)
June 19	Juneteenth (Commemorates the end of African American slavery)
July 4	Independence Day (Celebrates the Declaration of Independence)
First Monday in September	Labor Day (Honors ordinary workers and work ethic)
Second Monday in October	Columbus Day (Marks American exceptionalism)
November 11	Veterans' Day (Honors US military)
Fourth Thursday in November	Thanksgiving Day (Celebrates abundance and family)
December 25	Christmas Day (Honors consumption, giving, and Jesus)

In many ways, entertainment has conquered reality (Gabler, 2000). Hollywood used to be associated primarily with leisure and entertainment but, since the 1960s, the broadcast images have increasingly mixed fiction with documentary and informational material—"infotainment"—to the point that people refer to movies as if they were real history. For years, the Sunday night primetime Wonderful World of Disney opened with the soundtrack: "When you wish upon a star, makes no difference who you are. When you wish upon a star, your dreams come true." Hollywood gives life to the American dream and, particularly, to the viewers dreaming to recreate and reinvent life as seen in the movies. This can be a capitalist dream, a romantic dream, a religious redemption dream, or a democratic egalitarian dream.

In 2016, Hollywood released 718 new films and took in $11.4 billion, which was nearly one-third of global box office receipts of $38.6 billion ($6 billion higher than in 2011)—a fortune that is inestimable because of market tie-ins such as Netflix contracts, clothing, posters, music, games, and dolls (MPAA, 2017). In 2019 there were 800 films, but in 2020, due to the pandemic and to the rise of online streaming sites, only 329 films were released in theaters in the US and Canada (Statista, 2021c). Many viewers increased their pay TV subscriptions, resulting in a 26 percent increase and $233 billion

Illustration 7.2 Juneteenth National Independence Day

On New Year's Day 1863, in Washington, DC, in the second year of a four-year-long Civil War, President Abraham Lincoln announced "The Emancipation Proclamation" to free all slaves held in areas controlled by the Confederate States of America. While that was a "Day of Jubilee!" for four million people, it would take until June 15, 1865, before the last state, Texas, formally announced freedom for its slaves. Then, in 1870, Congress passed three constitutional amendments to free the slaves, provide citizenship rights, and open the voting booths to black voters. And still blacks were excluded in many places until the 1965 Voting Rights Act placed government supervisors at the polls. This act was overturned by Congress and the US Supreme Court in 2018. In 2022, the John Lewis Voting Rights Act was under consideration to reinstate protections for minority voters of every race, class, or condition, but it was defeated by congressional Republicans. On June 17, 2021, President Biden declared that June 19—Juneteenth—would be recognized as a public holiday.

Source: Drew Angerer via Getty Images

in sales (MPAA, 2021). Hollywood provides a soft power approach that complements US educational power to further foreign policy goals by presenting American culture writ large. US culture reaches into the world's living rooms in a variety of internet and traditional ways in the hundreds of made-for-TV sitcoms (situation comedies), dramas, mini-series, and movies. Since 2016, China, Japan, and India have been the top foreign markets for US films and TV programs. Conversely, globalization has had its effects on making movies, as high US production costs encourage producers increasingly to film scenes outside the United States. Overseas filmmaking also boosts sales and interest, as does the casting of non-American superstars like Zhang Ziyi, Gal Gadot, Gong Li,

Priyanka Chopra, Salma Hayek, Viggo Mortensen, Alexander Skarsgard, Javier Bardem, Christian Bale, Charlize Theron, Djimon Hounsou, Nicole Kidman, Marion Cotillard, Emma Stone, and Colin Firth. Hollywood must keep the international market in mind and play to global tastes for action movies and superheroes while they release films simultaneously worldwide.

Hollywood films have also functioned to help immigrants assimilate to American culture. Today, this assimilation is played out increasingly on a world scale, whether or not viewers immigrate to the US or live in McWorld. Fantasy America has been a country that could teach the rich humility, the poor to rise, the ignorant to study, the doubters to believe, and the foreigner to assimilate. Disney Studios expressed these themes in films including *Pinocchio* (1940), *Bambi* (1942), *The Lion King* (1994), *Finding Dory* (2016), *Beauty and the Beast* (2017), *Frozen II* (2019), and *Encanto* (2021) where ethnically diverse young humans, animals, robots, and children's toys face homelessness, lose and find parents, fall in love, and become heroes as they save themselves, adults, the community, or the world in the process. The Hollywood narrative for a superhero starts with a tragic experience—a great loss—that defines a child or young adult and becomes the central element inspiring her/him to fight the forces of evil. Superheroes and cartoon figures have long been intertwined but in the twenty-first century they are everywhere. In 2019, Marvel's *Avengers: Endgame* became the highest grossing film ever made, taking in $2.8 billion in global box office receipts (Statista, 2021b). Internet streaming services tie into the Marvel universe. For example, in 2021, the *Hawkeye* series told of a regular girl turned to idealism after a gang of villains killed her father. Superhero movies are insistent that inner beauty defeats outer appearances and that the Other can be heroic. Happy endings abound as tragedies are overcome and bad guys defeated.

Outside of Hollywood studios, independent filmmakers—Indies—are rising due to advanced technology and internet opportunities that require production costs. Annually, the Sundance Film Festival in Park City, Utah, accepts Indie submissions for evaluation and awards. For the 2022 competition, Sundance received 3,762 films. Juries selected eighty-two for the competition, with forty-three women directors and thirty-nine first-time directors (Sperling, 2021). Among the most common storylines were a focus on abortion, the nature of white male privilege, the fights for civil rights and racial justice, and the environmental emergency. The directors of the festival admitted selecting "a lot of films that are looking at the fight for democracy because we are in this age of reckoning, this age of accountability" (Sperling, 2021).

Sports

Americans love sports and have actively participated in organized games since the middle of the nineteenth century. The world's foremost yachting race, the America's Cup, began in 1851. Baseball, which can be traced to the English game of rounders, rose to prominence during the American Civil War. For the most part, Americans play the games of the world. Usually high in the medal standings in the Olympic Games, in 2020,

Contemporary United States

in Tokyo, the United States finished first with 113 medals, 39 of which were gold; China was second with 88 and 38. Certain sports are particularly associated with America, such as baseball, basketball, and American football. Ice hockey—more Canadian than American—is the fourth power in professional sports franchises just ahead of soccer and tennis. Since golf is a skill game like billiards where the ball stands still, it is not technically a sport and the players are not athletes. Still golf is played and adored by millions. With sporting figures and teams achieving hero status and salaries reaching alarming heights, each serious incident of drug abuse, cheating, or law-breaking is reported and discussed. Americans want their athletes to compete fairly, while they also want them to win at any cost. The hero status also provides a platform for the athletes to detail abuse, take up political causes, and be heard in social-justice cases (Illustration 7.3).

Baseball pits one man with a bat in his hands against a team of men ready to put him out. It represents the individual in competition against other men in one-on-one situations where no one can interfere to help the player succeed or fail. Baseball gives control of the ball to the defenders, something other sports do not. The game is highly nuanced and every play has a winner and a loser. The man who "wins" hits the home run, strikes out the batter, steals second base, or makes the game-winning catch near the wall in left field; the loser swings and misses, fails to catch the ball, shows bad judgment by throwing the wrong pitch or being caught off base. One team wins and one team loses, but the credit is given to a "hero." The size of the player is irrelevant but the skill of the player is all important. Time is not a factor and game length depends on how long it takes to play nine innings, as measured by the success or failure of individuals to get base hits or to make outs. Baseball is orderly and appeals to the American legal sense as an umpire rules on every single action of the game. Baseball is played on grass and the generally slow speed of the action reflects the pre-industrial pace of life and offers a respite from the hurried world of urban living. Softball has basically the same rules and is played by women as well as men.

Basketball began as a way to Americanize immigrants by organizing boys and girls into teams. It was invented in 1891 by James Naismith at a Young Men's Christian Association (YMCA) meeting in Springfield, Massachusetts, and quickly spread to Settlement Houses where immigrants lived. Basketball is more chaotic and represents a Rock & Roll society in the movement of players constantly in motion, racing up and down the court at extremely high speed. Time matters and is highlighted on the scoreboard, with stopwatch precision down to hundredths of seconds. Unlike baseball, physical size matters.

American football is played by precise rules on a field laid out in grids. Each play has been completely rehearsed in long days of practice and is activated in particular situations and against the opposing team's specific alignment and personnel. Football is very violent with head and other injuries fueling yearly calls for reforms. The game depends on the gain and loss of territory (Schrank, 1995). As in basketball, size matters. There is a certain lawlessness to the game, with twenty-two players all in motion, pushing and shoving, and trying to gain advantage by breaking the rules—something almost impossible to do in baseball. The corporate mentality of the team counts more, and

Culture, Media, Sports

Illustration 7.3 Olympic Athletes, Sexual Assault, #MeToo, and the US Senate

As #MeToo gained support as a movement whose time had arrived, women were encouraged to come forward against especially powerful males who had made inappropriate sexual overtures whether in language, touching, assaults, or misuse of their official positions in sexually predatory ways. Donald Trump's sexist language and the accusations of rape against him helped focus #MeToo. Many women found the courage to charge the abusers for recent and past outrages. Rich businessmen, Hollywood moguls, politicians on every level, Supreme Court Justices, college professors, medical doctors, and priests, among others, were called out as predators. Compensation for the victims came when the men did prison time, lost their reputations, were fired from lucrative jobs, and paid monetary fines to the women. In 2021, world-class gymnasts—including Olympic champions—proved that the US team doctor Larry Nassar had sexually abused 265 young girls and women through unwanted advances over a period of eighteen years. The US Senate Judiciary Committee investigated the charges, found the US Olympic Committee at fault for covering up the abuses, the FBI complicit in its failure to investigate complaints, and heard the powerful testimony of some of the nation's most admired and successful athletes. Pictured from left to right as they speak with Senator Diane Feinstein are Aly Raisman, Simone Biles, McKayla Maroney, and Maggie Nichols (partially obscured by Feinstein) (see also Illustration 5.1).

Source: Saul Loeb-Pool via Getty Images

individuals must submerge their own glory so that the group can penetrate most deeply into the opposing group's side of the field to score the most points and win the game. Movement is characterized in military terms as in "throwing the bomb," "the ground attack," and "shredding the defense" (Kanfer, 1995).

Baseball, basketball, football, and soccer are games played by a wide variety of Americans at many levels. To Americans, success in sports represents the faith that

Contemporary United States

individuals and teams have an equal opportunity to win, but that hard work and merit lift some above others. It is not rare for an underdog to beat the champion. The games are highly institutionalized rituals which combine religion, capitalism, and politics (Illustration 7.4). Every American school has weekly physical education classes organized around these and other sports—such as ice hockey, volleyball, tennis, and swimming. Every town of any size has organized baseball and basketball leagues where people aged six to sixty can compete. The Friday-night high school or Saturday-afternoon college football games, with their ferocious emphasis on winning, bring communities, social classes, and ethnic groups together to worship the home team at a level approaching religious belief in nearly all parts of the country. Teams and heroes in each sport become mythical, legendary, and historical. Writers often use sports in their novels, and Hollywood produces movies highlighting a particular team, league, and player, including a scene of a game or ballpark. On the individual and team levels, sports act as rallying points for civic pride, provide mass culture and Americanization, and fill media airways. And players' salaries and commercial endorsements make professional sports one of the most lucrative occupations in the world.

Sports have been central to definitions of American masculinity and have long been seen as crucial to the development of manliness. Until very recently, sporting women were stereotyped as unfeminine or lesbian. Women and men are still generally segregated by teams and leagues. Race has also been an issue, with African Americans and Native Americans historically excluded from participation and spectatorship at university and professional levels. For to include them—and to have them excel— questioned the rules of racial hierarchy and theories of manhood which long dominated American society.

Sports have become more political and have advanced equality in recent years as college and professional teams have been integrated or opened to African Americans and women. This rise in women's sports has given women the opportunity, not always successfully, to ask for equal pay and comparable worth with men (Illustration 7.5). Recent studies show that the chance to compete for status and income in sporting venues has kept many children focused on finishing high school. Minority groups and women have increasingly participated in the most class-based of sports—tennis—as evidenced by Venus and Serena Williams. Serena is the career leader in Grand Slam titles (39) and is the highest-earning American female athlete in the world, with $92 million in prize money and more than double that in product endorsements. In 2020, Serena won $30 million, a payday much lower than the top males in her sport even while ticket prices to see her play are the same.

Additionally, American sports spectatorship strengthens family by its orientation of adults attending games with children. This may help explain the lack of fan violence that punctuates sporting contests in other countries. The professional sports franchises are privately owned and each year presents the chance for everyone to win, although the teams with the biggest media markets and richest owners have an upfront advantage in recruiting the best players.

Culture, Media, Sports

Illustration 7.4 NFL Players, Racial Equality, and #BlackLivesMatter

In 2016, All-Pro Quarterback Colin Kaepernick (#7) of the San Francisco 49ers football team decided to use his notoriety to take a political stance to protest the daily police violence against African Americans. Every National Football League game begins with almost everyone in the stadium standing, many with their hands over their hearts or saluting the American flag and being quiet or singing the US national anthem to praise the nation, its mission, and its military. Kaepernick knelt instead, with arms folded, non-threatening, but openly defiant of tradition and infuriating those who believed that patriotism was more important than freedom of expression. President Trump was wishy-washy even if he had long said that players who knelt were "sons of bitches" who should be fired for disrespecting the United States. Kaepernick's action started a protest call-to-action taken up by many athletes at all levels including NBA superstar LeBron James. James went further, forming More Than a Vote to organize blacks to register and vote for progressive and liberal candidates. James increased his activism after the murder of George Floyd. Sports heroes who become activists have real power to persuade. James's nearly 140 million subscribers on Twitter, Facebook, and Instagram was equal to the total number of votes cast in the 2016 election and gave James an enormous outlet for his views. The photo includes Eli Harold (#58) and Eric Reid (#35).

Source: Michael Zagaris via Getty Images

Art

Few if any cities worldwide contain more art museums than New York City. The Museum of Modern Art, Metropolitan Museum of Art, Henry Frick Collection, Guggenheim Museum, J. P. Morgan Library, Brooklyn Museum of Art, Whitney Museum of

Illustration 7.5 World Champions Demand Respect and Fair Pay for Women

The US Women's National Soccer Team has been strong in world-class athletes who are great in international play. Among them, striker Megan Rapinoe (second row, fourth from the left) had an Olympic Gold Medal and had twice been a FIFA champion, with the 2019 award as leading scorer and best player in the World Cup. Rapinoe openly criticized the US Soccer Federation for paying male players more than female players, even though the women won more often. She and others filed a gender-discrimination lawsuit that a federal court dismissed. But the cause did not die and a general conversation erupted over gender pay inequities in all workplaces. President Joe and First Lady Jill Biden invited Rapinoe and two others to join them at the White House onstage to highlight "Equal Pay Day." Rapinoe was clear: "I have been devalued, I've been disrespected and dismissed because I am a woman. Despite all of the wins, I am still paid less than men who do the same job that I do" (Biler and Boren, 2021). Biden urged Congress to pass the proposed Paycheck Fairness Act (first proposed in 1997 and defeated more than twenty times) as part of the American Rescue Plan, saying "It's about justice." The House quickly passed the Act, but it foundered on four votes in the Senate, each time by votes of forty-nine in favor, fifty opposed, one abstention, and in the face of a filibuster that would require sixty yes votes. On February 22, 2022, despite the failed court case and the "no" decision by the US Congress, the US Soccer Federation reversed itself and granted a $24 million settlement to Rapinoe and twenty-seven fellow athletes for back pay equal to what the males made. Moreover, the organization agreed to an even wage disbursement from now on. It should be noted that FIFA does not pay women the same as men.

Source: Zhizhou Wu via Getty Images

Modern Art, and Museum of the American Indian are just a few of the better-known, world-class collections. While these museums reflect New York's tastes in high culture, the city by no means has a monopoly in that area. Every large American city has its own list of high culture sites.

American painting originally patterned itself after European models in the romantic landscape renderings of the Hudson River School. Most prominent American artists were traditionalists, such as Winslow Homer, Thomas Eakins, and James McNeil Whistler, who studied abroad and learned to combine portraiture with landscape. Georgia O'Keeffe focused on feminine forms, national myths, and landscapes. In the 1930s, the Ashcan School realistically painted the crowded streets and confusion of urban America. Later on, Edward Hopper's depictions of the solitude of city life and the loss of community reflected modernizing trends. American art came into its own in the 1940s, with public recognition and influence worldwide when Jackson Pollock began to drip paint and Andy Warhol depicted celebrities and consumer products. Pollock and others in the "New York School" who let their unconscious direct their creations came to be known as "abstract expressionists." Shunning all legible symbolism, Pollock claimed, "I am not aware of what is taking place ... It is only after [I have painted] that I see what I have done" (quoted in Tallack, 2000). Warhol's depictions of soup cans, Elvis Presley, and Marilyn Monroe, exploited popular culture icons and was dubbed "pop art." Louise Bourgeois challenged male supremacy and put forward Cold War anxieties in works that can be called "eccentric abstraction." Robert Rauschenberg used recognizable items—including tires, and toy animals, and pictures of John Kennedy—to construct collages mocking abstract expressionism but still asking for interpretation of a homophobic, racist, and materialist culture. Dissent is a key theme in the art-is-politics versus art-as-aesthetics debate (see Illustration 0.5).

American arts are primarily self-sufficient, supported mostly by private donations. Americans have long been resistant to the use of public funding for the arts, with the two notable exceptions. From 1935–1943, the Federal Programs for the Arts under President Franklin Roosevelt's New Deal supported thousands of artists who created hundreds of thousands of public art projects—most of them focusing on the themes of strong family and the heroic worker. Since its founding in 1965 as part of the Great Society Program of President Lyndon Johnson, the National Endowment for the Arts (NEA, 2021) continues to support innovation and "excellence." Overall, the NEA has granted over $5 billion and made 150,000 monetary awards in music, theater, dance, literature, education, and the visual arts to individuals and groups, such as historic African American colleges, American Indian tribal colleges, African American organizations, Hispanic institutions, Asian American and Pacific Islander communities, and organizations for people with disabilities (NEA, 2021). The NEA also selects honorees to receive the Medal of Arts from the US president. Because visual and performing arts can be so contentious during periods of conservative ascendancy, since 1996 there has been no direct funding to individual artists, but the NEA supports them indirectly through organizations. The Trump administration was strongly in favor of dismantling the NEA in its entirety. Upon taking office in 2021, the Biden administration increased the NEA's budget to a record

Contemporary United States

high of $201 million and participated in its award ceremonies, something Trump had shunned (McGlone, 2021).

Every year the Kennedy Center in Washington, DC, celebrates a handful of recording artists, writers, and actors who have made lifetime achievement contributions to the arts. For forty-three years, every president has hosted a White House reception and attended the annual ceremonies. Seeing this as "highbrow and liberal," Trump refused to participate. But Biden, at the first Kennedy Center event of his presidency, talked about "the critical role arts play in our nation" and pledged to advance the arts in "small towns and rural communities to made art more accessible for people at every age and every background, to lift up more voices and stories" (McGlone, 2021).

Overall, Americans insist that individual or corporate patrons support their own causes. There is also a deeply rooted idea of private giving to support public causes in the US and abroad. Contributions by philanthropic groups (19 percent of total giving) such as the Pew Charitable Trust, the John T. and Catherine D. MacArthur, John D. Rockefeller, Andrew Carnegie, George Soros, Bill and Melinda Gates, Henry Ford foundations, by corporations (4 percent), and individual or bequest donations (75 percent) raise most of the money needed to build theaters and museums and to fund cultural programs in the United States (GivingUSA, 2021). The Lincoln Center for Performing Arts in New York, which is home to the Metropolitan Opera and New York Philharmonic Orchestra, receives all but 5 percent of its funding from private gifts, advertising revenues, and ticket sales. In 2020, the total charitable giving by all Americans hit a record high of $474 billion (GivingUSA, 2021). The recipients varied, but for example, the arts received $22 billion, education $71 billion, religious groups $131 billion, human services including food banks and health agencies $166 billion, international aid $29 billion, and environmental causes $14 billion (GivingUSA, 2021). In 2020, the liberal MacArthur Foundation handed out $272 million in charitable grants, including money to support climate science, human rights, to combat global "anti-blackness" and to expand Covid-19 relief, to increase its total philanthropic giving since 1978 to $6 billion (MacFound, 2021). The Bill and Melissa Gates Foundation has dispensed more than $50 billion to global health, poverty and inequity in the United States and 100 countries, of which $5.8 billion was given in 2020 (GatesFound, 2021a, 2021c).

Even the museums and libraries in Washington, DC, which receive initial funding from the federal government—such as the American History Museum, National Air and Space Museum, Holocaust Museum, Natural History Museum, Library of Congress, and the National Portrait Gallery—are supported primarily by private donations, backed up with sales of articles in their museum gift shops and restaurants. The newest addition to "museum row" on the national mall is the Museum of African American History and Culture funded by $300 million from federal tax money, and half by private donations.

Among the reasons Americans distrust government funding of museums is because visual arts offer the irresistible temptation by politicians to censor art for personal reasons and political gains. In the 1990s, Robert Mapplethorpe, an NEA-funded artist, pushed the limits when his photographs of naked children, gays, and a particularly graphic picture of a man urinating in another man's mouth caused public outcry (Lewis,

248

2008). In February 2001, New York City Mayor Rudolph Giuliani announced that he was freezing the multi-million dollar subsidy to the Brooklyn Museum of Art because an exhibit contained a photograph by Renee Cox. "Yo Mama's Last Supper" depicted Jesus as a naked black woman surrounded by twelve black apostles as a way to highlight religion's refusal to recognize the deity of women and minorities. "Why can't a woman be Christ?" Cox asked (AP, 2001a). Another firestorm erupted over Andres Serrano's "Piss Christ," a photograph of a plastic crucifix submerged in a glass container of the artist's urine. Serrano was asking religion to support gays, call attention to the fluids of the AIDS epidemic, mix the fake with the real, and the otherworldliness with the common items of this world (Hartman, 2015). When these cases reached federal courts, the judges protected the artists' freedom of expression and asked Americans to choose for themselves whether or not to attend exhibitions. The National Coalition Against Censorship monitors all censorship activities in the United States and organizes support for artists and exhibitions that are under attack because of their political views depicting "discomforting" topics such as LGBTQIA+, sexism, slavery (NCAC, 2022).

Concert halls and major orchestras began with the New York Philharmonic (1842). By the beginning of the twentieth century, every major city had its own orchestra, dominated by European compositions. Today, the US has some 1,500 orchestras, including at least forty world-class symphonies and nearly as many Americans go to hear the orchestras as attend professional baseball games. There are also more than 400 ballet and 100 opera companies. Most cities also have theaters for live performances. Broadway is famous for the forty world-class theaters of more than 500 seats each and the year-round performances of old, new, foreign, and American plays. Long-term hits include *Cats*, *Wicked*, *Jesus Christ Superstar*, *The Lion King*, *The Phantom of the Opera*, *Chicago*, *Moulin Rouge*, and *Beauty and the Beast*.

Popular Music

Matching Hollywood, American popular music is a leading agent of globalization and cultural imperialism as the world is tuned in to American rhythms. The two world wars spread American music and dancing styles everywhere US soldiers went as young people accepted the modernity and utopian appeals of the American dream. The pop music craze exploded in the 1950s and 1960s as television brought stardom to musicians and bands, and as technology produced affordable record players and portable transistor radios for the baby boomers. Music Television (MTV) opened up a world of videos. In contemporary America, TikTok, Spotify, and YouTube lead the way and allow unknown artists to quickly become known to a global youth culture based on music and dance. For example, twenty-year-old, gay and black, Lil Nas X uploaded "Old Town Road" on TikTok. It went viral and became US Billboard Top 100's longest running number one song of all time (PBS, 2021). A few months later, nineteen-year-old Olivia Rodrigo's "Driver's License" was the most streamed download to Spotify, and quickly surpassed one million listeners (Odoom, 2021). The music industry is perfect capitalism, creating

Contemporary United States

a market and supplying the product. Storytelling and lyrics combine with strong visuals as music challenges power and helps people define their identity and activate protests.

In the first two centuries in America, there was Native American music, slave songs in the fields, and political tunes to help the country through the various wars, but mostly, music was confined to religious observances or played at large community gatherings. With the rise of American imperialism in the late nineteenth century, military music and marching bands played the nationalistic music of John Philip Sousa. Marching bands in New Orleans took up this movement, mixed in the Blues of slave songs and developed not only the modernity and urban styles of Jazz, but music with a special "ragged" beat, Ragtime. Blues and Jazz emphasized both the modern and the exotic. Jazz spread quickly to Europe after the First World War, developing from instrumental creations to the vocal patterns of Billie Holiday, Charlie Parker, Louis Armstrong and, a little later, B. B. King. The Depression and the Second World War brought in Swing, with the big band sound of Glenn Miller, Benny Goodman, and Duke Ellington. Patriotic folk ballads of hard work, heroism, and sacrifice were also popularized by the likes of Woodie Guthrie.

Country music—also called Southern Music—arose during the Great Depression in the 1930s in the poorest white sections of rural America in the Appalachian Mountain region of Tennessee and Kentucky. Tales of coal miners, cheating hearts, and "poor-white-but-proud" lyrics expressed the reality many lived. After Roy Acuff and his Smoky Mountain Boys became the pre-eminent live music radio show in America, the genre spread. Hank Williams, Sr. became the first true star with his songs about hard drinking and hard loving; his death at age twenty-nine from a mixture of alcohol and pills increased the fame of Country and Country Pop (HOF, 2002). Loretta Lynn, Hank Williams, Willie Nelson, Johnny Cash, Dolly Parton, Charley Pride, Garth Brooks, Alan Jackson, Taylor Swift, Billie Eilish, and Lil Nas X have so popularized the form that it remains the number one music format for radio stations in the twenty-first century.

A momentous change came when African American Blues patterns were combined with white Country music's lead guitar to produce the hybrid sound of Rock 'n' Roll. This emerged from the larger social prosperity, northward migration of Southern blacks, rapid expansion of the automobile culture, and revolutionary movements toward equality. The hip-grinding music broke from the "innocent and decent" 1950s (Hartman, 2015). The youth rebellion was on as Chuck Berry, Jerry Lee Lewis, Bill Haley, Little Richard, and Elvis Presley mixed sexual innuendo with a fast pace which crossed the Atlantic to inspire the Beatles and the Rolling Stones. Young people began to live for the music, an addiction that is still obvious. Rock 'n' Roll helped provide the vehicle for the counter-culture to protest both the Vietnam War and the conformity of the older generation. The music also changed dancing styles as steps and patterns turned into a liberation driven by the protest, desire, and pleasure of the music itself. Rock 'n' Roll—and, later, Rock—became as much an attitude as an art form.

Many conservatives criticized the beat and lyrics as immoral, depraved, and way too loud. Cultural critic Allan Bloom lambasted rock as a "barbaric appeal to sexual desire" which destroys the hearer's ability to reason due to its drug-like effects (Bloom, 1988).

Commentator George Will called rock "a plague of messages about sexual promiscuity, bisexuality, incest, sado-masochism, Satanism, drug use, alcohol abuse and constantly, misogyny" (Will, 1985). Young people responded with "Whatever!"

James Brown, Aretha Franklin, and Wilson Pickett sang the lyrics in a slower, deeper manner called Soul. Folk singers—including Bob Dylan, Joan Baez, Pete Seeger, Joni Mitchell and Jimi Hendrix—mixed ballads, spirituals, and rock into protest music. George Clinton, Rick James, and others mixed Soul with Jazz to produce an urban syncopation called Funk. In the 1970s and 1980s, Michael Jackson became the undisputed "King of Pop" with his dance steps, adolescent voice, and tender lyrics. Prince combined almost every musical genre into a style dominated by his voice and electric guitar. In the 1980s and 1990s, Madonna—with more number one hits than anyone ever—criticized the materialism, racism, sexual prudery, and religious hypocrisies of American culture while hooking the world on that culture. Lady Gaga mixed everything together into Electropop and Europop dance forms. Beyoncé challenged racism and sexism in her 2016 album "Lemonade."

The influence of Rap, or hip-hop, has been truly significant and the genre has changed dramatically since its early violent, racist, and misogynist days. Springing out of street culture in the 1970s and 1980s, rappers like Dr. Dre (Ice Cube) and Grandmaster Flash expanded the vocabulary of the inner-city antihero, expanded social criticism, and made rap into reporting, analysis—what Public Enemy called the "CNN of the ghetto" (Hartman, 2015). "Gangsta" rap played on the drugs and gangs in the "hood"—in the form of The Notorious B.I.G. and others. But rappers also aimed at white racism and "normative taboos," as did N.W.A.: "'Fuck tha Police' coming straight out the underground … Some police think They have the authority to kill the minority …" (Hartman, 2015). Many white conservative politicians attacked rap as obscene, but the US Supreme Court held firm for freedom of speech. rap was always performance art and developed into a dance style that expressed a "get outta my way" philosophy among American youth as a cultural expression of resistance and pride.

Music critic Hua Hsu cites Rap's rise in the international imagination as "hip-hop – the sound of the post-civil-rights, post-soul generation – found a global audience on its own terms" (Hsu, 2009). Rappers today have gone mainstream, and while they still "discuss" gay rights, the patriarchy, racism and poverty, they have moved away from gang and ghetto issues to themes of romance and lifestyle—to "say something significant" as Kanye West explained (McNulty-Finn, 2014). Social media and internet have freed and diversified rap in individual directions and a multitude of themes for different audiences that blend in with pop, rock, and other genres.

With the surge of Hispanic/Latino immigrants during the past decade, American music is making another change. Superstars have been around since the 1960s with Carlos Santana, José Feliciano, and Ritchie Valens leading the way. Selena, Pitbull, Gloria Estefan, Christina Aguilera, and Jennifer Lopez sang or sing in both English and Spanish, but there is a vibrant market for Spanish-language releases and superstars like Cardi B, Tom Morello, Becky G, Bad Bunny, Despacito, Camilla Cabello, and Ludacris (Illustration 7.6).

Illustration 7.6 Spotify Advances Latin Music and Hispanic Visibility

After YouTube gave anyone the opportunity to "broadcast yourself," the internet exploded with music from amateurs to professionals. Then came a multitude of other online vehicles by which aspiring singers could gain airtime and recognition. It is difficult to imagine the explosion of creative voices that has arisen and may yet arise as people can publish themselves. One of the key platforms has been Spotify, an almost purely capitalist venture to make the most money possible. Spotify holds online concerts and events promoting a variety of genres with cultural and multicultural advantages. In 2018, in a bow to the drawing power of Latin music, an online concert series, "Spotify Kicks Off ¡Viva Latino!" was broadcast. The concert cooperated with the 2018 Latin Music Awards in Las Vegas. The photograph features headliners, from left to right, Daddy Yankee, Becky G., Natti Natasha, and Bad Bunny, a combination of singers from Puerto Rico, Mexico, Dominican Republic, and Puerto Rico, respectively. They sing pop, rock, and rap in English and Spanish.

Source: David Becker/Stringer via Getty Images

Some critics worry over how this rapid expansion of Latin music might affect assimilation within national borders even though no one argues against the power English-language music has had in globalization. American culture is a created culture which relies on newness and change for vibrancy, something the world can dance to as well. The influences of the American music in the record-setting internet original and parodies by South Korean rocker Psy and his "Gangnam Style" are obvious. When Psy appeared with Madonna in Madison Square Garden, New York, in November 2012, his links to American music and the global stage highlighted the expansion of US cultural forms around the world (*Rolling Stone*, 2012). This connection has gotten stronger over the last decade.

American culture is a part of a transnational and multinational culture created from a diverse population and returned to a global audience, where it is changed and returned to Americans. This happens ever more rapidly with the advent of social media and internet technologies in a globalized arena that mixes domestic and international concerns over economics and global norms and makes culture available and adaptable to a wider audience. These themes will be explored further in Chapters 8 and 9.

Further Reading

Benshoff, H. and S. Griffin (2017) *America on Film: Representing Race, Class, Gender, and Sexuality at the Movies*, 3rd edn, Chichester, UK: Wiley-Blackwell.

Campbell, N. and A. Kean (2016) *American Cultural Studies: An Introduction to American Culture*, 4th edn, London: Routledge.

Gems, G., L. Borish, and G. Phister (2022) *Sports in American History: From Colonization to Globalization*, 3rd edn, Champaign, IL: Human Kinetics.

Orenstein, J. (2016) *Girls and Sex: Navigating the Complicated New Landscape*, New York: Harper.

Pohl, F. (2017) *Framing America: A Social History of American Art*, 4th edn, 2 vols., London: Thames & Hudson.

Putnam, R. (2015) *Our Kids: The American Dream in Crisis*, New York: Simon & Schuster.

Rapinoe, M. (2020) *One Life*, London: Penguin.

Sales, N. (2016) *American Girls: Social Media and the Secret Lives of Teenagers*, New York: Knopf.

Tolentino, J. (2019) *Trick Mirror: Reflections on Self-Delusion*, New York: Random House.

CHAPTER 8
THE ECONOMY

For a generation, the US economy has been shifting from industry to information and services and has tightly integrated into global marketplaces of goods, investment, and labor. Despite Covid disruption and four years of nationalist political currents, the US economy is inseparable from the global economy. In 2020 and 2021 the world was embroiled in the worst economic slowdown since the 1930s Great Depression, as pandemic globalization shook national economies. Prior to the Corona crisis, the US economy looked strong, showing greater rates of growth than comparable countries—though not as rapid as China or India. Median incomes climbed, mostly restoring decade-earlier losses during the 2008–2009 Great Recession. President Trump trumpeted the good times of higher employment, ballooning stock prices, juicy dividends, and rising real wages. But most people saw the pandemic pumping the brakes hard on the economic and social gains, depressing demand and sliding the economy into crisis. For voters, President Biden seemed a safer custodian as medical and economic crises played out, dooming Trump to the first single-term presidency since George H. W. Bush in the early 1990s.

Though the US economy is rebounding under Biden as relief packages come online, vaccines kick in, and pent-up demand sees Americans working and spending again, experience suggests that when Covid recedes people may be cautious of their economic prospects. Most people over thirty years old recall the debilitating 2008–2009 "Great Recession" when banks failed, nations teetered on the edge of bankruptcy, popular protests arose at corporate welfare, and millions at home and abroad suffered unemployment. People blamed growing and complex economic integration and rapacious financial markets for their troubles—while still enjoying the low prices offered by overseas producers of consumer goods. Economic imbalance threatened security, peace, and the domestic political order, and powered the economic nationalism that ultimately propelled Trump into office.

Even as the pre-Covid economy soared in 2019, 34 million Americans still subsisted below the poverty line (USCB, 2020a). Many people struggled to remain solvent, and the nation continued to run trade and spending deficits. Two years later, the economy contained chronic structural weaknesses and a growing national debt—as well as building inflationary pressures and rising prices.

From 2009–2019 comparative economic growth statistics suggested the economy was doing well, even though many ordinary people felt that they were struggling to stay solvent. Both Obama and Trump took credit for the booming economy and for reduced

Illustration 8.1 Joe Biden, Kamala Harris, and the American Jobs Plan

On April 7, 2021, President Biden presented his American Jobs Plan at a White House event, while Vice President Kamala Harris looked on. Biden called the plan the biggest single investment in American jobs since 1945. Seven months later, elements of the plan passed as the Infrastructure Investment and Jobs Act, promising over $1 trillion on new investment. Together with the $1.9 trillion Covid Relief Bill, around three trillion dollars total was pumped into the economy and unemployment fell to 3.3 percent. But in mid-2022, with inflation near 9 percent, some worried that deficit spending would cause the economy to overheat.

Source: Alex Wong via Getty Images

unemployment. Many on the right felt that Trump had supercharged the Obama boom by instituting tax cuts without making commensurate spending reductions. In January 2020, after a decade of growth, unemployment stood at a fifty-year low: 3.5 percent. Then Covid hit the global economy and damaged the overall system. Three months later, in April 2020, at least 14.8 percent of Americans were out of work: the steepest decline since the 1930s. Federal relief measures and a lull in the infection rate did soothe the economic shock—yet as the pandemic picked up speed, unemployment in November 2020 remained nearly double that of January (BLS, 2021e).

By comparison, America's strategic and economic rival, China, was less afflicted. Growing much faster for a generation, China looked likely to overtake the US as the world's premier economy more rapidly than projected—by 2028 (Reuters, 2020a). Economic power correlates with influence. China was pushing itself globally as a successful economic model, with strong internal governance, capable of meeting exceptional challenges more effectively than the US. Trump's economic nationalism construed trade in "I win, you lose" terms—very different from liberal "we all win through trade" ideas that had dominated for forty years. Trump's "renegotiation" of trade with China, Mexico, and Canada underlined this approach by looking for gains that would impress American voters. American wins presupposed foreign losses, which was a difficult proposition for US trading partners. While economic nationalism may have had limited effects on the economy before Covid, economic "America First" policies by the US threatened to make economic burdens worse. Nations traded free passage of labor for restrictions, by buttressing border controls and travel bans to protect their citizens from the virus and consequential economic dislocation.

American economic policy is usually poised between those who believe that the government has an important role to play in running and regulating the economy, and those who believe that government interference in economic matters is either ineffective or damaging for the economy. There are major nuances between these two views. Virtually no one maintains that government action is universally good or universally counterproductive. The Republican and Democratic parties are effectively coalitions promoting many, often conflicting, contours of economic thought. To name a few: Republicans include anti-taxers, defense-spending conservatives, moderate regulators, balanced budgeters, and Trumpian economic nationalists. Democrats span liberal promotors of environmental quality and economic equality, active bright-green utilitarian regulators, dark green preservation environmentalists, supporters of traditional industry and energy, defense hawks and centrist-balanced budgeteers.

On economic policy, once rhetorical passion has burned out, factions also have the ability to cross party lines—especially in a crisis—as witnessed by bipartisan Covid crisis legislation to keep the economy going and to support workers, employers, and state and local governments. Examples include the March 27, 2020, CARES Act, which injected $2.2 trillion into the economy (Werner, Kane, and DeBonis, 2020). CARES elicited virtually unanimous bipartisan support in both houses of Congress, as did the December 27, 2020, Corona relief measures, which provided an additional $900 billion to the economy suffering from Covid's second wave (Cochrane, Schwartz, and Friedman, 2020). The third relief measure, the American Rescue Plan (ARP) Act of March 11, 2021, passed on party lines, targeted Americans with lower incomes, and injected nearly $2 trillion more into the economy. Then, on April 7, 2021, Biden launched his American Jobs Plan which aimed to invest in infrastructure and training (see Illustration 8.1).

Keynesian "spend-in-a-crisis" economic methods have been used by the last three presidents in dealing with recessions—extending classic economic ideas of balancing tax and spending over the long term to manage economic life. Briefly, governments spend more than they tax to stoke the economy during hard times and balance budgets over the long term by spending less than they tax during booms. In practice, Keynesian methods call for governments to combat recessions by using tax and monetary policy, regulatory policy, and public investment to encourage business and citizens to spend again. Consumers buy more goods and services from corporations, which in turn have to hire more workers to meet demand, generating more private and corporate tax revenues

Contemporary United States

for government to collect and pay down the shortfall incurred in bad times The CARES Act and ARP Act fit this pattern, collectively injecting over $5 trillion into the economy.

Even with all the funding, Biden was blamed for a lack of radical ambition by all progressives and many liberals (as was Obama). Republicans condemned Biden for economic irresponsibility (as was Obama) for both ARP and upcoming bills proposing investments in physical and human infrastructure. While Biden prioritized efforts to preserve the economy, progressives believed that economic equality deserved to be served as much as economic stability. For Biden, the opportunity of transformative change altered his position and pushed him towards substantive change, including advocating human investment in higher minimum wages, expanded health care, pre-kindergarten childcare, family leave, and investments in community colleges—as well as in roads, rail, ports, internet accessibility, and other physical public goods. Intraparty debate among Democrats between progressives and liberals reaches back nearly a century to President Franklin Roosevelt's New Deal policies.

During the Obama administrations, strategic investments were made in clean energy to reduce the nation's exposure to unreliable oil producers and to lessen the impact of carbon emissions on the environment. These inducements helped bring success to electric auto manufacturer Tesla Motors—currently the most valuable US car company with a market capitalization of over $500 billion (Wayland and Kolodny, 2020). In 2021, major car companies turned to electric models as a significant percentage of all new cars. Other measures succeeded, including the job-saving auto industry bailout which initially cost nearly $80 billion in federal aid. Most of that money was recovered as auto production resumed. In 2009, while Republicans argued for the creative destruction of bankruptcy as a new start, Democrats insisted that government could help the market work better.

In 2020, federal government outlays were approximately $6.6 trillion—an amount nearly equal to one-third of the total gross domestic product (GDP represents the total value of goods and services produced in the country in one year). The government collected revenues of about $3.3 trillion, leaving a deficit of $3.3 trillion, or around 16 percent of GDP—a figure higher than at any time since 1945 (CBO, 2020a). The government has run a deficit yearly since 2002, effectively ignoring the Keynesian idea of "paying-down-debt" during boom times. On the one hand, the government is clearly increasing its debt unsustainably—to over 100 percent of GDP, leading to fears of too much monetary demand chasing too little supply—and thus inflation. On the other hand, most economists agree that extraordinary times require extraordinary federal action. Balancing budgets in 2021 would require either raising taxes or decreasing spending—both of which cause economies to shrink, with massive unemployment and growing poverty. What is economically rational is not always politically wise.

Biden believes that Keynesian policies involving short-term deficits will help the US out of the economic crisis, with deficits repayable through higher taxes and fees once the economy recovers. The magnitude of the spending needed to secure the health of the economy is unprecedented. Until recently, economists believed that borrowing more than 3 percent of GDP a year was profligate. Such near-budget balancing ideas—hegemonic since the early 1980s—are being re-examined. Politicians and central bankers are wary that borrowing costs could escalate as countries chase cash to keep their economies running, thus leading to a re-emergence of inflation and a return to small deficit budget orthodoxy. Despite these worries, the United States remains the capital of capitalism with the largest and most powerful economy in the world, a 2020 GDP of $20.8 trillion, and a per capita GDP of $55,837 (IMF, 2020, 2021).

The US economy benefits from geographic advantages, including several climate zones which provide an abundance of agricultural products to the internal market, and make the US the world's largest exporter of food and foodstuffs. Additionally, the nation's mineral reserves, timberlands, river systems, ocean harbors, and one of the world's largest fishing fleets strengthen its economic power. The US has nearly a quarter of the world's known coal reserves and 2.9 percent of the world's known oil reserves, amounting to over 38 billion barrels (EIA, 2022). With a 2019 production of 19.5 million barrels of oil a day (19 percent of global production) against daily consumption of 20.5 million barrels (20 percent of global consumption), and growing use of renewables, the nation seems energy secure (EIA, 2021c). Shale gas and tar sand exploitation have helped increase domestic production and decrease costs in recent years, despite efforts by OPEC countries to stifle the US domestic "fracking" industry. The US is already moving toward further energy self-sufficiency to include supplying more fuel to EU partners in response to the Russian attempt to conquer Ukraine and rebuild the old Soviet empire (see Chapter 9).

Domestic fossil energy suppliers, especially coal, had a friend in Trump. For Biden, environmental security had to be balanced with economic security. Biden moved to end the Keystone oil pipeline, and a return to global climate change mitigation through recognition of the Paris Agreement. Some progressive Democrats, including Alexandria Ocasio-Cortez and a growing legion of young activists push Biden further. "Green New Deal" programs involving reductions in fossil fuels and greenhouse gases, promotion of a high-tech green energy future, and advancing economic and environmental equality are possible. More conservative Democrats, including West Virginia Senator Joe Manchin, support clean energy but insist that an important place remains for fossil fuels. Proposed energy bans on Russian fuel have raised energy prices worldwide and at US gas pumps. Ensuring energy supplies is important for consumer well-being and thus for electoral reasons.

The US population enjoys one of the highest living standards in the world in relation to property and income. High levels of production, relatively low tax rates, and the intense competition of the world's largest single market (by value) mean that already-high incomes go further. Purchasing power parity (PPP) is a measure of what people in different countries can actually buy with their incomes, As Table 2.1 indicates, Americans surpass most other major economies in PPP (CIA, 2020). Income distribution tempers this positive picture because the gulf between rich and poor in the US is larger than in most other major countries, as depicted in the nation's high GINI coefficient (Horowitz, Ignielnik, and Kochhar, 2020). Still, this wealth combines with the sheer numbers of citizens to create a huge economy and market based on mass production and mass consumption. Americans have voracious appetites for all products, domestic and foreign.

Contemporary United States

The enormity of their purchasing power and rates of spending can cause a surge in the world economy if people are optimistic about the future or a recession if they close their wallets. In December 2020, the official labor pool consisted of over 160 million people, and strong immigration of legal and undocumented workers provided a supply of highly skilled and unskilled labor (BLS, 2021j).

The economy has benefited by the historical circumstances of a nation born in modern times, being physically removed from the arenas of two twentieth century world wars, enjoying the expansion of English as the global language, and through the technological inventiveness of thousands of immigrants who provide a "brain-gain." During the last two decades, scientists—especially from India and China—immigrated to the US, and advanced science, technology, and their personal fortunes. Other factors forming the American philosophy of the market include the Protestant or Puritan work ethic, a strong belief in education and research, 240 years of basically stable government—the Civil War notwithstanding—and the creative tension between individual freedom and state responsibility. Historically, the government has generally followed the laissez-faire and free-market principles of Scottish economist Adam Smith, whose 1776 book *The Wealth of Nations* shared the natural law philosophy of Thomas Jefferson's Declaration of Independence. Most Americans accept the notion that economic and political freedoms go hand in hand. Americans have agreed with Smith that individual self-interest would promote the general welfare, instead of regulation, intervention, and the high taxes required to support a bigger government, except in the most extraordinary times of protest or widespread, systemic economic crisis.

The US Domestic Economy

The American Work Force

Nearly 68 percent of working-age Americans were employed in December 2020—a similar percentage to most other major industrial nations (BLS, 2021j; OECD, 2021b). Almost 11 million people were unemployed, or 6.7 percent (BLS, 2021e). Among the unemployed, perhaps one-quarter were no longer looking for work (Strauss, 2020). The Bureau of Labor Statistics (BLS) estimated that perhaps an additional 5 percent of the workforce were either temporarily employed, marginally attached to work, or involuntarily working part time (BLS, 2021a). While unemployment rose quickly in 2020 due to Covid, the number of people unemployed fell sharply—to 3.3 percent in 2022—as crisis spending restored confidence. Table 8.1 shows significant differences in employment and unemployment rates for different demographic groups.

Currently women hold slightly less than half of all jobs, even though they hold more management and professional jobs than men (52 to 48 percent). The "glass ceiling" allows women to see the most senior positions without reaching them. In politics, other countries have elected women to the top political office. In 2016, Hillary Clinton fell short of presidency and, in 2020 Kamala Harris became the first female vice president.

The Economy

Table 8.1 Unemployment Rates, November 2016–December 2020 (unadjusted)

Category	UNEMPLOYMENT RATES (%) (labor market participation rate in brackets)			
	November 2016	February 2020	April 2020	November 2020
All workers	4.6 (62.9)	3.5 (63.3)	14.8 (60.2)	6.7 (61.5)
Adult men 20+	4.3 (16 + 69.2)	3.2 (71.6)	13.1 (68.6)	6.4 (69.7)
Adult women 20+	4.1 (16 + 57.0)	3.1 (57.4)	15.5 (56.3)	6.3 (57.2)
Teenagers, 16–19	14.1 (34.0)	11.5 (36.2)	32.1 (30.7)	16.0 (35.7)
White	4.0 (63.1)	3.1 (63.2)	13.8 (60.1)	6.0 (61.6)
African American	7.9 (61.2)	5.8 (62.7)	16.4 (58.4)	9.9 (59.8)
Hispanic/Latino	5.6 (66.1)	4.4 (68.1)	18.5 (63.1)	9.3 (65.3)
Asian	3.0 (63.6)	2.5 (64.4)	14.3 (60.5)	5.9 (61.8)

Source: BLS (2021e)

In economic crises, women often do better than men because they earn less than men overall and are employed in "essential" education, health care, and service jobs or professions that are more recession resilient. These factors make it cheaper for employers to retain working class women and fire males. Because they often work part time, women are probably overrepresented among the 10 percent of adults who still lack health insurance.

Wages differ substantially by educational level. Those with less than a high school degree average $556 per week; those with a high school diploma, $720; and those with a bachelor's degree, $1,198—as is shown in Figure 6.1 (BLS, 2019b). During a working career, a male college graduate earns around $900,000 more than a high school graduate, while women college graduates chalk up $630,000 more; a PhD or professional degree adds another $500,000 for both men and women (SSA, 2015). Despite slow improvements, a gender gap exists in 2021. Women make only 82 cents on every male dollar—$894 to $1072 a week (BLS, 2021g). Part-time versus full-time employment, pink-collar jobs, and historical factors of discrimination and less education account for this difference. Strikingly, the pay for "never married" women with full-time jobs is equal to that made by men. For American families in 2018, the median annual household income was over $60,000 before taxes (USCB, 2020a). However, there are many differences, as Table 8.2 indicates. Virtually all demographic groups saw their incomes rise significantly in the period 2010–2020—witnessing the return to prosperity during the Obama years and the deficit spending boom under Trump. Nearly two-thirds of all families had both partners working.

The United States has an unemployment insurance program paid for in combination by employers, and federal and state governments. The program does not apply to temporary, part-time, and self-employed workers and, to be eligible, workers must be unemployed through no fault of their own. The changes in welfare provisions from AFDC to TANF made the states primarily responsible for deciding how much money should be paid to individual recipients. As can be seen in Table 8.1, in November 2020, the unemployment rate amounted to 6.7 percent, nearly double the February 2020 pre-Covid crisis percentage. The 2019 average unemployment claim value of $378 a

261

Contemporary United States

Table 8.2 Yearly Median Household (Family) Income by Selected Characteristics (120 million households in 2018)

Group	Median Yearly Income		
	2010 (in $)	*2018 (in $)*	*Percentage Rise*
All groups	50,831	63,179	24.3
African American	33,317	41,361	24.2
Latino/Hispanic	38,679	51,450	33.0
White (non-Hispanic)	56,178	66,943	19.2
Asian American	66,286	87,194	31.5
Native-born	51,736	64,283	24.3
Foreign-born	45,354	58,776	29.6

Note: Race/ethnicity as reported by principal income earner.
Source: USCB (2019c)

week varies from state to state (Iacurci, 2020). The CARES and ARP Acts dramatically increased incomes for less-well-off Americans, though temporarily. On the right, some argue that Covid benefits have suppressed recruitment and inflated wages, making it harder for businesses to hire.

Laws prevent employers from discriminating in hiring on the basis of age, sex, race, religion, physical handicaps, or national origin. There are laws to maintain safe working conditions and to allow unpaid release time for childbirth, adoption, or to care for sick relatives. The United States introduced a federally mandated workweek and minimum wage in 1938, when the maximum an individual could be required to work was set at forty hours and the base wages put at $0.25 an hour. Since 2009, all full-time workers over the age of eighteen were guaranteed at least $7.25 an hour; those under eighteen, or those in jobs where tips made up a large part of their salaries, or who worked for small companies, might receive less. At minimum wage, a full-time (forty hours per week) worker would make $290 a week before taxes. Moreover, twenty-three states and the District of Columbia have laws putting minimum wages above the national requirement. For example, Washington, Massachusetts and Washington, DC, have set minimums at $10 an hour or more, and California and New York City minimum wages rose to $15 in 2022 (NCSL, 2017).

Most businesses pay higher wages than are required by law, usually about $9 an hour for beginners. In November 2021, the average hourly private-sector pay for US workers was $31.03 an hour (BLS, 2021d). Any work done beyond the forty-hour maximum is subject to overtime pay at a higher rate of 1.5 to 2 times the hourly rate. High wages increase pressure on the workers, as employers push them to be even more productive, a trade-off that most workers accept. Still, most recognize that minimum wages are too low. President Biden wishes to raise the federal minimum wage to $15 an hour to help the working poor who are oftentimes minorities. However, Senate Republicans and many moderate Democrats are likely to resist a one-step jump to double the minimum wage.

262

The Economy

Well over half (55 percent) of American workers say they are satisfied with their jobs. However, workers were less happy with levels of stress, opportunities for promotion, or the salaries they received (Gallup, 2020). Stress and salary dissatisfaction can be linked to acute competitive and productivity pressures. The intensity of work is has increased and the average workweek is fairly long. In December 2020, the average private-sector worktime was 34.7 hours per week (BLS, 2021c). This number includes part-timers so, with overtime, most full-time working Americans average over forty hours per week (BLS, 2020b). Technological advances increase the speed on assembly lines, and companies "downsize" the number of workers while "upscaling" the tempo and length of work in a continual striving for greater productivity and profit. Unlike the immediate post-1945 period, in recent years, productivity growth since 1980 has not translated into higher wages. Still, many firms are adopting forms of corporate social responsibility (CSR), whereby the well-being of workers, subcontractors, and environment sustainability are considered along with the economic bottom line. Critics counter that CSR without raises amounts to corporate window dressing.

However efficiently they work, Americans are keenly aware of competitive pressures from China, India, and elsewhere, leading to systemic "outsourcing"—sending jobs abroad in search of cheaper production costs. Iconic products such as Apple Computers and Levi's Jeans are mostly made abroad, though corporations have come under intense pressure from consumers and politicians, including Trump and Biden, to repatriate manufacturing jobs. Recent reductions in energy costs and rising wages abroad have led some companies to return to "near-sourcing"—bringing production back to the US.

Global competitive pressure may be lowering the differential between US and foreign workers, but relatively high US personal consumption—with high home mortgages and transportation costs—force workers to work harder to prove their worth. Those who work long hours hope to be among those retained when bad times hit. Technology is affecting work hours as the internet and smart phones allow work to push into home life. Additionally, the average two-way commute nationwide adds over fifty minutes to the workday (Ingraham, 2019). For those working in big cities like New York and living in the suburbs, commutes to affordable and attractive penurban—outer urban—homes can often total ninety minutes each way. The Covid-supercharged trend toward home working may encourage more Americans to move out of the cities.

Though older workers tend to be in more stable jobs than younger ones, about 15 percent of the labor force is in motion in any given year, offering their skills in the marketplace to the highest bidder as they change employers and geographical locations. These moves stimulate the economy but also increase stress, as most workers expect to profit on their old house to afford a new house. Around two-thirds of Americans own their homes (USCB, 2021b). Most workers sign yearly or long-term contracts and expect annual pay increases based upon inflation and merit. The notion of merit, not inheritance, is a long-standing tenet of faith, as Americans accept that there will be winners and losers.

The father of the Constitution, James Madison, called the unequal distribution of property a natural truth arising from disparities in human talent. That idea still resonates.

263

Contemporary United States

Often, Americans display more anger at welfare payments to poor families—especially those from minority groups—than to the extreme wealth of the privileged class. But, in times of economic recession, the bankers are vilified as "banksters"—part banker, part gangster—and the CEOs of major companies that contributed to the Great Recession were pilloried for high salaries, bonuses, and corporate privileges that seem to mock the working class and notions of fair play. This is especially true when companies fail and the government steps in to use taxpayer money to bail them out. CEOs now make over several hundred times the salaries of ordinary workers (FRED, 2018).

Some pundits speak openly of the rich and the rest. For white-collar jobs, a winner-take-all market has been the rule for a generation. This, as Robert Putnam noted in 2015, has hollowed out the middle class (see Chapter 5). An extended pay-pyramid exists where the few star performers at the top accumulate pay and prestige through lavishly high salaries and stock options that skew the distribution of wealth. This explains why median income statistics are lower than average incomes. The US has one of the most inequitable divisions of wealth among developed nations (OECD, 2018a).

For much of US history, land was the essential source of wealth. In contemporary America, human capital matters—people's skills and competences—in knowledge, ability, and "starpower." Stars attract money, so to pay high salaries for their talent does not dismay most Americans, even if it leads to a smaller pot to divide among the others. For the last generation, workers at the top have seen incomes advance and workers at the bottom have made less relatively, fueling the anti-elite resentment and the political upheaval that in 2016 saw Trump win traditionally blue-collar "Democratic" states Pennsylvania, Wisconsin, Ohio, and Michigan.

Taxes

Most Americans detest the idea of high taxes. "No taxation without representation" was a rallying cry that helped bring on the American Revolution. Since then, except in times of national economic distress, Americans have decided to keep as much of their income as possible and to accept limited government services. Historically, excise tariffs funded the government until federal income taxes came into being with the 16th Amendment (1913). Those first taxes were set progressively at 1 percent for incomes over $3,000, rose to 7 percent for those over $500,000, and created an ongoing debate over the fairness of a progressive tax system. In 1990 and several times afterwards, income tax rates were lowered—most recently in 2017 (see Table 1.1).

Currently, Democrats prefer to retain progressive rates, and are open to increasing the highest rates to pay for infrastructure investments, while many Republicans would prefer flat rates. At 37 percent, the current marginal rate is much lower than the 84 percent in 1950, 91 percent in 1960, 72 percent in 1970, 70 percent in 1980, and 50 percent in 1986. In addition to the national tax, the states levy income taxes—excepting Alaska, Florida, Nevada, New Hampshire, South Dakota, Tennessee, Texas, Washington, and Wyoming, which do not have state income taxes. Counties and municipalities also levy taxes. Together, state income tax (where applicable), county, and city taxes average about

The Economy

10 percent but vary between 7.2 percent (Alaska) and 13.8 percent (New York) (Stebbins, 2020). Consumers pay sales taxes on everything—up to 9.46 percent in Tennessee—and excise taxes on purchases of gasoline, alcohol, and cigarettes. While many Americans complain of high tax rates, combined taxes at the federal, state, county, and town level in the US remain lower than those in most other western countries.

President Reagan's Tax Reform Act of 1986 cut taxes on the highest income groups in line with his belief that high taxes and government regulations discouraged economic enterprise. Lavishly supporting the defense industry, Reagan considered the rising federal debt a small price to pay for starving the government of future spending. Whether his plan was correct or not is difficult to assess, but during the neoliberal (limited government intervention in the economy) period from 1983–2016, the United States enjoyed a huge business expansion. The country also had a greater national debt after eight years under Reagan than had been accumulated in its entire history. George H. W. Bush continued Reagan's policies, but when the economy hit a small recession as the Cold War ended and markets adjusted, Bush approved a tax increase. Voters disapproved, and Bush was voted out of office.

Clinton's presidency coincided with the longest period of continuous growth in US history. Some analysts credit this to continued Reaganomics and see the Clinton boom as part of a seventeen-year-long expansion (1983–2000). From 1998 to 2000, a booming economy provided huge tax revenues and three straight years of budget surpluses, totaling over $450 billion. The 1990s—a period bracketed by the fall of the Berlin Wall, the end of the Cold War in November 1989, and the onset of the "Age of Terrorism" in September 2001—have been described in books such as *The Fabulous Decade* and *The Roaring Nineties*. The collapse of the Soviet Union raised American faith in free-market capitalism to new heights. Some analysts spoke of an end of ideology as the market economy triumphed; others put forward ideas that economic recessions would fade into obscurity as globalization opened all markets to increased prosperity for all nations. While the 1990s was a decade of massive technological transformation and productivity gains, it was in hindsight also an age of reckless deregulation, deceptive corporate mega-deals and market manipulation, including insider trading, overvalued stocks, and investor spending exuberance.

Upon taking office in 2001, George W. Bush "returned" an inherited budget surplus to the people through a tax cut of $1.35 trillion. Six tax cuts during Bush's two terms benefited the wealthiest Americans and, proportionately, put more of the burden on the middle class. These tax cuts had a ten-year limit and required Congress to vote to extend or end them. The cuts expired in January 2013, meaning taxes would rise back to their earlier levels. In the ensuing American Taxpayer Relief Act, Congress voted to extend the cuts for all taxpayers earning less than $400,000 a year.

The changes in the tax rates, higher oil prices, and the costs of the wars in Iraq and Afghanistan had a massive impact on total tax revenues and spending, turning the budget surpluses into record deficits as the government experienced its most dramatic revenue drop since the Second World War. Even before the recession, the 2008 deficit reached $455 billion. Bush's "war Keynesianism" fueled the boom rather than managing

Contemporary United States

it by spending money which could have been used to dampen the effects of the recession. House prices rose as people felt confident about the future, and home ownership climbed—to over 69 percent. By 2009, as the recession truly took hold, the shortfall had risen to around $1.4 trillion. Deficits remained in excess of $1 trillion per fiscal year (FY) through Obama's first administration, then fell as growth resumed. And then came the Covid crisis. In February 2021, the deficit was projected to be $2.3 trillion, or 10.3 percent of GDP, several times the 3 percent that most economists consider responsible (CBO, 2021).

Usually property prices increase over time, for a number of reasons. However, when people feel less confident, home equity falls (the value left over once all loans have been paid). In late 2020, the homeownership rate was holding steady at around 65.8 percent due to the help the financial aid packages provided against a potential crash. While Bush and Reagan believed that deficits could "starve the beast" of government and leave it nothing to "feed" off, Obama and Biden believed in the use of deficits today as "investments" for the future. Both, however, faced opposition in Congress. Most economists accept that deficits stop economic collapse, allow for restructuring of industries, and advance new technology through direct investments, transport, and education.

Because Congress must authorize federal debt limit increases annually, differences in economic philosophy will emerge every time a vote is required. The 2012 Fiscal Cliff discussion exemplifies this: Congress refused to authorize increased borrowing and left the government facing the abyss of not being able to finance its activities. Twice, in January and December 2018, under Trump, the federal government shut down over disagreement between Congress and the administration as to how spending should be financed.

Labor Unions

Unless a person is self-employed, there is a built-in tension between management and labor over levels of production, work hours, benefits, and pay. Most employees negotiate individually with management. Trade unions represent about 14.3 million members (10.8 percent of all workers) (BLS, 2021i). Older workers and public sector employees are more unionized, while younger and private-sector workers are less unionized. The American Federation of Labor–Congress of Industrial Organizations (AFL–CIO) is one of the country's largest and oldest organized coalitions and includes workers in industrial, construction, or manufacturing plants who are members of around seventy affiliated unions (AFL–CIO, 2021). The rest are divided among independent unions, mostly composed of teachers, police officers, university professors, and government employees (BLS, 2021i).

Local craft unions existed before the American Civil War but the first major nationwide group was the Knights of Labor (KOL), which reached its zenith in the 1880s by accepting all workers into one organization. Because the KOL wanted to improve the immediate situation of pay inequities through strikes and violence, without a long-range

The Economy

program of reform, many craft workers who wished to maintain pay differentials based on skill differences founded a rival group, the American Federation of Labor (1886). The AFL represented skilled trade unionism and represented all groups that organized themselves and asked to join the federation. The AFL never enrolled more than 15 percent of all American workers because of the widespread fear of socialism and a view of unions as anarchistic or un-American. Federal and state police forces supported corporations against strikers. Additionally, the AFL suffered from a lack of cooperation from a heterogeneous labor pool of varying ethnicities, races, the sheer number of available workers—all of which were encouraged by employers, and a free-market ideology of individual responsibility. In 1890, Congress passed the Sherman Anti-Trust Act to stop big business from forming "conspiracies in restraint of trade" and to provide mechanisms for breaking apart monopolies. Later, this Act was turned against labor unions, which, when they went on strike, were seen as "conspiracies in restraint of trade."

From the 1870s to the 1930s, union members used strikes and violence to demand changes in safety conditions, benefits, and pay. Given the general level of violence in the country, it is not surprising that the United States has had one of the bloodiest labor histories among industrialized nations. Strikes were accompanied by the destruction of private property, or even the assault and murder of replacement—often immigrant— workers who dared cross the picket lines. Companies employed private detectives, state governors sent in police, and, sometimes, the president deployed federal troops to break up strikes. This era generally witnessed business expansion under laissez-faire rules of free-market capitalism. President Calvin Coolidge summed up the majority opinion that "The man who builds a factory, builds a temple. The man who works there, worships there." Hundreds of these "worshippers" died or were arrested trying to change conditions for the working-man and woman.

During the Great Depression, workers unhappy with the AFL, or not skilled enough to qualify for membership, created the Congress of Industrial Organizations (CIO). The New Deal's National Labor Relations Act of 1935 (Wagner Act) gave workers the right to collective bargaining, an action prompting 35 percent of the workforce—12 million workers—to join unions by 1945. Worried that labor would become too powerful, Congress passed the Taft–Hartley Act in 1947 to outlaw any "closed-shop" agreement which required employers to hire only labor union members. The Act also forbade agreements requiring workers to join, or be represented by, unions after they were hired. In 1955, the two biggest unions merged into the AFL–CIO. Collective bargaining tripled hourly wages between 1945 and 1970, and forced both unions and companies to accept the full enrolment of African American and women workers, who had been excluded by closed-shop conventions favoring a white, male workforce.

In the 1980s, the union movement foundered under deregulation, foreign imports, a recession, newer technology, downsizing, and hostile national administrations. Reagan was openly anti-union and effectively used executive power to stop strikes, keep wages low, and stunt union growth. Most Americans believe that big labor has been co-opted as management improved conditions in the workplace and made workers "part owners" by issuing stock to employees in a profit-sharing system in return for increased production

267

Contemporary United States

rates. In 2020, union members were in the middle-class. Median weekly earnings for full-time, non-union workers averaged $958—84 percent of the $1,144 that union members received (BLS, 2021i). One recent addition to the union landscape—a response to the no-hour contracts and job insecurity of the "gig economy"—is the 500,000-strong Freelancers' Union, founded in 1995 (Freelancers, 2021). Freelancer Union advantages include access to insurance and portable benefits that can be taken from job to job. Wages rose significantly in 2021, as employers looked to tempt workers back into jobs—with retail giant Amazon offering $18-an-hour starting salaries (Picchi, 2021).

Business and Industry

Foreign investment has been essential for American business since colonial times. For 150 years, British joint-stock companies, with the support of the Royal Navy and under the rules of mercantilism, poured money into the shipbuilding firms in the free-labor North and the plantation agriculture of the slave-labor South. By 1776, the United States possessed one of the world's largest merchant fleets and maintained ties with nearly every European nation along the North Atlantic rim. Except for the embargoes during the Napoleonic Wars and the War of 1812, trade continued uninterrupted as the European desire for American food products, cotton, and tobacco soared, and the money-making possibilities of America's westward expansion surged.

Beginning in the 1830s, European investment capital made the transportation revolution possible as American companies built hundreds of canals and new harbors and thousands of miles of roads and railroad lines. Railroad companies, entirely private, were the nation's first big businesses and, during the Gilded Age, were the keys to the expansion of steel and oil industries, the building of western cities, the moving of crops quickly from coast to coast to establish an integrated internal marketplace, and the rapid rise of a superpower. Once the Rocky Mountains had been conquered by rail, the entire Pacific was open for investment, from California to Asia.

The first factory in the United States was a textile mill built in 1793, in Pawtucket, Rhode Island. Gathering workers together into one building increased production, as did the development of a system of interchangeable parts in the handgun industry around 1800. The system was demonstrated to President Jefferson by bringing in ten guns, dismantling them, mixing the parts, reassembling, and firing each one. This mass production—called "the American System" by Europeans—revolutionized products, brought prices down, and all but eliminated the need for master craftsmen who built things one at a time. About mid-century, the growing need for machine tools that were used to make, package, or harvest other products spurred a whole new industry which made mechanical reapers, spinning and weaving machines, and precision tools.

By 1890, the value of the nation's manufactured goods exceeded agricultural production for the first time. Already the world's foremost agricultural nation, America became the leading industrial nation as the number of urban dwellers and industrial workers surpassed the rural population for the first time. In 2021, of the two million

The Economy

farms across the nation, less than half provided one or more full-time incomes. Most farms are thus either part-time or not commercial ventures at all. Many of these are pleasure or lifestyle undertakings—especially close to cities. Most of the nation's crops are produced by highly efficient giant agribusinesses which feed domestic and international marketplaces and are staffed by a rural working class reliant on foreign labor. The family farm of popular myth is relatively insignificant even among the remaining farms.

In the First World War, US factories made one-third of all industrial products produced worldwide and were implementing Henry Ford's idea of improving efficiency and lowering automobile costs by using continuously moving assembly lines. Ford's innovations and ideas of "scientific management" began to be taught in another American innovation, the business school. By the Second World War, American universities were turning out professional managers who had taken advanced courses in accounting, economics, finance, marketing, and management. Enhancing productivity, these managers quickly increased production to half of the world's total and, from the Second World War to the late 1970s, the US-dominated export markets. In 2020, the country still exported 8.5 percent of all global merchandise, while importing nearly 17 percent (Statista, 2021c).

During the Gilded Age, businessmen formed corporations, monopolies and oligopolies, and set up trusts and holding companies to control prices, production, and competition. When government regulation limited their size with the Clayton Anti-Trust Act (1914) and demanded that competition be fair and open, as supervised by the Federal Trade Commission (1914), businesses increased research and development, and expanded advertising and packaging of standard "name brands." Huge economies of scale meant lower costs per item.

Although China and others are catching up, the United States continues to lead the world in the development of high-technology products—especially in the aerospace and IT arenas. This is hardly surprising, given the headstart the country had with automobile, computing, and space shuttle industries. The US also puts great emphasis on acquiring bright young international scientists for US universities and companies through immigration-friendly rules. This practice mitigates the lead of emerging nations China and India in graduating nearly one million new engineers each year, compared with 70,000 in the United States. Perhaps five million engineers and scientists immigrated to the US between 2003 and 2013, helping make up for skill shortfalls. In 2015, nearly one-third of all science and engineering graduates in the US were foreign-born (National Science Board, 2018).

The World Economic Forum ranks the US first among larger developed countries in terms of competitiveness (Schwab, 2019). In 2020, American scientists won seven Nobel prizes (Nobel, 2020). Furthermore, the upgrading of weapons systems demands high-tech inventions to maintain military superiority, including supposedly clinical weapons like hi-tech drones that minimize boots on the ground. In 2016, President Obama remarked that the "spirit of discovery is in our DNA," an inquisitiveness that promised to aid technological and commercial competitiveness which could aid profits and benefit mankind such as a cure for cancer (Obama, 2016b).

269

Contemporary United States

The American space program is important to innovation and furthers America's scientific and military pre-eminence, yet it must compete for funds with other deserving programs. Most of the real gains have been made in unmanned flights—such as those putting the Hubble and Webb telescopes in position to explore the outer rim of the galaxy, or via the five successful missions to Mars. In February 2021, the Mars Perseverance Rover trundled across the Martian landscape in search of clues to past microbial life and climate on that planet. (NASA, 2020b). Over one-half (1,897) of the 3,372 satellites orbiting the earth are American, including 1,486 commercial and 212 military. In comparison, China has 412 and Russia 176 satellites of all types (UCS, 2021).

And yet it is the manned missions—with their promises of future colonies—that gain the most attention and prestige. In 2021, the National Aeronautics and Space Administration (NASA) celebrated sixty years and over 200 missions of manned flights (NASA, 2021). Current programs include the Mars Perseverance Rover missions, the Artemis project to send Americans back to the moon in 2024, and the Europa Clipper Mission to explore Jupiter's moon Europa. NASA is currently working with private corporations SpaceX (Illustration 8.2) and Boeing to develop rocket and space technology, as well as many other companies on the development of technologies in the Artemis program (NASA, 2020c). In recent years, space rivalry has increased. In 2012, North Korea launched a satellite into orbit. Four years earlier, India announced an ambitious program of manned flights. China landed on the moon in late 2020 and plans to have a space station operational by 2022 (Chang, 2020).

Government and Business

Regulation and Deregulation

Government and business cooperate, and the government has often intervened to promote or protect economic growth even if its leaders prefer free-market capitalism. From Reagan (1981–1989) until recently, deregulation replaced the strong interventionist and regulatory role that existed from the Great Depression to the 1970s. Some blamed the crisis of 2008–2009 on the unregulated nature of investment and banking infrastructure. Obama (2009–2017) pushed back, maintaining that regulation could provide "clear rules and basic safeguards that prevent abuse and check excess" (Obama, 2010). In stop-go policymaking, Trump followed Reagan in deregulation, but put levies on imports, especially from China. Biden followed Obama's economic intervention and regulation, but has retained many of Trump's trade tariffs (Lynch, 2021).

For most of American history, private interests have had relative freedom to control their own affairs. Even such necessities as telephone services, railroads, airlines, hospitals, and electric power have remained in private, not public, hands. The government procures goods and services for the public from the private sector, rather than providing utilities directly, and often partners with private business to provide new roads, schools, and other public services. While operating under a philosophy of laissez-faire and applying a

The Economy

Illustration 8.2 SpaceX: The Military Industrial Complex and the Space Race

Lifting off from Cape Canaveral on May 30, 2020, is the inaugural SpaceX Falcon-9 rocket which put the Crew Dragon capsule into orbit. The launch underlines the relationship between business and government. SpaceX founder Elon Musk had won out in the open competition for a government contract against Amazon CEO Jeff Bezos and his Blue Origin space company. Musk contracted to build the rockets, while the National Aeronautics and Space Administration (NASA) agreed to supply the personnel: astronauts Bob Behnken and Doug Hurley. Musk retained the right to put his own civilians on the space missions, charging huge sums for the experience, as does Bezos. Some critics fear that the US has ceded too much of its space program to private corporations even as it competes internationally with China and others for superiority in the galaxy. Others say that while NASA might be a better steward, Musk will advance the program faster due to the profit motive.

Source: Joe Raedle via Getty Images

Darwinian logic that systems which adapt best to changing conditions will survive and multiply, the American government uses taxes on imported goods (tariffs), subsidies, tax breaks, and a federal reserve bank to protect domestic enterprises. The American economy combines individual self-interest with a communitarian approach that serves the national interest. One example of this is the Affordable Care Act, which obliged people to be covered by health care insurance, while still allowing them to choose which health insurance plans they preferred. Biden's plans on providing a Medicare-like public option for healthcare, not a mandate, follow the same vein.

Contemporary United States

The idea that a liberal nation must be a limited nation with comparatively low levels of government direction has mostly held sway among the American populace. Whenever the government steps in to aid businesses, banks, or individuals, many critics complain that public money is being spent to rescue those who have been too greedy, imprudent, and dumb at the expense of those who have sought reasonable profits and lived within their means. The government is criticized when it tries to "pick winners" and support potentially profitable future industries, as the Obama administration was accused of doing in the alternative energy and car industries.

Yet, big industry and the industrial workforce have traditionally been the strongest advocates for protectionism at home. They generally ask the government to put tariffs on foreign imports so that their domestic products will cost less. The real fear is that if the market is flooded with cheaper imported goods, domestic wages will suffer and businesses will collapse. However, because American consumers want cheaper prices brought by open markets and lower tariffs, the United States has vacillated between periods of protectionism and periods of free trade. Since international trade demands goodwill and trust, tariff issues can damage relationships, or lead to retaliatory tariffs and quotas by trading partners. Some nations are favored and some pay more.

The Treasury Department received over $50 billion in tariffs from February 2017 to the end of 2018 (Heeb, 2020). Whether exporters abroad, or consumers at home covered these costs was a moot point. Tariff rates vary according to product and origin but average a relatively low 2 percent by value on industrial goods (USTR, 2021). Some, like Trump, argue that protectionist fair trade rhetoric boosts stocks and the nation. Others believe that a tariff trade war rattles markets and damages transnational corporations that rely on free trade. The Biden administration seems to straddle these divides.

The government also regulates business through acts designed to ensure that all products are safe. In 1906, the Pure Food and Drug Act put standards and restrictions on food processing and meatpacking and created the Food and Drug Administration (FDA) to test the safety of all prescription drugs. Today, because of the enormity of the American market, FDA rules are observed by pharmaceutical companies worldwide—making the FDA a global regulator. The Centers for Disease Control and Prevention (CDC) issues warnings and guidelines for what may be imported and exported. The Occupational Safety and Health Administration (OSHA) oversees workplace safety and health environments to reduce injuries and illnesses (2.8 million in 2019) and fatalities (5,333 in 2019) (BLS, 2021f). The National Safety Council (TNSC), a non-governmental agency with close ties to the government, is empowered to act for the benefit of the public. Its mission goals are the prevention of accidents and fatalities in homes, at work, and in the wider community via advocacy, research, leadership, and education (NSC, 2021).

The government mandates that all products are labeled with a list of ingredients or material composition and requires that all sellers mark prices clearly and advertise honestly. Any product claims that cannot be substantiated by government inspectors are illegal. Consumers have access to reimbursement through the legal system, but also by making complaints to state and local offices of the Consumer Protection Agency or the Better Business Bureau. Usually, companies show goodwill and business savvy by quickly refunding money or offering items in exchange.

Historically, the government helped settle the West by offering large acreages of public land to individuals who would "homestead" it and companies that would build railroads. In contemporary America, state governments continue this facilitator role by granting tax breaks and time-limited pollution exemptions to encourage companies to relocate to their states. The federal government also stands ready to prop up businesses which it holds vital to the national economy.

During the 2020–2022 Covid crisis, the government helped companies by providing $2.3 trillion, including tax breaks, market stabilization, and paycheck protection—around half the total value of Covid relief spending (Whoriskey, MacMillan, and O'Connell, 2020). Under the Trump administration, bipartisan consensus provided support for the first two relief bills, and helped many corporations stay in business. While voices on the Left would have preferred for aid to be directed at people, not corporations, on the Right many fiscal conservatives were uneasy about rising deficits and interfering with markets that would surely right themselves. On entering office, Biden sought a continuation of cross-floor cooperation. At the same time, Biden asserted that government help needed to be forceful and timely—a lesson learned from the Obama administration during the Great Recession. Biden wanted to avoid the "jobless recovery" that happened under Obama and hoped to bring well-paying jobs back to the underemployed and lowly paid. No quick consensus could be found, so Democrats, without even one Republican vote, passed the 2021 American Rescue Plan. In late 2021, that victory was not repeated as Democrat's internal divisions and a lack of bipartisanship saw Biden's human and physical recovery plans fail in the face of a threatened filibuster.

The Banking System

The central bank for the United States is the Federal Reserve (Fed), which consists of a board of seven governors who set policy, and twelve regional banks located around the country to handle the day-to-day operation of printing and circulating money to the 3,000 different banks that are members of the system (FRE, 2021). The Fed was established in 1913 and expanded its influence during the New Deal, when member banks were required to keep a certain amount of their total deposits on reserve in one of the twelve regional banks. This was to cover sudden credit needs and stave off financial panics that could lead to another great depression. The chairman of the Fed is appointed by the president to serve for four years. The primary function of the Federal Reserve is to establish a monetary policy that will enhance confidence and trust, encourage economic stability, administer consumer protection policies, reduce or increase inflation as needed, and limit unemployment by stimulating the market (FRE, 2021).

The US experiences boom-and-bust cycles like other market economies, as business expands or contracts. Congressional fiscal policy—taxation and spending programs— also affects the economy, as does any change in consumer spending patterns. Any disruption in the supply of oil, major terrorist assault, or natural disaster—forest

Contemporary United States

fire, hurricane, a bad harvest, Covid-disrupted supply chains—alters the economy in unpredictable ways. The Fed can moderate these fluctuations by adjusting the national interest rates for borrowing money: a high rate discourages borrowing and consumer spending, while a low rate does the opposite. Between September 2007 and December 2008, as the economy faltered, the Fed reduced interest rates nine times, from 4.75 percent to 0.25 percent to power the economy with cheap money. With interest rates at historically low levels the government can also encourage people to borrow for houses and thus inspire construction and related industries through "quantitative easing," which increases money in circulation by printing more of it. While this can cause inflation, quantitative easing was used several times from 2008 to 2014 to promote growth. There are 5,000 private banks that are not members of the Fed and are capitalized by other means (FRE, 2021). Whether or not a bank is part of the Fed, the Federal Deposit Insurance Corporation (FDIC) protects individual deposits in the event the bank collapses.

The Fed was not designed to fix speculation, negligence, fraud, and bad management by the nation's financial institutions and bankers, even though it has acted as a last resort to avert disasters. In the 1980s, the Fed bailed out the nation's Savings and Loans (S&L) banks by granting $150 billion over and above FDIC guarantees for individual depositors. The funding reimbursed the millions of average citizens who had put their life's savings into institutions that failed, a necessary action to restore trust among consumers and to prevent a financial panic leading to a run on bank deposits. In late 2008, guarantees were set at $250,000 for individual deposits (FDIC, 2020).

Wall Street, the Banks, and the Crisis of 2008/9

The New York Stock Exchange (NYSE) is located on Wall Street in New York City and is the world's leading organized market for the trading of stocks and bonds. The NYSE is the oldest and best-known stock market in the United States (established 1792), even though the American Stock Exchange (AMEX) and the Chicago Commodities Exchange handle nearly 25 percent of all transactions. The National Association of Securities Dealers Automated Quotations (NASDAQ) is an electronic stock market located in Times Square in NYC with ownership links to stock and derivatives markets worldwide.

Major corporations rely on investments to supply the capital required to develop their businesses more quickly than they could on profits alone. The stock market serves to encourage that investment and to provide a solid measure of a company's present and anticipated performance as stocks rise and fall. Famously, the stock market crash of 1929 signaled the beginning of the Great Depression and, in 1934, Congress established a regulatory agency, the Securities and Exchange Commission (SEC), to monitor the trading of stocks so that wildly inflated profit claims and speculative financing could be controlled to prevent future crashes. The 1933 Banking Act (Glass–Steagall) split investment banking from Main Street banking. Regulations separating different kinds of banking loosened in the 1990s and 2000s, a deregulation that some argued was a factor behind the 2008–2009 crisis—along with the increasing complexity of financial markets. The NYSE and other markets are privately run, but publicly supervised.

The SEC is responsible for monitoring traders by ensuring that real assets, such as property or cash reserves, are adequate to back purchases. It also regulates stock mergers and sets rules to disqualify persons from making profits by dumping or buying stocks before public announcements have been made—a practice known as "insider trading." The SEC also requires businesses to present standardized and accurate profit-and-loss disclosures to accounting firms who check the accuracy of their claims, both protecting investors and providing confidence in the American way of business.

At least it is supposed to operate that way. Capitalism works well when the players can trust one another and when companies act not only for their own benefit but also for the benefit of the economy at large, as Adam Smith argued. Ethical standards are fundamental to the American—and global—economic system. Any loss of confidence triggers a removal of capital into more trusted markets, thereby discouraging foreign investors—who own perhaps 40 percent of US stocks (Rosenthal and Burke, 2020). Greater government regulation and monitoring might increase confidence, yet support for it is limited.

The 2008 Great Recession made it crystal clear that the financial system had broken down. In analyzing the causes behind the 2008 financial crisis, economists point first to the mortgage lending system. The 1990s and 2000s provided boom times for many people as the economic scheme of Reaganomics—with its emphasis on deregulation, tax cuts, free markets, and deficit spending—became a "religion" under George W. Bush. Speculative capitalism increased and filtered through the system to middle-class citizens who did not want to be left behind in the good times. The American dream of homeownership combined with the belief that a house was a middle-class family's biggest investment/biggest asset to encourage a surge in real-estate purchases. Banks offered so-called "sub-prime" loans at low (but fluid) introductory rates to people who could not make deposit down-payments. As mortgage standards declined and as foreign capital invested heavily in the US stocks and bonds markets—especially in bundles of mortgage-backed securities—even cheaper money flooded in.

Financial institutions got caught up in the bonanza of profits as bank directors, board members, and mortgage specialists worldwide placed their corporations at risk by over-reliance on mortgages and mortgage-backed stocks. Financial derivatives which put tradable values on assets like mortgages, and which could be sold and "swapped" to reduce risk or increase potential returns, spread explosively. The collapse of insurer American International Group (AIG) in 2008 related directly to derivatives because the corporation could not cover (pay out on) the trades it had made. AIG survived only after receiving a $182 billion bailout from the US government, an amount close to $600 apiece from each of America's 325 million citizens (Keoun, 2012). Still, millions of Americans lost their homes as the housing market collapsed. Others remained in their homes despite owing loans which outstripped their property values.

Mending the "breakdown in our financial system" became an immediate goal of President Obama (Obama, 2010). In 2010, Congress passed the Dodd–Frank Wall Street Reform and Consumer Protection Act (known as "Dodd–Frank"). The Act set up a council to monitor financial stability and ensure that no bank became too big

Contemporary United States

or undercapitalized. It also split retail banking from investment banking by stopping banks from promoting, sponsoring, or owning hedge funds. Dodd–Frank also regulated the trade in derivatives, insisting that any and all trades must be transparent. The Act empowered the SEC to oversee the work of credit agencies so that they assess risk accurately. Finally, by empowering the Consumer Financial Protection Bureau, the Act protected ordinary customers from unscrupulous banking practices, including small-print conditions which lead to unexpected fees, overly complex loans, and arbitrary interest rate hikes (Koba, 2012). In the fourth quarter of 2020, around 2.7 percent of mortgages remained in technical default—much less than at their 11 percent recession peak in 2010 (FRED, 2021a). In 2019, Trump eased Obama-era restrictions on Wall Street "risk taking" and on consumer protection of financial products (Flitter, Smialek, and Cowley, 2020).

Managing the US economy in times of recession or growth is complicated. Money is transferred instantly, electronically, when investors chase the best possible returns. Corporate leaders can choose between workforces worldwide and taxation rules elsewhere to relocate and offshore wherever they see the greatest advantage. California-born Apple computer, for example, locates most of its manufacturing in China and houses its international tax paying divisions in low-corporate tax Ireland where effective rates are fractions of one percent. Meanwhile, Amazon's European operations and taxation are processed through Luxembourg for similar reasons. To combat corporate tax tourism, Trump reduced corporate taxes dramatically—from 38 to 21 percent. Biden has proposed to raise tax rates to 28 percent, to help rebuild infrastructure—a move which garners opinion poll support (Tankersley and Cochrane, 2021). Biden has also proposed global corporate tax cooperation at 15 percent of profits to avoid jurisdiction shopping by companies trying to avoid or lessen tax rates by relocating outside the United States, as Amazon has done.

Presidents are seen as economic managers—here the buck literally stops—yet corporate portability coupled with global financial fluidity limit the ability of a president or Congress to influence business behavior. Looking forward, the development of cryptocurrencies, such as Bitcoin, outside the power of federal government's control threaten to make corporate profits and wealth less transparent and diminish national government's economic policymaking.

Currently there is a global inability to manage financial anarchy. Many analysts believe that the best way to restore order lies not in the isolated actions of nations, but in the institutions of the global marketplace: the IMF, the WTO, the OECD, and the World Bank. While Trump worried that global and regional institutions and regulations would stifle growth and interfere with national sovereignty, Biden believes the opposite. Grassroots activists insist that raising the awareness of conditions in transnational American corporations abroad can modify corporate behavior and foster good corporate citizenship. Trump supported the repatriation of financial muscle to the US through tax holidays and competitive corporate tax reductions; Biden is promoting a carrot-and-stick domestic regulation approach fostering good corporate citizenship from business. Understanding the global economy is perplexing for voters, increasing the risks for policymakers in this field.

The Global Marketplace

World Trade Organization

From the time of its discovery, America has been involved in the web of commercial relations that stretched from Asia to Europe and beyond. What we call "globalization" began about 500 years ago with the advent of capitalism and has been expanding ever since, even if the immense worldwide economic changes brought about by the end of the Cold War together with the rise of the internet represent a significant acceleration. Issues concerning trade agreements, tariffs, subsidies, and agreements are central to US foreign policy. Even in its most isolationist periods, America has been strongly interventionist in promoting business interests and pursuing a "dollar diplomacy" of rewarding nations with monetary help in return for a favorable trade policy and in inflicting punitive economic sanctions on such "undesirables" as Cuba, Iran, and North Korea.

The US-dominated IMF and World Bank, which were set up as founding stones of the post-Second World War order, put requirements on nations that borrow money. This intervention into the internal affairs of other nations causes controversy as these nations need the money to bail out their economies or for development of new resources; however, they do not necessarily want the liberalization—the greater movement of jobs, goods, capital, and democracy across national borders—that is the price of the loans. Globalization can be seen as a destructive, exploitative system, especially when operated by the old colonial/imperial powers of the West who have proven untrustworthy in the past. At any rate, globalization is disrupting the economic linkages that influence people's lives.

Supporters of IMF and World Bank policies say that they will help close the gap between the wealthy Northern hemisphere and the under-industrialized Southern hemisphere through interconnection and trade. In 2020, many primary and general election voters rejected world economic equality in favor of the good life that had Americans atop the global economic pyramid. Former UN Secretary General Kofi Annan, from Ghana, acknowledged that "arguing against globalization is like arguing against gravity" (quoted in Crossette, 2000), and added that "The poor are not poor because of too much globalization, but because of too little" (quoted in DOHA, 2002). Domestic critics of globalization complain that it hurts American workers by creating a global labor market which suppresses wages and bleeds jobs abroad. Advocates argue that globalization makes everyone wealthier through competition and lower prices.

The World Trade Organization (WTO) is an international forum created to open markets, reduce tariffs (import taxes), and to expand free trade, particularly among developing countries. Established in 1995, the WTO is designed as the UN of the global economy and tries to resolve disputes among the 164 member nations (WTO, 2020). The WTO replaced the older General Agreement on Tariffs and Trade (GATT) conferences with a more permanent body of negotiators. It grew much stronger in late 2001 when China and Taiwan joined.

The WTO regulates trade, encourages fair competition, discourages domestic support to national businesses that distort trade, debates fair use of intellectual property, and promotes environmental standards. The WTO adjudicates complaints of unfair

Contemporary United States

practices—598 by 2020. Current cases include a dispute between the US and China over whether Hong Kong goods, labeled as Chinese products by the US, should be labeled as produced in Hong Kong (Reuters, 2020b).

Global trade has increased over the last decade or so, even without much progress on tariff harmonization, and despite Trump's promises to modify free trade to create more favorable trade for the US. Support for free trade has diminished among politicians in recent years, especially within the Republican Party—following the view that trade has geopolitical consequences. In 2019 Gallup polls suggested that up to three-quarters of Americans favored free trade (Saad, 2019).

Trade disputes with economically powerful China have become common. In 2009, the WTO agreed that China had hindered the import of cultural products such as film and music, in which the US is traditionally strong. In September 2012, the US brought forward a case asserting that China was illegally subsidizing automotive components via non-tariff measures. In 2016, Trump threatened to end alleged Chinese trade and currency manipulation—too-low exchange rates—by inflicting punitive tariffs, which were enacted in 2018. Meanwhile, Chinese companies continued to project their economic influence into Africa, Europe, Asia, and South America via loans and infrastructure in search of supplies of raw materials, suggesting that national policy could gain influence at the expense of free trade in future trade relationships. Biden sees his job as ensuring that premier rival China does not soon overtake the US in terms of influence: "That's not going to happen on my watch" (Renshaw, Shalal, and Martina, 2021). Trade friction is thus likely, especially as China is assertively taking up the reins of power.

In 2018, the United States exported $1.66 trillion and imported $2.6 trillion of merchandise, a deficit of nearly $1 trillion. Trade in services, etc., reduced this to about $620 billion (Statista, 2021c). American trade averages over $500 billion per year with each of four partners: China, Canada, Mexico, and the European Union (EU) (Statista, 2021f). The United States remains the world's leading developer and exporter of technology, despite outsourcing. Its manufacturing base is extensive. The US economy is increasingly global in outlook; more than one-quarter of GDP is traded—triple the level of 1960 (World Bank, 2021c).

Many firms have become "transnational," marshaling resources and labor while searching for favorable tax and regulatory regimes. Currently, design and innovation of Apple's iPhones and iPads remain in the US, even as their production has moved to subcontractors overseas. However, reports of poor conditions in factories abroad, such as those owned by FoxConn (a Taiwanese company based in China) and producing goods for Apple, or the slave-labor conclaves of Uighurs in western China, have raised ethical questions for American consumers (Bilton, 2014).

Blue-collar workers begrudge the migration of well-paid jobs overseas. Leading industries include steel, aerospace, textiles, automobiles, chemicals, telecommunications, semiconductors, biotechnology, and computers. Changes in technology and industrial organization continue to flow from US sources, although economies like China and India are increasingly innovative. Americans still make most of their money in the domestic market, as total exports make up only 11.7 percent of the GDP (2019). This compares

The Economy

Table 8.3 Top Fifteen US Trade Partners, Exports and Imports, 2020 (in billions of dollars)

Rank by total trade volume	Country	Exports	Imports	Total Trade	Balance
1	China	124.6	435.4	560.0	−210.8
2	Mexico	212.7	325.4	538.1	−112.1
3	Canada	255.4	270.4	525.8	−15.0
4	Japan	64.1	119.5	183.6	−55.4
5	Germany	57.8	115.1	172.9	−57.3
6	South Korea	51.2	76.0	127.2	−24.8
7	UK	59.0	50.2	109.2	+8.8
8	Switzerland	18.0	74.8	92.8	−56.8
9	Taiwan	30.5	60.4	90.9	−29.9
10	Vietnam	10.0	79.6	89.6	−69.6
11	India	27.4	51.2	78.6	−23.8
12	Ireland	9.6	65.5	75.1	−55.9
13	Netherlands	45.5	27.5	73.0	−18.0
14	France	27.4	43.0	70.4	−15.6
15	Italy	19.9	49.5	69.4	−29.6
	US Total Trade	1,431.6	2,336.6	3,768.2	−899.0

Note: 599.2 = $599,200,000,000. All numbers rounded up to nearest 0.1 percent.

Source: Statista (2021d, 2021e)

with China (18.5 percent), the UK (31.6 percent), Denmark (58.3 percent), Korea (39.9 percent), Japan (18.5 percent), and the Netherlands (83.3 percent) (World Bank, 2021a).

The United States is also the leading importer of world products, both in terms of raw materials to fuel factories and goods aimed at the consumer market. Since American imports far exceed its exports—the deficit amounts to over $600 billion per year—the country has a serious balance of trade problem (Statista, 2021e) (see Table 8.3). While the US imbalance is spread among the majority of the world's nations, the 2019 deficit was largest with China at around $200 billion, much more than other countries (USCB, 2021a). Since 2000, the connection of American consumers to Chinese producers has created a symbiotic economic relationship dubbed "Chimerica," which includes one-quarter of the world's population and one-third of its GDP.

Free Trade and Fair Trade

For forty years the world has worked towards freeing trade of tariffs and hindrances, in the belief that free trade benefits everyone by driving down costs, increasing economic efficiency, and improving security by drawing nations more tightly together. Put simply, it supposes that "if I sell you what I can make most efficiently at a good price and you

279

Contemporary United States

sell me what you can make most efficiently at your best price we both gain." This idea, "competitive advantage," has been shared by most leading nations, economists, most governing parties, and many ordinary people. The WTO is one general vehicle towards this end, but the difficulties of reaching consensus across borders where national interests are at stake has encouraged some nations to make regional deals.

Regionalization includes organizations like the EU, the now-defunct North American Free Trade Area (NAFTA), its replacement, the United States–Mexico–Canada Agreement (USMCA), and the Trans-Pacific Partnership (TTP). However, the 2016 election saw voters and politicians openly doubting that free trade meant fair trade—even as polls suggests large majorities nationally favor free trade and see it as an opportunity. Trump harnessed trade fears and drove new (mostly rhetorical) bargains with major trading partners Canada, Mexico, the EU, and China. While Biden is more sympathetic to free trade, the president must take free trade suspicion locally into account, as it is an energizing factor in rustbelt swing states. Here, pluralities felt

Illustration 8.3 USMCA and the Politics of the Border

In February 2022, "Freedom Convoy" protesters blocked the Ambassador Bridge crossing point between Detroit, Michigan, and Windsor, Ontario, a conduit accounting for 25 percent of all US/Canadian trade—or over $300 million a day. Trade is heavily focused on automotive components. Truckers were complaining about vaccine mandates for truckers crossing the border, soon joined by anti-maskers, evangelicals, vaccine skeptics, and lockdown resisters, and many others frustrated by the consequences of the pandemic. Protesters exerting pressure on a pinch-point demonstrated the problems of limited infrastructure for highly complex trade relations between two of the world's biggest trade partners.

Source: Cole Burston/Stringer via Getty Images

The Economy

that NAFTA had been bad for America, giving Trump backing to renegotiate the deal to form the USMCA in 2020 (USTR, 2020).

USMCA gathers the United States, Canada, and Mexico in one of the two largest free trade blocs in the world. Established as NAFTA in 1994, North American trade cooperation increasingly removed the investment and agricultural tariff barriers that restricted trade, with the final restrictions eliminated in January 2008. Originally, Congress strongly opposed the deal because of Mexico's failure to enforce environmental laws and from concerns that its cheap labor market would hurt American workers. Fearing that manufacturers might relocate to Mexico and take jobs with them, labor unions especially opposed NAFTA. Clinton used his position as "lobbyist-in-chief"—as well as the lobbying support of ex-presidents Ford, Carter, and Bush—to get sufficient votes for the agreement. US–Mexican trade rose dramatically under NAFTA, not least as US-based manufacturers established plants south of the border to take advantage of low wages—fueling blue-collar discontent at home, especially in the rustbelt. The US and Canada, meanwhile, have long had a close trading relationship based on similar wage, lifestyle, and regulatory levels, and aided by a border usually benefiting from limited practical friction—though this was not the case in February 2022 (see Illustration 8.3).

Trade inside USMCA benefits its members, even though China–US trade provides intense competition, as Table 8.3 indicates. Trump's support of the nationalist Right and need for a trade villain underlay the metamorphosis of NAFTA to USMCA. USMCA remains vitally important to the US, Canada, and Mexico, as it allows relatively low-risk near-sourcing instead of the more distant and precarious "outsourcing." Many observers saw few substantial differences between NAFTA and USMCA. Put simply, the three countries have an intertwined, complex, and transnational relationship where economic and social dimensions include the mobility of workers and capital seeking opportunity to create human and financial webs across borders. Earlier hopes that North American trade cooperation could grow into a massive continental Free Trade Area of the Americas (FTAA) have so far come to nought.

The Dollar and the Renminbi

In 2021, the US felt the results of a generation long trade imbalance where imports exceeded exports. The nation's $28 trillion national debt outstripped its $22 trillion yearly GDP (BEA, 2021; Statista, 2021a). From 1944 to 1971, under the Bretton Woods agreements, world currencies were tied to the dollar, with the dollar convertible to gold at a fixed rate ($35 per ounce). The dollar has remained the world's favored reserve currency and has vied with gold as a safe haven for international investors, a policy which gives the US access to foreign capital. However, with balance of payments deficits every year since 1974, and budget deficits every year since 2002, the rise of Asia, and the ebb and flow of world events, the dollar has fluctuated markedly in relation to most other currencies. In 2020, the dollar swung around 10 percent in value in relation to the Renminbi, the Chinese currency, and the European Euro currency.

281

Contemporary United States

Bucking a two-year trend, the Renminbi increased its value relative to the dollar in 2020, partially heading off US claims that the currency was strongly undervalued, and thus distorts US–Chinese trade balances—witnessed by the $210 billion 2020 trade surplus in China's favor (USCB, 2021a). The Renminbi's rise may have resulted from the lesser economic effects of the 2020 Covid recession on China than the US. Many pundits and politicians, including Trump, saw alleged currency manipulation as a deliberate strategy. With an undervalued currency, China could build up domestic strength at the expense of overseas economies. Trump imposed tariffs of 10–25 percent on selected Chinese goods, collecting over $60 billion in revenue in 2019 (Zumbrun, 2019).

The trading relationship between the US and China is certainly complex. Economic links benefit people in both countries. Americans gain cheaper goods and thus higher living standards, while Chinese wages have risen and Chinese lives have improved due to technology transfer and "insourcing." Yet, there are strains to this relationship. In 2011, when Obama asked Apple founder Steve Jobs what it would take to bring the firm's production back to the US, Jobs explained that Apple's locational preference was not primarily about costs, but about supply-chain flexibility. With transnational corporations expanding, work which relocates to China and elsewhere will not return to any real extent until market forces—costs, convenience, and corporate ethics—favor a return. Apple and others have been heavily criticized for using overseas assemblers whose wages and working conditions do not match domestic standards, inciting many green, humane, and labor organizations to insist that corporations show good "corporate social responsibility" (CSR) by fostering the same values abroad as they do at home. Huge employee-based pension funds like the California Teachers' State Retirement System, which manages over $290 billion for its members, have pushed CSR issues on companies they invest in (CALSTRS, 2021).

While free trade is beneficial to many, China's trade surplus signals a sea change in relative economic fortunes, as China is projected to become the world's largest economy within a decade. In 2020, both China and Japan each hold over $1 trillion of US debt (McBride and Siripurapu, 2021). Other countries have noted that China's economic success builds off a blend of strong governmental involvement, tight political control, and economic freedom, which all challenge US-inspired models of development that link economic and political freedom. China appears to offer other countries more prosperity and a path to development without chaotic Western-style democracy.

In the past, countries have been willing to lend America money because of the massive American consumer market and the acknowledgment that the US is the only "consumption superpower" (Schwenninger, 2004). Put differently, when the US sneezes, many other countries catch colds. Conversely, when the US experiences better growth rates and higher median incomes, countries around the world enjoy sunnier economic outlooks. Optimism breeds optimism. The value of the US dollar to a degree rises and falls on the back of American growth rates.

In spring 2021 as Covid vaccination rates accelerated and confidence returned to the economy, projections suggested that the US economy would grow a stunning 6 percent.

Biden's physical and human infrastructure bills promised more growth, but Congress sliced much of the plan and stalled its passage in mid-2022. Covid recovery packages helped fuel short-term growth—especially as they increase the purchasing power of poorer Americans. Some economists worried that inflation would return, after a generation of "Age of Reagan" austerity thinking which shunned federal government interference in economic affairs.

In the economy, global, national, and local factors combine. Economic policy must be seen through the transformation and global interconnectedness in business and social interactions. Interconnectedness of transnational corporate capitalism was obvious in the Suez Canal grounding of the massive container ship *Ever Given* in March 2021. Weighing in at around 200,000 tons and measuring nearly 300 meters from bow to stern, high winds caused the *Ever Given* to ground across both banks of the canal for a week. Well over a hundred ships were backed up at either end of the canal, blocking a trade worth nearly $10 billion a day (Harper, 2021). Meanwhile in California, supply lines creaked as gargantuan ships from Asia waited for berths to unload their products in harbors whose infrastructure was being stretched to the limits by a generation of new, super container ships (Kay, 2021).

Of course, huge ships promise savings for corporations. But this also causes destructive global competition among workers. Rising productivity and lower per unit labor costs have transferred greater shares to stockholders while employees received only limited bonuses. Until 1975, wages made up more than half of GDP; in the twenty-first century, this has fallen to 44 percent. Globally integrated Ford Motor Corporation, for instance, posted profits in the first quarter of 2021 of $4.8 billion (Ford, 2021). Apple, meanwhile, made profits of nearly $34 billion in the last three months of 2020, on sales of $95 billion, and paid out $30 billion to shareholders (Apple, 2021).

Clearly, the state of the US economy is spotlighted by the media—especially at election times—even though the rules of transnational economic globalization are not primarily concerned with national borders. Profits come first, with financial markets ruthless in their search to maximize value for shareholders. Economic competition among countries benefit the rich by reducing taxes on corporations and undermining labor rights, wages, and employment tenure for ordinary workers. The terms of overseas trade preoccupy the Biden administration as much as they did the Trump administration. Increasingly, economic and foreign policies interweave.

Further Reading

Gordon, R. (2016) *The Rise and Fall of American Growth: The US Standard of Living since the Civil War*, Princeton: Princeton University Press.

Krugman, P. (2021) *Arguing with Zombies: Economics, Politics, and the Fight for a Better Future*, New York: W. W. Norton

MacGillis, A. (2022) *Fulfillment: America in the Shadow of Amazon*, New York: Picador.

Piketty, T. (2014) *Capital in the Twenty-First Century*, Cambridge, MA: Belknap Press of Harvard University Press.

Putnam, R. (2015) *Our Kids: The American Dream in Crisis*, New York: Simon & Schuster.

CHAPTER 9
GLOBAL POLITICS

In 2021, Joseph Robinette Biden was a man in a hurry. The world needed guidance, assurance, cooperation, and to make a "pressure test" of the newest leader of the free world. Biden's predecessor, Donald Trump, had pursued a starkly different agenda for the global order. In 2017 Trump tossed out plans for win–win cosmopolitanism, insisted on "America First," and denounced his own foreign policy establishment. One of his supporters, a real nativist, defended Trump in an email to the editor of *Foreign Affairs*: "I'll simplify this for you. The average American rejects your Globalist, anti-American, anti-constitution, politically-correct VOMIT" (Rose, 2019).

Trump was antagonistic and he viewed the world in transactional terms, always looking for advantage over other nations. He believed that power was a zero-sum game where when one side won, the other lost. Most of the world grew restless with this blinkered thinking. As David Ignatius wrote, "Nobody loves a superpower in decline" (Ignatius, 2021). For Trump, world disorder was often the point. Biden saw the chance for the world order to be less of a competitive system and more of a cooperative society. Biden believed in an absolute or positive-sum game where compromises could be win–win. He rushed forward to repair alliances and international partnerships.

When Biden took office, tensions were growing over how to defeat the Covid-19 pandemic, its horrible mutations, the disagreement over vaccinations, and the disparity in vaccine availability in rich and poor countries. The increasing disruptions with the economic fallout of supply chains linked to rising inflation, and the security dilemmas involved as people died and refugees fled across national borders complicated his task. Authoritarian leaders saw opportunities to advance their own power. On top of this, America's longest war, in Afghanistan, was in its nineteenth year, and worse, the earth seemed to be failing, or at least humans had failed the world in terms of safeguarding it from manmade CO_2 emissions. In December 2021 at the world's largest-ever scientific conference on climate change, specialists unanimously agreed that "the weather of the past will not be the weather of the future" (Kaplan and Dennis, 2021). Earth had been transformed and 2021 was the hottest year on record. At one point, the globe seemed to be burning everywhere at once as forest fires set a record for the numbers of out-of-control fires and property destroyed. Simultaneously, drought, floods, tornadoes, typhoons, and hurricanes joined the observable melting of the icecaps at the North and South poles to push activists to organize as never before to save the planet and the life on it (Kaplan and Dennis, 2021; *NYT*, 2021). Around the globe, protesters were pushing leaders to do something quickly (Illustration 9.1).

Contemporary United States

Illustration 9.1 "All Mouth, No Trousers": The G7 Fail to Rein in Climate Change

The Group of Seven (G7: Italy, Germany, US, Canada, France, UK, Japan) Western powers meets annually to discuss international relations, especially finances and security, but also issues affecting cooperation across and around national borders. At the meeting in 2021 in England under the slogan "Build Back Better," guest countries included India, Australia, South Korea, and South Africa. The coronavirus, cybersecurity, and supply chain economic issues took central stage, but there was hope that the G7 would more-than-seriously consider steps to alleviate climate change and to address the skyrocketing public demand for cleaner skies, cleaner water, and provide a plan to help tame the extreme floods, wildfires, drought, melting glaciers and permafrost, hurricanes, and rising temperatures stemming from the use of fossil fuels. Much focus was on Biden who had already overturned thirty-one Trump policies including rejoining the Paris Agreement and added twenty-one of his own, including support for electric vehicles and a pledge to reduce greenhouse gases spewed by the US by 50 percent in 2030 (Eilperin, Dennis, and Muyskens, 2021). The G7 members made many pledges but no real immediate financial payments. In the photograph, members of the environmental action group, Extinction Rebellion, protested the lack of gender equality in the world and the impact of global warming on women and children. According to climate advocates, the ministers promised a lot but provided few details or specific measures to slow global warming. They were all talk and no action. They were "all mouth and no trousers."

Source: Jeff J Mitchell via Getty Images

An Upsurge of Nationalism

Compounding Biden's workload was the widespread anxiety of a world in disarray that had increased dramatically with the presidency of Donald Trump. The international system that had been in place since the Second World War was clearly outdated and nationalism loudly and rapidly returned to the world stage after three decades of movement toward a deeper global integration. Politicians everywhere recognized the growing discontent toward governing structures domestic and foreign. These jingoists led surging conservative parties whose election victories increased international tensions by questioning alliances, agreements, regional organizations and international institutions. Trump identified the enemy as cosmopolitanism (globalism), which, ironically, was the same enemy named by Islamic jihadists, Xi Jinping, and Vladimir Putin (Illustration 9.2). Political scientist Robert Kagan predicted that with the declining support for internationalism, the old order would collapse in the space of three to fifteen years, suddenly, with the coming of the Third World War (Kagan, 2017). He was not the only one predicting wars of one size or another as many political scientists believed an epoch was ending. The invasion of Ukraine by Russian President Vladimir Putin in 2022 attested to the realities of democracies in danger and authoritarian states eager to advance.

Economic fallout from the 2008 Great Recession (see Chapter 8) continued and class divisions widened. The world was in the second decade of a global war on terror and fears grew that a more destructive war could erupt between Islam and Christianity or expand into a global conflagration pitting civilizations against one another. Imperialism and colonialism were rising. China continued to gain strength by consolidating its control over minority groups within its borders and shutting down the open democratic government in Hong Kong. Hindu nationalism surged in India, Russia asserted itself in Ukraine, Syria, and the Baltics, and the large refugee and migration crisis in Europe was frightening to behold. People everywhere weighed the benefits of globalization against their needs for personal and tribal security. The ideological fault lines were no longer capitalism versus communism—capitalism had won. Increasingly, democratic governments were transitioning to soft authoritarianism or worse.

The sudden eruption of ethnocentric parties campaigning on fears of foreigners and demanding a return to national cultures, borders, and state sovereignty endangered the existence of the European Union. These parties included: France's National Front, Austria's Freedom Party, Britain's United Kingdom Independence Party, Holland's Party for Freedom, Slovakia's Slovak Freedom Party, Greece's Golden Dawn, Germany's Alternative for Germany, Italy's North League for Independence, Sweden's Swedish Democrats, and Denmark's Danish People's Party. In the United States, the election of Trump was a victory for the Alternative Right—called the "Alt Right"—and calls for law and order and the establishment of hierarchies that would "make America great again." Many European populists disagreed with Trump on a variety of issues, but they believed that with his willingness to ignore and erase global norms and institutions, their own dreams of independence would be furthered. Of course, this was a "double-edged sword" as people worried about a superpower freed from its commitment to defend the global order and the openings that the lack of leadership created for revisionist powers. Any transfer in American leadership raises questions over how much or how little US policy will change.

Contemporary United States

Illustration 9.2 The G7 Confronts Trump's "America First" Plan

In 2018, the Group of Seven (G7) held its annual meeting in Charlevoix, Canada. G7 leaders leaned forward on the table to press Trump to compromise his "America First" stances of non-cooperation and of his insistence that the US would dictate actions. From left to right are British Prime Minister Theresa May (second from left), French President Emmanuel Macron, and German Chancellor Angela Merkel. The tension is clear in the folded arms of Japanese Prime Minister Shinzo Abe and in the faces of everyone present. Trump is clearly the one being confronted and his posture reveals his intransigence to the demands of Merkel and Macron. One issue revolved around Trump's insistence that Russia be reinstated in what was the G8 before Russia was expelled due to the invasion of Crimea by Vladimir Putin in 2014. Trump also insisted that Crimea be formally recognized as part of Russia because the Ukraine "was one of the most corrupt countries in the world." When Trump's demands were not met, he left the meeting and isolated the United States from any decisions by the G7 (see also Illustration 9.4).

Source: Jesco Denzel/Bundesregierung via Getty Images

Since the Second World War, America's role in global affairs has been singularly important to maintaining world order through norms of international cooperation. These questions are compounded by the partisan polarization of contemporary American politics. In the twenty-first century, the foreign policy of George W. Bush centered on a neo-conservative unilateralism of aggressively dealing with "rogue" states and promoting democracy via regime change and nation-building. Obama's victory in 2008 brought more liberal leadership. Eight years later, in 2016, world leaders worried over Trump's lack of credentials, insistent jingoism of "America First," and what Jake Sullivan once described as "preaching predatory unilateralism" (Sullivan, 2019). Perceptions of fairness and trust play key roles in international relations and Trump began with large deficits in these areas, something neither his predecessor nor his successor faced. Trump was not a president who exemplified moral leadership.

His predecessor was. In 2008, Americans elected a man of mixed ethnicity and race to the world's most powerful office. Barack Obama seemed to defy gravity through his "Yes, We Can" optimism. UN Secretary General Kofi Annan noted "the dramatic change of leadership in the United States of America which I am witnessing with great emotion … [is] rightly celebrated around the globe, from the villages of Africa to the chancelleries of Europe" (Annan, 2009). Chinese political prisoner and soon-to-be Nobel Peace Prize winner Liu Xiaobo wrote: "the greatness of the American system" is that "every four years, the United States can, if it wants, turn itself around by means of a general election that is open to all. It sometimes does this, especially at moments of great crisis" (Xiaobo, 2012). The German newspaper *Der Spiegel* praised the "self-cleansing" American democracy and celebrated the new president as "a beacon of hope in a crisis-ridden world" (Steingart, 2009). Others proclaimed the coming of the first truly global president, a man who would lead the way to a better place (Brinkley, 2008). In fact, there were so many expectations placed on Obama, that just a few months after taking office, he was awarded the Nobel Peace Prize—not for having done anything particularly notable or heroic, but for his "vision" and in anticipation of what he might do.

Obama immediately used his approval ratings to try and reverse anti-American sentiments. He sought a meaningful dialogue about Iraq, Iranian nuclear ambitions, and the Palestinian–Israeli conflict. He believed in the power of reconciliation and insisted that "Americans are not your enemy." He offered to "extend a hand if you are willing to unclench your fist" (AP, 2009). Obama admired the European Union as a model for regional governance, reduced nationalism, and pooled sovereignty among states. He called for a broader understanding of national security that placed it with a framework of global cooperation and a multi-polar and multinational decision-making. His approach to world order gave more power to international bodies, including the United Nations, World Trade Organization (WTO), World Health Organization (WHO), and to international agreements such as the Universal Declaration of Human Rights, or agreements on climate change, such as the 2016 Paris Accords to reduce carbon emissions (see Chapter 2). US conservatives were appalled by these unforced giveaways of American supremacy and taxpayer monies.

Global politics employ different forms of power. Hard power—sometimes called "sharp" power—refers to military forces deployed in wars, used as a threat to coerce others to do what you want them to do, or to take over their country if they refuse to yield. Soft power is the persuasion achieved by advancing ideals and culture so attractive that others want to have what you have (Nye, 2015) (Illustration 9.3). US culture shows aspects of soft power in movies, tech, food, music, sports, clothing, and diversity. Soft power can also come from volunteering to work abroad, as more than 240,000 Americans have done in 142 countries since the Peace Corps was established by President Kennedy in 1961 (Peace Corps, 2019). Presidents also wield soft power if they are trusted actors on the world stage. Sticky power involves trade agreements, markets, globalization, and the economic institutions and policies that connect nations and non-state actors, such as

Illustration 9.3 Domestic Protests Heavily Influence America's Soft Power Advantages

For seventy-five years, since the end of the Second World War, the United States has benefited from its ability to influence others to follow its leadership in the global order. The country's military and economic power has provided hard and sticky components to achieving physical foreign policy outcomes. Just as important has been America's soft power in terms of its attractive culture of education, ideas, free society, and guarantees of individual freedoms in a democratic system. For centuries, immigrants relocated to America. They were not always welcomed with open arms. But despite the racism, sexism, white supremacy, and unequal treatment, most people endured. The election of Barack Obama was hailed as the beginning of a cosmopolitan world and a "post-racial" America. But the forces behind Donald Trump wanted an ethnically based America First and the number of hate crimes against minorities increased dramatically after 2017. The pandemic was blamed on China and Trump used "race-baiting" rhetoric that encouraged racists to lash out against Chinese and Asian Americans in response. Anti-Asian harassment and violence rose to highs not seen since the Japanese attack on Pearl Harbor in 1941. By 2021, the FBI reported that while hate crimes rose 6 percent nationwide against all groups, they jumped by 73 percent against Asian Americans, with 2,808 reported assaults, particularly on females and the elderly. America's soft power diminished as the world watched carefully. The photograph is of a "We Are Not Silent" rally in Seattle, Washington, in March 2021, denouncing racist violence and white supremacy against Asian Americans particularly and all non-whites generally.

Source: David Ryder/Stringer via Getty Images

multinational corporations, to control the flow of jobs and money. In 2013, Secretary of State John Kerry discounted hard and soft power in favor of sticky power, saying: "more than ever, foreign policy is economic policy" (Gearan, 2013).

Global Politics

In 2012, Secretary of State Hillary Clinton spoke of combining the three types of power into a liberal internationalist approach she called "smart" power. Acknowledging that the United States was being challenged by China, India, Brazil, and others, Clinton wrote that "it's a new world, and we all have to figure out how best to adjust to it" (Clinton, 2012b). She explained: "The test of our leadership going forward will be our ability to mobilise disparate people and nations to work together to solve common problems and advance shared values and aspirations ... into a multi-partner world" (Clinton, 2012a). Her ideas were completely in line with Obama's and Biden's beliefs in absolute gains but deviated from Trump's preference for a Hobbesian struggle of all against all—the rule of the jungle. Trump said that his inaugural speech would venerate the return of a patriot and the defeat of globalists. Trump spoke in zero-sum terms:

We assembled here today are issuing a new decree to be heard in every city, in every foreign capital, and in every hall of power. From this day forward, a new vision will govern our land. From this moment forward, it's going to be America First. Every decision on trade, on taxes, on immigration, on foreign affairs, will be made to benefit American workers and American families. We must protect our borders from the ravages of other countries making our products, stealing our companies, and destroying our jobs. Protection will lead to greater prosperity and strength ... America will start winning again, winning like never before. We will bring back our jobs. We will bring back our borders. We will bring back our wealth ... We will follow two simple rules: Buy American and Hire American.

(Trump, 2017c)

Trump saw only limited advantages in global alliances. For him, leadership was a heavy weight that hurt self-interested deal making. He scoffed at the rules-based international order (Daalder and Lindsay, 2018). In 2019, Trump spoke to the UN General Assembly and reiterated his nationalist rhetoric:

If you want your freedom, take pride in your country. If you want democracy, hold on to your sovereignty. And if you want peace, love your nation. Wise leaders always put the good of their own people and their own country first. The future does not belong to globalists. The future belongs to patriots. The future belongs to sovereign and independent nations.

(Trump, 2019)

Presidents have conducted an ambivalent foreign policy marked by a consistent belief in New World exceptionalism and the central idea of freedom. From the beginning, Americans have had a widespread distrust of other nations as places inclined toward war, conspiracies, class-based privilege, a lack of order and, increasingly in recent years, breeding grounds for terrorism. In 1776, Thomas Paine's pamphlet *Common Sense* proclaimed: "We have it in our power to begin the world over again." In another pamphlet, *The Crisis*, Paine called on the patriots to stand firm through "the times

291

Contemporary United States

that try men's souls." The United States began its national life with the *Declaration of Independence*, a document explicitly citing the need to ensure "a decent respect for the opinions of mankind" (see Box 1.1).

American history is marked by an adherence to "stand firm" in global affairs. Presidents are judged by whether they enhance or diminish the country's prestige, power, and global influence. In the twenty-first century, George Bush used his inaugural speech to warn: "The rulers of outlaw regimes can know that we still believe as Abraham Lincoln did: Those who deny freedom to others deserve it not for themselves; and, under the rule of a just God, cannot long retain it" (Bush, 2005). In 2009 Obama invoked God and duty: "Let it be said by our children's children that when we were tested we refused to let this journey end, that we did not turn back nor did we falter; and with eyes fixed on the horizon and God's grace upon us, we carried forth that great gift of freedom and delivered it safely to future generations" (Obama, 2009b). In 2017 Trump returned to Paine: "A new national pride will stir our souls ... It is time to remember that old wisdom our soldiers will never forget: that whether we are black or brown or white, we all bleed the same red blood of patriots, we all enjoy the same glorious freedoms, and we all salute the same great American Flag" (Trump, 2017c). For Biden, in 2021, "This is America's day. This is democracy's day. A day of history and hope. Of renewal and resolve. Through a crucible for the ages America has been tested anew and America has risen to the challenge ... Over the centuries through storm and strife, in peace and in war, we have come so far. But we still have far to go" (Biden, 2021d).

Separation of Powers and Foreign Policy

The United States operates under a federal system where states share power. This gives foreign interests multiple entry points to influence policy. Many nations have established lobbying groups in Washington and various state capitals to convince legislators to accept their proposals. Officially, the Constitution divides power over foreign policy between the executive and the legislative branches, but, in practice, Congress had most of the power in the nineteenth century and the president has had it ever since. In the twenty-first century, Bush, Obama, and Trump increased executive power in ways that alarmed the other two branches of government and, correctly, led to valid charges of being imperial presidencies who bypassed the people's representatives.

Presidents chafe under legislative controls and often sidestep them by using executive agreements, discretionary funds, undeclared wars, and other devices. A president can use an agreement between himself and a foreign head of state to make policy. Even though critics complain that this is ruling by fiat, these "executive agreements" are constitutional and the number of them outpaces formal treaties by almost 25 to 1. These agreements are only valid while the president is in office. A new president must renew, reject, or initiate his own agreements. "Executive orders" overlap with agreements but differ in that they are mandates. Bush issued 291 executive orders, Obama 275, and Trump 220 (in one four-year term). In his first year in office, Biden issued seventy-two orders, including mandates to re-join the Paris Climate Accords, the International Criminal Court, to focus on Covid-19, to closely monitor China cheating, international cybersecurity, Russian energy pipelines, and to keep an oversight on troubles in Belarus, the Balkans, Ethiopia, and Burundi.

Presidents also control a large amount of money for use in a crisis situation or to pursue pet projects. Called "discretionary funds," these expenditures make up about one-third of the entire budget. The other two-thirds is mandatory spending on programs that have been approved by Congress over time. In terms of spending aimed at global politics, Biden's 2022 budget was concentrated on the Department of Defense ($715 billion), State Department ($63.5 billion), and National Aeronautics and Space Administration ($24.7 billion).

The president is commander-in-chief of the military, has the power to make treaties, appoint ambassadors, and is head of state in affording diplomatic recognition to foreign heads of state. Only Congress can declare war, approve spending, raise an army, make rules regulating commerce, and create international programs—although these powers have been usurped by presidents over time. The Senate alone approves ambassadorships and must ratify all treaties made by the executive before they are legally binding. Congress struggles to control presidents. For example, the 1973 War Powers Resolution limits the president's ability to wage war by requiring him to notify Congress within forty-eight hours of sending in troops and by providing a limit of sixty days on their deployment, unless Congress specifically approves an extension. This has never worked very well and Bush, Obama, and Trump, while informing Congress, surpassed the sixty-day limit in Afghanistan and Iraq. The 1988 Arms Control Export Act restricts the president's ability to transfer arms approved for one nation to another nation although there are back avenues big enough to drive tanks through.

Beginning in 1974, Congress authorized a president to make "fast-track" trading agreements with foreign leaders. Known as Trade Promotion Authority (TPA), these agreements must be accepted or rejected by Congress, but they cannot be amended. A TPA helps a president open foreign markets by making foreign leaders more confident that the agreement will not be changed by congressional amendments. In 1997, in retaliation for Clinton's support of NAFTA (see Chapter 8), the Republican Congress ended fast-track agreements, then reversed course in 2002, giving Bush the power once again. In 2015, Congress approved Obama's request for TPA to seek cooperation and economic alliances in Asia. Obama wanted an Asia-wide free trade area, something overwhelmingly sought by multinational corporations. The Trans-Pacific Trade and Investment Partnership (TPP) was a key component of the administration's "pivot to Asia," an effort to compete effectively with China by forming the largest free trade organization in the world, including Japan, Mexico, Canada, Australia, New Zealand, Singapore, Vietnam and others. China was excluded from joining. Obama signed the TPP agreement, but it became highly political during the 2016 presidential campaign as both nominees claimed it would take jobs from American workers. On his third day in office, Trump signed an executive order removing the US from the TPP. Trump also rejected the use of fast-track agreements because he said he "didn't need them" and could make executive agreements and orders with or without congressional approval.

Contemporary United States

American policymakers must balance monetary costs against national security demands. They are aware of the danger of "imperial overstretch"—the condition of having too many properties and allies and too few armies and resources, or insufficient will to protect them all. For example, in 2021, the US had 50,000 troops stationed in Japan as part of a system of roughly 800 military bases worldwide and a powerful navy in every ocean. In 2021, the active-duty force of 2.25 million personnel and other costs totaled $778 billion, a figure estimated at nearly 40 percent of the total world military spending (DOD, 2021a). In 2017, Trump's first budget added a 10 percent increase for the Pentagon with Trump explaining: "It will be one of the greatest military buildups in American history." He added: "Hopefully we'll never have to use it, but nobody is going to mess with us. Nobody" (Tharoor, 2017). Trump's National Defense Strategy Report emphasized the competition with China in terms of America First, not in line with Clinton's admonition to defy history (DOD, 2018b).

The United States has enormous power to reward nations who conform to American wishes. The government grants access to the unparalleled American consumer market, distributes foreign aid in many forms, sponsors entry into international organizations, ignores violations of human rights, forgives debts, and adjusts economic sanctions. Presidents make political and economic decisions based on the relationship between each nation and the superpower. The United States tries to balance a realistic and sometimes harsh foreign policy with a pragmatic multi-polar cooperation that lessens criticism that American actions seem like "bossism." Still, whatever it does, the United States as the prime defender of the status quo both attracts and repels the international community.

History of Foreign Policy

Isolation and Expansion

In 1796, America's first president, George Washington, advised the nation to promote trade while being careful to avoid entangling political agreements: "'Tis our true policy to steer clear of permanent Alliances with any portion of the foreign world ... Our detached and distant situation invites and enables us to pursue a different course." America's third president, Thomas Jefferson, soothed fears stemming from the French Revolution and the competition between France and Britain by stating that America desired a policy of "peace, commerce, and honest friendship with all nations, entangling alliances with none." Yet, even while Jefferson held isolationist sentiments, his actions were interventionist. In 1801, Jefferson sent US marines to wage war against the Barbary Coast pirates who were raiding shipping lanes north of Algiers and, in 1803, he doubled the size of the nation by agreeing to purchase the Louisiana Territory from Napoleon. Expansion westward held the symbolic and real function of withdrawing from the Old World toward a new frontier.

Americans have rarely seen themselves as imperialists, maintaining a great myopia to their history in "colonizing their own nation" (colonizing themselves) by defeating

Indians, Mexicans, and others who occupied land they desired for themselves. In 1821, future president John Quincy Adams said that while America everywhere opposes tyranny and supports new democracies, "she goes not abroad, in search of monsters to destroy." Perhaps Adams overstated. In 1823, President James Monroe announced his Monroe Doctrine to claim a sphere of influence and hegemony over the Americas, closing them to further European colonization. Rapidly, the nation extended its boundaries to the Pacific Ocean.

During the Civil War (1861–1865), Abraham Lincoln insisted that the fate of global liberty rested on the outcome of that war when "this nation, under God, shall have a new birth of freedom – and that government of the people, by the people, for the people, shall not perish from the earth" (see Box 1.2). Lincoln's sentiment is often invoked by American presidents, as George W. Bush did: "The stakes for America are never small. If our country does not lead the cause of freedom, it will not be led" (Bush, 2001).

The 1890s witnessed a rising nationalism as America competed with Europe for overseas territories. The Reverend Josiah Strong preached that commerce always followed the missionary and Alfred Mahan's book, *The Influence of Sea Power on History* (1890), convinced Congress to build a modern navy. In 1898, President William McKinley ordered a war to liberate Cuba from Spanish control after the US battleship *Maine* exploded in Havana harbor. Secretary of State John Hay lauded "that splendid little war" which lasted three months but made America an imperial power. With the peace, the United States established a protectorate over Cuba and gained Guam, Puerto Rico and, after a three-year land war with Filipino nationalists in which 2,000 Americans and 200,000 Filipinos died, the Philippines. America became a Pacific Ocean power and forced Japan, Russia, and the European powers to allow free trade—the "Open Door"—in China.

In the twentieth century, America rose as both superpower and empire. President Theodore Roosevelt was an enthusiastic imperialist who intervened often in Latin America. His Corollary to the Monroe Doctrine made the United States an international police power claiming a "sphere of influence" over the Western Hemisphere. Where the Monroe Doctrine had pledged American power to ensure sovereignty for American nations, the Roosevelt Corollary committed the United States to intervene in the otherwise sovereign affairs of others.

A World Power

When war erupted in Europe in August 1914, a deeply divided and ethnically diverse American citizenry mostly insisted that the war was not their concern. President Woodrow Wilson declared US neutrality. Three years later, in 1917, American soldiers were fighting in France behind Wilson's new slogan to "Make the World Safe for Democracy." The next year, at the Paris Peace Conference, Wilson's "Fourteen Points" offered a way to secure lasting peace and proposed the establishment of a League of Nations, the rights of national self-determination, free trade, arms reductions, and open diplomacy.

Contemporary United States

Americans rejected the entangling alliances of Wilsonianism and the Senate refused to ratify the peace treaty or to allow the United States to join the League of Nations. Clearly unprepared for global leadership, America defined its security interests narrowly, restricted them to what a regional power could do, and removed itself as far as possible from European politics. Writer Ernest Hemingway captured the mood of the times: "We were fools to be sucked in once in a European war and we should never be sucked in again" (Hemingway, 1935).

With the Great Depression of the 1930s and the aggressive nationalism of Japan and Germany, Congress again passed a series of Neutrality Acts. In 1939, as the Second World War began, American neutrality became one-sided when President Franklin Roosevelt made executive agreements to ensure that Britain had the necessary supplies to fight Nazi Germany. Roosevelt called the US "the arsenal of democracy," lending and leasing supplies and equipment to those fighting totalitarianism while keeping its small 185,000-man army at home. Many Americans, once again, insisted on an "America First" policy of neutrality. That idea failed. On December 7, 1941, Japan erased isolationist sentiment by its powerful air strike against the US fleet at Pearl Harbor naval base in Hawaii. The United States entered and fought a two-ocean war and took the ultimate revenge against Japan by dropping atomic bombs on Hiroshima and Nagasaki to end the war in 1945.

Two superpowers emerged and an exhausted Europe and divided Asia took the consequences. The United States clearly had the most power—it produced half the world's steel, held a nuclear monopoly, possessed 70 percent of the world's ships and aircraft, and manufactured 50 percent of the world's goods. As the Soviet Union expanded into Eastern Europe and Asia, the United States helped rebuild Japan and Germany while consolidating its influence in Western Europe. Moreover, the US led an effort to build a system of international alliances and institutions to replace narrow nationalism and great power politics.

The Cold War, 1945–1990

For nearly five decades, the United States had a well-defined enemy to confront on every issue, anywhere in the world. The contest was ritualized and every encounter became a crisis. The main issue was democracy versus authoritarianism. Americans generally viewed communism as an evil system of godless, totalitarian, and anti-capitalist actions— an ideology obstructing the spread of freedom and free trade. America not only acted with an arrogance of power, it created consensus to wage wars in distant countries, stifle debate, prop-up Right-wing dictatorships, and enroll dozens of allies in the cause of anti-communism. The concepts of the "West" and the "Free World" were born. Mutual security and dependence intertwined the domestic and international affairs of Western Europe and America so tightly that it became difficult to separate national from international interests. As the USSR countered each move, the superpowers practiced mutual restraint and maintained order in a bipolar global system.

Global Politics

In 1947, President Harry Truman contrasted two ways of life and enacted a policy of "containment," the Truman Doctrine, to stop Soviet expansionism: "It must be the policy of the United States to support free peoples who are resisting attempted subjugation by armed minorities or by outside pressures." America thrust itself into the internal affairs of weaker nations, a role that meant ever-higher defense expenditures to support a massive military. That same year, the National Security Act expanded executive power by creating the National Security Council (NSC), Central Intelligence Agency (CIA), and Department of Defense (DOD). These agencies join with the Department of State (DOS) in collecting and analyzing information, and in dividing the administration of foreign policy into civilian and military spheres.

Historically, the DOS has had primary responsibility for foreign affairs and the Secretary of State has been the highest-ranking cabinet official, a key figure in formulating and implementing policy. The Secretary of State supervises all US ambassadors, who are mostly political appointees, including, in 2022, the nearly 4,000 permanent foreign-service officers. When the nation was formed, being Secretary of State was a path to the presidency, as Thomas Jefferson, James Madison, and James Monroe proved. In the twenty-first century, Secretaries Colin Powell, Condoleezza Rice, Hillary Clinton, and John Kerry were the country's top diplomats projecting the respective policies of Bush and Obama over sixteen years. Trump reduced the power of the Secretary of State by significantly cutting the DOS budget and relying instead on an inner circle of family members and political advisors over seasoned professional diplomats (Chollet and Smith, 2017). Trump often overturned statements made by his different secretaries. These reversals damaged the credibility of both the DOS and the president because foreign governments could not trust what they had just agreed to do. Biden re-established the power of the DOS in budget, staffing, and trust.

The DOD manages the armed forces and is situated under the leadership of a civilian, the Secretary of Defense, even though the "civilian" may have been a top general in the US military before taking the job. Trump appointed Jim Mattis, a former top-ranking Marine Corps general; Biden named former US Army Commander Lloyd Austin, the first African American to lead the DOD. The army, navy, and air force also have civilian heads who oversee the chairman of the Joint Chiefs of Staff (JCS) and the respective military commanders.

The Central Intelligence Agency is the official intelligence gathering arm of the foreign policy establishment. Since 1947, the CIA has collected, analyzed, and circulated information relating to national security to other agencies on a "need to know" basis. Most of the activities of the CIA are entirely mundane, collecting information from statistical reports and newspapers; but the agency is notorious for its covert activities, including wiretaps, assassinations, espionage, brutal interrogations of prisoners, and destabilizing governments.

The CIA is often blamed when presidential decision-making goes awry. The agency failed to predict the fall of the Soviet Union in 1989 and it took most of the blame for failing to stop the 9/11 attacks, and for the use of torture, specifically "waterboarding" in Iraq. In 2021 and 2022, the agency correctly analyzed and reported the Russian

Contemporary United States

buildup against Ukraine and the probability of invasion when the Olympic Games in Beijing ended. Because the CIA works at the direction of the president, there are flaws in intelligence reporting when an administration demands "proof" that supports its own view of a particular situation—something that clearly happened in the case of Iraq when the Bush administration needed to find weapons of mass destruction that did not exist.

The National Security Council (NSC) consists of two groups of advisors who help the president shape foreign policy. The NSC staff, headed by the National Security Advisor, provides a counterweight to the Secretaries of State, Defense, Homeland Security, and to the military brass in the JCS, and to CIA and FBI directors. The NSC discusses questions of armed intervention, "best-guess" scenarios, and other issues relevant to national security in order to recommend presidential action and persuade Congress to pass funding bills.

In 1948, the Cold War got colder when the Soviets tried to seize West Berlin by blockading all land routes. A massive airlift by American and British cargo planes kept the city free. Truman authorized the Marshall Plan, spending $15 billion in Europe over three years to provide humanitarian aid and tie the economies of the West into a common market. The General Agreement on Tariffs and Trade (GATT) helped stabilize currency rates, promoted free trade, and made the US the world's banker. In 1949, Mao Zedong won the Chinese Civil War, the Soviets exploded an atomic bomb, and twelve nations (Belgium, Canada, Denmark, France, Great Britain, Iceland, Italy, Luxembourg, Netherlands, Norway, Portugal, United States) formed the North Atlantic Treaty Organization (NATO). They agreed that an attack against any one of them would be considered an attack against them all. Even though this pledge has only been redeemed once—when the United States was attacked on 9/11/2001—it is a powerful deterrent against any outside attack on member states. NATO expansion includes its biggest increase in 1999 when ten former Warsaw Pact nations and four former Yugoslav republics were added. By 2022, NATO counted thirty members, with the newest members being Montenegro in 2017 and North Macedonia in 2020. With the Russian invasion of Ukraine in 2022 and Putin's threat to use nuclear weapons, Sweden and Finland joined NATO and Ukraine requested membership in the alliance. This indicates a great change in the thinking of the West, and nods toward the growing strength of a possible Chinese–Russian revision of the global order.

The two most recent US presidents took different stances on NATO. Trump had disdain for the alliance and liked to say that NATO did nothing for the United States. He criticized the member countries for failing to meet their defense spending obligations. In 2016, most NATO countries, with the exception of Greece, the UK, Estonia, and Poland failed to meet the 2 percent of GDP guideline. US spending was 3.6 percent of GDP. In dollars spent, the estimate for the US was $664 billion and Europe $239 billion (NATO, 2016). At the seventieth NATO Anniversary meeting in 2019, Trump's mercurial personality erupted against Germany, Britain, Canada, and France. He opened with a forty-minute finger-pointing speech to the delegates, participated in only two hours of meetings, and flew away angrily because, he said, the members disrespected him and thus disrespected the United States (Robertson, 2019). At the G7 meeting he repeated this same behavior (see Illustration 9.2).

Biden was warmer toward NATO and he actively reasserted US leadership on the world stage. At the June 2021 summit in Brussels, Biden asked for and got NATO support for his decision to withdraw from Afghanistan. Biden reaffirmed both America's need for and its "sacred obligation" to the military alliance: "I want to make it clear: NATO is critically important for US interests in and of itself. If there weren't one, we'd have to invent one … I just want all of Europe to know the United States is there" (Liptak and Sullivan, 2021) And, in a statement showing his own fears of a changing world order, Biden stated the need "to prove that democracy and our alliance can still prevail" (Liptak and Sullivan, 2021). Biden's belief in NATO was born out a year later when Putin tested the strength and will of the alliance to counter the Russian assault on Ukraine. Even though not a member, Ukraine would be supported by transfers of weapons and expertise from NATO.

The year after NATO was founded, National Security Council Memo NSC-68 put US power at the core of the Western coalition. Congress quadrupled military spending. That same year, an effort by North Koreans to occupy South Korea brought UN troops into a hot war that took 36,000 American and 3,100 allied lives, and a combined 2.8 million Korean and Chinese casualties. Chinese involvement escalated fears and created a new urgency for a more powerful weapon: the hydrogen bomb. It was the dawn of the Atomic Age as other countries joined the "nuclear club": Britain (1952), France (1960), and China (1964). Since then, the UN has attempted to stop nuclear proliferation and promote nuclear disarmament with a Non-Proliferation Treaty (NPT) in 1968 seeking to limit weapons solely to the permanent five members of the UN Security Council. The NPT has 191 signatories and remains in effect, even if it is imperfect (UN, 2021). By 2017, India, Israel, Pakistan, and North Korea had weapons. Iran has some capabilities (Table 9.1).

Table 9.1 Countries with Nuclear Weapons: Number of Warheads, 2021

Russia	6,375
USA	5,800
China	320
France	290
UK	215
Pakistan	160
India	135
Israel	90
N. Korea	40*

* Estimated.

Note: Key to military nuclear power are the delivery systems controlled by each nation. In 2021 the US controlled a powerful "nuclear triad" of nuclear submarine-launched ballistic missiles, land-based intercontinental ballistic missiles, and a large fleet of strategic bombers with nuclear bombs and cruise missiles. Russia was a distant second in delivery systems.

Source: WPR (2021a)

Contemporary United States

In 2015, Obama signed an executive agreement with Iran to lift economic sanctions in return for Iranian promises to give up about 98 percent of its stockpile of enriched uranium and freeze its nuclear weapons programs. In 2017 Trump decried this as "the worst deal" and added "The world is laughing at us" (Tharoor, 2017). Then Trump went to North Korea and met with the President Kim, giving the tyrant credibility as a legitimate leader who must be bargained with. Kim proved effective at "smile diplomacy" but doubled his nuclear capabilities while Trump was president. Coinciding with these moves, Trump approved plans for the US to produce new nuclear weapons, the first increase in its arsenal since the end of the Cold War (DOD, 2018a). In 2021, soon after taking office, Biden met with South Korean President Moon and reiterated the long-term US goal of denuclearizing the Korean peninsula (Wilkie, 2021). Biden did not go to North Korea but called Kim. Kim refused to accept the call and to emphasize his strength, launched three new ballistic missiles to showcase his nuclear delivery capabilities.

In 1953, to support NATO and NSC-68, President Dwight Eisenhower decided that the containment policy of the Truman Doctrine did not go far enough. The United States would help to liberate countries lost to communism. His policy included "roll back," "massive retaliation," and "brinksmanship." Any attack on the US or its allies would be met with an overwhelming counterattack, to include atomic weaponry. Enemies would be pushed to the brink of nuclear war and beyond. The new politics of deterrence rested on the fearsome technology of long-range rockets, bombers, and submarine-based atomic weapons that comprised the nuclear triad and provided "more bang for the buck."

The arms race accelerated when the Soviet Union created the Warsaw Pact in 1955 and launched an earth-orbiting space satellite named Sputnik two years later. Still, there were rules to the bipolar world, and when the USSR invaded Hungary in 1956 and Czechoslovakia in 1968, the US declined to intervene in an internal Warsaw Pact matter. Other nations were legitimate objects of interference, including Iran, Guatemala, Taiwan, and Vietnam. In 1961, the Soviet Union built a wall in Berlin that became a visible symbol of the Cold War division. The world feared threats of massive retaliation and mutual assured destruction (MAD), whereby any nuclear strike by one superpower against the other would result in a complete annihilation of both sides.

In October 1962, after the United States discovered Soviet missiles in Cuba, the superpowers raced to the brink of nuclear war, launching bombers and positioning navies with atomic weapons ready for firing. The Cuban Missile Crisis was also a domestic crisis challenging the American sense of security in North America and showing the nation's vulnerability. Having frightened the world and themselves before backing down, President John F. Kennedy and Soviet leader Nikita Khrushchev, and their successors, signed a series of test ban treaties and arms limitations agreements, even while they continued to build atomic bombs.

Vietnam

After the Second World War, nationalist movements in developing countries wrested control away from imperial powers. When the North Vietnamese forces under Ho Chi

Minh defeated the French army at Dienbienphu in 1954, the United States intervened, supported the division of Vietnam into North and South. As they financed the South, politicians expounded a "domino theory" that, if one nation fell to communism, it would create a chain reaction as others fell in turn.

In his Inaugural Address in 1961, Kennedy declared: "Let every nation know, whether it wishes us well or ill, that we shall pay any price, bear any burden, meet any hardship, support any friend, oppose any foe, in order to assure the survival and the success of liberty." After the assassination of Kennedy in 1963, Lyndon Johnson told the public, "We are not about to send American boys nine or ten thousand miles away from home to do what Asian boys ought to be doing for themselves." By 1965, Johnson reversed himself and ordered the first US combat troops to Vietnam. Things went sour but Johnson said that a great country could not just "cut and run" because it would create a credibility gap on the world stage. In 1969, President Richard Nixon had 543,000 soldiers in a war in which 2.5 million Americans served and 58,000 died. In 1973, Nixon claimed victory in achieving "peace with honor." The last American troops scrambled out of the country in 1975.

The impact of the Vietnam loss cannot be overstated. With the failure to win the war, the revelations that they had been lied to, and skyrocketing inflation, Americans lost faith in their ability to control world events. They became more reluctant to engage in foreign wars, a psychological condition analysts named the "Vietnam Syndrome." Still, the US pursued détente with Russia, entered into an Anti-Ballistic Missile (ABM) Treaty and Strategic Arms Limitations Talks (SALT), and initiated a joint space mission. Nixon explained the "friendship" as containment and he made simultaneous overtures to China as a way to deter a Sino-Russian great power alliance.

A Crisis of Confidence

President Jimmy Carter (1977–1981) rejected both containment and liberation approaches, concentrating instead on a liberal human rights policy. He hoped to normalize relations with the Soviet Union. The world focused on the violence between Israel and Egypt, the quadrupling of energy prices, the Soviet invasion and war in Afghanistan, and the overthrow of the Shah of Iran by Islamic fundamentalists, who escalated the situation by holding fifty Americans hostage in Tehran for 444 days. Carter declared Middle Eastern oil vital to American security interests and issued his Carter Doctrine that the United States would intervene militarily to protect the region. His threat was coupled with his greatest triumph. Through private talks with Israel's Menachem Begin and Egypt's Anwar Sadat, Carter ended the thirty-year-long Egyptian Israeli conflict.

But Carter's inability to free the hostages played a role in his failed re-election campaign. Republican Ronald Reagan spoke of America as "still a magnet for all who must have freedom, for all the pilgrims from all the lost places who are hurtling through the darkness towards home" (Reagan, 1989). He labeled the USSR an "evil empire" singularly responsible for the problems of the world. Reagan endorsed liberation, promised to help "freedom fighters" everywhere, and vowed never to compromise with terrorists. The

Contemporary United States

public later learned that the Reagan administration had approved a secret arms deal with Iran and that the money from the arms sale had been funneled to "Contras" in Nicaragua who were trying to overthrow the communist Sandinista government.

The End of the Cold War

Reagan expanded presidential power but his "Reaganomics" supply-side economic policy created huge deficits and made the US the world's largest debtor nation. He persuaded Congress to double appropriations for the military. He pressured NATO to deploy cruise missiles by threatening to decouple the US from Western Europe if it refused. He promoted a "Star Wars" Strategic Defense Initiative (SDI) of putting nuclear weapons and lasers in space. He sent US marines into Beirut and Grenada in 1983 and launched an air strike against Libya in 1986. Reagan also stopped American payments to the UN and rejected World Court jurisdiction over US actions.

In 1986, Afghanistan proved to be the "Russian Vietnam," as the fight against Islamic fundamentalists, with financial aid and military hardware from the US government, bankrupted the Soviet Union. Without warning, the Warsaw Pact disintegrated. Quickly, fantastically, the Berlin Wall fell, East and West Germany reunited, and the Soviet Union broke apart. The Cold War ended on November 19, 1990, when Mikhail Gorbachev agreed with Bush to declare that the East and West would no longer be adversaries. A quarter of a century later, in 2014, Russia seized Crimea and, in 2022, opened the Cold War again by invading the sovereign, democratic state of Ukraine (discussed at the end of this chapter).

The New World Order

President George H. W. Bush took an expansive view: "We stand today at a unique and extraordinary moment … A new world order can emerge … a world in which nations recognize the shared responsibility for freedom and justice, a world where the strong respect the weak" (McGrew, 2000). America would lead, Bush said, but in a multilateral way as a superpower, with support from the leading regional powers of Germany and France in Europe, Japan, China, and India in Asia, and Brazil in South America. There is no regional power in Africa although Egypt and South Africa have influence. Russia and Britain remained key players, sit permanently on the UN Security Council, and are consulted in every situation.

In response to Iraq's expansionist moves into Kuwait in 1990, Bush achieved a consensus—including among Arab states and Russia—before sending the largest expeditionary force since the Second World War into the Persian Gulf. "Operation Desert Storm" was a 100-day-long war, fought primarily by Americans and managed by JCS Chairman, General Colin Powell. His "Powell Doctrine" declared that any intervention by US troops be predicated on a threat to American strategic interests, that overwhelming force be used to accomplish results with the least risk to American lives, and that there be a clear timetable for withdrawal. The US quickly won the war, but Saddam Hussein remained in power, committing atrocities by using poisonous gas to kill ethnic and religious minorities, and putting up roadblocks to UN inspectors looking for chemical, biological, and nuclear weapons of mass destruction.

Enlargement and Engagement

In the 1990s, Americans hoped for a "peace dividend" and a safer, multilateral world. President Bill Clinton understood that economic policy is tied to national security and that the increased meshing of international and domestic—"intermestic"—markets created a complex interdependence. Clinton was reluctant to sacrifice American blood in conflicts where US interests were ill-defined. Called "zero casualty" or "Vietnam syndrome," this attitude surfaced during the 1990s in such flashpoints as Palestine, Somalia, Rwanda, Bosnia, Kosovo, and Macedonia.

Throughout the 1990s, the United States was a superpower in search of a coherent foreign policy (Huntington, 1999). Many of America's closest European allies worried of the dual possibility of abandonment and dominance. With the growing power of the European Union and without the Cold War to unite them, fundamentally different worldviews were exposed. Realist Robert Kagan explained: "Europeans see Americans as cowboys, belligerent and crude; Americans dismiss Europeans as decadent, spent and weak-willed" (quoted in Schmemann, 2003).

Clinton put forth a policy of "enlargement and engagement" to enlarge the numbers of democracies and to engage other leaders with different views. He rejected neo-isolationism and repeated the exceptionalist argument that "America must continue to lead the world we did so much to make … Our mission is timeless." GATT was reformed into the World Trade Organization (WTO). Clinton stressed humanitarian intervention even if no strategic interests existed: "Whether you live in Africa, or Central Europe, or any other place, if somebody comes after civilians and tries to kill them *en masse* because of their race, their ethnic background, or their religion, and it's within our power to stop it, we will stop it. We should not countenance genocide or ethnic cleansing anywhere in the world" (quoted in Korb, 2000). This commitment was in line with the UN's stated policy of R2P (Responsibility to Protect) which sets aside the principle of national sovereignty if a nation's government is slaughtering its own people. Clinton's promises lacked commitment, even if the US did finally stop the ethnic cleansing in Bosnia and Kosovo once it became clear that Europeans would not intervene. The US remained in Bosnia until 2004, when it ended its nine-year peacekeeping role.

Clinton did nothing to stop the genocide of half a million Tutsis in Rwanda. Bush's earlier use of American troops in Somalia, with the televised footage of a pilot being dragged naked behind a jeep, prompted Americans to demand that the troops be withdrawn. Without public support the US did not send troops to the civil war in East Timor or to the decades-long genocidal wars in Sudan and South Sudan. There were occasional airstrikes and the US has sent $11 billion in financial aid to South Sudan since 2005 and a sum of $481 million in 2019 alone (USDS, 2021).

Contemporary United States

Clinton acted primarily in the Middle East with low-risk, no-soldiers-on-the-ground air attacks. In his first week in office in 1993, he ordered a missile strike against the palace and military centers in Baghdad in an unsuccessful attempt to kill Saddam Hussein, who had been linked to an assassination attempt on former President Bush. For eight years, Clinton approved hundreds of air strikes against "perceived threats," including a failed 1998 strike in Afghanistan to kill jihadist leader Osama bin Laden.

The Twenty-First Century

In the first months of his presidency in 2001, George W. Bush denied the authority of the International Criminal Court, canceled US participation in the Kyoto Protocol on climate change, nullified the Comprehensive Nuclear Test Ban Treaty, and revoked the ABM Treaty with Russia. Bush took a muscular approach and many analysts worried as much about a "rogue superpower" as they did about rogue nations or terrorists. In what amounted to a "no-confidence" vote, the UN removed the United States from its seat on the Human Rights Commission, a seat it had held since 1947.

In just his third week in office, Bush authorized an attack on Iraqi air defense forces to keep the pressure on Saddam Hussein. The air strike sent a message that, while he might be inexperienced in foreign affairs, he would not be timid. Six weeks later, a Chinese fighter jet crashed into the South China Sea after a collision with US spy plane. The incident escalated into a crisis when the American pilot made an emergency landing in China and the Chinese gained access to sophisticated spyware. The situation cooled down when China released the aircraft and crew ten days later.

September 11, 2001

By mid-2001, international terrorism was a general threat to world peace and a particular threat to US interests. The number of anti-US attacks, most of them small-scale without casualties, rose from 169 in 1999 to 200 in 2000 (AP, 2001b). Previously, the bombing of the World Trade Center (WTC) in New York in 1993, the attacks on the US embassies in Kenya and Tanzania in 1998, and of the US destroyer *Cole* in Aden in 2000, were bold and frightening.

A congressional report, *Countering the Changing Threat of International Terrorism* (US Congress, 2000), concluded that the US would be the target of an increasing number of attacks. While Iran, Afghanistan, Iraq, Libya, and Syria continued to sponsor terrorism, the new threat consisted of individuals and groups who were "less dependent on state sponsorship and are instead, forming loose, transnational affiliations based on religious or ideological affinity and a common hatred of the United States" (US Congress, 2000). The al-Qaeda network and the fundamentalist Taliban government in Afghanistan were highlighted. Osama bin Laden, a Saudi who had once been an agent of the CIA, was encouraging terrorism against Americans worldwide, hating Israel, and declaring a "holy war" on Western influences in the Middle East. The congressional report suggested immediate action and coordination of all intelligence communities, recognizing that, with over one million visitors legally entering the US daily and with thousands of foreign students enrolled in universities, the risk was enormous (US Congress, 2000).

On September 11, 2001, a shockwave rocked the world when al-Qaeda terrorists hijacked and crashed four commercial airliners into the twin towers of the World Trade Center in New York City, the Pentagon building in Washington, DC, and a cornfield in Pennsylvania. Viewers worldwide watched live TV coverage as planes hit the WTC, people jumped to their deaths, and the towers collapsed into the streets. Nearly 3,000 people from eighty countries died. Bush responded quickly by assembling a global coalition against terror, even while his rhetoric of a "crusade," being "with us or against us," and putting a "Wanted. Dead or Alive" bounty on bin Laden alarmed many allies (Knowlton, 2001). Bush called for the immediate establishment of a cabinet-level position, the Department of Homeland Security (DHS) "to develop and coordinate the implementation of a comprehensive national strategy to secure the United States from terrorist threats and attacks" (Bush, 2001). The first major efforts in the war on terror focused on Afghanistan and Iraq.

America's Longest War

Before launching a military mission, the United States employed a successful diplomatic strategy against the Taliban and al-Qaeda factions in Afghanistan. The UN and NATO offered support for the "good war." Bush pushed a charm offensive which authorized millions of tons of food and clothing to be distributed among Afghan civilians, and greatly increased economic aid to Pakistan and Russia. Bush warned the Taliban government that it must stop harboring al-Qaeda or it would suffer the consequences. The Taliban refused and held up al-Qaeda as freedom fighters, not terrorists. More fundamentally, the culture of Afghanistan rests first and foremost on a history of proud resistance to foreign occupiers—this more than any other variable, including religion (Lamb, 2021). With US and NATO "infidels" in their homeland, the Afghan government was tainted and dishonorable, and, to many Afghans, "unjust" (Malkasian, 2021). On the other side, with overwhelming international outrage against the September 11 terrorist attacks legitimizing what it called a "just war" of self defense, US and allied forces from twenty-eight mostly NATO countries quickly routed the Taliban. A democratic election gave Afghanistan its first popularly elected president. But the Taliban proved resilient, civil war ensued, and bin Laden escaped into Pakistan (Haass, 2017). The Taliban were fond of saying "You have all the clocks, but we have all the time." They never believed the Americans would stay for the long haul (Lamb, 2021) (Illustration 9.4).

In January 2009, with insurgency on the rise and 644 US soldiers killed, General David Petraeus warned newly inaugurated Barack Obama that: "Afghanistan has been known over the years as the graveyard of empires … We cannot take that history lightly" (Whitlock, 2009). Obama had promised to end Bush's war and bring the soldiers home,

Contemporary United States

Illustration 9.4 American Soldiers Killed in Afghanistan

The United States based its soldiers in Afghanistan for twenty years in what became the longest war in American history. The war began in 2001 after the attacks on the World Trade Center in New York called for retaliation against those aiding the attackers. President Bush would hand the war over to President Obama, who passed it to President Trump, who left it to President Biden. No one seemed to know how to end the war without calling it a loss and taking the political domestic and foreign policy consequences. In 2021, Biden determined that enough was enough and wanted to bring the American troops home before any more soldiers died. Over the two decades of war, nearly 2,500 US soldiers were killed and nearly 21,000 were wounded in action (CRS, 2020b). The photograph shows an air transport plane about to return to the States with eight flag-draped caskets containing the bodies of American soldiers killed in an explosion in 2004.

Source: Brian Davidson/U.S. Air Force via Getty Images

but he could not accept the possibility of a resurgent terrorist threat again striking the US (Malkasian, 2021). After Petraeus argued that a surge of 100,000 combat troops could bring victory, Obama complied and increased the use of drone strikes and counter-insurgency raids. These measures failed. In 2012, while admitting that "We've still got much to do," Obama set a timetable for bringing the conflict to "a responsible end" by 2014 (Wilson and Nakamura, 2013). But the war went well past the deadline and the costs were unsustainable. Obama feared the political ramification of a withdrawal so he decided to downsize to a troop presence of around 10,000 troops.

Acknowledging that neither the US nor the Taliban could win the war as it was, Obama accepted a plan to "muddle through" with what he called "Afghan, good enough." And in a move that strengthened the US military and provided a bigger base from which to pull recruits, Obama ordered the armed services to allow female soldiers to take roles in combat operations.

The longest war in American history became "Mr. Obama's War" and, in turn, "Mr. Trump's War." The US strategy would be "hold-fight-disrupt" for as long as necessary (Landler, 2017). Americans seemed to have accepted the idea of "never-ending war" as a normal condition, especially when fought by a (non-drafted) all-volunteer, battle-hardened US military force made up of men and women who do multiple tours (Castner, 2017). The distinction between wartime and peacetime was also blurred because of drone strikes and the killing of terrorists anytime, anywhere—regardless of treaties, conventions, and international humanitarian law. Military strategist John Nagl said it best: "We live in the age of unsatisfying wars … messy and unsatisfying" (Nagl, 2012). The endings are untidy, lingering, and budget-breaking affairs. But superpowers must fight guerrilla wars as the string of ISIS initiated terrorist attacks in Germany, France, and Britain in 2016 prove.

Bush, Obama, and Trump had settled for a never-ending commitment as a better solution than to leave and have the country again become a staging point for terrorists (Malkasian, 2021). Trump was impatient to end the war, even more so than Obama had been (Whitlock and *WP*, 2021). His "America First" plan wanted nothing from Afghanistan, but the fear of electoral politics if another terror strike happened in the US, led him to increase troop strength (Lamb, 2021; Malkasian, 2021). Finally, Trump signed an agreement with the Taliban to have the last 2,500 US troops withdrawn by May 2021 if the Taliban cut all ties to al Qaeda. This set the stage for Biden.

Three months after becoming commander-in-chief, Biden announced that with a short extension to September 11, 2021, he would honor Trump's agreement if the Taliban stood down and no terrorist attacks occurred. The American part of the war was over. Afghan troops would have to stand or fall on their own. Biden spoke of endless "forever wars" and asked critics: "So when will be the right moment to leave?" and "How many more? How many thousands more of America's daughters and sons are you willing to risk?" (Zucchino, 2021). For twenty years the US had attempted nation-building and had some successes in establishing a Western-style government, helping 3.5 million women and girls attend schools and get jobs in law and law enforcement, supporting the growth of a diverse media, and building infrastructure (Lamb, 2021). With the US

Contemporary United States

leaving, some 7,500 mostly NATO troops and a large number of Afghanis who had close ties to the US Army had to be withdrawn. Biden's Pentagon advisors said that it would take two–three years for the Taliban to regain control. It took about two months. Afghan government forces refused to fight and Americans hastily and clumsily departed, on television, as they had done in Vietnam. Biden said that it was time to focus on the challenges of 2021, not those of 2001. These "bigger threats" included the rise of China, the decline of democracy worldwide, the pandemic, terrorism, and climate change. Even while saying "I do not regret my decision," the poorly planned and executed withdrawal had domestic political costs, with Biden's approval dropping overnight from above 52 percent to about 40 percent in most polls (Glasser, 2021). Most Americans agreed with the decision to end the war, but most were appalled at the lack of a face-saving "exit strategy" and a betrayal of Afghan allies.

Summarizing, the costs of the war including interest payments on the debt were estimated at $300 million per day for a total of $2.3 trillion, not including long-term medical care for veterans (Watson-Brown, 2021a, 2021b). The US spent $1.2 million to keep each American soldier in Afghanistan for one year (NPR, 2013). By 2021, allied fatalities totaled 3,609 and included 2,465 Americans, 455 Brits, and 689 others from Canada, France, Germany, Italy, Denmark, Australia, Poland, Spain, Georgia, Netherlands, Romania, NATO, Turkey, the Baltics, New Zealand, Norway, Czech Republic, Hungary, Sweden, Slovakia, Finland, Portugal, Jordan, South Korea, Albania, and Belgium (icasualties, 2021). The number of Americans wounded was 20,662. Afghan fatalities have been estimated at 241,000, including 71,000 civilians, a large number of them children (Watson-Brown, 2021a, 2021b).

The War on Terror

The war in Afghanistan merged with the war on terror to offer up only one true victory. On the night of May 2, 2011, a highly skilled commando team, US Navy Seal Team Six, hit a strongly fortified residential compound in Abbottabad, Pakistan, and killed Osama bin Laden. While the death of al-Qaeda's mastermind brought symbolic closure to the 9/11 attacks, it created a controversy because the Pakistani government had not been given advance notice of the raid. It is illegal under international law to target and kill someone in a country with which you are not at war. In fact, the Pakistani government was fully cooperating with the Taliban, providing money, running training camps, giving advice, and providing protection to continue the war against the US. At the same time the US was giving financial aid to the Pakistani government as an "ally" against terrorism (Malkasian, 2021).

Historian Samuel Huntington's "clash of civilizations" thesis that a modernizing world does not mean a Westernizing world, and that culturally conscious nationalism was rising in Asia, Africa, and the Middle East has been influential. Huntington dismissed notions of a New World Order or *Pax Americana* and predicted a religious cultural conflict (Huntington, 1996). For Huntington, the Cold War was insignificant when compared with the centuries-long struggle between the West and Islam, or maybe, "the West against the Rest." Historian Robert Lifton added that with the 9/11 attack on its homeland "the United States became an aggrieved superpower, a giant violated and made vulnerable, which no superpower can permit" (Lifton, 2003). Bush declared that a "war on terror" would go on indefinitely.

Six weeks after the 9/11 attacks, Congress passed the USA Patriot Act. Renewed in 2015 and 2019, the Act gives wide latitude for domestic and international surveillance, and for the arrest and treatment of suspected terrorists. It sets aside long-standing legal protections. Police are allowed to arrest suspects, snoop, secretly enter people's homes without notice, freeze bank assets, and compile dossiers on individuals. The government can open private letters, read email, use wiretaps, and request personal records from any source, including medical records. Clearly, this is dangerous to a democratic society. Many civil libertarians say that with this Act, the Bush, Obama, Trump, and Biden administrations promoted hysteria and paranoia. But most Americans agree with Republican Senator Mitch McConnell, that the Patriot Act has "kept us safe for nearly a decade and Americans today should be relieved and reassured to know that these programs will continue" (Abrams, 2011).

Bush approved the most disturbing and extraordinary tactics, including a systematic and widespread use of torture in secret "black ops" locations worldwide (Mayer, 2008). In Iraq, the abuse of detainees by American soldiers inside Abu Ghraib prison was universally condemned as a violation of the Geneva Convention rules on the treatment of prisoners of war (Danner, 2004). Photographs posted online of sadistic torture and pornographic poses scandalized the world. Additionally, from 2003 to 2009, 779 suspects were jailed in the US military detention camp at Guantánamo Bay, Cuba (ACLU, 2017). Bush denied violations of international law, snubbed world opinion, and ignored or silenced opponents in the CIA, FBI, Justice Department, Congress, and the military. Interrogations included the simulated drowning of prisoners known as "waterboarding," and "extraordinary rendition"—the kidnapping of suspects who are then turned over to governments in the Middle East and Asia for questioning and torture (Mayer, 2008).

Guantánamo prisoners were denied access to the courts. Historically, the judicial branch cedes power to the executive branch when the issue is one of national security. Still, in June 2008, the US Supreme Court ruled that "the laws and Constitution are designed to survive, and remain in force, in extraordinary times" (Robinson, 2008). The Court asked Bush to respect the law. Bush ignored the ruling.

Three days after taking office in 2009, Obama issued an executive order halting the CIA's "enhanced" interrogation program. He promised to close Guantánamo, but after the US Congress, US state governments, and foreign countries refused to allow prisoner transfers, Obama kept the facility open (Warrick and DeYoung, 2009). By the time Trump took office in 2017, forty-one "high risk" prisoners remained (ACLU, 2017). Trump immediately fully reopened the facility because "torture works," "whatever it takes," and "they deserve it anyway, for what they're doing" (Serwer, 2017). Biden decries torture and wants to close the facility but has done nothing for the remaining thirty-nine people (Callamard, 2022).

Contemporary United States

The War in Iraq and Syria

For decades, most analysts believed that the next big conflict, maybe a third world war, would erupt in the Middle East. Since 1948, when the state of Israel was created, the tension between the Jewish nation and its Islamic neighbors has been armed and dangerous. The Israeli–Palestinian conflict increases anti-Americanism among Muslims everywhere because of strong US support for Israeli security. Bush pointed out that American soldiers fought and died in non-Israeli places like Bosnia, Somalia, and Afghanistan, proving that the US is not anti-Muslim.

In 2003, Bush, with strong congressional support, believed that the war on terror, the protection of Israel, and the expansion of liberalism required a war in Iraq. The Bush administration overturned five decades of US multilateral cooperation with UN, NATO, and international law and set aside the doctrines of containment and deterrence to create a new strategic doctrine committing the United States to a unilateral use of military might—something analysts call "anticipatory self-defense" (Schlesinger, 2003) or "defensive imperialism" (Johnson, 2003). The Bush Doctrine of preventive war and pre-emption played into the psychological trauma many Americans felt after the September 11 attacks as the public accepted aggressive actions against a potential enemy before it could strike the US.

Bush made the case that Iraq was a breeding ground for terrorists, was "certainly" connected with al-Qaeda, and had weapons of massive destruction (Powers, 2003). He announced "a forward strategy of freedom in the Middle East" (Bush, 2003). Although Bush predicted that the Iraqis would welcome the American "liberators," many analysts disagreed and insisted: "No War for Oil." Western unity split, Russia and China opposed the actions, and anti-Americanism grew. In November 2002, Bush did convince the UNSC to vote 15–0 in favor of UN Resolution 1441, warning Iraq that it must comply with UN inspections or face the consequences. But, unable to get the support of NATO or the UN General Assembly, Bush assembled "a coalition of the willing" and ordered the attack to begin. The coalition consisted "on paper" of eighty countries, but the US would do the heavy lifting, with Britain, Spain, Denmark, Poland, and Japan in the main supporting roles.

The US implemented a "theory of rapid dominance" whereby highly mobile, highly informed forces of "Network-Centric Warfare" bring apocalyptic firepower to bear on many places at once (Danner, 2003). American air and ground power routed the Iraqi defenses and, on May 1, a jubilant President Bush landed on the aircraft carrier *USS Abraham Lincoln* under a banner declaring "Mission Accomplished." But the mission was not accomplished. A post-war insurgency brought a civil war that escalated beyond the ability of US troops to control, even with a constant force of 140,000 soldiers in-country and a total deployment of nearly 1.6 million American troops (Stiglitz and Bilmes, 2008).

The capture and execution of Saddam Hussein and his henchmen, and the discovery of mass graves of hundreds of thousands of Kurdish and Shiite victims of Hussein's rule, did little to reduce the resistance to the American occupation. Insurgents created internet spectacles by beheading foreign soldiers and civilians and by setting off suicide bombs in town squares. A few off-target US bombs and thousands of incidents between US occupiers, under stress, and the occupied Muslim population increased tension. Old grudges among Kurds, Sunnis, and Shia continue to be acted upon. The American people soured on Bush and spoke of a failed presidency in both domestic and foreign policies.

In his 2009 Inaugural Address, Obama set a different tone: "We reject as false the choice between our safety and our ideals ... our power alone cannot protect us, nor does it entitle us to do as we please" (Baker, 2009). Obama also believed in protecting the world from America—an obvious change from neoliberal and neo-conservative supporters of military intervention in the cause of democracy. Additionally, while Obama is a Christian, his father and stepfather were Muslims and he lived in Jakarta, where he attended school in an Islamic madrassa. Obama helped calm fears by using his life story to be an "honest broker" pushing for a two-state solution for Israel and Palestine and in refusing to use terms such as "Islamic terrorism" to describe ISIS or al-Qaeda. Israel's hyper-nationalist Prime Minister Benjamin Netanyahu had a tense relationship with Obama over Israeli settlement expansion into areas claimed by Palestine and for Obama's failure to veto a United Nations Security Council (UNSC) vote of 14–0 condemning Israel for these settlements. At the same time, Muslims disliked Obama's reliance on drone strikes, cyberwar, and traditional military tactics against Muslim-majority nations (Friedman, 2016a).

In 2010, Obama praised the soldiers who had fought in Iraq and announced that the US combat mission was over. It took another year before the "transitional exit force" of 50,000 soldiers was withdrawn. This proved to be premature and unwise. Iraq had not been completely stabilized and without a larger US presence, a vacuum was created which gave space for the establishment of another terror group. The Islamic State rose up, brought holy war and civil war to Iraq, and spread to Syria as the Islamic State in Syria (ISIS). Obama sent 9,000 soldiers back to Iraq. Under Trump and Biden, about 4,000 soldiers per year have remained to "advise and assist" the coalition forces. Biden did announce the end of US combat operations in 2021 but kept about 2,500 advisors in country just in case (*Barron's*, 2021).

Obama had rejected using US power for nation-building even while he supported democracy movements. When populist insurgents rose up in an "Arab Spring" revolution in Tunisia, Egypt, Libya, and Syria to depose dictators and establish democracies, Obama stood back. Only after Britain and France pledged to intervene directly in Libya, did Obama allow the US to "lead from behind," as his detractors put it, while using American airpower to support traditional allies and then protect Libyan rebels fighting to remove strongman Muammar Gaddafi. Obama said that he was decreasing the costs to the United States in terms of other nations "free riding" on the American military. Gaddafi was killed by Libyan rebels. But the "Arab Spring" stalled and Libya fell into chaos and civil war.

In Syria, the war that began in 2011 as an uprising against the government of Bashar al-Assad morphed into a multi-factional war when al-Qaeda and ISIS fighters organized

Contemporary United States

and gained strength. Turkey, Saudi Arabia, and Iran joined different sides of the civil war. Russia was heavily invested in supporting Assad because of the ties to oil and military bases and because of its commitment to Iran. Supporting the "Arab Spring" faction, Obama missed an opportunity early to help the democracy movement because he did not want to engage the US in another quagmire in an Islamic country (Goldberg, 2016b). In 2012, he announced that the US would intervene only if Assad crossed "a red line" by using chemical weapons. But when Assad used a poisonous gas to murder 1,400 Syrian civilians, Obama stood back. He did authorize the CIA to fund and train rebel groups. Obama believed that the war was a "trap" that would last for years and end badly. He acknowledged his support for the UN policy of R2P, but said he would send troops only if Congress approved a declaration of war (Goldberg, 2016b). Congress did nothing. Simultaneously, in Britain, Parliament refused Prime Minister John Cameron's request for war authority. ISIS grew stronger, the world saw Obama as a "bluffer," the US lost credibility, and the war tumbled out of control as refugees fled the war zone for Europe and beyond.

By 2021, with the war in Syria in its tenth year, between 500,000 and 700,000 civilians and fighters had been killed, and nearly six million desperate refugees escaped into adjacent states and one million more fled to Europe (Aljazeera, 2021). The US and Russian militaries carefully avoided each other while they supported different factions. Upon taking office, Trump followed the advice of his Defense Secretary to deploy nearly 1,000 combat advisors to Syria to support the rebels, but mostly to defeat ISIS. Trump gleefully ordered the use of a weapon called MOAB (Massive Ordnance Air Blast)—often called the "Mother of all Bombs"—the largest single non-nuclear weapon in the US arsenal against an ISIS tunnel and cave complex in Afghanistan (Mashal and Abed, 2017). One week earlier, when Assad unleashed poison again on civilians, Trump authorized a targeted attack of fifty-nine US cruise missiles against an airbase in Damascus. Critics worried about the growing perception that Trump was at war with Islam. Such a perception would radicalize many fighters to take the war into European and American cities, where as many as 7,000 people were known to have strong links to ISIS or al-Qaeda (Diehl, 2016; Goldberg, 2016a).

Like Obama, Trump preferred special operations teams, and the expanded use of drones and cyberwar capabilities over conventional methods of sending soldiers into land wars (Sanger, 2012). While these tactics are effective, the ethical implications are troubling as fighting becomes more like murder. The US Cyber Command had been established in 2009 to use the internet to direct operations through cyberspace (BBC, 2013). In 2010, the CIA created chaos within the Iranian nuclear program with the computer virus "stuxnet worm" (Sanger, 2012). Drones were developed as the major weapon of choice in the war against terrorists and are weapons of assassination hidden from public scrutiny. Obama budgeted $4 billion to buy an unspecified number of new drones. In 2017, Trump used discretionary funds to vastly increase the stockpile. But the use of these "unmanned assault vehicles" (UAVs) brings retaliation in kind from other countries. Some say that a Cool-turning-Cold War between the US and a Chinese–Russian alliance has already begun with cyberspace espionage raiding computer systems worldwide (Sanger, 2013). Cyberwar depends on "big data," and in the realm of collecting and using it for commercial, economic, and military advantages. China and Russia are far ahead of the West (Pottinger and Feith, 2021). Additionally, ISIS has been particularly adept at weaponizing social media with viral videos of announcements and uploads of beheadings and other acts of cyberterrorism.

The US "Pivot" to Asia

In February 2009, Obama's Secretary of State Hillary Clinton met with Chinese President Hu Jintao in the Great Hall of the People in Beijing. While disagreeing on, but downplaying, the issue of human rights, the bilateral economic relationship dubbed "Chimerica" would work to improve the three Es: energy, environment, and economy. Two years later, Obama announced that America would pivot from its focus on the Middle East and bring more comprehensive power to Asia. Clinton heralded the start of "America's Pacific Century" and a stronger alliance system with countries in the region (Clinton, 2011). Military resources were repositioned, including aircraft carrier task forces and army bases. These moves threatened China and led it to redouble its efforts to avoid America's "containment strategy."

Using the guiding principles of vigilance and uncertainty, US military superiority in the twenty-first century depends on the ability to protect economic shipping lanes and supply chains, support American national interests, and cooperate with allies worldwide. The National Military Strategy (NMS) has long held that the US must never be in a "fair fight" with anyone, especially with near-peer competitors like China and Russia. NMS entails an overwhelming military force of the most advanced kind, thus the largest military spending in the world, plus research and development funds, and nuclear superiority. In 2022, the military had thousands of drones and eleven powerful aircraft carrier task forces with another carrier under construction. Prototypes of flying aircraft carriers and submarine aircraft carriers are being developed.

The US war strategy is called "Air Sea Battle Concept" (ASBC) and is designed around the ability of US forces to control the world's oceans and airspace. ASBC connects US Space Command and US Cyberwar Command to Navy, Army, Marine Corps, and Air Force units to build an integrated battlefield. US war scenarios are always evolving through what is termed "a continuum of strategic direction" (DOD, 2019b). In 2019, Trump created the US Space Force—the first new military branch since the Second World War—which was a return to Reagan's idea for Star Wars and a bow to China's growing ability to use space for its own security interests (DOD, 2019a). These space-based military platforms provide overhead direct support for armies and navies operating worldwide. The DOD is prepared for "a transregional all-domain battlefield." That means, for example, that if a war breaks out between North Korea and South Korea, it will not be confined to the Korean peninsula because of North Korea's ability to extend the battlefield with ballistic missiles and nuclear warheads. Additionally, the US must be prepared to fight in multi-theaters worldwide as other nations seek to take advantage of US focus on one war to pursue their own ambitions against US interests elsewhere, such as if Russia attacked Ukraine and then China attacked Taiwan (DOD, 2019b).

Contemporary United States

The US and China have the most important bilateral relationship in the world and they will shape the long-term future of the international order. Their biggest hurdle is to overcome a seventy-year-old strategic distrust that has been heightened by the rapid ascendance of China to great power status and the relative decline of American power. Clinton acknowledged China's rise: "The goal for our relationship with China is to ensure that we defy history ... It has never happened that an established pre-eminent power and a rising power have been able to find a way to not only coexist but cooperate. We intend to make history with our relationship with China" (Clinton, 2011).

China is a strategic competitor, but it was also America's biggest trading partner before the Covid pandemic disrupted supply chains and boosted USMCA (NAFTA) partners Canada and Mexico ahead again. Trump and Biden wanted to scale back Chimerica, rejuvenate American manufacturing, and slow China down (Sanger and Crowley, 2021). Tensions have accelerated. The US calls China "the biggest geopolitical threat of the 21st Century." China says that "the biggest source of chaos in the present-day world is the United States" (Hudson, 2021).

Defying history is going to be difficult. In 2019, hyper-nationalist President Xi Jinping solidified power by overturning the ten-year limit on being president and taking control for life. By 2021, China was second in military spending ($252 billion), but the United States ($778 billion) spent more on its armed forces than the next nine countries combined (WPR, 2021b). Since 1945, American presidents have used the military 417 times against other nations. In comparing nuclear weapons (Table 9.1), it is worth noting that the US has greatly reduced its nuclear arsenal from the record high of 31,255 warheads in 1967 (Sheridan and Lynch, 2010). The argument for keeping a stockpile of nukes is to provide a "nuclear umbrella" to reassure and protect weaker allies and to provide long-range deterrence against enemies (O'Hanlon, 2019).

The arms race could be revived. China leads in the development of space lasers and has a highly accelerated space program putting more satellites into orbit since 2018 than any competitor. China has the stated goal of establishing bases on the moon and Mars. The US Space Force will accelerate the competition as will the private ventures of SpaceX and Horizon (Broad, 2021) (see Illustration 8.2). Differences over Taiwan, the seizing of Hong Kong, issues of human rights among the Uighur Islamic minority in western China, maritime access to the South China Sea, currency manipulation, trade, and the ownership of intellectual property continue to bedevil the US-China relationship.

Foreign Policy from Obama to Biden

On January 21, 2013, in his second Inaugural Address, Obama repledged the nation to its global commitments: "Engagement can more durably lift suspicion and fear. America will remain the anchor of strong alliances in every corner of the globe; and we will renew those institutions that extend our capacity to manage crisis abroad, for no one has a greater stake in a peaceful world than its most powerful nation."

Obama's foreign policy continued much along the lines Bush established. But where Bush was a crusader who alienated both allies and enemies with a "forward strategy" of US military might, Obama called for retrenchment and limits on American interventions (Ignatius, 2010). Some of the difference was in word choice and tone because US foreign policy is mostly declaratory. Policy begins in declaratory statements of support or warnings and ends in compromises, sanctions, or wars. Discussions that offer a "strategic reassurance and resolve" to come to terms without resorting to war go a long way toward lasting interdependence (Steinberg and O'Hanlon, 2014). A president's words must be consistent and trustworthy. Simply put, Obama had an eloquence and tone that Bush did not possess. Republicans painted Obama as a naive accommodator, whose reluctance to use force, and insistence on multilateral dialogue and action, put America in decline (Dumbrell, 2014).

Like Obama, Trump said "Free riders aggravate me" (Goldberg, 2016b). Trump insisted that allies pay their share of costs. NATO countries needed to raise their national budgets to cover the 2 percent of GDP mandate for NATO operations. Trump said that the UN cost too much and the 25 percent paid by the US must be reduced. Trump had no interest in being a non-partisan and he aligned completely with "a cherished ally" Israel, recognized Jerusalem (contested territory) as the capital of Israel, moved the US Embassy there, and appointed an aggressive Right-wing ambassador.

Obama had an informal, very direct slogan he lived by that expressed a cautious, think-before-you-act approach to all decisions: "Don't do stupid shit" (Goldberg, 2016b). Trump showed the opposite tendency and was quick to use intemperate words that had to be walked back by his advisors who clarified "what he really meant." One problem was Trump's trigger-finger quickness to use 140–280-character Twitter bursts. Another was his thin-skinned reaction to any suggestion that he may be mistaken. Trump's need to be great, right, and a winner made it impossible for him to apologize or admit to mistakes. For example, in his first hundred days in office, responding to three of America's closest allies, Trump hung up on the Australian Prime Minister, accused Britain of colluding with Obama to wiretap him, and openly insulted, mystified, and alarmed German Chancellor Angela Merkel during a joint press conference in the White House and elsewhere (Daalder and Lindsay, 2018). The Brits called this "utter nonsense" and said Trump was "peddling falsehoods," the Germans called him "the most dangerous man in the world," and the Aussies spoke of moving away from American leadership and toward China, while saying: "Donald Trump is not the United States of America" (Cave, 2017).

Obama (and Biden) believe that American exceptionalism requires a duty to compromise. Trump saw great power cooperation as squandering resources and sabotaging America by limiting the nation's ability to compete (Wertheim, 2017). Trump often set one nation against another and tried to get the best deals through bilateral talks. For example, in renegotiating NAFTA and renaming it USMCA, Trump insisted on separate concessions from Mexico and Canada before he would talk with them together. Often exhibiting a sense of persecution, grievance, and self-pity, Trump complained that other nations were only interested in exploiting US generosity, making the US "a wounded giant," a victim of bad deals and stealing by others: "we don't win anymore" (Daalder and Lindsay, 2018; Rucker and Leonnig, 2020).

Contemporary United States

In his book *Great Again: How to Fix Crippled America* (2017), Trump continued his oft-repeated praise of Putin as "the only effective leader in the world" (Trump, 2017b). One of Trump's key national security advisors, Sebastian Gorka, wrote that the president believes that international relations is a macho affair, with tough guys ruling the world (Glasser, 2017). Winning, not leading, was what Trump was all about (Daalder and Lindsay, 2018). To prove he was macho, Trump revoked Obama's policy of allowing transgender people to serve in the military. During his first week in office, Biden reversed this ban and issued an executive order: "This means no one will be separated or discharged, or denied reenlistment, solely on the basis of gender identity" (DOD, 2021b).

Trump wrote of himself as "the toughest guy. I will rebuild our military. It will be so strong, and so powerful, and so great" (Daalder and Lindsay, 2018). Trump approved drone strikes on a weekly level at increased levels surpassing what Obama had done. He authorized the CIA to proceed with strikes without briefing him beforehand. Trump ordered visa bans against travelers coming from seven majority-Muslim nations: Iraq, Iran, Libya, Somalia, Sudan, Syria, and Yemen. Even though the orders were suspended by US District Courts as unconstitutional, they dangerously offended America's most important allies in the war on terror: the millions of Muslims who reject ISIS and al-Qaeda and are fighting and dying on the front lines and in their homes. Presidents must be careful not to make more terrorists than they kill.

By 2017, US–Russian relations had reached their lowest point since the end of the Cold War, even though Obama and Putin agreed on a "Reset" in 2012 and a "New START" (Strategic Arms Reduction Treaty) to reduce their nuclear inventories. Tensions with Obama rose over Putin's takeover of Crimea and in disagreements over Iran, Syria, and Libya, Russian complicity in Wiki-leaks, new aggressions in moving military forces close to the Baltic States and Poland, and KGB interference in the 2016 presidential election. Despite the reset, Putin saw opportunities to expand Russia's influence over Central and Eastern Europe and Central Asia. He wanted to create a crisis of confidence and bring chaos to the world order. Putin's main goals aimed to destabilize NATO, breakup the EU, put Americans at odds with Europeans, and regain a top role among the great powers. But in comparing economic numbers, Russia produces only 10 percent of what America produces and is falling behind. Russia's GDP is half that of California and the Kremlin has nowhere near the soft power of American ideas and culture. Yet, Trump admired Putin's shrewdness and boldness in doing what he wanted.

Trump treated China differently. He met with representatives of the Uighur minority about their persecution, spoke directly to the Taiwanese president (something no US president had done since 1979), said he would rethink the ultra-sensitive "One China-Two Systems" policy and stated that maybe Japan and South Korea should develop their own nuclear strike capabilities (Ignatius, 2016; Landler, 2017). Beijing responded to Trump's provocations by saying that he was "playing with fire" and if this diplomatic imprudence continued, "Beijing will have no choice but to take off the gloves" (Erlanger, 2017). Trump's chief strategist Stephen Bannon talked openly of conflict: "no doubt … we're going to be at war in the South China Sea in five to ten years" (Wertheim, 2017). Trump continued to excoriate China over its currency manipulation, blaming it for stealing American jobs, of unfair tariff policies, and of creating the hoax that is called climate change as a way to scare liberals and gain advantage over American companies. Trump called for protectionist policies, including a 35–45 percent tariff on all Chinese goods imported to the United States. And when the pandemic hit in 2020, Trump relentlessly blamed China for what he called "the China virus."

The relationship between the US and China needs stability where red lines over "core interests" cross. This is particularly important in a time when the nativism sweeping the West is matched by Xi's revisionist dreams. In 2021, China was more controlled, repressive, and anti-foreign than five years earlier when Chinese specialist Orville Schell said "In my lifetime I did not imagine I would see the day when China regressed back to its Maoist roots. I am fearing that now" (Fallows, 2016). The difference is that Mao ruled a closed China. Xi believes the balance of power has shifted, the East has risen and the West has declined (Myers, 2021). The world is clearly at a "hinge moment" where too much militarism on the part of China and/or Russia and a US response could combine with the rise of nationalism to threaten world war. Complicating matters, during Trump's four years, and with no coherent policy toward China, the relationship with China has spiralled rapidly downward (Walt, 2021). In 2022, seeing an opportunity, Russian President Putin made overtures to Xi to consider a Sino-Russian alliance that would be a win–win for them and a strategic nightmare for the Americans.

A big question of our time is whether the political order dominant since the Second World War will fade into the past, or whether global cosmopolitanism may yet contain this nationalist anti-democracy moment. While often depicted as Manichean, a prominent American jurist argued that globalization and nationalism can instead complement each other as "well-functioning features of the modern world" (Breyer, 2018). Trump thought differently as one of his advisors explained: "The president embarked on his first foreign trip with a clear-eyed outlook that the world is not a 'global community' but an arena where nations, nongovernmental actors and businesses engage and compete for advantage" (McMaster and Cohn, 2017). Later on, citing the importance of national sovereignty and saying that the Paris Accord on CO_2 emissions was a "tremendous and debilitating disadvantage" for America, Trump pulled the US out of the agreement (Trump, 2017a). In so doing, the United States joined Syria and Nicaragua as the only non-signatories—against 190 others—and thereby ceded a great deal of leadership to China and the EU.

Political Scientist Richard Haass concluded that four years under Trump had done colossal damage to American democracy and thereby damaged America's global leadership position. Haass explained that "the hallmark of Trump's foreign policy" was the withdrawal from seventy years of alliance agreements, belligerence toward allies and to international institutions like the WTO, WHO, UN, and NATO (Haass, 2021).

American foreign policy is based on projections of costs and benefits. At present, the United States is in relative decline but still easily maintains its supremacy in every

Contemporary United States

arena of power: military, economic (per capita GDP), cultural, and technological. This primacy is likely to continue for a while. But primacy is not the same as hegemony and America cannot realize its ambitions without support from allies and regional powers. Confronted with resurgent ethno-nationalism, ethnic conflict, and religious fundamentalism, the US leadership role is as crucial as it is problematic. Any lessening of American primacy and collapse of the present world order are gambles because the balance of power approach did not work before or after the First World War. The two likeliest successors to American dominance, India and China, are so unlike the West that Europe prefers US leadership. At the moment, China is the only competitor that has comprehensive power in military, economic, and technological ways to dethrone the US (DOD, 2021a). Russia is a middling economic power with a super-sized military arm.

Biden took a firm stance against Russia and China. He understands that democracy is under attack everywhere and its restoration to legitimacy is a key to confronting authoritarian states (DeYoung, 2020). The 2021 Annual Threat Assessment Report (ATAR) highlighted China, Russia, Iran, and North Korea and transnational cross-border issues of the geopolitical instability caused by the Covid pandemic in terms of health, travel, national sovereignty, refugees, and global trade. The planet would suffer from global warming and pollution and there were major security threats from technological superiority, emerging biotechnology, artificial intelligence, computing, and cyberwarfare. Transnational threats also came from global organized crime networks, Islamic terrorism, increased immigration and migration from the displacement of refugees. ATAR noted the dangers stemming from the rise of violent white supremacy and exclusionary ethnocultural nationalists worldwide (DNI, 2021).

Biden faced up to these challenges but underlined his belief that democracy was at the crossroads. He stated:

> Democracies across the globe, including our own, are increasingly under siege. Free societies have been challenged from within by corruption, inequality, polarization, populism, and illiberal threats to the rule of law. Nationalist and nativist trends—accelerated by the COVID-19 crisis—produce an every-country-for-itself mentality that leaves us all more isolated, less prosperous, and less safe. Democratic nations are also increasingly challenged from outside by antagonistic authoritarian powers. Anti-democratic forces use misinformation, disinformation, and weaponized corruption to exploit perceived weaknesses and sow division within and among free nations, erode existing international rules, and promote alternative models of authoritarian governance. Reversing these trends is essential to our national security. The United States must lead by the power of our example, and that will require hard work at home to fortify the founding pillars of our democracy, to truly address systemic racism, and to live up to our promise as a nation of immigrants.
>
> (Biden, 2021b)

The Invasion of Ukraine and a More Powerful Western Alliance

Perhaps the greatest foreign policy dilemma for Biden was in overcoming the reality that the world cannot unsee what it saw with Trump at the helm. Trust in America to do the right thing most of the time had fallen. The US was deeply scarred and the world alarmed by how quickly one US president can shred decades-long alliances, treaties, agreements, norms, conventions, and the belief in democracy itself. While almost every world leader preferred Biden over Trump, the botched US withdrawal from Afghanistan also lowered confidence in Biden's competency in international relations. It would take an extraordinary threat to revitalize the Western coalition with America in the lead.

Vladimir Putin provided that threat. During the last week of February 2022, Putin brought the largest land war to Europe since 1945, invading Ukraine, attacking military bases—and kindergartens, hospitals, residential areas, and two active nuclear plants—and placed his nuclear strike forces on high alert to demonstrate his resolve. These actions were crimes against humanity and Putin is being investigated as a war criminal by the International Criminal Court. He told French President Emmanuel Macron that he was determined to achieve his goals, "no matter what" (Bostrup, 2022). This was not a war of necessity for Putin. No military threats were being made against Russia. Putin's war of choice against Ukraine was an unprovoked, predetermined, and savage attack aimed at regime change. Putin sought to regain a sphere of influence—a resurgence of empire—in great power politics that had been lost when the Cold War ended in the breakup of the Soviet Union (Michel, 2022).

It was a macho venture by a megalomaniac, pushed along by Putin's recent cooperation pact with Xi Jinping, and making it difficult for Putin to back down in the face of Ukrainian, Western, and global reactions. His neo-imperialism rests on the idea that "the strong do what they will and the weak suffer what they must," as Thucydides defined imperialism 2,000 years ago. But Putin made a wider gambit aimed at splitting NATO and the EU into factions and trying to demonstrate that autocratic nations will overcome alliances and democratic world leadership. Many Eastern European nations fear that they are next, even while they are comforted by their memberships in the EU. Certainly, the war was aimed at deepening America's relative decline and at ending the liberal world order. Putin had long worried about NATO expansion but he worried more about EU soft and sticky power to attract even more states and to expand democracy and the rules of international law concerning sovereign nations—as exemplified by the UN, World Bank, International Criminal Court, and WTO. It was just those fears, according to political scientist Anne Applebaum, that made Ukraine an existential ideological threat that endangered Putin's rule. In the Ukrainian people's determination to create a liberal state and to join the EU lay the seeds for domestic discontent among Russians who wanted the same (Applebaum, 2022).

Thus, Putin miscalculated and overplayed his hand even though his armies occupied the big cities, killed thousands, and installed a reign of terror. To control the narrative, Putin censored all Russian media outlets, blocked Facebook, Google, and Twitter, took up a misinformation campaign, closed down the last outlets of a free press, and arrested

Contemporary United States

thousands of anti-war "We stand with Ukraine" protesters in Moscow. Putin ordered anyone using the words "war," "invasion," or "attack" jailed for fifteen years. The war was to be called "special military operation." But because this war highlighted the struggle for freedom and democracy in Europe, and with strong Ukranian resistance, Putin looked weaker—a madman really—as suddenly, the democratic world coalesced around sanctions, stood unified, and punished Russia with strong weapons of soft and sticky power, and promises of hard power weaponry in the service of Ukrainian resistance fighters.

The battle for Ukraine became a transformational struggle for the future structure of the world order. Journalist Thomas Friedman wrote of "the most dangerous confrontation … since the Cuban missile crisis" (Friedman, 2022a). Friedman also noted that this war was different because smartphones and social media (TikTok, Spotify) initially covered the brutality of missile strikes, Russian army depravations, and, most importantly, because of the heroic stance taken by ordinary Ukrainians and by President Volodymyr Zelenski in defense of their country and its democracy. Friedman said that while Putin had made an eighteenth-century style imperial landgrab, he overlooked the interconnected world, making this a "wired war" with Russian atrocities open to a global audience (Friedman, 2022b).

American leadership, and Biden particularly, helped unite the Western response. Beginning in November 2021, Biden supplied leadership by alerting the global media to the Pentagon and CIA analyses on the probability of an invasion. His even-temper, broad perspective, and deep reverence for his Western partners kept down any overreaction that may have come from another president. Biden pressed European leaders to put together a set of coordinated sanctions. The US suggested economic measures, sent officials to European capitals and made thousands of phone calls. Putin insisted that Russia would not invade and was simply performing "routine military exercise." Biden called him a liar and warned the EU and NATO that any war against Ukraine could quickly expand across Europe. Europeans knew this already, of course, but they seemed unable to believe that a dictator would start a war in Europe, and perhaps a world war, as Adolf Hitler had done not so long ago. Maybe appeasement could work? (Illustration 9.5).

Then, suddenly, after Putin ordered the invasion, the EU and NATO acted rapidly to impose the strictest economic sanctions ever used against a sovereign state, its businesses and banks, and the properties of its oligarchs in Russia and abroad. Europeans awakened to a common threat and called Putin's attack "a 9/11 moment" (Ioffe, 2022). It all happened so quickly, underlining a verity from Vladimir Lenin during the Russian Revolution: "There are weeks where decades happen." Biden was at the center of things, encouraging and compromising with allies in a way that Trump had refused to do. The US joined the other NATO countries in sending military equipment and soldiers to support military activities that might be necessary. By March 1, Biden ordered troops to Germany and Poland and offered $1 billion in strategic support, with more to come—$13.6 billion was approved by Congress on March 10 (Cochrane, 2022). Six weeks later, Biden sought $33 billion more—which Congress raised to $40 billion—the largest amount ever offered in a war where US troops were not actively fighting (Baker and Levenson, 2022). Biden did not

Global Politics

Illustration 9.5 Two Dictators, Same Results: A Stronger Western Alliance

Adolf Hitler and Vladimir Putin were/are aggressive megalomaniacs and war criminals who saw their opportunities in Europe—and took them. From 1939–1945, Hitler led Nazi Germany to occupy its neighbors in pursuit of *lebensraum* (geographical expansion), revenge (for the treaty of the First World War), ideology (Master Race white supremacy), and totalitarian government (fascism). After 1945, the United States constructed a global system with multinational institution building from which sprang the UN, NATO, EU, WORLD BANK, and a vast number of power-sharing agencies. In 2022, President Putin launched the first major land war in Europe since Hitler was defeated. Putin sought to expand Russia (grab Ukraine), get revenge for losing the Cold War (when the USSR split apart), regain great power status (breakup the EU, disrupt NATO), and overturn the liberal world order led by America (building autocracies, destroying democracies). Putin's war created a reaction and a recommitment to the Western alliance and global cosmopolitanism that had been in decline. In the ongoing struggle between authoritarians and democrats, the liberal world order has survived another challenge to its hegemony as protests erupted worldwide in support of Ukraine. In the photograph from Amsterdam, a Ukrainian protester demonstrates the link between Hitler and Putin and the need for decisive EU and NATO support for a democratic state ravaged by a brutal tyrant.

Source: Romy Arroyo Fernandez/NurPhoto via Getty Images

respond to Putin's initial threat of a nuclear exchange. Instead, he aimed at de-escalation by not ordering the US to "DefCon 3" (a fifteen-minute response time) or higher and declaring that US soldiers would not enter Ukraine to directly fight Russians. German Chancellor Olaf Scholz filled a vacuum in European leadership by significantly cutting the vast German-financed Nord Stream 2 Oil pipeline from Russia, declaring a new push for German energy self-sufficiency, increasing the German defense budget to equal

Contemporary United States

2 percent of GDP as NATO suggested (an amount equal to 150 billion euros extra for Germany alone), and exporting weaponry to Ukraine, a move that overturned seventy-five years of post-Second World War policy. Denmark sent anti-tank weapons, Canada sent rocket launchers, hand grenades, and thousands of individual meal kits, France included aircraft, the US poured in anti-aircraft missiles, tank killers, and powerful state-of-the-art howitzers, and Sweden and Switzerland, both of whom had been neutral throughout Second World War, sent weaponry to Ukrainians. Parliaments in Finland and Sweden voted to join Nato in May 2022. There were applications for immediate acceptance into NATO from Ukraine, Georgia, and Moldova. Quickly, big oil companies with ties to Russian Gazprom Oil cut corporate ties, including BP, Shell, and Exxon. Japan, Singapore, South Korea, Taiwan, Brazil, and others imposed sanctions and the UN General Assembly condemned the invasion by a vote of 141–5 (Russia, Belarus, North Korea, Eritrea, and Syria), with forty-seven abstentions including China and India (Fassihi, 2022). There was talk of a new Iron Curtain falling in Europe and "doomsday" fears when Russian troops set fire to the biggest nuclear power plant in Europe, a facility six times the size of the plant at Chernobyl that had exploded in 1986 in the world's largest nuclear accident.

Within ten days, the entire Western alliance and most of the free world joined Europe in speaking in a unified voice, loudly condemning Putin and Russian oligarchs. Everywhere, in real time, TikTok, Facebook, and smartphones streamed images worldwide. Ukrainian bloggers posted pictures of the Russian dead along with lists of the names of those killed. When Putin doubled down and talked again of nuclear weapons, Biden kept the US nuclear capabilities at normal status. But the World Bank removed Russia from the ability to use the crucial international finance system SWIFT and targeted the Russian Central Bank—two actions that immediately shut Russia out of the global market and caused the Russian currency to collapse. Overnight, Russian Central Bank stock fell from $14 a share to less than one cent a share. Inflation inside Russia soared past 30 percent. And still Putin pushed on. History teaches that when an aggrieved and ambitious leader has a fundamental nationalist vision as a core interest, economic sanctions fail to stop a war.

The world continues to progress through uncertain times. Foreign policy planners sketch out scenarios and make detailed plans to forecast "if they do this, then we do that." For Putin, the plans to split the West and exploit a weak Joe Biden failed spectacularly. Rarely does realpolitik follow pre-planned scenarios. An alliance of democratic nations supported by strong-willed democratic populations looks to be the best way to build a community of nations that can stand up against the law of the jungle (Bremer, 2022). Germany found a new strength as the EU's strongest nation among many that had re-learned the importance that in togetherness is security. The US regained much of the world's confidence that Trump had tossed aside and Biden had damaged with the withdrawal from Afghanistan. The EU realized a unity and reason for being that had not been attained since its founding. Even the UK and the EU looked past the Brexit quarrel to cooperate again on vital issues. The question is whether the US has the will as the world's strongest superpower to defend the core principles of the system it built. American prestige is on the line. A commitment to NATO is one thing, but to lead, as journalist Susan Glasser stated, "the US must address the broader world order and the principles of international law" (Glasser, 2022). In line with this sentiment, on March 10, the US Congress appropriated a $42 billion increase for military spending, for a total military spending of $782 billion in early 2022 alone (Cochrane, 2022). Clearly, the American public accepts the high costs of maintaining its unrivaled military power. But it is unknown how long the people will support a foreign war, or the policy consequences of possible Republican victories in upcoming elections.

What China might conclude is another matter. It seems likely that if Russia had achieved a clear, quick victory, soon, China would have been encouraged to push its own advantages in Asia. If Russia loses or the war continues for years, caution will likely restrain Chinese military adventures (Cohen, 2022). President Xi was unsettled by the heroic Ukrainian resistance, the West's unity, the lightning speed and highly damaging economic sanctions by nations and private corporations, and the failure of a quick Russian victory (Burns, 2022). The war cost Russia much of its status as a great power as the world saw a pariah state. In the end, Putin's war could add some distance between Xi and Putin because of the great emphasis on its own reputation and the fear that sanctions could migrate to focus on China as well. Xi is not Putin. China is not Russia. Nader Mousavizadeh of the World Resources Institute put it clearly: "China wants to compete with America in the Superbowl of economics, innovation, and technology, and thinks it can win. Putin is ready to burn down the stadium and kill everyone in it to satisfy his grievances" (Friedman, 2022a). Some forty years ago, when asked about the future of liberal democracy, Chinese President Deng Xiao Ping answered: "It's too early to tell." That answer reflects the reality of the contemporary world order.

Further Reading

Bremer, I. (2022) *The Power of Crisis: How Three Threats—And Our Response—Will Change the World*, New York: Simon & Schuster.
Burns, W. (2019) *The Back Channel: A Memoir of American Diplomacy and the Case for Its Renewal*, New York: Random House.
Daalder, I. and J. Lindsay (2018) *The Empty Throne: America's Abdication of Global Leadership*, New York: Public Affairs.
Haass, R. (2017) *A World in Disarray: American Foreign Policy and the Crisis of the Old Order*, New York: Penguin.
Haass, R. (2020) *The World: A Brief Introduction*, New York: Penguin.
Kagan, R. (2018) *The Jungle Grows Back: America and Our Imperiled World*, New York: Knopf.
Malkasian, C. (2021) *The American War in Afghanistan: A History*, Oxford: Oxford University Press.
Nye, J. (2005) *Soft Power: The Means to Success in World Politics*, New York: Public Affairs.
Nye, J. (2015) *Is The American Century Over?* New York: Polity.
Osnos, E. (2021) *Wildland: The Making of America's Fury*, New York: Gerard, Straus, & Giroux.
Shambaugh, D. (2013) *Tangled Titans: The United States and China*, Lanham, MD: Rowman & Littlefield.
Whitlock, C. and *WP* (2021) *The Afghanistan Papers: A Secret History of the War*, New York: Simon & Schuster.
Zakaria, F. (2012) *The Post American World: The Rise of the Rest, Release 2.0*, New York: W. W. Norton.

CHAPTER 10
PROSPECTS

Twice a year, in Spring and Fall, the Institute for Politics at Harvard University conducts a nationwide poll of young Americans aged eighteen to twenty-nine years old. This age demographic had voted in record numbers in the 2020 presidential election and gave notice of their growing power in future contests. In fall 2021, these young adults said, by a margin of 55 to 44 percent, that they were more fearful for their nation's democracy than at any time in the past. They gave Biden a 46 percent approval rating (Trump got 30 percent) with the highest marks for his handling of Covid vaccines and masks (51 percent) and the lowest for gun violence (34 percent), crime (37 percent), and the economy (38 percent). Only 7 percent agreed that America had "a healthy democracy" with 52 percent rating it "in trouble" or "failed." Just 57 percent believed that it was "very important" for America to be a democracy at all. Twenty-one percent chose "somewhat important," 7 percent "not important," and 13 percent "didn't know." Fully one-third of these young Americans expected a civil war to erupt "in their lifetimes" and one-quarter expected one or more states to secede from the union. In terms of national pride, 31 percent ranked America as the "greatest country on earth," but more than half answered that there were "other nations as great or greater than America." Finally, these young adults were asked to pick where the primary focus of US foreign policy should be. The top results were "promoting international peace and human rights" (27 percent), ensuring US national security (18 percent), focusing on "climate change" (12 percent), and promoting US economic interests (11 percent) (Harvard Kennedy School, 2021a) (Illustration 10.1).

Four months later, another poll asked Americans eighteen and older to pick the single most pressing current problem in the United States (Table 10.1). Their answers reveal bipartisan agreement over the economy/jobs and war/foreign affairs, but double-digit disagreement over health, immigration, and environment/climate. When viewed in combination with the Harvard poll, there are many prospects on which Americans can cooperate and many issues to tear at the social fabric. Discord and free expression are expected in all democracies, but compromise and civility are essential to hold the country together in an era when many fear the decline or fall of democracy and are convinced that civil war, or world war, might come rather sooner than later.

In terms of conflicts and wars, every year the Director of National Intelligence releases a "Threat Assessment of the US Intelligence Community"—NSA, CIA, FBI, and Pentagon—as a primer for politicians to use to increase military spending and surveillance activities to safeguard the nation. In the report released on March 7, 2022,

Contemporary United States

Illustration 10.1 A Generational, Racial, Gender, and Power Question

Increasingly, with growing demographic strengths in the numbers of young people, racial and ethnic diversity, sexual and gendered identities, and political activism, the protester in the photograph has asked an important and encompassing question about the nation's historical hierarchies and the failures to gain the aspirational promises of the US Constitution for equal treatment under moral law. The question was asked in Texas in October 2021 during a rally against the new Texas abortion law that banned abortions after six weeks of pregnancy and which was allowed to stand for the time being after an appeal to the US Supreme Court. The Court also allowed any private citizen to bring charges against anyone who aided a person in getting an abortion—a decision criticized as "vigilante justice." Beyond the abortion application, the question being asked is one with larger implications for the prospects of the people and the country as the twenty-first century unfolds. As we have noted in this book, the new social movements involving young people, women, LGBTQIA+, immigrants, and the baby boom among minority groups might bring great changes in power relationships that will bring the long arc of the moral universe bending toward justice, finally, as Martin Luther King, Jr. prophesized years ago.

Source: Montinique Monroe/Stringer via Getty Images

the assessment cited the usual suspects: Russia, China, North Korea, Iran, and Syria with the "capability and intent to advance their interests at the expense of the United States and its allies." China was a "near-peer competitor … pushing to change global norms and potentially threatening its neighbors" with the most modern military, cyber, and space technology. China and Russia were forming a cooperative alliance to challenge the liberal world order (DNI, 2022). Russia was described as a most "malign influence," a huge threat to the US and its partners in the cyber realm and in military confrontation. There were strong strains put on governments to work together and not to blame the

Prospects

Table 10.1 What's the Most Urgent Problem in America Today? (percentage)

Issues	Republicans	Democrats	Independents	All
Economy and Jobs	22	20	26	22
Other Issue or Don't Know	23	16	20	18
Healthcare and Health Issues	6	20	15	14
War and Foreign Affairs	14	12	15	14
Crime, Corruption, Terrorism	16	9	9	12
Environment/Climate	2	13	6	8
Immigration	15	2	5	7
Inequality and Unequal Treatment	2	8	4	5

Note: This poll was taken before Putin invaded Ukraine and before SCOTUS overturned *Roe*. Poll of 1,005 Americans over eighteen years old taken February 28–March 2, 2022. Respondents self-identified: 389 Republicans, 428 Democrats, 118 Independents, 70 Unspecified.

Source: Ipsos (2022)

others for international tensions. The political instability of Covid, global warming, and the effects of migrations, food scarcity, water security, and the ramifications of technologies to disrupt institutions and corporations needed special attention. Other transnational threats came from new disruptive technologies, global crime rings, refugee crises, and ISIS/al-Qaeda/Hezbollah terrorism.

In the same time frame in which the two opinion polls and threat assessment appeared, President Biden was required to stand before the nation, explain his decisions on the issues he most cared about, and give a progress report on the condition of the American union. On March 1, 2022, Biden appeared before a Joint Session of Congress, in front of Supreme Court Justices, the top military leaders, his entire cabinet, and various leaders, invited guests, and media representatives. Much of the nation watched on TV or online, and the speech was broadcast in many countries. This was the annual State of the Union Address given by every president (see Chapter 3). The purpose has always been to gain support for domestic affairs and the executive's actions. The presidents offer up their spin on the present condition of the union and on the need to continue the course or change direction to advance national priorities. Biden had prepared to address those issues—and he did—but another item pushed up its ugly head and demanded immediate attention (Biden, 2022a).

Six days before the speech, the world order was challenged violently when Vladimir Putin used his considerable war machine to strike into the independent country of Ukraine to gain land and status for Russia and himself (see Chapter 9). CIA Director William Burns would later testify that Putin brought war to Europe because he believed he held advantages that made this the moment to strike. He believed Ukraine was "weak and easily intimidated." He thought the EU was "risk averse," especially with France in the throes of an election and Germany dealing with a change in government after years of steady guidance under Angela Merkel. Putin believed he had "sanctioned-proofed his economy" with a $650 billion "war chest" in foreign currency reserves. He was convinced of military superiority through a large and modernized army that would win "a quick

Contemporary United States

decisive victory" over Ukrainian opposition. He concluded that US global military power was in decline, uninterested, or impotent due to the recent loss in Afghanistan, and with an inability to act due to its domestic infighting on almost everything.

"He's been proven wrong on every count," Burns said. "His assumptions were flawed" (Burns, 2022). The Ukrainians were "fierce," NATO and the EU showed "remarkable resolve," and the US proved its leadership role at a time in which many people had "justifiable doubts" that domestic politics and four years of "America First" would allow Biden to lead (Daalder, 2022). Putin had argued time and again since his 2014 invasion of Crimea, that Ukraine was not a real country, but "He was dead wrong about that," said Burns. "Real countries fight back and that's what the Ukrainians have done, quite heroically" (Daalder, 2022). Burns expected that Russia would eventually prevail in taking the cities and setting up a puppet government, but only by increasing civilian casualties as leverage to do so. History shows that an occupying power is a temporary power that sooner or later will be forced aside by resolve and resistance.

Biden's actions after Putin's invasion confirmed that he was the leader of the free world. He rose to the occasion. He gave a war speech, a mild one but still unequivocal, in his support for Ukraine and in his call for US allies, and others, to stand before the bar of history (see Chapter 9). Biden spoke to a higher moral purpose: "In the battle between democracy and autocracy, democracies are rising to the moment, and the world is clearly choosing the side of peace and security" (Biden, 2022b). He was judicious, he hoped diplomacy could prevail, but he resolutely worked for economic sanctions at the same time he sent military hardware to Ukraine. Simultaneously, remarkably, NATO and the EU rallied. Biden's domestic approval ratings rose slightly—before quickly falling again—and he had the short-lived opportunity to get more programs through Congress before political partisanship eroded the gains.

Strikingly, just as the war began, Donald Trump had praised Putin for his buildup against Ukraine. Trump called Putin "savvy" and "a genius" to be admired. Fox News, especially top-rated talkshow host Tucker Carlson, backed Putin's actions and sneered at Biden's response. Meanwhile the images of dead children, the bombing of a maternity hospital, the dangers of fighting around active nuclear power plants, and the threats of using nuclear weapons to achieve victory caused a rupture in the Republican Party. What that meant for future elections was not immediately clear.

Political sociologist George Packer looked to the prospects of the 2024 presidential election. He rightfully asked, "Are We Doomed?" (Packer, 2021). Packer argued that unless the Republican Party changed course, democracy would fail because the US Constitution has "no answer" for a major party that "functions like an insurgency" with "a legal legitimate wing that conducts politics as usual and an underground wing that threatens violence" (Packer, 2021). The underground wing makes the Republicans a party that refuses to lose an election, a central tenet in a functioning democracy that depends on winners and losers. A political party that is half democratic and half authoritarian encourages Republican governors and state legislatures to enact new voting laws that make it almost nearly impossible for the party to lose the Electoral College vote. Packer concluded that Republicans have recognized the simple fact that in a free and fair

Prospects

Illustration 10.2 One Person, One Vote—Cast, Counted, Certified

During the five presidential elections in the twenty-first century, the Republican nominee has received the most popular votes nationwide only once—the re-election of George W. Bush in 2008. Bush lost the vote count in 2000 and Trump lost in 2016 and 2020. The Electoral College system made Republican candidates winners in the first two cases, and only barely failed in 2020 in the face of the attempt to overturn Biden by allowing state governors and legislatures to submit their own Electoral College winners even if their states showed that voters had selected another winner. Legal and extra-legal challenges are likely to multiply in the 2024 election in many states, such as rewriting voting laws, gerrymandering districts, limiting the numbers of ballot boxes, reducing mail-in ballots, cutting the number of voting days, empowering partisan legislatures to decide winners, changing residency requirements, and demanding stricter voter identification cards. Reliable studies of the 2020 election showed it to be the most secure and honest election in history. But the institution of the Electoral College and Constitutional provisions giving the states the power to decide electors is at the root of the democratic and political crises. The system is broken and in desperate need of repair to ensure, as the protesters marching in Philadelphia, Pennsylvania, say, that every person's vote is counted.

Source: Bastiaan Slabbers/NurPhoto via Getty Images

election, they would lose the presidency and control of Congress (Illustration 10.2). The question is whether or not the rupture over Trump and Putin will be enough to convince enough Independents and disaffected Republicans to vote to salvage the system (Packer, 2021). Rising oil prices, the pandemic, Court decisions, and inflation will have an effect.

Clearly, the single biggest threat to American democracy is in its internal divisions. But how do Americans get past their mistrust and animus to engage those with different agendas? A moral approach could work, as Michael Sandel and David Brooks have long argued (Sandel, 2010, 2020; Brooks, 2015). Americans must return to an idea of republican virtue whereby everyone, or most, are focused on the good of the whole,

Contemporary United States

believe in each other, and help each other, the nation, and the world to reach a better place. In the Second World War the national slogan "We Do Our Part!" summed up the social contract inherent in virtuous citizens in a democratic system (Peters, 2019). In contemporary America, the prospects for a more unified democracy revolve around the reality of revitalizing community fair play and supporting social-justice issues in terms or race, class, and gender. This cannot be done through legislation—although that would help. The people must demand that their parties stop the demagogues during the nomination process. If that is impossible, the American democracy will remain in an existential crisis, and could collapse.

The 2021 PEW research center's report "Beyond Red vs. Blue: The Political Typology" divided the voting population into nine groups and showed the differences and similarities among them, even when they are in the same party. Republicans fell into four groups, all with large white majorities—and with only one group being more than 1 percent African American. Faith and Flag Conservatives support religious values and think political compromise is "selling out." Ninety-four percent of people in this group strongly agrees that "White people do not benefit much or at all from advantages in society that Black people do not have." Committed Conservatives, believe in free markets, states' rights, and limited government regulation. They are "softer" on immigration and racial issues. A third group, the Populist Right are rural and less educated. They are highly critical of immigrants, big corporations, and social engineering. Finally, the Ambivalent Right has more young people and they favor legal abortion and legalized drugs but want limited government, a free market, and racial and gender traditions upheld. Still, 25 percent of Ambivalents voted for Biden in 2020. Those who voted for Trump say that they prefer not to do so again.

PEW grouped Democrats into four categories, all highly racially and ethnically diverse. The biggest faction is the Democratic Mainstays who are older and are "unshakeable" loyalists. Group 2, the Establishment Liberals, differ from Group 3, the Progressive Liberals in being more willing to compromise with Republicans over the rate of change. Progressives are the only Democratic group with a white majority (68 percent). They promote rapid and "sweeping changes" to achieve racial and economic justice, a fairer and more equal society, and immediate attention to save "Mother Earth" (Illustration 10.3). Group 4, the Outsider Left, is the youngest group. They are highly suspicious of both parties but are "deeply negative" toward Republicans. If they vote, they hold their noses and vote for Democrats (Doherty, 2021).

PEW identified one other political group: Stressed Sideliners. This group represents about 15 percent of the voting age public but were only about 10 percent of the actual vote cast. They shy away from politics. PEW sees the biggest possible gains in voting among this group of Stressed Sideliners, the Ambivalent Right, and the Outsider Left. If these groups up their percentages slightly and in the same political direction, they could determine the outcome in 2024 (Doherty, 2021). If this doesn't happen, it would support David Brooks's prospect of a "Dark Century" with liberalism in steep decline, "history reverting toward barbarism," with Putin and Xi and a gaggle of "thuggish populists across the West undermining nations from within" (Brooks, 2022).

As gloomy as Brooks's conclusion is, he is right that the survival of American democracy is at stake. In 2021, the International Institute for Democracy and Electoral

Illustration 10.3 The Youth Movement Understands the Connections

Climate Justice and Racial Justice are intrinsically linked because overwhelmingly the poor and discriminated against suffer environmental injustice by being forced to live in more highly polluted places than those occupied by more affluent citizens. Simply stated, the most vulnerable people do not have the financial resources to save themselves from damaged living spaces. In September 2020, during International Climate Week, a crowd of young people were joined in Manhattan by Swedish activist Greta Thunberg (not pictured) to demand politicians worldwide to "protect the sacred"—Mother Earth and humans of all races and ethnicities. The protesters wanted strong reductions in CO_2 emissions that caused global warming and made life on earth more precarious. In what sometimes seemed a "youthquake," Millennial and Gen Z activists have thrown themselves into #MeToo, #BLM, March for Our Lives gun protests, voter registration drives, support that has been called "socialism" in the past, and the protests stressing that there is no "Plan-et B" when it comes to climate change. The intersections of these causes are obvious to a generation that has now passed the baby boomers in sheer numbers of people. Older politicians have recognized the potential power of the youth vote and are adjusting platforms accordingly. The youth vote points in a liberal direction.

Source: Erik McGregor/LightRocket via Getty Images

Assistance (IDEA) in Stockholm, Sweden, called the US "a backsliding democracy." IDEA did not mince words: "The United States, the bastion of global democracy, fell victim to authoritarian tendencies itself" (IDEA, 2021). Political Scientist Barbara Walter writes that "We (USA) are no longer the world's oldest continuous democracy" but are an "anocracy"—the transition from democracy to autocracy (Walter, 2022). Sweden, New Zealand, and Canada are now the oldest continuous democracies. For Walter, "social media is every ethnic entrepreneur's dream" when aided by partisan mainstream media outlets like Fox and a president and political party who refuse to respect vote counts and to accept loses or voting rights.

Contemporary United States

America's turmoil and partisan distrust happened, according to political scientist Robert Kagan, because of a long "bubble of the liberal order" stretching from the Second World War to the twenty-first century. Westerners came to believe that progress was "normal and inevitable" even though history is full of law of the jungle realism where the wolves devour the weak through wars, taxes, ethno-nationalism, and authoritarianism (Kagan, 2018).

Summarizing the disruption and loss of order, the takeover of the Republican Party occurred hyper-rapidly with Trump's surprising win in 2016, four years of increasing partisanship capped by a rising authoritarianism, the appointment of three hard-Right, activist Justices, and a massively frightening pandemic that overturned all aspects of normal, daily home lives, jobs, and work activities. The legal precedents of the US Constitution, and the political processes of expanding rights and freedoms were put in reverse. Democracy suffered as Electoral College distributions and a determined political minority of activists and media outlets used technical procedures, such as gerrymandered districts, the filibuster, and new restrictions on voting rights to subvert the will and power of the majority. The vigilante insurrection of January 6, 2021, the massive increase in gun violence nationwide in 2021 and 2022 including lone assassins and racist police actions, and a white power and male power movement vowing that immigrants, minority groups, and women "will not replace us!" gave rise to more civil unrest. All of this fed into the growing evangelical movement working in concert with strong political action committees and SCOTUS to overturn the First Amendment protection separating church and state and to establish Christianity as the bedrock political power and identity of the United States.

It is in this atmosphere of what has been and what might be that demands balance as the country and world move forward toward and beyond the 2024 election. American democracy is under siege and at risk because of the social, political, and constitutional crises being compounded by fears over the pandemic, climate change, a changing world order, global financial instability, and a loss of cohesion in family, community, and institutions. There is much that could be lost, or won. There are possibilities for recovery exemplified by citizens' groups, including #Black Lives Matter, #MeToo!, and the growing numbers of young people organizing to save the planet, regulate guns, accept different sexual identities, and protect immigrant rights. A youthful, liberal and progressive majority may still join with independents and traditional non-Trumpist Republicans to restore a *zeitgeist* that would return America to its more balanced ideals of respect and fair play for a diverse population spread over fifty states.

In 2021, at President Biden's inauguration, a twenty-two-year-old African American poet, an optimist from the young adult generation, delivered her poem, "The Hill We Climb." Amanda Gorman reflected patriotically on the past, present, and future. She asked Americans to keep the faith in their country and in themselves: "Somehow we've weathered and witnessed a nation that isn't broken but simply unfinished …" (Gorman, 2021). The presidential election of 2024 will give a clear judgment on whether we are set for a "Dark Century" as David Brooks warned, or might move toward "a more perfect Union," as the preamble to the US Constitution, Abraham Lincoln, Barack Obama, and Amanda Gorman believed possible. The betting odds for either outcome are presently 50–50.

Further Reading

Brooks, D. (2015) *The Road to Character*, New York: Random House.

Burns, W. (2019) *The Back Channel: American Diplomacy in a Disordered World*, London: C. Hurst & Company.

Diamond, L. (2019) *Ill Winds: Saving Democracy from Russian Rage, Chinese Ambition, and American Complacency*, London: Penguin.

Greenblatt, J. (2022) *It Could Happen Here: Why America Is Tipping from Hate to the Unthinkable*, New York: HarperCollins.

Hill, F. and C. Gaddy (2015) *Mr. Putin: Operative in the Kremlin*, Washington, DC: Brookings.

Kagan, R. (2018) *The Jungle Grows Back: America and Our Imperiled World*, New York: Knopf.

Peters, C. (2017) *We Do Our Part: Toward a Fairer and More Equal America*, New York: Random House.

Sandel, M. (2013) *What Money Can't Buy: The Moral Limits of Markets*, New York: Farrar, Straus, & Giroux.

Sandel, M. (2020) *The Tyranny of Merit: What's Become of the Common Good*, London: Allen Lane.

Walter, B. (2022) *How Civil Wars Start: And How to Stop Them*, New York: Crown.

BIBLIOGRAPHY

Abbreviations

AJC	*Atlanta Journal-Constitution*
AP	Associated Press
ATL	*Atlantic*
BBC	British Broadcasting Corporation
BI	*Business Insider*
CSM	*Christian Science Monitor*
FT	*Financial Times*
ECON	*Economist*
IHT	*International Herald Tribune*
LAT	*Los Angeles Times*
LRB	*London Review of Books*
NPR	National Public Radio
NR	*New Republic*
NYRB	*New York Review of Books*
NYT	*New York Times*
PEW	Pew Research Center
TNR	*The New Republic*
WP	*Washington Post*
WSJ	*Wall Street Journal*

AACC. American Association of Community Colleges (2021) "Fast Facts."

AARP. American Association of Retired Persons (2021) "About AARP: Social Impact."

ABA for Law Students (2019) "Where Do Women Go to Law School? Here Are the 2018 Numbers," Feb. 28.

Abbott, B. (2019) "About One Million Species Face Risk of Extinction, U.N. Report Says," *WSJ*, May 7.

Abrams, J. (2011) "Patriot Act Extension Signed by Obama," *Huffington Post*, Jul. 22.

ACLU. American Civil Liberties Union (2010) "Everything You Always Wanted to Know about Redistricting but Were Afraid to Ask."

ACLU. American Civil Liberties Union (2017) "ACLU Annual Report 2015."

ACLU. American Civil Liberties Union (2021) "About Us."

Adamy, J. and P. Overberg (2019) "Immigrants Propel Population Growth in 10% of U.S. Counties," *WSJ*, Apr. 18.

AFL–CIO. The American Federation of Labor and Congress of Industrial Organizations (2020) "Press Release: AFL–CIO Endorses Joe Biden for President," Mar. 26.

AFL–CIO. The American Federation of Labor and Congress of Industrial Organizations (2021) "Our Affiliated Unions."

Bibliography

AFT. American Federation of Teachers (2022) "About Us."

Aguilera, J. (2019) "Here's What to Know about the Status of Family Separation at the U.S. Border, Which Isn't Nearly Over," *DHS*, Oct. 25.

AHA. American Hospital Association (2021) "Infographic: Children's Health Insurance Program (CHIP)."

AICF. American Indian College Fund (2021) "Our Purpose."

AIHEC. American Indian Higher Education Consortium (2017) "About AIHEC."

ALA. American Library Association (2017) "About Us."

ALA. American Library Association (2021) "The State of America's Libraries, 2021: Special Report, Covid 19," Mar. 20.

Alexander, M. (2012) *The New Jim Crow: Mass Incarceration in an Age of Colorblindedness*, New York: New Press.

Aljazeera (2021) "New UN Death Toll: At Least 350,000 People Killed in Syria's War," *Aljazeera*, Sep. 24.

Alter, C., S. Haynes, and J. Worland (2019) "2019 Person of the Year," *Time*, Dec. 4.

Alterman, E. and K. Mattson (2012) *The Cause: The Fight for American Liberalism from Franklin Roosevelt to Barack Obama*, New York: Viking.

America's State Parks (2021) "About Us."

Anbinder, T. (2016) *City of Dreams: The 400-Year Epic History of Immigrant New York*, Boston: Houghton Mifflin.

Annan, K. (2009) "America Will Re-Engage with the World," *The Independent*, Jan. 21.

AP (2001a) "Giuliani Angered by Nude Female Exhibit," *AJC*, Feb. 16.

AP (2001b) "Powell: Terrorists More Isolated," *NYT*, May 1.

AP (2002) "Bush Defends Pledge on 4th of July," *NYT*, Jul. 4.

AP (2009) "Obama on Arab TV: 'Americans Are not Your Enemy,'" *USA Today*, Jan. 27.

AP (2017) "Arkansas Executes Killer for Fourth Lethal Injection in Eight Days," *Telegraph*, Apr. 28.

Apple.com (2021) "Apple Inc. Condensed Consolidated Statements of Operations (Unaudited) (In Millions, except Number of Shares which Are Reflected in Thousands and Per Share Amounts)."

Applebaum, A. (2018) "A Warning from Europe," *ATL*, Oct.

Applebaum, A. (2020) *Twilight of Democracy: The Failure of Politics and the Parting of Friends*, London: Penguin.

Applebaum, A. (2022) "Calamity Again," *ATL*, Feb. 24.

Arango, T. (2008) "World Falls for American Media, even as It Sours on America," *NYT*, Dec. 1.

Aratani, L. (2008) "Catching Up to the Boys, in Good and Bad," *NYT*, Feb.10.

ASPE. Office for the Assistant Secretary for Planning and Evaluation (2021a) "2021 Poverty Guidelines," Feb. 1.

ASPE. Office for the Assistant Secretary for Planning and Evaluation (2021b) "HHS Poverty Guidelines for 2021," Jan. 13.

Astor, M., C. Caron, and D. Victor (2017) "A Guide to the Charlottesville Aftermath," *NYT*, Aug. 13.

Baker, P. (2009) "With Pledges to Troops and Iraqis, Obama Details Pullout," *NYT*, Feb. 28.

Baker, P. and M. Levenson (2022) "Biden Digs In on Ukraine Strategy, Seeking $33 Billion More in Aid," *NYT*, Apr. 28.

Baldwin, R. (2016) *The Great Convergence: Information Technology and the New Globalization*, Cambridge, MA: Belknap Press.

Ballotpedia.org (2021a) "Ballot Initiatives."

Ballotpedia.org (2021b) "2020 Ballot Measures."

Ballotpedia.org (2021c) "States with Initiatives or Referendum."

Banks, D., and Hendrix, J. (2016) "National Sources of Law Enforcement Employment Data," US Dept. of Justice, *NCJ* 249681, Oct. 4.

Bibliography

Barnes, R. and D. Eggen (2010) "Supreme Court Rejects Limits on Corporate Spending on Political Campaigns," *WP*, Jan. 22.

Barron, L. (2018) "'A New Low.' The World Is Furious at Trump for His Remark about 'Shithole Countries,'" *Time*, Jan. 12.

Barron's (2021) "Timeline: US Involvement in Iraq Since 2003 Invasion," Dec. 9.

Barroso, A. (2020) "61% of U.S. Women Say 'Feminist' Describes them Well; Many See Feminism as Empowering, Polarizing," PRC, Jul. 7.

Bazelon, E. (2008) "The Next Kind of Integration," *NYT*, Jul. 20.

BBC (2013) "US Cyber Command in 'Fivefold' Staff Expansion," Jan. 28.

BBC (2020) "Breonna Taylor: Lawsuit after US Health Worker Shot Dead by Police," May 13.

BCJ. Brennan Center for Justice (2019) "New Voting Restrictions in America," Nov. 19.

BCJ. Brennan Center for Justice (2020) "The Equal Rights Amendment Explained," Jan. 23.

BEA. Bureau of Economic Analysis (2020) "State Personal Income," Mar. 24.

BEA. Bureau of Economic Analysis (2021) "Gross Domestic Product, First Quarter 2021 (Advance Estimate)," Apr. 29.

Benefits.gov (2021) "State Children's Health Insurance Program."

Bennett, J., R. Fry, and R. Kochhar (2020) "Are You in the American Middle Class? Find Out with Our Income Calculator," PRC, Jul. 21.

Benshoff, H. and S. Griffin (2017) *America on Film: Representing Race, Class, Gender, and Sexuality at the Movies*, 3rd edn, Chichester, UK: Wiley-Blackwell.

BIA. Bureau of Indian Affairs (2016) "Frequently Asked Questions."

BIA. Bureau of Indian Affairs (2021) "About Us."

Bialek, C. (2019) "State of the Union 2019: How Americans See Major National Issues," PRC, Feb. 4.

Biden, J. (2020) "The Greatest Commandment Has Guided My Politics," *Christian Post*, Oct. 29.

Biden, J. (2021a) "A Proclamation on Juneteenth Day of Observance, 2021," Whitehouse.gov, Jun. 18.

Biden, J. (2021b) "Biden's Speech to Congress: Full Transcript," *NYT*, Apr. 29.

Biden J. (2021c) "Interim National Security Strategic Guidance," White House, Mar. 20.

Biden, J. (2021d) "Inaugural Address by President Joseph R. Biden," Whitehouse.gov, Jan. 20.

Biden, J. (2022a) "Remarks by President Biden in State of the Union Address," Whitehouse.gov, Mar. 1.

Biden, J. (2022b) "Remarks by President Biden Announcing Response to Russian Actions in Ukraine," Whitehouse.gov, Feb. 22.

Biden/Harris (2020) "The Biden Plan for Education Beyond High School," Fall.

Bieler, D. and C. Boren (2021) "At White House, Megan Rapinoe says She's Been 'Disrespected and Dismissed because I am a Woman,'" *WP*, Mar. 25.

Bilton, R. (2014) "Apple 'Failing to Protect Chinese Factory Workers,'" BBC, Dec. 18.

Birt, J. and D. Frost (2002) "The Nixon Tapes, Part 1," Discovery Communications.

Bishop, B. (2008) *The Big Sort: Why the Clustering of Like-Minded America is Tearing US Apart*, Boston: Houghton Mifflin Harcourt.

Bishop, B. (2017) "Americans Have Lost Faith in Institutions," *WP*, Mar. 3.

BJS. Bureau of Justice Statistics, Department of Justice (2017) "Factsheet on MS-13," Apr. 18.

BJS. Bureau of Justice Statistics, Department of Justice (2019) "Firearm Commerce in the USA: Annual Statistical Update."

BJS. Bureau of Justice Statistics, Department of Justice (2020a) "Violent Victimization by Race or Ethnicity, 2005–2019," NCJ 255578, Oct.

BJS. Bureau of Justice Statistics, Department of Justice (2020b) "Jail Inmates in 2018," Mar. 31.

Blanck, D (2002) "'We Have a Lot to Learn from America': The Myrdals and the Question of American Influence in Sweden," Duncan, R. and C. Juncker, eds., *Angles on the English Speaking World*, 2, Copenhagen: Museum Tusculanum Press, 129–45.

Bibliography

Bloom, A. (1988) *The Closing of the American Mind*, New York: Touchstone.

Blow, C. (2017) "Trump, Archenemy of Truth," *NYT*, Feb. 27.

Blow, C. (2021) "Is America's Democracy Slipping Away?" *NYT*, May 30.

BLS. Bureau of Labor Statistics (2019a) "American Indians and Alaska Natives in the U.S. Labor Force," Nov.

BLS. Bureau of Labor Statistics (2019b) "Data on Display: Education Pays," Feb.

BLS. Bureau of Labor Statistics (2020a) "News Release: USDL-20-0815," May 8.

BLS. Bureau of Labor Statistics (2020b) "Persons at Work in Nonagricultural Industries by Age, Sex, Race, Hispanic or Latino Ethnicity, Marital Status, and Usual Full- or Part-Time Status," Jan. 22.

BLS. Bureau of Labor Statistics (2021a) "Economic News Release: Table A-15. Alternative Measures of Labor Underutilization," Dec. 6.

BLS. Bureau of Labor Statistics (2021b) "Table A-2. Employment Status of the Civilian Population by Race, Sex, and Age," Dec. 6.

BLS. Bureau of Labor Statistics (2021c) "Table B-2. Average Weekly Hours and Overtime of All Employees on Private Nonfarm Payrolls by Industry Sector, Seasonally Adjusted," Dec. 6.

BLS. Bureau of Labor Statistics (2021d) "Table B-3. Average Hourly and Weekly Earnings of All Employees on Private Nonfarm Payrolls by Industry Sector, Seasonally Adjusted," Dec. 6.

BLS. Bureau of Labor Statistics (2021e) "The Employment Situation," USDL-21-2075, Dec. 3.

BLS. Bureau of Labor Statistics (2021f) Employer-Reported Workplace Injuries and Illnesses – 2020," USDL 21-1927, Nov. 3.

BLS. Bureau of Labor Statistics (2021g) "Usual Weekly Earnings of Wage and Salary Workers-Third Quarter 2021," USDL-21-1871, Oct. 19.

BLS. Bureau of Labor Statistics (2021h) "Earnings and Unemployment Rates by Educational Attainment," BLS Statistics: Employment, Apr. 21.

BLS. Bureau of Labor Statistics (2021i) "Union Members—2020," USDL 21-0081, Jan. 22.

BLS. Bureau of Labor Statistics (2021j) "Labor Force Statistics from the Current Population Survey."

Booth, W. (2001) "A Slow Start to an Environmental End-Run," *WP*, Jan. 13.

Bostrup, J. (2022) "'No Matter What,' Putin Wants to Achieve His Goals in Ukraine," *Politiken*, Mar. 4.

Bote, J. (2020) "George Floyd Told Officers He 'Can't Breathe' Nearly 30 times, Newly Released Body Cam Transcripts Show," *USA Today*, Jul. 9.

Boyle, K. (2021) *The Shattering: America in the 1960s*, New York: W. W. Norton.

Bremer, I. (2022) The Power of Crisis: How Three Threats—And Our Response—Will Change the World, New York: Simon & Schuster.

Brenan, M. (2019) "40% of Americans Believe in Creationism," *Gallup*, Jul. 26.

Brenan, M. (2020a) "Support for Stricter U.S. Gun Laws at Lowest Level since 2016," *Gallup*, Nov. 16.

Brenan, M. (2020b) "New High 54% Want Government to Solve More Problems in U.S.," *Gallup*, Sep. 28.

Breyer, S. (2018) "America's Courts Can't Ignore the World," *ATL*, Oct.

Brinkley, A. (2008) "In Search of Bush," *NYT*, Mar. 2.

Brinkley, A. (2009) "Worse than Hoover," *TNR*, Jan. 13.

Broad, W. (2021) "How Space Became the Next 'Great Power" Contest between the US and China," *NYT*, Jan. 24.

Brockwell, G. (2020) "The 10th President's Last Surviving Grandson: A Bridge to the Nation's Complicated Past," *WP*, Nov. 29.

Brooks, C. (2019) "Federal Law Enforcement Officers, 2016 – Statistical Tables," US Dept. of Justice, *NCJ* 251922, Oct.

Bibliography

Brooks, D. (2004) *On Paradise Drive: How We Live Now (And Always Have) in the Future Tense*, New York: Simon & Schuster.

Brooks, D. (2011) *The Social Animal*, New York: Random House.

Brooks, D. (2015) *The Road to Character*, New York: Random House.

Brooks, D. (2016) "The Shame Culture," *NYT*, Mar. 15.

Brooks, D. (2021a) "Abortion: The Voice of the Ambivalent Majority," *NYT*, Dec. 2.

Brooks, D. (2021b) "The Terrifying Future of the American Right," *ATL*, Nov. 18.

Brooks, D. (2022) "The Dark Century," *NYT*, Feb. 17.

Bruni, F. (2016) "How Facebook Warps Our Worlds," *NYT*, May 21.

Buchanan, L., Q. Bui, and J. Patel (2020) "Black Lives Matter May Be the Largest Movement in U.S. History," *NYT*, Jul. 3.

Budiman, A. (2020) "Key Findings about U.S. Immigrants," PRC, Aug. 20.

Budiman, A. and P. Conor (2018) "Migrants from Latin America and the Caribbean Sent a Record Amount of Money to their Home Countries in 2016," PRC, Jan. 23.

Burke, S. (2017) "How Many Social Followers Does Trump Actually Have?" CNN, Jan. 17.

Burns, A., J. Martin, and K. Glueck (2020) "How Joe Biden Won the Presidency," *NYT*, Nov. 7.

Burns, W. (2022) "Testimony to House Intelligence Committee amid Russian Attack on Ukraine," Mar. 8.

Bush, D. (2019) "Religious Liberals Want to Change what it Means to Be a Christian Voter," *PBS Newshour*, Jul. 8.

Bush, G. (2001) "Executive Order Establishing Office of Homeland Security," Oct. 8.

Bush, G. (2003) "In Bush's Words: 'Iraqi Democracy Will Succeed,'" *NYT*, Nov. 6.

Calfire (2021) "2021 Incident Archive," CA.gov.

Callamard, A. (2022) "20 Years On, Biden Must Close Guantánamo Once and For All," Amnesty International, Jan. 11.

Calmes, J. and P. Baker (2012) "Obama Says Same-Sex Marriage Should Be Legal," *NYT*, May 9.

CALSTRS. California State Teachers' Retirement System (2021) "Current Investment Portfolio."

Campbell, J. (1998) "Clinton: I Did Not Have Sex with Lewinsky," *Evening Standard* (London), Jan. 26.

Campbell, N. and A. Kean (2016) *American Cultural Studies: An Introduction to American Culture*, 4th edn, London: Routledge.

Carlisle, M. (2020) "Here's What the Massive Amount of Smoke Created by West Coast Wildfires Looks Like from Space," *Time*, Sep. 12.

Carrington, D. (2016) "The Anthropocene Epoch: Scientists Declare Dawn of Human-Influenced Age," *Guardian*, Aug. 29.

Carson, E. (2020) "Bureau of Justice Statistics: Prisoners in 2018," BOJ, *NCJ* 253516, Apr.

Carter, J. (1979) "Address to the Nation," Jul. 20.

Casselman, B. (2019) "Why Wages Are Finally Rising, 10 Years after the Recession," *NYT*, May 2.

Castner, B. (2017) "Still Fighting and Dying, in the Forever War," *NYT*, Mar. 9.

Cave, D. (2017) "In Australia, a Call for Closer Ties to China Gains Support," *NYT*, Mar. 16.

CBO. Congressional Budget Office (2020a) "An Update to the Budget Outlook: 2020 to 2030," Sep.

CBO. Congressional Budget Office (2020b) "Education." CBP.

CBO. Congressional Budget Office (2021) "The Budget and Economic Outlook: 2021 to 2031," Feb. 11.

CBPP. Center on Budget and Policy Priorities (2020) "Policy Basics: Where Do Our Federal Tax Dollars Go?" Apr. 9.

CC. Christian Coalition (2016) "About Us."

CDC. Centers for Disease Control, Department of Health and Human Services (2016) "NCHS: Mean Age of Mothers Is on the Rise: United States, 2000–2014." NCHS Data Brief, no 232.

CDC. Centers for Disease Control (2017) "Health-the United States: Table 15. Life Expectancy at Birth, at Age 65, and at Age 75, by Sex, Race, and Hispanic Origin: United States, Selected Years 1900–2016."

Bibliography

CDC. Centers for Disease Control (2018) "Provisional Number of Divorces and Annulments and Rate: United States, 2000–2018."

CDC. Centers for Disease Control (2021a) "National Center for Vital Statistics: Birth Data," Dec. 9.

CDC. Centers for Disease Control (2021b) "Adult Obesity Facts," Sep. 30.

CDC. Centers for Disease Control (2021c) "Reproductive Health: Unintended Pregnancy," Jun. 25.

CDC. Centers for Disease Control (2021d) "Drug Overdose Deaths," Mar. 3.

CDC. Centers for Disease Control (2021e) "National Center for Health Statistics: Unmarried Childbearing, 2019," Mar. 2.

Chang, K. (2020) "Watch the Moon Landing of China's Chang'e-5 Spacecraft," *NYT*, Dec. 17.

Chavez, N. (2020) "'There's No Such Thing as the Latino Vote.' 2020 Results Reveal a Complex Electorate," CNN, Nov. 9.

CHE. Chronicle of Higher Education (2021) "Major Private Gifts to Higher Education," Dec. 17.

Cheeseman Day, J. (2020) "88% of Blacks Have a High School Diploma, 26% a Bachelor's Degree," USCB, Jun. 10.

Chinni, D. (2021) "The GOP Is Rapidly Becoming the Blue-Collar Party. Here's what that Means," *NBC News*, Feb. 21.

Chollet, D. and J. Smith (2017) "Bannon's Strategic Initiatives Cabal inside the NSC is a Dangerous Hypocrisy," *FP*, Feb. 1.

Cohen, R. (2017) "Am I Imagining This?" *NYT*, Feb. 20.

Cohen, E. (2022) "This is the War's Most Decisive Moment," *ATL*, Apr. 13.

CFR. Council on Foreign Relations (2020) "Demographics of the U.S. Military," Jul. 13.

CIA World Factbook (2020).

Clinton, H. (2011) "America's Pacific Century," *FP*, Nov.

Clinton, H. (2012a) "An Interview with Hillary Clinton," *Economist*, May 22.

Clinton, H. (2012b) "The Art of Smart Power," *New Statesman*, Jul. 18.

CMS. Center for Medicare and Medicaid Services (2018) "National Health Expenditure Projections, 2018–2027."

CNN (2020) "2020 Exit Polls."

Coates, T. (2015) *Between the World and Me*, New York: Spiegel & Grau.

Coates, T. (2017a) "My President Was Black" *ATL*, Feb.

Coates, T. (2017b) *We Were Eight Years in Power: An American Tragedy*, London: One World.

Cochrane, E. (2022) "Congress Clears $1.5 Trillion Spending Bill, Including Ukraine Aid," *NYT*, Mar. 10.

Cochrane, E., N. Schwartz, and G. Friedman (2020) "Trump Signs Pandemic Relief Bill after Unemployment Aid Lapses," *NYT*, Dec. 27.

Cohen, A. and W. Codrington (2020) "The Equal Rights Amendment Explained," Brennan Center, Jan. 23.

Cohen, R. (2016) "Thanks to No-Drama Obama, American Leadership Is Gone," *WP*, Dec. 26.

Cohen, R. (2017) "Am I Imagining This?" *NYT*, Feb. 10.

College Board (2016) "Big Future – College Costs: FAQs."

College Board (2020) "Trends in College Pricing 2020."

Collins, B. and B. Zadronzy (2021) "Twitter Permanently Suspends President Donald Trump," https://www.nbcnews.com/tech/tech-news/twitter-permanently-bans-president-donald-trump-n1253588.

Confessore, N. (2022) "American Nationalist, Part One: How Tucker Carlsen Stoked White Fear to Conquer Cable," *NYT*, May 4.

COPSPCU: Center on Poverty and Social Policy – Columbia University (2020) "Monthly Poverty Rates in the United States during Covid-19," Oct. 15.

Bibliography

Corchado, A. (2020) "What's Gone Wrong in America? An Outsider Explains," WP, Jul. 3.

Corcoran, K, S. Baker, and D. Choi (2019) "The FBI Has Closed its Investigation of the Las Vegas Mass Shooting that Killed 58 People and Injured Hundreds More. Here's Exactly how the Nation's Worst Modern Gun Massacre Unfolded," *Business Insider*, Jan. 30.

Court Statistics Project (2020) "State Court Caseload Digest: 2018 Data. National Center for State Courts."

Craig, T (2020) "'The United States Is in Crisis': Report Tracks Thousands of Summer Protests, most Nonviolent," *WP*, Sep. 3.

Craigie, T., A. Grawert, and C. Kimble (2020) "Conviction, Imprisonment, and Lost Earnings," Brennan Center for Justice, Sep. 15.

Crèvecoeur, J. (1782) "Letters from an American Farmer."

Crossette, B. (2000) "Globalization Tops Agenda for World Leaders at UN Summit," *NYT*, Sep. 3.

CRR. Center for Reproductive Rights (2016) "Whole Woman's Health v. Hellerstedt."

CRS. Congressional Research Service (2020a) "Membership of the 116th Congress: a Profile."

CRS. Congressional Research Service (2020b) "American War and Military Operations Casualties: Lists and Statistics," RL32492, Jul. 29.

CRS. Congressional Research Service (2021a) "The Temporary Assistance for Needy Families Responses to (TANF) Block Grant: Frequently Asked Questions," Dec. 14.

CRS. Congressional Research Service (2021b) "Membership of the 117th Congress: A Profile Congressional Research Service," R46705, Aug. 5.

CRS. Congressional Research Service (2021d) "Juneteenth National Independence Day," July 1.

C-SPAN (2021) "Presidential Historians Survey, 2021."

Cunningham, P. (2020) "The Health 202: Funding for Planned Parenthood Went up – Yes, up – During the Trump Administration," *WP*, Oct. 21.

Daalder, I. (2022) quoted in Cave, D. "The War in Ukraine Holds a Warning for the World Order," *NYT*, Mar. 4.

Daalder, I. and J. Lindsay (2018) *The Empty Throne: America's Abdication of Global Leadership*, New York: Public Affairs.

Dailygreen (2012) "BP Oil Spill, Gulf of Mexico Update," Jan. 1.

Danner, M. (2003) "Iraq: The New War," *NYRB*, Sep. 25.

Danner, M. (2004) *Torture and Truth: America, Abu Ghraib, and the War on Terror*, New York: NYRB.

Davis, J. (2017) "How the Presidency Changed Obama," *NYT*, 17 Jan.

Dawkins, R. (2006) *The God Delusion*, Boston: Mariner Books.

DeBonis, M. (2021) "'Lefty Social Engineering': GOP Launches Cultural Attack on Biden's Plan for Day Care, Education and Employee Leave," *WP*, Apr. 30.

DeParle, J. (2012) "Harder for Americans to Rise from the Lower Rungs," *NYT*, Jan. 4.

DeSilver, D., M. Lipka, and D. Fahmy (2020) "10 Things We Know about Race and Policing in the U.S.," PRC, Nov.

Desjardins, J. (2020) "All of the World's Wealth in One Visualization," *Visual Capitalist*, Jan. 16.

Desmond, M. and M. Emirbayer (2020) *Race in America*, 2nd edn, New York: W. W. Norton.

DeYoung, K. (2020) "Biden Faces a Changed World and No End of Foreign Policy Challenges from China to Iran," *NYT*, Dec. 9.

DHS. Department of Homeland Security (2016) "About DHS," Jun. 29.

DHS. Department of Homeland Security (2020a) "Budget in Brief: Fiscal Year 2020."

DHS. Department of Homeland Security (2020b) "Yearbook of Immigration Statistics, 2018," Table 1, Jan. 6.

DHS. Department of Homeland Security (2020c) "Yearbook of Immigration Statistics, 2018," Table 3.

DHS. Department of Homeland Security (2021) "Naturalization Fact Sheet," Aug. 24.

Bibliography

Diamant, J. (2019) "With High Levels of Prayer, U.S. Is an Outlier among Wealthy Nations, PRC, May 1.

Diamond, L. (2019) *Ill Winds: Saving Democracy from Russian Rage, Chinese Ambition, and American Complacency*, London: Penguin.

Dickler, J. (2019) "Tuition-Free College Is Now a Reality in Nearly 20 States," *CNBC*, Nov. 12.

Didion, J. (2017) *Slouching towards Bethlehem*, London: 4th Estate.

Diehl, J. (2016) "Trump's Coming War with Islam," *WP*, Dec. 11.

Dietz, R. (2016) "Eye on Housing: Little Change for New Single-Family Home Size."

Dinan, S. (2020) "Oregon Gov. Kate Brown Says National Guard Not Needed," *Washington Times*, Sep. 4.

Dionne, E. (2008) *Souled Out: Reclaiming Faith and Politics after the Religious Right*, Princeton: Princeton University Press.

Dionne, E. (2012) *Our Divided Political Heart: The Battle for the American Idea in an Age of Discontent*, New York: Bloomsbury.

Dionne, E. and J. Dilulio (2000) *What's God Got to Do with the American Experiment?* Washington: Brookings Institution Press.

Djordjevic, M. (2021) "21 Extraordinary Newspaper Statistics You Should Know About in 2021."

DNI. Office of the Director of National Intelligence (2021) "Annual Threat Assessment of the US Intelligence Community," Apr. 9.

DNI. Director of National Intelligence (2022) "Annual Threat Assessment of the U.S. Intelligence Community," Homeland Security Digital Library, Feb/Mar.

DOD. Department of Defense (2018a) "Nuclear Posture Review," Feb.

DOD. Department of Defense (2018b) "2018 National Defense Strategy," Jan. 19.

DOD. Department of Defense (2019a) "Trump Signs Law Establishing US Space Force, Dec. 20.

DOD. Department of Defense (2019b) "National Military Strategy Addresses the Changing Character of War," Jul. 12.

DOD. Department of Defense (2021a) "Military and Security Developments Involving the People's Republic of China, 2021," Mar.

DOD. Department of Defense (2021b) "Biden Administration Overturns Transgender Exclusion Policy," Jan. 25.

DOD. Department of Defense (2021c) "Interim National Security Strategic Guidance," March.

DOE. Department of Education (2020) "Fiscal Year 2021 Budget Summary."

DOHA, Doha, Qatar (2002) Conference of the WTO "Economic Perspectives: Trade in the Post-Doha Global Economy," *An Electronic Journal of the U.S. Department of State*, Jan. 7.

Doherty, C., ed. (2021) "Beyond Red vs. Blue: The Political Typology," Washington, DC: Pew Research Center.

DOL. Department of Labor (2022) "Unemployment Insurance Relief During COVID-19 Outbreak."

Dolan, K. (2021) "Forbes 400: The Definitive Ranking of the Wealthiest Americans in 2021," *Forbes*.

Dos Passos, J. (1979) *The Big Money*, New York: New American Library.

Dowd, M. (2022) "Can Dems Dodge Doomsday," *NYT*, Feb. 19.

DPIC. Death Penalty Information Center (2019) "End of Year Report, 2019," Dec. 17.

DPIC. Death Penalty Information Center (2021a) "Executions by Race and Race of Victim," Dec. 9.

DPIC. Death Penalty Information Center (2021b) "Innocence," Dec.

DPIC. Death Penalty Information Center (2021c) "Women," Jul.

DPIC. Death Penalty Information Center (2021d) "Facts about the Death Penalty," Apr. 21.

DPIC. Death Penalty Information Center (2021e) "Time on Death Row."

D'Souza, D. (2014) *America: Imagine the World Without Her* [film], Lionsgate Films.

DuBois, W. (1903) *The Souls of Black Folk*, Chicago: A. C. McClurg & Co.

Bibliography

Duffin, E. (2021) "U.S. Defense Outlays and Forecast as a Percentage of the GDP 2000–2030," Statistica, Dec. 6.

Dumbrell, J. (2014) "Foreign and Security Policy," in Peele, G. et al. (eds.), *Developments in American Politics* 7, 244–62, Basingstoke: Palgrave Macmillan.

Duncan, R. (2015) *The Dragon and the Eagle: Cultural Comparisons of China-US Relations*, Xi'an: Shaanxi University Press.

Dunkelman, M. (2014) *The Vanishing Neighbor: The Transformation of American Community*, New York: W. W. Norton.

Dyson, M. (2016) *The Black Presidency: Barack Obama and the Politics of Race in America*, Boston: Houghton Mifflin Harcourt.

Earthjustice (2020) "Judge Orders Dakota Access Pipeline to Shut Down," Jul. 6.

EDI. Education Data Initiative (2020) "Research and Resources to Tackle the Rising Costs of Higher Education."

Edsall, T. (2016) "How the Other Fifth Lives," *NYT*, Apr. 27.

Edsall, T. (2021) "The Capitol Insurrection Was as Christian Nationalist as It Gets," *WP*, Jan. 28.

Edweek. *Education Weekly* (2021) "School Shootings in 2021: How Many and Where," Mar. 1.

Ehrenfreud, M. (2015) "The Stunning – and Expanding – Gap in Life Expectancy between the Rich and the Poor," *WP*,Sep. 18.

EIA. Energy Information Administration (2021a) "Energy and the Environment Explained: Outlook for Future Emissions," Nov. 8.

EIA. Energy Information Administration (2021b) "US Energy Facts Explained, May 15.

EIA. Energy Information Administration (2021c) "FAQ."

EIA. Energy Information Administration (2021d) "FAQ: What Countries Are the Top Producers and Consumers of Oil?"

EIA. Energy Information Administration (2022) "U.S. Crude Oil and Natural Gas Proved Reserves, Year-end 2020," Jan 13.

Eilperin, J., B. Dennis, and J. Muyskens (2021) "Tracking Biden's Environmental Actions," *WP*, May 3.

Emily's List (2022) emilyslist.org.

EPA. Environmental Protection Agency (2021) "Inventory of U.S. Greenhouse Gas Emissions and Sinks."

EPA. Environmental Protection Agency (2020) "EPA's Budget and Spending."

EPIC. Electronic Privacy Information Center (2008) "ACLU v. Mukasey," Jul. 22.

Erlanger, S. (2017) "As Trump Era Arrives, A Sense of Uncertainty Grips the World," *NYT*, Jan. 16.

Everett, B. and S. Kim (2015) "Judge Not: GOP Blocks Dozens of Obama Court Picks," *Politico*, Jun. 7.

Evers-Hillstrom, K. (2020) "Outside Spending Reaches Record $2 billion as Super PACs Hammer Trump," OpenSecrets.org, Oct. 19.

Evers-Hillstrom, K. (2021) "Most Expensive Ever: 2020 Election Cost $14.4 Billion," OpenSecrets.org, Feb. 11.

Fadel, L. (2018) "How Muslims, Often Misunderstood, Are Thriving in America," *National Geographic*, May.

Fagan, M. and C. Huang (2019) "A Look at How People around the World View Climate Change," PRC, Apr. 18.

Fallows, J. (2016) "China's Great Leap Backwards," *ATL*, Dec.

Fassihi, F. (2022) "Several U.N. Security Council Members Condemn Russia's Attack on a Nuclear Power Plant," *NYT*, Mar. 4.

Faulkner, W. (1948) *Intruder in the Dust*, New York: Modern Library.

FBI. Federal Bureau of Investigation (2015) "National Gang Report."

FBI. Federal Bureau of Investigation (2018) "Uniform Crime Report: Hate Crime Statistics, 2018."

Bibliography

FBI. Federal Bureau of Investigation (2021a) "About."

FBI. Federal Bureau of Investigation (2021b) "National Instant Criminal Background Check System."

FBI. Federal Bureau of Investigation (2021c) "What We Investigate: Violent Crime—Gangs."

FBP. Federal Bureau of Prisons (2021) "Inmate Gender," Dec. 18.

FDIC. Federal Deposit Insurance Corporation (2020) "Understanding Deposit Insurance," Jul. 12.

Feeding America (2019) "2019 Annual Report."

Feeley, J. (2020) "US Wants $11 Billion in Purdue Pharmaceutical Bankruptcy Case," *Bloomberg*, Aug. 4.

Ferguson, N. (2012) "College Becoming the New Caste System," *Daily Beast*, Aug. 27.

Fightback (2021) "About #Fightback."

Fieldstadt, E. (2019) "James Alex Fields, Driver in Deadly Car Attack at Charlottesville Rally, Sentenced to Life in Prison," *NBC*, Jul. 28.

Fieldstadt, E. (2018) "America's Biggest Megachurches, Ranked," *NBC News*, Nov. 26.

Flegenheimer, M., and K. Glueck (2020) "Joe Biden's Non-Radical 1960s," *NYT*, Oct. 17.

Flitter, E., J. Smialek, and S. Cowley (2020) "How the White House Rolled Back Financial Regulations," *NYT*, Nov. 6.

Flynn, M. and A. Chiu (2020) "Trump Says His 'Authority Is Total.' Constitutional Experts Have 'No Idea' Where he Got That," *WP*, Aug. 14.

Fogel, R. (2000) *The Fourth Great Awakening and the Future of Egalitarianism*, Chicago: University of Chicago Press.

Foner, E. (2020) *Give Me Liberty! An American History*, 6th edn, New York: W. W. Norton.

Ford, G. (1974) "Gerald R. Ford's Remarks on Taking the Oath of Office as President," Gerald R. Ford Library and Museum.

Ford.com (2021) "Enhanced Execution, Fresh Portfolio of Exciting Vehicles Drive Ford's Strong Q1 Profitability, As Trust in Company Rises," Apr. 28.

Fox, J., L. Tierney, S. Blanchard, and G. Florit (2019) "What Remains of Bears Ears," *WP*, Apr. 2.

FRE. Federal Reserve Education (2021) "The Structure and Functions of the Federal Reserve System."

FRED. Federal Reserve Bank of St. Louis (2018) "The FRED Blog. Corporate Profits versus Labor Income," Aug. 9.

FRED. Federal Reserve Bank of St. Louis (2019) "FRED Adds Wealth Distribution Data," Jul. 2.

FRED. Federal Reserve Bank of St. Louis (2021a) Delinquency Rate on Single-Family Residential Mortgages, Booked in Domestic Offices, All Commercial Banks," Dec. 27.

FRED. Federal Reserve Bank of St. Louis (2021b) "Personal Saving Rate," Nov. 24.

FRED. Federal Reserve Bank of St. Louis (2021c) "Housing Inventory Estimate: Occupied Housing Units in the United States," Nov 2 (EOCCUSQ176N).

FRED. Federal Reserve Bank of St. Louis (2021d) "Housing Inventory Estimate: Total Housing Units in the United States," Nov. 2 (ETOTALUSQ176N).

Freelancers Union (2021) "About Freelancers Union."

Friedman, T. (2008) *Hot, Flat, and Crowded. Why the World Needs a Green Revolution – and How We Can Renew Our Global Future*, London: Allan Lane.

Friedman, T. (2016a) "Bibi Netanyahu Makes Trump His Chump," *NYT*, Dec. 28.

Friedman, T. (2016b) "Social Media: Destroyer or Creator?" *NYT*, Feb. 3.

Friedman, T. (2021) "Is There a War Coming Between China and the U.S.?" *NYT*, Apr. 27.

Friedman, T. (2022a) "I See Three Scenarios For How This War Ends," *NYT*, Mar. 2.

Friedman, T. (2022b) "We Have Never Been Here Before," *NYT*, Feb. 25.

Friedman, Z. (2020) "Student Loan Debt Statistics in 2020: A Record $1.6 Trillion," *Forbes*, Feb. 2.

Frosch, D. and R. Levy (2020) "Cities Were Filled with Mass Protests in the Summer of 2020. They Are Different Now," *WSJ*, Sep. 15.

Bibliography

FWS. US Fish and Wildlife Services (2012) "Endangered Species Report," Dec.22.

FWS. US Fish and Wildlife Services (2016) "National Wildlife Refuge System – Overview."

Gabler, N. (2000) *Life the Movie: How Entertainment Conquered Reality*, New York: Vintage.

Gabler, N. (2016) "My Secret Shame," *ATL*, May.

Gallup (2017) "Trust in Government."

Gallup (2020) "Work and Workplace," Aug. 17.

Gallup (2021a) "Presidential Job Approval Center," Dec.

Gallup (2021b) "Congress and the Public," Nov. 16.

Gallup (2021c) "Death Penalty," Oct. 19.

Gallup (2021d) "Guns," Oct. 19.

Gallup (2021e) "Supreme Court," Sep. 17.

Gallup (2021g) "Presidential Approval Ratings – Donald Trump," Jan. 15.

Garger, K. (2020) "Trump Says He Now Identifies as a Non-Denominational Christian,"
New York Post, Oct. 23.

Garrison, J. (2020) "Voter Turnout 2020: Early Voting Tops 100 Million Ballots Cast,"
USA Today, Nov. 3.

Gates Foundation. Bill and Melinda Gates Foundation (2021a) "Committed Grants," Dec. 13.

Gates Foundation. Bill and Melinda Gates Foundation (2021b) "Foundation Fact Sheet."

Gates Foundation. Bill and Melinda Gates Foundation (2021c) "Introduction."

Gearan, A. (2013) "Kerry Sails through Senate Confirmation Hearings on Secretary of State Bid,"
NYT, Jan. 24.

Gecewitz, C. (2018) "'New Age' Beliefs Common among both Religious and Nonreligious
Americans," PRC, Oct. 1.

Geller, A. and J. Har (2021) "'Shameful': US Virus Deaths Top 400K as Trump Leaves Office," AP,
Jan. 20.

Gellman, B. (2022) "January 6 was Just Practice," *ATL*, Jan/Feb.

Gems, G., L. Borish, and G. Phister (2022) *Sports in American History: From Colonization to
Globalization*, 3rd edn, Champaign, IL: Human Kinetics.

Gerstein, J. (2020) "In a Video from the White House, Trump Once More Suggests He Won't Let
Go of the Presidency, Saying Maybe the Next Administration 'Will Be Me'," *Business Insider*,
Dec. 23.

Gessen, M. (2020) *Surviving Autocracy*, New York: Riverhead.

Gessen, M. (2021) "Trump's Defense Was an Insult to the Impeachment Proceedings and an
Assault on Reason," *New Yorker*, Feb. 14.

Giannarelli, L., L. Wheaton, and G. Acs (2020) "2020 Poverty Projections," *Urban Institute*, Jul.

Giffords Law Center (2021) "Gun Laws Save Lives."

Gilbert, D. and S. Kent (2015) "BP Agrees to Pay $18.7 Billion to Settle Deepwater Horizon Oil
Spill Claims," *WSJ*, Jul. 2.

Giridharadas, A. (2021) "Welcome to the New Progressive Era," *ATL*, Apr. 14.

Gitlin, T. (2012) *Occupy Nation: The Roots, the Spirit, and the Promise of Occupy Wall Street*,
New York: HarperCollins.

Gitlin, T. (1995) *The Twilight of Common Dreams: Why America Is Wracked by Culture Wars*,
New York: Henry Holt.

GivingUSA (2021) "Giving USA 2021 Report: Charitable Giving Trends."

Gjelten, T. (2020) "2020 Faith Vote Reflects 2016 Patterns," NPR, Nov. 8.

Glasser, S. (2017) "Trump's Alpha Male Foreign Policy," *Politico*, Feb. 27.

Glasser, S. (2021) "'Not Our Tragedy': The Taliban Are Coming Back, and America Is Still
Leaving," *New Yorker*, Aug. 12.

Glasser, S. (2022) "The Fallout from Russia's Nuclear Power Plant Attack," Comments to Michel
Martin, CNN "Amanpour," Mar. 4.

Bibliography

Goldberg, J. (2016a) "The Lessons of Henry Kissinger," *ATL*, Dec.

Goldberg, J. (2016b) "The Obama Doctrine," *ATL*, Mar.

Goldberg, J. (2017) "Political Panel Comments, on TV program 'Face the Nation,'" Jan. 22.

Goldstein, D. (2020) "Two States. Eight Textbooks. Two American Stories," *NYT*, Jan. 12.

Goodwin, D. (2006) *Team of Rivals: The Political Genius of Abraham Lincoln*, New York: Simon & Schuster.

Gordon, R. (2016) *The Rise and Fall of American Growth: The US Standard of Living Since the Civil War*, Princeton: Princeton University Press.

Gorman, A. (2021) "The Hill We Climb," *CNBC*, Jan. 20.

Graham, A, et al. (2019) "An Oral History of Trump's Bigotry," *ATL*, Jun.

Gramer, R. (2019) "State Department Vacancies Increase Embassy Security Risks, Report Warns," *Foreign Policy*, Mar. 7.

Gramlich, J. (2019) "What the Data Says about Gun Deaths in the U.S.," PRC, Aug. 16.

Gramlich, J. (2020a) "What the Data Says (and Doesn't Say) about Crime in the United States," PRC, Nov. 20.

Gramlich, J. (2020b) "Black Imprisonment Rate in the U.S. Has Fallen by a Third since 2006," PRC, May 6.

Greenhouse, L. (2001) "Justices Clarify Role on Using Race in Redistricting," *NYT*, Apr. 19.

Gross, J. (2020) "Far-Right Groups Are behind Most U.S. Terrorist Attacks, Report Finds," *NYT*, Oct. 24.

Grynbaum, M. (2017) "Trump Calls the News Media the 'Enemy of the American People,'" *NYT*, Feb. 17.

Guardian (2020) "Trump Administration Revokes Tribe's Reservation Status in 'Power Grab,'" Mar. 31.

Guardian (2021) "What's Actually in Biden's Build Back Better Bill? And How Would it Affect You?" Oct. 18.

Guarino, M. (2020) "Kyle Rittenhouse Released from Jail after Posting $2 Million Bail," *WP*, Nov. 20.

Guo, J. (2016) "The Asian American 'Advantage' That is Actually an Illusion," *WP*, Dec. 9.

Guttmacher Institute (2017) "Induced Abortion in the United States," Jan.

Haag, M. and R. Fausset (2017) "Arkansas Rushes to Execute 8 Men in the Space of 10 Days," *NYT*, Mar. 3.

Haass, R. (2017) *A World in Disarray: American Foreign Policy and the Crisis of the Old Order*, New York: Penguin.

Haass, R. (2020) *The World: A Brief Introduction*, New York: Penguin.

Haass, R. (2021) "Donald Trump's Costly Legacy," *Council of Foreign Relations*, Jan. 11.

Hanc, J. (2019) "The Military's New Retirement Option," *NYT*, Sep. 12.

Hannah-Jones, N. and *NYT* Magazine (2021) *The 1619 Project*.

Hanson, M. (2021) "U.S. Public Education Spending Statistics," Educationdata.org, Aug. 2.

Harari, Y. (2018) *21 Lessons for the 21st Century*, New York: Random House.

Harper, J. (2021) "Suez Blockage Is Holding up $9.6bn of Goods a Day," BBC, Mar. 26.

Hartman, A. (2015) *A War for the Soul of America: A History of the Culture Wars*, Chicago: University of Chicago Press.

Hartocollis, A. and Y. Alcindor (2017) "Women's March Highlights as Huge Crowds Protest Trump: 'We're Not Going Away,'" *NYT*, Jan. 21.

Harvard Kennedy School (2021a) "Youth Poll," 42nd Edition, School of Politics, Dec. 1.

Harvard. T. H. Chan School of Public Health (2021b) "Harvard Injury Control Research Center: Homicide."

HBO. Home Box Office (2021) *Four Hours at the Capitol*, HBO Documentary, Oct. 22.

Heeb, G. (2020) "The Government Has Collected an Extra $50 Billion in Tariffs since the Start of the China Trade War, According to New Data," *Business Insider*, Feb. 10.

Bibliography

Heilemann, J. (2017) "Remarks to Stephen Colbert. The Late Show with Stephen Colbert," Mar. 8.

Hemingway, E. (1935) "Notes on the Next War," *Esquire*, Sep.

Hess, A. (2019) "Graduating in 4 Years or Less Helps Keep College Costs Down—but Just 41% of Students Do," *CNBC*, Jun. 19.

HHS. Department of Health and Human Services (2021a) "HHS FY2021 Budget in Brief."

HHS. Department of Health and Human Services (2021b) "Head Start Program Facts: Fiscal Year 2019," Apr. 20.

Higgins, A. (2017) "Trump Embraces 'Enemy of the People,' a Phrase with a Fraught History," *NYT*, Feb. 26.

Hillstrom, K. (2020) "Outside Spending Reaches Record $2 Billion as Super PACs Hammer Trump," OpenSecrets,org, Oct. 19.

Hinton, E. (2017) *From the War on Poverty to the War on Crime: The Making of Mass Incarceration in America*, Cambridge, MA: Harvard University Press.

Hirschfeld-Davis, J. and M. Shear (2019) *Border Wars: Inside Trump's Assault on Immigration*, New York: Simon & Schuster.

HOF. Country Music Hall of Fame (2002) "The Rise of an Industry: Country Music Comes of Age."

Horowitz, J., A. Brown, and K. Cox (2019) "Race in America," PRC, Apr. 9.

Horowitz, J., N. Graf, and G. Livingstone (2019) "Marriage and Cohabitation in the U.S.," PRC, Nov. 6.

Horowitz, J., R. Igielnik, and R Kochar (2020) "Trends in Income and Wealth Inequality," PRC, Jan. 9.

Howard University (2019) "The Howard University Consolidated Financial Statements for Fiscal Years ended June 30, 2019 and 2018," Dec. 23.

Howard University (2020) "Howard University Receives Transformative Gift from Philanthropist MacKenzie Scott," Jul. 28.

Hrynowski, Z. (2019) "How Many Americans Believe in God?" *Gallup*.

Hsu, H. (2009) "The End of White America," *ATL*, Jan.

Hudson, J. (2021) "Biden Administration Shows Appetite for High-Profile Fights with China and Russia," *WP*, Mar. 20.

Hughes, L. (1994) "Let America Be America Again," in *The Collected Poems of Langston Hughes*, New York: Knopf.

Hulse, C. (2021) "After Success in Seating Judges, Biden Hits Resistance," *NYT*, Dec. 5.

Hunter, J. (2021) "Divided America: An Interview with James Davison Hunter," *PBS Newshour*, Nov. 26.

Huntington, S. (1996) *The Clash of Civilizations and the Remaking of the World Order*, New York: Simon & Schuster.

Huntington, S. (1999) "The Lonely Superpower," *Foreign Affairs*, Apr.

Huntington, S. (2004) *Who Are We? America's Great Divide*, New York. Free Press.

Iacurci, G. (2020) "How Much Unemployment Will I Get? That Depends on Your State," *CNBC*, Apr. 10.

icasualties (2021) "Fatalities by Year and Country," icasualtics.org, Aug.

ICPR. International Centre for Prison Research (2018) "World Prison Population List," Nov. 5.

IDEA. International Institute for Democracy and Electoral Assistance (2021) *The Global State of Democracy, 2021, Building Resilience in a Pandemic Era*, Stockholm: IDEA.

Ignatius, D. (2010) "Obama's Foreign Policy: Big Ideas, Little Implementation," *WP*, Oct. 17.

Ignatius, D. (2016) "Trump Flunks His First Foreign Policy Test," *WP*, Dec. 6.

Ignatius, D. (2021) "Opinion: Biden's First 100 Days in Foreign Policy Have Been about Undoing. Here's What Comes Next," *WP*, Apr. 28.

IIE. The Power of International Education (2019) "Number of International Students in the United States Hits All-Time High," Nov. 18.

Bibliography

IMDB. International Movie Database (2021) "Best TV Shows, 2021."

IMF. International Monetary Fund (2020) "World Economic Outlook Database," Oct.

IMF. International Monetary Fund (2021) "GDP Per Capita, Current Prices U.S. Dollars per Capita."

Ingraham, C. (2015) "There Are Now More Guns than People in the United States," *NYT*, Oct. 5.

Ingraham, C. (2019) "Nine Days on the Road. Average Commute Time Reached a New Record Last Year," *WP*, Oct. 7.

Ioffe, J. (2022) "Europe's 9/11," *Puck*, Mar. 3.

IOP. Institute for Politics. Harvard Kennedy School (2021) "Youth Poll," 42nd edn, Dec.1.

Ipsos. (2022) "Core Political Data: 'In Your Opinion, What Is the Most Important Problem Facing the US Today?'" Feb 28–Mar. 1.

Ipsos/Reuter (2021) "Majority of Republicans Still Believe the 2020 Election Was Stolen from Donald Trump," Apr. 2.

Irfan, U. (2019) "Trump's EPA Just Replaced Obama's Signature Climate Policy with a Much Weaker Rule," *Vox*, Jun. 19.

IRS. Internal Revenue Service (1964) US Federal Income Tax Brackets for Tax Year 1963.

IRS. Internal Revenue Service (2020a) "IRS Provides Tax Inflation Adjustments for Tax Year 2020," Oct. 26.

IRS. Internal Revenue Service (2020b) "US Federal Income Tax Brackets for Tax Year 2019."

Issa, E. (2022) "2021 American Household Credit Card Debt Study," *Nerdwallet*, Jan. 11.

Jamieson, A., S. Jeffery, and N. Puglise (2016) "A Timeline of Donald Trump's Alleged Sexual Misconduct: Who, When and What," *Guardian*, Oct. 27.

Janda, K., J. Berry, J. Goldman, D. Schildkraut, and P. Manna (2022) *The Challenge of Democracy: American Government in Global Politics*, 15th edn, Boston: Cengage.

Jaschic, S. (2017) "The Numbers and the Arguments on Asian Admissions," Inside Higher Ed., Aug. 7.

Jefferson, T. (1787) "Letter to Edward Carrington," *The Works of Thomas Jefferson*, vol. 5 (Correspondence 1786–1789).

Jenkins, J. (2020) "2020 Faith Vote Reflects 2016 Patterns," *America: The Jesuit Review*, Aug. 24.

Jenkins, P. (2002) "The Next Christianity," *ATL*, Oct.

Jones, J. (2021) "Biden Job Approval Steady at Lower Level," *Gallup*, Oct. 22.

Jones, N. (2021) *The 1619 Project: A New Origins Story*, London: One World.

Johnson, P. (2003) "America's New Empire for Liberty," *Hoover Digest* (4).

Jordan, G. and C. Weedon (1995) *Cultural Politics: Class, Gender, Race, and the Postmodern World*, Oxford: Blackwell.

J. P. Morgan (2020) "Research: A Breakdown of the CARES Act," Apr. 4.

Judis, J. and R. Teixeira (2002) *The Emerging Democratic Majority*, New York: Scribner.

Julian, K. (2018) "The Sex Recession," *ATL*, Dec.

Kagan, R. (2017) "Backing into World War III," *FP*, Feb. 6.

Kagan, R. (2018) *The Jungle Grows Back: America and Our Imperiled World*, New York: Knopf.

Kakutani, M. (2017) "Donald Trump's Chilling Language, and the Fearsome Power of Words," *Vanity Fair*, Jan. 21.

Kamarck, E. (2016) *Why Presidents Fail and How They Can Succeed Again*, Washington, DC: Brookings.

Kammen, M. (1987) *A Machine That Would Go By Itself: The Constitution in American Culture*, New York: Knopf.

Kanfer, S. (1995) "The Greatest Game," in M. Petracca and M. Sorapure (eds.), *Common Culture: Reading and Writing about American Popular Culture*, 380–3, Englewood Cliffs, NJ: Prentice Hall.

Kaplan, S. and K. Dennis (2021) "2021 Brought a Wave of Extreme Weather Disasters: Scientists Say Worse Lies Ahead," *WP*, Dec. 17.

Bibliography

Karl, J. (2021) *Betrayal: Final Act of the Trump Show*, New York: Dutton.

Karp, A. (2018) "Estimating Global Civilian-held Firearms Numbers," Small Arms Survey, Jun. 18.

Kaufman, S. (2015) "Why Obama's Singing of 'Amazing Grace' Is so Powerful," Jun. 26.

Kay, G. (2021) "The US Shipping Crisis Is Not Going Away as 33 Cargo Ships Float off the Coast of LA Waiting to Dock," *BI*, Jul. 26.

Keoun, B. (2012) "A Shortage of Bonds to Back Derivative Debts," *Businessweek*, Sep. 20.

Kessler, G. (2020) "The 'Very Fine People' at Charlottesville: Who Were They?" *WP*, May 8.

Kiersz, A., I. De Luce, and M. Hoff (2020) "This Map Shows the Most Commonly Spoken Language in Every State," *BI*, Aug. 12.

King, M. (1963) *Why We Can't Wait*, New York: Mentor.

Klein, E. (2022) "Elon Musk Got Twitter because He Gets Twitter," *NYT*, Apr. 27.

Knowlton, B. (1999) "Wired World Leaves Millions Out of Loop," *IHT*, Oct. 9.

Knowlton, B. (2001) "Bush Says He Wants bin Laden Brought to Justice 'Dead or Alive,'" *IHT*, Sep. 18.

Koba, M. (2012) "CNBC Explains: Dodd-Frank Act," *CNBC*, May 11.

Koerth, M. and A. Thomson-DeVeaux (2020) "Many Americans Are Convinced Crime Is Rising in the U.S. They're Wrong." *FiveThirtyEight*, Aug. 3.

Koppelin, Z. (2014) "Was Moses a Founding Father?" *ATL*, Nov. 25.

Korb, L. (2000) "Defense," Council on Foreign Relations.

Kornacki, S. (2018) *The Red and The Blue: The 1990s and the Birth of Political Tribalism*, New York: Echo Press.

Kramer, S. (2019) "U.S. Has World's Highest Rate of Children Living in Single-Parent Households," PRC, Dec. 12.

Krogstad, J., M. Lopez, and J Passel (2020) "A Majority of Americans Say Immigrants Mostly Fill Jobs U.S. Citizens Do Not Want," *Pew*, Jun. 10.

Krugman, P. (2021) *Arguing with Zombies: Economics, Politics, and the Fight for a Better Future*, New York: W. W. Norton.

Krugman, P. (2004) "The Death of Horatio Alger," *The Nation*, Jan. 5.

Kurtz, H. (1998) *Spin Cycle: How the White House and the Media Manipulate the News*, New York: Simon & Schuster.

Lakewood (2021) "About."

Lamb, C. (2021) "Chronicles of a Defeat Foretold: Why America Failed in Afghanistan," *Foreign Affairs*, Jul./Aug.

Landler, M. (2017) "Trump Foreign Policy Quickly Loses Its Sharp Edge," *NYT*, Feb. 10.

Landler, M., K. Bennhold, and M. Stevis-Gridnef (2022) "How the West Marshaled a Stunning Show against Russia," *NYT*, Mar. 5.

Law.gov (2008) "United States: Gun Ownership and the Supreme Court," Library of Congress.

Lee, M. (2020) "Gen Z, Millennial Voters Embrace Activism and Voting, as Youth Turnout Surges Ahead of Election Day," *WP*, Oct. 29.

Leip, D. (2021) *Atlas of US Presidential Elections*.

Levine, A. and M. Funakoshi (2020) "Most Expensive Ever: 2020 Election Cost $14.4 Billion," *Reuters*, Nov. 24.

Levine, P. and R. McKnight (2020) "Three Million More Guns: The Spring 2020 Spike in Firearm Sales," *Brookings*, Jul. 17.

Levine, P. and H. Papasotiriou (2010) *America since 1945: The American Moment*, Basingstoke: Palgrave Macmillan.

Levitsky, A. and M. Ziblatt (2019) *How Democracies Die: What History Reveals about Our Future*, New York: Penguin.

Lewis, J. (1998) *Walking with the Wind: A Memoir of the Movement*, New York: Simon & Schuster.

Bibliography

Lewis, M. (2008) "After the Art Wars," *Commentary*, Jan.

Lifton, R. (2003) "American Apocalypse," *The Nation*, Dec. 22.

Lilly Endowment, Inc. (2021) "Education and Youth Programs."

Lind, D. (2018) "Sanctuary Cities, Explained," *Vox*, Mar. 8.

Lindsay, J. (2020) "The 2020 Election by the Numbers," *Council on Foreign Relations*, Dec. 15.

Lipka, M. (2017) "Muslims and Islam: Key Findings in the U.S. and Around the World," PRC, Aug. 9.

Liptak, A. (2018) "Supreme Court Avoids an Answer on Partisan Gerrymandering," *NYT*, Jun. 18.

Liptak, A. (2019) "Rancor and Raw Emotion Surface in Supreme Court Death Penalty Ruling," *NYT*, Apr. 1.

Liptak, A (2020a) "Supreme Court Won't Block Ruling to Halt Work on Keystone XL Pipeline," *NYT*, Jul. 6.

Liptak, A. (2020b) "Supreme Court Strikes Down Louisiana Abortion Law, with Roberts the Deciding Vote," *NYT*, Jun. 29.

Liptak, A. (2021) "Supreme Court to Hear Abortion Case Challenging Roe v. Wade," *NYT*, May 17.

Liptak, A. and A. Parlapiano (2020) "The Supreme Court Aligned with Public Opinion in Most Major Cases This Term," *NYT*, Jul. 9.

Liptak, K. and K. Sullivan (2021) "NATO Leaders at Summit Back Biden's Decision to Pull Troops out of Afghanistan, CNN, Jun. 14.

Livingstone, G. (2018) "The Changing Profile of Unmarried Parents," PRC, Apr. 25.

Lynch, D. (2021) "Biden Keeps Many Trump Tariffs in Place, Confounding Businesses Hoping for Reprieve," *WP*, Aug. 17.

M-Live (2016) "Flint News: How the Flint Water Crisis Emerged," Jan. 17.

MacFound (2021) "John D. and Catherine T. MacArthur Foundation: Financials," https://www.macfound.org/about/financials/.

MacGillis, A. (2022) *Fulfillment: America in the Shadow of Amazon*, New York: Picador.

MagazineLine (2021) "The Most Popular Magazines of 2020."

Mahshie, A. (2020) "Trump Echoes Reagan and Nixon in Law-and-Order Tack," *Washington Examiner*, Jun. 5.

Mak, T. (2020) "New York Attorney General Moves to Dissolve the NRA after Fraud Investigation," NPR, Aug. 6.

Malkasian, C. (2021) *The American War in Afghanistan: A History*, Oxford: Oxford University Press.

Malloy, A. (2021) "Obama Breaks Ground on Presidential Library in Chicago," CNN, Sep. 28.

Manjoo, F. (2016) "Social Media's Globe-Shaking Power," *NYT*, Nov. 16.

Manjoo, F. (2021) "The Year America Lost Its Democracy," *NYT*, Dec. 8.

Marikar, S. (2019) "You Won't Find Your Self-Worth on Instagram," *NYT*, Nov. 2.

Maruschak, L., and T. Minton (2020) "Correctional Populations in the United States, 2017–2018," US Dept. of Justice, *NCJ* 252157, Aug.

Mascaro, L. and M. Daly (2020) "Biden Seeks Swift Cabinet Votes, but GOP Senate Stays Silent, AP, Nov. 24.

Masci, D., B. Mohamed, and G. Smith (2018) "Black Americans Are More Likely than Overall Public to Be Christian, Protestant," PRC, Apr. 23.

Mashal, M. and F. Abed (2017) "'Mother of All Bombs' Killed Dozens of Militants, Afghan Officials Say," *NYT*, Apr. 14.

Mayer, J. (2008) *The Dark Side: The Inside Story of How the War on Terror Turned into a War on American Ideals*, New York: Doubleday.

Mayer, J. (2016) *Dark Money: The Hidden History of the Billionaires Behind the Rise of the Radical Right*, New York: Doubleday.

Bibliography

McBride, J, and A. Siripurapu (2021) "Backgrounder: The National Debt Dilemma," Oct. 1.

McCain, J. (2017) "Interview," Meet the Press with Chuck Todd, Feb. 19.

McCann, A. and T. Johnson (2022) "Where Abortion Could Be Banned without Roe v. Wade," *NYT*, May 3.

McCarthy, J. (2018) "Americans Still More Trusting of Local than State Government," *Gallup*, Oct. 8.

McCrummen, S. (2021) "An American Kingdom," *WP*, Jul. 11.

McElwee, S. (2015) "Why Non-Voters Matter," *ATL*, Sep. 15.

McGlone, P. (2021) "Biden Vows His Support for the 'Critical Role' the Arts Play in America," *WP*, Jun. 4.

McGreal, C. (2018) *American Overdose: The Opioid Tragedy in Three Acts*, New York: Public Affairs.

McGrew, A., ed. (2000) *The United States in the Twentieth Century*, London: Hodder & Stoughton.

McIntosh, K., E. Moss, R. Nunn, and J. Shambaugh (2020) "Examining the Black-White Wealth Gap," Brookings Institution, Feb. 22.

McKay, B. (2018) "U.S. Life Expectancy Falls Further," *WSJ*, Nov. 29.

McKenzie, R. (2021) *We the Fallen People: The Founders and the Future of American Democracy*, Westmount, IL: IVP Academic.

McMaster, H. and G. Cohn. (2017) "America First Doesn't Mean America Alone," *WSJ*, May 30.

McNulty-Finn, C. (2014) "The Evolution of Rap," *Harvard Political Review*, Apr. 10.

McPherson, J. (1982) *Ordeal by Fire: The Civil War and Reconstruction*, New York: Knopf.

Meacham, J. (2018) *The Soul of America: The Battle for Our Better Angels*, New York: Random House.

Meckler, L. and H. Natanson (2021) "As Schools Expand Racial Equity Work, Conservatives See a New Threat in Critical Race Theory," *WP*, May 3.

Memmott, M. (2012) "Only 'A Good Guy with a Gun' Can Stop School Shootings, NRA Says," NPR, Dec. 21.

Menand, L. (2019) "Is Meritocracy Making Everyone Miserable?" *New Yorker*, Sep. 30.

Mervosh, S. (2019) "Gun Ownership Rates Tied to Domestic Homicides, but Not Other Killings, Study Finds," *NYT*, Jul. 22.

Mesch, G. (2009) "The Internet and Youth Culture," *The Hedgehog Review* (11:1, Spring): 50–60.

Meyer, R. (2016) "Obama Abandons Plan to Drill in the Atlantic Ocean," *ATL*, Mar. 16.

Michel, C. (2022) "Vladimir Putin's Empire of Delusions," *New Republic*, Feb. 22.

Milbank, D. (2022) "How Fox News and Republican Officials Devised One Biden Smear," Jan. 22.

Milkis, S. and M. Nelson (2019) *The American Presidency: Origins and Development*, 1776–2014, Los Angeles: Sage.

Miller, C. and Bui, Q. (2016) "Equality Grows, and So Does Class Divide," *NYT*, Feb. 27.

Montellaro, Z. (2020) "Georgia Senate Candidates Raise a Record-Smashing Amount of Money, *Politico*, Dec. 28.

Morgan, E. (1995) *American Slavery, American Freedom: The Ordeal of Colonial Virginia*, New York: W. W. Norton.

Mounk, Y. (2019) *The People Versus Democracy: Why Our Freedom Is in Danger and How to Save It*, Cambridge, MA: Harvard University Press.

Mounk, Y. (2022) *The Great Experiment: Why Diverse Democracies Fall Apart and How They Can Endure*, London: Penguin.

MPAA. Motion Picture Association of America (2017) "Global Box Office Remains Strong in 2016, Reaching $38.6 Billion," Mar. 22.

MPAA. Motion Picture Association of America (2021) "Theme Report 2020."

MPI. Migration Policy Institute (2020) "Top 25 Destinations of International Migrants."

Bibliography

Müller, J. (2016) *What Is Populism?* Philadelphia: University of Pennsylvania Press.

Murdock, J. (2021) "Why Joe Biden Has Millions Fewer Twitter Followers than Trump Did One Month into Office," *Newsweek*, Feb. 22.

Myers, S. (2021) "Testy Exchange in Alaska," *NYT*, Mar. 19.

NAFSA. Association of International Educators (2016) "Trends in U.S. Study Abroad."

Nagl, J. (2012) "The Age of Unsatisfying Wars," *NYT*, Jun. 6.

NAM. National Association of Manufacturers (2016) "Advocacy Programs."

NASA. National Aeronautics and Space Administration (2020a) "2019 Was the Second Warmest Year on Record," Jan. 16.

NASA. National Aeronautics and Space Administration (2020b) "Mars 2020 Mission Overview."

NASA. National Aeronautics and Space Administration (2020c) "New NASA Partnerships to Mature Commercial Space Technologies, Capabilities," 20–113.

NASA. National Aeronautics and Space Administration (2021) "60 years and Counting: Human Spaceflight."

Nash, E. and J. Dreweke (2019) "The U.S. Abortion Rate Continues to Drop: Once Again, State Abortion Restrictions Are Not the Main Driver," Guttmacher Institute, Sep. 18.

Native Partnership (2021) "Living Conditions."

NATO. North Atlantic Treaty Organization (2016) "Defense Expenditures of NATO Countries (2009–2016)," Graph 2 and Table 2, Jul. 4.

NCAC. National Coalition Against Censorship (2022) Homepage.

NCAI. National Congress of American Indians (2020) "Language."

NCAI. National Congress of American Indians (2021) "Veterans."

NCES. National Center for Education Statistics (2016a) "Digest of Educational Statistics – Figure 1."

NCES. National Center for Education Statistics (2016b) "Fast Facts."

NCES. National Center for Education Statistics (2018) "Digest of Educational Statistics," Table 318.30, Sep.

NCES. National Center for Education Statistics (2019a) "Status and Trends in the Education of Racial and Ethnic Groups: Indicator 3–Children's Living Arrangements," Feb.

NCES: National Center for Education Statistics (2019b) "Status and Trends in the Education of Racial and Ethnic Groups,"Indicator 27: Educational Achievement," Feb.

NCES. National Center for Education Statistics (2019c) "Digest of Education Statistics 2018," (Ch. 3. Postsecondary Education).

NCES. National Center for Education Statistics (2020a) "Condition of Education: Racial/Ethnic Enrollment in Public Schools," May.

NCES. National Center for Education Statistics (2020b) "Common Core of Data: America's Public Schools," Table 1.

NCES. National Center for Educational Statistics (2020c) "Digest of Education Statistics 2019," Table 104.20

NCES. National Center for Education Statistics (2021a) "Condition of Education: English Language Learners in Public Schools," May.

NCES. National Center for Education Statistics (2021b) "Graduate Degree Fields," May.

NCSL. National Conference of State Legislatures (2016) "Federal and State Recognized Tribes," Oct.

NCSL. National Conference of State Legislatures (2017) "State Minimum Wages 2017 by State," May 1.

NCSL. National Conference of State Legislatures (2020a) "Self Defense and "Stand Your Ground," May 26.

NCSL. National Conference of State Legislatures (2020b) "The Term Limited States," Mar. 13.

NCSL. National Conference of State Legislatures (2021a) "Full and Part Time Legislatures." Aug. 7.

NCSL. National Conference of State Legislatures (2021b) "Felon Voting Rights," Jun. 28.

Bibliography

NEA. National Endowment for the Arts (2021) "NEA 2021 Guide."

Nelson, C. (2017) "Moving Away from Data Invisibility at Tribal Colleges and Universities," American Council on Education, Nov. 20.

Nelson, M. (2019) *Trump: The First Two Years*, Charlottesville, VA: University of Virginia Press.

Nelson, S. (2020) "White, Male and Conservative: Trump's Damaging Legal Legacy," *USA Today*, Mar. 7.

Neustadt, R. (1990) *Presidential Power: The Politics of Leadership from Roosevelt to Reagan*, New York: Free Press.

Newport, F. (2016) "Most Americans Still Believe in God?" *Gallup*, Jun. 29.

Newport, F. (2020) "American Attitudes and Race," *Gallup*, Jun. 17.

Nichols, T. (2017) *The Death of Expertise: The Campaign against Established Knowledge and Why It Matters*, New York: Oxford University Press.

NIGC. National Indian Gaming Commission (2020) "FY14–FY18: Gaming Revenues by Range."

Nobel Prize.org (2020) "Nobel Prizes 2020."

NPR (2009) "46 Million Uninsured: A Look behind the Numbers," Aug. 21.

NPR (2010) "Do You Believe In Miracles? Most Americans Do," Feb. 23.

NPR (2013) "Post Afghan Mission, How Many Troops Will Stay There," Jan. 10.

NPR (2016) "In Commencement Speech, Obama Advises Howard University Grads on Creating Change," May 7.

NPR (2021) "Whistleblower's Testimony has Resurfaced Meta's Instagram Problem," Oct. 21.

NPS. National Park Service (2022) "About Us," Dec. 16.

NRA. National Rifle Association (2022a) "A Brief History of the NRA."

NRDC. Natural Resources Defense Council (2021) "About."

NSC. The National Safety Council (2021) "About the National Safety Council."

NSF. National Science Federation (2018) "Science and Engineering Labor Force: Immigration and the S&E Workforce." Jan.

Nye, J. (2015) *Is the American Century Over?* New York: Polity.

Nye, J. (2005) *Soft Power: The Means to Success in World Politics*, New York: Public Affairs.

NYT (2016) "Transcript: Donald Trump's Taped Comments about Women," Oct. 8.

NYT (2020) "National Exit Polls: How Different Groups Voted."

NYT. Editorial Board (2021) "Postcards of a World on Fire," *NYT*, Dec. 18.

Obama, B. (2004) "A More Perfect Union," Jul. 27.

Obama, B. (2009a) "Address to Congress," Feb. 24.

Obama, B. (2009b) "Inaugural Address by Barack Obama," *NYT*, Jan. 20.

Obama, B. (2010) "Remarks by the President at Signing of Dodd-Frank Wall Street Reform and Consumer Protection Act," *The White House – President Barack Obama*, Jul. 21.

Obama, B. (2012) "Transcript of President Obama's Election Night Speech," *NYT*, Nov. 7.

Obama, B. (2016a) "Barack Obama: Now Is the Greatest Time to Be Alive," *Wired*, Oct. 12.

Obama, B. (2016b) "Remarks of President Barack Obama – State of the Union Address as Delivered," *The White House – President Barack Obama*, Jan. 13.

Obama, B. (2020) *A Promised Land*, New York: Generic.

Odoom, L. (2021) "The Singer behind the World's Greatest Song Has Released a Great Sour Youth Work," *Politiken*, Jun. 1.

OECD. Organization for Economic Cooperation and Development (2018a) "Statistics and Data Directorate: Inequalities in Household Wealth across OECD Countries: Evidence from the OECD Wealth Distribution Database," Working Paper 88, Jun. 20.

OECD. Organization for Economic Cooperation and Development (2018b) "Pisa 2018 Results: Snapshot of Student Performance in Reading, Writing, and Arithmetic."

OECD. Organization for Economic Cooperation and Development (2021a) "Income Inequality (Indicator). DOI: 10.1787/459aa7f1-en.

Bibliography

OECD. Organization for Economic Cooperation and Development (2021b) "Employment Rate-Q3."

O'Hanlon, M. (2019) "Can America Still Protect Its Allies," *Foreign Affairs*, Sep./Oct.

Oliphant J. (2018) "Public Support for the Death Penalty Ticks up," PRC, Jun. 11.

Olson, E. (1998) "UN Report Assails US Death Penalty," *IHT*, Apr. 8.

OpenSecrets.org Campaign for Responsive Politics (2020a) "2020 Election to Cost $14 Billion, Blowing away Spending Records," Oct. 28.

OpenSecrets.org Campaign for Responsive Politics (2020b) "Small Donor Donations as a Percentage of Total Fundraising, Current Candidates Only," Oct. 22.

OpenSecrets.org Campaign for Responsive Politics (2021a) "AFL-CIO: Outside Spending Summary 2020," updated Oct. 29.

OpenSecrets.org Campaign for Responsive Politics (2021b) "American Federation of Teachers," updated Mar. 22.

OpenSecrets.org Campaign for Responsive Politics (2021c) "National Association of Manufacturers," updated Mar. 22.

Oppel, R. (2002) "Bush Extols Military Service and Expedites Citizenship," *NYT*, Jul. 5.

OPS. Office of the Press Secretary (2004) "President Bush Meets with Michigan Judicial Nominees," Jul. 7.

Orenstein, J. (2016) *Girls and Sex: Navigating the Complicated New Landscape*, New York: Harper.

Osnos, E. (2014) *Age of Ambition: Chasing, Fortune, Truth and Faith in the New China*, London: Bodley Head.

Osnos, E. (2021) *Wildland: The Making of America's Fury*, New York: Gerard, Straus, & Giroux.

Otterson, J. (2017) "Fox News Pulls Judge Andrew Napolitano over Trump Wiretap Claims," *Variety*, Mar. 20.

Overby, P (2012) "NRA: 'Only Thing That Stops a Bad Guy with a Gun Is a Good Guy with a Gun,'" NPR, Dec. 21.

Packer, G. (2013) *The Unwinding: Thirty Years of American Decline*, London: Faber & Faber.

Packer, G. (2014) *The Unwinding: An Inner History of the New America*, New York: Gerard, Straus, & Giroux.

Packer, G. (2021) *The Last Best Hope: America in Crisis and Renewal*, New York: Gerard, Straus, & Giroux.

Paik, N. (2020) *Bans, Walls, Raids, Sanctuary: Understanding U.S. Immigration for the Twenty-First Century*, Los Angeles: University of California Press.

Palazzolo, J., N. Hong, M. Rottfeld, R. O'Brian, and R. Bullhaus (2018) "Donald Trump Played Central Role in Hush Payoffs to Stormy Daniels and Karen McDougal," *WSJ*, Nov. 9.

Parker, K., N. Graf, and R. Igielnik (2019) PRC, Jan. 17.

PBS. Public Broadcasting System (2017) "PBS Newshour," Feb. 2.

PBS. Public Broadcasting System (2021) "What Lil Nas X's 'Montero' Says about Black Queerness," Apr. 1.

Peace Corps (2019) "Fast Facts," Sep. 30.

Pearce, M. (2020) "Trump and Biden on Guns: Far Apart on Policy and Perspective," *LAT*, Aug. 19.

Peele, G., C. Bailey, B. Cain, G. Peters, and J. Herbert, eds. (2018) *Developments in American Politics 8*, Basingstoke: Palgrave Macmillan.

Pells, R. (2012) *Modernist America*, New Haven: Yale University Press.

Pells, R. (2000) "Who's Afraid of Steven Spielberg," *Diplomatic History*, 24:3, 495–502.

Peters, C. (2019) *We Do Our Part: Toward a Fairer and More Equal America*, New York: Random House.

Pew (2015a) "2014 Religious Landscape Study," Nov. 20.

Pew (2015b) "U.S. Public Becoming Less Religious," Nov. 13.

Pew (2015c) "Social Trends 2015."

Pew (2016) "6 Takeaways about How Parents Monitor Their Teen's Digital Activities," Jan. 7.
Pew (2017a) "Americans Say Religious Aspects of Christmas Are Declining in Public Life," Dec. 12.
Pew (2017b) "Digital Divide Persists even as Lower Income Americans Make Gains in Tech Adoption," Mar. 22.
Pew (2018a) "Teens' Social Media Habits and Experiences," Nov. 28.
Pew (2018b) "Public Support for the Death Penalty Ticks up: Gender, Racial Differences in Opinions about the Death Penalty," Jun. 8.
Pew (2018c) "When Americans Say They Believe in God, What Do They Mean?" Apr. 25.
Pew (2018d) "Muslims in America: Immigrants and Those Born in U.S. See Life Differently in Many Ways," Apr. 17.
Pew (2019a) "In U.S., Decline of Christianity Continues at Rapid Pace," Oct. 17.
Pew (2019b) "Two Decades of Change in Federal and State Higher Education Funding," Oct. 15.
Pew (2019c) "Political Independents: Who They Are, What They Think," Mar. 14.
Pew (2020) "Americans' Views of Government: Low Trust, but Some Positive Performance Ratings," Sep. 14.
Pew (2021a) "Few Americans Blame God or Say Faith Has Been Shaken Amid Pandemic, Other Tragedies," Nov. 23.
Pew (2021b) "News Consumption across Social Media in 2021," Sep. 20.
Pew (2021c) "Newspapers: Fact Sheet," Jun. 29, https://www.pewresearch.org/journalism/fact-sheet/newspapers/.
Pew (2021d) "A Third of Large U.S. Newspapers Experienced Layoffs in 2020, More Than in 2019," May 21.
Pew (2021e) "Public Trust in Government: 1958–2021," PRC, May 17.
Picchi, A. (2021) "Amazon Boosts Average Starting Pay to $18 an Hour for 125,000 New Hires," *CBS News*, Sep. 14.
Piketty, T. (2014) *Capital in the Twenty-First Century*, Cambridge, MA: Belknap Press of Harvard University Press.
Pinsker, J. (2019) "Why Are American Homes So Big?" *ATL*, Sep. 12.
Pohl, F. (2017) *Framing America: A Social History of American Art*, 4th edn, 2 vols., London: Thames & Hudson.
Pottinger, M. and D. Feith (2021) "The Most Powerful Data Broker in the World is Winning the War against the US," *NYT*, Dec. 1.
Powers, R. (2018) *The Overstory: A Novel*, New York: W. W. Norton.
Powers, T. (2003) "The Vanishing Case for War," *NYRB*, Dec. 4.
PPF. Planned Parenthood Foundation (2021) "Mission Statement."
PRB. Population Reference Bureau (2019) "Fact Sheet: Aging in the United States," Jul. 15.
Pressman, S. (2018) "New Data Paint an Unpleasant Picture of Poverty in the US," *The Conversation*, Sep. 12.
PRRI. Public Religion Research Institute (2021) "Competing Visions of America: An Evolving Identity or a Culture Under Attack? Findings from the 2021 American Values Survey," Nov. 1.
Putnam, R. (2000) *Bowling Alone: The Collapse and Revival of American Community*, New York: Simon & Schuster.
Putnam, R. (2015) *Our Kids: The American Dream in Crisis*, New York: Simon & Schuster.
Quintana, C. (2018) "With $1.8-Billion Gift to Johns Hopkins, Michael Bloomberg Sends a Message on Affordability," *The Chronicle*, Nov. 18.
Rabin, R. and T. Arango (2022) "Gun Deaths Surged During the Pandemic's First Year, the C.D.D Reports," WP, 10 May.
Rapinoe, M. (2020) *One Life*, London: Penguin.
Rauch, J. (2021) The Constitution of Knowledge: A Defense of Truth, Washington, DC: Brookings.

Bibliography

Ray, R. and J. Schmitt (2017) "No-Vacation Nation USA – A Comparison of Leave and Holiday in OECD Countries," European Economic and Policy Brief (3:2007).

Reagan, R. (1989) "Farewell Address," *Congressional Quarterly Weekly Report*, Jan. 14, 95–7.

RealtyTrac (2017) "US Real Estate Statistics & Foreclosure Trends Summary," Jan.

Reeves, R. (2017) *Dream Hoarders: How the American Upper Middle Class Is Leaving Everyone Else in the Dust, and What to Do about It*, Washington, DC: Brookings.

Reiley, L. (2020) "Anti-Hunger Groups Call on Biden to Reverse Some of Trump's Signature Initiatives," *WP*, Nov. 13.

Remnick, D. (2010) *The Bridge: The Life and Rise of Barack Obama*, New York: Vintage.

Renshaw, J., A. Shalal, and M. Martina (2021) "Biden Says China Won't Surpass U.S. as Global Leader on His Watch," *Reuters*, Mar. 25.

Reuters (2020a) "China to Leapfrog US as World's Biggest Economy by 2028 – Think Tank," Dec. 26.

Reuters (2020b) "Hong Kong Launches WTO Trade Dispute against U.S. over Labelling," Nov. 3.

Revesz, R. (2017) "Steve Bannon Says Media Should 'Keep Its Mouth Shut' after It Was 'Humiliated' by Surprising Election Result," *Independent*, Jan. 26.

Robertson, N. (2019) "Leaders Learn the Hard Way That Trump will be Trump at NATO Meetings," CNN, Dec. 19.

Robinson, E. (2008) "A Victory for the Rule of Law," *WP*, Jun. 13.

Rolling Stone (2012) "Madonna Performs 'Gangnam Style' with Psy in New York," *Rolling Stone*, Nov. 14.

Romm, T. and A. Chiu (2020) "Twitter Flags Trump for 'Glorifying Violence' after He Says Minneapolis Looting Will Lead to Shooting,'" *NYT*, May 29.

Roosevelt, F. (1941) "State of the Union Address," National Archives, Jan. 6.

Rose, G. (2019) "The Fourth Founding: The United States and the Liberal Order," *Foreign Affairs*, Feb.

Rosenbaum, D. (2005) "Bush to Return to 'Ownership Society' Theme in Push for Social Security Changes," *NYT*, Jan. 16.

Rosenbaum, D. and B. Keith Jennings (2019) "SNAP Caseload and Spending Declines Have Accelerated in Recent Years," Center on Budget Policy and Priorities, Jun. 6.

Rosenthal, S. and T. Burke (2020) "TaxVox: Business Taxes," Tax Policy Center, Oct. 20.

Rothaker, R. and D. Ingram (2012) "Wells Fargo to Pay $175 Million in Race Discrimination Probe," *Reuters*, Jul. 3.

Rubin, R. (2017) "Next Tax Battle: Trump's Bid to Ax a Favorite Blue State Deduction," *WSJ*, Apr. 27.

Rucker, P. (2017) "To Trump, the Russia Matter Is a 'Cloud' that Hangs over His Presidency," *WP*, Jun. 7.

Rucker, P. and C. Leonnig (2020) *A Very Stable Genius: Donald J. Trump and the Testing of America*, London: Bloomsbury.

Ruiz, V. (2008) *Unequal Sisters: An Inclusive Reader in U.S. Women's History*, 4th edn, London: Routledge.

Saad, L. (2019) "Americans' Views on Trade in the Trump Era," Oct. 25.

Saad, L. (2021) "Americans' Political Ideology Held Steady in 2020," *Gallup*, Jan. 11.

Safire, W. (1978) *Safire's Political Dictionary*, New York: Random House.

Sales, N. (2016) *American Girls: Social Media and the Secret Lives of Teenagers*, New York: Knopf.

Sandel, M. (2010) *Justice: What's the Right Thing To Do?*, New York: Farrar, Straus, Giroux.

Sandel, M. (2020) *The Tyranny of Merit: What's Become of the Common Good?*, New York: Allen Lane.

Sanger, D. (2012) *Confront and Conceal: Obama's Secret Wars and the Surprising Use of American Power*, New York: Random House.

Bibliography

Sanger, D. (2013) "A New Cold War in Cyberspace, Tests US Ties to China," *NYT*, Feb. 24.

Sanger, D. and M. Crowley (2021) "As Biden and Xi Begin a Careful Dance, a New American Policy Takes Shape," *NYT*, Mar. 17.

Santayana, G. (1905) *The Life of Reason*, vol. 1.

Savage, D. (2019) "Supreme Court Says the Constitution Does Not Ensure a 'Painless' Execution," *LAT*, Apr. 1.

Schatz, A. and B. Kendall (2012) "Indecency Fines Tossed Out," *WSJ*, Jun. 21.

Schlesinger, Jr. A. (2003) "Eyeless in Iraq," *NYRB*, Oct. 23.

Schlosser, E. (2001) *Fast-Food Nation: The Dark Side of the All-American Meal*, Boston: Houghton Mifflin.

Schmemann, S. (2003) "'Of Paradise and Power: The Divergence Thesis," *NYT*, Mar. 30.

Schneider, M. (2020) "Gay Marriages Rise 5 years after Supreme Court Ruling," *ABC*, Sep. 17.

Schomer, A. (2021) "US Adults Will Consume almost as Much Media in 2021, but TV Viewing Will Backslide," Insider Intelligence, Jun. 6.

Schrank, J. (1995) "Sport and the American Dream," in M. Petracca and M. Sorapure (eds.), *Common Culture: Reading and Writing about American Popular Culture*, 358–61, Englewood Cliffs, NJ: Random House.

Schwab, K. (2019) "The Global Competitiveness Report 2019," World Economic Forum.

Schwenninger, S. (2004) "America's Suez Moment," *ATL*, Jan.

ScienceDaily (2016) "Costs of US Prescription Opioid Epidemic Estimated at $78. 5 Billion," Sep. 14.

Semega, J. (2019) "Pay is Up. Poverty is Down. How Women are Making Strides," USCB, Sep. 10.

Sengupta, S. (2019) "Protesting Climate Change, Young People Take to Streets in a Global Strike, *NYT*, Sep. 20.

Serwer, A. (2017) "Can Trump Bring Back Torture?" *ATL*, Jan. 26.

Shambaugh, D. (2016) *China's Future?*, Cambridge: Polity Press.

Shear, M. and Y. Alcindor (2017) "Jolted by Deaths, Obama Found His Voice on Race," *NYT*, Jan. 14.

Shearer, E (2021) "More than Eight-in-Ten Americans Get News from Digital Devices," PRC, Jan. 12.

Sheridan, M. and C. Lynch (2010) "Obama Administration Discloses Size of US Nuclear Arsenal," *WP*, May 4.

Sheth, S., M. Hoff, M. Ward, and T. Tyson (2021) "These 8 Charts Show the Glaring Gap between Men's and Women's Salaries in the US," *BI*, Mar. 24.

Shubber, K. (2020) "How Trump Has Already Transformed America's Courts," *FT*, Sep. 25.

Shultz, G. (2017) Interview with John Dickerson, CBS, "Face the Nation," Mar. 26.

Silver, L. (2021) "Amid Pandemic, International Student Enrollment at U.S. Universities Fell 15% in the 2020–21 School Year," PRC, Dec. 21.

Silver Ring Thing (2017) "About Us."

Silverstein, J. (2021) "The 1619 Project and the Long Battle over U.S. History," *NYT*, Nov. 9.

Singer, P. (2012) "Washington's Think-Tanks: Factories to Call Our Own," *Brookings*, Washington, DC, Aug.

Singh, A., J. Skerrett, and R. Hogan, eds. (1994) *Memory, Narrative and Identity: New Essays in Ethnic American Literature*, Boston: Northeastern University Press.

Skowronek, S. (2011) *Presidential Leadership in Political Time: Reprise and Reappraisal*. Lawrence: University Press of Kansas, 145–46 and Chapter 5.

Smith, W. (2016) "Will Smith: Racism is Not Getting Worse, It Is Getting Filmed," *The Late Show with Stephen Colbert*, Aug. 3.

Snyder, T. (2017) *On Tyranny: Twenty Lessons from the Twentieth Century*, London: Penguin Random House.

Bibliography

Snyder, T. (2021) "The War on History is a War on Democracy," *NYT*, Jun. 29.

Spector, M. (2020) "U.S. States Seek $2.2 Trillion from OxyContin Maker Purdue Pharma: Filings," *Reuters*, Aug. 17.

Spencer H. and M. Stevens (2017) "23 Arrested and Tear Gas Deployed After a K.K.K. Rally in Virginia," *NYT*, Jul. 8.

Sperling, N. (2021) "Sundance Film Festival Unveils 2022 Lineup That Reflects Age of Reckoning," *NYT*, Dec. 10.

SPLC. Southern Poverty Law Center (2021) "SPLC Reports Over 160 Confederate Symbols Removed in 2020," Feb. 23.

SSA. Social Security Administration (2015) "Education and Lifetime Earnings," Nov.

SSA. Social Security Administration (2020) "Factsheet." Jul.

SSA. Social Security Administration (2021) "Cost of Living Adjustment."

Stalley, O., A. Ossola, K. Palmer, M. Bain, A. Epstein, and A. Campoy (2020) "What We Know about Biden's First-Day Checklist," *Quartz*, Nov. 7.

Statista. The Statistics Portal (2020) "Mean Earnings in the United States in 2020, by Highest Educational Degree Earned and Gender."

Statista. The Statistics Portal (2021a) "Public Debt of the United States of America from November 2020 to November 2021, by Month," Dec. 8.

Statista. The Statistics Portal (2021b) "Movies Released in North America, 2000–2020," Nov. 17.

Statista. The Statistics Portal (2021c) "U.S. Trade – Statistics & Facts," Oct. 13.

Statista. The Statistics Portal (2021d) "US Book Industry: Statistics and Facts," Sep. 10.

Statista. The Statistics Portal (2021e) "Leading 15 Trade Partners with the United States in 2020, by Country," Mar. 24.

Statista. The Statistics Portal (2021f) "Total Value of U.S. Trade in Goods Worldwide 2004–2020," Mar. 10.

Statista. The Statistics Portal (2021g) "US Magazine Industry, Statistics and Facts," Feb. 18.

Statista. The Statistics Portal (2021h) "Leading Countries Based on Meta Audience Size, January 2021," Feb.

Statista. The Statistics Portal (2021i) "Number of Monthly Active Meta Users Worldwide as of 2nd Quarter 2021."

Stracqualursi, V. (2020) "Rep. Ilhan Omar on Trump's Racist Attack: 'He Spreads the Disease of Hate,'" CNN, Sep. 23.

Strauss, D. (2020) "Hidden Joblessness Threatens Economic Recovery in US and Europe," *FT*, Oct. 7.

Stebbins, S. (2020) "Which States in the US Have the Highest Tax Burdens? Many Can Be Found in North, Northeast," *USA Today*, Apr. 19.

Stebbins, S. and E. Comen (2020) "How Much Do You Need to Make to Be in the Top 1% in Every State? Here's the List," *USA Today*, Jul. 1.

Steinberg, J. and M. O'Hanlon (2014) *Strategic Reassurance and Resolve: US-China Relations in the 21st Century*, Princeton: Princeton University Press.

Steingart, G. (2009) "The New American Feeling," *Der Spiegel Online*, Jan. 21.

Stewart, K. (2020) *The Power Worshippers: Inside the Dangerous Rise of Religious Nationalism*, London: Bloomsbury.

Stiglitz, J. (2012) "Of the 1%, by the 1%, for the 1%," *Vanity Fair*, May 31.

Stiglitz, J. (2015) *The Great Divide: Unequal Societies and What We Can Do about Them*, New York: W. W. Norton.

Stiglitz, J. and L. Bilmes (2008) "The $3 Trillion War," *Vanity Fair*, Apr. 1.

Stockman, F. (2017) "Who Were the Counterprotesters in Charlottesville?" *NYT*, Aug. 14.

Sullivan, J. (2019) "Yes, America Can Still Lead the World," *ATL*, Jan./Feb.

Sullivan, K. (2008) "US Again Hailed as Country of Dreams," *WP*, Nov. 6.

Bibliography

Sutton, B. (2016) "Monkey Cage: 8 Questions about the Future of Banking Regulation under Trump," *WP*, Nov. 23.

Sutton, M. (2016) *American Apocalypse: A History of Modern Evangelicalism*, Cambridge, MA: Belknap.

Swisher, K. (2021) "Emily Ratajkowski Isn't Quite Ready to Quit Profiting off the Male Gaze," *NYT*, Nov. 29.

Talev, M. (2021) "Midnight Is Approaching to Pass Voting Rights Protections," *NYT*, Nov. 21.

Tallack, D. (2000) "Architecture and Art," in R. Maidment and J. Mitchell (eds.), *The United States in the Twentieth Century: Culture*, 2nd edn, 235–69, London: Hodder & Stoughton.

Tanenhaus, S. (2021) "Jan. 6 Wasn't an Insurrection. It Was Vigilantism. And More Is Coming," *WP*, Dec. 10.

Tankersley, J. and E. Cochrane (2021) "Biden Wants to Pay for Infrastructure Plan with 15 Years of Corporate Taxes," *NYT*, Mar. 30.

Taylor, A. and M. Smallberg (2020) "How Biden Might Change Trump's Immigration Policies," *WP*, Sep. 25.

Tharoor, I. (2017) "Trump Presidency Ushers in a New Age of Militarism," *New Zealand Herald*, Mar. 2.

THE. Times Higher Education (2020) "World University Rankings 2020."

Thernstrom, S. and A. Thernstrom (1999) *America in Black and White: One Nation, Indivisible*, New York: Simon & Schuster.

Thomas, D. (2020) "As Family Structures Change in U.S., a Growing Share of Americans Say It Makes No Difference," PRC, Apr. 10.

Thompson, A., B. Sarlin, and S. Dean (2021) *NBC*, Oct. 14.

Thurston, A. (2016) "Inside US Islamic Schools," *The Brink*, Apr. 26.

Time (2015) "Transcript: Read the Full Text of the Primetime Republican Debate."

Tindera, M. (2020) "Biden Pulls Away in Race for Billionaire Donors, with 131 To Trump's 99," *Forbes*, Aug. 8.

Tocqueville, A. (1994) *Democracy in America*, London: The Everyman's Library.

Tolentino, J. (2019) *Trick Mirror: Reflections on Self-Delusion*, New York: Random House.

Toobin, J. (2007) *The Nine: Inside the Secret World of the Supreme Court*, New York: Doubleday.

Totenberg, N. (2020) "The Supreme Court Extends a Life-Support Line for Dreamers," *NPR*, Jun. 18.

Traister, R. (2016) *All the Single Ladies: Unmarried Women and the Rise of an Independent Nation*, New York: Simon & Schuster.

Trent, S. (2020) "At 88, He is a Historical Rarity – the Living Son of a Slave," *WP*, Jul. 27.

Trump, D. (2015) "Donald Trump's Presidential Announcement Speech," *Time*, Jun. 16.

Trump, D. (2016a) "Transcript: Donald Trump's Victory Speech," *NYT*, Nov. 9.

Trump, D. (2016b) "Donald Trump: I Could Shoot Somebody and I Wouldn't Lose Any Voters," *Guardian*, Jan. 24.

Trump, D. (2017a) "Statement by President Trump on the Paris Climate Accord," whitehouse. gov, Jun. 1.

Trump, D. (2017b) "The Fake News Media," Feb. 17.

Trump, D. (2017c) *Inaugural Address*, Jan. 20.

Trump, D. (2019) "Trump's Full U.N. Speech at the 2019 United Nations General Assembly," Sep. 24.

Trump, D. (2020) "Remarks at the National Prayer Breakfast," Archived at The American Presidency Project, Feb. 6.

Turner Enterprises, Inc. (2021) "Turner Ranches."

Turner, F. (1966) *The Significance of the Frontier in American History*, Ann Arbor: University of Michigan Press.

Bibliography

UCS. Union of Concerned Scientists (2020) "Each Country's Share of CO2 Emissions," Aug. 12.

UCS. Union of Concerned Scientists (2021) "UCS Satellite Database."

Uhing, C. (2020) "Biden Campaign Releases Child Care Proposal as COVID-19 Pushes Industry to the Brink of Collapse," First Five-Year Fund, Jul. 21.

Unaltered Ministries (2021) https://www.unaltered.org/.

UN. United Nations (2021) Office of Disarmament Affairs, "Treaty on the Non-Proliferation of Nuclear Weapons (NPT)."

UNEP. United Nations Environmental Program (2022) "Spreading like Wildfire: The Rising Threat of Extraordinary Fires," Nairobi: UNEP, Feb. 23.

USCB. United States Census Bureau (2012) "Census Bureau Reports There Are 89,004 Local Governments in the United States."

USCB. United States Census Bureau (2016) "Educational Attainment in the United States: 2015," Mar.

USCB. United States Census Bureau (2017) "More Children Live with Just Their Fathers than a Decade Ago," Release CB17-187, Nov. 16.

USCB. United States Census Bureau (2018a) "U.S. Census Bureau Releases 2018 Families and Living Arrangements Tables," Release Number CB18-TPS.54, Nov. 14.

USCB. United States Census Bureau (2018b) "Current Population Survey, 1968 to 2018 Annual Social and Economic Supplements," Fig. 1.

USCB. United States Census Bureau (2019a) "Health Insurance Coverage in the United States: 2018," P60-267, Nov. 8.

USCB. United States Census Bureau (2019b) "America's Families and Living Arrangements: 2019," AVG-1.

USCB. United States Census Bureau (2019c) "Median Household Income and Percent Change by Selected Characteristics," P60-266.

USCB. United States Census Bureau (2019d) "Languages Spoken at Home," Dec.

USCB. United States Census Bureau (2020a) "Income and Poverty in the United States: 2019," Report Number P60-270, Sep. 15.

USCB. United States Census Bureau (2020b) "Quick Facts."

USCB. United States Census Bureau (2021a) "Trade in Goods with China," Dec. 7.

USCB. United States Census Bureau (2021b) "Quarterly Residential Vacancies and Homeownership, Third Quarter 2021," Release Number: CB21-166, Nov. 2.

USCB. United States Census Bureau (2021c) "Age and Sex Composition in the United States: 2019," Oct. 8.

USCB. United States Census Bureau (2021d) "Foreign Trade: Top Trading Partners," Oct.

USCB. United States Census Bureau (2021e) "Quick facts: California," Jul. 1.

USCB. United States Census Bureau (2021f) "Current Population Survey: November Supplement, 2000–2020," Apr.

USCB. United States Census Bureau (2021g) "Annual Social and Economic Supplements," Figure MS-2 Median Age at First Marriage: 1890 to Present.

USCB. United States Census Bureau. (2021h) "Housing Vacancies and Home-ownership (CPS/HVS)."

USCB. United States Census Bureau (2021i) "Quarterly Residential Vacancies and Homeownership, Third Quarter 2021," Release Number: CB21-166.

USCB. United States Census Bureau (2021j) "Quick facts: Wyoming."

US Congress. National Commission on Terrorism (2000) "Countering the Changing Threat of International Terrorism," Jun.

US Congress (2021) "Committees of the U.S. Congress."

USCBP. United States Customs and Border Protection (2022) "CBP Enforcement Statistics Fiscal Year 2022."

USCIS. United States Citizen and Immigration Services (2022) "Naturalization Statistics."

Bibliography

USDA. United States Department of Agriculture (2017) "Expenditures on Children by Families, 2015," Mar. 15.

USDA. United States Department of Agriculture (2020) "The Cost of Raising a Child," Feb. 19.

USDA. United States Department of Agriculture (2021a) "Snap Data Tables National School Lunch Program," Dec. 10.

USDA. US Department of Agriculture (2021b) "National School Lunch Program," Dec. 7.

USDA. United States Department of Agriculture (2021c) "What Is Electronic Benefits Transfer (EBT)?," Jul. 7.

USDA. United States Department of Agriculture (2021d) "Snap Eligibility," Jan. 10.

USDS. United States Department of State (2021) "US Relations with South Sudan," Aug. 31.

USDV. United States Department of Veterans (2020) "Women Veterans Health Care."

USDV. United States Department of Veterans (2021a) "VA Benefits: Education and Training."

USDV. United States Department of Veterans (2021b) "VA Benefits for Service Members."

USEP. United States Election Project (2020) "2020 November General Election Turnout Rates," Dec. 7.

US News (2020) "Colleges: Top 100 – Lowest Acceptance Rates," Fall.

United States Senate (2021) "Vetoes by President Donald J. Trump."

United States Supreme Court (2019) "2019 Year-End Report on the Federal Judiciary," Dec. 31.

USTR. Office of the US Trade Representative (2020) "United States-Mexico-Canada Agreement."

USTR. Office of the US Trade Representative (2021) "Industrial Tariffs."

VA Blog (2018) "Silver Star Recipient to Represent the More than 300,000 Women Who Have Served in Iraq and Afghanistan," May 24.

Valdes-Dapena, P. (2016) "Ford Moving All Small Car Production to Mexico," CNN, Sep. 15.

Vasquez, M. (2020) "Trump Rails against the 'Liberal Indoctrination of America's Youth' in Latest Culture War Salvo," CNN, Sep. 17.

Vasquez, M. and B. Klein (2020) "Trump Signs Conservation Funding Law that Will Aid National Parks," CNN, Aug. 4.

Vespa, J., L. Medina, and D. Armstrong (2020) "Demographic Turning Points for the United States: Population Projections for 2020 to 2060," USCB, Table P25-1144, Feb.

Vogue (2017) "Celebrities Share Stories of Sexual Assault for #MeToo Campaign," Oct. 16.

Wagner, P. (2012) "Incarceration is not an Equal Opportunity Punishment," Prison Policy Initiative.

Walsh, K. (2020) "Early Voting Hits Historic Numbers in 2020," *ABC*, Nov. 3.

Walt, S. (2021) "Trump's Final Foreign Policy Report Card," *Foreign Policy*, Jan. 5.

Walter, B. (2022) *How Civil Wars Start: And How to Stop Them*, New York: Crown.

Walzer, M. (1992) *What It Means to be an American*, New York: Marsilio.

Warrick, J. and K. DeYoung (2009) "Obama Reverses Bush Policies on Detention and Interrogation," *WP*, Jan. 23.

Watson Brown. Watson Institute, Brown University (2021a) "Afghan Civilians, Cost of War," Aug.

Watson-Brown. Watson Institute, Brown University (2021b) "US Costs to Date for the War in Afghanistan, FY2001-FY2022," Aug.

Wayland, M. and L. Kolodny (2020) "Tesla's Market Cap Tops the 9 Largest Automakers Combined—Experts Disagree about if that Can Last," *CNBC*, Dec. 14.

Webster, N. (1783) "Dissertations on the English Language," in M. J. Adler and C. V. Doren (eds.), *The Annals of America*, Chicago: Encyclopedia Britannica, 1976, 3: 375–79.

Webster, N. (1789) "Dissertations on the English Language," in M. J. Adler and C. V. Doren (eds.), *The Annals of America*, Chicago: Encyclopedia Britannica, 1976, 3: 375–9.

Weisberg, J. (2019) "Bad News: Can Democracy Survive if the Media Fail?" *Foreign Affairs*, Sep./Oct.

Weiss, B. and J. Pasley (2019) "Only 3 Countries in the World Protect the Right to Bear Arms in their Constitutions: the US, Mexico, and Guatemala," *BI*, Aug. 6.

Bibliography

Werner, E., P. Kane, and M. DeBonis (2020) "Trump Signs $2 Trillion Coronavirus Bill into Law as Companies and Households Brace for more Economic Pain," *WP*, Mar. 27.

Wertheim, S. (2017) "Trump and American Exceptionalism," *Foreign Affairs*, Jan. 3.

Williams, K., T. Craig, and M. Iati (2020) "Kentucky Grand Jury Declines to File Homicide Charges in Death of Breonna Taylor," *WP*, Sep. 23.

White House (2021a) "Briefing Room: Paris Climate Agreement," Jan. 20.

White House (2021b) "Executive Order on Protecting Public Health and the Environment and Restoring Science to Tackle the Climate Crisis," Jan. 20.

White House Briefing Room (2021) "Fact Sheet: The Bipartisan Infrastructure Deal," Nov. 6.

Whitlock, C. (2009) "National Security Team Delivers Grim Appraisal of Afghanistan War," *WP*, Feb. 9.

Whitlock, C. and *WP* (2021) *The Afghanistan Papers: A Secret History of the War*, New York: Simon & Schuster.

Whoriskey, P. D. MacMillan, and J. O'Connell (2020) "'Doomed to Fail': Why a $4 Trillion Bailout Couldn't Revive the American Economy," *WP*, Oct. 5.

Wikipedia (2021) "Twitter."

Wilkie, C. (2021) "Biden Rejects Trump's Approach to North Korea, Says He Won't Give Kim Jong-Un 'International Recognition,'" *CNBC*, May 21.

Will, G. (1985) "No One Blushed Anymore," *WP*, Sep. 15.

Williams, J. (2020) "10 Percent of Open Congressional Seats Changed Party Hands in 2020," Ballotpedia News, Oct. 18.

Wilson, S. and D. Nakamura (2013) "Obama Announces Reduced US Role in Afghanistan this Spring," *WP*, Jan. 11.

WMFC. West Midland Family Center (2017) "Generational Differences Chart."

Wolfe, A. (1999) *One Nation After All: What Middle Class America Really Think About*, New York: Penguin.

Wolfe, A. (2006) "The Politics of Immigration: Getting In," *TNR*, May 1.

Wood, G. (1969) "The Whig Science of Politics," in J. Kirby Martin (ed.), *Colonial America: Selected Readings*, 330–47, New York: Harper & Row.

Woodward, B. (2002) *Bush at War*, New York: Simon & Schuster.

Woodward, B. (2020a) *Fear: Trump in the White House*, New York: Simon & Schuster.

Woodward, B. (2020b) *Rage*, New York: Simon & Schuster.

Woodward, B. and R. Costa (2021) *Peril*, New York: Simon & Schuster.

World Bank (2016) "Military Expenditure (% of GDP)."

World Bank (2020a) "Per Capita GDP (current US$)."

World Bank (2020b) "Population Density (People per Square Kilometer of Land)."

World Bank (2021a) Exports of Goods and Services: United States."

World Bank (2021b) "GINI Index (World Bank Estimate) – United States."

World Bank (2021c) "Trade (% of GDP) United States."

WP (2012) "President Obama's Speech at Prayer Vigil for Newtown Shooting Victims (transcript)," Dec. 17.

WP (2021) "910 People Have Been Shot and Killed by Police in the Past Year," Dec. 16.

WPR. World Population Review (2021a) "Countries with Nuclear Weapons, 2021."

WPR. World Population Review (2021b) "Military Spending by Country, 2021."

Wright, E. and J. Rogers (2015) *American Society: How It Really Works*, London: W. W. Norton.

WSJ (2020) "Money: As Stimulus Check Uplift Wanes, Vulnerable Workers Are at Risk," Oct. 22.

WTO. World Trade Organization (2020) "The WTO's 25 Years of Achievement and Challenges."

Xiaobo, L. (2012) *No Hatred, No Enemies: Selected Essays and Poems*, Cambridge, MA: Harvard University Press.

Yassky, D. (2016) "Unlocking the Truth about the Clinton Crime Bill," *NYT*, Apr. 9.

Yonatan, R. (2016) "Which Countries Have the Most Vacation Days?" *NYT*, Sep. 4.

Younis, M. (2020) "Americans' Approval of ACA Holds Steady," *Gallup*, Mar. 9.

Zakaria, F. (2012) *The Post American World: The Rise of the Rest, Release 2.0*, New York: W. W. Norton.

Zakaria, F. (2020) *Ten Lessons for a Post-Pandemic World*, New York: W. W. Norton.

Zhao, C. (2021) "59% of GOP Voters Say 'Believing' Trump Won 2020 'Important' to Being a Republican: Poll," *Newsweek*, Sep. 12.

Zhou, L. (2020) "Attention Has Faded on the More than 20 Sexual Misconduct Allegations against Trump," *Vox*, Nov. 3.

Zucchino, D. (2021) "The War in Afghanistan: How It Started and How It Is Ending," *NYT*, Aug. 13.

Zumbrun, J. (2019) "U.S. Collected $63 Billion in Tariffs through June," *WSJ*, Aug. 7.

INDEX

abortion rights 108, 163, 188
  see also Roe v. Wade (1973)
Abrams, Stacey 42, 172
Abu Ghraib prison 309
accountability 142
Acuff, Roy 250
Adams, John Quincy 5, 85, 295
Adams, Stacy 148
advertising 31, 138, 139, 224, 269
  negative 141
Affirmative Action policies 195, 202–204
Affordable Care Act (ACA) 40, 208, 271
  see also Obamacare
Afghanistan 302, 305, 306, 312
  botched US withdrawal from 319
  see also Taliban
African Americans 60, 71–72, 80
  Civil Rights Movement 35, 71, 143, 165
  crime and punishment 171
  and gerrymandering 141
  historical perspective 30, 31, 32
  "passing over" for promotion 167
  post-slavery stress syndrome 169
  religion 185
  stereotypes 235
  voting behavior 132
  in workforce 32
  see also blacks; Civil Rights Movement
    (1954–1968); ethnic minorities; race;
    slavery
Agent Orange 52
agnosticism 184
Aid to Families with Dependent Children (AFDC),
    1962 206, 212, 261
Air Sea Battle Concept (ASBC) 313
Akoato-Bamfo, Kwame 14
Alaska 25, 45, 47, 48, 50, 64, 65
  Alaskan Arctic Refuge 49
Albright, Madeleine 163
Albuquerque, New Mexico 62
Alito, Samuel 109
Allen, Woody 146
al-Qaeda terrorist network 304, 305, 307, 308, 310,
    311–312, 316, 327
Altidor, Kenny 8
Amazon 65

Amendments, constitutional 90
  see also Constitution of the United States of
    America
"America First" philosophy 7, 32, 41, 188, 257, 285,
    288, 307, 328
America Online (AOL) 223
American Association of Retired People (AARP)
    210, 231
American Bald Eagle 52
American Bar Association (ABA) 123
American Birth Control League (ABCL) 163
American Civil Liberties Union (ACLU) 31, 123
American Civil War (1861–1865) 23–25, 266, 295
American College Test (ACT) 195
American Community Survey, Census Bureau
    158–159
American Constitution see Constitution of the
    United States of America
American Creed 148, 152, 220
American culture 215–222
American Dream 3, 149, 152, 160, 197, 216, 237,
    249
American Enterprise Institute 124
American exceptionalism 204, 315
American Federation of Labor (AFL) 123, 267
American Federation of Labor–Congress of
    Industrial Organizations (AFL–CIO) 266
American Federation of Teachers (AFT) 121, 122
American football 242–243
American Health Care Act (AHC) 208
American History Museum 248
American International Group (AIG) 275
American Medical Association (AMA) 123
American people 66–72
  African Americans 71–72
  immigration 72, 73t, 74–81
  Native Americans 67–68, 69f, 70f, 71
American population see population, American
American Recovery and Reinvestment Act (ARRA)
    40
American Recovery Plan Act (ARPA) 205, 207
American Rescue Plan (ARP), 2021 257, 258, 273
American Revolution (1765–1791) 18–20, 85, 193,
    264
American Stock Exchange (AMEX) 274
"Americanization" 219

Index

Anasazi culture, Colorado 68
"Ancestor Project" 14
Anglican Church, separation from 17
Annan, Kofi 277, 289
Annual Threat Assessment Report (ATAR) 318
Anthony, Susan B. 29
"Anthropocene" age 51
anti-Americanization 219
Anti-Ballistic Missile (ABM) Treaty 301
appeal courts 110
Apple 66
Applebaum, Anne 5, 319
Arab Spring 311, 312
Arizona, Navajo Indian reservation 48
Armory Modern Art Show 221
Arms Control Export Act (1988) 293
arms race 300, 314
  see also atomic weapons; nuclear weapons; wars
Armstrong, Louis 250
Arquette, Rosanna 146
Arrests for DWB (Driving While Black) 171
art 245–249
artists 221
ASBC *see* Air Sea Battle Concept (ASBC)
Ashcan School 247
Asia 64, 268, 283, 293, 309, 313–314
  Central 316
  historical aspects 67, 296
  immigrants from 74, 76, 80
  nationalism 308
  rise of 281
  students 196
  Trump on 316–317
  see also Asian Americans; China; India;
    Japan; North Korea; South Korea;
    Taiwan
Asian Americans 76–77, 80, 141, 151, 167, 195
atheism 184
atomic weapons 33, 300
  bombing of Hiroshima and Nagasaki, Japan
    32, 296
  see also arms race; nuclear weapons; wars
Attorney General 110
Austin, Lloyd 297
authoritarianism 5, 20, 332
  anti-authoritarianism 18
  democracy distinguished 296
  soft 287
  technological 7

Baby Boomers 226, 249, 331
Baez, Joan 251
Ballmer, Steve 154
Bank of America 167
Banking Act (Glass-Steagall), 1933 274

banking system 57, 273–274
Bannon, Stephen 230, 316–317
Barrett, Amy Coney 108, 163, 182, 188
baseball 241–242
Bears Ears monument 52
Begin, Menachem 301
behavior
  business 276
  conventional 121–122
  corporate 276
  effect of television on 235–236
  interest groups 121–122
  police 165
  political 121
  sexual misbehavior 162
  suspicious 171
  voters 126, 128, 143
Bellamy, Francis 29
Berlin Wall 35
  fall of 37, 265, 302
Berry, Chuck 250
Beyoncé 165
Bezos, Jeff 138, 154, 198, 271
Biden, Hunter 103
Biden, Joseph Robinette (Joe) 1, 5, 7, 49, 83, 182,
    185, 217, 256, 259, 280, 285, 318
  appeal to voters 255
  approval ratings 94, 116, 328
  and the arts 247–248
  border enforcement 81
  "Build Back Better" policies 32, 42, 83–84, 114,
    116, 117, 143, 148, 149, 163
  Covid policy 9, 181
  environmental protection 48, 49, 50, 51, 52
  at G.H.W. Bush funeral 97, 98
  Inauguration Day 49, 51, 113, 332
  oath of office 113
  and Obama 41, 43, 182, 217
  1776 Commission, disbanding of 14
  Paris COP-21 climate protocol agreement,
    rejoining 51 receiving Covid 19 vaccine 9
  State of the Union Address (2022) 327
  unlikely choice for presidency 113–114
  as Vice President under Obama 114
  see also presidential election of 2020 (Trump/
    Biden)
"Biden-Pelosi-Schumer Gun-Ban Agenda"
  123
Bierstadt, Albert 221
Bill, G. I. 194
Bill and Melinda Gates Foundation 197
Bill of Rights (1791) 85, 86
bin Laden, Osama 39, 304, 305, 308
Bipartisan Campaign Reform Act (BCRA), 2002
  140

365

Index

bipartisanship 40, 101, 115, 155, 171, 273
  Bipartisan Campaign Reform Act (BCRA), 2002 140
Birx, Deborah 84
Bishop, Bill 153
Black Lives Matter (#BLM) movement 3, 7, 8, 14, 66, 72, 92, 173, 225
  see also African Americans; blacks; ethnic minorities; Floyd, George (murder of); race
Black Panthers 35
"Black Wall Street," Tulsa (Oklahoma) 31
blacks 60, 72, 118, 141, 150–152, 159, 164–166, 172, 177, 179f, 195, 201, 215, 240
  historical perspective 25, 26
  Historically Black Colleges and Universities (HBCU) 198
  incarceration of 166–167
  "New Negro" 30
  non-Hispanic 164
  socioeconomic precariousness 166
  Universal Negro Improvement Association (1919–1927) 30
  see also African Americans; Black Lives Matter (#BLM) movement; Civil Rights Movement (1954–1968); ethnic minorities; race
Bloom, Allan 250
Bloomberg, Michael 140, 198
Blow, Charles 231
blue-collar workers 278–279
Boeing 65–66
Booker, Corey 117
boom-cycle deficit spending 83
Border Patrol officers 79
Bourgeois, Louise 247
branches of government
  executive 83, 85, 93–99
  judicial 83, 85, 106–112, 111f
  legislative 83, 85, 99, 100, 101–106
  overlapping of 88
Breyer, Steven 109, 178
Brin, Sergei 75, 154
Britain
  and history of the US 18, 20, 28
  Navy 28
  Whig Party 18, 23
Broadcast Decency Enforcement Act (2005) 236
broadcast media 233–236
Brookings Institution 124
Brooks, David 5, 153, 184, 329, 330, 332
Brooks, Preston 24
Brown, James 251
Brown, Michael 66
Brown v. Board of Education (1954) 33, 202, 203
Bucklew v. Precythe (2019) 178
Buffett, Warren 154

Bureau of Labor Statistics (BLS) 260
Bureau of Land Management 71
Burns, William 327–328
Bush, George Herbert Walker 37, 98, 109, 114, 144, 255, 265
  funeral 97, 98, 109
Bush, George Walker 29, 39, 52, 188, 189, 265, 304
  and Electoral College 87
  Farewell Address 219
  and federalism 90–91
  foreign policy 292
  at G.H.W. Bush funeral 97, 98
  and government 92, 95, 96, 109
  Inaugural Address 219
  "war Keynesianism" 265–266
business 268–270
  and government 270–276
Business-Interest PAC (BIPAC) 123

Cable News Network (CNN) 234
Calhoun, John C. 24
California 32, 45, 65, 66, 136
Cameron, John 312
campaigns, electoral, finances 139–141
Cancel Culture 7
Cape Canaveral, Florida 56, 271
capital punishment 169, 177
  and Arkansas 178, 180
  death row 178
  differences of opinion 179f
capitalism 17, 204, 236, 259, 277, 287
  anti-capitalism 54
  corporate 219, 283
  and the economy 275
  finance 58
  free-market 37, 265, 267, 270
  industrial 23, 221
  managerial 26
  manufacturing 54
  and music 249
  perfect 249
  speculative 275
Capitol building, storming of (January 6, 2021) 1–2, 24, 103
Carlsen, Tucker 7, 328
Carnegie, Andrew 26, 27–28, 58
Carter, Jimmy 36, 37, 52, 110, 189
  Carter Doctrine 301
  and federalism 90
  at G.H.W. Bush funeral 97, 98
  and government 95, 96
Carville, James 2
Cassidy, Bill 115
Catholic Church 184
Cato Institute 124

366

Index

Census Bureau, American Community Survey 158

Center for Disease Control and Prevention (CDC) 208, 272

Center for Responsible Politics 139

Central Intelligence Agency (CIA) *see* CIA (Central Intelligence Agency)

Chang, Jeff 220

Charlottesville, protests in 173

Chauvin, Derek 8

Chavez, Cesar 35

checks and balances 84, 85, 88, 89f

Cheney, Dick 98

Cheney, Liz 117, 125

Cherokees 20, 53

Chicago, Illinois 60

Chicago Commodities Exchange 274

Chicanos (Mexico, immigrants from) 76

Children's Health Insurance Program (CHIP) 207

China
    Civil War 298
    connection of American consumers to Chinese producers 279
    economy 256–257, 269, 270
    "One China-Two Systems" policy 316
    perceived threat of 43, 314
    relations with the US 279, 316–317
    and Russia/alliance with Russia 310, 313, 317, 319, 323, 326
    Tiananmen Square killings (1989) 37
    Trump's policy towards 316–317
    see also Asia; People's Republic of China

Chopin, Kate: *The Awakening* 221

Christian Coalition (CC) 122

Christie, Chris 125

Church of England 17

CIA (Central Intelligence Agency) 297–298, 312, 316

cities 28, 45, 47, 60

Citizens United v. Federal Elections Commission (2010) 140

citizenship 25, 39, 91, 191, 240
    corporate 276
    "fetal" 4
    and immigration 74, 75, 78
    permanent 80
    and race 164–165
    second-class 33
    see also immigrants

civic violence 1

Civil Rights Act (1964) 35, 161–162

Civil Rights Movement (1954–1968) 35, 71, 143, 165

civil society 123, 181, 191–192

class 148–156

    and demography 141–142
    middle classes 149–152
    poverty and affluence 153–156
    rural and urban America 152–153

class action suits 111, 124

Clayton Anti-Trust Act (1914) 269

Clean Air Act (1970) 52

Clean Power Plan (2015) 53

climate/climate change 47–51
    conference 285
    deniers 204
    House Select Committee of Climate Crisis 104
    International Climate Week 331

Clinton, George 251

Clinton, Hillary Rodham 38, 40, 41, 87, 97, 125, 148, 161, 163, 233, 260, 297, 313
    defeat by Trump in 2016 election 41, 75, 87, 106, 114, 132, 136, 260
    under investigation in 2016 170
    as a Methodist 185
    nomination of 211
    and Obama 182
    as Secretary of State (2009–2013) 163, 170
    as "smart" power 291

Clinton, William (Bill) Jefferson 39, 110, 170, 171
    Affirmative Action policies 202–203
    character 93–94
    known as "Comeback Kid" 95–96
    and the economy 265
    extra-marital affairs 98
    foreign policy 303
    and government 90
    impeachment of 95, 103
    Lewinsky affair 38, 95, 103
    presidential style 93–94
    problems faced by 95
    known as "Slick Willie" 95

Clipper Mission 270

Clyburn, Jim 42

Coates, Ta-Nehisi 41, 165, 216–217

Cold War (1945–1990) 32–38, 75, 96, 194, 296–302
    end of 97, 188, 265, 302

Cole, Thomas 221

collective bargaining 267

"college preparatory" schools 201

colleges
    community 68, 194, 198, 258
    elite 196
    elite college tuition 195
    Historically Black Colleges and Universities (HBCU) 198
    junior 194
    private 195
    public 195
    state-supported 194

Index

tribal 198, 247
vocational training 194
see also universities
Collins, Susan 115
Columbus, Christopher 16, 53, 184
colonial America (1607–1763) 16–18
Columbian Exposition, Chicago (1892) 29
Comey, James 170
common law 110
Communications Decency Act (1996) 235
"compassionate conservatism" 39
competitive advantage 280
Comprehensive Nuclear Test Ban Treaty 304
concert halls 249
Confederate States of America (CSA) (1861–1865) 23, 54, 240
confidence, crisis of 301–302
confirmation bias 231
Congress 8, 76–77, 80, 99, 101–106
  and Affordable Care Act 208
  bicameral legislature 99
  constitutional powers 102
  and delegation of powers 96
  establishment by Founders 85
  impeachment power 103
  Library of Congress (LOC) 232, 248
  male domination 106
  officeholders 106
  on presidential term 95
  profile of the 117th Congress 100t
  and separation of powers 88
  size 136
  synthesis of government models 106
  see also House of Representatives; Senate
Congress of Industrial Organizations (CIO) 267
conspiracy theory 18
Constitution of the United States of America 6, 85–88, 92
  1st Amendment 107, 122, 137, 140, 183, 186
  2nd Amendment 175
  8th Amendment 177
  10th Amendment 89
  11th Amendment 86
  12th Amendment 86
  13th Amendment 25, 87, 91
  14th Amendment 25, 87, 107, 162
  15th Amendment 25, 87
  16th Amendment 87, 264
  17th Amendment 87
  18th Amendment 31, 87
  19th Amendment 29, 87
  20th Amendment 87
  21st Amendment 31, 87
  22nd Amendment 87, 95
  23rd Amendment 87

  24th Amendment 87
  25th Amendment 87
  26th Amendment 87
  27th Amendment 87
  and American Revolution (1765–1791) 18–20, 85, 193, 264
  Article I 86, 91, 102
  Article II 86, 95
  Article III 86, 107
  Article IV 86
  Article V 86, 89
  Article VI 86, 91
  Article VII 86
  Bill of Rights 86
  briefness 110
  Congress, constitutional powers 102
  "cruel and unusual" clause 178
  degrees of faith in 5–6
  federal system set up by 18
  and federalism 93
  founding document of American government 85
  necessary and proper (elastic) clause 91
  Preamble 86
  and presidential elections 87
  and Republican Party 328
  separation of powers 84–85, 88, 89f, 292
  summary 86–87
  supremacy clause 91, 107
constitutional law 110
Consumer Financial Protection Bureau 276
Consumer Protection Agency 272
Coolidge, Calvin 267
Coronavirus Aid, Relief, and Economic Security Act (CARES ACT), 2020 105, 151, 155, 205, 257, 258, 262
corporate social responsibility (CSR) 282
Country music 174, 233, 250
county commissioners 93
court system 111f
Covid 19 pandemic 5, 43, 83, 226, 227–228, 232
  and 2020 presidential election 9, 80, 83–84, 132, 133
  Biden on 181
  Coronavirus Aid, Relief, and Economic Security Act (CARES ACT), 2020 105, 151, 155, 205, 257, 258, 262
  Covid Task Force 84
  death toll 84, 114
  and the economy 255, 273, 282–283
  and federalism 92
  geopolitical instability caused by 318
  and government 95
  mishandling by Trump 9, 116, 149, 181
  politicizing 84
  relief packages 152

Index

Cox, Renee 249
craft unions 266
Crane, Stephen, *Maggie* 221
creationism 203–204
creeping socialism 33
Crèvecoeur, Hector St. John de 220, 221, 222
Crime Act (1994) 171
crime and punishment 168–178, 179f, 180
  capital punishment 169
  common crimes 169
  drug wars 171
  gangs 173–174
  homicide rates 175
  incarceration rates 171
  law and order as electoral issue 172
  non-white American males, focus on 171
  rates of crime 170
  silence, right to 168
Crimean invasion (2014) 288, 302, 316, 328
Critical Race Theory (CRT) 7, 14, 15, 164, 238
  see also Black Lives Matter (#BLM) movement;
    race
cruise missiles 302, 312
Crusades 16
Cruz, Ted 117, 125
Cuba 35
Cuban missile crisis 320
culture 215–222
  literature 221–222
culture wars 4
Custer, George Armstrong 26
Customs and Border protection agents 79
Cuyahoga River, Cleveland 60
Cyber Command, US 312
cyberwar 312–313

DACA (Deferred Action for Childhood Arrivals)
    80, 112, 182
dance 251–252
Daniels, Stormy 146
Darwin, Charles/Darwinism 27, 30, 187, 203
Davison, James 4
death penalty *see* capital punishment
Declaration of Independence
  equality in 23
  excerpt from 19
  and global politics 292
  written by Jefferson (1776) 18
"deep state" 83
Deepwater Horizon Oil Well disaster (2010) 49
DefCon 3 (fifteen-minute response time) 321
Defense of Marriage Act (DMA), 1996 158
Deferred Action for Childhood Arrivals (DACA)
    79, 112, 182
Delevingne, Cara 146

democracy 4–5
  and authoritarianism 296
  evaluation of problem in the US 325–332
  "hyper-democracy" 143
  liberal 5, 80, 323
  participatory 119–124
  pluralistic 141–144
  "Twitter Democracy" 230
  US seen as backsliding 331
Democratic National Headquarters, Watergate:
    burglary of 1972 36
Democratic Party/Democrats 4, 6, 23, 27, 83, 85,
    126
  and California 65
  on capital punishment 177
  categories of Democrats 330
  core values 127–128
  and the economy 257
  elections 133
  ethnic minority voters 13
  and federalism 92
  on homosexuality 158
  and presidential election of 2020 83–84
  Progressives 330
  public lands, protection of 52
  and race 166
  see also Biden, Joe; Clinton, William (Bill)
    Jefferson; Obama, Barack Hussein
Deng Xiao Ping 323
Denmark 322
Department of Defense (DOD) 294, 297, 300, 313,
    316
Department of Education (DOE) 198
Department of Health and Human Services (HHS)
    programs 207
Department of Homeland Security (DHS) 7, 39, 78,
    90, 145, 305
Department of Justice 110
Department of the Interior, Bureau of Indian
    Affairs (BIA) 68
dependency culture 205
deregulation 270–273
DeSantis, Ron 117, 125
DHS *see* Department of Homeland Security (DHS)
DINKS (double income no kids) 160
Dionne, E. J. 148
Director of National Intelligence 325–326
discrimination 14, 15, 38, 195, 203
  gender 13, 161, 162, 246
  housing 7
  race and gender 13, 162
  racial 30, 35, 72, 152, 165, 167
  reverse 202
  workplace 112
Disney Studios 241

Index

districts, electoral 141, 142
    see also gerrymandering
division of powers *see* separation of powers
DOD *see* Department of Defense (DOD)
Dodd-Frank Wall Street Reform and Consumer
    Protection Act (2010) 275–276
dollar, and renminbi 281–283
domestic economy 260–266
Dos Passos, John 31
Douglass, Frederick 15
"DREAM Act" (Development, Relief, Education for
    Alien Minors) 80
D'Souza, Dinesh 215
Dual federalism 90
DuBois, W. E. B. 30, 164
Dunkelman, Eric 152–153
Dylan, Bob 222, 251

"e pluribus unum" (from many, one), national
    motto 3
Eakins, Thomas 247
Easley v. Cromartie (2001) 141
economic nationalism 255, 256–257
economy 255–283
    American work force 260–264
    business and industry 268–270
    comparative growth statistics 255–256
    dollar and renminbi 281–283
    government and business 270–276
    labor unions 266–268
    pre-Covid 255, 257
    stock market 274
    taxes 264–266
    US domestic economy 260–266
    Wall Street 274
education 193–204
    blacks 195
    colleges and universities 193–198
    integration and Affirmative Action 202–204
    school districts and boards 200–202
    state responsibility 198, 199f
    US educational system 198, 199f
Edwards, Jonathan 17
egalitarianism 149
eighteenth century
    from 1765 to 1791 (American Revolution)
        18–20, 85, 193, 264
    and federalism 91
    interstate commerce 91
Einstein, Albert 186
Eisenhower, Dwight D. 33
elastic clause 91
elections 133–136
    adversarial tone 143
    campaign finances 139–141

caucuses 134
districts 141
exit polls 132
gerrymandering of voters *see* gerrymandering
to House of Representatives 135–136
insurgent campaigns 125
midterm 3, 9, 79, 83, 101, 114, 116, 133, 144
primaries 133, 134
split tickets 101
winner-takes-all system 124, 126, 141
see also parliamentary election of 2016
    (Trump/Biden); political parties; politics;
    presidential elections
Electoral College
    and Constitution 87
    Obama electoral victory (2008) 40, 66
    Reagan electoral victory (1980) 37
    and Republican Party 328
    and storming of the Capitol (January 6, 2021) 24
    Trump electoral victory (2016) 41, 75, 114
    votes in 39
electorate 119–121
Ellis Island 58, 76
Ellis Island Immigration Museum 57
Ellison, Larry 154
Ellsberg, Daniel 36
Emily's List 106
Endangered Species Act (ESA), 1973 52
enlargement and engagement 303–304
Enlightenment 184
Environmental Impact Statements 49
environmental protection 49–52
    see also climate change; national parks
Environmental Protection Agency (EPA) 49–51
    Superfund program 52–53
Epstein, Jeffrey 146
equal opportunity 27, 72, 121, 165, 193, 220, 244
    and class 149, 152
    education 200
    integration and Affirmative Action 203
Equal Rights Amendment (ERA) 161
Espionage Act (1917) 30
ethnic cleansing 303
ethnic minorities
    enclaves 28, 58
    support for the Democrats 13
    see also race
ethno-nationalism 43, 318, 332
Euro-Americans 17, 23, 67
European settlements 53
evangelism 33
evolutionary theory 27
executive branch of government 93–99
    administrative roles 98
    delegated powers 96

370

Index

department heads 99
and election of 2020 83–84
influence on judicial branch 110
presidential influence 93
presidential style 93–94
and separation of powers 85, 88
Trump on 90
vice presidency 98
see also presidency; presidential elections
Executive Office of the President (EOP) 98
executive orders 40, 80, 94
expansion
and isolation 294–295
map (eighteenth- and nineteenth-centuries) 21
westward 20–23
expressionism 247
Extinction Rebellion 286

Facebook/Meta 122, 138, 171, 227, 319, 322
and Biden 133
and Obama 94
and Trump 116
fair trade 279–281
fake news 7, 138, 139, 230, 231
families/American family 156–160
Family and Medical Leave Act (1993) 163
fast-track trading 293
Fauci, Anthony 84
Federal Bureau of Investigation (FBI) 170
Federal Bureau of Prisons (FBP) 170
Federal Communications Commission (FCC) 235
Federal Deposit Insurance Corporation (FDIC) 274
Federal Election Campaigns Act (1971) 140
Federal Election Commission 140
Federal Reserve 273
Federal Trade Commission (1914) 269
federalism
Dual 90
federal courts 107, 110
federal system 89–93
and judicial branch 110
Layer Cake 90
local government 93
Marble Cake 90
"New Federalism" 35, 90
as a process 89, 90, 91
Rhetorical 90
state government 93
twentieth century 91
twenty first century 92
Feeding America 154
Feliciano, José 251
feminism 4, 106, 161, 162, 187, 194
Fields, Barbara 165
Fields, James Alex 173

financial derivatives 275
financial institutions 57, 274, 275
First Great Awakening 187
First World War (1914–1918) 30–32, 269
Fisher v. University of Texas (2016) 203
Fitzgerald, F. Scott 31
Fletcher v. Peck (1810) 91
Florida 39
anti-racism laws 14–15
Cape Canaveral 56
Disneyworld 56
purchase by the US (1819) 20
Universal Studios 56
Floyd, George (murder of) 8, 13, 66, 145, 172, 226
see also Black Lives Matter (#BLM) movement; police
Floyd, Philonise 8
Folk music 250
Food and Drug Administration (FDA) 272
football 242–243
Ford, Gerald 36, 95, 96
Ford, Henry 31, 269
Ford Motor Corporation 283
foreign policy
becoming a world power 295–296
history 294–302
isolation and expansion 294–295
and separation of powers 292–294
see also global politics
forestry, Pacific Rim 66
fossil fuels 259
Founders 85, 88, 99, 106–107, 119, 183
Fourth Awakening 189
Fox, Vicente 76
Fox News 4, 6, 7, 328
FoxConn 278
France 234
Franken, Al 146
Franklin, Aretha 251
Franklin, Benjamin 85
"Free America" group 4
free market 27
free press 229–233
free trade 279–281, 282
Freelancer Union 268
Freeman, Morgan 165
French Revolution 294
Freud, Sigmund 31
Friedan, Betty 29
The Feminine Mystique 160
Friedman, Thomas 320
frontier thesis 26
Fuller, Margaret: *Woman in the Nineteenth Century* 23

371

Index

fundamentalism 187, 189, 301, 304
Furman v. Georgia (1972) 177

Gaddafi, Muammar 311
Galbraith, John Kenneth: *The Affluent Society* 33
Gardener, Eric 66
Garland, Merrick 110
Garvey, Marcus 30
Gates, Bill 154, 223
Gellman, Barton 2–3
gender equality 160–164
General Agreement on Tariffs and Trade (GATT)
    277, 298, 303
Generation Alpha 226
Generations Y and Z 226, 227, 228, 331
Germany
    emigration by Jewish people from 186
    ethnocentric parties 287
    as EU's strongest nation 322
    imperialism 30–31
    language 30
    navy 28
    Nazi Germany 296, 321
    and New World Order 302
    post-war rebuilding of 296
    reunification 37, 302
    terrorist attacks on 307
    war material 32
    see also Merkel, Angela
gerrymandering 43, 130, 131
    partisan 142
    racial 141
Gessen, M. 3
get-tough-on-crime policy 171
Giant Sequoias 66
gig economy 268
Gilded Age 268, 269
Gilman, Charlotte: *Women and Economics* 29
Gingrich, Newt 105
GINI coefficient 259
GINI Index 159
Ginsburg, Ruth Bader 83, 108, 109
Gitlin, Todd 27
Giuliani, Rudolph 249
Gladstone, William 18
glass ceilings for promotion 163, 167, 260
Glasser, Susan 322–323
Glen Canyon Dam, Colorado River 50
global marketplace 277–283
global politics 285–323
    Cold War (1945–1990) 32–38, 296–302
    confidence, crisis of 301–302
    enlargement and engagement 303–304
    New World Order 302–303
    9/11 terrorist attacks 304–305
    separation of powers 292–294

supremacy of the US, evaluating 317–318
twenty first century 304
Vietnam *see* Vietnam War (1954–1975)
wars 305, 307–308
see also foreign policy
global village 91
global warming 49–51
globalization 92, 188, 191, 194, 265, 277, 317
glocalization 219
Glorious Revolution (1688) 18
Goldberg, Jeffrey 225
Google 66
Gorbachev, Mikhail 302
Gordon, Robert 150, 157
Gore, Al 39, 87, 97
Gorman, Amanda 332
Gorsuch, Neil 109, 178, 188
government
    assistance from 205–210
    branches 93–112
    and broadcast media 235–236
    and business 270–276
    divided 101
    governing structures 84–85
    local government 93
    separation of powers 84–85
    state government 93
    strong 91
    trust in 91, 151
    see also Constitution of the United States of
        America; federalism
Graduate Record Exam (GRE) 197
Graham, Billy 33
Gray, Freddie 173
Great American Desert 61
Great American Outdoors Act (2020) 52
Great Awakening 18
Great Depression 32, 36, 39, 75, 90, 94, 255, 267,
    270, 274, 296
Great Lakes 58, 60
Great Plains 61
Great Recession (2008) 151, 264, 273, 275, 287
Great Revival (1830s) 185
Great Society Program 35, 37, 90, 247
Great War for Empire (French and Indian War),
    1754–1763 18
greenhouse gas emissions, reducing 51
Group of Seven (G7) 286, 288
Gulf Wars 37–38
gun crimes/gun ownership 174–175
    school shootings 176, 177
    see also National Rifle Association (NRA)

Haass, Richard 317
habeas corpus 96
Haley, Bill 250

372

Index

Hamilton, Alexander 85
handguns, concealed 175
hard power 289
Harlem Renaissance 30
Harris, Kamala 42, 77, 95, 113, 126, 148, 152, 161,
  165, 185, 256
  first female Vice President 260
Harvard University, founding of (1636) 17, 58
Hawaii 45
Hawthorne, Nathaniel, *The Scarlett Letter* 221
Hay, John 295
Hayes, Rutherford B. 25–26
health care policies 27, 35, 38, 41, 79, 124, 149,
  204–208
  Clinton on 95
  complementary 163
  costs 208, 210
  expanded 40, 258
  inadequate 68
  insurance 271
  interest groups 123
  Obama on 90, 92, 94
  premium 208
  problems 208
  reproductive 163
  universal 165
Hearst, William Randolph 229
Heilemann, John 41
Hendrix, Jimi 251
Henry H. Huntington Library, San Marino 232
Heritage Foundation 124
Hispanics 75, 76, 80, 151, 167–168, 195
Historically Black Colleges and Universities
  (HBCU) 198
history of the US 13–44
  from 1607 to 1763 (colonial America) 16–18
  American vs. United States history 15–16
  birth of America 16–17
  eighteenth century *see* eighteenth century
  Native Americans 15, 16, 26
  nineteenth century *see* nineteenth century
  twentieth century *see* twentieth century
  the twenty-first century *see* twenty first century
Hitler, Adolf: compared with Putin 321
Holiday, Billie 250
Hollywood 238–241
Holocaust Museum 248
home ownership 150
Homer, Winslow 247
Homestead Act (1862) 58
homicide 4, 31, 110, 171, 173–176, 179f, 312
  of African Americans 72, 177
  of Floyd 8, 13, 66, 67, 172, 245
  lynch mobs 26
homosexuality 158
Hoover, Herbert 233

Hoover, J. Edgar 31–32
Hoover Dam, Colorado River 61
Hopper, Edward 247
horizontal integration 26
House of Representatives 99, 126, 135–136
  committees 105
  and Constitution 85
  elections to 135–136
  House Agriculture Committee 104
  House Subcommittee on Livestock and Foreign
    Agriculture 104
  impeachment powers 103
  legislative agenda 102
  main responsibility 102
  majority party 102
  making of law 102
  and separation of powers 88
  Speaker 102, 105
  working atmosphere 101
  see also Congress; Senate
House Un-American Activities Committee
  (HUAC) 33, 235
Hsu, Hua 251
Hu Jintao 313
Hubble Telescope 270
Huerta, Dolores 35
Hughes, Langston 30
Huntington, Samuel 76, 308
Hurricane Katrina (2005) 47, 51
Hurricane Sandy (2012) 51
Hussein, Saddam 96, 304, 310
hydraulic fracturing (fracking) 48, 259

identity 85, 216, 220, 250
  controls 120
  gender 162, 316
  national 4
  Native American 68
  play 227
  progressive 213
  regional 53
  symbolic 72
  white Southern 54
identity politics 15
identity theft 72
ideological self-placement and party identification
  128t
Ignatius, David 285
immigrants 72, 73t, 74–81
  billionaire 75
  chain migrations 58
  colonial America (1607–1763) 17
  Ellis Island Immigration Museum 57
  from Europe 58
  first-generation 75
  "fresh-off-the-boat" 28

373

Index

Green Cards 72, 73t, 75
illegal 75
immigration reform 80
Mexican 79, 168
"Old Immigrants" and "New Immigrants" 74
quota system 75
from Russia 58, 186
undocumented 79
US as a nation of 216
US policy 74–75
see also ethnic minorities; Hispanics; Latinos
Immigration Act (1986) 75
Immigration Act (2000) 75
Immigration and Customs Enforcement (ICE) 170
Immigration and Nationality Act (1965) 35
impeachment of presidents 8, 95, 103, 113
imperialism 249
income tax brackets 34t
India 51, 78, 227, 291, 302, 322
and economic issues 255, 260
film market 240
Hindu nationalism 287
perceived threat to the US 240, 263, 318
technological innovation 269, 270, 278
individualism 188
Industrial Revolution 23, 57
industry 28, 268–270
"infotainment" 230, 239
insider trading 275
Instagram 224, 226, 227, 245
Institute for Policy Studies, Washington DC 124
Institute for Politics, Harvard University 325
insurrectionists 1–2
interest groups 121–124
open and closed 122, 123
International Institute for Democracy and Electoral
Assistance 330–331
International Monetary Fund (IMF) 277
Internet 222–225
interstate commerce 91
iPhones 278
Iraq war 95, 310–313
see also Afghanistan; al-Qaeda terrorist
network; ISIS (Islamic State); 9/11 terrorist
attacks; Syria, war in; terrorism
ISIS (Islamic State) 307, 311–313, 316, 327
Islam 186–187
isolation and expansion 294–295

J. Paul Getty Museum, Malibu 232
Jackson, Andrew 20
Jackson, Ketanji Brown 42, 108, 163
Jackson, Michael 165, 251
James, Letitia 174–175
James, Rick 251

Jamestown, Virginia 16, 53
Japan
atomic bombing of Hiroshima and Nagasaki
32, 296
and film industry 240
nationalism of 296
post-war rebuilding of 296
troops in 294
and US foreign policy 282, 295, 302, 310, 316
"Jazz Age" 31
Jefferson, Thomas 5, 15, 18, 20, 53, 96, 294, 297
Declaration of Independence 260
Jobs, Steve 282
John F. Kennedy Airport, NYC 76
John Hopkins University 193, 198
Johnson, Lyndon Baines (LBJ) 35, 301
Great Society Program 35, 37, 90, 247
as an "imperial" president 94
presidential style 94
War on Poverty 206
Joint Session of Congress 126, 127
Jolie, Angeline 146
Judaism/Jewish people 186
judicial branch of government 106–110, 111f, 112
access to the courts 111
appeals courts 110
common law 110
constitutional law 110
dynamic nature of judicial politics 108
elected judges 110
and election of 2020 83–84
federal court system 110
inferior courts 110
influence by executive branch 110
lower courts 108–109
method 108
restraint 108
and separation of powers 85, 88
superior courts 110
Supreme Court see Supreme Court, US
(SCOTUS)
judicial review, principle of 107
June Medical Services v. Russo (2020) 107, 112
"Juneteenth National Independence Day Act"
(2021) 238
justice, obstruction of 103

Kaepernick, Colin 245
Kagan, Elena 109, 163
Kagan, Robert 287, 303, 332
Kavanaugh, Brett 109, 188
Kennedy, Anthony (Justice) 109
Kennedy, John F. 34, 35, 102, 137, 300
assassination of (1963) 2, 301
election to presidency (1960) 185

Index

as an "imperial" president 94
Inaugural Address 300–301
presidential style 94
Kennedy, Robert 35
Kennedy Center, Washington DC 248
Kerry, John 290, 297
Key, Francis Scott 20
Keynesianism 257–259
Keystone XL pipeline, construction plans 49–50
Khrushchev, Nikita 300
Kim Jong-un 300
King, B. B. 250
King, Martin Luther 2, 33, 35, 71, 185, 189
Kinzinger, Adam 117, 125
Knights of Labor (KOL) 266–267
Korean War (1950–1953) 33, 76
Ku Klux Klan 25, 31, 75, 235
Kuwait, invasion of (1990) 37
Kyoto Protocol 39, 304

labor unions 266–268
Lady Gaga 251
LaHaye, Tim 188
laissez-faire philosophy 27, 270
land 45–66
country and state comparisons 46t
Environmental Protection Agency (EPA) 49–51
and global warming 49–51
the Midwest 58, 59t, 60
national parks 51–53
natural resources 48–49
the North see the North
the Pacific Rim 64–66
protections 52
regions 53
the South see the South
topographical features 45, 47
the West 60–64
language 76, 98, 174
Apache 71
biblical 189
clear 176
English 194, 221, 251, 260
foreign 75
German 30
and "Gettysburg Address" 24–25
lack of official national language 216
national 193
nationalist 215
native 71, 200
primary 218t
sexist 147
Spanish 53, 75, 251
unintelligible 184
violent 235

Las Vegas, Nevada 61–62
Latinos 75–76, 77, 80, 119, 141, 184
Lauer, Matt 146, 147
Layer Cake federalism 90
League of Nations 295
Leary, Timothy 218
Lee, Mike 125
Lee, Robert E. 173
"legacy Americans" 7
legislative branch of government 99, 100, 101–106
bills 104, 105
committees 103–104, 105
division of labor 103
and election of 2020 83–84
ideas for legislation 105
lawmaking process 104f, 105
"pork-barrel" legislation 103
procedural changes 105–106
and separation of powers 85, 88
subcommittees 104, 105
see also Congress; House of Representatives; Senate
legitimacy crisis 5
leisure time 236–241
Lenin, Vladimir 320
Lesbian Gay Bisexual Transsexual (LGBT) community 158–159
Lewinsky, Monica 38, 95, 103
Lewis, Jerry Lee 250
liberal democracy 5, 80, 323
liberalism
cultural/multicultural 148
economic 148
expansion of 310
extreme 189
possible decline of 330
see also liberal democracy; Liberals; Progressives
Liberals 7, 13, 149, 188, 215, 330
libraries 232–233, 248
life expectancy 156
Lifton, Robert 309
Lilly Endowment 197–198
Limbaugh, Rush 233
Lincoln, Abraham 5, 15, 23, 292, 295
"Emancipation Proclamation" 24, 96
"Gettysburg Address" 24–25
literature 221–222
and rise of a nation 221–222
Little Big Horn River, Montana 26
Little Richard 250
Liu Xiaobo 289
local government 93
Locke, Alain 30

375

Index

Loeffler, Kelly 136
Louisiana, purchase by Jefferson (1803) 96

MacArthur Foundation 248
McCain, John 40, 231
McCarthy, Joseph 33, 34
McCarthyism 230
McConnell, Mitch 2–3, 108, 126, 309
McDougall, Karen 146
McKinley, William 295
McNeil, James 247
Macron, Emmanuel 288, 319
Madison, James 20, 53, 85, 263–264, 297
Madonna 251
magazines 231–232
Major League Baseball Players Association
(MLBPA) 123
majority rule 1
Makah people, Washington 16
Make America Great Again (MAGA) 51, 181, 316
Malcolm X 35, 71–72
male privilege 160–161
Manchinn, Joe 115, 117, 259
"Manifest Destiny" 22
Manjoo, Farhad 225
Mao Zedong 298, 317
Mapplethorpe, Robert 248
Marble Cake federalism 90
Marbury v. Madison (1803) 91
Marshall, John 107
Marshall Plan 298
Martin, Travyon 66, 171, 173
mass culture 234
mass media 235
Massive Ordnance Air Blast (MOAB) 312
Mattis, Jim 297
"McDonaldization" 219
Meacham, John 148
Medal of Arts 247
media 137–139
    broadcast 233–236
    gatekeeper role 138
    influence by politicians 138
    newspapers 138
    print 229–233
    radio 137, 233
    and Trump 139
    see also social media
Medicaid 35, 121, 152, 210
Medicare 35, 38, 207–208, 210, 271
megachurches 191–192
Melville, Herman 221
meritocracy 3
Merkel, Angela 288, 315, 327
Mesch, Gustavo 226

#MeToo movement 3, 4, 7, 13, 100, 225
    and position of women 160–161, 162
Mexico
    border wall 75, 76, 79, 80, 164, 167, 168
    immigrants 79, 168
Microsoft 65
middle classes 149–152
midterm elections 101, 116
    of 2018 79, 83
    of 2022 3, 9, 114, 133
the Midwest 58, 59t, 60
Milano, Alyssa 146
Millennials 151, 188, 226, 331
minimum wage 160
"Miranda Rights" 168
mobile phones 227
modernization 89
Monroe, James 53, 295, 297
Monroe, Marilyn 247
Monroe Doctrine 295
Moon Jae-in 300
Mormon Church (Church of Jesus Christ of Latter
    Day Saints) 186, 187
Mousavizadeh 323
movie industry 239–241
"muckraking" 28
multiculturalism 37, 159, 203, 215, 220, 222, 252
    and cosmopolitanism 224
    and liberalism 148
    multicultural society 17, 75, 168
    and revivalism 187, 188
    and transnationalism 216
multimedia privatization 226
Murkowski, Lisa 115
Murrow, Edward R. 230
Museum of African American History and Culture
    248
museums 69, 245, 247, 248
music 169, 221
    American/Native American 249, 251, 252
    Blues 250
    and capitalism 249
    concert halls 249
    Country (Southern) 174, 233, 250
    English language 252
    Folk 250
    hip-grinding 250
    Hip-Hop 251
    Jazz 250
    Latin 252
    live 250
    military 250
    nationalistic 250
    popular 249–253
    protest 251

Index

Rap 251
Rock 222, 250
Soul 251
Swing 250
Music Television (MTV) 249
musical theater 249
Musk, Elon 75, 154, 226, 271
Muslims 186–187
mutual assured destruction (MAD) 300
Myrdal, Gunnar 193

NAFTA (North American Free Trade Area) 280, 281, 293, 314, 315
Nagl, John 307
Naismith, James 242
Napoleonic Wars 268
National Aeronautics and Space Administration (NASA) 55, 270, 271, 293
National Air and Space Museum 248
National Archives (NA) 232
National Association for Gun Rights 177
National Association for the Advancement of Colored People (NAACP) 30, 202
National Association of Manufacturers (NAM) 121–122
National Association of Securities Dealers Automated Quotations (NASDAQ) 274
National Coalition Against Censorship 249
national debt 281
National Defense Education Act (1958) 194
National Endowment for the Arts (NEA) 247
National Labor Relations Act (1935) (Wagner Act) 205, 267
National Military Strategy (NMS) 313
National Organization for Women 29
National Origins Act (1924) 31, 35, 75
National Park Service (NPS) 51
national parks 51–53
National Portrait Gallery 248
National Prayer Breakfasts 190
National Public Radio (NPR) 233
National Resources Defense Council (NRDC) 122–123
National Rifle Association (NRA) 122, 123, 174–175
National Science Foundation 222
national security 92, 289
National Security Act 297
National Security Council (NSC) 98, 297, 298, 299
National Wildlife Refuges (FWS) 52
nationalism 106, 188, 286–294, 317
    "America First" philosophy 7, 32, 41, 188, 257, 285, 288, 307, 328
    "Americanization" 219
    Asia 308

Christian Right 190
economic 255, 256–257
ethno-nationalism 43, 318, 332
of India 287
of Japan 296
"Keep America Great" 83, 143
Make America Great Again (MAGA) 51, 181, 316
"McDonaldization" 219
nationalistic music 250
"100 percent Americanism" 75
symbols of, location in the North 56
of Trump 7, 13–14, 41, 114, 215
white (of Trump) 7, 13–14
White Millennials 151
xenophobia 75
Native Americans 53, 61, 67–71
    cultural survival 69
    historical perspective 15, 16, 26
    poverty 153
    reservations 70
    shamanism 183
    tribes 16, 53, 68, 69, 71, 212
        historical perspective 17, 20, 26
        partisan 5
        tribal colleges 198
    see also Black Lives Matter (#BLM) movement; blacks
NATO (North Atlantic Treaty Organization) 39, 298–300
    members 298
    and the Ukraine 43, 299
    and US foreign policy 302, 305, 315, 316, 319–322, 328
natural disasters
    Hurricane Katrina (2005) 47, 51
    Hurricane Sandy (2012) 51
Natural History Museum 248
natural resources 48–49
necessary and proper (elastic) clause 91
Netanyahu, Benjamin 311
Neutrality Acts 296
New Atheism 188
New Deal (1933–1939) 32, 33, 37, 90, 96, 211, 247, 258
    and social services 205, 206
    Wagner Act 205, 267
New Orleans, Louisiana 53
New Religious Movement, "Fourth Awakening" 183
New World Order 37, 291, 302–304, 308
New York City (NYC) 23, 45, 93
    Broadway theaters 249
    as a financial center 57
    John F. Kennedy Airport 76

377

Index

museums 245, 247
New York Public Library 232
as a port 58
New York Philharmonic 249
New York Stock Exchange (NYSE) 57, 274
News Corporation 6
Newsmax 6
newspapers 138, 231
Niebuhr, Reinhold 41
9/11 terrorist attacks 95, 304–305
nineteenth century
  from 1803 to 1850s (westward expansion and reform) 20–23
  from 1803 to the 1850s (westward expansion and reform) 20–23
  from 1861 to 1865 (American Civil War) 23–25
  from 1870 to 1900 (late nineteenth century) 26–28
  citizenship 91
  rural lifestyle 28
Nixon, Richard 24, 33, 34, 95, 230, 231, 301
  on executive failure 98
  and federalism 91
  "Great Silent Majority" 35
  as an "imperial" president 94
  "New Federalism" 35, 90
  presidential style 94
  resignation of 36
  Watergate affair 90, 96, 97
Non-Proliferation Treaty (NPT) 299
the North 20, 23, 56–58
North American Free Trade Area (NAFTA) see
  NAFTA (North American Free Trade Area);
  USMCA (United States–Mexico–Canada Agreement)
North Atlantic Treaty Organization (NATO)
  see NATO (North Atlantic Treaty Organization)
North Korea 270, 277
  and US foreign policy 299, 300, 313, 318
nuclear weapons 35, 36, 62
  Comprehensive Nuclear Test Ban Treaty 304
  Iranian programs 289, 300, 312
  North Korean threat 300, 313
  Putin's threats 298, 319, 321
  stockpiles 314
  Trump's policy towards 316–317
  UN action 299
  and uranium use 48
  and US foreign policy 296, 303, 312, 322, 328
  see also arms race; atomic weapons
NYC see New York City (NYC)

Obama, Barack Hussein 5, 41, 42, 49, 53, 66, 80, 92, 94, 109, 148, 158, 165, 181, 189, 219, 261, 269, 289, 305, 314–318

Biden as Vice President under 114
compared with Trump 8
on economy 256, 273
electoral victory (2008) 40, 66, 95, 130
foreign policy 292, 293, 315
at G.H.W. Bush funeral 97, 98
and government 83, 90
Howard University Commencement Address (2016) 72
Inaugural Address 311, 314
see also Obamacare
Obama, Michelle 161
Obama Presidential Library 233
Obamacare 83, 114, 182, 208
  see also Affordable Care Act (ACA); health care policies; Medicaid; Medicare; Obama, Barack Hussein
obesity 208
Ocasio-Cortez, Alexandria 51, 100, 117, 148, 211, 259
Occupational Safety and Health Administration (OSHA) 272
Occupy Wall Street movement 149
Office of Management and Budget (OMB) 98
O'Keeffe, Georgia 247
Omar, Ilhan 187
One America 6
1619 Project 13, 17
1776 Commission 13–14
Operation Desert Storm 37, 302
opinion polls 130–131, 139
Osnos, Evan 3–4
Ossoff, John 136
Oval Office 35, 98

the Pacific Rim 64–66
Packer, George 4, 150, 328
Paddock, Steven 174
Page, Larry 154
Paine, Thomas 291, 292
Paltrow, Gwyneth 146
Paris Accords (2016) 289
Paris Peace Conference (1918) 295
Parker, Charlie 250
participatory democracy
  interest groups 121–124
  voters and voting 119–121
Patriot Act 39, 309
Paul, Alice 29
Paul, Rand 125
Peace Corps 35
Pearl Harbor, Japanese attack (1941) 76
Pells, Richard 218
Pelosi, Nancy 1, 126, 127, 132, 163
Pence, Mike 97, 98, 113
  and religion 185, 190
  threats to hang 1, 24

378

Index

Pentagon 320
Pentagon Papers 36
Pentecostal groups 189
people *see* American people
People's Republic of China 36
Perdue, David 136
periodicals 231–232
Perot, Ross 37–38
personal computers 223
Petraeus, David 305, 307
Pew research center, 2021 report 330
philanthropic groups 248
Phoenix, Arizona 61
Pickett, Wilson 251
Planned Parenthood Federation (PPF) 163
plea bargain agreements 169
Pledge of Allegiance 29, 33, 183
Plessy v. Ferguson (1896) 26, 33
pluralistic democracy 141–144
pocket veto 105
police brutality 8, 145, 165
    see also Black Lives Matter (#BLM) movement
Political Action Committees (PACs) 139, 140, 141
political parties 118, 124–128, 129–130t, 130–133
    ethnocentric 287
    and history of the US 28
    ideological self-placement and party
        identification 128t
    partisan realignment 117
    party affiliation 103
    small 124
    two-party system 117
    Whig Party, UK 18, 23
    see also Democratic Party/Democrats; Liberals;
        Progressives; Republican Party/Republicans
politics
    bipartisanship 40, 101, 115, 140, 155, 171, 273
    global 285–323
    identity 15
    Left wing 7, 127
    partisan 15
    racial analysis of voters 13
    Right wing 7, 127
        Alternative Right 287
    see also Congress; democracy; Democratic
        Party/Democrats; elections; electorate;
        government; Liberals; political parties;
        Republican Party/Republicans
Polk, James K. 20–21, 22
Pollock, Jackson 247
polyvocality (hybrid) 216
popular culture 220, 247
popular music 249–253
population, American
    African Americans 72
    by age and sex 156t

California 65
and the economy 259–260
growth in colonial period (1607–1763) 17
and immigration 74
New York City 23
populism 106
Populist Party 28
Portman, Rob 115
post-modernism 188
post-slavery stress syndrome 169
poverty
    and affluence 153–156
    Trump on 155
    War on Poverty 206
Powell, Colin 165, 302
presidency
    cabinet 98–99
    and executive branch 93–99
    Executive Office of the President (EOP) 98
    "interregnum" 98
    legal power 95
    limitations on power 94
    newly elected and outgoing presidents 95
    path to 134
    powers 96
    presidential style 93–94
    terms of office 95
    see also individual presidents
presidential election of 2020 (Trump/Biden) 9,
        41–42, 83–84, 113–119
    Biden's appeal to voters 117, 118
    Biden's policy intentions 114–115
    campaign 138–139
    desire of Trump to overturn results 42
    law and order issue 172
    media use 115–116
    opinion polls 139
    partisan realignment 117
    presidential preference in 2020 129–130t
    progressivism of Biden 116, 117
    state ballot issues 191
    stolen, Trump and Republicans' belief as to
        113, 142
    voting behavior 139
    see also Capitol building, storming of (January
        6, 2021)
presidential elections 129–130t, 135t
    of 2008 40, 66, 95, 130
    of 2016 41, 75, 87, 106, 114, 132, 136, 170, 260
    of 2020 *see* presidential election of 2020
        (Trump/Biden)
    complexity of election process 133–134
    and Constitution 87
    cyber hacking, Russian 170
    no gerrymandering in 141
    see also midterm elections

Index

Presley, Elvis 247, 250
print media 229–233
privatism 192
Programme for International Student Testing (PISA) 202
The Progressive Era (1896–1916) 7, 28–30, 91
Progressive Policy Institute 124
Progressives 7, 29, 120, 173, 211, 330
    see also Democratic Party/Democrats; Liberals; The Progressive Era (1896–1916)
Prohibition 31
proportional voting 141
Protestantism 31
Prynne, Hester 221
Public Broadcasting System (PBS) 235
public health guidelines, politicizing 84
Pueblo Indians 16
Pulitzer, Joseph 229
purchasing power parity (PPP) 259
Pure Food and Drug Act (1906) 272
Puritans 17, 57
Putin, Vladimir 6, 43, 287, 288, 316
  and 9/11 320
  attitudes to the West 322, 327–328
  censoring of media 319–320
  character 316
  and China 317, 319, 323
  Crimean invasion (2014) 288, 302, 316, 328
  goals 316
  Hitler comparison 321
  investigating as a war criminal 319
  miscalculations by 319–320, 327–328
  neo-imperialism of 319
  and oligarchs 322
  pact with Xi Jinping 319
  praising by Trump 288, 328
  preparations for Ukraine war 319
  relations with Trump and Obama 288, 316, 328
  threat to use nuclear weapons 298, 319, 321
  see also Russia; Ukraine invasion (2022)
Putnam, Robert 157, 223, 264

R2P see Responsibility to Protect (R2P)
race 4, 164–168
  anti-racism laws 14–15
  and citizenship 164–165
  diversity 166
  and frontiers 25–26
  massacre of 1921 31
  racial discrimination 30
  racial equality 35
  white nationalism 7
  see also African Americans; Black Lives Matter (#BLM) movement; Civil Rights Movement

(1954–1968); Critical Race Theory (CRT); ethnic minorities; Native Americans; slavery
Race-To-The-Top (RTTP) education policies 92
radical conservatism 189
radio 137, 233
Rauschenberg, Robert 247
Reagan, Ronald 33, 37–38, 39, 41, 165, 212, 231, 301
  and the economy 270, 271–272
  and federalism 90, 91
  "The Great Communicator" 37, 83, 93
  photo opportunities 98
  presidential style 93
  "Teflon President" 95
Reaganomics 265, 275, 302
realpolitik 322
"Red Scare" (1919–1920) 30, 31, 33, 230, 235
Reform Party 125
regulation 270–273
Reisman, David: *The Lonely Crowd* 33
religion 182–192
  Catholic Church 184
  Christian Right 190
  creationism 203
  dissenters 17
  evangelism 33
  God, belief in 184
  megachurches 191–192
  National Prayer Breakfasts 190
  Pentecostal groups 189
  portable civil society 192
  Protestantism 31
  religious freedom 183
  religious groups 184–187
  Religious Right 188
  revivalism 187–191
Religious Freedom Act (1978) 187
Remnick, David 40
renminbi, and dollar 281–283
representative democracy 141
Republican Party/Republicans 4, 6, 7, 23, 38, 278
  on capital punishment 177
  categories of Republicans 330
  core values 127–128
  and the economy 257
  elections 133
  and federalism 92
  on homosexuality 158
  and race 166
  "Stop the Steal" campaigns 120
  Trump's takeover 191
  and US Constitution 328
  white male voters 13
  see also Trump, Donald

Index

Responsibility to Protect (R2P) 303, 312
reverse discrimination 202
revivalism 187–191
Rhetorical federalism 90
Rice, Condoleezza 163
Rice, Tamir 173
Ringgold, Faith 10
Rittenhouse, Kyle 177
Roberts, John 109, 113
Roberts Court 108
Rock & Roll Hall of Fame, Cleveland 60
Rockefeller, John D. 26, 58
Rockefeller, Nelson 98
Rodrigo, Olivia 249
Roe v. Wade (1973) 108, 164, 188
see also abortion rights
Romney, Mitt 40, 115, 117, 125, 140
Roosevelt, Franklin Delano 32, 137, 148
  "fireside chats" 233
  New Deal (1933–1939) 32, 33, 37, 90, 96, 205,
    211, 247, 258
  "past is prologue" 15
  power 94
Roosevelt, Theodore (Teddy) 30, 96
Rose, Charlie 146
Rubio, Marco 125, 182
rural America 152–153
Russia
  Alaska purchased from (1867) 25, 64
  atrocities committed by 320
  Central Bank 322
  and China/alliance with China 310, 313, 317,
    319, 323, 326
  Crimean invasion (2014) 288, 302, 316, 328
  cyberhacking and interference with 2016
    election 170, 225
  and energy/fuel 259, 293, 322
  immigrants 58, 186
  inflation in 322
  and New World Order 302, 327–328
  oligarchs 322
  perceived threat of 43, 317
  relations with the US 18, 35, 301, 305, 310,
    316
  and Trump 288, 328, 329
  sanctions against 322
  seen as a malign influence 326
  seen as a pariah state 323
  and Syria 312
  see also Cold War (1945–1990); Putin,
    Vladimir; Soviet Union (USSR); Ukraine
    invasion (2022)
Russian Revolution (1917) 30–31, 320
"Rust Belt," Midwest 60
Rwanda genocide 303

Sadat, Anwar 301
Saint Augustine, Florida 53
Salem witch trials (1692) 17
Salt Lake City, Utah 62
San Diego, California 65, 77
San Francisco, California 45, 65
San Juan, Puerto Rico 53
Sanctuary Cities 79, 92
Sandel, Michael 3, 329
Sanders, Bernie 117, 125, 132, 149, 211
Sanger, Margaret 30, 163
Santa Barbara, California 65
Santana, Carlos 251
Scalia, Antonin 107
Schama, Simon 231
Schell, Orville 317
Scholastic Achievement Test (SAT) 195
Scholz, Olaf 321
school districts and boards 199–202
school shootings 176, 177
Schulz, Howard 140
scientific management 269
Scopes, John 31
Scopes Monkey Trial (1925) 187
SCOTUS *see* Supreme Court, US (SCOTUS)
Seattle, Washington 65
Second Great Awakening 187
Second World War (1939–1945) 32, 60, 75, 94, 269,
  288
  female labor 161
  Pearl Harbor, Japanese attack (1941) 76
  social contract 330
Securities and Exchange Commission (SEC) 274,
  275
Seeger, Pete 251
Senate 79, 113–114, 116, 131, 136, 142, 172, 186,
  246, 296
  ambassadors, approval of 293
  Committee on Foreign Relations 104
  and Constitution 83, 85
  and executive branch 93, 95
  impeachment powers 103
  and Judicial branch 107, 108
  Judicial Committee 243
  and legislative branch 99, 106
  majority party 102, 105
  making of law 102
  President 105
  Republican-controlled 103, 107, 114, 262
  and separation of powers 88
  Standing Committees 103
  working atmosphere 101
  see also Congress; House of Representatives
Senators 136
seniority principle 105

381

Index

separation of powers 5, 84–85, 88, 89f, 292–293
Serrano, Andres 249
Sessions, William 170
sexual harassment 162
Shaheen, Jeanne 115
shamanism 183
Shaw v. Reno (1993) 141
Shelby v. Holder (2013) 141
Sherman Anti-Trust Act (1890) 267
Shinzo Abe 288
Shirky, Clay 225
Shultz, George 231
Sierra Club 49, 52
silence, right to 168
Sinema, Kyrsten 115
slavery
    1619 Project 13, 17
    in the South 20, 26, 55
    Trump on 14
    see also African Americans; blacks; ethnic
        minorities; race
"Smart America" group 4
"smart" power 291
smartphones 67, 227, 229, 322
Smith, Adam 275
    The Wealth of Nations 260
Smith, Dan 16
Smith, Will 5
Snyder, Timothy 15, 230–231
social class *see* class
Social Darwinism 27, 29, 40
    see also Darwin, Charles/Darwinism
social media 5, 6–7, 11, 43, 67, 75, 102, 137–138,
        153, 158, 162, 251, 253, 313, 320
    and Biden 133
    fake news 224
    interconnectedness 171
    interest groups 122
    and Obama 94
    personalized 137
    platforms 122, 224, 226
    sites 2, 15, 229
    and Trump 98, 115, 121, 230
    and youth culture 225–229
    see also TikTok
Social Security programs 35, 206, 210
    see also government
Social Security Trust Fund 206
social services 204–213
socialism 149, 331
society 145–180
    American family 156–160
    class 148–156
    crime and punishment 168–178, 179f, 180
    race *see* race

women 160–164
    see also American people; population,
        American
soft power 290
solicitor general 110
Sotomayor, Sonia 109, 163
Soul music 249, 250
Sousa, John Philip 250
the South 53, 54t, 55t, 56
    crops 54
    language and dialect 53
    map 54
    slavery in 20, 26, 54
    and the United States 20, 23
South Korea 299, 313, 316
Southern music *see* Country music
Soviet Union (USSR)
    and Cold War 32–33
    Reagan on 37, 301
    see also Cold War (1945–1990); Russian
        Revolution (1917)
space program 270
SpaceX Falcon-9 rocket 271, 314
Spacey, Kevin 146
SPAM filters 223
Spencer, Herbert 27
sports 241–245
Spotify 4
Staircase Escalante monument 52
Standing Rock pipeline dispute (2016) 71, 187
Stanton, Elizabeth Cady 29
Starbucks 140
state government 93, 111
State of the Union Address (2019) 100, 106
state responsibility, for education 198, 199f
Statue of Liberty 57
statute law 110
Stiglitz, Joseph 153
stock market 274
storming of the Capitol *see* Capitol building,
        storming of (January 6, 2021)
Strategic Arms Limitation Talks (SALT) 301
Strategic Defense Initiative (SDI) 302
Strong, Josiah 295
subcommittees 105
Sullivan, Andrew 40
Sullivan, Jake 288
Sumner, Charles 24
Sumner, William Graham 27
Sundance Film Festival, Utah 241
"Super PACs" (Political Action Committees) 139,
        140, 141
superdelegates 134
Supplemental Nutrition Assistance Program
        (SNAP) 206

382

Index

supremacy of the US, evaluating 317–318
Supreme Court, US (SCOTUS) 3, 4, 20, 80, 107,
    163–164, 235
  appeals to 169
  Brown v. Board of Education (1954) 33
  Chief Justice 103
  choosing own cases to hear 109
  conservative nature 108–109
  criticism of 111–112
  and election of 2020 42–43
  and executive branch 96
  flexibility of 109
  Founders on 106–107
  and freedom of speech 30
  on homosexuality 158
  indecency acts 224
  justices 93, 95, 107–108, 109, 111, 188, 243, 327
  and Keystone XL pipeline, construction plans
    50
  and Pledge of Allegiance 29
  Plessy v. Ferguson (1896) 26, 33
  predominant role 111
  on religion and education 202
  and solicitor general 110
  and Trump 83
  women appointed to 40
survival of the fittest 27
Sutter, John 65
Swing music 250
symbolic identity 72
Syria, war in 310–313
    see also Afghanistan; al-Qaeda terrorist
      network; Iraq war; ISIS (Islamic State); 9/11
      terrorist attacks; terrorism

Taft, William Howard 30
Taft–Hartley Act (1947) 267
Taiwan 314
Taliban 39, 304, 305, 307, 308
    see also Afghanistan
taxes 264–266
Taylor, Breonna 145, 171–2
Taylor, Frederick W. 31
technological determinism 226
Telecommunications Act (1996) 235
television 234
  global 2
Temporary Assistance for Needy Families (TANF)
    212, 261
terrorism 159, 164, 189, 291
  Age of Terrorism 265
  cyberterrorism 313
  international 304
  ISIS/al-Qaeda/Hezbollah 304, 305, 307, 308,
    310, 312, 313, 316, 318, 327

Taliban 304, 305, 307
  war on 78, 189
Tesla Motors 258
Tester, John 115
The National Safety Council (TNSC) 272
the twenty-first century 39–43, 92
The Gilded Age (1870–1900) 26–28
think-tanks 124
Thomas, Clarence 109, 165
Thunberg, Greta 146, 331
TikTok 4
Timberlake, Justin 235–236
Tocqueville, Alexis de 121
toxic masculinity 160
Trade Promotion Authority (TPA) 293
Traister, Patricia 162
TransCanada (oil company) 49–50
transnationalism 76, 215, 216
Trans-Pacific Partnership (TTP) 280
Transpacific Trade and Investment Partnership
    (TPP) 293
Truman, Harry S. 93, 95, 297, 298
Trump, Donald 3, 6, 14, 52, 53, 60, 67, 71, 81, 83,
    88, 90, 92, 96, 105, 108, 113, 121, 125, 139,
    155, 162, 198, 208, 226, 247, 257, 315
  behavior/character 139, 190, 243, 298, 315
  communication skills 94, 114
  compared with Obama 8
  construction of wall between the US and
    Mexico 75, 76, 79, 80, 164, 167, 168
  Covid crisis, mishandling 9, 116, 149, 181
  "Drain the Swamp" rhetoric 117
  economic nationalism of 255, 256–257
  election victory of 2016 41, 75, 87, 106, 114,
    132, 136, 260
  and Electoral College 87, 113
  foreign policy 315, 316–317
  at G.H.W. Bush funeral 97, 98
  and global order 287
  and immigration 75, 76, 80
  impeachment of 8, 103, 113
  Inaugural Address 41
  "Keep America Great" 83, 143
  Make America Great Again (MAGA)
    philosophy 51, 181, 316
  National Defense Strategy Report 294
  on NATO 298
  1776 Commission 13–14
  populism 148, 210
  and Putin 288, 328–329
  religion 185, 190
  scandals concerning 8–9, 103
  and social media 98, 115, 121, 230
    Twitter 37, 94, 116, 133, 138, 226
  State of the Union Address (2019) 100, 106

383

Index

and storming of the Capitol (January 6, 2021) 1–2, 24, 103
on the Ukraine 288, 328
visit to North Korea 300
white nationalism of 7, 13–14, 41, 114, 215
see also Capitol building, storming of (January 6, 2021); nationalism; presidential election of 2020 (Trump/Biden); Republican Party/Republicans
trust in government 91
breakdown of 151
Turkle, Sherry 227
Turner, Frederick Jackson 26
Twain, Mark 26
Adventures of Huckleberry Finn 221
Tweed, William M. 27
twentieth century
from 1914 to the 1920s 30–32
from 1933 to 1945 (New Deal and the Second World War) 32, 33, 37, 90, 96
from 1947 to 1991 (Cold War) 32–38, 296–302
the 1950s 32–33
the 1960s and 1970s 34–36
the 1980s (Reagan era) 37–38
the 1990s 38
business regulation 91
global village 91
stronger government 91
trust in government 91
urban machinery 28
twenty first century 39–43, 92, 304
Ukraine invasion (2022) 5, 43, 302, 319–323
Twitter 122, 224, 227, 234, 315, 319
and Obama 94
and Trump 37, 94, 116, 133, 138, 226
"Twitter Democracy" 230
Tyler, John 16

UAVs (unmanned assault vehicles) 312
Ukraine invasion (2022) 5, 11, 43, 192, 259, 287, 298, 299, 302, 319–323, 327, 328
called "a special military operation" by Russia 320
and Putin 298, 299, 327
miscalculations by 319–320
see also Putin, Vladimir; Russia
United Farm Workers Union 35
United Nations Commission on Human Rights 177
United Nations Environment Programme (UNEP) 63
United Nations Headquarters 57
United Nations Security Council (UNSC) 311
United States Supreme Court (SCOTUS) *see* Supreme Court, US (SCOTUS)
United States–Mexico–Canada Agreement

(USMCA) *see* USMCA (United States–Mexico–Canada Agreement)
universities 193–198
fees 197
Georgia 194
Harvard 17, 58
Historically Black Colleges and Universities (HBCU) 198
Howard University Commencement Address (2016) 72
John Hopkins 193, 198
North Carolina 194
private foundations 197–198
rankings 196
scholarships 197
tests 197
see also colleges
unmanned assault vehicles 312
urban America 152–153
urban machinery 28
US Customs and Border Protection (UCBP) 170
US Support for the Death Penalty 177
USMCA (United States–Mexico–Canada Agreement) 280, 281, 314, 315
see also NAFTA (North American Free Trade Area)
US–Spain War (1898) 28

vacation law 238
Valens, Ritchie 251
"Values Generation" 4
vertical integration 26
veto power 105
vice presidency 98
Vietnam War (1954–1975) 90, 96, 143, 209, 250, 300–301
historical perspective 35, 36, 37
and immigration 79
Vietnam Syndrome 301, 303
vigilantes 1, 2, 67, 313
private 13
"vigilante justice" 326
violence 2, 5, 6, 10, 35, 38, 173, 225, 226, 229, 235, 266, 267, 290
civic 1
domestic 23, 175
fan violence 244
language 235
Middle East 301
mob violence 184
police 8, 14, 245
racial 13, 290
representative 175
school shootings 176, 177
sporadic 202
see also gun crimes/gun ownership; homicide

Index

voters and voting 119–121
   in 2020 118–119, 139
   African Americans 132
   age factors 132
   gerrymandering 43, 130, 131, 141, 142
   media influence on education and political
     socialization 139
   "median" voter theory 126–127
   opinion polls 130–131, 139
   referendum, calls for 120
   voter fraud, Trump's accusations of 113, 120
   see also elections; parliamentary elections;
     political parties; politics; presidential
     election of 2020 (Trump/Biden)
Voting Rights Acts 35, 120, 141

Wagner Act (1935) 205, 267
Wall Street 274
Walter, Barbara 331
Walton, Alice 154
war on property 35
War on Terror 39, 92, 308–309
War Powers Resolution (1973) 293
Warhol, Andy 247
Warner, Mark 115
Warnock, Raphael 136
Warren, Elizabeth 149, 211
wars 305, 307–308
   American Civil War (1861–1865) 23–25, 266,
     295
   anti-war protest 30
   in Iraq and Syria 310–313
   Korean (1950–1953) 33, 76
   US–Spain (1898) 28
   Vietnam (1954–1975) 35, 36, 37, 96, 143, 209,
     250, 300–301
   see also Cold War (1945–1990); First World
     War (1914–1918); Second World War
     (1939–1945)
Warsaw Pact 37, 298, 300, 302
Washington, Booker T. 30
Washington, DC 55, 88
Washington, Denzel 220
Washington, General George 18, 20, 53, 96, 221, 294
Water Pollution Control Act (1972) 52
Watergate affair 90, 96, 97
weapons of mass destruction 39
Weinstein, Harvey 146
Wells, H.G.: *The War of the Worlds* 233
Wells Fargo Bank 167
the West 60–64
West, Kanye 251
Wheeler, Andrew 53
Whitefield, George 18
Whigs, UK 18, 23

Whistler, James McNeil 247
White House 24, 51, 60, 83, 107, 113, 135, 165, 183,
   191, 248, 315
White House Staff 98
White Millennials 151
white nationalism, of Trump 7, 13–14, 41, 114,
   215
   see also Republican Party/Republicans; white
     supremacy
white supremacy 7, 24, 28, 146, 290, 318
Whitefield, George 187
Whole Women's Health v. Hellerstedt (2016) 107
Wilderness Society 52
wildfires, American West 63
Will, George 251
Williams, Hank 250
Williams, Venus and Serena 244
Wilson, Woodrow 30, 103, 295
Winfrey, Oprah 165
winner-takes-all system, elections 124, 126, 141
Winthrop, John 17
Wittenhouse, Kyle 145–146
WOKE culture 7
Wolfe, Alan 80, 184
women 160–164
   female Secretaries of State 163
   glass ceilings for promotion 163, 260
   organizations 29–30
   in workforce 32
   see also feminism
Women's March 162
Women's National Soccer Team 246
Women's Rights Convention (1848) 23
women's suffrage 29
Wood, Lin 177
Woodhull, Victoria 29–30
Woods, Tiger 220
workforce 210–212, 260–264
Works Progress Administration 205
World Bank 159, 223, 277
World Economic Forum 269
world power, becoming 295–296
World Trade Center 2
World Trade Organization (WTO) 277–279, 303
Wyoming 136

Xi Jinping 287, 317, 323

yellow journalism 229
Yellowstone national park, Montana 51
youth culture, and social media 225–229
youth rebellion 250

Zelenski, Volodymyr 320
Zuckerberg, Mark 154